THE DOUBLE LIFE OF
PAUL DE MAN

Books by
EVELYN BARISH

Emerson in Italy
(photographs by Evelyn Hofer)

Emerson: The Roots of Prophecy

Arthur Hugh Clough:
The Growth of a Poet's Mind

THE DOUBLE LIFE OF
PAUL DE MAN

EVELYN BARISH

LIVERIGHT PUBLISHING CORPORATION

A Division of

W. W. NORTON & COMPANY

NEW YORK · LONDON

For information about permission to reproduce
selections from this book, write to Permissions,
Liveright Publishing Corporation, a division of
W. W. Norton & Company, Inc.,
500 Fifth Avenue, New York, NY 10110

For information about special discounts for bulk
purchases, please contact W. W. Norton Special Sales
at specialsales@wwnorton.com or 800-233-4830

Manufacturing by RR Donnelley, Harrisonburg
Book design by Barbara M. Bachman
Production manager: Anna Oler

ISBN 978-0-87140-326-1

Liveright Publishing Corporation,
500 Fifth Avenue, New York, N.Y. 10110

www.wwnorton.com

W. W. Norton & Company Ltd., Castle House,
75/76 Wells Street, London W1T 3QT

1 2 3 4 5 6 7 8 9 0

Dedicated to
Micheline de Braey,
Esther Sluszny,
and the brave women
of the Belgian Resistance

CONTENTS

NOTE ON
TRANSLATIONS

Because many documents written in French by Paul de Man and others are archival and unpublished, unless otherwise noted the translations are by this writer. This applies equally to de Man's published, formal essays in *Wartime Journalism* (1992) and to informal, unpublished manuscripts. Texts in Dutch, the written form of Flemish, have been translated by commission or by friends and colleagues to whom this writer is most grateful.

INTRODUCTION

All his life he was very secret.

—FRIDA VANDERVELDEN, FRIEND

**Paul the personal man was very
different from the public one.**

—PATRICIA DE MAN, WIDOW[1]

A CULTURAL GIANT OF EPIC PROPORTIONS IN THE 1970S AND 1980S, PAUL de Man no longer seems to exist. In the second decade of the twenty-first century, the onetime "masters of thought," intellectuals like Jean-Paul Sartre and Hannah Arendt, who by sheer force of mind made themselves the dispensers of great social power and influence, are gone, and have not yet been replaced. Paul de Man was just such a man, known by some as the "father of deconstruction," although he said the term was coined by Jacques Derrida. He was indeed a star.

Born in 1919 into wealth in Belgium in the aftermath of World War I, he arrived in the United States in 1948 as a penniless immigrant without connections or a profession. It would be one of the many paradoxes and reversals that marked his life that in just three decades de Man would create a new philosophy, a way of looking at the world that redefined America's cultural point of view. Influential in both the academic world and the broader social one, de Man wielded more influence on intellectual ideas than any other voice either here or abroad. Clothing that wore its seams inside out was suddenly "deconstructed": so, too, was architecture when its pipes and staircases were exposed in full view as external elements. A popular line of clothing, Theory, was named after his work. Even de Man's fleeting comment about the famous 1970s TV bigot Archie Bunker (who, when asked by his wife whether to arrange his sneakers' laces outward or inward, had replied, "What difference does it make?") was cited as the power of Paul de Man's thinking to find and reveal the truth of deconstruction in us all. In 1983, when de Man died at the age of sixty-four, the *New York Times* reported his death on page one, and many articles appeared in foreign newspapers, as well. Later, Yale University held a solemn memorial service attended by scholars from many countries, and its university press published a volume weighing almost two pounds, titled *The Lesson of Paul de Man*. The renowned French poet Yves Bonnefoy spoke lyrically to his assembled friends of having met the man with the intense blue eyes—the light of the sun, the light, he implied, of being itself.

De Man, who held the prestigious position of Sterling Professor of the Humanities at Yale, had been a man of extraordinary charisma. In his youth, as the scion of a leading Belgian family led by an uncle who was a brilliant, if controversial, politician, Paul was a golden boy, blond, blue-eyed, handsome. Intellectually, he was a prizewinner, gifted equally in mathematics and languages. At age nineteen, during the pre–World War II years, he coveted an open sports car, and, his father being rich, he got one and tooled around Antwerp in it with his girlfriend. Yet, paradoxically, he also helped run a political journal established by Trotskyist friends. He was the great love of the three main women in his adult life: Frida Vandervelden, his first intimate woman friend; Anne Baraghian Jaeger de Man Brajatuli von Orland-Ipsen, his first wife (who married several times); and Patricia Kelley de Man, his second wife and widow. Forty-five years after separating, Frida remained "haunted" by his memory, Anne was still angry at his abandonment, and Patricia spoke of their "forty-year love affair." Mary McCarthy pursued information about him even on her deathbed; she had been his protector and perhaps his lover before he ended their relationship.

By the time his American colleagues knew him in his middle years, when I also met him, he had the look of a highly cultivated European intellectual. He had a Flemish face, with a high, wide brow, penetrating eyes, a strong, irregular nose, and cheeks marked by deep furrows, suggesting unspoken anxieties. His expression was austere and his manner quietly reserved, yet almost imperceptibly insouciant. He was at once not to be approached, untouchable, and magnetically attractive. De Man seemed to embody the highest ideals of the profession of literature, and his graduate students followed him, as if magnetized, at first from Harvard to Cornell, then from Cornell to Johns Hopkins, and lastly from Hopkins to Yale, while would-be apostles from elsewhere made pilgrimages merely to audit his courses.[2] Although Paul was secretive, he became the subject of several romans à clef, even one conceived while Paul was still a graduate student at Harvard.[3] In the 1970s, his long-separated cousin Li (Elise LeCocq-de Man) tracked Paul de Man down when he gave a talk in Geneva, Switzerland, and recalled with pleasure "how those professors looked on him as a god."[4] To know him was a privilege; to have been his student, even in the professionally lean years of the 1970s and 1980s, virtually assured a candidate of one of the few good university jobs available.

Yet five years after his death, de Man was again on the front page of the *New York Times*, although in a very different light. Suddenly, he became the focus of a scandal that had erupted concerning his wartime activities. Until then, he had been seen, as his colleague Geoffrey Hartman said in an interview of December 1997, as merely another refugee professor like himself. In 1987, however, a young Belgian scholar named Ortwin de Graef, looking for a dissertation topic, discovered that during World War II de Man had collaborated as a journalist and a book reviewer—and had written at least one anti-Semitic article.[5] Given de Man's preeminence and the power of his intellectual legacy, the revelation in 1988 rocked the academic world, becoming so significant an issue that *Newsweek* put the story on its cover, together with a picture of a Nazi prewar march.[6]

He was reviled, and a great many people regretted their past connections. By some of his newly declared enemies, he was labeled a "Nazi." At a 1988 conference in Antwerp, originally organized to celebrate de Man, he was publicly and without warning accused by an early friend and respected historian, Georges Goriély, of committing astounding transgressions—bigamy, forgery, theft.[7] Uproar broke out as his American friends and colleagues objected and refused to believe the charges. "One would have thought," Jean Stengers, the dean of Belgian historians, remarked later, "that their lives were at stake," adding ironically, "and professionally, perhaps they were."[8] In the long run, although Goriély submitted his essay, it did not appear in the collection the American editors later published. Early in his career, the writer and editor James Atlas attended the conference and learned of some of the purported scandals, but although Atlas quoted Goriély in the magazine of the *New York Times*, it was undoubtedly among the several pieces that de Man's highly placed defenders continued to dismiss as mere "journalism."[9]

Yet the scandal refused to abate for years. As the accusations sank in, de Man's friends and colleagues, Jews and non-Jews alike, felt deeply betrayed. Before the revelations, as the issue came to be called, standard teaching anthologies of literature had lengthy index entries under "de Man." A few years later, the entries were very brief; then his name sometimes disappeared from the indices entirely. A scholar who had been his student said publicly that de Man had been a "baby-burner." Yet it was hard to discover facts about de Man himself. In the period that followed the scandal, a great many angry essays and letters were published, but they focused on de Man's wartime writings and this single anti-Semitic article in particular. Little or nothing appeared to explain what lay behind his journalism, or to examine his roots, or to understand the factors that had influenced him and the culture from which he derived. Like his own approach to literature, he seemed to have virtually no history. What had really happened in Belgium in the 1930s and early 1940s, and who de Man had been before and after he wrote for its newspapers, what kind of family and social position he came from—all the details of life that might give context to his attitudes as a young man—were left uncertain, supported only by hearsay. A well-written and searching book by David Lehman appeared in 1991, but it focused on de Man's American years, on the scandal, and on deconstruction, saying little about his prior life.[10]

One awaited the publication of his two hundred reviews, a considerable work of scholarship by a collective band of editors, that appeared in 1992, together with a second volume of commentary.[11] Although these volumes were valuable, many, though not all, of those who wrote about de Man were themselves involved with deconstruction or theory, as it came to be called, and eschewed biographical and historical research. *Context* came to be an acceptable term, but there was no longitudinal study of de Man, particularly one that focused on his formative years.

I was haunted by the contradictions. I had known de Man slightly as a colleague when I began teaching at Cornell in 1964, first as an instructor and then as an assistant professor for five years. He was the star of the humanities faculty, and like everyone else, I admired him. His occasional lectures were difficult, even impossible, to understand, but he had a magnetic pull in this already-glittering group. He was the smartest person around, all the older colleagues agreed, while the leaders of the younger group wanted to be his friends. In fact, Paul de Man had been brought to Cornell to revive the study of comparative literature, according to M. H. Abrams, the revered American literary critic, whose book *The Mirror and the Lamp* redefined Romanticism for the postwar period. The study was essentially an American invention pursued more at Harvard than in Europe, but one dear to Mike Abrams's heart.[12]

How could de Man, a person of such austere temperament, occupying a position of such respect, seeming to personify the highest professional and even ethical achievement, have had such a past? This book, the result of my attempt to answer those questions, ultimately provided two kinds of perspective, one focused on de Man himself, one more general and historical. Research, which was fascinating but became very time-consuming, unearthed a set of facts that related a biographical narrative that was often hard to believe. De Man's lifelong habits of secrecy made every new fact a surprise. Many crucial events in his life were unknown either to his widow or to many of his friends. Initially I found it impossible not so much to believe what I was learning as to comprehend it. Old reverences are surrendered with difficulty, and my subject was turning out to have been an entirely different man than most of us had thought. Simultaneously, there appeared another narrative, for it became clear that de Man could only be understood in the context of his country, his own and his family's social history, and Belgium under the occupation during World War II. In Europe between the wars, numerous socialist leaders turned their coats and, as Hitler rose to power in the 1930s, became fascists themselves. One gains an intimate view of this process in Paul's life history, for he was especially close to one of these men, his brilliant uncle Henri de Man.[13]

Another topic, collaboration itself, has been much discussed, but what did it mean to be a "collaborator"? Paul de Man was no mere book reviewer, as has been thought. As the facts gradually came to light, I learned that as a young man in Belgium de Man had had a stellar career, one that was totally unknown even to his friends during that period, but it put him at the heart of the collaborationist publishing world during the occupation. (The word *collaborate* is a contested one.[14] It was used by Henri de Man, Paul's politically dominant uncle, when at the beginning of the war he urged other Belgians to "*collaborer*," or work with the occupant. As the war and its oppressions were felt more deeply, it carried more and more opprobrium.) The documents from the Military Court that I unearthed, working through summers under the sun-heated, leaden roof of the Palace of Justice and elsewhere, provide a rare picture of how literary and commercial collaboration proceeded inside the media. In fact, de Man was employed simultaneously by the three major media companies in Belgium during this time, and one forms a picture not only of de Man's activities but of a highly corrupted world in which the managers caroused with the enemy officers set to watch them, lined their own pockets by plundering the company coffers, and managed the black market. De Man, needless to say, profited handsomely, as well. In that world, de Man now appears to have embodied the "velvet-gloved" seduction—meaning seduction of his readership—that was far more effective, according to Gérard Loiseaux, historian of literary collaboration, than the gross impostures of Nazi propaganda.[15]

Personal sources were also important. Given the fact that I began to investigate de Man's world in 1990, while many people who had been associated with him were still alive, I did not have to rely on archives alone. More than one of de Man's relatives, hearing I was in Brussels, tracked me down and telephoned before I even knew who they were, eager to provide information. One literally took me by the hand and introduced me to others who had been in de Man's circle. Not everyone wanted to talk, but many did and wanted their side of the story to be heard. The leads were too interesting to turn down, and gradually I realized that the book was shaping my life quite as much as I was making a book. I surrendered to what felt like a deep and fast-moving river of new work with a multiplicity of insights into a fascinating world. My field was English, but I had always loved languages, and I was able to resurrect my French. Gradually, I learned much—for example, by questioning and understanding who among de Man's friends took the same path as he, and who chose different routes. His contacts ranged widely. On the one hand, he was close to Louis Carette/ Félicien Marceau (1913–2012), a propagandist for the Nazi occupant, who was so notorious he had to flee Belgium and go into exile in Paris in 1942—only to become a world-famous writer of French farces— while on the other hand, de Man showed himself a good friend to a Jewish couple whom he briefly sheltered from arrest, and who disappeared at roughly the same time as Carette, but into the maquis and a life as *réfracteurs*, or resisters.

A third area touched on here is the question of how anti-Semitism could be so quickly triumphant in a world whose members, when interviewed, universally declared—always voluntarily and unasked—"I am not anti-Semitic," and "Paul was no anti-Semite." Jan de Man (1912–1994), Paul's cousin, was one such correspondent, who yet wrote a surprising letter to this writer in the last year of his life.[16] This book, *The Double Life of Paul de Man*, was not intended to study the historically enormous subject of anti-Semitism, with its inevitable complexities, but such discussions are unavoidable to some extent, for it became clear that even in the context of the pervasive anti-Semitism of the 1930s, many of de Man's friends *and* relations were entirely or partly Jewish by birth. This fact was also regularly imparted sotto voce, always about someone else, to a writer who had not asked the question.

YET WHAT DE MAN had taught or stood for seemed to be unclear. At Cornell, in fact, we arrived in the 1960s at the center of what had become an intellectual hurricane, but it was very quiet in the eye of it. Ours was a generation trained rigorously in New Criticism, and only "the words on the page" were supposed to matter. We thought that what we professed was important, that the values of our culture, tested and rethought but precious, were embodied in the literature in which we were immersed, and we taught, spoke, and wrote of it obsessively. That literature was uncontaminated by politics or philosophy. The primary demand was to speak truthfully: Good writing grew clear by the disciplined use of language. The essential rule was that one must define one's terms and stick to them. New Criticism had become boring and mechanical, but it purported to achieve logical truth telling. And truth was the highest of values; there was nothing ironic about it. Larry McMurtry wrote that his "deepest conviction" was "the belief, common in the Fifties, that the highest possible aspiration was to somehow connect with literature, and then to live for it, in it, near it." Writing and writers at their best were sacred.[17] Lionel Trilling, who was formed in the politics of the 1920s and '30s, was rare in doubting this when he challenged a graduate student: "You don't really believe that literature has nothing to do with psychology, with biography or society or history?" Cynthia Ozick, to whom that question was addressed, commented later, "I did believe it. I had been trained to believe it."[18]

Suddenly, we arrived at our first teaching posts, only to learn that something called structuralism, very important, might or might not be passing away. We were referred to structural linguistics, an entirely other discipline, and if we inquired further, we were told to study the analysis of a poem ("*Le Chat*") by Roman Jakobson. That commentary, though interesting, was short, even undeveloped, and did not suggest general application. Other names were invoked, especially those of foreign scholars in various fields. Claude Lévi-Strauss and Mircea Eliade were shibboleths, although few Americans had read them yet. As for personal contacts, it seemed to be a game of catch-up, but it had no umpires, no rule book, and no playing field except for the Faculty Club, where the varsity, seated around de Man after lunch, was a team unto itself.[19]

In 1964, de Man was strengthening his position at Cornell while establishing a foothold in Europe, where he also had begun teaching around 1960. Only in the course of this research did I learn that he had tenure at two universities at once, at Cornell and at the University of

Zurich. This was double-dipping, and a primary crime against professional ethics, but the deans of both universities facilitated it while keeping mum.[20] That was one of the most consistent aspects of de Man's
success: the ability to enlist the protection of his superiors as he and
they silently bent or broke the rules that governed others.[21]

I began this study of Paul de Man in the early 1990s, knowing virtually nothing of this intellectual history, but with the aim of understanding simply, as I thought, what had happened to de Man in Belgium, a small country unknown to most Americans, including myself.
I was haunted by the questions suddenly surrounding him. No one I
had known at Cornell had been able or was willing to explain what de
Man was actually teaching. His occasional lectures were impenetrable
but were accepted with a certain degree of bewildered wonder. I went
on to other institutions but followed de Man's career from a remove,
and was stunned, like so many others, by the seemingly unthinkable
news that came out, almost like a bombshell, in 1988. Having finished
another book the following year and doing some tag-end summer
research in France, I planned in 1990 just to run up to Belgium, spend a
short time, and learn what I could briefly, with the aim of writing perhaps a couple of articles. In fact, each step forward produced new and
more tangled mysteries; yet they also were leading into other issues that
were both more interesting and deeply serious. No archive devoted to
de Man existed at that time.[22] In the long run, I traveled to five countries on both sides of the Atlantic—Belgium, France, the United States,
Switzerland, and Canada (the latter two briefly)—and worked with
four languages: French, English, Dutch (which is the written version of
Flemish), and to a small extent German, the last two with the help of
translators. I lived for extended periods in Belgium. Yet when I first
arrived in the capital city of Brussels, I did not know if evidence of the
more bizarre allegations about de Man even existed. There were so few
leads that I had first to imagine the nature of the documents I needed
before I could pursue them, in a language that was uncertain and in
locations I had to conjecture.[23] In addition, because Belgium is a linguistically variegated country, its official records are very complicated.
Research was sometimes impeded by official reticence that sprang from
the profound split in Belgium between the Flemish and Walloon (Fran-

cophone) populations and the anxiety that information would be used for "political" purposes by one group against the other.[24] I took a year off to go to that country (and much more time later), but in the beginning I waited through precious months to gain access to archives, although in due course I received significant help from many Belgian librarians and scholars, to whom I remain very grateful.

Face-to-face meetings were essential, and I conducted interviews in places stretching from Zurich in the east to California in the west, and from a northern city in Nova Scotia to Palm Beach, Florida. The subjects included men who had worked with de Man and, unlike him, had been imprisoned for collaboration. This was a touchy matter. The process was time-consuming, but eventually in the course of conducting close to two hundred interviews (and many more ongoing, informal contacts), I was able to speak with both of de Man's wives, his cousins and other relatives, with all the surviving members of his circle of university friends, and with some of the collaborators who had known him at *Le Soir*, always called during the war *Le Soir (volé)*, or *The Stolen Evening*, a big Brussels daily that had been taken over by the Nazis. In the United States, I contacted his friends and acquaintances among the New York Intellectuals, as they are known, and colleagues from his years at Cornell, Harvard, Bard, Johns Hopkins, and Yale. Many of my subjects, such as the influential professor Harry Levin, de Man's mentor at Harvard, told me that I was the first person they had agreed to speak with in detail because I was willing to travel to meet them and told me that I was going about it the right way.[25] The fact that I intended to ground the book in the context of Belgian society and its history, especially its experiences of World War II, was keenly appreciated. On the other hand, a few others, Americans close to Paul—whom I had not contacted—sent word that I should *not* contact them.

Since I began this biography, a study whose complexity I had not anticipated, much less the inordinate amount of time it would take, excellent work on once-taboo subjects, such as that by Paul Aron, Ortwin de Graef, and other Belgian postwar scholars, have appeared,[26] adding new dimensions to the important studies by earlier scholars.[27]

Eventually, my forays turned up a great deal, including family mementos, like a photograph of Paul's paternal great-grandfather, Jacob

Deman, a butcher in Antwerp. A lot of material thought to be missing or nonexistent, like the transcript of de Man's postwar interrogation by the king's prosecutor, came to light. Most interesting and surprising was the discovery of de Man's plan as a Belgian journalist to create an entirely Nazi journal, one dedicated to promulgating Hitler's ideology, from his views of race to his notions about nutrition—and even his cosmology.[28] Equally troubling was finding—and deciphering—the records of de Man's criminal dealings with the finances of his own postwar publishing company. Perhaps the most unexpected but remarkable results came from following him, as they say, down *both* sides of the street, and recognizing that he occasionally gave assistance to the Resistance, while simultaneously, and stealthily, promoting his own meteoric rise within one of Belgium's biggest collaborating media companies. In the postwar records of the Military Court, de Man's name ran like a red thread as he worked directly with the Nazis, aiming ever higher in his attempt to control the levers of power that corrupted Belgian publishing.

The image I began with, that of Paul de Man as an austere, self-contained, aloof intellectual, proved misleading, to say the least. Instead, there emerged a chameleon who changed colors when prodded, holding his ground when necessary, slipping and turning to escape time and time again, to reemerge triumphantly somewhere else, as something or someone else. His second wife, Pat, moving her hand to simulate a roller coaster, said Paul compared himself to Icarus, except that his own meteoric flights and disastrous falls were trajectories he repeated again and again. These transmogrifications were very curious, but for a considerable period it was difficult even to believe and assimilate the facts.

The work stretched on. Whenever it appeared that I had brought de Man to a juncture in his life from which I could move swiftly toward the book's close, I discovered some new and significant false claim, such as a divorce whose dates showed it hadn't happened, or a questionable graduate record. There was evidence of a ménage à trois, of a luxurious apartment of suspect provenance (was it seized from deported Jews?), of bigamy, blackmail, forgery, and suspicions about how he got into Harvard. Research was like the crossing of a great mountain range: Each time one reached a crest, what at first seemed to be the horizon disappeared and one discovered that further ranges and peaks lay ahead—

and from them, once attained, more ranges and more crests appeared, seemingly without end. I came to understand the spirit in which his father wrote his sister after Paul had secretly left Antwerp to go into exile that the departure had been achieved in his son's accustomed "style of mysteries and contradictions," and that it had all resulted in "the radical exhaustion of my wallet." The exhaustion, which in Bob de Man's case was also physical and not limited to his finances, was probably shared by many who had had to deal intimately with Paul's many metamorphoses.[29]

Yet everywhere Paul went throughout the forty-odd years covered in the present biography, however impoverished, for he was spendthrift with money, he was rich in friends, who did not care about what they did not know. He was somehow impervious to detection or even suspicion. Even in gaining his last position, the Sterling Professorship at Yale, his friends there, among them Geoffrey Hartman, provided the energy for assembling de Man's essays into a book that would suffice to meet the academic rules. He was at the time over fifty years old and had published significant essays, but never a book.[30] In short, as one of his Swiss colleagues and friends remarked later with conscious irony, de Man "was double in every way," with a "completely cynical view of life and the world in general."[31]

At Cornell, an older colleague and friend once advised me to "stay away from the theorists . . . except for Paul de Man. He, I think, is a great man." Were we all wrong? I wondered. And how could we have been so misguided? What was it, particularly in the United States, that had made this man, however personable and intelligent he seemed, so overwhelmingly influential, catnip to many of the most prominent intellectuals in the world? Or was all this unimportant, his behavior separate entirely from what de Man taught, from the doctrines and practices that continue to enlist followers and are held in high regard by some?[32] Certainly, de Man's friends and intellectual heirs—and they still have a voice—would say so and dismiss the idea that a writer's life or indeed the existence of a "subject" are stable enough to be worth attention, or that they have any bearing on what he or she proposes.

———

THE SUBJECT OF DE MAN'S later, academic theories goes beyond the scope of this study. It was not until the 1960s that de Man, by then over forty, began to develop the controversial ideas that would become known as theory and deconstruction, making a turn toward a stance of ironic "undecidability," in which reality is an endless hall of mirrors and writing is a necessarily "perverse" enterprise based on human lies, or the inability of language itself to express truth. I came to realize that deconstruction and theory had proved to be not another crest in my journey across the Rockies, but so distinct an issue, separated by time and space from his early life, as to be another range of mountains. There is a profound connection between the man who secretly fled from Belgium, exiled in 1948 and never publicly to return, and the one we knew for generations later as our intellectual and cultural leader. Drawing out those links is a task I hope others will take up as they see de Man's mature intellectual development in the context of his life and formative experiences.

Yet while I fully acknowledge the influence that de Man's theories had on late twentieth-century academicians and on the cultural gate-keepers who once had been his students, a study that concentrates on the first two-thirds of de Man's life offers something that yet another discussion of his theories—and there are probably thousands of them—cannot do. His early life and ideas were significantly constructed by a unique social context. He interests us now because of his capacity to invent leading roles for himself—"narratives"—and then to play them out against a constantly changing diorama that reflects the historical vicissitudes of a tortured century. The success of his career reflects both the turbulence of the era and our own vulnerabilities. De Man was famous among his students for his little shrug, the gesture with which he dismissed what was too trivial to matter, and for the stance with which he recommended only a handful of books: In an interview of February 2001, a former member of a class recalled him saying that his limited list would give them all that an accomplished student had any need to absorb; that if they had read it, they would count, but if not, they'd be nobodies. It was a doubtful assertion, considered damaging to his students and the profession by several of his colleagues, but such assurance in itself, coming from him, was unquestionably seductive.

Paul de Man's teachings have been fruitful for some in their radical skepticism. They did not, however, spring merely from the abstract philosophical ideas he developed after he passed that chronological milestone of forty. They were deeply rooted in what he had lived through, indeed suffered. De Man's intellectual accomplishments need to be grasped in the context of his early life, and the cast-iron doubts that formed his many defenses. The great men of Paul de Man's generation have now slipped away, sinking beneath the horizon along with his favorite ocean liner, the *Normandie*, the three-martini lunch, and, perhaps, much of our trustfulness concerning assertions of "greatness." Before he and his world disappear from sight, it is important to look with a steady gaze if we are to understand what he stood for, what was delusive, and what remains as teachable and powerful in this iconic figure.

PART ONE

BELGIUM

1.

THE BUTCHER'S BOY

A S AN ADULT, PAUL DE MAN HAD A HABIT OF STARING AT HIMSELF FOR long periods in the mirror. Apparently, he had done this throughout his life, and so often that his second wife, Pat, once made a joke of it, ordered a mirror from a Wheaties box, and gave it to him: he used it. He once called himself, she said, "the butcher's boy."[1] His remark was almost literally true, for both his grandfather and great-grandfather had been butchers, and the family fortune was built on their trade. Patricia loved to hear her husband's stories of his early life, for they seemed to her "all sunshine." That was hardly the case. While he had indeed had many triumphs, deep anxiety and misfortune surrounded his family from his earliest years.

Paul's origins went deep into Flemish soil. Named after his two grandfathers and christened Paul Adolph Michel Deman—his surname means simply "the man" in Flemish—he came from a family not long removed from its roots in the artisanal and working classes of nineteenth-century Belgium. His paternal great-grandfather, Jacobus Philippus Deman (1816–1866), called Jacob, was a Freemason, a tough man famous in family lore for having beaten up a priest when the cleric forbade his wife to eat meat during Lent. Jacob's son, Adolphus Léo (1859–1936), known as Adolph, was even more brutal, so abusive that he beat his son Bob beyond bearing and tried without success to break his son Hendrik (1885–1953) in the same way. Adolph got his start by delivering meat to the family's customers, working at first on the docks of Antwerp, then a great port city, and later rising to become head of the provisioning department of the Red Star Line, a company that specialized in shipping poor emigrants to the New World.[2]

By the time Paul was born, on December 6, 1919, just a year after the armistice, the Demans were prominent among the new bourgeoisie in Antwerp, many of whom had grown rich on the rising tide of nineteenth-century industrialization. The family culture by then was shaped by two major forces. On the domestic side, it was governed by four aunts who stuck together, married well, and kept their many children close. These were the Van Beers sisters, daughters of the Flemish "national poet," Jan Van Beers (1821–1888). Noticeable on the other side was the growing influence of Paul's uncle Hendrik Deman, soon known as Henri (or "Rik") de Man, who survived Adolph's attacks, challenged his father, and became a brilliant, but ungovernable, world-famous socialist politician who envisioned and wrote about a new world so vividly that for generations he carried all before him.

Henri's younger brother and Paul's father was Bob de Man (1890–1959). A gentle, artistic man, he was Adolph's special victim. The older brother boasted that although Adolph's violence had been more terrible to him than to his brother, it had not broken him, but made him stronger, and helped him become a success. But Bob, he said, had been too weak to withstand the abuse. This claim reflected the ideology Henri de Man was serving when he wrote a memoir in 1941, years after he became a spokesperson for what is not called "appeasement" in Belgium. Although he began as a socialist, by the end of that anguished decade he had shifted to fascism, and his party, which celebrated violence, saw the contemporary world as degenerate and soft: purification and power could come only through the purgation brought about by the renewal of the warrior spirit and dedication to change by violent means.[3]

All the Van Beers women were strongly Flemish in orientation. The close bond formed by these sisters was important, for they lived near each other in Antwerp and shared the duties of rearing their many children, managing the extended family as a unit, so that more than a dozen cousins grew up together essentially as a clan, running in and out of one another's houses, going to one aunt's home for meals and then to another's for baths, and protecting each other against the world.

The de Man family created its own myths, some truthful, others embellished, as is true in so many families, but these stories spoke of family pride and cohesiveness at the core. When Josepha, the third sister, married Adolph and became a Deman, that sense of importance became more marked in their branch of the family: As one of the cousins remarked to his son, "The Demans have strong personalities—and are aware of it. The only good people in the world are Demans."[4] These children were also encouraged to see themselves as dominant.[5]

The criticism of Deman self-importance came from Jan De Braey, Paul's uncle and brother to Madeleine, Paul's mother. Their father, Michel De Braey, had been a cultivated man, by profession an architect. On the Deman side, the fact of their shared Van Beers heritage—the artistic side—was as important as the Deman family's wealth and Henri's political prestige. Paul de Man told Pat that it was a happy world, stressing that the Demans spent their leisure time in a charming, remote northern village near the Netherlands. Called Kalmthout, it was situated in a Brueghelian landscape discovered and colonized by nineteenth-century artists, surrounded by rich farmland, and peopled by family and friends from the well-to-do set of Antwerp. Paul's mother was beautiful, if sad, and her father was a talented architect.

There was indeed a lot of sunshine in that upper-middle-class world. Nevertheless, Paul omitted a great deal from his stories. Shaped by the bourgeois, upwardly mobile mercantile world of Belgium in the late nineteenth and early twentieth centuries, he was the product of a deeply divided, if striving, country. Belgium was, in fact, overrun by Germany in both the world wars, only twenty-five years apart, and it has always been squeezed economically and geographically by its much larger, more powerful neighbors: The Netherlands lies to the north, France to the south, and Germany to the east. Even its coastline, still marked by an old-world tranquillity, is short, less than forty miles.[6]

For the non-European reader, it is important to realize that as a European nation, Belgium is new, for it was cobbled together in 1830 by the Great Powers, several decades after the end of the Napoleonic Wars, as a buffer state made up of numerous small principalities. Their individual histories went back to the medieval era, and to this day the major cities retain a deep sense of individuality. A woman who lives in Namur will identify with that city and be proud of and fascinated by its history, which goes back to the eighth century and the reign of Charlemagne, but while she may work in and commute every day to Brussels, she will say that beyond working there, she has essentially nothing to do with the capital city. With no animus toward the idea of country per se, she is a Namuroise. Against this particularized sense of identity, Belgium developed into a land that is existentially divided, both linguistically and culturally. Some of the new Belgians (called Walloons, although even this is a disputed term) living largely in the south of the country had been French in orientation, while others were Flemish-speaking. To complicate the situation, Flemish is a spoken language with almost as many dialects as there are towns; Dutch, however, is the written language. (There are actually three official languages, for after World War I, Belgium annexed a small area of Germany, and German was added to the list.)

De Man's own life, like that of his family, was marked by these linguistic disputes. During the nineteenth century, under the thumb of landowning powers and the Church, Flanders, primarily agricultural, kept its populace undereducated and close to the land as peasants; in an unwritten agreement, the French-speaking southern peoples dominated, and their governments ruled from Brussels. Among these linguistically divided peoples (many of whom believed there were "racial" differences as well), there was ongoing ill will, for the law of the land—of courts and even the army—was French. If a Fleming wanted to get ahead, he had to learn French, but the Francophones did not return the compliment. Paul de Man's family became one of those rich Flemish clans that assimilated and spoke French "even in the home," a custom that later scandalized young historians. A Fleming could be judged in court and yet be unable to speak even to his own lawyer. Low-ranking Flemish soldiers in World War I were commanded by officers who could not even speak to them directly because they possessed only French.[7] In earlier centuries, Flanders had been Europe's center of riches, art, and culture, but those days were long past.[8]

Paul's surname epitomizes this history of social conflict. It changed as the family fortunes rose. Jacob, the butcher of Antwerp, went by the name of Deman, as did Adolph, Paul's grandfather. Yet the business run by Paul's father, begun in 1920 and financed by Adolph and his circle, used the French cognomen, Etablissements de Man, and Bob signed the contract as Robert de Man.[9] And when a decade later Hendrik Deman, Bob's older brother, became a prominent politician, he renamed himself Henri de Man and published his memoir, *Après Coup*, in 1941 under his new name.[10] In Brussels, this de Man had entered the French-speaking world of the court. He was thought to be the lover of Queen Elisabeth of Belgium and known to be the close adviser of her son, King Léopold III. The change of surname reflected his higher social status.[11] With that social promotion, the Flemish particle "De" was simply changed into the genitive or French "de," denoting noble ancestry, and the name that had once suggested "the people" now implied aristocratic descent. Bob de Man, Paul's father, followed his older brother in this, as in other matters. (Paul de Man, it should be noted, always pronounced the name Man as the Flemish do, which uses a flat syllable similar to the English word *man*.)

Within that thin layer of upper-middle-class society, those who were ethnically Flemish but used French as their common tongue, the de Mans grew prominent. They lived between these two worlds, while the larger country profited greatly from its ownership of the Congo.[12] The Francophone part of Belgium controlled the coal and steel industries and produced industrial goods until the mines were exhausted in the early twentieth century. In the heyday of its industrial power, however, when Belgian engineers traveled worldwide installing railroads and other infrastructure in less developed lands, its engineers enjoyed higher status than physicists. Paul's father, Bob de Man, was an engineer who manufactured X-ray tables, and Paul seemed destined for the same career.

Antwerp, where Paul was born, was a major port on the North Sea, situated only a few miles from Holland and not far from Germany. This part of Belgium considered itself Germanic rather than French in culture, and valued a Flemish ideal of strong family ties, close and supportive relationships with the serving or working classes, and cheer-ful, industrious self-respect. This, at any rate, was the social vision that Paul's uncle Henri de Man promoted vividly in his wartime memoir. An important theorist of socialism and a charismatic professor before he entered what eventually became a disastrous political career, he was a master of narrative and persuasion. The Antwerpen world he depicted of Flemish virtues rooted in folk culture is warm and invit-ing. But it is also mythopoeic: His aim was to glorify and justify him-self to the German occupant, and the best way to do this was to construct the de Man-Van Beers family as embodying the folk—indeed to some extent the *völkisch*—qualities then prized by the "Ger-manic ideology."[13]

There was another side to the family story, however, which Henri omitted but which research has revealed. In that world, still governed by Victorian mores, hypocrisy might be essential when families had pulled themselves into the upper classes by hard work and perhaps hard deeds. Respectability slammed shut its doors on family secrets like rape and suicide, while artistic yearnings among family members were sub-sidized by profits derived from rough-edged trades, like butchery, metal fabrication, and the transport of emigrants.

Henri's memoir contains many distortions and even lies written to serve the German occupant. Cross-checked with other sources, how-ever, it provides useful information about the family culture. Henri de Man chose to stress the warlike and dominant traits of the de Man side of his heritage, but he omitted the fact that Jacob—whom he described riding to hounds over family property—was a Freemason.[14] That orga-nization, which provided an upward social path and organized itself in secret cells, was anathema to both the Catholic Church and the Nazis, who persecuted it slightly less than the Jews and Gypsies.[15]

Paul's grandfather Adolph, also a Freemason, belonged to the Lib-eral party, the party of big business. He became the head of the provi-sioning department of the Red Star Line, but he was neither a director nor a politician. (It was Michel De Braey, Paul's maternal grandfather, who was an alderman.) By the time Adolph retired in 1924, he was a wealthy man. The family liked to stress that he also specialized in a more luxurious product, as he was the company's purchaser of cigars.

Adolph was rigid and punitive: One of his grandsons recalled him as "very strict, very law-abiding. As children, if we had a knife he'd say, 'Ah, it's not authorized and you go in prison.'"[16] The lack of mercy Adolph showed to his children extended to his workers. Henri, who rebelled against him when still young, first showed his socialist politics when the workers on the waterfront staged a strike against his father, and he went out among them on the dock, took their side, and harangued their bosses. One of Adolph's brothers, Felix, was shut up in an institution.[17] Given the problems of emotional instability that would dominate the family, that was an ominous fact.

Henri's memoir included Bob's story, and related how the family of Van Beers sisters and their husbands, in order to save the boy from his father's attacks, had removed him from his home and "loaned" him to one of them, his aunt Ida Kemna-Van Beers (1852–1925). This spared the boy at least his health, but he grew up rejecting combativeness and identified with the poets and artists on his mother's side of the family. He loved music, played the violin, and kept a classical record library at home. He was unassertive. His niece Elise, Henri's daughter, always known as "Li," described Bob as "soft . . . a weak character—too good, too soft. Amiable. Just the opposite of my father."[18]

Henri wrote that the "loan" to Ida of this child was meant to replace Ida's real son, who had died "in an accident." In fact, that removal was one of the secrets on which Henri's memoir founded the family myth. For the son of Ida and Adolph Kemna did not die by happenstance. Born on April 23, 1877, in Antwerp, the Kemnas' son, named Adolph after his father, was what is now called a "challenged youth," and the young man was institutionalized from the age of twenty-three. Beginning in 1900, he was sent to live with the Alexian Brothers in the city of Mechelen in an asylum they maintained for men who, though not insane, were incompetent to live in society. He died there nine years later. Two monks from the Godhuis de Cellebroeders on Nokersstraat, reported his death in 1909.[19] No hint of these facts appeared in Henri's text. Only the Antwerp census of 1900 recorded Adolph's existence, for it shows the young Adolph as living at home in that year, while the records of the Cloister of the Cell Brothers in Mechelen inscribed his death on June 11, 1909.[20]

This pattern of concealment is important, for discovering the facts and becoming "knowing" would be central to Paul's behavior all his life. Indeed, Paul did know this family secret, for he told his first wife, Anne, that this cousin of his father had been "a Mongolian." This was the term formerly used for what is now known as Down syndrome.[21] Henri and Bob de Man (and their parents) judged this illness too shameful to be admitted. In 1941, Henri falsified the reality of Adolph's life and death. Handicapped persons were being exterminated by the Nazis, and, as with the family's Freemasonry, Henri avoided trouble through prevarication. The young Paul, who very much loved and admired his uncle, was being given a double message: To survive, one must find out what is being hidden, but to prosper, one must lie and conceal.

Another, more horrifying family story was one that Henri simply erased. This was the tragic life and death of young Adolph's sister, Ida Kemna (1878–1897), who at nineteen committed suicide by hanging herself. She was never mentioned, and Henri pretended she never existed, but Paul knew, and he told his first wife she was "a very bright girl. One afternoon the governess or maid said her uniform was dirty, and the girl went into another room and killed herself by hanging."[22] Only the Antwerp census records her brief life.[23]

It thus goes without saying that this was not a happy family. However, among the group of cousins who played in that inward and shadowed household, there were two, Bob Deman and Madeleine De Braey (1893–1937), who would marry and become Paul's parents. Just three years younger than Bob, Madeleine, nicknamed "Talenteke," was quiet, shy, gentle, blond, and very pretty.[24] The daughter of a successful architect, she was also intelligent and likable—that is, except for her moods.[25] A studio photograph taken at the seaside resort of Ostend in 1902 shows some of the cousins when Bob was twelve. They are dressed as if for the beach, wear miniature sailor's caps, striped and tasseled, and are posed in a studio stage set surrounded by fishnets, pails, and shovels. The others look stiff, but only Yvonne, the third child of Josepha and Adolph, is smiling, as if only she could obediently look agreeable under such peculiar circumstances.[26] The setting speaks volumes, for the Demans later looked down on Simone, Madeleine's sister-in-law, for her family sold fish; Paul told Patricia they called her a "mussel wife." Perhaps

transmuting their own working-class origins into picture-postcard tab-
leaux was one way the second generation solidified their status.

Equally shy, Bob and Madeleine grew close. By the time they were
young adults, they became engaged, and over the strong objections of
their families they wed when he was twenty-four and she twenty-one.
No one approved of the marriage of first cousins, although it was legal,
but in this case the older generation felt they had reason to be anxious.
The existence of the "perfectly harmless" but institutionalized Felix
Deman, brother of the Red Star manager, may have added to their con-
cerns, for with Ida Kemna's short life in the back of their minds, it
showed there was mental instability on both sides of the family. Madeleine would, in fact, have known her older cousin during the first years
of her life and certainly knew of her suicide. The elders must have
looked with foreboding at the young bride-to-be, clearly delicate in her
emotional makeup but determined to marry a first cousin who carried
so many of the same genes. One relative remembered hearing that the
family was "absolutely against" the marriage, "because they were first
cousins and they were afraid about the children." But when they consulted doctors, they were told there was no legal ban.[27] The couple prevailed, and they married in June 1914, the same month that Archduke
Franz Ferdinand was assassinated, an attack that precipitated the outbreak of World War I just one month later. The rising socialist Henri
was then working as a journalist and living in Germany, a country he
said he "loved" deeply, but when Kaiser Wilhelm attacked his home, he
returned to Belgium at once and donned its uniform to fight the adopted
land in which he had flourished. The gentle, "musical" Bob, on the
other hand, joined the National Guard and stayed in Antwerp. Belgium
took the brunt of the German attacks during the next four years, and its
land became a battleground engulfed in blood. Men died by the hundreds of thousands in single battles, and whole cities were destroyed.
The glorious medieval city of Ypres (later rebuilt house by house like a
kind of Belgian Williamsburg) was leveled to smoking black stumps of
bricks and rubble.

The country was subject to heavy aerial attacks, and these took a
toll on Madeleine's health. She had become pregnant immediately
after her marriage, and she was sent to England to be out of harm's

way, with her brother's wife, Simone,[28] to take care of her. In fact, both young women were pregnant, but Madeleine suffered emotionally from the heavy bombardments. Times were hard: A photograph taken at the time shows Simone in a utility room, using a scrub board to do the laundry; her arms are covered with suds to the elbow, and she is looking out the window as if waiting—perhaps for the photographer to finish, perhaps for her ordeal to be over. Since their families usually employed servants for such labor, the pose carried the message of pluckiness in hard times.[29]

Madeleine returned to Antwerp for the birth of her first child, but the birth took place during continuous bombing. She was never the same after that ordeal. It was, said her niece Li, a "terrible shock" from which she never recovered. "The shock was more the bombing than the birth. The shock of bombing and war can be something terrible." Li reported that she had "heard more than once from [her] grandparents [and] family that she'd been affected." Paul's first wife understood that Madeleine "had a very bad pregnancy and . . . a big fever . . ." after which "she changed completely" and the relations between the couple changed also.[30]

Paul's older brother, Hendrik, was born March 3, 1915, eight months and three weeks to the day after his parents married.[31] Named after his uncle and nicknamed "Rik," he would always be his mother's favorite, but he learned slowly and lagged behind his age-mates. Her family blamed the trauma of the war. Within the next five years, the young woman bore two more children. One was a girl who was stillborn.[32] That loss, it seems, was the greatest blow of all. Soon afterward, however, came Paul Adolph Michel Deman, born December 6, 1919, her third and last child.

TO OUTSIDERS, THE ATMOSPHERE in the home of Bob and Madeleine appeared serene and calm.[33] But for Madeleine, the loss of her second child, a much-hoped-for daughter, was more than she could bear. Shortly afterward, she had a breakdown and attempted suicide. It was the first of several attempts. It was also, it appears, exactly what her family had feared. For the next twenty years of Madeleine's life, her husband (at least initially), her parents, her brother, his wife, and even her nieces—and finally Paul—were enlisted in watching closely over her as she suffered through a condition they would not have called clinical depression but whose etiology and dangers were well known as melancholia. Although Paul was always far brighter and more successful than his older brother and loved his mother dearly, he never felt, according to Patricia de Man, that he had her full attachment.

A young niece was sent to "cheer up" Madeleine, but Paul's mother grew increasingly depressed. Madeleine understood the reasons for these visits, and Paul came to realize that she felt suffocated by always being under surveillance.[34] This niece, Micheline De Braey (b. 1921), known as Minime, would find her sitting alone, apathetic, withdrawn, and tired. Sometimes her aunt would cry uncontrollably. At first, the crying spells happened once or twice a year; then they began to occur every three or four months. Later, they came more often, perhaps every month, and nothing could lift them. The intimacy between the aunt and the niece who loved and observed her extended from around 1925 until Madeleine's death in 1937. Of course, she had little of herself to spare for her younger son. The man who obsessively needed to seek himself, Narcissus-like, in a mirror all his adult life was certainly preceded by the infant and boy who had lacked the close and loving attention of his first caregiver. One need not be a Lacanian to perceive that Madeleine's condition was wounding to Paul as he struggled to gain an identity through experiencing the presence, or what Lacan named the "gaze," of the Other, to whom he should have meant so much. De Man would grow into a talented man, but the "mirror stage" described by Lacan was clearly a halting place for him as a child. In psychoanalytic terms, there can be little doubt that profound damage to his sense of self would underlie much of his subsequent development. And one may venture to guess that what was unstable in himself, which he called the abyss, or *abîme*, would become the instability of language. The unfulfilled hunger of narcissism that Lacan associates with damage at this early stage of development would paralyze de Man in many ways, and it would mark him, both with the effortless and indifferent charm typical of this sort of personality and with self-centeredness and a private sense of lack, a damaging emptiness that he would try disastrously to fill by money and acquisitions.[35]

Decades later and continents apart, two men who knew Paul de Man well at different times of his life used almost the same word to sum up his most striking characteristic. "Knowingness" was how M. H. Abrams described the special quality of his protégé.[36] He was "knowing," agreed his cousin Bob De Braey. This was evident in Paul de Man's look as a grown man and it was part of his attraction: a penetrating, quick, and amusedly complicit glance that said without words that he knew and shared one's own perceptions. He sent that message even in the beginning; it was evident in Paul's childhood and was read by his cousins and by the ordinary Belgian boys around him. It was the only defense of a sensitive, perceptive child who needed to understand the silent conflicts that shaped his world.

2.

KALMTHOUT:
THE RULES OF
THE GAME

EXPLAINING BELGIUM TO HIS AMERICAN WIFE, PAUL DE MAN WOULD say "the church was in the middle of the village," a French expression evoking the sense of bourgeois order he loved, which was provided by a central authority that kept its doors open to all quarters of the town. Constructing order, authority, and traditions—even if they concealed disorder—was important to the newly arrived family, which not only remembered its games from one generation to the next but photographed its children playing them. Around 1900, Paul's father, Bob de Man, and his first cousin Jan De Braey were photographed as little boys: faded brown images of creatures wearing big hats and playing Boer War, with the English as the enemy. Seventy years later, Paul's younger cousin Bob De Braey (1922–) looked at an old photograph of himself and Paul playing as children. Paul was wearing a hat. "He always liked to take my hat from me," Bob recalled.[1] The remark was made without animus; Paul and the doors he had opened for Bob De Braey had great meaning.

Little Bob adored the older boy and followed him around. He, his older sister, Minime, and Paul were all grandchildren of the architect Michel De Braey and belonged to the branch "who had wit and style."[2] Playing together was encouraged; it was "normal," and *c'est normal* has a strong, positive meaning in Belgium. In a country less than a hundred years old, always angrily divided by religious, linguistic, and political issues, stability was highly valued.

The Demans were less cultivated than the De Braeys, but richer, and once they had arrived among the bourgeoisie, they gripped tightly to conventions and to one another. Bob de Man and Jan De Braey had been born within two days of each other in 1890. They went to the same university (Ghent), majored in the same subject (engineering), lived in the same district of Antwerp, and passed their holidays together in Kalmthout, a village where Bob's father, Adolph Deman, was to spend his retirement years. It was natural that Michel De Braey, Paul's maternal grandfather and Jan's father, should design Adolph's gracious country house, a handsome dwelling, and normal that Michel himself should retire in the same town.[3] In the summers, the de Man family lived together in their impressive home, which is set well back from the road with an imposing facade, but is actually smaller than it appears, with two comfortable reception rooms below but only three bedrooms on the second floor. Until 1930, Bob's parents, Adolph and Josepha, had live-in servants, a gardener and a maid. In Antwerp, Jan and Simone De Braey and Bob and Madeleine Deman went together to football matches; in the country, they belonged to the same tennis club and attended the same parties. Origins and class, however, were not forgotten. Paul's later competitiveness was part of his family's culture. Michel De Braey might be an architect, but his son Jan married Simone, who came from a different background. Perhaps it was from his mother, Madeleine, that Paul learned to dismiss his too-helpful aunt as a "mussel wife"—an attitude based, Patricia said later, on the fact that Simone's family had "made their money in the fish business."[4]

Young Paul was successful in everything he tried, for he was tall and athletic, eager and effective in competitions. Always the leader, he was smart, talented, good-looking, and, above all, amusing to be with. (His competitiveness was "killer," as his friends and second wife attested. Patricia reported that once he'd learned to play baseball in the United States, the first time he had run to first base, he hit her in the stomach and knocked her down—and she was pregnant.)[5] Yet although

Paul's stories of his youth were "all sunny" and his second wife said she "love[d] to bask in the sunshine of his childhood," he also told her that his upbringing was "rough." His father did not beat him, but he was harsh. When Paul later became a father himself, he employed "sarcasm" in dealing with his own children. " 'This,' he told his family, 'is how I was made strong.' Sarcasm brought you up, not tenderness."[6]

In summers, the family visited the seashore at Ostend, but most of their leisure time was spent in Kalmthout, where the many children played tennis and football (soccer to Americans), sports where Bob De Braey's hero worship of Paul was shared by Minime and another cousin, Li (Elise, Henri de Man's daughter). Paul did not always win, of course, and he told one story about his mother that indirectly illustrated that treats from her were rare. "He related it with both humor and feeling," recalled his widow. "He saw himself as an outstanding soccer player. [Once when] he had told everyone he would be [the] champion, even he could see he'd done badly. . . . Having lost a game, he was taken by his mother as a special treat for an ice-cream soda."[7]

There were not many such comforting moments. The effect of these on Paul, though important, was probably inaccessible to him, but he was certainly aware of the differences between his mother and other mothers.

Minime remembered that as a boy of eight not only was he already the arbiter of their own gang but that the grown-ups also made him the umpire for their tennis games. "He was already grown-up for a child. I can remember him being eight . . . sitting on the tennis court when the parents were playing, writing down all about the game, about every-body doing it. What he thought about the service of one. What he thought about the vocabulary of the people."[8] It is a charming picture of a precocious child, seizing language and teaching himself new words, something he would do all his life.

To young Bob De Braey's innocent eye, Paul's parents were happy, and his admiration of Paul extended to his uncle and aunt, a couple who seemed to create an ideal world, more peaceful, cultivated, and musical than any he had known. "For me," he said, "it was like going to heaven when we made a visit to Pijnenberg [the house in Kalm-thout]." There, family life was tranquil. No one ever shouted. There were no quarrels—it simply wasn't done. Little Bob especially loved Madeleine because she was so gentle. They "always talked about music, literature, art. My father never talked about music. It's in that family that I learned to appreciate classic music."[9]

The best part of those visits, however, was playing the games Paul invented with full scenarios and thrilling intrigues. In describing their relationship, De Braey put his finger on one of the qualities Paul had all his life and that was to be central to his success as a critic and teacher: "I appreciated the way he made me appreciate life." It was Paul who taught him how to hear music, playing *Boléro* and *Prince Igor* on the phonograph, and explained "what was happening behind the music. . . . He was the one who made things interesting."

Seeing Paul at his games gives the key to some of the more puzzling aspects of his development. Most enchanting to others was his performance as a storyteller, a weaver of fascinating mysteries. He especially liked reenacting parts of *The Three Musketeers*, and he directed their play of this story for years and so intensely that half a century later Bob remembered their hours with a kind of muscle memory, waggling and beckoning with his fingers as he reproduced Paul's impression of Milady and her mystery. "When Milady appeared," Bob remembered, "that was something special. She was very dangerous, but more because she was a spy than because she was a woman."

The plot of the novel turns on more than the famously close friendship of a band of young soldiers, united in their service to their king in the era when France was threatened by the English. Its major themes are adultery, betrayal, spying, and murder, and the leading villain is Milady, a cold and beautiful blond spy employed by Cardinal Richelieu. Branded before the novel opens as a thief, she has deserted her first husband to dwell bigamously with her second, and probably has murdered her third, an Englishman. (Oddly enough, Paul himself was to repeat two of her crimes.) Glamorous and daring but motivated by hidden rage, revenge, and greed, she slips on nefarious missions between France and London, stabbing and poisoning her enemies, men and women alike. Her strength lies in her beauty and unparalleled powers of seduction.

The novel was important to Paul because it enabled the young boy by role-playing to try to work out an understanding of the world in which he found himself. He enjoyed playing D'Artagnan, but when he took the part of Milady he could at once identify with a cold and distant mother whom he loved "too much" but could not reach, and also defend her by becoming her, but a stronger, more aggressive, even murderous version, able to revenge herself. Was the knife she wielded in his fantasy turned against not the band of soldiers but against the man whom the child perceived as Madeleine's real enemy, her unfaithful, often absent husband? The game solved nothing, but like guided therapy today, its fluidity let young Paul represent what he could not consciously penetrate. By bending his energies, Paul could enact in Milady's mystery his own bewilderment and anger.

Sex, however, was under some kind of ban. Bob De Braey was aware that he himself was in fact "more interested in girls than [Paul] was," although his cousin was older. His memories stretched from about 1926 to 1936, when Paul would have been between six and sixteen and Bob four to fourteen. According to Bob, "Paul was never interested in girls. I was surprised when they told me he was married. I never had any experience of my cousin going with a girl or having any interest in them except in literature."[10]

Paul's indifference to sex was an anomaly that a friend from his high school years would also bring up as a puzzle. Bob did not think his cousin was homosexual. He was in no position, however, to have insight into the complexities of Paul's developing sexuality and what was, in fact—and for good reason—an extended period of latency. Certainly Bob did not understand the fear and anguish his cousin felt on behalf of his mother or his close identification with her suffering. Bob did not recognize the anxieties and sense of loss or absence of self that his older cousin expressed so vividly in his lifelong habit of mirror gazing, but one of his earliest memories of Paul is how in the elevator of his house there was a mirror, and when they rode up and down in it together, Paul would stare and make faces at himself.

As time went on in the 1930s, it became generally known that Bob de Man had become habitually unfaithful, that he was away at night most of the time, and that Madeleine was hurt by this, which would have added to her underlying depression. How did Paul reconcile this reality with the apparent peace of their household? Perhaps in his games the young boy was tentatively and unconsciously trying to reach out toward the immaterial limits that surrounded him, to touch the glass walls of self that were beginning to hem him in. He had a part to play, but he could ask no questions. Self-control was everything. He was obedient, or tried to be. When he had an appendectomy at age eight, the doctor commented to Paul's mother, "He's a nervous type, but controls himself."[11] Yet the uncertainties were excruciating. Why was there a mother who could not protect him but whom he wanted to defend? What was going on between his parents, who preserved an appearance of such serenity but secretly were so unhappy? Who was his father, so accessible to others but closed to his wife, who was equally closed off, and tender perhaps only to young Rik, if even to him? What should be his own developing role in this family and in the world?

The main game that Paul invented at Kalmthout was organizing his tribe to spy on the adults, a practice the band of children did by night as well as by day. Little Bob was an eager member. The environs were lovely in summer, for the lawns of the village were set close beside fields of golden grain that rolled richly away. The Brueghelian countryside was cultivated by peasants indifferent to the behavior of the wealthy businessmen who came in the summer to relax and enjoy their own version of a way of life caught later by Ingmar Bergman in his *Smiles of a Summer Night*. They were manufacturers like Bob de Man, brokers, wool merchants, politicians like Henri de Man, and others from the upper-middle class of Antwerp society who had probably followed the set of artists who had discovered and painted the village at the end of the preceding century.

Kalmthout was a place where these people could play tennis, give parties, flirt, and have affairs with one another's wives and husbands without being called to account by Antwerp society, perhaps because it was not only a geographical site but a state of mind, valuable precisely because there they could play more colorful and agreeable roles. Adolph Deman had helped to build Kalmthout, but the village developed a tone and way of life quite different from his pre–World War I world. In that class and time, freedom and sexual liberty, if pursued with regard for appearances, were the rules of the game. Sexual behavior was free, "adans un sens positif," as one of them, Marlene de Man-Flechtheim, emphasized, for she was a psychologist and shared the enlightened thought of her time and place. Freedom was the theme, and it was understood that they were entitled to claim it because they saw themselves as being not so much bourgeois as unconventional, "bohemian" and "artistic." Sexuality and *jouissance* (sexual pleasure) were good things among the advanced thinkers of this class and generation. Adolph's three adult children, Bob, Henri, and Yvonne, all perceived themselves in this way.[12]

The fields, riverbanks, and promenades were open to the prying eyes of Paul's little gang, and the children studied and decoded the intrigues of this sexually charged atmosphere assiduously. In young Bob's detailed memories, one hears the hours of patient observation that he, tutored by Paul, spent learning the rules of this particular game. There were "erotically beautiful" women, there were their affairs, and especially the all-night parties, which ended with a "promenade" outdoors by the river. "Some might think something happened," he remarked euphemistically, because the participants were "always happy and large [free]. Paul noticed, too," and he talked to his younger cousin about it. Paul's father was active in these games. He liked to give parties, and, as Bob De Braey recalled, there was "always a very funny party. Bob de Man was always very gallant to all the women. [One of these was] . . . really sexy. She could . . . maybe have been in a very good relationship with my uncle Bob. I remember that when Madeleine died, she paid a visit to him that was very compassionate. Before he died, she paid him visits, as well."[13] Bob De Braey knew that the woman's visits were not innocent, and later he was more direct in discussing the love affairs of Paul's father.

Young Bob's curiosity about the grown-ups' behavior seems to have arisen simply from a child's need to learn about sex and from the enjoyment of following his leader, Paul. It was the older boy who initiated the games of spying, but his motives were different and more complicated. To Paul, finding out what was going on was crucial for other reasons, not merely because the activity was amusing or titillating. Bob remembered that his cousin had criticized all the people engaged in the ongoing sexual play. One thing that the advanced thinkers of the era probably did not anticipate is that at least one of these children, Paul, would, after he reached the United States, turn out to be far more puritanical than they. There is abundant evidence that he blamed his father for his attentions to other women.

Paul expressed his dislike of that liberated atmosphere and of his father's behavior pointedly and clearly. Throughout the era in Antwerp and Kalmthout, Bob de Man played chamber music in a small group, and over a period of years one of the women in this group was his mistress (and he had more than one).[14] This "especially sexy" woman would appear at the family home on Wednesdays with her violin to play duets with Paul's father. Her presence was covered by its musical excuse, but Paul felt it was an invasion. When those visits occurred—and they began long before his mother's death—Paul would leave the house and refuse to return, not reentering his home until the other woman was gone.[15]

Anger at his father and unspoken sympathy for his mother's humiliation ran deep. Undoubtedly, this long exposure to her pain and his identification with her would later underlie the estrangement between himself and his father. Paul's confusion and ambivalence about sex was evident in the way he changed his social practices from one decade to the next. In the 1940s, during the war, he became much freer in his attitude, but later, when living in the United States in the 1950s, trying to shuck off his past, although he would have many friends, he kept his home life rigidly private, telling Pat that he "did not want [her] even to dance in public."[16] Even during the war, however, he was ambivalent about sexual freedom; while enjoying it himself, he nevertheless told Anne Ipsen, his first wife, of his distaste for the behavior that went on when he was a child, which she paraphrased with equal distaste, saying disdainfully that at Kalmthout, "each . . . . husband was with the wife of the [other]."[17]

Eventually, Madeleine replied in kind to Bob's behavior. More than one person remembered hearing that at some point she, depressed as she was, had also taken a lover, a Spanish diplomat. That affair may have been short-lived. By the late 1930s, it was common knowledge that Bob and Madeleine de Man were unhappy together. Even Frida Vandervelden, who later became a close friend of Paul at the university in Brussels, had heard this, although not from Paul himself.[18]

In a turn of the wheel worthy of Schnitzler, Bob de Man's partner in love and music did ultimately divorce her husband, but only to marry another man; at which point, Bob became the lover of the wife abandoned by his rival for the "especially sexy" violinist. The amusement with which this game of sexual-musical chairs was recalled over fifty years later suggests that even in Kalmthout, this had been a well-noted scandal, perceived virtually as a stage comedy. But Madeleine had stood on one side, withdrawn and mute, while the quartet played on. Paul, who saw it all, shared both her feelings and her silence.

Until the war brought Bob new German customers under the occupation in 1940, his business was not exceptional. He was a likable man but not a dynamic businessman. Trained as an engineer, when he was thirty, not long after Paul's birth, he was set up by his father, Adolph, not as the owner but as the chief employee and director of his Etablissements de Man. The terms of his contract were very unfavorable, but he had the satisfaction of running a business that bore his name and drew on his training.[19] He made a niche for his company by manufacturing X-ray tables. Still, the small company gave Bob the free time he liked to devote to other interests.[20]

Minime De Braey, Bob's sister, was a favorite with both Paul and his father. A tomboy, always very attractive to men, she grew up to be beautiful. After the onset of World War II, the De Braey and de Man branches of the family separated politically, and she undertook daring rescue missions for the Resistance. Yet she never lost her love of her fascinating relative, whom she later defended against criticism, collaborator though he was. Once when Paul was given a bike and she was not, she had poked holes in his tires out of sheer jealousy. He didn't care: He was forbearing—and he knew that he'd get new tires. His reaction illustrates one aspect of Paul that helped draw people to him throughout his life: He was easygoing, understanding of others' impulses, and not judgmental. But he resented his father, as she saw very clearly one day when, her own bike needing paint, she got Paul to go with her to his father's factory to get it painted white, like Bob de Man's X-ray tables. When they came upon her uncle, however, he was in the midst of an altercation with his employees, manual laborers, and Bob was getting the worst of it. He could not manage his men. Minime remembered how disgusted Paul was by the scene, contemptuous of his father's lack of authority.

THE DE MAN FAMILY had other serious and concealed troubles. For almost a decade, the income from Bob's little company enabled them to live in Antwerp in an apartment at 193 Markgravelei, a handsome street, and close to the impressive house of Madeleine's father. But in September of 1929, Bob moved the family to live with the retired Adolph and Josepha in Kalmthout.[21] It was a major and disruptive change in their way of life. Antwerp was the capital of Flanders, a busy, cosmopolitan port city, rich in art, architecture, and with a history going back to the sixteenth century and well before. Rubens and other artists had flourished there, and its citizens loved the pleasures of its winding cobbled streets and generous harbor on the river Scheldt. It has a quality of being at once its own place and yet connected promisingly to the great world across the sea. Kalmthout, on the other hand, was a tiny village, served by a single railroad track, with one main street lined by charming but small rural homes.

To move an entire family and reverse its way of life so completely was a major decision, and although no records exist to tell the story, there must have been compelling reasons. It probably was Madeleine's fragility that suggested to the family that they should live with Josepha and Adolph in Kalmthout. Bob was thirty-nine, Madeleine three years younger, and their growing sons Rik and Paul were, respectively, fourteen and nine. Yet after fifteen years of marriage, they arrived in Kalmthout, to live in cramped quarters with Bob's parents, and stayed there for almost five years, as long as Josepha lived. From age nine to thirteen, Paul regarded Kalmthout as his home. The building at 25 Putsesteenweg, though attractive, was built for two adults and their help; it had only three bedrooms.[22] Now it had to shelter four additional people, and there was very little privacy.[23] Even when Adolph lay dying of cancer in the summer of 1936, Paul had to share the bedroom of the old man, then seventy-seven, and hear his cries of pain rend the house.[24] Living there also meant that from the age of eleven Paul had to commute to high school, for he attended the Royal Athenaeum in the city. No doubt he and his father commuted together.

Saving money cannot have been the main reason for their change of life, for Bob de Man was consistently seen as a rich man. Madeleine's emotional instability had worsened throughout the 1920s as her attacks came more often and lasted longer.[25] Henri's daughter Li was just two years older than Paul, a cousin she loved and admired always. As an adult, she understood that Paul had loved his mother deeply and "too much." In her seventies, Li recalled the ominous instructions her grandmother Josepha gave when she was sent to the seashore at Ostend with Madeleine and a group of her cousins. Then aged around eleven, the girl had to "look after Madeleine." In addition, she was to watch the children, keep an eye out for the luggage, and, in short, perform what should have been Madeleine's duties. Her aunt sat alone. To pass the time at the resort, she would sew for herself, then dress up and walk down into town, looking at the shops. "She was treated as a child, that woman," Li recalled. "She was the child of her sons and her husband."[26] Madeleine "was always outside everything. . . . She wasn't a mother. All the family pitied her and treated her very carefully."

Madeleine's other niece Minime remembered her wearing suits, reading a lot, and being seen as an intellectual. She didn't socialize with the other women or take active part in guarding the several children. She also recalled seeing her aunt repeatedly "cuddling [the] twelve-, thirteen-year-old Paul on her lap."[27] Paul permitted it, but the girl knew it was inappropriate, and he probably sensed it was meant for his mother's own comfort more than his. Madeleine needed physical contact, and perhaps in fantasy she identified her son with her lost infant, a stillborn daughter, though now gone fourteen or fifteen years. In a way, Paul was not fully Paul for his mother, but someone else, and the aporia he later talked about, the abyss, was his early recognition of the gulf between who he was in fact and the ghostly infant she may sometimes have imagined him to be.

In Josepha's home, the household duties and child care would be shared and perhaps supervised by the older woman, and Madeleine would have the companionship of close relatives to buffer her from harm. This is probably part of what Li meant when she said that Madeleine was the "child of her sons and her husband." Bob, on the other hand, after some years, evidently found life with a woman whose depressions and continuous tears could last for months something he could not abide. Undoubtedly his multiple affairs were at least in part a response to his own frustrations. To turn the management of the household over to his mother would have been welcome to them both. Given Madeleine's history and contemporary testimony that she had made repeated attempts on her life both before and during the 1920s, it is possible that this major upheaval was suggested by a new crisis, perhaps a new attempt at suicide. The family must have recognized that Madeleine was "irritated," as Paul told Patricia, by their hovering attentions.[28] But they were trying to keep her alive.

It could not last forever. Paul's grandmother Josepha died, as it happened, on his own fourteenth birthday, December 6, 1933. The young family moved back to Antwerp five months later, leaving Adolph behind.[29]

Paul perceived quickly what the others feared for his mother. Minime said, "Of course. The whole family was always afraid of what she would do."[30] When essential facts in a family are repressed and banned from discussion, they do not become invisible to the children, but are felt by them only more deeply. If we look for the roots of Paul's silence and secrecy, and also his need to penetrate the mysteries of others, they must lie to some extent in these years of distress. It would be years, until he was in his twenties, before he regained the social poise to conceal the obsessive secrecy that governed him, and show again the warmth and charm that he invariably possessed.

THERE WAS ANOTHER SECRET family disaster about which Paul would have known. Rik, his older brother, had serious problems, which grew worse with every passing year. Madeleine made a favorite of her firstborn son, but according to Bob De Braey, young Rik was small, slow, and did not have friends his own age; he played with younger children.[31] Perhaps an additional reason for the move to Kalmthout in 1929 might have been to send Rik to the local high school, so that in the country he could receive a simpler, less mystifying education than at the Royal Athenaeum, an elite high school that Paul was attending and where his father, an alumnus, was on the board of governors. The decision was made to train Rik in a prestigious trade with a long history in the Netherlands, and one pursued by a wealthy branch of the family, the Buschmanns. So Rik was sent to the Printers' High School in Utrecht. Unfortunately, there, too, he could not keep up. The demanding curriculum required courses in publishing, which were beyond the boy's capacity. Rik failed, and he returned to live, it seems, in Kalmthout. "I think," said Bob De Braey, "he was not so happy working at this Drukkerij because he was finding out he did not have such a good future." Rik's low opinion of himself reflected the judgment of his family and others in their world.

Rik was unlike Paul in another way, for he was openly interested in girls, though he could find no girlfriend. This had a tragic result. In 1933, apparently in Kalmthout, when he was eighteen, Rik raped his beautiful young cousin Minime, then twelve years old.[32] He was probably in his last, failing year of high school. More than that, according to Minime, he had also attacked other young girls. She was not the first: Rik was a serial rapist.

She told her parents. The experience was highly traumatic, and it was made worse by the fact that her father, Jan De Braey, refused to believe it. Her mother did, however, and took her to the hospital. It was supposed to have been a great secret, entirely hushed up. That, however, is unlikely, given the circumstances, for too many would have had direct or indirect knowledge of the event.[33] No doubt, out of respect for the prominent families involved in that small town, it would have been spoken of only in whispers, but since Rik had been active already in the same violent way, the news would have spread quickly.

Paul was thirteen or fourteen when the rape occurred. The family could only guess at Rik's prospects, or how they could provide for his future. Whatever they showed in public, they must have been near despair, especially Madeleine, for Rik had been her favorite. What is clear is that Paul was about fourteen when the family returned to Antwerp, with Rik still unsettled and in disgrace, his grandmother dead, and Adolph left alone back in Kalmthout. They returned on visits, but Kalmthout was never again his permanent home. During the next several years, when Paul was in high school, he seemed a different person to his contemporaries. Undoubtedly, the excruciating family problems contributed to his sense of solitude. As he turned his attention to the Royal Athenaeum, he took with him memories of the sunny joys of that Flemish village, but now there grew up about him an almost palpable habit of silence, a distance from others, and perhaps the sense of being, like Milady, a spy in a universe whose secrets, once discovered, were best kept dark. He would learn to "play the hero," he told his second wife; that acting would become ingrained in his character.

3.

PAUL AND
HIS TEACHERS

A DECADE AFTER PAUL DE MAN'S DEATH, HIS NAME WAS NOT IN GOOD standing in Belgium, even in his old school. Yet when two headmasters of the prestigious high school he had attended looked at the records of his academic work sixty years earlier, they exclaimed with virtually one voice, "With these grades, especially in mathematics, he could have done anything he wanted."[1]

Between 1931, when he enrolled a few months short of the age of twelve, and 1937, Paul was a brilliant student at the demanding Royal Athenaeum. His intellectual accomplishments at this young age were formidable. In addition, he bathed in the glow of his uncle Henri, who also seemed in that decade able to "do anything he wanted" and was moving—with a distinct right-wing cant—at a meteoric rate through Belgium's political firmament.

In spite of his accomplishments, the boy's private existence was hellish, for he lived in a home whose crises were quickly reaching a tragic denouement. By most accounts, Paul had only one friend at school, Julien Vandiest, and he knew nothing of these problems. In short, Paul kept his secrets even at an early age. It was a lonely life.

Getting away from home and going to school was probably a relief, even a pleasure, for it took him away from the emotional imprisonment of his home. The Royal Athenaeum was and remains a highly competitive but nondenominational academy. An Antwerp institution founded in 1807, it cherished its reputation as the best in the province. The school building, which covers an entire city block, rises severely from treeless sidewalks, its high-ceilinged and colorless classrooms probably little changed since de Man's day. Paul's uncle Henri de Man had hated it: He, too, had been enrolled at the age of eleven, but he was a natural rebel and had found its "large and mixed population, impersonal instruction, and mechanical discipline" intolerable. It "resembled a prison," he wrote, and at the end of a few weeks he had run away from both school and home.[2] Yet Paul's great-grandfather, Jan Van Beers, the poet, had taught literature there, and to belong to its board of governors, as Bob de Man did, was an honor.[3]

Hard to get into and even harder to exit in good standing, the Athenaeum was meant, like certain leading French high schools, to produce an elite. To that end, it set prizes, assigned students unalterable curricula, and ranked them annually by thousandths of decimal points in published lists, or *palmares*, which became part of the school's archives. The young de Man excelled all the others and there is no question that he got first-class training in a narrowly specialized field. Nevertheless, the school had its limitations. Paul de Man's career throughout high school was triumphant. When he enrolled on September 15, 1931, he was one of thirty-eight Flemish-speaking students admitted.[4] When he graduated almost six years later, on July 14, 1937, two-thirds of the students had flunked or withdrawn; he, however, had led his class for four years and come in second the first two years. His family was accustomed to seeing Paul come home on Prize Day loaded down with the books that were his honors.

The school day, which started at 8:00 A.M., was long, the course offerings identical every year, with no choices permitted. A student, on entering, elected from among three curricula: classical, Latin-mathematics, or scientific. And there he had to stay (no girls were admitted at the time). Paul chose science because his father intended him to be an engineer like himself and engineering was highly prestigious. Every year he took mathematics, two physics courses (one more advanced than the other), geography, history, and four languages: German, English, French, and

Dutch. German and English would have been new to de Man; the other two he spoke already.

The mathematics courses, in which he placed first, as he did in almost all other work, were especially demanding, requiring eight class hours a week. Much later, readers of de Man's essays who were impressed by their "rigor" may well have been responding to the training he had eagerly absorbed in framing and demonstrating a theorem given him during some eighteen course years of studying mathematics and physics. These topics enforce the defining of a problem while paring away its inessentials, and it was a similar approach that lent his writing a sharpness and elegance of focus that came to be characteristic. The only subject in which he consistently got the equivalent of a B was German—and while his reading skills were very high, his command of spoken German would never be outstanding.[5]

An important fact yielded by this academic record is that de Man's officially managed study of literature, as distinct from his private reading, which must have been extensive, was somewhat thin, if not superficial. The several languages studied necessarily included training in writing and speaking, but this very multiplicity, together with the curricular emphasis on science, indicates that probably only the high points of each culture could be touched upon. Scientists needed to be able to deal with other Europeans; classical or historically remote literatures were for those in the classics curriculum. In fact, although Paul devoted a great deal of his time to literature, he never officially focused on it in high school or at the university level until he reached Harvard at the age of thirty-two—by which time he had already been both a professional book reviewer and a publisher. He was essentially an autodidact in this area, apart from the probable influence of his uncle. Nor did he officially study philosophy.[6]

Clearly, from the beginning de Man knew how to study what he needed to know and above all how to delimit an area of knowledge and site himself in it. But as his widow said repeatedly, "He never read anything he didn't intend to use." The corollary of this, of course, was that he knew how to use everything he did read. What he didn't need, he ignored. That is why all but the most superficial references to the classical languages are absent from his writings; equally, one looks in vain for a range of reference to Renaissance or even most eighteenth-century materials—or indeed to history in general. He hadn't had the time, and the materials didn't interest him enough for him to pursue them.

As a competitive institution, the Athenaeum was open to Protestants and Jews as well as to Catholics, and it employed six instructors, two from each faith, to teach in both Flemish and French the required weekly two-hour religion classes every student had to attend.[7] Paul had little personal contact with his classmates. Perhaps school was already a public sphere where he perceived that competition, rather than comradeship, ruled. His one friend, Julien Vandiest, recalled Paul de Man vividly and with admiration, if not complete approval.[8] Like Paul, Vandiest came from a family of Freemasons, and their shared background may have made them more skeptical of received ideas. What Vandiest recalled most warmly about de Man was his humor, which was constantly in play even over serious issues: "He always, even in dramatic instances, found a way to make us laugh. A jolly good fellow." But the humor was contradicted by an aloofness that emanated from him already. According to Vandiest, "Paul was a kind of mystery all by himself. Pupils who didn't talk to him felt about him as not belonging here. He wasn't really interested in studying. Perhaps that explains his failing [at the university—a fact that shocked Vandiest] later on. But perhaps he didn't need to be. It all came naturally."

At this time, for Paul to have a friend meant that it must be on his terms, a contact entirely without intimacy. He knew what boys talked about, and he knew that sex was of paramount interest, but after his intense period of preoccupation with the sexual activities going on around him at Kalmthout, once he reached adolescence, with its more powerful instinctual demands, he removed himself entirely from the issue, entering a period of latency. He "never spoke about girls," said his classmate. "Not once. I was interested, but I sensed that he was not. In my opinion, it was the last thing he ever thought about."

It was not just sexuality he repressed. He was healthy, amusing, highly intelligent, good-looking, physically strong, and socially connected at the highest levels of the upper bourgeoisie. But the other boys did not like him. In a telling memory, Vandiest recalled that even when attacked physically, Paul was too remote to be drawn into the fray. "Once he was knocked down on the playground and his jaw was bleeding. Yet he merely shrugged and said, 'Boys are stupid.'" He did take part in sports actively enough to break his leg playing hockey when he was fifteen.[9] Paul alluded casually to having broken a leg, and limped a bit at the time, but only for two or three weeks. But he did not explain. It is a rare adolescent who is able to be coolly dismissive when physically assaulted. For good or ill, de Man showed preternatural self-control at an early age. Emerging from Vandiest's memories is someone already recognizable to the world that knew him thirty or more years later: a witty, aloofly indifferent figure who gave the impression of being too intelligent, sure of himself, and arrogant to care what others thought of him. The charm well known in his family circle he did not bother to generate for schoolboys, and the general run of his peers resented him, probably seeing him as a snob.

Not a popular figure at the school, he lived, said Vandiest, "in a kind of aristocratic loneliness. As if he did the world a favor just by living." The tone of grudging admiration was strong as Vandiest looked back: "I ask myself if he really cared much about anything. No. Or at least he made that impression." Summarizing his adult sense of what de Man had been like as a boy he said. "He would have liked very much to be a Junker. He would have enjoyed that status." (A Junker was a young Prussian aristocrat; the term in Belgium was uncomplimentary, implying exclusiveness and chilly arrogance.)[10]

Paul's silences are not difficult to understand. During his first three years at the Athenaeum, the family continued to live in Kalmthout, and it would have been impossible to bring friends home, even if he had wanted to. One problem was Rik, who was four years older and not in good form. Besides Rik, there was Grandfather Adolph's slow death from cancer, which occurred after Josepha's demise, not to mention Bob de Man's nightly disappearances either to his technical school or to a rendezvous with his mistress. Darkening everything else was Madeleine's gradual loss of psychic strength. Paul would do nothing that would make himself vulnerable. The best defense was to stay clear of danger by avoiding intimacy. Humor was a barrier, and wit came naturally to him.

Julien had no inkling of any of this. He was tolerant enough to accept Paul and his touch-me-not stance for what he was and could offer. While he "couldn't imagine him ever having talked to anyone else," the two, although they never met outside the school building and never intended to, "had a kind of not-avowed brotherhood." What they did share was an intense interest in literature, ideas, and the questions of belief that become sharp and new at that stage of life. Vandiest went on to become an administrator and much later a published writer—a talent suggested by the precision of his observations and language. According to him, not only were they not taught literature but reading was discouraged by their teachers, who might remark, "You read too much."[11]

De Man turned away from the rigid curriculum of this world. "The only question that matters," he told his friend Vandiest, "is whether God exists." More specifically, he cultivated an interest in certain mystics, including Jacob Boehme and Meister Eckhart, a thirteenth-century theologian who was the author of the concept of the indwelling spark and considered the founder of written vernacular German. Eckhart had famously been tried for a heresy whose essence the youths perceived as "Without me, God could not exist."[12] Paul disliked the two great icons of English literature, abhorring Milton and saying Shakespeare " 'wrote too much.' " He admired Blake, however: " 'Now there's a real mystic.' "[13]

This was high praise, for de Man's real interest throughout these years and for some time to come was in German mysticism. It would be a mistake to dismiss his implied expertise ("Now there's a real mystic") as braggadocio. He seems to have felt an innate yearning for a kind of preverbal illumination that was to form a suppressed but long-term theme in his writings. "Mystery in general had a certain appeal to him," Vandiest commented. "One could give it many names. The Ungrund [abyss] of Jacob Boehme, we both had read him. We spoke a few words to make sure we had the same opinion of Boehme: 'One of the greatest mystics of the West,' de Man said." It was "a real interest," the onetime friend insisted, "not trivial. Paul was a kind of mystery all by himself."

These were arcane figures for an adolescent to discover on his own, and how the boy came on them is a question. Was it rebellion against the interests of his father and teachers? Mysticism as a mode of knowing was in diametrical opposition to the world of X-ray tables, the small factory of busy technicians, and the cheerful frivolity of Kalmthout society that his father inhabited. Ideas, however, usually have mediators, and for Paul there was a powerful one. In a certain sense, he went to two schools as an adolescent: the one concretely in the center of the city, and the other emanating from his uncle's mind and presence.

Henri de Man entered his nephew's life at this crucial time, bringing with him all the glamour and information a highly placed intellectual with an international reputation could command. If there was a "habitus," to adopt Pierre Bourdieu's term, surrounding the avant-garde socialist thinkers of the interwar years, Paul's uncle was an integral part of it. He struck his contemporaries, in fact, as a charismatic genius.[14] Indeed, more than fifty years later the former socialist and American intellectual Alfred Kazin described him as a "great man,"[15] using the same tag that was later applied to Paul de Man by his own contemporaries.

Henri was a classic European politician-intellectual: a writer, adventurer, and a dashing leader who had lived an exciting life in the turbulent political world of the Continent between the wars. As a boy, he claimed, he had helped lead an Antwerpen dockworkers' strike in the face of his own oppressive father, Adolph. Later, he ran away to Germany, became a journalist for a left-wing Leipzig newspaper, and grew close to the leaders of the social democrats. With the outbreak of World War I, he returned to Belgium, enlisted, and fought against Germany, a country he loved—having a good war, he wrote, although it was an experience that made him doubtful of the proletariat he championed. Later, he established himself in Frankfurt as a professor in the new field of social psychology. Not an early Hiterlian, he returned to Belgium, and by 1935 he was a minister of state. At once a professor and an economic historian, he was also the author of a highly influential book, translated into thirteen languages (*Beyond Marxism* in English), a teacher who attracted students from afar, and a representative of the prefascist avant-garde German culture.[16]

As he rose in social circles, he came into contact with the court, and by the end of the 1930s he was both a close adviser to the young King Léopold, and, rumor had it, lover of the queen mother, Elisabeth. The fact that his surname evolved from Deman to de Man, was a token less of pro-French feeling than of identification with the conventions of the Belgian ruling classes and their marks of status. His politics were decidedly anti-French. As a minister, he replied to enemies who criticized his upper-class athleticism—he skied in the Alps and galloped in the Royal Park of a morning—by attacking his opponents as despicably Francophile, part of a degenerate Belgium, sunk in sensuality,[17] not hard and warlike like himself—and the fascists. Writing his memoir in 1941 as chief collaborator during the occupation (technically, he was still a minister of state), Henri represented France as contemptible in the eyes of Germanic culture; he was called to a higher, colder ideal, the warrior culture of fascism.

It was immensely exciting to be this man's nephew, and the relationship was the more valuable because from an early date Henri, who maintained close family ties, liked his nephew and, according to his son Jan, "respected Paul's intelligence." In spite of his long absences, it was Henri who was the natural head of the family and set its course. When he visited Kalmthout in the summer with Jan, they all crowded together into Adolph's house, and the stories of the four Van Beers aunts would be told and retold.[18]

As a politician, Henri was adept at cutting corners and playing both sides of the street. Not a Flemish nationalist of the extreme sort, he knew how verbally to privilege his Flemish heritage at the same time that he adopted French customs and manners, even while avowing his love for Germany. *Internationalist* for him was a word of praise. In this world, already long fractured along the quasi-ethnic lines of Fleming and Walloon, Paul was thus following his uncle when he considered himself to be part of the "Germanic culture." In trying to explain Paul's collaboration with the Nazi occupant in World War II, his close friend Frida Vandervelden said, "He was Flemish and he felt deeply his German roots."[19] In fact, because so much of Paul's mature writing dealt with French literature, some of his followers in later years, as Paul's second wife noted, were surprised by his dislike of aspects of French culture. Yet this ambivalence was typical both of the family and of the particular class of well-to-do Flemings from which it came.

When one asks, then, who mediated figures like the German mystics Eckhart and Boehme to the young Paul, the answer is clear, for Eckhart had become an iconic figure in the movement of ideas known as "the Germanic ideology." That medieval priest had been used since the early nineteenth century by proponents of German romanticism as they fought to construct a purely Germanic cultural tradition with which to oppose the dominance of France.[20] The person most likely to have introduced a figure like Eckhart to the adolescent Paul was, of course, his uncle, whose own publisher was Eugen Diederichs, the same important neoconservative who had printed Eckhart's highly reconstructed "works." Other "spiritual" or illuminated thinkers were being rediscovered at that time by certain non-Marxist intellectuals throughout western Europe; a new emphasis on spiritual values, especially as opposed to Marxist materialism, was in the air. Henri de Man was a true weather vane in these winds of change. In the 1930s, this onetime socialist took an interest in contemporary experiments with religious ideas and described himself to a leading French monk as being sympathetic to thirteenth-century Thomism.[21] Previously, before he was forced out of Germany, where he was teaching at Frankfurt University, he had created a sort of people's mass on religio-socialist principles called *Wir* (Us). It was performed, he said, by two thousand devoted citizens; it was a sort of street theater.

To have such an uncle was an immense advantage to a budding intellectual. And it must have been a pleasure for Henri to recognize in his nephew a mind not unlike his own and a temperament that echoed his own independent rebelliousness. The boy was proud of his uncle and must have been glad to find at last a family figure on whom he could model himself. From such a man a passing question—"What are you reading?"—and a suggestion tossed out would have a profound effect. One need look no further, then, to find where Paul picked up his admiration for such arcane figures as Boehme and Eckhart.

As for Paul's friend Julien Vandiest, he, too, went on to the same university as de Man, the Free University of Brussels (ULB), but after they left the Royal Athenaeum, the two never met again. At the university, de Man would go on to find a new circle. Vandiest once attended a lecture given by Henri, who continued to function as a professor. The talk was interesting, but Vandiest remembered that he "allowed not one question. [He was a] very authoritative man. His last words were, 'No questions.' He knew he was right and you had to agree with him."[22]

For the young Paul, such agreement was easy and natural. Only much later would he grasp how disastrous were its consequences.

4.

LE ROUGE
ET LE NOIR

PAUL WAS PRECOCIOUS. AT ONLY SIXTEEN, HE PUBLISHED HIS FIRST
article, long thought lost, which appeared on September 9, 1936, in a
Belgian journal called *Le Rouge et le Noir*.[1] While it would be remarkable
if only for having been published in an adult journal when its author
was so young, it is the more surprising that he could have written it at
all, for it appeared immediately after the deaths of his brother and then
his grandfather.

By the summer of 1936, Rik had turned twenty-one, but he had not
yet found his place in the world, nor would he. A disturbed young man,
he would die in Kalmthout on June 20, 1936, almost Midsummer Eve,
usually a long and happy day, when the sunlight lasts till late and colors
grow brilliant. He was on his bicycle and returning from Antwerp with
a friend. It was an easy distance,[2] and they stopped at a little railroad
crossing just outside the village to wait for the Rotterdam–Antwerp
train to pass at its normal time. As it moved away, Rik darted out ahead
of his companion and was hit by an onrushing train coming from the
opposite direction. Its approach, people said, had been hidden by the one
directly in front of it. Rik died instantly.[3] There was no evidence that the
tragedy was anything but an accident caused by the rush of an impulsive
youth. Yet, perhaps because of the aura of failure that hung around him,
a few people felt it might have been a suicide. Even some in his family

were not certain, including Bob De Braey and Paul, who wondered about it, but concluded that the death was "accidental, not suicide."[4]

That same summer, Adolph Deman lay on his deathbed. The family kept the news of Rik's death from him; as a result, they lived in fear that he might discover it in the newspaper, which they concealed. He finally expired in unrelieved pain on August 19, 1936, two months after Rik's death.

The tension in the house was great. Paul must have felt considerable, if suppressed, guilt at the death of his brother. It was in his successful rivalry with Rik that he had first practiced the competitive habits that would bring him triumph throughout his life. He did not show it, however; evidently, he steadied himself by working at his writing, and it was during these months that he wrote his first published essay, a piece of fewer than seven hundred words, "Humanity and Mankind," a smoothly written, anodyne article by a well-taught, idealistic adolescent who hoped literally for world peace: His recipe for social ills was moral reform by all the warring classes. In tone, it turns its back on the bloody struggle and dark political choices that marked his family life and the politics of his era. He must have composed it in July and August, between Rik's death and the demise of Adolph. The writing reflects none of that. The message of the essay was simple, but showed sophistication about the underlying social issues. Theories, parties, and nations were engaged in a merciless struggle. Was social and international understanding impossible?

The boy was publishing in one of the most fluid and fateful years of that ominous decade, as the fascists gradually won the balance of power. With the Bolshevik Revolution less than twenty years past and Stalin in power, the Continent was more frightened of communism than of Nazism, and Hitler's ever-expanding policy of anti-Semitism, long endemic in Europe as well as in the United States, was not regarded as a reason for even moderates actively to resist his aggression. Robert Paxton has referred to "the ambient anti-Semitism of the 1930s,"[5] and one sees this in the private journals and letters even of such a figure as Simone de Beauvoir.[6] The Nuremberg Laws, forbidding social commerce with Jews, who were now deprived even of citizenship, had been passed in 1935; the violence and gross humiliations of Kristallnacht lay ahead in

1938, but the issue in Belgium was not so much how to stop Hitler as how to avoid again being devastated by Germany in another war.

While volumes have been written about the violence that rent German politics in the 1930s, less is known about Nazi expansion in other European countries in that era. It is important, then, for the English and American people to realize that in May of 1936 the new fascist Rex party suddenly gained a foothold in the Belgian Parliament, winning twelve seats and bringing to prominence Léon Degrelle, who in a few years would become an out-and-out Nazi. Supported for a time by many conservative Catholics, Degrelle was born to a father who had renounced France and moved to Belgium in 1902 rather than countenance the French state's suppression of some of the Church's privileges. (The word *Rex* stood for Christ the King.) In France, the coalition Popular Front came to power when the left and center parties combined, but the election of Léon Blum—France's first Jewish prime minister—was so contested that during the same year he was dragged from his car—while in office—and beaten nearly to death by anti-Semitic rioters. A few months later in Spain the Civil War broke out. Only twenty miles across the Channel in England, Oswald Mosley, who had founded the British Union of Fascists in the early 1930s, was at the height of his strength, leading his black-shirted "stewards," as they were called, through London in violently anti-Communist and anti-Semitic marches.[7]

Everywhere, people were frightened, and many—like Pierre Fontaine, Paul's editor—announced themselves as pacifists, crying, "Non! Non! Non!" to the idea of war.[8] Paul-Henri Spaak, now a socialist minister and a leader of the pacifists, announced that even if the rest of the West fought, Belgium would not. For if the country was "entirely disarmed, they'll leave us in peace," he confidently predicted.[9] Spaak and Henri de Man, architects of appeasement (not known as such in Belgium), were quickly sweeping away old treaties to clear the way so that Hitler should recognize their goodwill when inevitably he marched onto their soil. Other Belgian politicians protested, but they did not prevail.

The young Paul de Man did not refer directly to these events in his essay. In a voice that was not partisan, but, rather, removed, he briefly summarized the shortcomings of the three contending currents of thought. Since the nineteenth century, the bourgeoisie had given merely lip service to humanitarianism and the rights of man, while looking only after their own interests. Nationalism, by which Paul alluded both to Hitler's and Mussolini's programs, promised charity and protection of the workers, but internationally it meant egotism and grandeur bought at the expense of "other peoples." (This was a euphemistic allusion to Hitler's grab of the Rhineland and aggression toward France.) "But that's another question," Paul added, hurrying on to his third point, Marxism. That, in theory, meant the complete realization of man's duty toward man—but alas, men as they were presently educated were only egotists, not ready to sacrifice themselves for their brothers. What was the answer to these deep divisions? Moral reform. Men's duty was to "*humanity*" [emphasis his]. And he hoped it might proceed toward "better times and true progress."

The essay was not fascist in tone, but its idealistic "humanitarianism" was precisely the stance that de Man later derided. If it reflected anything, in its contempt for the bourgeoisie, its dismissal of the working class, and its stress on moral reeducation, it represented the influence of Henri de Man's evolution and his present turn toward the spiritual, a temporary posture that would give way to active collaboration when the Nazis did, in fact, march into Belgian territory. In a subtle way, it also reflected perhaps Henri's connection to other contemporary searchers, such as the unorthodox group of Catholics in France, the Personalists, led by Emmanuel Mounier, who struck a not dissimilar tone in mid-decade, as John Hellman has shown, and with whom Henri had established an understanding.[10] Such groups, with their calls for spiritual awakening, were taking root in the despondency of the economic depression, the supposed failure of parliamentary democracy, the strength of communism, and especially the pressure of Nazism. But those movements proved impotent and would not last. The sixteen-year-old's ideas about politics grew in that soil, and he would remain a pacifist for a few more years. Under the occupation, however, those notions would quickly melt away.

5.

MADELEINE'S DEATH

———————

AFTER THE DEATHS OF RIK AND ADOLPH, MADELEINE, GIVEN HER fragile psychological composition, went into a tailspin. She had identified with Rik's suffering as his unpromising life had unfolded. The family returned to Antwerp in the fall of 1936 and to the shell of their normal life as Paul went back to finish his last year at the Athenaeum. But his mother had changed. Small things irritated her.[1] Bob de Man, who had lost his son and his father almost at the same time, had no emotional energy to spare for his stricken wife. Unable after decades of an unhappy marriage even to pretend to fill his role as protector, he resumed his normal routine: work at his business, some evenings at his night school, some playing with fellow musicians, and some hours alone with his mistress.

Bob thus left Paul, who was still only sixteen that autumn, alone in the evenings with his mother. Nothing helped lighten her mood. It was the husband's function to help her, not the son's, but Bob, who never showed his feelings, avoided what he could not sustain. He probably had refused to see and had no insight into the effect his absence would have on Paul, whom he left continually as company for a mother who could not be comforted.

Years later, Paul commented to Patricia de Man that his mother "did not find me sufficient." Yet surely it was not that Madeleine found Paul not "sufficient," but that nothing sufficed, and perhaps nothing really ever had. "Plenitude," nostalgia for it, and the sense of its "absence" became thematic elements of Paul de Man's early linguistic pursuits, and he wrote about them with a moving and lyrical sadness.[2] One cannot doubt that they had roots in personal experience long prior to his reading of Heidegger. According to Patricia, "He said in relation to his father that his father was incapable of expressing feelings. Maybe he was seeming to say without saying that there was a greater sensitivity in [his] mother—I think he felt some bitterness about his mother's preference for the older brother. It would seem to have been confirmed by the fact that she took her life."[3]

Madeleine had, as previously mentioned, attempted suicide several times.[4] The adults in the family, seeing her prolonged suffering, had long dreaded but did not mention that possibility. The tradition of keeping children ignorant of family troubles prevailed. Yet such silences are never a true secret, but become gnawing, internalized questions within the minds of the children they are meant to protect. Undoubtedly, Paul's juvenile obsessive play at mystery, the need to reenact and penetrate it, whether through the fiction of Milady or the quasi-fictions of the mystical Eckhart, are likely to have taken root precisely where most obsessions are born—in the family center, the family romance. What made his mother unhappy? What had happened in her past? Above all, why was she sometimes so withdrawn, so unwilling to cope, to smile, to give? Where did she go, psychically, and what had he or Rik or their father done to merit this absence?

Paul's second wife recalled that he spoke with her about the events leading up to the catastrophe. "Paul asked me to tell no one about it— the bourgeois idea. He spoke—she'd wanted a daughter. There'd been a child lost between the two brothers. A child born dead perhaps—or a miscarriage. They were worried. Bouts of melancholia. I think he blamed his father about it a little. He'd be alone with her in the evenings. She'd be distraught because the father would be off—[with] a musician."

It was a mild spring evening, May 12, 1937, less than a year after Rik had died, when Paul and Bob sat down to dinner and saw that Madeleine was missing. In one version, they asked a servant where she was and were told she'd gone to the attic. In another, Madeleine had dismissed the maid for the afternoon. They were understandably alarmed. The night before, they had gone to see a movie of Gogol's *The Lower Depths*, a film of great tragedy that includes a graphic suicide by hanging.[5] Had Madeleine previously threatened to hang herself in the attic, a laundry room where the windows were open to the wind and clotheslines stretched across the space? Bob apparently feared the worst, and, perhaps suspecting what would be found, "he told Paul to go and look."

The building has nine floors. Paul would have taken the elevator, the one with the mirror. There in the late afternoon light of a northern spring, Paul saw the lifeless body of his mother hanging in the wind, her face and eyes perversely distorted. How he told his father, how they removed her, how he informed the family—nothing of that is known, but it was and must have remained the worst and most traumatic experience of his life. A friend was to find after Paul's death a pattern of imagery in his writing—the trope de Man called *prosopopoeia*—turning on the staring face, which he linked to what Paul saw when he went to find his mother.[6]

Although he would speak of his mother's death to Frida Vandervelden a year later, Paul never mentioned her suicide, and he never got over it. The long years of caring for her and finding himself unable to hold her back would unalterably shape his thinking. He had lived for a long time with her on the edge of the abyss, the *"abîme,"* as he called it later, and this threat became a fixed idea for him.

It all happened in one year, his seventeenth. In less than ten months a family that with his grandfather had numbered five had become a pair of two single men, related but uncomfortable with each other. One must surmise that in addition to grief, there was guilt, and the repressed anger of those who are abandoned. For Paul to have survived them all, even his rival, Rik, was a great burden, and one he could not set down. Moreover, by her suicide, Madeleine may well have seemed to signal, to son and husband alike, that Rik had won after all: For it was her eldest she had followed into the night; it was not the living who could command her love. If Paul's passion for competition was about his mother, about winning this lovely, remote, sensitive woman who was never quite accessible, then in so leaving the world did Madeleine signal to her younger son that he would never really win? The sadness of his later summary, as well as the "bitterness" sensed by his widow, implies that this may have been the case: not to be "sufficient" in so deep a relationship is to be radically lacking.

However the losses affected Paul, he did not show his feelings directly. Madeleine's death came two months before he graduated from high school, but Paul told no one, not even his friend Vandiest; he dutifully took his examinations and remained at the top of his class. That stoicism matched the ideal of family behavior. Paul de Man much later expressed to his wife his own view of how he played his role: "He said to me, 'Oh, you know how it is at this time: You are the object of great sympathy and you become the hero of the story.' It might have crushed somebody else, but he could keep his mind on college."[7]

6.

"MY FATHER,
HENRI DE MAN"

EVEN BEFORE MADELEINE'S SUICIDE, HENRI DE MAN HAD BECOME THE central intellectual figure in Paul's life, a position he would occupy until Paul was over thirty, and in many ways his career would mimic his uncle's. This was true of his talents as well as in respect to his rebellion against his father and his bourgeois values; in fact, as will be discussed, Paul de Man, by his twenties, appears to have played out a fantasy that he was the son, not the nephew, of Henri, who always played a protective role toward Paul. In the summer after Madeleine's death and before Paul entered the university, Bob and Henri, concerned about the boy's deep depression, took their sons and Bob De Braey on a long tour, driving in a magnificent car through Germany and Austria. En route, they fished in the king's trout preserve and they also sang, Jan belting out the marching songs of Nazi Germany. Songs apart, this was not a naïve journey. When a public intellectual and member of the government such as Henri visited Germany in that era, he would inevitably be seen as making a statement.[1]

The minister operated in the turmoil of a world driven by the ascendency of Nazi Germany, and Paul's choices were prefigured by those of the older man. Politically, Henri was notorious for following a zigzag path before arriving at fascism and anti-Semitism, but in private life he created for himself serious marital confusions, which again strangely foreshadowed some that were replicated much later by his nephew.

Paul's style was always quieter and more subtle; he displayed neither his uncle's almost crippling egotism nor his great élan and public flamboyance. Yet if it is possible to learn how to be a "great man," then Paul had the best of mentors.

How Henri moved from the socialism of his youth to full-blown fascism in 1940 is a central issue, for he was followed in that trajectory not only by the leading segment of his party but also by the royal house. Both the young King Léopold and his widowed mother, Queen Elisabeth, were caught up by Henri's charisma. So were successive leaders of his party, including Emile Vandervelde, whose protégé Henri had been, and Paul-Henri Spaak. The word *charisma* certainly pertained to Henri, and he knew his power. When reflecting on his great success as a political speaker, he wrote that he, too, if he had so wished, could have become, like Hitler, a "demagogue."[2]

Spaak, himself active in appeasement and an adroit politician who managed to be prime minister of Belgium both before and after the war, first met Henri de Man when he assisted him as a teacher in a workers school de Man directed in the early 1920s. Both then and later, he always felt "seduced" and "a little subjugated" by the "genius" of a man who was "the most authentic political thinker of the twentieth century." Spaak thought it ironic that Henri's political errors arose from the surprising lack in this social psychologist of an understanding of people: "His intellectual superiority led him to despise them."[3] Strangely, all the characteristics Spaak attributed to Henri—"seduction," power, "rigor," "logic," coldness, genius, contempt for ordinary minds, extraordinary powers of persuasion—would be used to describe Paul de Man in a different time and place many years later.

Henri de Man was short, dark, and, by all accounts, intense. He liked to be photographed with a pipe jutting out from under his mustache and pointed nose. Vigorous and magnetic, he gathered crowds of eager listeners around him whether in large meetings or elite salons as he laid out his analyses and plans. Personally, he was a bundle of contradictions, and he played many roles. He thought of himself as ascetic, but he liked the grand gesture: skiing in the Alps, morning gallops in the King's Park, while living at an excellent address in Uccle, near the castle. He was sought out there by Raymond De Becker, a young radical right-wing Catholic, who had named himself a "Social Nationalist" (meaning a Belgian version of the German National Socialist—Nazi—party) and who wanted Henri to take charge of his new group. Henri received him and personally prepared a simple supper for them in his apartment. The rising journalist, seeking a leader, was ravished. De Becker would soon become Paul de Man's boss as the Belgian Nazi who became publisher of the occupant's version of *Le Soir*. But whatever he served for dinner, the minister had adopted other sports and now moved among the wealthy. Accurate or not, however, that such a dinner was plausible indicates something of his aura.[4]

Henri was considered more a dreamer or theoretician than a practical man of politics, and his colleagues resented his morning rides while they worked at their negotiations. For his part, Henri despised them as party hacks,[5] and linked himself to the young king and the queen mother.[6] Alice Cook, later a distinguished sociologist who as a young American came to "sit at his feet" at the University of Frankfurt in 1930, described him as "very outgoing, rather handsome in a roughcut way. I found him very charismatic. . . . He had a commanding presence, and spoke several languages almost perfectly. Socially he was very welcoming—informal and direct. He didn't stand on ceremony—and he thought of himself as very American in that sense."[7]

Henri had led an unsettled, adventuresome life. After finding his own way to socialism, he had continued moving toward the Left, leaving the university at age twenty for Germany, home of social democracy and birthplace of both Marx and Engels.[8] There he supported himself by journalism and translating, his quick mind, aggressiveness, and charm gaining him influential friends among the socialists while he earned a doctorate in history. When World War I broke out, he returned to Belgium, enlisted in the army, and defended his own country, one of his more comprehensible acts of reversal. During the postwar era, he lived for a time in the United States, settling among the Wobblies in Seattle, and thought of obtaining citizenship, but was declared persona non grata because of his radical politics. Again he returned to Belgium, where he capitalized on his alliances with the socialist leaders.[9]

During the 1920s, once again in Germany, Henri de Man became a professor of sociology among the predominantly left-wing sociologists at the University of Frankfurt. In 1926, he published the book *The Psychology of Socialism*, which would make him internationally famous and draw students to him from other countries as a socialist opponent of conventional Marxism. In the turbulent years following World War I, Henri de Man gave up any belief that Marxist class struggle would occur, least of all from a proletarian source. He had come to believe that the mass of men would choose embourgeoisement, identification with the classes that oppressed them. He worked instead to develop a form of "corporatism" (not his term) in which workers, owners, and government, theoretically but not practically equals, would be forced by law to cooperate in running the country. Tastes and ideas would be formed from above, and it was undoubtedly toward this end that he set up his workers' camps to train an "elite" force that would lead cadres of lesser workers.[10] Clearly, the workers would be indoctrinated in Henri de Man's own brand of education and culture. This in itself marked his doctrine as rightward in tendency and a departure from orthodox Marxism. Alice Cook explained that at the time all culture was divided into socialist and bourgeois types. "You couldn't be a socialist and a bourgeois, and to be interested in bourgeois culture—literature, poetry, or art [was] *not* to identify with the worker culture."[11]

For the rest of the 1920s, he rooted himself in German life, taking up his ties to the right-wing, avant-garde intellectuals who surrounded his publisher, Eugen Diederichs. After Hitler took control, Henri returned to Belgium once again. There he became active in the POB (Parti Ouvrier Belge, or Belgian Workers' party) and taught at ULB, whose name meant it was free of religious ties. Enormous changes began that would resonate throughout Europe.[12] The Nuremberg Laws of 1935 were deplored by some, but the Jews had no general base of support, and no country wanted to risk confronting Nazi aggression.[13] Anti-Semitism was pervasive at every social level, and Jews were expendable.

In 1938, Henri de Man, having moved upward like a meteor in Belgian politics, was active in managing the policy known elsewhere, although not in Belgium, as appeasement. At the epicenter of the geopolitical tornado created by Hitler, Henri was on his way to becoming "the most important man in Belgium."[14] Henri, who said Germany was the country he "loved" most,[15] was not a Hitlerite, but he foresaw the war, as many did, and imagined Belgium could avoid Nazi aggression if with his help it removed all barriers to Hitler's aggressions. In fact, not so to act would make Belgium a victim once again. It was also Henri de Man's path to ultimate power. To that end, with Paul-Henri Spaak and others he courted the equally seductive Otto Abetz, then leader of the German contingent from the Nazi Foreign Office. When in 1936 Hitler retook the Rhineland, Belgium and other Western powers broke the treaties they had made precisely to prevent future German expansion, and did nothing.

By the time Paul entered the university, his uncle was minister of finance and determined to impose on a reluctant but governing Socialist party his personally crafted economic reformation, known as the Plan of Work, or "the de Man Plan." The rank and file of his party resisted the corporatism he defended as benevolently authoritarian. They saw it as essentially a form of fascism, a reactionary economic policy that deflected power from labor to give it to the state and the bosses.[16] In 1938, the battle grew more fierce and Henri increasingly angry. He evoked without irony a society where opinion would be perfectly free but where the government would control what could be published and thus there would be no freedom of the press. In his "dictatorial regime," those "who were at the head of things" must know and decide "what is good for others."[17] His enemies knew Henri de Man was moving steadily toward adopting a fascist ideology. They were not wrong: It became a fact by 1940. For the results of his misjudgment, and probably for his long-held and public "love" of the country under whose occupation they would suffer for almost five years, he would be exiled in 1941, rejected by the Germans and Belgians alike.

A strange and little recognized aspect of Henri de Man's life was how he lied about his intimate ties to Jews. Because the revelation of Paul de Man's anti-Semitic article of 1942 was central to the destruction of Paul's reputation, the place of that doctrine in Henri's thought—and life—is relevant. In fact, Henri's attitudes were extraordinarily contradictory. In his memoir, which cannot be taken at face value, written, as it was, to strengthen his failing standing with the occupant, he repeatedly expressed his "visceral" dislike of Jews and his innate Aryan contempt for them. He spoke of Jewish incapacity for leadership, of the need to "protect the race" (a veiled allusion to supporting the Nuremberg Laws), and of the "unhealthy atmosphere," the pandemonium that had surrounded other professors while he was a professor at Frankfurt. He did not say that the excitement was generated by his more important rivals, Theodor Adorno, Max Horkheimer, and Karl Mannheim, all Jews, whose reputations have long since eclipsed his own.

He was also at pains to conceal the fact, although it was well known in the family, that he had married and divorced at least one Jewish woman, Lily Reinemund, and that both of his children had subsequently married persons fully or partly Jewish.[18] In addition, Hendrik Brélaz, Henri's respected biographer, points out that long before that second marriage, while Henri de Man wrote of his poverty during his early years in Germany, he did not credit his wife for her help. Elvire Lotigiers was a working-class woman, whom he married in 1910 and who gave him two children, Jan and Elise ("Li"), while working as a seamstress to support them all.[19] Brélaz reports his mistreatment of her in 1922, when he literally kidnapped their children and took them to live with him and Reinemund in Germany. (Jan de Man did not like his biological mother and frequently said of Elvire Lotigiers, "*Mère est merde*.")[20] He went further when, in 1928, he forced a divorce on Lotigiers at a time when she was poor and not defended legally. She was not even present at the divorce trial, of which she later said she was kept in ignorance. She was left bitter and impoverished and died in an institution.[21]

His second wife was "a friend of [his] youth," and he wrote that with her he had known a "true marriage."[22] He was silent, however, about her name, occupation, and origins. Brélaz was also silent about Lily's ethnicity, but it was well known within the family, particularly by Marlene de Man-Flechtheim, that Lily Reinemund came from a wealthy Jewish Antwerpen family connected to the shipbuilding industry. (Reinemund was a Jewish surname well-established in Germany.)[23] Marlene, born Flechtheim, offered the information and was herself half Jewish.[24] Lily evidently filled the difficult role of stepmother very well, and she may have provided a model for her husband's children, both of whom went on to marry people who were Jewish—by Nazi standards—or half Jewish, as others counted them—when to do so in that era was very dangerous. Henri was therefore multiply related to the Jews he despised, including his own grandchildren—who would have been targets for Nazi extermination had their ancestry been known.

The story illustrates the tight imbrications long existing between the upper levels of enlightened Belgian and Jewish social circles. When Paul later befriended Jews at the university, he was doing as his uncle and many others had done. Mixed marriages were not rare in that class, but the blatant anti-Semitism of Henri's proclamations in his memoir, which stand in stark contrast to the intimacy of his relations with Jews, suggests not only hypocrisy but the extremes of his ambition. Henri's erasure of Lily's origins to fit the genocidal policies of the Nazis was identical to his elimination of the life of his cousin Ida, a suicide, and the falsehood he invented about another cousin, her institutionalized brother. To be close to Jews, the mentally defective, or Freemasons—all meant risking oblivion or worse under the regime he was courting. Such lies were nothing when his goals and policies were in play. Truth was a dog that must be whipped out and kenneled.[25]

What did it mean to Paul in his youth that one of his revered uncle's wives had been Jewish and that this was a fact that must be suppressed? Did he also understand that the second marriage was evidently bigamous? He shared the information about her background with his own second wife, Patricia, which shows that the fact had some significance to him. From an early age, he knew that relations with Jews could be intimate and privately beneficial but had to be concealed and were even dangerous. It was one more family secret he had to keep, and in time he himself would become a bigamist.

A distinguished publisher remarked to this writer toward the end of his career, "You tell people what they want to hear for as long as you can, and one day they don't want to hear it anymore." For Henri, the day when the socialists no longer wanted to hear him occurred when Paul was in his second semester at the university. The politician was in full cry, arguing passionately in parliament for his Plan of Work in February 1938, when, facing shouts that his proposals were "barely disguised fascism" and would lead to dictatorship,[26] he fell to the floor, paralyzed by a severe stroke that left him speechless, bedridden, and unable to return to work for three months.[27] Henri recovered from his stroke and for some years became ever more important, especially to his nephew. Yet one wonders how much of that paralysis came from the inner conflict of a man, once an idealist and optimist, who now was being forced to face how far grandiosity had taken him, and how many doomed compromises he had made with a country already bent on evil.

The depth and endurance of Paul's fantasy about Henri's being his father was captured later in a remarkable conversation with Alice Cook, who went on to become a distinguished sociologist at Cornell University, where Paul de Man also taught in the 1960s. As colleagues, both were invited to a dinner given for the visiting French political philosopher Raymond Aron, and she found herself seated across from Paul. She asked him if he was related to Hendrik de Man, and Paul, then in his forties, "said very straightforwardly and immediately, 'He was my father.'" Thinking of her own evenings at Henri's home in Frankfurt, she replied, "Then we met when you were a child." Certainly the youth she had met was Jan, who was then living with his father in Germany, but Alice did not doubt Paul's assertion. Years later, however, when visiting Belgium, she met the former chief secretary of the Socialist party in Belgium. "I said [Hendrik de Man's] son was at Cornell. [He replied,] 'He is not. He's lied again. He tells everybody lies.' Then a note came from him: 'I've talked with aunt somebody [probably Aunt Yvonne, Henri's sister], and she said, "Yes, that's our unfaithful one."'"[28]

Years earlier, as a graduate student at Harvard in 1955, Paul had elaborated on the same falsehood when trying to clear himself from accusations of dishonesty. At the time of the dinner for Aron, however, he was a full professor at Cornell and had no need to tell the same old story.

7.

A BROKEN
RUDDER

ON RETURNING FROM HIS TOUR OF GERMANY AND AUSTRIA, PAUL MATRIC-
ulated at ULB in the fall of 1937. Change is normal in college, but for
Paul, only seventeen, still grieving and unready, and with the world in
turmoil, the transformation would be like a hurricane. In just two
years, he would finally make friends, fall in love, or what seemed to be
love, embrace a series of new ideas, and become entangled in a relationship, scandalous even in those circles, that would affect the rest of his
life. In Antwerp, his image had been one of poised success; now for the
first time, he would fail. Above all, he would not know who he was or
why he felt so fluid.

The era he was living through gave him no chance to grow into
experience; time was being compressed by the oncoming war. Europe
lived in fear of Hitler, and, uncertain about what the dictator would do
next, people made forced choices. Fathers sent their daughters to live
abroad, or let them marry prematurely, just to escape. Jews who could
afford it either emigrated or hesitated, sometimes too long. Patriot Germans like Thomas Mann had gone into exile in 1933, some wandering
first to Switzerland, then to Spain, and then onward, perhaps to Mexico
or the United States.[1] The world was revolving like a fun house, and
Paul was caught by force on its turning wall. A few years later, as a
book reviewer, he described adolescence as a thoughtless, easy time,

during which a youth has no forewarning of the life-changing moment when he will sustain a "violent emotional shock . . . lose his personality" and become shipwrecked, gyrating with every wind and swell.

At first, he commuted to the university in Brussels, only forty minutes by train from Antwerp, but little remained there for Paul. Now it held bad memories. Brussels, still largely French-speaking, was the nation's capital and possessed a very different culture from that of the Flemish city. Henri lived there, and although no love was lost between Jan and Paul, Henri made sure that his son made room in his apartment for the boy, who seemed uprooted. And with this, Henri brought Paul into his circle. He undoubtedly knew that the two young men disliked each other, but his word was law. There was jealousy between them. Jan resented Paul's "indifference" and arrogance. An instance of this, Jan said, was his cousin's behavior when his courtship of Marlene Flechtheim succeeded and he had officially posted the banns, the necessary legal announcement of the impending marriage. At home, Jan expressed his deep feelings by pinning up a map of the world on his wall. Paul, however, seized the map and took it away as a prop for a talk he was giving at the university. He considered himself "cock o' the walk," he told Patricia, and believed he had won the battle for his uncle's affection. Henri seems to have accepted Paul's idiosyncrasies— his indifference to norms and others' feelings, his already-spendthrift extravagance—without prejudice. "When Paul comes, he wants to borrow money," he told his daughter, Li. The world had changed. Henri described the new habits of contemporary youth, no doubt from observing Paul's behavior. Now children kept their belongings in valises, moved out with rucksacks on their backs, and were satisfied when their friends gave them a night's shelter, let them sleep on the sofa, and came up with a meal ticket for their breakfast.[2] The boy was in trouble, Henri loved him, and he would grow out of it.

Henri seemed cold to Paul-Henri Spaak, but he was perceptive and warm toward Paul, whose intellect even Jan granted his father had "respected," and he was playing the role of head of the family. The boy showed many of his own talents. Even in the tone of perfect good humor with which the uncle reproved the younger generation, he and his nephew resembled each other. It was that temperamental similarity, an innate savoir faire and self-confidence, that enabled both de Mans to move so effectively through their social worlds. Knocked down on the playground at the Athenaeum, Paul had merely wiped his bloody jaw and remarked, "Boys are stupid." Vandiest's comment that his friend would have liked to be a Junker could have applied to both men, coolly aristocratic and superior in manner, armored alike by good humor and indifference to others' opinions.

Paul may have thought that after his mother's death he was playing "the hero's part," but in fact he had been badly derailed, and those around him could see it. He bore his suffering silently, but his stoicism based on repression did not open the borders of his growing self to the needs of others or his own need of them. Rather, he kept an armored distance, tempered with wit, from most people, moving through existence as if in an intangible no-man's-land. It also became a prison house.

The strained relations with his father worsened. To Paul, Madeleine's death was Bob's fault. Traumatized, he was too young to empathize with his father's limitations and blamed him greatly. He probably felt that if her husband had not been so consistently unfaithful and indifferent, Madeleine could have survived, damaged perhaps, but alive. Now Bob's relation wih his mistress was open; he would have others, but he would never remarry. Paul wanted to be out of his house. They continued to meet over the next years, and Bob would unfailingly provide generous funds to his only remaining son for as long as he lived in Belgium. For the most part, however, they went their separate ways. Paul de Man's disapproval and judgment would underlie his second marriage, when, trying to change his own life, he evidently determined that the habits of sexual freedom he had so long observed at Kalmthout were destructive. In the United States, he adopted a style of life that was perceived as admirably but puzzlingly "ascetic."

Henri was the person he greatly admired and loved, for by him he felt nurtured. Henri literally fed his nephew and indulgently and regularly supported him with "loans" even for his extravagances.[3] Frida Vandervelden attested later that while Bob de Man was "sweet," it was Paul's uncle who had the greatest influence on the youth.[4] Henri now made a point of holding a family dinner every week at which just he, Paul, Jan, and sometimes Bob De Braey were present. The leader, then approaching the height of his career, was single at this point, but he took the time to arrange these intimate masculine family gatherings at his ministerial residence at 90 avenue de Boetendael, which were marked by much talk and joking. It was also a way of keeping tabs on the boy. To a precociously intelligent seventeen-year-old, evenings spent with a man who was the Socialist party's leader, a minister of state, a charismatic professor at his own university, and also an uncle whose respect he possessed were immensely valuable. Moreover, with such a leader, those dinners constituted a virtual seminar, one that ran for years and undoubtedly took politics and political philosophy as ongoing themes. Here Paul de Man also learned the rules and nuances of social behavior at a high level. This privileged contact was something a rising working-class fascist like young Raymond De Becker would have given his right arm to enjoy.

Jan, an electrical engineer, six years older than Paul, was sympathetic, but he did not like the spendthrift youth who so casually showed up to throw his bedding on the floor and make use of his space. Jan recalled, "One thing Paul said to me—he thought he was being clever—is that 'principles are [what] the idiots substitute for intelligence.'" Undoubtedly, they were rivals for Henri's affection. Jan had suffered an injury in high school and could not take part in the skiing and other sports his father and Paul gloried in.[5]

Paul was certain that Henri disliked his son and preferred himself.[6] The history is important in view of Paul's later claim, made more than once over a period of years, but most famously in 1955, that Henri was actually his father, an assertion that not only scandalized the American intellectual community when it was published in 1992 but offended his relations in Belgium even more. Was it possible? Born on December 6, Paul would have been conceived early in March 1919. Dates are often vague in the writings concerning Henri's whereabouts, but it is known that he was away in the United States for two periods lasting years after World War I ended, and it is also certain that he was in Belgium for a Socialist party conference on April 20, 1919.[7] There is no evidence, however, that Paul's uncle was in Belgium a month and a half earlier. On more general grounds, the assertion is not credible. Henri, for all his failings, had a strong sense of personal honor, functioned as head of the family, and he and his brother, Bob, were close. It is highly unlikely that he would have seduced his sister-in-law, an unstable young woman (and his own first cousin), while she was still mourning the death of her stillborn girl. This political leader was very attractive to women, especially glamorous ones. When he sought relations, he found them readily and had no need for such deeply damaging behavior.

PAUL WAS NOW ESTABLISHING a breach between himself and the conventions of good bourgeois behavior. At the university, he enrolled in the engineering faculty, a prestigious program, but he had no taste for the discipline. That it was also his father's subject made it even less appealing.[8] The evidence of his total academic failure in that first year suggests that however he thought he appeared, in others' eyes he was visibly consumed by unspoken grief and confusion. Toward the end of his second semester, at Easter of 1938, he took a solitary hiking trip, intending to study for his exams. Perhaps he felt exhausted, uncertain of being able to change, hopeful by habit but at the same time hopeless from recent experience about what he might accomplish. He had not been going to class, he hated engineering, and he was toying with the idea of skipping the year-end exams completely. He took along his books, but he probably did not really believe he would read them, or that the journey would change anything.

In fact, at a small country inn deep in the mountains, he found something he had not expected at all, a woman under whose influence he would begin to stir from his paralysis. Frida Vandervelden (1913–1993) was beautiful, deeply kind, and as intelligent as he was; meeting her would prove to be a turning point in his life. She was also both rich and a Communist. Frida remembered the exact moment she first saw Paul. She and the innkeeper were expecting him and aware of his reflected celebrity. Sasha, the innkeeper, shouted, " 'Come see, the little de Man—look at the boy. It's extraordinary.' " Running to the window, she beheld only Paul's characteristic blond forelock, rising straight up and falling, Flemish-style, "like Tintin," his body hidden as he moved behind a hedge, his shoulders set in the slight forward hunch that his friends recalled and relatives saw also in his father, Bob. "He came in, his head tilted to one side, blond hair flowing."[9]

Paul was not so little. In fact, by the standards of the day in Belgium, he was tall and always described as such.[10] Now he was entering a nest of strong leftists, and yet he was the nephew of Henri de Man, once a hero of the Left, but now the man who was leading Belgium into accommodation with German aggression. As graceful and attractive as the young man was, Frida was his match, for she exemplified the classic Flemish image of beauty with her blond hair, blue eyes, and porcelain skin. Even in old age, she was magnetically attractive, preserving until her death, at eighty, both her personal beauty and a quality of luminous, warm intelligence and charm. Paul would have been less than human if he had not fallen in love with her. Unlike a Madonna painted by Memling, however, she also had a square jaw and great strength of character. Within the disciplines she imposed on herself, she did what she wanted.

Frida later denied that they were lovers, but that may not have been the whole truth.[11] Her eyes still glowed when she produced a postcard from the 1930s showing the inn and pointed out her own room in one corner and Paul's just underneath it on the floor below; she had long ago marked both windows with an X.[12] "I am still haunted by him," she said. "I met him when he was between eighteen and a half and nineteen and I was twenty-five."

For her, their friendship had been both deep and undying. Even after many decades of absence, when Paul had become internationally known and was based at Yale, she tried twice to contact him, once through her daughter, a visiting academic; she was still saddened in the 1990s that he had refused all contact. She had married, pursued her career, had children, been divorced, and lived a full life, but even as the end approached in her late seventies, this early relationship and its unresolved questions were still alive for her.

The spring when she first met Paul had brought personal problems to her also, and she was in "near despair." Hoping to shake off her mood, she had gone alone to the remote hostelry in the village of Monthouet,[13] a place known in her circle.[14] The obstacles she faced may have been connected to the fact that she had just received her doctorate in chemistry, an unusual achievement for a woman of her time and class, and was preparing to take a job in that industry. She did not need to work, which in that era may have been part of the problem "relating to [her] immediate family," for her father, who had risen from office boy to become the director of the Générale de Banque, one of Belgium's largest financial institutions, was high-handed. She respected him but had long battled with him, and their determining confrontation hardened a fundamental rebelliousness that would shape her life.[15] Like Henri and Paul, she came from that class of self-made Flemings who in creating their own fortunes helped to build Belgium's wealth in the early twentieth century but whose money paradoxically permitted their offspring, if they wished, to choose directly opposite paths. Frida had a powerful social conscience and, aware that the Great Depression, unemployment, and social misery seethed everywhere, she was determined to use her money creatively to further greater justice. By the time Paul met her, she had already joined the Communist party.[16]

Stubborn and fiercely proud of her independence and integrity, Frida chose her friends for their intelligence and originality rather than for their social status. It was unusual for a bourgeoise, but not for a leftist, to be friends with numerous Jews, some of them new immigrants and relatively poor, but interesting people. One of these was Alexander Schor, the innkeeper, who probably hoped to relieve his illness by living quietly in the mountains.[17]

Paul was happy in his uphill trek to the inn on that sunny day. While he was a devoted hiker, he preferred climbing mountains to descending them. This was a trait that Pat de Man later remarked epitomized his character, implying not only his lifelong energy but also his fecklessness and resistance to completing a task. Frida and her friends, gazing through the glass of the veranda, must have wondered what he intended by joining them, a group that, however pacifist, would certainly have despised the De Man Plan. The prospective guest was still a cipher.

This soon did not matter, however. Paul was good-looking, charming, and already emanated a unique air of intelligence and knowingness. Yet he was also very needy and racked by loss. It was almost the anniversary of Madeleine's suicide and his discovery of her hanging body on the evening of May 12, 1936. He had come to the Ardennes—small mountains on the southwestern border of Belgium—for the same reason as Frida: to deal with a private grief he could not master. They would take their books and walk together into the fields, but instead of reading, they would talk. Yet he did not then tell Frida about his mother's death or Rik's. "All his life," she said, "he was very secret."

He did, however, show signs of distress. "One evening he had been very silent." Since they shared a passion for music, she procured a record of Bach's sonata for violin and piano and played it for him. After it was over, he stood up, silent for a little, and said, "I think that's exactly what I needed." Yet the retreat to the mountains, though healing, did not move him to prepare for his examination. Rather, he failed by not showing up for the exam at all, and he wrote Frida that he had decided to "take another direction."[18] In fact, following her example, he would now study chemistry. He was surely Erik Erikson's alienated youth before such a term existed.

He confided his intellectual and emotional state of crisis.[19] His earlier questions about the existence of God had given way to a focus on "elementary pleasures." He wrote:

> I'm evolving almost in the direction you extol. That is to say that
> if for some time I've already abandoned the hope of depending on
> any sort of theory or doctrine to conquer the anguish of doubt,
> neither do I count on any individual to stabilize my internal sense
> of direction. . . . I can get along without that individual—more,
> that person would irritate and upset me. This is to declare, rather
> pretentiously, that I'm in a condition to bear, to defy doubt while
> contenting myself solely with elementary pleasures: (that is to say,
> material, esthetic, and intellectual ones.)[20]

He would live in accord with the zeitgeist. His announcement had bravado and was a bit pretentious, but it was not false, and from then on he would almost always follow his own interests as he saw them. Henri remarked of Paul, Jan said, that he was "amoral." Frida interpreted Paul's "anguish of doubt" to mean not only metaphysical questioning but also a questioning of "people and things beyond metaphysics." She was expressing in a more positive way a judgment like Henri's. It reflected Paul's new attitude about moral decisions, including political and vocational ones.

In the next years, he would work on Frida's journals, but he could neither master his studies nor take a serious political position. He liked to go to the Ardennes and take a kayak out on weekends. Cut by meandering rivers bordering rich meadows and rolling fields of wheat, it was ancient country and had been Charlemagne's domain in the eighth and ninth centuries. Belgians love this remote and peaceful region, and in summer they still float in canoes down the placid, sunlit curves of its streams. It was a good place to seek peace. Perhaps, drifting down the sunny Semois River, flanked on one side by tall cliffs and on the other by green valleys shimmering in the summer light, de Man found some balance. He was competitive, but not a battler. Open conflict repelled him. Although enormous events were reshaping the world, he largely avoided polemics. When he wrote later of youths who had lost their moral compass, he knew this state of mind firsthand. The engineering test he refused to take was only his first experience of a lifetime pattern of balking at exams. ULB transcripts show that he would get the report "*ajourné*," meaning he had failed.[21] When later he did take exams, his best grade would be "distinction," approximately a B or B+.

Something had broken in him. The superb schoolboy who could make no errors, who shut out the world by burying himself in his studies and came home every prize day overloaded with the awards of special books, who "with these grades could have done anything he wanted," could no longer study for an examination. His brain, as he explained later to his wife while he was at Harvard, would simply turn "to mush" at exam time. In the long run, he became a kind of intellectual entrepreneur, who would do only what he chose to do—and do it on the whole quite well. Exceptional ambition, intelligence, and other talents remained and eventually brought him great renown. But doing the tasks that institutions would set for him on their terms became essentially impossible.

He adopted the posture of a dilettante:

> I spend my evenings at home and consume a fabulous amount of tobacco. It's not the same story with my studies, but my own good will astonishes me. On weekends I escape as fast as I can (camping on the Semois over Pentecost holiday was excellent)

and forget almost at once everything I learned during the week. That makes a mixture in my brain of countryside, sun, and organic chemistry which is not without charm.[22]

He was planning to buy a little roadster, open to the wind.

It was apparently not a fully conscious refusal, this balking, but something deeper. He became an autodidact. Everything he knew that particularly impressed and even inspired others, from his youthful book reviews in Le Soir (volé) to his use of Hegel in the 1960s and 1970s, came from his self-chosen agenda of study, and he would not hesitate to change the rules of whatever game he was playing. In fact, when he later wrote about Heidegger's sometimes abusive use of the same freedom, it amused de Man, who admired Heidegger's access to higher insights.[23] Ortwin de Graef, among others, has shown how Paul de Man later altered texts to suit his own ends, and his students, as will be discussed, noticed the same thing.[24]

Throughout this era, he and Frida were at least half in love, or perhaps more than that. They met a great deal, corresponded when apart, and, equally important, she soon brought him into her circle of friends, a group that was centered at ULB and was devoted to a publication its members issued three times a year, Cahiers du libre examen—a journal that explored ideas, art, and all things sacred and profane. Its skeptical, freethinking approach reflected the Freemasonic, rationalistic heritage of the university's founding. Nothing was forbidden; they were free-thinkers, at least by the standards of the day. Freedom, however, had enemies, and their skepticism did not embrace either Catholic dogma or fascism. Frida said she had founded the publication with another engineering student, Charles Dosogne. That probably meant she met its costs, for in his student years, Dosogne had little money.

Over one summer, Paul spent some time in Brittany in a state of withdrawal, a condition that had become habitual. Frida warned him seriously not to lapse into a state of "moral solitude." He acknowledged the justice of her reproach but denied that his condition was necessarily dangerous or likely to lead to psychological catastrophe. He preferred this state of being, not because—as she thought—he was afraid of being deceived by others, but because he was afraid of attaching himself while knowing that his fickleness or instability of spirit would inevitably lead him to abandon that which (or who)[25] had once been useful. He must remain "free" and not put himself and a friend "of either sex" through such laceration. He would keep his contacts objective and detached. Behind a frieze of complicated, impersonal diction, Paul was warning Frida off.[26]

A revealing essay he wrote on André Gide crystallized his defense of his "moral solitude."[27] By then, Gide was a cult figure and liberating force, unquestionably the most influential of French writers on the youth of the period between the wars, and every one of Paul de Man's friends, when queried, cited Gide as an important writer for them during their youth.[28] No phrase of his was more resonant than the cry of the young protagonist in one of his early novels, "I hate the family!" which was quoted again and again by young intellectuals struggling to distance themselves from the iron grip of nineteenth-century bourgeois customs. Gide used his novels to examine the variety of ways in which one might assert one's sexual, social, and religious freedom, especially by abandoning the patterns of bourgeois behavior.

Paul embraced Gide wholeheartedly, stressing the famous "*morale gidéenne.*" This he defined as the refusal to follow a single line of conduct, an insistence on one's liberty: "Everything is justifiable at the moment that one wishes it, because 'there is profit in desires, and profit in reassessing desires.'" There is no morality that holds, Paul paraphrased, because morality is something rigid, while our needs vary incessantly. "One must act without judging whether the act is good or bad. Love without worrying if it's good or evil."[29]

His readiness to maintain his "moral solitude" was partly bluff. He simply wasn't ready for a deeper relation with a serious woman. Yet Frida had put her finger on a profound tendency in his nature, and they both knew it. He stayed away from the university for most of the fall term of 1939, following an operation for appendicitis. Frida paid him a visit during those months, but meanwhile she was growing closer to her friend Dosogne. He was an engineer who had already graduated from ULB but had been very active as a Trotskyist leader of the socialist student group and effective at confronting—indeed frightening—

the university administration. Both he and Frida were Communists at that time, but with customary stubbornness she did not break with her position until 1968, according to Dosogne. He, more hardheaded, saw through Stalin from the time of the purge trials, as they both acknowledged, and renounced his allegiance in 1939.

That autumn was a turning point for both Paul and Frida, and they found—or accepted—other partners. Paul told Frida that he had a girlfriend, and she, at more or less the same time—just before mid-December—became engaged to Dosogne. She told Paul this, and that was the only occasion in their decade of friendship that he got angry. She later recalled this incident: "He stood up and made his fists so [she gestured, thrusting her hands into her pockets] and said, '*Nom de Dieu!*' and I was so struck. Because [I] had no idea that this could have some meaning or importance for him. Nothing had made this clear before." In speaking of this passage in their lives, Frida returned repeatedly to his gesture and questioned it, one might think disingenuously, "What could it have meant?"

On December 15, Paul wrote an extended critique of Dosogne (unnamed). He admitted that he himself was in a "continual state of instability" and that he was jealous of the other man. But his rival, although forceful, was naïve, lacked critical sense, suppleness, and objectivity. Evidently, de Man found something crude about those who could "sincerely believe that there are good and bad causes, and who have chosen or constructed a firm doctrine and have made it their goal in life to defend and impose it on others."[30]

Dosogne was locally famous for having successfully raised the funds to drive two trucks, intended for use as ambulances, to Spain to assist the Republicans during the Spanish Civil War.[31] By his own account, he was a self-made man, a natural leader who liked to do battle with the university's beer drinkers.[32] Toward de Man, Dosogne, who had been head of the Cercle du Libre Examen, was dismissive. Paul de Man, he said later, was considered a worthy kid ("*un garçon de valeur*"), but personally he found him a weakling ("*un faible*"), while "I was the leader surrounded by my guard."

Paul, too young and too ambivalent, lost that battle. Less than a month later, Frida wed Dosogne, in January 1939. Yet just a few days before that, Paul sent her a letter: "He had a girlfriend. In his last letter, he tells me he is leaving her. [The] date was a few days before my marriage." In retelling her romantic story, Frida remained seemingly puzzled that Paul's offer to break off with another woman had any relation to her impending marriage. "I should never dare to think so. Why should he have spoken to me of his girlfriend? [He] spoke not very enthusiastically."

A few weeks earlier, however, on December 3, 1938, however, Paul had gone to a party, where he met a highly attractive, dark, and sparkling young woman, who fell in love with him on the spot and engaged him almost at once in an affair. She was newly married to one of his friends, but to her this was irrelevant: She knew what she wanted. It was within the next few weeks that Paul wrote Frida his last letter, just before her wedding, offering to break off with a girlfriend, but her marriage took place anyway. She and Paul remained close but platonic friends.

Perhaps in their long dance of mutual uncertainty, no moment would have been the right one. Very likely, Frida, though drawn to the boy who was just turning nineteen, also understood from the beginning that his age made him taboo, for the six-year difference in their ages constituted for women at that time and possibly even now an enormous gulf. Perhaps she intuited also that the very similarities that drew them together, their tastes for solitude and sensitivity, meant they needed the counterweight of different, more extroverted companions.

It was a tale of misunderstanding and missed opportunity, yet to their credit, they were able then to maintain and deepen their friendship. Although denying that their feelings were romantic and sexual was a ritual that Frida began in 1938 and did not end even when she was near the end of her life in the 1990s, she was able to say at the age of seventy-eight that it had been the "most impressive" relationship of her life. There is no question that she had loved Paul de Man from the moment they met, and never stopped. She would not be the only woman of whom this was true.

8

UNIVERSITY:
TAKING SIDES

BRUSSELS IS A RICHLY LAYERED CITY. BELOW IT IS MEDIEVAL WITH cobbled plazas, gabled houses, and crooked streets that are thick with tourists and named after the poultry and grass markets the passages once contained. Above, on heights guarded by the massive shoulders of the Palace of Justice, stretch leafy boulevards evoking the nineteenth century. They are solid, inviting, and lined with cut-stone facades which let nothing out and are careful about what they let in. Trams run along with a steady click. These are the discreetly charming precincts of the bourgeoisie at its most reassuring.

The university lies off to one side in a more prosaic quarter. The Free University of Brussels, with its Freemasonic origins, was hospitable to immigrants. Quite different from the exquisitely Gothic Catholic University of Louvain, ULB was a leader in modern subjects. Its architecture breathes the city-planning notions of the late nineteenth and early twentieth centuries: It has a campus, its central library suggests college Gothic, its main classrooms might in a smaller setting be low-key office buildings. The cloudy skies of northern Europe sometimes make for treeless streets, but the surrounding district, suitable for a comfortable professoriat, is marked by wide avenues of attractive and solid edifices, varied by the occasional porte cochère.

EDOUARD COLINET WAS THE son of a Belgian general, but he was part of the editorial board of *Cahiers du libre examen* and felt comfortable with the crowd around the Cercle du Libre Examen, whose politics in American terms could be called generally left-liberal. He was a photographer, and a group portrait he made of the writers shows them in a bare classroom with large windows as they stand and sit around a long worktable, probably literally their editorial board. Colinet supplied the names: among them are Jean Burgers, Benjamin Pinkus, Gilbert Jaeger, Adella Englert, and Anne Gilbert, her head down, and smoking, with Paul de Man on the extreme right. Colinet, who wanted, like de Man's other friends, to make the point that Paul de Man was not anti-Semitic, stressed that at least three of these colleagues were Jewish; another, Jean Burgers, became a leader of the Resistance and died a hero's death. The date of this image is not precise, but it was taken between 1939 and 1940. Paul wears a well-cut jacket and sits composedly, a cigarette in hand, his face full, his expression open, if not communicative, a handsome lad, with thick hair, large eyes, and well-marked eyebrows. He looks like a well-brought-up schoolboy with Flemish, perhaps even rather English features. But he is unlike his friends in style, by far the youngest among the more finished and determined-looking young men around him. They live in this world, and to state their place in it and assemble for this group portrait, they have put on their good suits. From Paul, there emanates something else. It is apparent not only in the English tweed he wears or even in his features; in eyes and body, he seems to come from a different place.

In 1938, during his first summer at the university, the newspapers were ablaze with the events that led to Hitler and Chamberlain reaching their now inglorious agreement in Munich. Yet although the English prime minister returned home to proclaim that there would be "peace in our time," it was only a day later that Hitler sent his army into Czechoslovakia: This was the price of such peace. The following summer, while Paul floated down the Semois in his kayak, the Soviet Union and Germany were negotiating their hideously misnamed

Non-Aggression Pact. Their talks were secret, but tension was enormous; ever since Munich, everyone knew that Hitler meant to continue seeking his lebensraum, claiming dominion, which men like Henri de Man, allies both by force majeure and some degree of personal inclination, were ready to justify.

In the midst of this, Paul failed again at his studies. Facing his examination in chemistry, he balked once more and was marked *ajourné*. The fateful Non-Aggression Pact was finalized in late August 1939. And in a reprise of 1938, a week after signing this new pact, Hitler sent his troops into Poland.

The world was splitting up, and people were taking sides, huddling by their radios. Paul was devoting most of his time to two journals, *Jeudi* and *Cahiers*. There were open fights with the Communists, while outside the university at least, the right wing was gaining ground. Yet for a time, he and his group managed to steer a course of their own. Among his own relatives, matters came to a head. Bob De Braey was an eyewitness to the rage that would soon break even families apart. He and his father, Jan De Braey, regarded themselves as patriots, a term meaning that they loved their country and resisted its enemies without being nationalists, a designation too closely linked to National Socialism, or Nazism. Young Bob vividly remembered a family meeting in the summer of 1940 called by Henri, by then the most important Belgian, the intermediary of the occupant, and virtually Belgium's prime minister. He wanted to tell his family why he had taken to the airwaves, calling on Belgians to "collaborate"—work with—the occupying Germans for the sake of Belgium itself. (The word *collaboration* took on a progressively darker meaning as the years of occupation went on.) Bob recalled Henri's impassioned defense at that gathering in Antwerp and also Jan de Man's antics, for he "was applauding when the German bombers were going against England," jumped onto a table and sang a German war song, which Bob remembered as "*Vaterland gegen Engeland: Bang! Bang!*"[1] Hearing Henri's words, Jan De Braey was scandalized. He felt betrayed, and insisted angrily that as for his branch of the clan, the Germans had always been and would remain the enemy. "All of the men," Bob De Braey reported, "felt betrayed . . . by Henri de Man. . . . From that time on we had nothing to do with him except that he was from the family." Bob de Man, however, Paul's father and brother to the minister, followed what Jan de Man called the "king's" policies "impeccably." Those policies, of course, were Henri's own.[2]

Meanwhile, at the ULB and in and around Brussels, a distinct group of "de Manians" had formed, young admirers of Henri de Man who would follow him into collaboration. Only two were members of the Cercle du Libre Examen. Paul knew and was on amicable terms with many of the de Manians, meeting them either at the university or in venues friendly to Belgian fascism. They were a mixed group and not without talent. (Paul Aron has discussed the intellectual asymmetry in this period between the Belgian intellectuals of the Left and the Right, with the latter including a greater number of strong and influential thinkers, a situation opposite to that in France.)[3] Their number included Jean Barthélémy, Pierre De Ligne, Louis Fonsny, and Louis Carette, who later adopted the pen name Félicien Marceau. De Ligne, a tall, distinguished-looking man who was a few years older and had studied law, would become Paul's direct boss as managing editor of Le Soir (volé). Jean Barthélémy, known as JIB, a talented cartoonist (one of his sketches of a frowning Paul de Man was published at the time), would go much further than any of the others, enlist in Léon Degrelle's battalion, and fight side by side with the Nazis in Eastern Europe. Raymond De Becker, Henri's follower and before long Paul's boss, did not attend university, but he was active in the political circles of Brussels and already publishing his own right-wing journal. Just seven years older than Paul de Man, De Becker would soon be tapped by the German Foreign Office and his friend Max Liebe to become editor in chief of Le Soir (volé), where he would employ Paul de Man, beginning on December 24, 1940. Fonsny, erstwhile adherent of the Trotskyist Charles Dosogne, moved in a few years to the right and wrote a novel—which Paul de Man reviewed—of the sort that exemplified the "Literature of Defeat."

Paul and this group were denounced in 1941 in an anonymous flyer typed on red-colored paper. This document exemplifies the tone of rage that prevailed among opponents of Henri de Man's faction. It accused Paul of being ambitious for advancement, someone who knew which side his bread was buttered on—and also alluded to the person who was dispensing the bread. This was a clear reference to Henri de Man, who was the ultimate target of this attack. The source was *L'Etudiant*, a clandestine organ probably issuing from the extreme Left or from Communist circles with which De Ligne and the others had skirmished before the war. It attacked four men by name: Paul de Man, Pierre De Ligne, Louis Fonsny, and JIB (J. I. Barthélémy), all of whom by 1941 were employed at *Le Soir (volé)*. They were, according to the flyer, "bootlicking flunkies" of the occupant. The document revealed a knowledge of their new status and of the ULB, and asserted that out of 2,800 students, only these four had "seen the light" and made themselves "disciples of [Alfred] Rosenberg and the great Céline"—two of the most notorious anti-Semites of the era. This privileged group, the broadside raged, despised the "foul, mangy baseness of the stinking cowards of a university of Yids and foreigners." Only these four, the denunciation asserted, had thought so well of themselves that they could write that university youth would trumpet "grandiose and just conceptions of the realities that were on the march." This was probably a reference to something written by Paul de Man. He, it asserted, had gotten his politics directly from his uncle, with whom he had met the very day after the war began. The document also foretold—and not wrongly—that Henri de Man, who was notorious for abandoning his political ties, would surely shift his position again.[4]

The flyer was correct in claiming that Paul was following Henri's line to a large extent. He did not, however, go as far as De Becker and Henri de Man in supporting the notorious "Thirteen," a coalition of right-wing intellectuals who called for an extreme form of conciliation with Germany, which would leave Hitler's hands free to do whatever he wanted in Eastern Europe.[5] Yet Paul de Man certainly had a choice, for countermanifestos were also published, nuanced but clear and signed by numerous university professors and socialist leaders.[6] These Paul ignored. He was a de Manian by birthright. He identified himself at this time as a neutralist, and his relationship gave him considerable luster in the early days of the war.

He was not alone in clinging to this position till the last possible

moment. This was the period when many, including Simone de Beauvoir, decided that they were not prepared "to die for Danzig"—that is,
that they would not defend Poland and live up to the mutual defense
agreements their countries had signed to limit Hitler's aggression.[7] The
public, already endemically anti-Semitic, was now whipped up against
Jews and all foreigners. Few even on the Left retained faith in parliamentary government—that is, in democracy itself—which had been
widely denigrated for years as "failed" and utterly "*pourrie*," corrupt. In
England, Churchill was campaigning for the preservation of that form
of government, but in the thirties his voice had little influence. His
famous dictum that "Democracy is the worst form of government,
except for all the others." is much quoted now, but he was almost alone
among European politicians when he defended it.[8] Even Paul's leftist
friend, Esther Sluszny, who was a Jew and became a Resistance member
during the war, was still vehement when she was interviewed in the
1990s. Democracy in Belgium, she said, had shown itself to be utterly
corrupt and impotent before the war.[9]

Paul's writing for the *Cahiers* and *Jeudi* (Thursday), which appeared
weekly, first appeared as signed articles on March 23, 1939. He had
begun at *Jeudi* in 1938, where he was willing to work at everything,
from making up the pages and soliciting articles to proofreading and
similar tasks, according to a colleague.[10] More to the point, Dosogne
testified that de Man wrote the unsigned literary chronicles for *Jeudi*
throughout this period, long before he became editor of the more ambitious *Cahiers*, which they published three times a year.[11] Undoubtedly,
this is where all Paul's real energies were going—into writing and literary work, not the sciences.

His first article dealt with the health-service needs of university students and was illustrated with conscious irony by a photograph of an
ominous white X-ray table ready for use and captioned "The indispensable instrument of medical verification: the X-ray machine." Though
not irrelevant to an article that touches on tuberculosis, this strange
"appareil" (apparatus), highlighted against a dark background, seems to
have been lifted from an Expressionist film—or more likely his father's
sales catalog—and its disconcerting presence winks at the reader like a
Surrealist joke.[12]

When it came to politics, Paul developed a "neutralist" position, opposed to Hitler but also to democracy as a failed system that needed to be replaced. The humanitarianism of the essay he had written at age sixteen was gone. There was no time left for the West to fine-tune democratic systems in the face of surrounding aggression; the proximate villain—as in much pro-German or fascist polemic—was democracy itself. A "revision of values" was what was needed internationally, as well. The problem of recurring war in Europe would not go away. Using euphemistic terms, but undoubtedly referring to Hitler's aggression, he wrote that the problem would be "insoluble" if one allowed a country ambitious for world domination to grow "at the expense of the weak."[13]

Paul's closing remarks in this article were probably meant to blame not only Germany but also Great Britain, whose dominance as a colonial power was resented on the Continent—a resentment kept hot by German propaganda. Other European nations also would fit some portion of this impeachment. But though he was overtly critical of Hitler, Paul de Man's language simultaneously found reasons, as it were, to dilute the blame by implicating Germany's victims as creators of their fate.

His summary was ambiguous: While it justified passivity, it may also have been a muffled call for Henri to assume leadership.

> To sum up, this war will only have a justification if it serves as a prelude to a complete and sudden reversal in the foreign and domestic politics of all European countries. If it doesn't find anyone who can understand this necessity and reflect its practical realization, we will have lived, once again, through a carnage both horrible and sterile.[14]

How could a self-proclaimed pacifist find any reason to justify war? His language foreshadows the pro-German position he would later take. The sweeping away of the clutter of decadent democratic practices that such a reversal would carry with it was exactly what his uncle looked for, and it was the reason Henri de Man would regard the socialist revolution as having reached its culmination in June 1940 under the

German occupation. Clearly, if one wanted to identify a defender of Western democracy at ULB in late 1939, one should not look to the nephew of Henri de Man.

EDOUARD COLINET, WHO TOOK the group photograph mentioned at the beginning of this chapter, pointed out a significant feature of Paul's set of friends and coworkers, which is reinforced by the masthead of *Cahiers*. When Paul joined, the group was politically and ethnically heterogeneous and included numerous students who were either Jewish or of partly Jewish extraction. The editorial board when Paul de Man became director in 1940 was made up of twelve members: Jean Burgers, Edouard Colinet, Pierre De Ligne, Paul de Man, Charles Dosogne, Adella Englert, Paul Hiernaux, Gilbert Jaeger, Jacques Kupissonoff, Christian Lepoivre, Youra Livchitz, and Marcel Sluzny. Of these, three or four were Jewish, and another had a Jewish father. Georges Goriély, part of the same group, was also Jewish.[15]

But the circle did not hold. The directions they took once the war started were wildly various. Jean Burgers became a hero of the Belgian Resistance, heading an important network before he was caught and executed by the Gestapo. Early in the war, Colinet followed his father to unoccupied southern France, where the latter had been given a command that was of necessity largely titular, but the son soon joined the French Resistance and fought underground. Pierre De Ligne, on the other hand, initially considered himself a socialist (as a matter of political advancement and ambition, according to Colinet). When war came, he enlisted and fought with the rank of lieutenant. Yet by the end of June 1940, he went to work on *Le Soir (volé)* and was soon an indispensable administrator at the right hand of Raymond De Becker, in charge of domestic political affairs, and active in Rex, the Nazi party in Belgium.[16] When JIB returned to Belgium from the Eastern Front, he worked for a time both on the collaborating radio station and on the publications of Paul Colin, the archcollaborator and hated model of Belgian Nazi journalism. In 1944, JIB went into exile in France, as Carette, the Didiers, and Henri de Man himself had already done or soon would do.[17] As for Fonsny, in March 1943, he would be shot by the

Resistance as a collaborator—not, according to Dosogne, for any particular act, but "just because he worked for *Le Soir*, more or less by chance."

One thing is clear: These were articulate, intelligent men and women with distinct political points of view, and they would have said that admission to their group was based rather on personal and intellectual merit than on adherence to particular political or religious creeds. If there was a Louis Fonsny, there was also Jean Burgers, who died as a hero of the Resistance. Dosogne was an avowed Trotskyist; while Colinet, his successor, was a general's son, for whom thwarting a Communist takeover of the group was a matter of family pride and class loyalty. The university was a meeting place for women and men of diverse origin. At the Cercle and *Cahiers* they were able to mingle and exchange ideas for a few years. The war would change all that. Family origin, the particular layer of the particular class from which one sprang, and, of course, pure ambition—for one could rise fast in the Nazi regimes, which gave power to youth and advanced it over older, experienced men—these more than anything else seem to have determined the diverse paths Paul de Man and his friends would soon take.

9.

THE DIDIER CIRCLE:
SERVANTS TO POWER

DOWN A LITTLE HILL FROM THE AVENUE LOUISE LIES A SET OF SMALL ponds planted with willows and dotted by swans and geese. The watercourse wanders through the city as the centerpiece of a string of half-hidden plazas whose fountains and decorative lakes give the nineteenth-century part of the city a peculiarly gracious air. In a country where uncounted numbers of medieval castles rest deep in the countryside, untouched but open to those who seek them, as if part of some shared public dream, the little ponds of Brussels mark some of its differences from French culture, for one must slow one's pace to go around and not through them, and in their tangle of light and wind one takes more time to see and feel.

It was in this section of the city that Henri de Man would meet his mistress, the wealthy and beautiful Lucienne Didier, an ardent supporter of the Nazis and their representative Otto Abetz. Her political salon provided Henri with the setting he needed to promulgate his ideas. Paul did not like his uncle's glamorous mistress, thinking her "too worldly," according to his friend, the writer Paul Willems, but he attended her political salon nevertheless.[1] She received in spectacular style at her house at 37 avenue de la Hippodrome, a curving street backing up to one of the swan-filled ponds in fashionable Ixelles. Guests found her lying on a chaise longue, her blond hair flowing, two Afghan hounds at her feet, and a Chinese manservant at her shoulder. According to the sexualized account of Léon Degrelle, she met her guests in her boudoir, reclining on a lion skin, clothed in a flowered and fragile gown. Her skin, legs, and back were divine and exquisite. There, she was accompanied by the German diplomat Otto Abetz, with whom she "gave birth to Young Europe."[2] Léo Moulin, a minor historian, friend, and follower of Henri de Man, recalled Lucienne as "one of the most beautiful women of Brussels, who served as a model for sculptors, painters. She got it into her head to have a political-literary salon where she would receive the young elite."[3]

It was all political theater, and men loved it; few women were known to attend. Paul appeared at Henri's behest while he was still writing for the moderately left-wing journals run by his friends at the university, thus entering the precincts of the right wing, a dichotomy that presaged his future life. Unaccompanied by Frida and certainly without the Jewish Georges Goriély, he was being inducted by his uncle into the fascist social network of Brussels, an important part of which was known collectively as "the Didier circle," a group in which Henri was the star.[4] Lucienne Didier was also a publisher. Socially, her salon was elitist and intellectual; politically, it was largely, although not always, fascist. The tone was overwhelmingly pro-German.

There was no opposing circle on the left side. Paul Aron has pointed out in a detailed analysis the unfortunate failure of opposing Belgian intellectuals to cohere and speak with a united voice against the oncoming German hegemony, as their French counterparts were doing.[5] France had Sartre and others as intellectual leaders. In Belgium, however, the talent had been absorbed by many forces: conservative Catholicism; an overwhelming fear of Bolshevism; the sense of a history of betrayal that many Belgians felt vis-à-vis their Western allies; and, among some Flemish, a sense that they belonged to a "Germanic culture"—the words used by Frida Vandervelden to describe both Paul and herself, Communist though she was. Above all, perhaps, the lifeblood of Belgian intellectuals had long been being drained off by the great magnet of Paris, where publishers openly insisted that even the best Belgian writers must move before they would bring their works to the public. Otherwise, they would not be reviewed. Willems told this writer that the powerful French publisher Gallimard had directly made such a demand, but that on grounds of love of country, he had refused the offer, an act of self-denial some other Belgians considered both unusual and praiseworthy.[6]

Willems's younger friend Paul (whom his testimony consistently sheltered) may have disliked Mme. Didier, but he certainly knew her, and he profited greatly by his entrée, for he would find many of his wartime colleagues and friends among the members of the salon. There his uncle held forth every other week as, pipe in hand and wreathed in smoke, he laid down the lines of argument and policy his followers might debate but ultimately would follow. Henri's influence was never greater than at this period preceding and at the beginning of the war, before Belgians recognized how fully the occupation was a disaster under which they would endure long suffering. In Lucienne, Henri had wisely chosen both a lover and supporter, for she was not only a seductive woman but also an energetic and very intelligent one. Her friends remembered that her chic had resulted in her image appearing in the pages of French *Vogue* during the 1930s,[7] but she is also credited with the idea of creating the publishing house Editions de la Toison d'Or (Golden Fleece Publishers) to bring out works friendly to the Nazi regime. Its first book, in fact, was Henri's self-justifying memoir, *Après Coup*, while she also published the first two books by the young Willems.[8] The venture was secretly subvented by Mundus, an arm of the German propaganda ministry. While those who knew the couple well, such as Pierre De Ligne, believed that she was the actual force behind the business, the company was managed by her husband, Edouard.[9] She generally read manuscripts at home and corresponded on an equal footing with authors and directors of the company through little notes handwritten on blue paper.[10]

Her salon, which was one among several others, was cosmopolitan and renowned for its range of guests.[11] To those who would have termed themselves *patriots*, during and after the war it was a hotbed of Nazi subversion. As André Molitor put it, there one met, "among others, members of the German embassy charged with cultural propaganda whom one was to see again in Brussels under the occupation."[12] Many

French intellectuals on the Right visited, for Brussels is but a couple of hours by train from Paris.

Her object was political men, and she emanated fascination especially to Otto Abetz, von Ribbentrop's good-looking deputy and later Nazi ambassador to occupied France, and to his attaché Max Liebe, blond and blue-eyed, a "*diplomate de charme*" who was known as Abetz's "man in Brussels."[13] Others susceptible to her were fascist journalists like the still little-known Raymond De Becker, the rich and popular journalist Pierre Daye, and, of course, Henri de Man himself. "All the core Belgian intellectuals revolved around her."[14] The foreign minister, Spaak, either showed up on a few occasions or was a frequent guest (depending on whether the witness was Léo Moulin or Pierre Daye), and even Emile Vandervelde, head of the POB (the Belgian Socialist party) and for a period prime minister, came once or twice. Also present among the smaller fry were a variety of lesser journalists and followers of Henri de Man. Many of those guests became important figures in the media world in which Paul would shortly make his career. The ambitious Didiers courted such people, for control of the press and radio was an essential element of German propaganda.

Paul de Man certainly attended, for the Didiers became his employers. Ortwin de Graef has inferred his presence at least once from one of Paul's articles mentioning a gathering at the Toison d'Or.[15] His uncle, with his watchful eye and close sponsorship, would certainly have introduced him there. Paul also soon developed a tight network of friendships among some of the salonistes. Whatever his private opinion, at least occasional appearances by Paul at Mme. Didier's gatherings would have been de rigueur, for there was far too much to be gained for Paul to snub Lucienne Didier. She would surely have engaged him, if only as a favor to his uncle, but it is most unlikely that the Didiers would have taken him on as a reader for their publishing company if he had not already passed the test of those quasi-social evenings when the political sheep and goats were certain to be separated.

The couple's prominence began in the early 1930s when Edouard, Lucienne's complacent husband, had responded when the Germans were making a determined push for political and social entrée, by founding a friendship circle called "Jeune Europe." Otto Abetz was the point man in Belgium of Joachim von Ribbentrop, the German foreign minister, and Didier had sponsored Abetz, for whom Jeune Europe was an early accomplishment. The Belgian was attractive in the "English style," according to Paul Willems.[16] England was still in the ascendant socially, and Lucienne had been educated there, although her clothes and friends came from Paris.[17] Léo Moulin, interviewed in July 1993, agreed that Didier was "very distinguished," tall and elegant—like an "Afghan." But he was "always in the shadow of his wife," according to Pierre De Ligne. Of De Becker, who became both his own boss and Paul's as publisher of the widely read newspaper Le Soir (volé), De Ligne said, "De Becker talked only of her, but not of him [Edouard]. She was a singular woman, worldly; men were impressed. She had class."[18]

Abetz was said to have underwritten the expenses of the salon. Both he and Max Liebe were regarded as spies, employed by Joachim von Ribbentrop, as the Belgian ambassador to Berlin, Jacques Davignon, attested.[19] The Nazis aimed to influence the opinion leaders and were successful. While certainly not everyone who attended, even regularly, would become a collaborator, there is no doubt that the circle provided valuable information and contacts.

Paul de Man would have multiple roles in the heart of the collaborating media, more than has been known, and his publications in Le Soir (volé) beginning at the end of 1940 were merely the opening of his career. Briefly noting who some of his compeers were, men he was already in touch with or soon would be in 1940–1942, provides valuable insights. Abetz was central, and the strongly fascist journalist Pierre Daye (who notoriously reaffirmed his Nazi sympathies when he put on the German army uniform in 1942 and became commissioner of sport) described the German spy with admiration: his powerful shoulders, his thick chestnut hair. According to a Frenchman sympathetic to Abetz and present at the German's war-crimes trial, who wrote an introduction to his hero's memoir, he was handsome as Siegfried, and blond. By the clear look in his eyes—his humor, irony, and his contempt for routine—he showed all the marks of superiority. Abetz was also rumored to be the wartime lover of Lucienne Didier—that is, after Henri de Man's disappearance.[20] His role, according to Léo Moulin, was to defang the image of National Socialism.[21]

Born in 1903 near the French border, with memories of Napoleon's occupation a hundred years earlier drummed into him from childhood, Otto Abetz had begun life as an instructor of design.[22] He joined the Nazi party in 1931 and was considered sympathetic to the Nationalist Socialist (Nazi) left wing.[23] He became an organizer of youth congresses and worked for the violently anti-Semitic Baldur von Schirach. In 1932, he met Henri de Man at a Franco-German friendship conference he had organized in Mainz.[24] These transnational friendship conferences were an important feature of German foreign policy, and many French and Belgians with liberal views participated in them, hoping to heal the wounds of World War I and forestall the outbreak of new hostilities. André Gide, for example, was a frequent visitor to the Pontigny conferences in France, which were often shaped around the same theme in the 1920s. The meetings were often youth-oriented, but young German participants had to be members of the Nazi party. Raymond De Becker, born to poverty, got his first taste of the intellectual and social high life at a Pontigny gathering in 1934, when at twenty-two he was dazzled by a display of wealth, power, and intellect he had not seen before.[25]

Abetz was effective with these conferences, and in 1934 he became an adviser to Ribbentrop, the ex–champagne salesman, on matters French, making these contacts an instrument of state policy. Married to a Frenchwoman, he was briefly embarrassed when he was deported as a spy to France, but the next year he returned to Belgium. Once Germany had overrun France in 1940, he came back as ambassador to France and in effect became the wartime ruler of both occupied France and Belgium. With a keen sense of how to manipulate intellectuals, he published a bilingual journal, which, under the guise of bilateral dialogue, was closely controlled to push the basic positions of German cultural hegemony.[26] Michel Grunewald has shown that lip service was given to the value of certain French qualities, but the political lines of Abetz's publication reflected the current German position: rejection of the "universal" values of 1789 (the rights of man, reason, individualism, liberty, etc.) and acceptance of Hitlerian policy as the sole source of hope for peace. In addition, his journal rejected French claims to be the source of "civilization," and promoted the division of Europe into

"Germanic" and "Latin" historical elements. His line was the moral superiority of contemporary Germany, whose time for dominance had come. France and its culture were unhealthy and decadent. Most of these themes, stripped of reference to Hitler, were to be expressed in Paul de Man's wartime journalism.[27]

Although crucial as underwriter and manipulator of the Didier salon, Abetz was not its main player. In that European world, no line was drawn between writers and politicians, or journalists and statesmen. It was assumed that all writers and journalists had political positions and that these would be reflected in what they wrote. Henri de Man himself wrote journalistically even while serving as a minister of state.

Pierre Daye, a Belgian to whom Paul would later pay obeisance, was born to a great insurance fortune, and he made himself a highly visible man-about-town. He was also a journalist present at the Didier salon and very active in fascist politics. In his postwar memoirs, written in exile, he chronicled that world vividly, but he greatly sanitized the story. Daye had joined the Belgian fascist Léon Degrelle and his Rexist party early and, clad in morning coat and dove-gray top hat, he led his group into parliament when they first took their seats after the party's sudden success in 1935. Himself gay, he liked to emphasize his "athleticism," which enabled him to take the position under the Nazis in 1942.[28] He was a tender older friend toward the young Raymond De Becker, whom, in 1932, he urged not to depart from Brussels on a religious retreat: "We need your courage," he told the twenty-year-old fascist in the making, "your dynamism." De Becker left anyway.

Daye also befriended Robert Brasillach, the violently anti-Semitic editor of the French fascist journal *Je suis partout* (I Am Everywhere), for which the Belgian frequently wrote. The fascist world privileged male dominance and placed "extreme stress on the masculine principle."[29] As such, it did not overtly encourage gay men, but there was room for them under its aegis, providing they remained secret. Like Daye, both De Becker and Robert Brasillach (who came up from Paris for these meetings) were said by members of the circle to be homosexual, but closeted—essential for survival in that era, and the more so for De Becker, who for a time was an ardent Catholic.[30] Paul de Man would review Brasillach's work as well, although critically, for Brasillach was too French for de Man: The Frenchman was not sufficiently moved by the mass frenzy at the Nuremberg games.

In his days of popularity, Daye kept an apartment in Paris, and followed the pattern of a certain cosmopolitan literary type of that era, using his wealth for worldwide voyages, which he then exploited and incorporated in his image of cosmopolitan writer. He avoided political invective when possible, and in Daye's discourse, his friends were not fascists, but good writers, thoughtful Catholics, friendly to "Europe" and to peace, impressed by German energy and health, and opposed to Bolshevism. Paul de Man admired his political acumen, he wrote in a review, and repeated the praise in some correspondence they exchanged.[31]

Daye's protégé De Becker was also a regular guest at the salon. Although there is nothing comic about the power and position De Becker assumed in a few years, his career during the 1930s has a bizarre flavor not rare in the lives of other National Socialists. Born in 1912 and only seven years older than Paul de Man, Raymond De Becker was himself secretly half Jewish, the illegitimate son not of the concierge turned wine salesman who raised him, but of a Jewish father whom he hated, facts known to certain of his colleagues but which he did not commit to his autobiography.[32] A consistent anti-Semite, he changed his other alliances continually throughout the 1930s, going through phases of socialism, monastic Catholicism, the Personalism of the Frenchman Mounier, and Rexism, before abandoning them all for national socialism.[33]

After an abortive two years in a French monastery, De Becker, then twenty-two, yearned to establish a new Catholic ascetic order of his own to "re-christianize" the profane modern world of art, culture, and politics. He was a valuable ally of Mounier, the mystically inclined but unorthodox Catholic founder of Personalism, a vaguely defined "spiritual" movement whose members were antibourgeois and anticapitalist, which John Hellman has studied closely. In these tightly overlapping circles, Henri de Man, himself ideologically ever in flux, was a natural ally of the Personalists. Already a minister of state, he wrote for their journal *Esprit* and was praised by Mounier as "inspired by a spiritualism so close to being Christian" and "nourished by the German experience yet immune to its faults."[34]

One of De Becker's friends in Louvain was Louis Carette, then an ardent Catholic. Carette was to become one of Paul de Man's friends during their collaborationist days of the war, becoming well known—indeed notorious—through his wartime radio broadcasts, which emanated from a Nazi-controlled station and were considered at the time and later to have directly served German propaganda.[35] The farceur's description of De Becker, then about twenty-three years old, hints at the slightly crazy quality others perceived in the failed monk. De Becker sought Carette out to announce that he had chosen Louvain following "certain signs in the sky or elsewhere." There he set up a monastic household by ordering four identical wooden beds, tables, chairs, and crosses, the latter each six and a half feet tall.[36] In fact, he was in Louvain at least in part to help his widowed mother establish a boardinghouse.[37] De Becker soon gave up his religious yearnings and turned full time to journalism and political ideology.[38]

Many, if not most, of the right-wing French and Belgian intellectual leaders attended the Didier salon at one time, and this was the world into which Paul de Man was inducted at an early age, one overflowing with glamour, money, and odd, often gifted, sometimes deservedly hated individuals.[39] Among them were writers whose work Paul de Man would review, often very favorably. It goes without saying that many were fascists, anti-Semites, and Nazis. Some of the men he met there would remain part of his network and the source of his social and intellectual position. When the war ended, many of its members fled into exile or were imprisoned.

10.

ANNE

PAUL WAS ALWAYS LUCKY IN ATTRACTING BEAUTIFUL WOMEN, ALTHOUGH some might say it was not sheer luck. In December 1938, he was in the midst of losing Frida to Dosogne, but an exciting and exotic foreigner had fallen in love with him on sight and determined to make him her own. Anaide Baraghian (1919–2000) was born in Tiflis, or Tbilisi, the capital of Georgia. In Belgium, she soon adopted the name of Anne, by which she will be known in this work. In her native country, her mother's family owned what she called "immense latifundia," or vast border-crossing properties that stretched into what is now northern Iran, but she had moved with her wealthy family at an early age to Romania. That country, however, was, like others in Europe, caught in the grip of the increasingly bloody struggle of fascists against the monarchy, as the Romanian demagogue Corneliu Codreanu led the fascist party known as the Iron Guard, aiming to wrest power from King Carol II. Anne's father was a highly placed antiques dealer who was decorator to the king; as such, he was a member at some level of the court circle.[1] In 1937, the Iron Guard gained strength in the parliamentary election. Then came the Munich Pact in September 1938. The upper classes in Romania, caught between Nazi and home-grown fascism, knew they were living under the gun, and Baraghian determined to get his daughters to safety and continue their education in Switzerland.

Just then, however, salvation, or at least a solution, arrived for Anne. An eligible visitor from Belgium named Gilbert Jaeger (1918–2009) met and fell in love with the dark-haired and strikingly attractive young woman with flashing black eyes, only eighteen but already very seductive.[2] By wedding this youth who had immediately become her suitor, she could escape to the West. She said later that she had proposed to Jaeger that they should have a *"marriage blanc"*—unconsummated. This statement was always denied by her husband, who is unlikely to have taken her with him to Belgium on such terms, especially given the several years they would remain legally wedded. Anne got her mother to encourage the match, although Baraghian père objected. The lovely, if hot-tempered, Anne, however, used to being doted upon by her family, had moved in high circles and was accustomed to having money and getting her own way.[3]

Gilbert was twenty years old, the son of Norbert Jaeger, a Belgian engineer working in the Romanian oil business, and he had come to visit his father.[4] He was mature for his years, had sufficient money, a first-rate mind, and Belgian citizenship; simply on practical grounds, there was much to recommend him. Soon the two women overcame the father's resistance, and Anne married the love-smitten Belgian in Bucharest in 1938. Slightly older than Paul de Man, Jaeger was an unusually intelligent man who had a wide circle of friends, and in some ways he remained a leader of the group throughout his life. He later became an economist, and in his postwar career he would become director of protection for the United Nations High Commissioner for Refugees, based in Switzerland.[5] Undoubtedly, the young husband understood that his wife would bring him prestige and shine brightly in his set in Brussels, where he was active in the Cercle du Libre Examen.

The couple came to Brussels on November 17, 1938. Like most upper- and also middle-class women in Europe in that era, Anne already spoke French, but she wanted to learn German, which was obviously going to be increasingly important for all Europeans.[6] No doubt encouraged by Jaeger, she began at once to take lessons from the mother of Georges Goriély, Mme. Temmerman, an émigrée who had created work for herself as a private tutor in German before gaining an appointment at ULB. It was natural for both Paul and Georges to meet her bewitching new student.[7] The young Romanian woman was very small and dark, with regular features, large, lustrous eyes, shining black hair, and a warm, ebullient manner that won her friends easily. In many ways, she was the opposite of Frida, and so perhaps the more attractive to a man on the rebound. Goriély, an outstanding student who would later become a highly respected historian and was a German-Jewish émigré, had been a little in love with Anne, whom he later described as having been "one of the most beautiful women in Brussels."[8]

While her social qualities helped sweep most people into her circle, they did not count with everyone. The astute Paul Willems was a lawyer—tall, handsome, and distinguished in appearance; for thirty-six years, he would work for and then preside over one of Belgium's major cultural institutions, the Palace of Beaux-Arts. He knew Anne well but appreciated her only moderately. She was a charmer, he remembered, and quite pretty. The parties she gave were very pleasant, but she "wasn't very intelligent. . . . She never made a remark worth taking the trouble to remember." Implying a certain self-centeredness and smallness, he added, "She also didn't bear hardship well," and was "sometimes a little difficult to manage if she was hungry, or had lost something."[9]

Tant pis. She was indifferent to criticism. The occasional high-minded intellectual might not like her, but Anne had exceptional social intelligence, which would help her climb out of desperate situations throughout her life, enchanting men, pushing them always, by her own account (and that of others), to provide her with the money her extravagant tastes demanded, needs she readily admitted. She had plenty of faults, but her later life would reveal that from her own point of view she overcame serious obstacles by shrewdness and skill—and no little courage. Intelligent but not an intellectual, she enjoyed managing her friends—for their own good, of course. However, her temperament was "fiery . . . she could turn on a dime," according to her eldest son, and as both mother and wife, she could be harsh and physically abusive.[10] But that lay ahead.

These were the central figures in Paul's circle. Gilbert Jaeger, who would graduate from ULB in 1941, worked, like Paul, on its *Cahiers*. Georges was an intimate. All of them loved and respected Frida and respected Dosogne, whether or not they loved him. To be one of them was to be accepted by the most intellectual group of the mixed but essentially liberal-left set of friends at ULB, who sprang largely from middle- and upper-middle-class Brussels, especially those who regarded themselves as freed from the shackles of conventional religion. Appearing together, the four comrades looked radically different. Paul, cool, ironic, and charming, was an athletically built young man with thick blond hair and piercing, deep blue eyes. Anne was as short as she was pretty, her dark coloring showing her Middle Eastern origins. Goriély, tall, big-boned, and somewhat awkward, was not handsome, but it was easy to read the sincerity, high intelligence, good will, and vulnerability that marked his face.

November 1938 was a bad month. In Germany, Kristallnacht occurred on the ninth. A night of horrors prevailed when all over Germany Jewish shops were broken into and the glass from store windows lay strewn on the streets. Jews were attacked and publicly humiliated; some were arrested and sent to Dachau.[11] The newlywed young couple arrived in Belgium from Bucharest just a week later, on November 17, barely in time for safety, for eleven days after Anne and Gilbert left her home, a bloodbath began, in which over the next years the members of Romania's royal house and the fascist Legionnaires fought one another to the death in a battle that included the strangulation in prison of a party leader.[12]

International politics, though horrific, did not stop life from going on. The four young friends, an original-looking bunch, all appeared at a Christmas party at the university on December 3, 1938. Anne always remembered the fateful date, not because of the bloody turmoil in her homeland, but because it was the night that she met Paul. For her, it was a thunderbolt, a *"coup de foudre."*[13] He would not be nineteen for three more days. Unfortunately for her, he did not share her feelings. For Anne, however, it was to be the romance of her life, the only relationship that gave her children (although she was to marry four times), and the one about which her anger and sense of loss persisted almost till the end of her life. "I met him in the dark," she said, speaking in a mixture of French and English, meaning perhaps that Paul was still mourning for his mother but also that it was night and midwinter, both in fact and in his heart. She made up her mind instantly, she reported, to begin an affair. "His eyes became really like fire [when he saw me]. I saw the sad, incontrollable soul coming from the darkness. I had such a happy childhood—joyous, happy. . . . I said, I will give happiness to this person. I met Paul de Man and I said to Gilbert, 'Look, this is my life. There is nothing to do.' "[14]

Undoubtedly, Anne began to invite Paul to grow closer at once, and he seems to have responded, perhaps halfheartedly, for he was still tied to Frida. Unable to commit himself to anything except his work at *Cahiers*, certainly not to his studies, he was fearful of "lacerating" both his own feelings and those of another person. Haunted by an uncertain and fluid sense of self, of which he had earlier written to Frida, he was emotionally in limbo. But events were getting ahead of him, and the women were moving faster than he was.

Frida told him she was marrying Dosogne. When he wrote her desperately in January that he had broken off his other tie, undoubtedly referring to Anne, it was too late, and Frida and Dosogne were wed a few days later.[15] The pins were knocked out from under Paul, and there returned what can only be called existential suffering. He accepted that he would have no one to help him gain a sense of direction. He wrote Frida that he would live for those things that pleased him. Soon he planned to buy a convertible, in the fall, a "small car, but open."[16]

This was a decisive moment and an important letter. It was full of hurt, but the determination he was announcing to live for the pleasures of this world—material, esthetic, and intellectual, but without personal ties; in short, to be an alienated man (and in the full Ericksonian sense)—these would not pass, but would become deeper as he struggled through these difficult years. To paraphrase Gertrude Stein, there would be "no there there"; he would live in an Oakland of the spirit. For him, Frida had been a moral compass; now he had none. The troubles Paul de Man would make for himself, both in Belgium and the United States later on, are undoubtedly in part the result of the turn he decided to take at this time. Knowing himself to be unstable and lacking a consistent sense of self, as he said in the letter of December 15, 1938, to Frida, he would become a shipwreck. Later working for *Le Soir (volé)*, he would consider a novel by his friend Louis Fonsny and reflect on the devastation caused by "violent emotional shocks" that could turn a man into a shipwreck and cause him to break his rudder, lose his personality, and gyrate morally with every wind and swell. De Man's apparent topic was the effect of war; the subtext was his own life and many losses. Indeed, in the three collaborating media companies he would work for in Brussels, in his own publishing company, Hermès, in Antwerp, and at Harvard once he was in the United States, there would appear a consistent pattern, a sort of wake left by the trail of his own broken rudder. Paul took the chemistry test again in October 1939 and this time he passed, his first academic success of this nature at the university. The grade, however, was the equivalent of a B, "*distingué*."[17]

Something had broken, or perhaps developed in the mind of this once-promising student. (Even years later, as a graduate student at Harvard, he would again have grave difficulties with examinations.) His indifference to the judgment of others, whether people or institutions, had hardened. He would become self-sufficient, an intellectual, always humorous and amusing among his friends—indeed delightfully malicious and catty about them, as many testified—and intellectually independent. He was reading Sartre, as his reviews would later show, and probably eagerly consuming all the literary journals from Paris. If he was going to shape a new self in the literary world, the man-made shackles of conventional behavior must be broken. From Nietzsche to Gide, he had nineteenth- and twentieth-century intellectual forebears who pointed the way. He would become at a very early age not precisely learned or widely erudite, but an autodidact with deep knowledge of the topics that interested him and command of a magisterial written tone.[18]

And so he began an affair with Anne. Probably at first he thought it was just a fling, given her married state and his evident readiness to break it off, of which he wrote to Frida. Yet he was flattered, for the young Romanian beauty was "much courted" in his circles, and being seen with her was "something of a coup," as he explained to his second wife.[19]

Their motives and characters were fatally different. To Anne, an affair with Paul was her heart's desire—and he was also an excellent catch in the practical sense. She was an émigrée, and politics were threatening. The greater the fear of German invasion grew, the more valuable a lover Paul became as the nephew of Henri de Man, with the latter's position and close ties to the court. Such a connection gave added protection.

As for Paul, he, too, was learning. He might have seemed weak in the opinion of more extroverted and aggressive men, but socially and intellectually he was finding his feet and moving in quite a different direction from the one his father had planned. The younger man already had subtle social skills and knew that he did not need to assert himself loudly: His intelligence, aristocratic manner, ability to provide a stream of entertaining humor, as well as his good looks and high social status, already made him a magnetic figure, able to find his way into the center of any situation he wished. He might have had some passing sexual experience before Anne, but she represented his first real affair. She was a passionate woman, and at first she offered powerful rewards.

He was twenty. Did he argue with himself that it was more "healthy" to enter a supposedly immoral relationship than to let himself be pushed by the changing winds of "mystical doctrines" he would later deplore? As an adolescent, he had disapproved of his father's infidelities, but now he was an adult, a young one, still mourning his mother and on the rebound from Frida. Paul came from a sophisticated world where married women often had affairs without arousing much hostile comment, providing they were discreet. He drifted into Anne's orbit. Later, he said of the relationship with Anne that he had been "trapped. [And that] 'My father told me that I'd regret it, and I did.' "[20] He could not foresee how profoundly his life would be altered by the affair he entered into lightly with the seductive young woman who sparkled and intrigued him on that dark December night.

11.

EXODUS

ALTHOUGH HE HAD LOST FRIDA, PAUL, AN ATTRACTIVE AND TALENTED young man, continued to have a full life, for his ongoing work on *Cahiers* led to a growing circle of literary friends, with whom he shared serious literary interests. These included Georges Lambrichs, a man of the Left who would become important to him. Above all, he was becoming more intimate with Anne and her husband.

How did Gilbert Jaeger deal with the increasing closeness of his wife and Paul de Man? Gilbert was in some ways wise beyond his years. He saw Paul as intelligent, but not as the most intelligent man in their circle, and he thought him a luftmensch, a dreamer. If, as Anne testified later, she told her husband at once about her feelings, he may have thought it was an infatuation that would pass, or even that Paul himself would grow tired of the affair. An entirely serious person himself, though only a little older than his wife and his friend, he loved Anne and wanted to hold on to her. Moreover, an important aspect of her personality was that she had very extravagant tastes, as all her friends testified and as she admitted herself—always specifying that Paul was equally a spendthrift. Her young husband, a man who perhaps knew that he was destined for the success he did achieve not only in business but in the world of international relations, probably supposed that she would go on needing him when the feckless Paul was only a memory. By comparison to himself, the nineteen-year-old de Man, still clearly racked by mourning and known to have so recently been attached to Frida, was a youth unable even to pass his examinations. Gilbert may have told himself that Anne, young and recently uprooted, separated from her family, needed time to settle down. If so, events would show that he underestimated the steely determination that underlay the nineteen-year-old's public persona as a warm and intriguing social butterfly.

Whatever the emotional currents swirling around him, Paul liked the attention he was getting from Anne. He remained close to Frida, who was entirely different but nevertheless attractive and influential. He had money, and his father left him alone. He was envied by other men. He could keep his grief to himself and maintain his seductively aloof distance from most of the world, while entertaining his friends with his flow of ironic wit and good-natured, accepting stance. He didn't judge others. On the contrary, he emanated toward the world a quiet and amused sense of complicity in its foibles and venial sins. At the same time, he was highly secretive about himself, as Frida knew, and always "discreet," a watchword he would utter even in his fifties. With perfect manners and an instinctive knowledge of how to manage others, he was well equipped to occupy his increasingly complex social role. Despite this facade, he also seemed vulnerable.

Paul Willems met him during these years, when he, Lambrichs, André Souris, and other young writers frequented a café at the Port Louise in the center of Brussels. Paul was not only very young, the other recalled, but always seemed even younger. This, together with his air of being a supergifted youth, gave him an "irresistible allure." Like de Man, Willems sprang from a wealthy, intellectual, and socially prominent family, and after the war he was interrogated for having served in an official position under the occupant.[1] As a widely praised writer, he was an excellent observer, and his descriptions are valuable.[2] They must be taken with a grain of salt, however, for the testimony of others shows that at times he aimed to forestall and soften criticism of Paul de Man.[3]

De Man's faults were already well established. He never had enough money, in spite of his father's generosity, and he always spent more than he possessed. And while his discretion saved him from social mistakes, all of his friends, including those from his later years in the United States, testified that he not only loved to gossip but also was consistently, if amusingly, malicious about whatever person had just left the room. His put-downs were not confrontational, but funny and insightful. That, however, was seen as a minor peccadillo, common enough, though evidently more noticeable in Paul. With his wide reading, capacity for rare insights, and his direct, physical energy, he was able after the Athenaeum to make the world more interesting for those around him, as he had done for his cousin Bob De Braey. With Paul, life was theater, and he was always ready to slip into character.

He was reading voraciously, developing his taste for Surrealism, which would be evident to the wider public once he began publishing his reviews in 1941, and he was also establishing friendships on both ends of the political spectrum. On the one hand, he entered a long-term and valuable period of debate with Georges Lambrichs, who would later play a marginal role in the literary Resistance, and debate with him such matters as the relative importance to literature of psychology and formal values. Modernism was in full flower, though the movement was not then called by that name. Reading and "culture"—always understood as high culture—held respected, if not dominant, places in the minds of even the general public (a respect that has essentially disappeared, especially in the United States but also in Europe). It was in this arena that Paul was orienting himself during his years on *Cahiers* at the ULB. To become an influential figure in the world of high culture was a goal open to few, but it was worth achieving, as great prestige came with it. A well-placed, highly cultivated, and ambitious young man of talent could go far. Even political power could follow, for in European countries, and especially the Francophone world, one could become a minister of state, managing the national offices for culture or education, or running a plum, state-supported institution, such as a theater or great library. That was what the future had in store for Paul Willems, who continued to write throughout his career and would thrive in the center of Belgium's highest cultural bureaucracy after he emerged from World War II. (His first two novels would be published by the Didiers' Nazi-subvented Toison d'Or.)

Yet while Paul de Man and many other youths were enjoying life, the world around him was almost literally imploding. Hitler was privately planning war while publicly denying it. With his invasion of Poland, the cry went up: "I will not die for Danzig"—the Polish port on the Baltic Sea, its sole direct access to shipping and the wider world. But the Western powers could not ignore the fate of Poland as they had done with Czechoslovakia, and on September 3, 1939, England and France declared war. This was soon called the Phony War, for they took only minimal action. The Maginot Line had been constructed in the north of France and Belgium, and Britain moved a large number of troops, the Expeditionary Force of over 200,000 men, to the northwest portion of France and its coast.[4] But these were passive acts, and Hitler used the winter of 1939–1940 to plan his biggest, most decisive campaign yet against the West, beginning with the occupation first of Denmark and Norway and then of Holland and Belgium. These small, flat lowland countries would be relatively easy to pick off, and he could thereafter march unimpeded into France, a larger and richer prize and Germany's traditional enemy.

Paul's uncle, meanwhile, was approaching the apex of his career. In 1939, he came back with great force as minister without portfolio in the Pierlot government, always promoting pacific relations with Hitler. By then, he was an increasingly close adviser to the young King Léopold III, and when he abandoned Pierlot's government at the end of that year—no doubt seeing what lay ahead—he continued to be identified as the official "protector" of Queen Elisabeth during the dangerous months just before and during the arrival of German troops.

Eight months after the war began, Hitler fulfilled his plans and his troops moved into Norway. That finally brought Britain, led by a renascent Churchill, to attention, but by then the situation was beyond control. On April 9, 1940, the German army reached Denmark. For Belgium, that signaled the end. From then on, the only hope of those on the Left was that the United States would join the war.[5]

IN THIS PERIOD OF terrible suspense, Paul, on or around April 11, 1940, borrowed Jan de Man's keys, went to bed with Anne, and conceived his first child.[6] It was probably not their first such encounter, but it would be the most consequential. Oddly, it would prove to be part of what might be called a "generative pattern," for this would not be the last time Paul would respond to a major crisis, public or private, by starting a new child into life. A month later, the Nazis were at the border of Holland, and that country fell in the next several days. Then, on May 10, the German army crossed into Belgium. The sound of tanks and trucks could be heard rumbling down the roads to Brussels, and the little country was engulfed in war. By trying to pacify Hitler and by not arming against him, the country was also unprepared to deal with invasion even organizationally. Because of their suffering in the war of 1914–1918, its citizens knew and feared what was coming. They were still demoralized by the results of the Great Depression of the 1930s, and the country had long been divided by linguistic, quasi-ethnic strife. Certain elements of its Flemish population—though only a minority— had actively assisted the German conquest in World War I. Some now welcomed the renewed entry of the Germans. For many reasons, the country had no stomach for a new war it was certain to lose.

Now Paul de Man was caught up in what was called the "*pagaille*" (shambles) following the invasion. Bitter quarrels erupted between the ministers and King Léopold III, who, after years of pursuing the rigidly "neutralist" policy of Henri de Man, now tried, albeit unsuccessfully, to arrange a last-minute mutual defense league with the French and British, only to be stymied by his cabinet. (Similar treaties had actually existed after World War I but had been canceled in the 1930s to signal to the Nazis that Belgium would not deserve punishment if war should come.) Simultaneously, the government was under attack by the French, who were themselves surrendering but blaming Belgium as traitor for its part in the shambles. Within days, Belgium lost its government entirely, for all the serving ministers of state fled the country, with the exception of Henri de Man alone.[7] Only four Belgian ministers went on to London to form a tiny and symbolic government in exile, among them Paul-Henri Spaak. It was typical of the time that when the then prime minister, Paul-Emile Janson, addressed the nation on the radio from "somewhere in Belgium," he was actually over the border in Le Havre.[8]

Suddenly, the king took it upon himself to lead his troops into war, but then he reversed himself, and on May 28, after only eighteen days, he declared, again acting alone—except perhaps with advice from Henri de Man—that he was "capitulating" to the enemy, using a term that has since been a bone in the throat of a plenitude of Belgians. Meanwhile, the disappearance of the ministers from the country made them contemptible in the eyes of the populace. Soon German propaganda would mock their flight, and its army would capture large numbers of troops, imprisoning them as POWs in Germany for much of the war.

Immediately after his capitulation, the king, a widower, shut himself up with his children and their governess in a castle outside of Brussels, declared himself "a prisoner of war," and refused to communicate or appear in public again. Then he married the governess. These were strange decisions, to say the least. How could one become a "prisoner of war" of one's own volition, especially while living in the comforts of one's castle (just outside Brussels) with one's family? Léopold was so resented that he would lose his throne after the war and be forced to abdicate in favor of his son, Prince Baudouin. The people would have been much more angry had they seen the photograph that historian Jean Stengers later discovered.[9] During the war, the king was so eager to curry favor with Hitler that he flew secretly to Berchtesgaden, donned the uniform of a Nazi officer, and in that dress posed with the Führer as the two relaxed on a sunny terrace against the background of the Bavarian Alps.

The confusion, indiscipline, and lack of planning at the highest levels in both Belgium and France were reflected downward. Paul de Man and his friends became harbingers of an immense movement of millions of people that from mid-May through June washed south over France in a tidal wave, or exodus (known as the *exode* in France), a flight of refugees of biblical proportions. The youth of Belgium had to save themselves as best they could. Early in the eighteen days of war, the government issued an order directing all males aged eighteen to thirty-five to equip themselves with a blanket and at least two days' food and gather in two cities in the south to be "mobilized." Because the war was a lost cause, it was probable that the nation's youth would be sent to German POW or forced-labor camps, and so on the eve of Léopold's capitulation, the government ordered its young men to flee the country, theoretically to be organized for battle elsewhere, but actually to avoid imprisonment.[10]

Paul faced the same threat. His uncle was the avowed friend of Germany and Otto Abetz, and Henri de Man would be repaid for a time with greatly increased importance. Henri did not, however, try to keep his nephew apart from the rest of his generation. Perhaps he joined Bob de Man in supplying the young man with money; certainly he gave Paul invaluable advice about when, where, and how to go, for it was crucial to move quickly to get ahead of the great wave of refugees that would soon flee from the oncoming war, and at once to to find a remote, comfortable refuge. And so at dawn on the morning of May 14, Paul de Man checked his backpack for food, clothing, and water, stashed his money safely about his person, and, shouldering his heavy load, set off for the earliest possible train. He did not go alone, but was joined by his mistress, already one month pregnant, and her husband, both equally burdened. As they made their way to the railway station, they could hear the guns of the artillery on the outskirts of the city. But—crucially—the country's borders were still open. Eagerly and with sharp elbows, they stuffed themselves onto an already-overcrowded train headed for Lille, at the northern edge of France. There they transferred to another train, and then to another, and another, till they were riding in cars with wooden slats for seats. Discomfort, however, was bearable at their age, and they were heading for the south of France, far from the oncoming troops and bombs.

Their timing was good. Paul and his friends were members of that human tsunami that swept millions out of their homes to suffer and sometimes die on the impossibly overloaded roads of France.[11] From Paris alone, two million took to the roads during the second and third weeks of June.[12] In a country of fewer than sixty million, approximately ten million persons were displaced.[13] The Germans were ruthless in trying to prevent the people's escape, and for seventeen days, until France surrendered, their planes flew low, mercilessly strafing both highways and railroad tracks. Only two days after Paul departed, by May 16 trains were halted so frequently by bombardments that passengers frequently had to get off and walk; by the twentieth, no train could leave Calais, on the northern coast of France, for the south.[14] The attacks came so fast that finally the warning sirens could not be distinguished from the all-clear signals. The fleeing populace did not know precisely where they were going or what would happen—only that the men must avoid capture and German conscription. Many died on the roads, for when the aerial guns attacked, the refugees had no cover and could run only to the ditches.[15] Many on foot could not move along roads blocked by impassable traffic and tried to walk through the woods, only to be assaulted there by hungry people, compatriots who had turned criminal.

By June 1, having concluded the Belgian campaign, the Germans were in France. The Maginot Line yet again failed to hold, and the Wehrmacht swept through the industrial area where Belgium and France meet, an area that was to be governed as part of greater Belgium once the occupation had begun. There would be plenty of finger-pointing on both sides, but in the end France resisted for one day less than Belgium had; it declared an armistice with Germany on June 17.

After four torturesome days, Paul and his friends reached their haven, a small, sparkling spa town on the French slopes of the Pyrenees, Bagnères-de-Luchon. It was perfectly situated near the crest of the wooded mountains, almost at the end of a minor road, and the terminus of the tertiary rail line. There was nothing there but pine woods, thermal springs, and bright, clear air, nothing the Germans wanted to possess, too distant and insufficiently fashionable to attract officers on holiday. Along the short and sunny main street lay little boutiques, a few hotels, and some restaurants. One did not travel to these mountains for remarkable food, but it was excellent and piquant, due to the abundant game from the surrounding forests. The local people were used to visitors and would ask few embarrassing questions, for Spain was only fifteen kilometers away, or some nine miles over the crest of the mountains, and the street through town and the little paths through the surrounding forest had undoubtedly long been known to smugglers.

This was the first brush that Paul and Anne had with adult life in the sense of having to manage their own lives without family or friends to back them up, but the Belgian government gave all these young escapees a small daily subsidy. In Bagnères-de-Luchon, the men registered with the local official recruiting center for the Belgian army (CRAB, its French acronym), which allowed each man and members of his family ten francs a day, plus free accommodation. In fact, the group of three lived rather well. At first, they stayed in a local hotel, where, in a corridor on June 18, one of them heard Charles de Gaulle's famous "*Rappel*"—his radio call from London—rallying France to his side and promising the eventual return to his country both of himself and of freedom.

Then they found a charming villa, rented part of it, and settled in. They got a garden as well, where a little creek ran below, glittering in the sun. It was nothing short of idyllic. The summer of 1940 was beautiful and sunny, a good time, at least for them, to be in the mountains. Some have speculated that it was Paul de Man's intention to escape to Spain by stopping close to the border and then crossing it. Geographically, this might seem likely, but the facts make that implausible. Even apart from political considerations (for his close friends hated Franco), there was a more important issue: The crossing would have been dangerous for Anne. Safety was central, and the unborn child, as all acknowledged, was Paul's. He could afford to wait peacefully until he received his uncle's signal to return.

Meanwhile, the occupation had begun. Henri de Man was in the saddle with the occupant. On June 28, he issued first a printed manifesto and then made a radio speech. He intended to pacify both his German bosses and the Belgian people, but in the long run he failed in both aims. His published document was addressed to militant socialists, and as the de facto prime minister and the actual head of the Socialist party, he urged the workers and party members to accept the occupation and work with the Germans peacefully because it represented a "national resurrection." They were not only to give up the idea of democracy but also must renounce the Socialist party, for its role had ended: The socialist revolution, long awaited, had been realized![16] This was scandalous: A lifelong socialist leader was telling them that Nazi rule represented the culmination of the socialist revolution, something that shocked all socialists who had not turned against democracy and toward that dictatorship by the elite that Henri de Man favored. Then Henri took to the national airwaves and told the country essentially the same thing, that they must work with the occupant, and had to "collaborer"—a term that at this period was already quite contentious but did not yet carry the deeply ominous meaning it developed as the war's sufferings and hatreds grew deeper.

Now Otto Abetz, the German "ambassador" to occupied France but actually its political ruler, decided to celebrate the moment and savor his victory. On August 10, he invited Henri de Man to join him at a dinner party in Paris, together with other Belgian friends. Two years before, Abetz had been expelled by France as a dangerous spy. Now he was the most powerful man in the country. On that hot summer evening, the group relaxed and feasted, for they were men of hearty appetites, and the dinner was luxurious. He and his guests, all men except for one woman, would later have much to atone for and would pay for their decade of subversion with exile, judicial condemnation, and assassination, but at this gathering all were at the top of their form. For almost a decade, they had worked the levers of power to manipulate public opinion and persons of influence, and now their time had come: after just eleven months of war and and with relatively few casualties. Germany had conquered or was dominant in all the countries of western Europe.[17]

Henri de Man traveled to France in the same eccentric way that his nephew Paul had done three months earlier, taking with him both his mistress and her husband, Lucienne and Edouard Didier. Also present that night were Léon Degrelle and Pierre Daye. The bullyboy Degrelle enjoyed playing the role of salacious aesthete, for from his exile in Spain he wrote retrospectively of how the evening sky had glowed over Paris with green-tinted lights, a place of refinement and pleasure. Lucienne looked resplendent, Degrelle wrote, describing the "consummate art" of the little veiled hat, which made her skin seem exquisitely delicate, even "immaterial"–and concealed the tiny wrinkles about her eyes— her long and graceful huntress's legs and "divine haunches"—and her intelligence, he added—all of which contributed to Degrelle's ironic pose of fainting admiration.[18] As they visited France that August, the de Mans, uncle and nephew alike, could look forward to a promising future.

The ambassador's alleged purpose for arranging the meeting—to induce Henri de Man and Degrelle to work together—did not bear fruit, but it did put the stamp of approval on the present arrangement among the two countries and the occupant that had defeated them. Now the signal could be given for Belgium's youth to return home. This was crucial to Paul, for Anne was now five months pregnant, and his first child would be born on January 11, 1941, a month and five days after his own twenty-first birthday. Paul, to his credit, would both acknowledge his responsibility and take it seriously.

The three young people returned to real life in Brussels on August 23, 1940. Across the Channel, meanwhile, Germany had begun bombing Britain in July and would continue with heavier attacks in August. On September 7, it launched the infamous Blitz, which over the course of fifty-seven consecutive nights reduced parts of London and other cities to rubble and death. So far as the Belgians knew, whether they later joined the Resistance or were active in collaboration, the war was already over, lost definitively. Every one of Paul de Man's friends stressed this as fact, including the Jewish Esther Sluszny, who went into the maquis after remaining in contact with Paul for years, and Frida, who withdrew in her own way.[19] There was no question of that for Paul. Occupation meant different things to different people; and for him the coming years were a time of opportunity.

12

PAUL COLLABORATES

———————

WHEN PAUL DE MAN RETURNED WITH HIS MISTRESS AND HER HUS-
band to Brussels in late August 1940, they found a city already struggling under German oppression.[1] Unlike London, it had not been
damaged by aerial bombardment, but the occupation would last four
years, until September 1944. The ruler was Gen. Alexander von Falkenhausen, a Prussian who managed Belgium and northern France; side by
side with his army, the Gestapo also reigned.

During the next few months, Paul moved in with Gilbert Jaeger and
Anne, and together they formed a ménage à trois. They inhabited an
apartment at 65, square des Latins, a solid, prominent building in a
comfortable middle-class district adjacent to the university. For one so
naturally secretive, openly entering this arrangement was surprisingly
flamboyant. It would be one of the several oddities in Paul's early life
that his friends remembered with amusement. Yet they did not criticize. They had even more to laugh at when, after the birth of Paul's son
on January 11, 1941, Paul and Gilbert were seen daily together, deep in
conversation, pushing the infant in his carriage around the square.[2]

Paul was at loose ends that autumn. He had at least learned that science held no attraction for him. Without enthusiasm, he enrolled for a
fourth time at ULB, but now he entered the School of Political and
Social Sciences. The discipline he chose was his uncle's field, and good
preparation for living under the New Order (then a polite cognomen

for Nazi rule and ideology). Required at one time to write a paper on political philosophy, he instead asked Goriély to write it for him. The obliging Georges complied, but Paul did not bother to present it and was marked as having failed all the numerous courses for which he had signed up.[3] Soon he dropped university work entirely.

Later, he accurately wrote on his application to Harvard that he had achieved "Candidature" at ULB. The word had an official sound to American ears, but in Belgian terms, it meant merely that he had spent three undergraduate years without achieving any academic status. That problem, however, lay ahead. In late 1940, he was twenty-one years old and would soon be a father, but he had taken no steps to define his future. Compared to his friend Gilbert Jaeger, who as a young engineer had a job and would soon be rising in heavy industry, Paul was not impressive. For some months, he was idle.

In the meantime, von Falkenhausen consolidated his power, holding sway through most of the war, until his friendships with members of the anti-Hitler putsch brought him to a Nazi prison. A Prussian aristocrat and a soldier of the old school, he sported a monocle and a shaved head, and was said, out of contempt for Hitler, to leave his office to walk his dog just at five, the hour when the Führer gave his daily radio address. He had served for many years in China, and in his memoir he presented himself as a cultivated man and a connoisseur of orchids and jade.[4] When Paul de Man became a reviewer, he wrote favorably about the opening of the Exhibition of German Books, which von Falkenhausen mentioned he also attended, including in his memoir a photograph of himself flintily quizzing a text through his single eyeglass.

Von Falkenhausen perceived his mission as being to pacify, not destroy, Belgium, for he needed the country to remain productive, and he pressed from it as much production of foodstuffs and heavy goods as possible in order to send to them to Germany. His army, of course, was nevertheless always ready to shoot to kill when the Resistance threatened. On the whole, however, the populace noticed that the German soldiers were well behaved, following policies that were set in deliberate contrast to their brutal practices in World War I. The general boasted famously that he had succeeded so well in persuading Belgians to continue working and producing in their normal, prewar jobs that he ruled the country with only four hundred German officers in place. He did not add that under his governance much of the populace was near starvation and that in order to feed their families, Belgians went to work in factories, making weapons for war. Some traveled voluntarily for this employment to Germany, where they were better paid, as Jan de Man did late in the war; others were forced to go.[5]

For the occupant, control of the media was crucial, for it meant controlling information and, they hoped, public opinion. Such management was the cornerstone of what began as a relatively peaceful occupation, although the Resistance soon made itself felt. *Le Soir* had long been a widely circulated newspaper that appealed to the middle and managerial classes, and influencing those opinion makers was part of von Falkenhausen's strategy. All the old staff there who had been loyal to democratic ideals had quit or been fired the day after the German army marched into Brussels. Once the army was in the saddle, new jobs suddenly opened in the summer of 1940 for younger men in the media, providing they were pro-Nazi. It was typical of the ad hoc style of the early days of collaboration under the occupation that Raymond De Becker was hired on the street in Brussels one summer day when he ran into Max Liebe. De Becker, who would become Paul de Man's boss, had fled the country in May when the war began, as Pierre Daye and other "neutralists" had done, for they had pushed pro-Nazi policies and suddenly feared internment for treason. A few weeks later, however, once the Germans had won, they returned. De Becker and Liebe had long been friendly; the latter was Abetz's sidekick. He was also considered a spy. Now the friendship paid off, for Liebe had become chief of the Press Section of the German embassy.[6] When the two men encountered each other, Liebe simply offered De Becker the job of running *Le Soir (volé)*, and the young Belgian Nazi vaulted immediately into a position of immense power.

Paul de Man was making only token appearances throughout the autumn at ULB and spent his time with his friends. Anne, very popular, loved to give parties, which were so well attended that Nellie De Ligne, the wife of Paul's first boss, remembered that at one of them she had "eaten sausages in the bathroom," so crowded were the other rooms at the house on square des Latins. Throughout the war, the couple would entertain lavishly, even when others were in need and had to spend their days hunting "for potatoes and coal," as Marlene and also Li attested. For Paul, who had grown up in a household that at its best was lonely and depressed, this new life with the cheerful, sexy, and highly social Romanian woman was undoubtedly a revelation. It was his first experience of ordinary worldly pleasures and a warm home life. Anne could be very difficult, with her bad temper and incessant demands, but in some ways she was a balance wheel. Paul dealt well enough with the world on his own terms by keeping others at a distance; Anne brought people into her circle.

De Man also decided publicly to acknowledge his child and to support him, an honorable decision. Many men would simply have refused responsibility and walked away, knowing that his offspring would be born in wedlock and that neither the child nor its mother would suffer. But when Anne invited Paul to share her home with Gilbert and establish a ménage à trois, she made it easier—almost obligatory—for Paul to stand by her and her child. Perhaps she pointed out that if he moved in, it would be only a continuation, almost a formalization, of the same pleasant relationship that the three had enjoyed since May. The only difference would be that their unconventional arrangement would be known widely among their friends in Brussels.

Paul's conflicts resemble in many ways the stance that Erik Erikson, drawing in part on his own adolescent experience in northern Europe in this era, would later attribute to the "alienated man," the adolescent fundamentally in rebellion who expresses it passive-aggressively by dropping out, refusing commitments, prolonging "latency," and showing a low level of affect, rather than through overt anger. Paul's repeated refusal to appear for his examinations was undoubtedly part of this condition. The *morale gidéenne* was still vital for him, and he undoubtedly enjoyed flouting conventions. After all, the arrangement did no harm to others, while benefiting himself. He was not made for bachelorhood, had no flat of his own, had never lived alone, and never would. Anne, showing her skills in managing people, understood this and was able to make a shared life very agreeable to him even while handling her husband's objections, if indeed he raised any.

One motive, of course, would have been that it was in Anne and her husband's own interests to join with Paul, for as Henri de Man's nephew, he was not merely Anne's lover but a powerful ally. Moreover, with the uniformed soldiers of the German army already everywhere on the streets, it would not have escaped the married couple's attention that after Anne gave birth, the four of them could, in turn, expect protection from the occupant. Such special treatment suited her tastes well. No doubt, however, the primary motive for Anne was that she was in love and knew that for Paul the child and his own ongoing residence with her was her best means of holding him. Nevertheless, as she never forgot, on one occasion, the Gestapo did enter their apartment and search it without explanation.[7]

Bob de Man, however, well versed in managing sexual liaisons and careful in spite of numerous affairs to keep free of all legal ties after his wife's death, foresaw what might lie ahead, and at some point he warned his son against the marriage that later ensued. But when he spoke out, Paul probably took his objection merely as a reason to do the opposite.

Equally dramatic were the entanglements that swirled outside the bedroom. At the journal that Paul de Man would soon join, Raymond De Becker was a force to be reckoned with, and De Becker's story throws light, by contrast, on Paul's. Only twenty-eight, he was editor in chief and sometimes known as the publisher (although a "Germanophile" Belgian named Schraenen technically held that post).[8] He was a man with certain gifts, in addition to his passionate adoption of the violent and oppressive ideas of Belgian Nazism. He and Pierre De Ligne were close; he dedicated his memoir, written in the summer of 1942, to both De Ligne and Louis Fonsny, the young novelist with whom De Ligne said the editor in chief was in love.[9] De Ligne considered him a "good boss" and a "good friend: friendly, intelligent, and interesting. A deep thinker [and] a self-made man" with a "very clear vision, [and] great political, cultural, and philosophical culture acquired on his own."[10] What De Ligne omitted was any hint of how deeply De Becker was driven by personal hatreds and resentment.

Untested at any large institution when he was given the position on *Le Soir (volé)* but long a publisher of small, extremely right-wing Catholic journals, De Becker had moved upward very quickly from working-class origins into sophisticated circles. Described by his political cartoonist, the unsparing Paul Jamin, as an ugly man, dark, with Semitic features, he was a popular, respected, highly intelligent boss. De Becker was also strongly anti-Semitic, and some might speculate that this perhaps resulted from his looks, or even from his being the illegitimate and rejected son of a Jewish businessman father who did not acknowledge him.[11] He made a hero of Edmond Picard and his bizarre and hateful ideas. (Jamin, like De Becker, was sentenced to long years in prison for helping the Nazi ideology "penetrate" Belgian culture—the classic collaborationist crime.)[12] The publisher's own origins and those of his opinions echo the pattern already discussed of the close admixture of Jewish and non-Jewish Belgian marriages and other relationships even among active anti-Semites who conveniently forgot those connections. The publisher himself attributed his inflamed fascism to the harshness of his early life. Impoverished, at age five he was evacuated to a brutal camp in Holland, where hordes of unsupervised children were crammed together, barely fed, and kept in unheated barracks. There he was starved and bullied mercilessly by the older boys. His foot was injured and then froze, leaving him crippled for life. Greatly traumatized, he returned to Charleroi carried by another child, unable to speak, and he lived as a mute for an extended period. He had gained, he wrote in his memoir, the conviction that everywhere in life, "the strong tyrannize over the weak."[13] A more generous socialism proved inadequate; only a National Socialism could satisfy him. De Becker had little formal education and had to leave school at fifteen. Most of his self-education evidently began during the years when he attached himself to a variety of Catholic leaders as he wandered on his own through France and Belgium.

In the autumn of 1940, De Becker began to devote a series of front-page articles to anti-Semitic tirades, and there can be no question that Paul was aware of the temper of the journal he was joining in December 1940. Perhaps anticipating the laws that in January 1941 would exclude Belgian Jews from all professions, De Becker assigned Léon Van Huffel, whom he had hired in September 1940 to promote his views, and bracketed his essays with a series of extracts from one of De Becker's foundational heroes, the writer-lawyer Edmond Picard, whom the publisher described approvingly as "Socialist and Nationalist and equally anti-Semite and racist." In his book, *L'Aryano-Sémitisme* (1899), Picard had stated, among other things, that Christ had been an Aryan. From the twelfth through the eighteenth of December, lengthy front-page extracts from Picard, probably selected by De Becker, composed of fake history and calumnies, represented the Jews as fearful ravagers of the goods and privileges of innocent and vulnerable Aryans.[14] His message was comparable to that of the fallacious Russian work (published in 1903 but composed in Paris) *The Protocols of the Elders of Zion*.

Paul would become for a while something of a protégé of the publisher, but his sufferings had not been material. De Becker certainly recognized the contrast between himself and Paul, but he didn't waste energy resenting the golden boy when he presented himself. He gave him an opening; it would be up to the other to prove his value.

THAT WINTER OF 1940–1941 was one of the coldest in memory. In spite of having its own coal mines, Belgium had little fuel or food, as these were being gobbled up by the occupant. As a result, widespread hunger and poverty set in. Under De Becker, however, *Le Soir (volé)* mixed strong doses of kitsch and determined optimism with its pro-German politics, running photographs of medieval castles, peasants plowing behind mighty oxen, and Dutch fishermen clad in clogs and "pittoresques costumes." Their *völkisch* appeal did not conceal the reality.[15] Morale was falling fast, and in the paper a leading article reproved Belgians for negative gossip, for beginning to doubt German victory—worse, for talking openly of "waiting" for German defeat. ("*Attentisme*"—the wait-and-see attitude of fence-sitters—was to be a particular target of the collaborating press, a line that Paul de Man was to echo.) Yet the same front-page article granted that everywhere people were mourning the dead, thinking of broken homes, of missing relatives—the men in POW camps in particular—and of their own hunger, sorrows one could read in the tight-lipped smiles and drawn faces of the people on the street.[16] What had become a national obsession with food invariably appeared also in the columns of the newspaper. People fled the city, and apartments, even in good neighborhoods, were renting at "prix de crise" minimal levels caused by the crisis. One could readily find two-

and three-bedroom apartments in such neighborhoods for between three hundred and four hundred francs per month. And that, as the books of the Agence Dechenne—where Paul de Man was later employed—were to show, was the weekly salary of a cleaning woman.[17] As the winter went on, the paper's pro-Nazi messages grew more explicit. Hitherto taboo, pictures of Hitler himself now appeared as he received Norwegian Girl Scouts on page one, or the plaudits of a crowd in Florence, or looked heavenward in "une attitude."[18] Princess Marie, of Belgian origin, was shown in Italy, receiving the Nazi salute from a double row of celebrants.

By the end of the year, a job was essential for Paul de Man. He enjoyed shocking those he saw as hypocritical moralists, but he also knew that he could not continue to live on an allowance, and Anne, who always pressed the men in her life to provide well for her, very strongly encouraged him to make money. In fact, she demanded it. Nellie De Ligne, who remained Anne's lifelong friend, recalled with a mixture of amusement and disapproval hearing her repeatedly shout at all her men, especially Paul and her fourth and last husband, the German ex-army officer Gerhard Ipsen-von Orland, that they must make more money, and that von Orland in particular must not retire for that reason.[19] Of course, Paul would never have joined his own father in making X-ray tables, although it was an enterprise that, as Philippe Burrin has shown, was just the sort of industry that profited considerably from German orders during the war.[20]

In December, Paul de Man arranged it: On Christmas Eve 1940, he published his first article, a short report on a concert, which appeared on the front page of Le Soir (volé). Paul was hired to assist the regular music critic, Oscar Esplá, he told his postwar interrogator, Roger Vinçotte. How Paul got the job has been debated. During his procès-verbal, the record of questioning (a document long thought to be lost or else nonexistent), he said that his old friend from university days, Pierre De Ligne, who on returning from the war had changed sides and at age twenty-six gone to work for De Becker, had provided entrée. "To help me, Pierre De Ligne, whom I had known at the university, suggested me as someone to help [Oscar] Esplá with the music column of Le Soir. At the same time, I continued my studies."[21] (It was not true that he went on studying, but saying this was probably meant to minimize his commitment to the journal.)

De Ligne, however, denied that he had helped de Man. He granted that he had known him from both the ULB and the Cercle du Libre Examen. As with all the respondents, his testimony must be taken with a grain of salt. He did not mention that as one who knew Lucienne Didier well, he would have met Paul at her salon as well. Like Paul de Man when he defended himself in 1955 at Harvard, Pierre De Ligne later claimed to have originally been a "socialist." His justification for his five years of work on *The Stolen Evening* was the standard one for collaborating intellectuals in Belgium who wanted to present themselves as being of the less extreme sort: He was a de Manian, a Europeanist. According to him, Paul de Man had just turned up in the office one day, and he had assumed that De Becker had taken Paul on as a favor to his uncle. De Ligne said later, "He knew I was at *Le Soir*. I didn't take the initiative—he had the idea by himself. He presented himself to De Becker. [It was] *'un jour de surprise'* when I saw his article there."[22]

However their contacts started, De Ligne and Paul de Man soon became professional allies and grew close socially during the war, although it appears from conflicting elements of their postwar testimony that the two fell out. De Ligne made domestic and agricultural news his special province while working at the newspaper, and after the war he used his wartime contacts to enter the food business.[23]

The former managing editor, who went to jail for collaborating, was certain that Paul was as fully guilty as he and that it was unjust that the other went free without a trial. Jan de Man expressed the same resentment. De Ligne, a onetime lawyer, thrived as a businessman after his release from prison, but forty years later no one in his old circle of friends admitted to seeing him. Like Jan de Man and the cartoonist Paul Jamin, equally sentenced for collaboration, De Ligne lived on with his wife in the same district as the others from ULB—although more opulently than they—but there was an invisible wall between them. He was no longer accepted or known within the circle that had stuck together through peace and war all their lives. He had no motive to soften his memories of de Man, and little or nothing left to lose, unlike some who had better survived the war and had more reason to be discreet.

If one asks why Paul de Man chose to collaborate, there is little mystery, especially in the context of his social and political worlds. *Collaboration* was a term whose meaning seems to have shifted and become more opprobrious during the course of the war.[24] Nevertheless, from de Man's own point of view, the case was clear. He was a birthright de Manian, tied by conviction and affection to his uncle's policies. He was eager—and needed—to make a lot of money, and he was convinced both of the Flemish cause, as he saw it at the time, and of his own great opportunity to "take a place"—a prominent place—in the future life of his country, where under German aegis, the Flemings would be important. In the early days of the occupation, before the United States had joined the war, when Hitler had not suffered a single defeat—or even a delay—the war, in the opinion of everyone around Paul de Man, simply was already lost. To Frida Vandervelden, who chose a different course from the one taken by her friend, he made the most idealistic case he could. "Paul told me when he began his collaboration with *Le Soir*, he saw that there was a possibility to create a Europe after the war—where let us say the nationalities, to be sure under German hegemony, would regain a degree of independence. A certain autonomous life," she recalled. He "knew what the risks were," he told her, but he said, " 'There's a place to take in the life of the country.' If our people didn't take these places, the Germans would. He may have seen a role for himself with a future. But he also felt cultured, intellectual men should create an intellectual structure ready to work when the culture should become to some degree free."

She defended him not as a "dreamer" but as a "visionary, one who can see things constructed in the future," comparing him to Henri: "Like his uncle." She stressed the reality that the war was over, definitively ended: "Everyone in the summer of 1940 considered that the war was over. And we had to cope with a future where Europe should be under German influence."[25] Frida shared Paul's allegiance to the autonomy of Flanders and his belief that they belonged to what they considered to be "the Germanic race." She was therefore the more open to his nationalistic self-justification, although she acted quite differently.

Others, however, had more nakedly self-interested reasons for joining and furthering Nazi rule. Pierre De Ligne argued his own and de

Man's case for joining the collaboration by saying there were important distinctions to be made: "We weren't Nazis, but merely disgusted with corrupt and inefficient democracy. We felt that within the ideology we could choose a nuanced position." One was free, he said, to choose the more "honest" elements of the Nazi ideology, the ideas with more "grandeur," indeed the more "socialist" ones.[26] The wealth they gained, he failed to mention. As for the anti-Semitism that was so central to Hitler's policies, De Ligne and men like him simply ignored it. No doubt many condoned it.

Yet, whatever the arguments put forth by Henri de Man and his nephew, collaborating was not a foregone conclusion. Some who had a private income simply disappeared, as Frida and Charles Dosogne did. "You did nothing," Frida said. "You refused to do anything. That was our position, my husband and I."

Young men who might have been seized by the occupying army to be sent to its wartime factories in Germany, like Paul's cousin, Bob De Braey, also disappeared. He was sheltered by his father, Jan, and stayed out of sight in Antwerp, avoiding the eyes of the enemy. Georges Goriély, too, managed to disappear, even while living on in Brussels. Active resistance was rare, but it did occur. In Frida's words, "Resistance—that [was] for the few who said, 'No, it's not over.'" Resistance was the brave choice of Paul's cousin Minime, Bob De Braey's older sister, who played a heroic, still unheralded role in it.[27] Yet she was one of a small minority at the beginning of the war.

Did Paul have other choices? Of course. Yet to him, entering his father's world of commerce would have been safe but pedestrian. Always a risk taker, Paul was now aware he was essentially a man of letters. He preferred the glamour and the potential for social and intellectual power offered by the intellectual world. Journalism might not be the nicest of callings, but that portal had been wide enough for his uncle Henri in 1905 (also a year of revolution) to turn his early freelance work for the *Leipziger Zeitung* into entrée into the highest levels of twentieth-century socialism.

While there were many contributing factors to Paul de Man's decision to join the collaboration, there is only one primary inference to be drawn. The words of one of New York's most famously corrupt politicians, Boss Tweed, are apropos: "I seen my opportunities, and I took 'em." De Man chose freely and opportunistically, knowing that he could succeed and would be aided by family connections. His friends placed blame for Paul's actions on Anne and her incessant demands for money, and she did not deny that she pressed him for it. Both of them believed, Anne said later to more than one person, that once Germany had won the war, Paul could become "an ambassador or minister of culture."[28] (It would surely have been de Man and not Anne who found that definition of future success word for word in Flaubert's novel, for in Frédéric Moreau, the irresolute young dreamer of *A Sentimental Education*, Paul could have seen in its first chapter a parallel self.) The decision, however, was his. The Third Reich regarded itself as a revolutionary movement and liked to promote young men to positions of power that formerly would have been out of their reach. Paul, more gifted and skillful than most, was one of those often intelligent, unscrupulous youths who favored Nazi ideas in general, if not always in their totality, and had the ability to make use of their social skills and privileged status and get rich. Paul told Frida he wanted to have a place in the new world, and that to do that, he must join at once. With that assertion, he began the first of the many shifts in identity he would make during his lifetime. In December of 1940, the good schoolboy vanished; only the attractive youthful shell remained. But no one who knew him would have been surprised when they saw his first byline appear in *Le Soir* *(volé)* on that Christmas Eve.

13.

"THE JEWS IN
PRESENT-DAY
LITERATURE"

———————

ONCE HE WAS ENGAGED BY *LE SOIR (VOLÉ)*, PAUL DE MAN SAW A DIFFERENT future and his sense of direction changed perceptibly. Outwardly, he was unobtrusive. He did not have an office, and his first assignments were drawn from the cultural desk and in particular the musical scene that was usually covered by the composer Oscar Esplá. In the city room, Paul Jamin, not a sensitive spirit, remembered the novice as an unimpressive figure who sat quietly aside; he thought him "timid."[1] But Paul was not playing to the cartoonist or his mass audience, and he was content to be misperceived by some of those around him.

The policies of *Le Soir (volé)* were essentially the creation of the German Foreign Office in Brussels, after an internal struggle for power was resolved between Joachim von Ribbentrop's group and the army.[2] That force, according to both De Becker and Max Liebe, had organized a group of journalists to run the paper, but these two men saw the others as an ill-assorted group of little-known figures, "a bunch of incompetents who hired the first Belgian journalists to appear."[3] With his diplomat friend, De Becker planned the tactics by which he would assume control of *Le Soir (volé)* and institute a "national" policy—that is, a Nazi one. Between them, they arranged for the embassy, a branch of the Foreign Office with its own Press

Section, to persuade the army's Propaganda Division to let them name the newspaper's censors. With their longer experience in Belgium, they were able, Liebe claimed, to prevail. Thus the journal's minder, seconded from the German Foreign Office, sat in his own office on the city-room floor, wearing an army uniform. At first he read everything before it was printed and could see everything that transpired.[4] Later, he trusted the editor and his deputy so implicitly that he did not bother to check the copy, reading the paper only after the fact. De Becker and Liebe made censorship an arrangement among friends. De Becker explained it away to readers of *Le Soir* *(volé)* by making an analogy to traffic lights: One must organize even liberty.[5]

It wasn't long before De Becker put his new recruit Paul de Man to the test and gave him his first opportunity. On March 4, 1941, the publisher devoted the whole of page 10 to anti-Semitic attacks. This was the back page, normally dedicated, in rotation, to news of culture, sports, labor, and agriculture. The entire sheet was headed "The Jews and Us: The Cultural Aspects." Paul signed one of the articles, titled "The Jews in Present-Day Literature."[6] He came to write it, Mme. Ipsen asserted, because he had to: Her husband had come home late one night and said that the other reporters had combined to force him to write a "bad" article with them, but he had done his best and told her, "Now they cannot put me out." She, however, told him that he had done a bad thing.[7]

One may see her comment as essentially self-exculpating. Yet it does remind one that the essay could not have been perceived as innocent at the time it was written. The Nuremberg Laws of 1935, Kristallnacht of 1938, and other acts of violence and Nazification had already taken place and were widely publicized. No one in Paul's circle could have been unaware of what was happening, and with his numerous and close Jewish contacts, he knew what was at stake in siding with the German occupant. While the wholesale roundups of Jews did not begin until the next year, the existence of concentration camps in "the East," if not the deathly work that would be planned for them, was known. Belgium and France already had their own holding camps: Breendonck, an ancient prison, functioning in Belgium from September 1940,[8] and Drancy, outside Paris, were gathering points from which Jews and political prisoners would be shipped to the better-known concentration camps created by Germany.

Since his essay of March 4, 1941, by itself brought down on de Man the wrath and pain of large numbers of people who had hitherto invested him with a particularly high moral stature, it seems appropriate to look at it, not merely in and of itself but also in the setting of the other essays of the day. By early 1941, *Le Soir (volé)*'s anti-Semitic articles were a consistent, though not a daily, element of its coverage. On January 1, the occupant promulgated new laws, throwing Jews out of their professions, an event for which the essays by De Becker and Van Huffel had prepared the way in mid-December. Attitudes in Brussels were evidently being aroused to favor the new measures, and it was probably not accidental that *Jud Süss*, one of the most hate-filled of Goebbels's films, was showing in the city on New Year's Day. Frequently, anti-Semitism, pure and without any triggering episode, was the subject of the lead editorial articles that were printed on page one in the left two columns, and often continued farther back in the paper. These were signed by Léon Van Huffel or De Becker himself. Van Huffel returned to the attack on January 29 with "Toward a Racial Anti-Semitism." In Germany, Hitler was showing his hand more openly; he announced to the military on January 30 that this was to be a war of extermination and that plans had been made to kill massive numbers of POWs and Russians in the East as well as Jews.[9] De Becker, perhaps inspired by information from his friend Max Liebe at the embassy, would have had time to digest that speech.

Sometime in February, De Becker began to plan the frontal attack, which he launched on March 4, 1941, using his heaviest artillery. Again, he chose Van Huffel to lead it, but also called on his other columnists, Georges Marlier, the regular art critic, and V. d. A., an occasional contributor.[10] Their topics, respectively, were "The Two Faces of Judaism," "Jewish Painting and Its Repercussions," and "A Jewish Doctrine: Freudianism." Until then, Paul had not been a columnist; now, suddenly, he was given space on that page to write about literature. It was his first opportunity to be noticed.

Because it affords a clear example of racism at its most virulent, Van Huffel's essay is worth looking at. It led with the assertion that Jews through ruse and tenacity had gotten hold of the levers of power in politics, the economy, and the press; they had profited from their privileged situation to the detriment of the people who had welcomed them, leading them into a catastrophic policy whose issue could only be war. The largest part of the article was an attack on traditional Jewish solidarity and the refusal of Jews to assimilate into Christian culture from the time of the Babylonian captivity. Exclusivity and pride were at the basis of their political-religious position; their God was avid for justice but without love: They were racists. They were also nationalists, and highly political in their religiosity. As for assimilated Jews, they were still Jews, motivated by a hunger for power and domination. Quoting a supporting source, Van Huffel held that if Jews claimed to be internationalists (a code word here for socialists and Marxists), this amounted only to "enlarged nationalism," an "ideological imperialism" aimed at pushing a purely Jewish idea of justice, handed down for millennia. It was a philosophy that despised human limits and diversities, was contemptuous of traditions, and aimed through its prophetic voice to realize the "proud and impossible dream of Israel." Van Huffel's article was illustrated with two shocking photographs of bearded, unkempt, wild, and aged male faces (presumably power-seeking prophets), one showing snaggleteeth, a fantastic visage courtesy of the rubber gum and glue of movie makeup, as it was an unattributed image of the villain from the hate-filled movie *Jud Süss*. As usual, Van Huffel offered no evidence. Accusations, buttressed by other accusations quoted from allies, were all he needed.

If to Van Huffel the Jews in their deceitfulness were responsible for the war, to Georges Marlier they had produced the degenerate state of contemporary French art. This so-called degeneracy of what elsewhere was called "modern art" was already a powerful point of attack for right-wing and Nazi ideologues. Expressionist works—"avant-garde"—which for years had puzzled or angered some of the public unaccustomed to its new, nonrepresentational language and signs, were constructed as "degenerate," and entire exhibitions were paraded around Germany in traveling shows to demonstrate to the public how low its practitioners, especially Jewish ones, had sunk.[11] Marlier recognized that another critic had pointed out that most modernist artists were not, in fact, Jewish. But that was not the point: Art dealers were, he asserted. Moreover, the "influx" of Jews from Russia, Poland, Spain, and the Balkans into Montparnasse had "turned French art from its natural objects." Marlier was following the Nazi party line when he deplored the failure of "authentically French" artists like Braque and Leger to "contribute to the renewal of monumental art" (probably a tacit allusion to sculptors favored by Goebbels, such as Arno Breker).[12] If Cubist painting had been "animated by a constructive spirit, it would have been able to adapt itself to the new architectural style." Not attaching names to these misdeeds, Marlier described avant-garde art as pushed by a "secret sadism"—sarcastic, morbid, pessimistic, and nihilistic. Cubism, Negro art, Surrealism—all could be traced to unnamed Jews who had given it this "violently subversive and destructive character which had to lead finally to the most total anarchy."

By contrast, Italian art had regenerated, become vital and dynamic, and the creators of the new Italy—that is, Mussolini and the fascists— had naturally paid homage to Futurist works as the "forerunner of fascism." Flemish art happily was not "contaminated" by the atmosphere of Paris and lacked its "perversion of spirit"; it had "preserved unharmed its freshness of soul." The Jewish spirit had not "raged" among Flemish artists, who largely remained deeply rooted in the soil of the country. Interestingly, the essay was illustrated with three photos, all of works by Picasso—a Spaniard, of course, long working in Paris—who was not a Jew.

The third article, on Freudianism, by V. d. A., was shorter. Freudianism was a "subtle poison," a destroyer of morality, fermented by decadence. It was a "Jewish production, foreign to the Western mentality," seductive because it promised liberation from moral constraints. This said, however, the author interestingly went out of his way to exempt Freud—who had died in London in 1939—from his attacks, which he aimed instead at his "disciples." He also gave a rather dispassionate account of ideas of the unconscious, the libido, and a very sanitized version of the Oedipus complex, omitting all references to Oedipus himself or to incest. He returned to the set theme, however, by criticizing this product of "particularly mordant Jewish intelligence" and "Jewish hyperanalysis," attacking the Freudians for teaching a doctrine that held law and order to be "superstitious, pathological and contemptible."

Any reading of Paul de Man's article must be made in this context. ("The Jews in Present-Day Literature" is not, however, his only expression on this topic; his passing return to the subject will be discussed later.) While it is true that he voluntarily joined in this intellectual gang attack and is accountable for it, the difference between his remarks and those of his colleagues is striking. His essay was the shortest, appeared in the least prominent part of the page, at the lower right corner, and was the only one without its own illustration, perhaps because the editors deemed it the least interesting in view of its unexciting tone. Its stance, briefly, is the shrug: The Jews don't matter very much in our literature. But it was also, and this has perhaps not been sufficiently noticed, a challenge to his elders and to their "vulgar anti-Semitism"— one might add, the vulgarity of their argument qua argument. In a rhetorical sense, his target was precisely the kind of intemperate ranting that appeared on the page above his article. His aim was not so much to spare the Jews (although one cannot dismiss this as a motive, given the contrast between his language and that of his colleagues) as to maintain respect for contemporary literature.

He began by pointing out, sarcastically, that the "lapidary judgment" that all postwar art (art that followed World War I, especially Surrealism) was polluted and wicked, reached simply on the basis that one had discovered some Jewish writers publishing under Latinized pseudonyms, carried dangerous consequences. First, it condemned a whole generation of writers, undeservedly. And secondly, it hardly flattered Western writers to suggest that they were merely imitators of a Jewish culture that was foreign to them.

Jews themselves had contributed to expanding this myth of their influence, he granted. He conceded also that Jews had played an important role in the disordered life of Europe since 1920—so that a novel written in this atmosphere might, up to a point, be considered Jewified [enjuivé]. But in fact—and this was a position that he would expand on over the next two years—esthetic evolutions obey their own laws, and the art forms we know are actually the logical and normal developments of what came before them.

As to the novel—here he quoted Stendhal—it should be a mirror held up on the road of life. More, it should go searching into the most secret corners of people's souls. To this process, Gide, Hemingway, and Lawrence had all made their contribution, not as destroyers of past traditions, however, but simply by carrying on and deepening the realist tradition, now more than a century old. In naming these avatars of modernism, de Man's tone implied he was merely listing the names most familiar to his audience, with the exception of the fourth, Kafka's. Yet all he named were somewhat ambiguous politically in that era of the Nazi campaign against "degenerate art." Gide was the modernist par excellence, the harbinger of the movement, and notorious among the *bien-pensants* for his anti-Catholic and almost overtly homosexual writings. Ernest Hemingway and D.H. Lawrence had both explored themes of violence interesting to the fascists. The French literary figure Pierre Drieu La Rochelle, a strong fascist and editor under the Nazis of *La Nouvelle Revue française* (NRF)—which the occupant had taken over—had already given his stamp of approval to Hemingway, whom he found pleasingly in touch with his animal nature, like a "happy rhinoceros who has taken his bath in the small hours and is rushing toward his first meal."[13] Lawrence's obsession with themes of "blood" and violence had culminated in his late work (including *The Plumed Serpent*), and de Man had been reading him since high school. Members of his circle were familiar with these writers also.[14] However, the American Hemingway and the English Lawrence represented countries that were being attacked daily on the front pages of the newspapers as enemies of the Reich. As often is the case with de Man, what seems innocent may be loaded with subversive meanings.

De Man's inclusion of Kafka in this group has caused the most comment. The misspelling of his name in itself is meaningless: the names of Proust, Chardonne, and Stendhal were rendered elsewhere as "Prouest," "Chardonnie," and "Dendhal," and numerous other typographical errors appeared in the paper.[15] There is a question, however: Was Kafka well enough known as a Jew to bring down reprisal against de Man by the Germans, and was he taking a chance in mentioning him, as some have suggested? The Czech-born author, who wrote in German, enjoyed a *succès d'estime* in France and was well known as a writer among the cognoscenti. It is of course possible that Paul de Man did not command this biographical fact and threw in the name of an exotic and avant-garde figure merely to strengthen his authoritative stance. On balance, however, given the decade or so of Franz Kafka's success among the intellectuals in France and elsewhere, it seems likely that they—Sartre, de Beauvoir, and Camus in particular—would have known his antecedents, for "Who is this person? And where did he come from?" are likely to be the first questions readers ask about a great new discovery. In fact, Kafka visited Paris twice, first in 1910 with Max Brod, and mingled there with the Czech expatriate Jewish community.[16] One may tentatively infer that de Man, probably aware of Kafka's antecedents, referred to him for more than one reason. First, he was a brilliant writer and a forerunner of the Surrealists. In addition, by including him with his three other provocative choices, de Man could assert a claim to sharing in esoteric knowledge of the leading writers without running much risk. Kafka was certainly caviar to the general and the other three were too popularly accepted to draw fire. Perhaps Paul also wished secretly to thumb his nose at the ignorance of his masters—men like Jamin and De Becker—about high-level intellectual culture.

In general, de Man followed the party line, albeit in a minor key. He added that, in fact, the Jews should have played a more brilliant role, given what was recognized as their "cerebrality" and capacity to assimilate doctrines. At the same time, he maintained a certain coolness toward them: These qualities should have made them better at the lucid analysis required by the novel. But their role had been rather "mediocre." He concluded, dismissively, that one could have little hope for Western literature if it had let itself be invaded by a foreign force—but happily, in spite of Semitic interference in all aspects of European life, literature had remained healthy. His final suggestion was the now-notorious position that a solution to the Jewish problem that involved creating a colony isolated from Europe, would not carry deplorable consequence for the West. If it took place, he wrote, the West would lose some personalities of mediocre worth and would continue to develop according to its own evolutionary laws.

It is clear that de Man's attack was not comparable in tone to that of

Van Huffel, Marlier, Streel, and others. There was not the animus, the sense of being threatened, or the paranoia that attached to their anti-Semitism. It did not aim to create hatred. On the contrary, he went out of his way to minimize the threat. He was not abusive. He did not feel he or his people had been cheated, tricked, misled, and undermined by a satanic other. They had been "meddled" with by a nuisance that claimed more influence than it really had; it was a problem to be resolved by moving the nuisance elsewhere.

Having said that, one cannot ignore the anti-Semitism of this essay. That Jews had played an important role in the artificial and disordered quality of existence in Europe since 1920, that they had interfered with European life, that they were uniquely cold and cerebral and were a "problem" to be solved by having them colonize some non-European domain—one thinks of the "Madagascar solution" not yet abandoned by Hitler—not to mention the standard attribution to them of their own mental characteristics: There is no question that all this contributed to the newspaper's attack on the Jews and shared its underlying ideology. In itself, the essay helped Nazi policy makers to prepare the populace for its eventual "Solution" to the "Jewish problem" they had invented. He accepted De Becker's basic policy: to establish the Jews as a "race" with negative influence on Europe (and Belgium) and one from which the West must be freed.

De Man's anti-Semitic expressions were more suave than the others', but they had the special strength of giving an upper-class imprimatur to their crudity. More skeptical and educated persons might have found Van Huffel's obsessive racial mythopoeia both tedious and fantastic. De Man's remarks, more nuanced and composed, could have signaled that there was a respectable and low-key way to be anti-Semitic. The audience to which his measured remarks appealed was very important to the Germans, for this was the managerial class, the businessmen who were the proxies through whom von Falkenhausen's four hundred German officers ruled the country. The occupant was closely attuned to the importance of this group.

This shows in the episode when the extremist Belgian Nazi leader of Rex, Léon Degrelle, tried to persuade Berlin to let him establish a new paper, to be called *Le Jour* (The Day). The military administrator, however, Egbert Reeder, opposed Degrelle and scuttled Degrelle's grab for more power by telling Berlin that *Le Soir (volé)* with its 250,000 readers reached precisely the Anglophile, educated, bourgeois class who would be offended by Degrelle's violent Nazism, and these were the people the army needed to do their work.[17]

A similar point was expressed by Gérard Loiseaux, the scholar who studied the lists of forbidden books written by the censors working for Alfred Rosenberg and his violently anti-Semitic Office of Foreign Policy. Loiseaux reached an interesting, counterintuitive conclusion about the dynamics of propaganda: "Contrary to received opinion," he wrote, "the most virulent writers of the collaboration were [the] . . . sophistical and prudent ones." That was because the most clearly committed French Nazis struck too hard and wrote too violently to be credible to the general public. "One needed a tone that Brasillach or a Drieu did not have." (Robert Brasillach was the only writer to be executed postwar in France for collaboration. Pierre Drieu La Rochelle chose to commit suicide rather than stand trial.) That necessary tone was one of "velvet-glove solicitation."[18] This was precisely the voice that de Man commanded. Many have commented on the flatness of his style in the hundreds of reviews he wrote at this time, but he sounded the note his public wanted to hear. In an era of darkness and anxiety, dullness and certainty were reassuring. Paul de Man's stance as cultural critic was knowing, staid, and law-abiding, exactly calibrated for his purposes. As the subsequent success of his career demonstrated, he knew instinctively what he was doing, whom he wished to reach, and how to address that audience.

14.

THE YOUNG WOLF

———————

THAT FIRST ESSAY WAS A CRITICAL STEP IN DE MAN'S CAREER AS HE began to adopt the ideology favored by his employer. Just two weeks after Paul produced "The Jews in Present-Day Literature," De Becker, clearly pleased by his young protégé's writing, created for him a new, regular weekly column, "Our Literary Chronicle," which began on March 18, 1941, and for some weeks ran on page six. Six weeks later, the editor in chief moved it, on May 6, to a more prestigious space and gave Paul de Man a byline, which appeared over the title. The column appeared thereafter every Tuesday on page two for a year and a half, until the end of November 1942, when long-festering but self-inflicted wounds would lead to Paul's downfall. His essay was almost always printed in the prominent upper-left position, surrounded by heavy leads that gave it added visibility. When he did contribute additional articles, they appeared with few exceptions on page one. Without a doubt, he was a favored person.

No one around him perceived that he would soon rise with astonishing speed into the heart of the collaborating media, or guessed how munificently he would be paid. Like many in publishing, such as Gaston Gallimard and Jean Paulhan, he learned to be comfortable playing both sides of the street. Leftist friends whom de Man continued to see on occasion, such as the Dosognes or, more rarely, Goriély, would have been shocked to know to what extent he was not merely writing book reviews, as they supposed. Paul de Man was actually becoming the protégé of leading Nazis, Belgian and German both. In terms of pay, he would outstrip even his boss, Pierre De Ligne, the managing editor, who was astonished when he learned many years later that his friend Paul, with his multiple jobs, had earned more than he.

Over the course of the next two years, de Man would publish about three hundred reviews, including brief summaries for trade papers.[1] Censorship, centered in Paris, was powerful and governed not only what he could write but which books would cross his desk. On August 5, 1940, the occupant had informed publishers and booksellers that they could no longer sell the works it had placed on an early index. Three weeks later all the bookstores and libraries were invaded by police, the stock tossed, and great quantities carted away.[2] Another two thousand books were banned in September. De Man had no problem with these events and followed the party line, especially as it was supported by his uncle and the newspaper itself, although he did not go as far as some who wrote for it. He had a wide readership. When his column appeared, its author's youth was invisible but his name and tone were impressive. The paper had much useful information for the common reader, and in Belgium the rate of reading of all printed works during the war, when life was so constricted, was phenomenally high. From 1941, Paul de Man also wrote for publications put out by the Agence Dechenne, a book distributor that had been taken over by the Nazis and had a stranglehold over what books Belgians could purchase. Its monthly publication to the trade was small in circulation but influenced what was bought by bookstores, and hence had real leverage.

Paul de Man's position was not unvitiated Nazism, nor did it extol particular deeds of the German army; he stayed away from current victories and defeats, except in passing allusions. There was no hero worship of the Führer of the sort one finds in the writings of Bernhard Payr or Alfred Rosenberg, for example.[3] In fact, de Man never mentioned Hitler's name. Instead, he provided for his readers a cultivated, staid, and consistent tone that would have appealed to many. What he wanted at this time of his life were rules by which to judge both literature and life. It became a permanent search. Ten years later in United States, the critic and editor Ted Weiss, Paul de Man's friend, noticed that the peculiarity in de Man's thinking was that "he was the kind of man who wanted to write one small thing that would change [the] world."[4] Already in 1941 de Man had begun to seek that "thing" onto which he could build a grand scheme that would explain particular works and schools of writing. The historian of literature, he opined—meaning himself—should be more interested in the evolution of the genre than in particular authors. Not beauties, but laws interested him.[5] Criticizing a history of French literature, de Man complained not only that it generalized too little but that what mattered above all were

> not the subtle differences of expression between two authors, [but] their common submission to implacable rules. . . . Every period makes . . . its own esthetic laws. . . . One might wish to write a literary history in which only a very few names would be cited, these serving as a point of landmark to mark . . . a formula or style.[6]

De Man was looking for general principles and abstract theories of aesthetics into whose niches he could fit literary works; their particularities did not matter. That longing for a Grand Theory would mark his thought for life: "implacable rules . . . Individuals have little importance." Much later, commentators on de Man wrote of the "violence" of his tropes. It is nascent here already. There are laws—they are impersonal and inalterable—and he wanted to be the historian who would find them. Cutting away what was merely "individual" and showing how writers "submitted" to those supposed aesthetic regulations shifting with the ages would be the task of the historian.

If you have a knife, you go in jail, Adolph had told his grandsons. Paul had laughed with his cousin at the old man, but he did not forget the lesson. A successful critic must have a knife, and he would be a danger to some, but totalizing ideology was in good odor in 1940, and Paul was one of those who aimed to shape it.

His search led him assiduously to support all the prevalent ethnic and racial stereotypes and prejudices of the day. He emphasized the virtues of books that ennobled the supposed Germanic virtues of soul, deep culture ("*Vernunft*"), and willingness to sacrifice for the cause of the war, while also praising what he constructed as the Flemish racial qualities of simplicity, love of mystery, and imagination. Simultaneously, he denigrated French civilization, culture, and history with a steady drumbeat of criticism. It was "degenerate," like the French themselves, "cerebral," heartless, frivolous, and historically aggressive toward other countries and cultures. His adherence to the fascist ideology deepened over time as the war turned more difficult for the Germans, and he took up the cry against sitting on the fence—*attentisme*—or doubting the triumph of the Nazi cause. De Man's agenda was to place Belgian—and Flemish—culture where the French had been, and he underscored his message by saying that in future, literature would belong not to so-called intellectuals (that is, French ones) but would be the province of those with "a frame of mind that fits more especially peoples having a very developed collective sense and who have come spontaneously to less individualistic modes of life." That frame of mind, it went without saying, would be Germanic. Obviously, a French work did not exhibit Germanic qualities, nor a German work French elements. German works were rarely truly inferior, but usually possessed praiseworthy moral qualities. French works were often good in their way—for all their evidence of decadence—but the best were so precisely because they acknowledged that France had gone wrong, wandered, become soft and immoral, and must change its ways. Applying these distinctions became the master trope of de Man's enterprises.

Always resentful of French intellectual dominance, he had a competitive attitude toward the two dominant French Nazi journalists, Pierre Drieu La Rochelle and Robert Brasillach; about the latter, Alice Kaplan has written a groundbreaking study.[7] Both were prized by the German censor, but to Paul de Man, neither was sufficiently pro-Nazi.

Brasillach was one of France's most active political propagandists on behalf of Hitler. A long-term fascist, he was still young when made an editor of the hated *Je suis partout* and became notorious for denouncing by name the opponents of the occupation. He had enjoyed Hitler's Nuremberg games—but not enough for de Man (who had not attended). The young reviewer found ambivalence in Brasillach's praise of this notorious mass propaganda meeting: Brasillach thought that the German rituals were eastern and foreign.[8] (The term *eastern* was an insult, as it referred to lands Germany was conquering, peopled by Poles and others whom Ernst Jünger referred to in his wartime journals as despicable "yellow" men when he fought on the Eastern Front.) The French journalist was considered a political boy wonder, but to Paul he was too "aesthetic," had lived an "apolitical life," had a frivolous "French mentality," and was given to "poetic joys."[9] Perhaps de Man saw a rival in the wealthy young Frenchman. Ironically, Bernhard Payr appreciated Brasillach much more. In his report to the Rosenberg Office of Foreign Policy, the censor reported that the French Nazi, far from "lacking political sense," was an excellent friend of Germany, a young fascist to be credited with creating "the anti-Semitic journal, *Je suis partout*." The censor's reputation was already established.[10]

Another important French Nazi, as already noted, was Pierre Drieu La Rochelle, one of the French fascists who had emerged from World War I in love with the idea of violence. De Man took a different tack toward him. As a prominent writer with a long history of extreme anti-Semitism, he was named editor of the *NRF*, of which Otto Abetz had said, "There are only three powers in France: the Catholics, the Communists, and the *NRF*. Let's begin with the *NRF*! He took it."[11] Drieu was nostalgic for his country's medieval past and yearned for a mystical Church and a warrior-dominated feudal order that would negate modernity.[12] De Man argued that such a plan would not return alienated man to a desirable "primitive grandeur." Drieu's retreat to the past would undercut the "unfolding of an ethical evolution." Here again, de Man's teleological vision of culture was at work: This unfolding was the function of art. At stake for de Man was control of the high ground of intellectual fascism, and he pressed the idea that art must be at the service of social engineering.[13] Under the New Order, Drieu's antimodernist nostalgia should join the dust heap of history. As the prospects for German triumph worsened, de Man urged greater, less rational emotional commitment to the cause: calling for a Nietzschean "suffering, exaltation, and drunkenness" of spirit as times got worse.[14]

Novelists, too, de Man discussed ideologically: If a fiction by the well-respected Hans Fallada adopted an Expressionistic, cinematic technique, it was because he was German; the rationalistic French were too cerebral to accept this avant-garde mode.[15] On the other hand,

Expressionism itself constituted "a veritable theoritization of . . . decadence." De Man praised it in this aging writer but carefully added that his work was outdated.

In the scandal four decades later surrounding the discovery of Paul's essay "The Jews in Present-Day Literature," another much shorter essay critical of "Jewish" thought was overlooked. The worst moment of Jewish history in Belgium began in late July 1942, with the deportation of many thousands of Jews into train cars loaded at Mechelen, in Flanders.[16] While Nazi soldiers were using Antwerpen volunteers to help in the capture, de Man, no doubt merely by coincidence, published in a Flemish newspaper an essay attacking Expressionism, which he identified with Jewish artists.[17] De Man asserted that while German writings since 1933 were profoundly moral and showed "deep spiritual sincerity," some other German productions since that date were bad—and mostly Jewish: "cerebral . . . founded upon abstract principles, remote from all naturalness. . . . in open conflict with the proper traditions of German art." Who were the perpetrators? "Small wonder . . . that it was mainly non-Germans and specifically Jews, who went in this direction."[18] This was Paul de Man's passing contribution to the notorious *"Entartete Kunst"* attack by Nazis on what they labeled "degenerate art."[19]

He was careful never to criticize a French publisher, for Paris was still the great magnet that drew ambitious Belgian writers. Bernard Grasset, a favorite of Payr and head of an esteemed French publishing house, had produced a particularly anti-Semitic series titled "In Search of France."[20] De Man singled out Grasset as "one of those men who have understood that it is necessary to break definitively with the past if one wishes France still to play a certain role in Europe."[21]

Paul de Man used his position for more than reviewing books. It also allowed him to open doors and make new friends in the fascist world. He sought opportunities not only to review their works but to meet in person, interview, and praise notorious pro-Nazi intellectuals like Pierre Daye; Abel Bonnard, the French minister of education; and Friedrich Grimm, an important, very aggressive Nazi historian, active in politics and an ardent friend of Hitler's Germany.[22] Grimm even appeared on the city-room floor of *Le Soir (volé)*, an unheard-of intrusion, and lectured the staff. De Man also showed up in Antwerp at the

Exhibition of German Books, where General von Falkenhausen proudly demonstrated the literary fruits of his culture.[23]

Aiming to consolidate his support of Nazi intellectuals, de Man in another unnoticed piece extolled the now forgotten but then notorious Weimar Literary Congress. (Postwar de Man's notice was identified by Frans De Coster, the auditor working for the Military Court on the Agence Dechenne.)[24] Organized by Goebbels in 1938 to promote Nazi writing, that annual congress brought together the best-known and strongest pro-Nazi writers from different countries, partly to demonstrate how closely they hewed to the Nazi party line.[25] Paul de Man wrote that Goebbels's congress strengthened ties among the European literatures and described the presence and reactions of Brasillach, Drieu, and the Flemish collaborating writer Filip de Pillecyn, one of whose books Paul himself had translated. "An immense step forward has been made toward a deep agreement" by their "learning what their differences and similarities were," de Man wrote. The congresses were notorious enough that postwar the *nonappearance* of certain writers, or their refusal to attend this gathering, would be counted in their favor by De Coster if later their "civic spirit" was in question.[26]

Paul reserved his strongest, most consistent praise for his collaborating friends, especially when he could show they dealt with political issues in correct fascist fashion. He was most flattering toward Pierre Daye, the man-about-town turned Rexist leader and then an open Nazi. Daye was inheritor of an immense insurance fortune, which he used to travel the world and print encomiums to his mediocre writing, and that, in turn, got him admitted to a prestigious academy. The cover of one pamphlet showed a portrait of himself gazing down at a globe representing the earth, which he literally held in his hands. De Man found Daye's reflections "pertinent and judicious." A "European society"—code for a Europe dominated by Germany—would be more equitable. It was the "duty" of those who believed in such a change not to "abstain" from the "present condition"—that is, from support of the occupant and the German war effort.[27] When the indefatigable Daye was overcome at Nuremberg by the "magnificent" spectacle and surpassing emotions it inspired, de Man wrote that Daye had a "gift" of swift understanding of what mattered, "such as the

Nuremberg Congress, whose significance he has very clearly seized"[28] (unlike the imperceptive Brasillach). The courteous Daye responded to this praise with a note of thanks, and within a few months the reviewer, no doubt working with De Becker, had made him one of the judges of a literary prize that Le Soir (volé) sponsored in its search for some Belgian literary talent.[29]

He also tried to help the novelist Louis Fonsny, a colleague in the newsroom, by making his book appear more pro-German than it actually was. After the war, both Le Soir (volé) and the Agence Dechenne were tried for collaboration, and the expert examiner Frans De Coster was appointed to study the files. About de Man's writing, he noticed accurately:

> The articles are those of a critic who is convinced of the quality of the ideas and creations of the New Order. Better: when the book is not sufficiently anti-Belgian the critic takes it on himself to separate all he can find there which is hidden and favorable to the German propaganda.[30]

In September 1942, Le Soir (volé) announced the winner of the prestigious literary award, the Prix Rossel (which brought with it ten thousand Belgian francs), a matter studied by Paul Aron and others.[31] De Man was on the award committee, and undoubtedly he had influence in making up the jury, which included, among others, the two notorious collaborators, Pierre Daye and Louis Carette, who was Paul's friend and a novelist himself.[32] The prize was great and comparable to the Prix Goncourt in France. Everyone on the jury with the exception of de Man was a well-known collaborator and a member of what might be called the Belgian literary establishment. It was in this context that Aron described Paul de Man as "a young wolf" (un jeune loup).[33] The book so honored, entitled Hohenmoor, was the kind of conversion narrative that revolutionary movements cherish. In it, a leftist Belgian soldier, taken prisoner and held on a farm, sees the light of German life and culture, so superior to his own, and eventually dies, but in a state of grace. It was part of the "Literature of Defeat" that later was criticized during the Epuration (Repression) for having caused German ideology to "penetrate" Belgian culture. In organizing the prize and choosing this novel, Paul de Man showed how adroitly he was forming bonds with the top echelons of literary collaborators in Belgium and also how the tools of criticism could help one's friends while sweeping others away.

15.

DRINKING FROM
THREE SPOUTS

AFTER THE WAR, THE PROSECUTING ATTORNEY FOR WARTIME COLLABORATION searched in the Didiers' offices and found a file containing a prospectus for a new journal so egregiously Nazi in its aims that he called it "treason."[1] Focusing his pursuits on the major offenders, Roger Vinçotte attributed the *Cahiers Européens* (European Notebooks) only to Raymond De Becker and made it part of a successful prosecution that condemned De Becker to death. However, the idea for the journal appears to have been written and originated at least equally with Paul de Man. It was part of his meteoric, if temporary, success in the heart of the collaborating media.

The years 1941–1943 saw enormous changes for Germany, as it went from seemingly total conquest to the approaching defeat that followed its loss at Stalingrad. Paul's brilliant if secret career followed the same arc, even though early on he lost the protection of his uncle when Henri de Man lost favor with the occupant and was forced into exile in Paris. Throughout, the young de Man seemed to his friends to be just a book reviewer whose eccentric living arrangements were emphasized by the baby carriage he and Gilbert pushed around the square.[2] But that was merely a cover.

Amid the swirl of contending forces, Paul de Man found his feet and focused his ambition. His friends were mistaken because he hid the fact

that from 1941 to 1943, he pursued a secret career. He held three positions simultaneously in the very heart of the collaborating media, and
he rose very fast in each. This appears clearly in the postwar records of
the Military Court, which prosecuted collaborators; there his name
runs like a red thread throughout the three dossiers of the Agence
Dechenne, the Editions de la Toison d'Or, and *Le Soir (volé)*. Each institution was tried and found guilty of treason; some of their leaders were
sentenced to death (judgments that were commuted after several years).
De Man began as a dogsbody in their offices but moved up fast in all
three, becoming an aspirant for governing power and, for a time,
achieving it. Publishing in Belgium was a small world ruled by interlocking directorates. *Le Soir (volé)* gave him a stepping-stone. From
there, he gained a foothold at Belgium's biggest distributor of books
and magazines, the Agence Dechenne. Meanwhile, he was reading
manuscripts for the Didiers. By the first part of 1942, de Man had
become secretary of the Agence Dechenne, was planning a coup to take
over the Toison d'Or, and, with Raymond De Becker's help, almost
succeeded in starting a luxurious art journal whose raison d'être would
be to promote the entire range of the most bizarre Nazi ideologies. Its
editor in chief would be Paul de Man.

This last venture was the one Paul pursued first. He was not a member
of the exclusive Association of Belgian Journalists (AJB), a Nazi-created
trade organization, but he wanted to be. Apropos of this, some have suggested in defense of de Man that he was not a member of the association.[3]
However, in March 1943, when membership of the group was finalized,
Paul de Man's name was on the first typescript list when De Becker, who
was active in forming the group, considered some forty-odd eligible
journalists. De Man didn't make the cut, perhaps because it was largely
the province of older men, but that he was on the first list showed he was
held in esteem.[4] In early 1942, Paul de Man and De Becker began planning their new journal. Internal evidence suggests that the idea probably
originated with de Man. Having succeeded in organizing the Prix Rossel and bringing major intellectuals on board its jury, de Man was now in
a position to persuade the editor in chief of *Le Soir (volé)* to present to the
Mundus group a project for a serial publication—tentatively titled *Les
Cahiers d'Europe* (Notebooks of Europe). Mundus was a powerful Slova-

kian group located in Berlin and actually controlled by von Ribbentrop and the German Foreign Office. De Becker evidently got a welcoming reception, and they tossed about many names before settling on *Cahiers Européens*. De Becker would be publisher and Paul de Man secretary of the editorial board—that is, its editor.[5]

What the prospectus explained was a plan that the angry prosecuting attorney for the Epuration/Repression would later call simply "treason." Its aim, De Becker had written, was to make "German culture penetrate further into Wallonia and France." It would help create a "vital center" that would "spring forth" and "energize the work" of this penetration. It would be a "laboratory" in which Francophone writers would "confront Nordic and German authors and savants."[6] The goal of this sexualized encounter was that "works impregnated with the new conception of life will be able to spring forth among them." De Becker himself drafted this statement of purpose, and his handwriting in the original document was clear and unhesitating.

To have assisted in such "penetration," however, was to prosecuting attorney Vinçotte the very definition of treason because it would have destroyed Belgian culture by making it part of Germany's, and that was the essential aim of the Third Reich and its "thousand-year empire." Until now, little has been known about this incriminating plan, but it shows clearly the marks of de Man's ambitions and characteristic methods of operation. Vinçotte was shocked. On September 24, 1946, in his "Summary of the Facts," he compared the magazine's announced "penetrative" purpose to the goals set by the German army's Office of Propaganda. One could "measure" the "gravity of the treason" committed by the Toison d'Or and its Belgian directors (of whom De Becker was one) by reading the prospectus and comparing it, he wrote, with the written aims of the Propaganda Abteilung (the German Office of Propaganda) in turning Belgian public opinion toward dependence on Germany. That, he asserted, would change Belgium into a German colony. In particular, he faulted the project for using German funds to pretend to be a Belgian publication.[7]

However, although he assigned all blame to De Becker for this prospectus, the holograph manuscript of the first draft is extant, and Paul de Man's own handwriting shows that he wrote at least half of it, the portion that describes the magazine's content. The first pages of the draft of the prospectus are clearly in De Becker's hand, which Pierre De Ligne recognized instantly fifty years later.[8] Belgians, De Becker wrote, knew too little about Germany. A "great cultural effort" was indispensable to insert into ordinary Belgian thinking "all the notions issuing from the science of life and which are at the base of the new worldview (*sciences of heredity, race, ethnology, hygiene, and of food, of geopolitics, of cosmobiology, etc. . . .*)" (emphasis added).[9]

These ideas were precisely the notions promulgated by men like Alfred Rosenberg, who regarded Hitler as the founder of something like a new religion. However, the journal would not deal overtly with politics. "It would be a question of really giving an orientation to literary, artistic, and scientific questions that would conform with the new conception of life"—that is, to Nazi ideology.

Vinçotte chose to ignore or did not notice that the closing pages of the original draft of the document were in a different handwriting, which was that of Paul de Man. The most noticeable thing about his contribution is its contrast with De Becker's style, which was lucid and direct. De Man, on the other hand, wrote loosely; his writing was careless in expression and conceptualization. Produced in pencil and with words crossed out, his manuscript is a first draft (which was reproduced without touch-up in the typed copy), marred by gaps of thought. There were few details about content, readership, or influence. Contributors would include his friends Louis Carette and Paul Willems, and to these he added Robert Poulet, a notorious, if gifted, pro-Nazi who wrote for Paul Colin, and other collaborators. Under the rubric of "The national character of culture" de Man wrote:

> The goal of this study is to define precisely what factors are in play, how and to what extent they are determining for the orientation of different cultures, and to illustrate these theoretical considerations by examples drawn from the cultural activity of this era.

He was looking once again for a Grand Theory that would provide a framework for cultural stereotyping, a deterministic or sociological explanation for how artistic genres develop. It is in the style physicists call "hand-waving"—a notional theorem one cannot yet prove. However, about the expensive journal's appearance, he was explicit. It should appear "monthly, or every two months at a minimum," and its format would be about seven by eight inches and 150 pages; some of these pages would be on costly coated paper for the plates that would accommodate the essays on art. It would "be classy, with a high intellectual and European range of reference." The prospectus offered some general titles, all stressing the idea of interconnectedness, either of Europe itself, or Belgium as a "Crossroads."

The project at first looked like a sure thing, and initially those in Berlin encouraged them strongly. On March 10, 1942, the Paris office of Mundus, S.A., agreed to the title *Cahiers Européens*. Unfortunately, so far as the documents go, this was the end of the story. Like many other proposals for new publications, it died stillborn, and there is no other trace of these "Notebooks." Perhaps Berlin realized that after more than two years the war had begun to go badly and that this was not the time to underwrite a "classy" publication printed on coated paper stock. After all, it would appeal to only a small fraction of a fractional population, the rich, French-speaking Wallonians of Belgium. At the time, the Germans were waging war on the Eastern Front and experiencing devastating losses, while at home, too, they were beginning to suffer from shortages. Some no doubt thought, as Admiral Canaris privately told a friend in that same month of March, that there were signs that the war could not be won.[10]

Who thought up the idea for *Cahiers Européens*? It is more likely to have been de Man than De Becker. De Becker was a successful executive and a manager of men, but he had no background in the creative arts, the habitus Paul had made it his business and passion to know very well. De Becker had eventually turned from Catholicism, but the working-class youth, who left school at fifteen, who made a pilgrimage on a permanently damaged foot through France to seek enlightenment from right-wing Catholic monks, who admired the austerity of the simple supper Henri de Man had prepared just for them—this was a man who sought influence and power rather than luxury. Moreover, once its political lines were set, the journal in appearance and content was clearly going to be essentially literary and aesthetic: Writers, cinéastes, and art historians would be its contributors. De Becker's work as publisher would be to set policy and use his influence to get the project under way. Highly intelligent, he had advanced through adopting Nazi ideology and personal force, seeking out important people, getting invited to Nazi-sponsored peace conferences, and impressing rising men like Abetz or leaders like Henri de Man. But Raymond De Becker was not yet thirty years old and only self-educated, the son of an alcoholic father, who had been a wine salesman, and a working-class mother.

On the other hand, the proposed *Cahiers Européens* do bear the traces of Paul's signature approach. Paul was not a committed Nazi in the same sense that De Becker was. He was not interested in the wilder elements of Nazi ideology; one cannot imagine him giving more than lip service to the New Order's cosmobiology and precepts on hygiene. He merely accepted these as the price of achieving his ambition. It was a given, and politics he could and must leave to De Becker. Creating a magazine that exemplified high culture was his aim. He wanted *Cahiers Européens* to be a luxury item, costly and narcissistic, just as his own life was soon to become. The kind of cultural capital needed to imagine this publication, not to mention forming its creative staff, was not within De Becker's purview.

In the long run, although Vinçotte mentioned the prospectus in summing up the case against De Becker, it does not seem to have figured in his list of charges, no doubt because the project—however vitally to be impregnated—never came to birth. Neither did de Man face consequences for the scheme. One could not prosecute bad intentions (unless they were those of the Jews). Nevertheless, the document's language, with its description of the penetration of Belgian culture by racist and "ethnological" National Socialist doctrines, is shocking to Belgian scholars. "That is pure Rexism!" remarked a Belgian historian on first hearing the language from this writer, and Rexism among Belgians represents true treason.[11] The Rexist party under Degrelle was the only one that overtly promulgated the submersion of Belgian culture by the Nazi one, and the only one that actively recruited young men to fight with the German army in the war on the murderous Eastern Front.

———

THE FAILURE OF THE NOTEBOOKS to take root did not matter. Paul was simultaneously making great strides at the biggest of the three companies that employed him, the Agence Dechenne, and there he rose by means that came naturally to him. Already he possessed if not the "charisma," at least the "aura," the glittering attractions that later brought him so many followers. His tactic was evidently first to draw himself to the attention of the top men and, using his personal gifts, befriend them. That would be a normal goal for most young people hoping for advancement, but few realize that goal. To establish such contacts from an inferior position in a big company is difficult; yet for Paul, it was easy. He was skillful and did not let personal friends or men he did not like see him as a rival, but toward the associates he displaced, such as J. Bauwens, whose job he took as reviewer at the Agence Dechenne, he had sharp elbows.

The records suggest that de Man's process was to work quietly for a while, letting his plans mature, and when he had grasped the situation and understood what motivated his bosses, to present them with a daring plan by which, working together in secret, they could enlarge their field of action, greatly increase their power, and make vastly more money. In each case, Paul's boss, an older man, would be the titular leader of a coup of some sort. His role was to take the initiative publicly and use his prestige and contacts to persuade his masters in Berlin to provide permission and funds for a new publishing venture. Paul, the mastermind of the project, would then be able to make a quick upward leap and be named to a high position in the company, perhaps becoming chief editor of a new publication or taking over an existing one. The repeated process was not an accident. For de Man's name to figure in this way in two of his employers' histories might be coincidence; three times looks like planning.

De Man already had a foothold reviewing books for a little monthly the Agence Dechenne distributed to the trade, but soon he supplanted Bauwens and began writing also for the more widely circulated *Bibliographie Dechenne*.[12] In the process, he was successful in drawing himself to the attention of the director-general. On June 27,

1942, Lothar von Balluseck sent a memo to the company's 750 employees, announcing that he had named Paul de Man to be secretary in charge of reorganizing the French Book Department, with responsibility for purchasing, sales, and the smooth running of that department.[13] Paul would report to the directors, meaning himself and Charles Peeters, who was secretary-general. In addition to very high pay, de Man was also given the right to sign correspondence in his own name, a signal honor, which De Coster noted: "[T]his privileged situation of Paul de Man resulted from the good relations that he had personally with von Balluseck."[14] De Man made sure everyone heard of this, for he sent out a letter saying, "Henceforth all communications pertaining to the AGENCE DECHENNE as a member of the Belgian Circle of Booksellers must be addressed to me by name."[15]

The Agence Dechenne lacked panache, but it had great commercial power, especially in a world starved for reading matter, where all books and other public sources of information had to pass through censorship. With a total of four thousand points of sale and a monopoly on the kiosks at railroad stations, it had a stranglehold over the distribution of printed media in Belgium. The French Book Department bought books heavily in Paris as well as in Brussels and sold them to both bookstores and stationers. In addition, it also published some texts. It also owned vital material assets: trucks—with access to gasoline—railroad cars, and paper. The original owners had been pushed out and the company taken over by the Nazis and their straw men at the beginning of the war. Being able to move goods on this scale, denied to most people, would make its officers rich as major purveyors on the black market.

Von Balluseck was effective, engaging, and slippery, a Nazi officer who, though only thirty-five years old, knew how to impose himself on others and ran the Agence Dechenne with "extreme skill," according to De Coster. With his title of minor nobility, von Balluseck was a real Junker; perhaps he recognized in de Man a simulacrum of himself. Able to swim in any waters, he had successively joined the Communist Red Shirts, and then the conservative German National People's Party (DNVP) while working for two Jewish firms (one of which made theater scenery) before finally connecting with the Nazi party.[16] By 1940, von Balluseck had a commission and arrived with the German army in Brussels, where he had a special mission. He was not only Mundus's envoy to run the Agence Dechenne but was also to oversee the sales of *Signal*, a popular magazine modeled on the American magazine *Life*. Max Ammann, head of Mundus, was determined that *Signal* would make his old army friend Adolf Hitler rich, for the Führer received the profits from the magazine. When an internal Nazi party spy met the director-general, he found him "in the biggest and best building, in the best and biggest room under a giant portrait of Hitler and seated in an accordingly appropriate throne."[17] Paul de Man would have consulted with his boss there under the swastika of the Nazi flag.

Von Balluseck was often away on diplomatic "illnesses," actually missions to Spain, where he oversaw the successful publication of its own version of *Signal*.[18] In his absence, the company was run with great efficiency by Charles Peeters, the secretary-general, who cooperated with the Germans almost from the beginning.[19] Under him, Dechenne made great profits, but these were never distributed to the shareholders. Yet the company's books were kept so accurately that Frans De Coster, the examining expert, determined that nothing had been falsified: All the bills had been paid, the bills had been true ones, and there were no hidden accounts or amortizations. The defalcations, and these were immense, could be found duly recorded and may have been technically correct. The company's profits had gone instead to grossly inflated salaries and the personal enrichment of upper management through expenses and inappropriate purchases.[20] It was white-collar crime at its orderly best. Peeters was later judged to be by far the most active and culpable of the pillagers of the company. He died of a heart attack in jail while awaiting indictment—the classic fate of some dishonest CEOs—but seven other managers were tried and found guilty.[21]

The company where Paul de Man first learned business practices was highly corrupt. Peeters set his own salary at 300,000 Belgian francs annually. Also powerful was the supersalesman Albert Pletinckx, the adjunct secretary, who had a penchant for denouncing his enemies to the Gestapo. Théophile Daras, who ran the fleet of trucks, used them to become a major vendor on the black market, supplying everything from hams to seaside villas to the higher-ups, who profited from his work. That black market flourished under the Wehrmacht, both as a

supplier of scarce goods and as a means of control. No doubt Peeters
was drinking liqueurs he got from Daras when, after entertaining the
German officer Hauptmann Pichler at an expensive restaurant one
night, he took the whole party back to his office at Dechenne, where
they continued a binge that left behind so many empty bottles that his
staff counted them by the tens when they cleaned up the next morning.[22] Another underling, a man named De Haas, was a particularly
convinced Nazi, actually a Dutchman, who in his enthusiasm for
Nazism had renounced his country during World War I to fight on the
German side. He boasted proudly to von Balluseck that in fulfilling his
job of promoting *Signal* in Belgium, he had caused its sales far to outstrip those achieved in Holland, a much larger nation.[23]

De Man would have known these men and their notorious stories.
Von Balluseck got along with most of them but didn't care for a
too-eager Nazi sympathizer named Reiss, though he worked well
pushing *Signal*.[24] Reiss liked to sign his letters to the Belgians in the
Agence Dechenne with "Heil Hitler!" a closure the more tactful von
Balluseck omitted except when corresponding formally with other
Germans.

This cast of characters might at first have been strange, perhaps even
unsavory to Paul de Man, but he adapted and learned fast. One of the
most powerful figures in the Belgian media, a man close to the Nazis
and much feared, was the publisher Paul Colin, with whom Peeters
especially curried favor.[25] Paul de Man would also seek the approval of
this powerful Belgian Nazi, and he courted him in a letter he wrote
soliciting his presence at a luncheon with von Balluseck in exceedingly
polite terms:

Sir and dear colleague,

I have the pleasure to transmit to you the invitation of M. von
Balluseck, director of the Agence Dechenne, for lunch together
one day next week. M. von Balluseck would like very much to
see you again and eventually to discuss certain questions concerning the Nouvelle Société d'Edition that you direct. I suggest
for example that we meet Wednesday 23 July for lunch. Would

you have the goodness to give me a phone call to confirm if this date is agreeable and to fix the exact hour and place of the meeting. Accept, dear colleague, the assurance of my distinguished consideration.

Paul de Man.[26]

At roughly the same time, Paul de Man asked De Becker to tell Colin that he, de Man, on his "honor" as a literary critic, would never use his new position at the Agence Dechenne to favor one publisher over another, and in a peculiarly ambiguous set of phrases, he implied that he either already was a member of the AJB or that he was promising to act as if he were one.[27] It did not matter to Paul that Colin was deeply hated as "personally vicious" by noncollaborators, one of whom described his "porcine profile" rising eternally above a "green loden coat."[28] Pierre Daye, on the other hand, found Colin to be an extremely intelligent man, aggressive perhaps, but an art collector—and "adored" by his staff.[29]

Paul aspired to have the income that would allow him to run with the big boys, and he almost did. By the time he left nine months later, in April 1943, with raises and severance pay he had received a total of 100,000 Belgian francs, plus expenses.[30] This was in addition to remuneration from both Le Soir (volé) and the Toison d'Or. His monthly salary surpassed Pierre De Ligne's at the newspaper, a fact De Ligne resented when he learned of it, even many years later.[31] One notes that at the other end of the pay scale, a daily cleaning woman at Paul Colin's Nouvelle Société d'Edition got between thirteen hundred and seventeen hundred Belgian francs per month, and a messenger received even less.[32] Despite his earnings, the young de Man was always in debt. "How can one explain that?" asked his friend Georges Goriély.[33] On hearing of de Man's multiple employers and sources of income, Goriély exclaimed, "But he was drinking from three spouts!"[34]

Having reached his powerful new post in July 1942, de Man was ready to alter his way of life. On August 20, he and Anne left Gilbert Jaeger behind at the humdrum square des Latins and moved with their little son to a grand address, 151, boulevard Saint-Michel, on the other side of the city. The ménage à trois was over, and Paul and Anne now lived together, though unmarried, as man and wife.

De Man returned to work in September with new ideas. Not one to plan painstakingly, he liked to seize the moment intuitively, and his timing was usually excellent. First, he went to Paris to purchase books. The Agence Dechenne had long had a buyer there, but de Man had another agenda: to meet the French publishers. He spent lavishly entertaining these vendors, who deeply impressed him. Reporting later to von Balluseck, he wrote that he had made a tour of all the publishing houses and had learned that the Agence Dechenne was held in low esteem. It was a *"grossiste"* (a mere wholesaler), and was systematically discriminated against by its suppliers, who were "very often very fine and cultivated people who do not sacrifice commercial needs to cultural needs [*sic*]."[35] The war gave new power to the publishers: Their sales were up and they had more readers than they had stock. Dechenne was at a disadvantage in dealing with them, for these refined persons had "the impression of feeding a simple machine which has no consciousness of the work that it accomplishes." Psychology was needed: "A publisher is sensitive to the fact that one buys his merchandise with discernment, knowing what it is worth and appreciating its contents." Discernment and taste were what de Man intended his company should now exhibit. The French publishers "regret that wholesalers like us do not profit from the chance . . . to exploit the literary appetite of the public [and] to raise the natural bad taste of the mass."

De Man had a plan of action: on the one hand, a new "policy of purchase," involving active search for the best new works, and on the other, the creation of a new post, that of "literary director," a man who would be sited in Paris itself. Out would go the old, undiscriminating system of standing orders. And out also would go a certain M. Petitdidier, the current purchasing agent. This was an opportunity for everyone, even the public weal. Freiherr Von Balluseck may have been less concerned than de Man about "rais[ing] the natural bad taste of the mass," but the director-general agreed to everything, including Paul's repeated demand for a "representative in Paris" and that person's "enormous role." He penciled a comment into the margin beside this, urging the "condition that he should have a sufficient knowledge of the Belgian market."

With that, Georges Lambrichs, Paul's friend from ULB days, a fellow writer for the *Cahiers du libre examen*, and a figure who eventually made an important mark as an editor of the *NRF*, got his start in French publishing, for it was he who filled this role.[36] De Man knew how to help a friend and himself at the same time. Placing his colleague in this position was a great coup, for through this astute and active man, Paul saw a direct way into the heart of the intellectual circles in Paris they both admired and yearned to join. Clearly, even a French publisher of refined sensibility would welcome as a friend and supporter an intelligent, appreciative buyer of his carefully nurtured creations. Paul was close to both Lambrichs (who soon dropped the *t* from his Flemish name, Lambrichts) and his wife, Gilberte, who became a translator.[37] In fact, they soon formed the nucleus of a group that the French poet and Resistant Jean Lescure later said was known in publishing circles there as the "Belgian Mafia."[38] Paul carried the day with his new purchasing policy, his literary director was installed, and the unfortunate M. Petitdidier continued to be blamed for problems with bad stock. Meanwhile, de Man's request for 3,500 Belgian francs in travel expenses was honored.

As the volumes de Man had ordered in large numbers began to arrive, he had a new idea, and he made a mysterious, urgent request to speak with von Balluseck about a "project" he had conceived in regard to the Toison d'Or—an idea that was "too complex to be described" in his report.[39] Probably this "complex" endeavor was the coup they soon launched, by which the two of them, acting under the aegis of the Agence Dechenne and using the power of Mundus, would take over Les Editions de la Toison d'Or. The plan of attack was daring but simple. Paul would write a damaging report on Didier's management of the Toison d'Or, and von Balluseck would sent it to Berlin, where he was in favor as a great moneymaker. The director-general had disliked Didier from the beginning and reminded his correspondent that he had frequently mentioned his low opinion of Didier's meager capacities.[40] Paul Willems described Edouard Didier as elegant and generous, but said the idea for founding the house had been Lucienne's. Pierre De

Ligne thought Edouard resembled a "greyhound," suggesting someone elegant and quick on his feet, rather than acute at his business.[41]

The campaign almost worked. Its opening salvo was the straightforward letter written by von Balluseck mentioned above. In it he sent a report "by my colleague Mr. de Man, who is a great connoisseur of French literature [that] perhaps will interest you." Von Balluseck continued:

> The report naturally does not turn on the political tasks and the cultural policy of the publishing house, but limits itself to an exposé purely of the issue of publishing. The negative judgment of M. Didier by de Man is shared not only by me, but by everybody in the field of books in the country. Without wishing to involve myself in the business of the publishing house, I would like to propose all the same a change of direction. The Propaganda Office of Belgium . . . will certainly be able to give you the names of appropriate persons to replace M. Didier.[42]

Von Balluseck had long had his eyes on the Toison d'Or and wanted to monopolize its sales.[43] Since Mundus supplied Didier with his funds, and especially his stock of paper (control of which was a central method by which Germany controlled all publishing), the Agence Dechenne was likely to have had the advantage, since it was a source of profits and the Toison d'Or was not. The latter was, in fact, deeply in debt to Mundus.[44]

The attempted coup went forward. Mundus asked for "practical proposals," and on November 19, von Balluseck responded. Didier should be replaced by two men: a commercial director and a literary adviser. For the latter position, he suggested none other than Paul de Man.

> I do not know however if, because of his overload of actual work with Dechenne, he is in a position to be ready for that. Because the course of the cultural policy of this publisher is largely set by the German Services of Brussels, the designation of a commercial director would seem especially important to me.[45]

One notes the carefully casual tone of the reference to de Man's position and the implication of its relative unimportance: If the plan proceeded but Paul's age was revealed and in question, the German could argue that de Man's contribution would be a minor issue; at the same time, he hedged his bets by writing of de Man as perhaps too busy for the work.

Thus when Paul de Man was still only twenty-two, he was close to becoming the editor in chief of one of Belgium's most active publishing houses, already subsidized by National Socialism with many millions of francs. It must have been a moment of high anticipation for both men. Their power and income would be greatly increased, and for de Man, the days of anonymity would be over. It was not a coincidence that in September he had published in the *Bibliographie Dechenne* a little essay on the publishing profession. He was giving it serious thought.

But it was not to be. There were spies everywhere, and the Agence Dechenne was no exception. Just a month later, on December 19, a Herr Seidel at Mundus wrote von Balluseck in effect that his bluff had been called and the game was over—not without penalty to the Agence Dechenne for losing.[46] De Man's report had been communicated to Didier, and the long-legged greyhound had raced directly to Berlin to defend himself. There, armed with a loose-leaf book filled with press clippings, he had successfully established the value of his press.[47] Ironically, a significant number of the favorable notices he was using to save his company were reviews of Henri de Man's *Après Coup*, his company's first published work, written by Lucienne's lover. Edouard Didier, cuckolded by the uncle, now was being attacked by the nephew. He was determined this time to prevail and destroy his enemy.

Addressing himself to Paul de Man's report, Seidel stated, "The criticisms formulated by your collaborator were highly exaggerated. In the given circumstances, the question of a change in the management of the publishing house is no longer a burning one, a fact which I beg you to note well."

To make matters worse, Mundus also informed von Balluseck that now the Agence Dechenne could not have the monopoly on book sales they'd been negotiating for, either for the Toison d'Or or for another publishing house. They were checkmated.

Von Balluseck nursed his wounds for a while, and then, to judge by

Seidel's reply, wrote again on January 15, 1943, asking how it had happened that Didier had been invited to write a reply to de Man's charges. Seidel responded that "Mr. Didier was never invited by anyone in Berlin to take a position in writing about the reproaches." Instead, "Didier showed it [Paul de Man's report] . . . when he arrived in Berlin in mid-December and therefore must have had knowledge of your report already from a Service [that is, a spy] in Brussels."[48]

No doubt because he had now met Didier, Seidel could add that "I entirely share your opinion on this matter, and I assure you that there will be equally another opportunity on our part to nominate someone else in place of M. Didier." The man was indeed a weak reed; Berlin would relent, and even though Didier's self-defense had prevailed at the time, their star manager, von Balluseck, was to be mollified. Unfortunately for Paul, however, the failure of his coup did not end there.

16.

THE BOULEVARD
HAD TWO SIDES

ANNE AND PAUL, WHO WERE STILL ONLY TWENTY-TWO, LIVED A VERY good life in Brussels while de Man was "drinking from three spouts," as Georges Goriély put it. These were the years of the wolves. Collaborators flourished in a darkened Brussels from 1940 through early 1943, and many of them learned to play both sides of the street. For Anne, though still unmarried, crossing the city was at least a step in the right direction. She reported on her pleasure in their beautiful new space on the boulevard Saint-Michel, where they could entertain on a scale approaching that of their neighbors, for they lived in a luxuriously furnished apartment on an avenue lined by embassies and the mansions of the wealthy. That the apartment was magnificent all but one who saw it agreed. It was not far from the square Montgomery and the elegant end of the avenue Tervuren,[1] and its appointments included both a Bechstein grand piano and a library. Only Paul Willems demurred; the famed writer and cultural impresario said that the flat was ill-furnished and that he had sat there on packing crates. He, however, had his own reasons for not incriminating his friend.[2] Perhaps he had been a very early visitor and had indeed once sat on packing crates. Nevertheless, as a good friend of the party-giving Paul, he certainly also saw the dwelling in its later glory.

How de Man acquired a home already so richly furnished is not clear. Pierre De Ligne, who was a close friend of Paul de Man at the time, believed–rightly or wrongly–that the apartment had been spoliated from deported Jews and was a payoff from his bosses. In fact, 151, boulevard St. Michel was just across the street from the Gestapo headquarters—the Germans also knew how to live. De Ligne remembered being told by de Man that the apartment had been "loaned" to him by his German boss at the Agence Dechenne, Lothar von Balluseck.[3] "Loaned" was a euphemism. As von Balluseck was only a temporary resident of Belgium and traveled a great deal, he is not likely to have actually owned the apartment, but to have acquired it as a perquisite of his outstanding work in enriching Hitler and holding a lofty place in the Nazi hierarchy. A great many dwellings and their contents had been stolen from Jews who were being sent to the concentration and death camps. The massive deportations began in July 1942, just after de Man's elevation to secretary, and were in full operation in August. This was the prime time for the army, in which von Balluseck held officer rank, to seize its prey.[4] Bob De Braey independently voiced similar suspicions about the provenance of his cousin's new home. He knew it well, for he had stayed in the apartment and met a girlfriend there. It contained "very nice carpets and furniture. [It was] high-class—very good. What I'm afraid of is that [there] were a lot of Jews who had been ousted—it's troubling me."[5] Young Bob himself spent the war years, like many young men his age, lying low in Antwerp to avoid impressment into the German munitions and other factories.

On the other hand, de Man's first wife explained that the apartment had been rented from a friend of Paul de Man's father, a man named Mansion, and that they paid 3,500 Belgian francs per month for it.[6] This is open to question. Thirty-five hundred francs was a great deal more than the most expensive, large, and furnished apartments rented for in Brussels at that time. The wealthy who could afford it had fled from the city, and two- and three-bedroom apartments were readily available for between five and seven hundred francs; even ten or eleven rooms were not advertised for over eleven hundred francs.[7] De Man, always short of money, is not likely to have spent one-third of his salary on rent when he did not need to. Rather, his habit was not to pay rent at all, and this would later repeatedly and seriously damage his career.[8]

Paul and Anne entertained lavishly. Nellie De Ligne remembered that the couple had always treated their friends in high style. But they also always had a lot of debts, and Anne needed more than ordinary amounts of money, an opinion widely shared in their circle. Mme. Ipsen herself did not deny this, but she pointed out that her husband in fact had the same desires as she and that he habitually approved her purchases and even suggested some. In those good years early in the war, she had everything she wanted, including, she specified, never fewer than two servants. That number probably applied only to the later, leaner years spent in hiding. And why not? With so many guests, an infant, and a large establishment to care for, with the need to purchase and maintain a beautiful wardrobe and her bedrock expectation of luxuries, she undoubtedly needed more than just two in help. A nursemaid and a cook certainly, but also a housemaid and a general scullion would have been essential for one brought up in the traditions of her wealthy Middle Eastern background with the family's great "latifundia" and abundance of servants. Nellie De Ligne remembered running into Paul by chance in Paris. He was shopping on the Champs-Elysées and looking, he told her, for "slippers to fit Anne's tiny feet."[9]

Paul now had friends who were leading intellectuals and he was intimately connected to the powerful. Moreover, he could pass freely back and forth to Paris—a great and rare privilege. For the most part, the collaborating and non-collaborating populations drifted apart, but lines were often crossed.[10] In this world, Paul's characteristic "doubleness" served him well. Sometimes he could help his friends on the Left; more often, he courted figures on the Right. When the war concluded, the pan-European German Reich would need loyal representatives and governors in its provinces, and Paul, as Frida Vandervelden and Anne Ipsen both said, intended to be one of them. In that era, he would have been at the top of his form—cool, hip, and victorious. It was his success in working on both sides of the boulevard St.-Michel that gave them reason to hope for that ambassadorship they had dreamed of.

Among their many visitors were the Jewish brothers Marcel and Nahum Sluszny, and Nahum's wife, Esther. They had all known each other "very well" from ULB days.[11] Esther and her husband when caught suddenly by the curfew had reason to spend several days with

Paul and Anne, and Esther observed well what went on. She described the apartment as "*magnifique*," "*très belle*," large, very well heated, with all the food one could want—everything set out. They kept "open house" and people came and went. Most inhabitants of Brussels spent their days hunting for enough coal and potatoes to keep at bay the cold and chronic illnesses that were attacking them and sickening, sometimes killing their children, as Anne Somerhausen, Marlene de Man-Flechtheim, and even Li LeCocq-de Man testified. At Anne's place, however, life was luxurious. "Europe was in the process of falling apart," Esther reported, but the de Mans had everything. Paul de Man was very well paid—highly paid, she thought.[12] Anne explained to this writer that the copious supplies of food she offered their visitors came in packages sent by her father from Romania. This, however, would have been unlikely in that era of total war.[13]

From now on something of the flavor of the Antwerpen social mores his father had enjoyed became noticeable in Paul's life. He had despised that behavior as a youth, and much later he would avoid it in his second marriage. But in his twenties, the angry adolescent gave way to a worldly young man who was enjoying the same sexually liberated social dance. The Georges Lambrichs were often guests, for they lived just across the boulevard from the de Mans. (Georges moved from that elegant address, said Gilberte Lambrichs—his second but later divorced wife—only when he learned that he was living next door to the Gestapo.) That couple once gave a very strange party whose result typified some of the anomalies of collaboration. Gilberte, alluring, slim, and dark, who later became one of the several translators whom Paul employed but did not pay for their work, recalled the particular evening when her husband had invited Paul along with "all [Georges's] friends from the Resistance." They were horrified. "When they saw Paul, they went completely white. They thought it was a trap. They looked at each other like *chiens de faïence* [china dogs facing each other on a mantelpiece]."[14] Lambrichs had crossed a line. Although a talented editor and a good friend to Paul—who, in Gilberte's words, was "after all his employer"—he did not always show good judgment.

Also part of de Man's circle were his cousins, the De Braey siblings, although not Jan and Marlene de Man. Jan was away for a time in Germany, working voluntarily in a munitions factory.[15] Jan De Braey, Bob's father, however, wanted none of these jaunts to Brussels, and he told his son not to see Paul after the war began, saying it was " 'because I know Paul writes infamous lies, and I do not agree—therefore I consider Paul working . . . for, with the enemy.' "[16] The same warning was given by a family friend, Jan Eeckels, who was an important printer in Antwerp and was part of the group that later helped finance Paul's publishing company. The printer told Minime (Micheline De Braey) to avoid Paul and Anne because "he knew what Paul was doing and told me it was dangerous."[17] The targeting of collaborators by the Resistance had begun.

Perhaps the well-informed Eeckels had also begun hearing of Minime's own exploits. These profoundly contrasted with Paul's political choices and show how families might on principle choose opposite sides and yet remain in close personal contact. The adoring and spirited young cousin who had punctured Paul's tires because his bike was so much better than her own had grown up to be a ravishing woman and also a committed member of the Resistance, courageous beyond the point of daring, a genuine hero. Quite young, she married a man who was half Jewish. When her father-in-law was imprisoned by the Gestapo in Antwerp for wearing the Star of David because he "said he was proud to be Jewish" and would not deny his faith, Minime thought this a stupid act. Yet she went in person to the deportation camp in Mechelen and, using all her arguments and wiles, persuaded the dreaded police to release him. Nor was this the first such rescue she pulled off. Already in 1940, carrying false papers, she had penetrated Breendonck and succeeded in freeing the same family, three people—her fiancé and his parents—who were being held there after arrest on some unknown charge. She evidently enjoyed the danger of moving between two worlds. Soon she took on one of the most dangerous jobs of the Resistance, often carried out by women, the rescue of British soldiers who parachuted into France at night behind enemy lines. She would search for them in the dark fields, help them bury their white parachutes, then stealthily lead them to safe houses, where she would clothe them in local garb. Later, posing as a girlfriend, she would accompany the airmen on the train to the Swiss border while buying the tickets and chatting up the inspectors.[18] With this kind of character, nothing could have stopped her from remaining in Paul's circle, however compromised he might have become.

The atmosphere that surrounded Paul became sexually charged, and he was having his own affairs. One of these was with the wife of a good friend who, when she later met Pat de Man, wordlessly but deliberately let his second wife know of her previous intimacy with Paul. Pat de Man felt the insult. Anne, too, had at least one lover, a man named Wedelund, who later was a minor Belgian diplomat in Paris, and in the 1950s Paul would take ironic pleasure in pressing him into providing irregular assistance with his visa: He was owed the favor. David Braybrooke, a young American soldier whom Paul befriended at the end of the war in 1945, was delighted by the number of beautiful and intelligent women he found clustered around his new acquaintance. From his visits to Kalmthout, he remembered both Minime's looks and one detail of her hair-raising way of life: "Another very beautiful girl—had been strafed on the road while biking by U.S. air forces: Micheline."[19] (He did not know of her exploits in France, of which she told no one.) Braybrooke, who went on to become a professor of both government and philosophy, made it clear that he had enjoyed the tone of the place and had observed numerous sexual liaisons. In particular, he remembered that de Man had a mistress, the elegant wife of one of his friends.

Dominique Rolin, who later became a very well known French novelist, was also part of Paul's circle. She was another darkly exotic woman, unhappily married, but so beautiful, her biographer reported, that when she worked in the library at ULB, young men would come there just to stare at her.[20] She was unknown when de Man very favorably reviewed her first novel, *Les Marais*, but for some time she had been a protégée of the publisher Paul Colin, who had brought out many of her stories, a connection, as Frans De Haes wrote, that "placed her clearly, if not consciously, in the hard right of the Belgian literary world."[21] De Man soon profited by her connection to a notorious publisher in Paris, Robert Denoël, a man once Belgian, now French, who had actively put out many pro-Nazi works, many of them anti-Semitic. One of these, a manual, was forthrightly called *How to Recognize a Jew*. Paul established himself in Denoël's good graces when he carried manuscripts, love letters, and copies of Rolin's newly printed books for them back and forth between Brussels and Paris when such movement was forbidden to all but the favored few who, like himself, possessed a treasured *Ausweis*.[22] Paul made such a trip in July 1943, and Denöel reported to his lover that he had been "ravished" by Paul's "excellent" review of her book, and that "the visit of Paul de Man gave me the most lively pleasure. We talked of you at length, as we had to."[23] It was always in de Man's interest to be in touch with a French publisher, whatever his politics.[24]

Anne testified that she was rarely jealous of other women, and in particular not at all of Frida Vandervelden, whose relationship with Paul she understood. She did, however, despise and hold a grudge against "that woman at the university: ugly," she said.[25] Moreover, Paul had wanted her to befriend the woman and her husband, but Anne had refused. They lived badly and were not her social equals. In fact, the woman's husband had paid her an unwelcome and offensive visit. There were probably few women other than Rolin who met the criteria of knowing Paul and being admired by him, working at the university, being married, living in sordid circumstances, and yet being one whom he wanted to promote socially. For Paul's part, intellectual and dark-haired women were his classic choice.

Rolin, interviewed in the early 1990s, immediately remembered de Man warmly as a "tall blond boy, very young"—and as the son of Henri de Man. "That was the rumor. The name de Man was very well known at the time."[26] They belonged to the same world and would meet at cocktail parties, she said. Interestingly, Henri's fatherhood was also taken for granted more widely, for it was assumed to be a matter of fact by the Military Court's auditor, De Coster.[27] This could have been contradicted by Paul, but it was not in his interest to do so.

For Anne, this was the high point of her life. Just twenty-three, she was creating for herself the role of society belle. Her character was contradictory. Generous in some of her impulses, loving to manage her friends' affairs, she had courage and élan, especially while the money was rolling in. Yet she was distinctly bad-tempered. As her grown son Rik put it, "She could turn on a dime," from charm to rage, and she would physically abuse those around her—showering blows on her husband and servants alike.[28] Nellie De Ligne spoke more than once of how Anne would scream in anger first at Paul and later at her last husband, Gerhard von Orland-Ipsen, demanding that they bring her more money and refusing to let the older man retire. With Paul's child just a year and a half old, a little boy, dark like his mother and already very bright and forthcoming, Anne hoped sooner or later to make the relationship legal. When among friends, she liked to sit at her companion's feet and embrace him, gestures Frida thought not false but exaggerated and those of an actress. Minime, however, thought Anne evil and blamed on her all Paul's mistakes of collaboration.

ON THE OTHER SIDE of the boulevard, meanwhile, Paul's childhood role as Milady was coming back to life, along with his taste for secret games. He learned to use his position to help both collaborating friends and friends in the Resistance. The most often cited episode took place when he and Anne gave shelter to Nahum and Esther Sluszny one night when they found themselves on the streets of Brussels after curfew, with nowhere to go. Clearly, this was very dangerous. Nahum, a violinist, had papers showing he was half Jewish and therefore theoretically safe from arrest, but Esther did not. The streets were patrolled, and if they were detained, prison and deportation would follow. They rang the de Mans' bell, and their friends kept them hidden for a few nights while the couple decided what to do. On the subject of Paul de Man's articles in *Le Soir (volé)*, Esther Sluszny specified that she and her Jewish friends had read them: "We thought he had gone crazy." She believed there was more than one anti-Semitic article. "We laughed about it. But he had not become crazy. He was dangerous."[29]

Anne reported with justified pride that she herself had directly done good for the Jewish community when she and Paul once gave a benefit performance for Jewish musicians, at which Nahum had played. Very likely, she was following the example of Queen Elisabeth, for she, unlike her son, mixed in society and had previously arranged for Nahum to play during an evening at the palace. The Slusznys went as M. and Mme. Fauconnier (a word meaning "Falconer," but also a pun on *faux connâitre*, or false knowledge), and the queen knew exactly who

M. Fauconnier was. The Germans, however, who were at the door checking identity papers, were hoodwinked. Had the couple been caught, they would have been sent to Auschwitz. "You had to be brave, or you died," said Esther.[30]

One of Paul's good friends, the collaborating Louis Carette, was especially despised among Paul's noncollaborating circle. It was his presence and that of men like him among de Man's friends, Esther Sluszny testified, that made her realize, even before the episode of missing the curfew, she must go into hiding. Carette, the writer who later took the pen name Félicien Marceau, was already notorious because as a broadcaster he had his own program on Radio Brussels, an overt organ of Nazi propaganda. A very small, very clever man, fundamentally serious but exceptionally amusing as a writer, he would become rich and so internationally successful as a farceur that a casual French restaurant in the theater district of New York was and still is named La Bonne Soupe after one of his plays. As a youth growing up in the mid-thirties in Louvain, Carette was, he wrote, a somewhat fanatically right-wing Catholic and a friend of Raymond De Becker. Prewar, he took a job at Radio Brussels, left it to do his military service, but returned to the national station *after* it had been taken over by the Nazi Propaganda Office. He rose in the ranks of the station, created programs for it, and on one occasion interviewed his good friend Paul de Man.[31] Two Belgian scholars, Paul Aron and Cécile Vanderpelen, quoted Carette's words in an interview de Man himself published. Carette told Paul of his aim as a novelist: He had "made conquerors" of his heroes because "it is . . . above all a question of a will completely directed toward happiness, which resides in the affirmation of the self."[32] This expression of a Nietzschean will to power reminds one of de Man's own affirmation of Frida of his intention to live only for his own pleasure; the two friends shared certain fundamental ideas.

Paul helped Carette in an important way, which Marceau only implied in his memoir, *Les Années courtes*. Fearing assassination, he had fled into exile in Paris, but when he discovered he could not find a publisher there, he returned briefly to Brussels in 1942 and went to Paul de Man for help. He was not disappointed, and de Man secretly used his position at the Agence Dechenne to distribute Carette's book. The playwright confirmed to this writer that de Man was indeed the conduit whom he had not named in his memoir.[33] Their meeting was clandestine because, threatened with assassination by the Resistance, Carette had not waited for the defeat of Germany at Stalingrad at the end of 1942 to abscond. In Paris, he lived in fashionable Neuilly into his nineties, attended by a white-gloved butler, who guarded him and his wife in a small, elegant mansion with a tiny salon embellished by tall polished stone pillars.[34]

Frida avoided Paul's circle in Brussels, but she invited him for frequent visits to her country home just outside Villers-la-Ville, where she remained for the duration of the war. This picturesque village was built around the immense ruins of a twelfth-century Cistercian abbey, and her dwelling was a restored two-hundred-year-old stone mill, whose thick walls she surrounded with terraces and softened with ivy, roses, and hanging beds of lavender.[35] Frida remembered that Paul had gotten angry at her there only for the second time in their friendship. They had brought their son, and she had a daughter a year older. "It was terribly difficult to keep the house going during the war and find food," she recalled. "I was busy morning to night. He sat one morning on [the] verandah and I [sat down and] said, 'I am so tired, worn-out, but at least I got the necessary things.' He stared at me so—'This is not a reason to be everybody's servant.' He was disgusted because I was the housemaid of the whole house. With such an aggressive tone. He never apologized. I stood up and went away, crying." She told this story with emotion, miming their gestures, living it over, while appearing to be still mystified by its content.

Frida was taking a chance in visiting with the de Mans during the war, and it led to punishment afterward when she and the Jaegers, Gilbert and his new wife, Josette, were called before a tribunal in 1945. They faced somewhere between six to ten accusers. "Why did you see de Man during the war?" Gilbert was asked. Protecting him, Frida had, she recalled, interjected with fervor, "'You don't have to answer that.' And he did not." She went on: "It was a question of what they'd *done*, and they'd done nothing unpatriotic." She noted with bitterness that there had been no criticism of de Man during the war because no one had dared: He was too well connected and might soon have real power.

"They said it *afterward*, after the war. They criticized the Dosognes and Paul afterward."[36] Frida preserved her idealistic picture of Paul de Man partly by remaining ignorant of behavior that lay outside her village and also because she rarely read *Le Soir (volé)*—in her circle, it wasn't done. She knew her friend only as a reviewer for the newspaper.

De Man would never have asked her for a loan, as he did Goriély at least once, but money was already a big problem despite his large income. Anne and other relatives reported an episode that had embarrassed her and damaged his ties, already strained, with his family. On one of his trips to Paris, his aunt Yvonne, sister of Bob and Henri, entrusted her nephew with a considerable quantity of linens to sell for her. These had a market value during wartime, and she needed funds. He took them but came back with neither the money nor her basket, saying only that he had forgotten them en route. Yvonne did not believe him, and she remembered the tale when later he was involved in more serious defalcations. He told his second wife that he had fallen asleep in the station.

The strongest evidence of Paul de Man's willingness to help the other side was his help in distributing in Belgium the fourth volume of a Resistance journal name *Messages*.[37] This journal was published irregularly and with great difficulty. Each volume of the journal bore an individual title. *Messages* was started in Paris by the French poet Jean Lescure, a man of the Left. The volume brought to de Man by Georges Lambrichs for distribution was entitled "Exercice de Silence."[38] Hence the paradox that at the same period when Paul was praising the aggressively propagandistic Weimar Congress in the *Bibliographie* and plotting with von Balluseck to take control of the Toison d'Or, he was secretly distributing *Messages*—which he then reviewed favorably in his weekly column, using his office in the same way as he had used it to help Carette. *Messages* was mild enough not to have incurred the full wrath of the German censors in Paris; rather, the message to which its title alluded was the injunction to be silent. This stance combined intellectual passive resistance toward the occupant with open support of the "uninterrupted mission of France." Lescure trod a fine line, and without openly resisting the occupation, he stood for the survival of French culture and the refusal to accept intellectual German domination. Jean

Lescure, a respected, careful member of the Resistance (and an aristocrat who had renounced use of his title), had already hatched three
issues of his journal, but the fourth was still in the nest.[39] The poet said
he knew Lambrichs only slightly, not as a friend, but was glad to have
his offer of help. He never met de Man; but he thought of Georges
Lambrichs as one of the first members of what he called "the Belgian
mafia" because of their numbers in Parisian literary circles. This volume of the journal was published in December 1942—and thereupon
Paul reviewed it favorably in *Le Soir (volé)*. Shown those comments in
1998, Lescure liked them, saying they were "extraordinarily free" of
bias, judging that "Paul de Man was not at all one of the aggressive literary collaborators." Lescure, however, had read nothing else by de
Man, either during the war or later, and was unaware, for example, of
his urging Belgians as the war got worse to give up their "wait and see"
attitude and support Germany's victory more strongly.[40]

Keen on continuing with *Messages* and probably elated at an idea he
now had for opening a new avenue into the center of the French literary
world, de Man wanted to bring out a fifth volume.[41] To that end, he left
Brussels for Paris on January 18, no doubt in high spirits. De Man
intended, Lambrichs wrote to André Souris, to round up works by
Paulhan, Bataille, Queneau, Quincy, Béalu, Fardoulis-Lagrange—all
the biggest names from the stable of the dominant French intellectual
publisher Gallimard, whose editor in chief was Jean Paulhan himself.[42]
Paul had not succeeded with the plan for *Cahiers Européens*, and the plot
to take over the Toison d'Or had also come undone, but this was a better idea entirely; it would save and even enlarge his ambitions. He
would be the editor and publisher, the facilitator of the only editors and
publishers who really mattered.

It was an enchanting prospect, but what Paul de Man, in his normal
haste, did not understand was that he was leaving his flank unprotected
against Peeters. His enemy seized the moment. Two days after de Man
set off for Paris, the secretary-general wrote the director-general of the
Agence Dechenne, Lothar von Balluseck, and laid out in damning
terms an account of serious mismanagement of the French Book
Department by its secretary. Icarus, as Paul liked to think of himself,
was about to find his wings clipped.

17.

ICARUS FALLS

THE FAILURE TO LAUNCH *CAHIERS EUROPÉENS* WAS LESS IMPORTANT TO PAUL than his now lofty position at the Agence Dechenne and his relationship to the increasingly influential Raymond De Becker. Yet suddenly in both places de Man was in serious trouble. It began not long after he and von Balluseck lost their campaign to take over the Didiers' publishing house, Editions de la Toison d'Or. Unfortunately for Paul, the always suave Edouard Didier was able to punish the upstart with little effort.

Back from Berlin, Didier now went directly to his friend Raymond De Becker, with whom he was tightly allied. The working-class head of *Le Soir (volé)* had been dazzled in his youth by attending some of the Pontigny conferences where he met highly placed intellectuals who gathered at an ancient abbey to promote reconciliation among the still-divided European Nations. Later, the older man sought De Becker's advice on political matters, putting him on his board of directors and even giving him his own office at the Toison d'Or.[1] On December 4, 1942, Didier sent De Becker a memo that was the more devastating because its attack on de Man was measured, judicious, and factual. Avoiding any reference to the plot against himself—why publicize that?—Didier related a series of failures and falsehoods in an employee from whom, in simple "prudence," he must separate himself. Lies, irresponsibility as a translator, lateness of the work he did do, and, above all, de Man's loss of not one but two manuscripts that had been entrusted to him were cited. He had produced as his own translations ones that had only been partly done by him—a fact he had "carefully concealed"—and yet these were of poor quality. Their lateness was compounded by his demands for extra sums over what he'd been paid in advance—still without his producing the work itself. Worst of all, de Man had been entrusted with a "UNIQUE" manuscript of a novel. De Man had lost it. It was just gone—"*égaré*"—irrecoverable. The novelist had been doubly damaged, for a French publisher wanted to read it. Didier asserted:

> The collaboration of this person was valuable in what concerned foreign literature and his advice was always judicious, but unfortunately for several months (more exactly since his appointment at the Agence Dechenne) his work has been absolutely zero.[2]

De Man was guilty of "dangerous negligence . . . and in spite of the sympathy that I might have for him, in spite also of his unquestionable talent, it seems to me more prudent, henceforth, to renounce his services." He was a publisher's nightmare.

Some of what exasperated Didier as carelessness and deceit would show up as a pattern in de Man's subsequent career, after he himself became a kind of publisher and later a Ph.D. candidate. Even Paul's loving second wife, in a parallel instance, was the writer who translated the famous edition of the classic novel *Madame Bovary*, for which de Man got sole credit; it was her translation, not her husband's, which so many American students read as Flaubert's. Loyal to a fault, Patricia de Man told this writer in 1990 that she had done the work simply because she'd had to, explaining, "Paul's English wasn't good enough."[3] Indifference to facts and what Charles Peeters would call "lightness" would continue to be Paul's ongoing problems.[4]

When De Becker received Didier's damning indictment of his protégé, he knew it was time to part company. Effective and efficient himself, it would not have escaped the editor's notice that de Man was ambitious but could not follow through on his grand plans. Paul's uncle and protector, Henri, had been in exile for some time, perhaps because in part he had shown himself too hard for the occupant to handle. The siege of Stalingrad had stalled, and the Germans no longer needed the de Mans. De Becker fired Paul, and *Le Soir (volé)* printed his last contribution on November 28–29, 1942.

THERE WAS WORSE TO COME. Asked by the prosecutor postwar why he had left the Toison d'Or, Paul de Man told Vinçotte that Dechenne had made him a "better offer." That was false. He had lost his job there as well, and in a way that was drawn out and humiliating.[5] Charles Peeters undoubtedly had been waiting for his chance ever since de Man's star had begun to rise at the rue de Persil (Parsley Street). Now he had been tipped off by his henchman Pletinckx that de Man had made a wasteful and possibly nepotistic purchase—a mistake that was going to cost the company a lot of money—and that Paul's department was in trouble.[6] With that, Peeters started looking for the evidence that would allow him to emerge openly as the enemy of von Balluseck's so-called golden-haired boy. He made sure as he ferreted out the details that the process would be torturesome.

The retribution began on January 20, 1943, a bad time for collaborators everywhere. The war had reached a turning point that winter when the Germans had been finally forced to retreat in December after their unsuccessful besiegement of Stalingrad. The United States and Great Britain were now on the ground in North Africa, and the Resistance was suddenly active everywhere, gaining numbers with each passing week. (Even the young François Mitterrand, who had long worked for the Vichy government, changed sides in 1943, paving the way for his re-emergence later as a socialist.) These events were signals De Becker did not ignore, although his newspaper had long been publishing the same warmongering and racial fictions. Like many others, he foresaw what was coming, and in January he resigned from Rex, together with his deputy, Pierre De Ligne.[7] Meanwhile, the British, supported by the Americans in North Africa, took Tripoli on the same day that De Becker sent his letter, three months after the attack at El Alamein. Rommel was about to be defeated.[8]

Nowhere, however, do the records of the Agence Dechenne show that its waters were roiled by such events. What bothered Charles

Peeters were wasteful expenditures—at least those not benefiting himself. Perhaps he also had gotten wind of de Man's humiliating dismissal at the Toison d'Or, for Didier would have had no reason to keep that silent. Although Peeters must have been offended by de Man's "policy of purchase" and unbusinesslike attempt "to lift the bad taste of the mass," he chose not to attack him on those grounds. Instead, he focused on a clear example of mismanagement.

On January 20, two days after Paul had raced off to Paris to solicit the great Parisian writers and engage them in his new volume of *Messages*, Peeters sent von Balluseck a memo, warning him that the head of the French Book Department had committed the company to buying twelve thousand calendars from the Union of Manual and Intellectual Workers (UTMI), a so-called union based on the corporative, essentially fascistic model created by Henri de Man. Because Paul de Man hadn't placed the order until late November, these calendars were basically unsalable. Moreover, he hadn't had the business sense to make the order subject to confirmation, and so the company was committed to the purchase. It was going to be a virtually complete loss and would cost Dechenne fifty thousand Belgian francs, the equivalent of more than four years of Paul's salary. The whole matter showed a "complete absence of even a sense of maneuver," the kind of language required to get out of the contract. In particular, Peeters was irritated by how de Man and Lambrichs had responded to his inquiries: "This business has been treated by the Librairie Française (Messieurs de Man and Lambrichts [sic]), with a great deal of lightness."[9]

The negligence that Didier reported had also shown up at the book distributor. The stakes, however, were much higher. Most likely, Peeters had been watching Paul, as the sudden emergence of this inexperienced but favored figure had attracted attention and open jealousy at the lower levels. Two weeks after the secretary-general sent his memo to von Balluseck, a new order went out over their joint signatures. From now on, de Man, whose freedom had hitherto been unlimited, could not order more than one thousand copies of anything without first clearing it with Peeters or von Balluseck.[10]

That was essentially the end of Paul's career there, and it left him in no position to cultivate his friends in Paris. The loss of this unique chance was undoubtedly a great disappointment to de Man, but now he had worse problems, for Peeters made the process of fixing blame long and drawn out.[11] From then until the day the twenty-three-year-old left the company, his superior delved into exactly what he had been doing, how many books he had ordered, from whom, and at what price they had been bought and sold. With every discovery Peeters was undoubtedly more appalled, for the situation was, in the words of the duc d'Enghien, "worse than a crime, it was a blunder."

Peeters might have been a white-collar criminal, but he did not make stupid mistakes; at the Agence Dechenne, when it came to money, one might be a knave, but not a fool. On February 14, he asked de Man for a list of everything he had ordered but had not yet received from the publishers, together with the price and the Agence Dechenne's discount.[12] A week later, de Man replied in a three-page single-spaced memo, which he may have made up from memory alone. He heard nothing further for over a month.[13] But on March 24, Peeters, in a memo headed "Personal," showed that he had spent the time checking de Man's accounting both against company records and the figures he had secured from the vending publishers themselves (an exercise that would certainly have tended to humiliate de Man with his suppliers). His indictment took the form of more questions, and it was devastating.[14]

Out of eight texts, all but one of Paul's entries had been erroneous in some way. Evidently working from memory, for the most part, de Man had simply named a completely different book from the one shipped by the vendor. In one case, he forgot to mention buying thousands of copies of a book—and at an excessive price. Other complaints followed. Finally, Peeters demanded, "Are we going to get satisfaction in making the other reductions?"[15]

De Man must have balked at this point. Nothing appears in the files for two weeks more, but obviously the secretary-general must have been communicating directly with the director-general whenever he had proof against the young upstart. On April 5, Peeters, in another private memo, informed de Man directly that he had personally reduced the past orders from various vendors by almost one-half. The only publisher virtually untouched was the Toison d'Or—the publishing house of Didier—in whose inventory, of course, Mundus and the German Foreign Office, sponsors of Agence Dechenne, were heavily invested.

The next day, Paul de Man must have had a painful talk with von Balluseck. The German may have been sorry to separate from his young protégé, whose social class and fluid, not to say unstable, character may have reminded him of himself at the same age. Had Hitler been successful, von Balluseck undoubtedly would have risen high and Paul very possibly might have moved upward with him. Von Balluseck, an unscrupulous man, probably would have cared little about Paul's shenanigans as long as he could have denied knowledge of them and the company made money. (That was no doubt why Paul had been able to distribute Carette's novel.) But the figures of loss presented by the secretary-general left him no choice, and de Man had to go.

And so on April 7, Paul de Man sent his resignation to his friend, a handwritten note on his personal stationery, offering as explanation his desire to take up once more the literary work he had abandoned but which some other (unnamed) position open to him would give him liberty to pursue. He added warm personal thanks: "I am infinitely thankful for what you wished to do for me and for the confidence that you have shown in me" and closed with "all my gratitude and my regrets."[16]

Peeters lost no time announcing mordantly to the staff that while formerly the company had pursued a "policy of purchase," it must now pursue a "policy of sales." There would be weekly sales meetings, the books in stock would be supported by the office, and things would return to so-called normal. "Raising the natural bad taste of the mass" was off the agenda; getting rid of the overbought stock was the order of the day.

After the war, an expert tried to determine if the "rossignols" ("nightingales") purchased by de Man—meaning unsalable books—really did, as Pletinckx charged, both cost the company great sums and reflect the interests of German propaganda. He came to the conclusion that, in fact, it was true that the distributor had lost a large amount of money. As late as December 1943, for example, eight months after de Man's departure, the directors of the Agence Dechenne were planning to offer the French publisher Colbert 200,000 Belgian francs as a settlement on the cost of books they wanted to return. There were many other publishers with whom they had to deal.[17] De Coster, who was by profession originally an auditor, wrote:

> The presence of Paul de Man in the Librairie Française of the Agence Dechenne showed itself above all in the excess by several millions of purchases over sales. These were thoughtless purchases that, moreover, led the Agence Dechenne to separate itself from the subject. [However, in his monthly purchasing report,] Paul de Man does not overtly show an intention of especially supporting the sale of works of propaganda.

Politically, the auditor was inclined to exculpate de Man, rather than the reverse. On one occasion, he pointed out, de Man had resisted buying a work pressed on them by one of the German propaganda bureaus because it was unsalable, and von Balluseck himself stepped in to order only three hundred, not five thousand.[18] De Coster judged de Man's role based not only on what he purchased but also on broader issues, placing him in the context of his more odious companions.[19] If he had reordered a book rather than initiated its purchase, for example, De Coster did not hold it against him.[20] He compared de Man's behavior favorably to that of Reiss, head of the German Book Department, who had purchased *Mein Kampf* and the books of Goebbels for sale in his bookstalls and elsewhere. Works by active collaborators like Degrelle, Delaisi, and Doring appeared among de Man's purchases, but not *Mein Kampf*, and in general De Coster saw de Man using discretion during a buying trip to Paris, which he appears to have made in July or August.[21]

On the other hand, De Coster took offense at several of the brief reviews he read in the *Bibliographie Dechenne*.[22] He also came down hard on de Man's work on Pillecyn, who had pushed the notorious Weimar Congress, discussed earlier. De Coster credited de Man with writing the article praising that meeting of literary propagandists, or implied credit. Although the article is unsigned and is not included in *Wartime Journalism*, de Man probably was indeed its author, for the literary knowledge and tone it displayed were certainly beyond the competence of J. Bauwens.[23]

The Agence Dechenne did what it could to recover from its encounter with Paul de Man, and even De Coster seemed to find the history somewhat comic. Peeters set out Bauwens's policy: De Man bought, Bauwens must "*sell*." They sent quantities of de Man's unpopular purchases of French propaganda works to Germany—where they would go to prison camps—but even there they did not sell.[24]

WHEN THIS ICARUS FELL into the North Sea, he was pulled down not as much by overweening ambition as by his own incompetence, the weight of tens of thousands of unsold books and calendars. What de Man thought he was doing during this era of compulsive buying, it is hard to say. His wife testified that in private life his spendthrift ways were as great as her own and that this was also his pattern in his later career as a businessman. Examination of de Man's records suggests that he purchased something like double the normal quantities of stock on his first interaction with these "refined" and "sensitive" French publishers. Had they swept him off his feet? Or did he, like Dr. Lydgate, the unfortunate bankrupt protagonist of George Eliot's *Middlemarch*, have an unappeasable hunger simply for buying, for surrounding himself with goods that would tell him of his power, and how far he was removed from the abyss below.

While concealing from friends the reasons for his departure, Paul de Man understood that it was essential now to make his retreat. He remained officially registered in his apartment in Brussels until just after D-day, in June 1944, but he retreated to the country soon after leaving the Agence Dechenne in the spring of 1943. For him, it was already the end of the war, or at least of his collaborative work. He acted none too soon: The spring of 1943 had become the era not of wolves, but of retribution. Only a week after de Man disappeared, Paul Colin was shot to death one pleasant spring evening by one of three young men who were waiting for him in the bookstore he kept below his office, situated near the Palace of Beaux-Arts and close to the Royal Library.[25] A few days later, Dominique Rolin paid a consolation call on Colin's widow at 8, square Marie-Louise, where he had a house that overlooked the graceful fountains of a tranquil park. The publishing magnate and art critic who had denounced resisters and enemies by name was assassinated by the Resistance—all men of ULB—who were caught, tortured at Breendonck, and executed. Later, Arnaud Fraiteur, the leader, was acclaimed as a hero and martyr, and his name was given to several public venues in Brussels. Pierre De Ligne told this writer that he and De Becker took this event very seriously and understood that it was a sign they must begin to withdraw from public life.[26] Paul de Man meantime settled into a little cottage in the village he had always loved, kept out of sight, and meditated his future plans.

18.

HIDING IN
PLAIN SIGHT

After his precipitous fall, de Man spent almost three years, between 1943 and 1946, in Kalmthout, a period of retreat that laid the groundwork both for the creation of his publishing house, Hermès, and for the eventual collapse of his relationship with Anne. The glory years of collaboration and easy money were over. As soon as D-day occurred, he removed himself from the register for the suspect apartment in Brussels. He had to rethink himself. All the collaborating media would become defunct, and all the companies he had worked for would be tried and found guilty of collaboration. Their chief managers would be sentenced to prison and even death. Paul de Man would be banned from returning to the university because of his own past. He would have to become his own boss. One consolation was that many of his circle were also living very quietly nearby in Kalmthout, for some who had been on the same side politically as the de Mans had also repaired to the village near the border of Holland.

Important figures like Henri de Man were being targeted. Henri had been living in exile in Paris, but in the spring of 1945, he had to flee from there as well, sometimes on foot through France and into Switzerland just ahead of the Resistance, which was eager to bring him to trial in Belgium. He was never able to reappear publicly, and he lived out the eight remaining years of his life in a remote mountain village. Ernst

Jünger, the talented but notoriously cold-blooded German writer, now old but once again attached to the army in Paris, was expecting a morning visit in April 1945 from his friend Lucienne Didier—who had turned sculptor and was making a bust of him—but instead he received only a brief word that she must leave at once to help Henri in his immediate flight.[1] Paul maintained some kind of contact with his uncle at least until 1948, when he gave Georges Goriély a note of introduction to Henri, but it is not clear that they ever met again.[2] Henri would die in 1953 outside the village of Ardez, in the Grison Alps, when his car collided with a train, his death most likely a suicide.[3]

Paul, always able to adjust, made himself part of the social world of Kalmthout hamlet, visiting its pub and befriending the village elders. He was all right: He had a companion, a child, a family name respected in those quarters, and undoubtedly money from his increasingly wealthy father. The liberation of Brussels took place on September 19, 1944. After a year and a half, with his plans for his publishing house going forward, Paul wrote Marlene de Man-Flechtheim in November 1945, inviting her to visit. He knew that she was overworked and supporting two children in poverty because of the absence of Jan, who was now imprisoned (a fact Paul did not mention). He and Anne were "well settled, thanks to an advantageous arrangement," he wrote. The country was good for the children, and he was subletting the apartment that he'd rented for himself in the same building as his father on Langeleemstraat in Antwerp. They planned to stay in the village all winter and the following summer.[4] Marlene did not visit, however, and he never provided the work he also promised her.

For Anne, village life was a comedown, and the elegant woman took it hard. On July 1, 1943, three months after settling in Kalmthout, she and Jaeger were divorced.[5] Yet even then, the reluctant Paul did not marry her. Instead, she found herself crammed into a small country cottage with their son, lacking all the amenities, much less the luxuries, to which she was accustomed. She later said proudly that she had never had fewer than two servants even during the war, but one of these evidently was Paul's cousin Minime, who mostly helped with little Rik. Cooking, cleaning, laundry—these tasks were new for Anne, and she did not care for them. Moreover, she spoke French; Flemish was her third and not her best language, and although she did get involved with local people, the contacts were not always successful. She missed her circle of friends. Paul could lose himself in books, but she was trapped, suddenly living the life of a lower-middle-class housewife.

Apparently, they were also chronically short of money, even though they were undoubtedly supported to a large extent by Paul's father. X-ray tables were always needed by the Wehrmacht, and his sales increased significantly during the war.[6] Madeleine had left Paul a considerable amount of money, but her estate was not yet settled, and Bob's subventions were not enough. Paul got into the habit of asking friends for loans. Georges Goriély loaned him ten thousand Belgian francs, which were not repaid, and other friends also were called on for money. He asked Walter Van Glabbeek's father for some three months' living expenses at one point, but Walter, a younger friend, who knew him very well, reported that Paul made the sum good.[7]

Yet while Anne always needed money, that was not, for her, fully the point. What was there to buy even with cash? In the words of Paul Willems, "She did not bear adversity well." She had outbursts of temper. Minime De Braey remembered with astonishment fifty years later that once Anne had beaten her—literally picked up a broom and struck her repeatedly with the handle because of some perceived error in the kitchen.[8] As an adult, Rik remembered Minime with affection, but he also recalled clearly his mother's violence and the rages that blew up like squalls, then subsided. Both parents, he said, not only argued but struck each other, his father as well as his mother. Once as a child, he had interposed himself between them to shield his mother. Yet while they shared this behavior, Paul was the less violent.[9]

Bob de Braey also recalled the fights, which the relatives of the couple found distressing. The de Man and De Braey men suppressed their anger, he said, and when it did come out, it was not about the real cause, but about trivial things. "We hate vehement discussions—we are prepared to suffer and will do everything to avoid [them]. . . . From time to time, [Paul] got angry—shouting—it was always a little bit ridiculous—it was not [in the family's] character. But from her to him, it was very vehement. I remember Anne shouting—more explosively."

Anne became unpopular. According to Bob, the people of Kalmthout liked her at first but changed their opinion over time, finding that she wasn't "tolerant" of others or their opinions, enjoyed pitting one person against the other, and "gossiped about the sexual affairs of others. A troublemaker."[10]

Minime, who worked closely with Anne, went further. Devoted to Paul and not one to mince her words, she said Anne was a "very bad woman" and blamed her entirely for Paul's collaboration: "Whatever happened to Paul during the war is his wife's fault." She considered Anne "very intelligent" but capable of "mak[ing] Paul do what she needed," because, Minime held, "he was frightened of her." As a young person of around twenty, so was Minime. "I was frightened of her in the end because she would kill me otherwise."[11] Undoubtedly, the strong animus in this judgment came from Minime's anger not merely at having been physically abused by Anne but also from her sorrow at Paul's failures and the catastrophe that came later. Those disasters, she believed, need never have occurred. To those who were not intimates, the couple appeared to get along well enough. That may have been merely the impression they created, and many saw through it.[12] Both Frida and Marlene considered Anne an actress, and Jan de Man said Paul was "the slave of his wife."

Anne succeeded, however, in achieving two important goals. The first was to move out of the little cottage into "a sizable brick house with many bedrooms," at 311, Stardnerslei, probably the home David Braybrooke visited in 1945, which Paul rented from his great-aunt Henrietta ("Jet") Buschmann, whose second husband, a printer, had left her a wealthy widow. According to Walter Van Glabbeek, her son, Jan Buschmann, Paul's cousin and his junior, became close to de Man in these years and later his business partner.[13]

The other imperative issue for Anne was to regularize her status. In the spring of 1944, after a year of this difficult retreat and with a child of three growing up fast, she still was not married. Technically, she was a mistress and the mother of an illegitimate son. Though they lived in a permissive society, property rights and legal status still mattered. Paul could console himself by sinking into books, but Anne was a woman rooted in ever-present reality, and hers was an immediate problem. Around them, history was literally changing fast, and people compulsively guessed about or hoped for what was coming. The Allies had not yet landed in western Europe, but their arrival somewhere on the coast of France, contiguous to Belgium, was widely expected. In May, the Allied forces fighting in Italy were on the point of victory, and Rome would be captured on June 4, just two days before the invasion of Normandy began. Perhaps Anne knew intuitively that if she did not get Paul to agree to marry before such a great upheaval, it would be much more difficult, perhaps impossible, to persuade him once the Americans, in whose written culture he was immersing himself, arrived and, in some unpredictable but certain way, changed everything.

The result she sought took place. Against Paul de Man's better judgment and his father's advice, he and Anne were married in Antwerp on May 17, 1944. Three months later, she became pregnant with their second son, Marc, even before the liberation—which meant not the end of the war, but the arrival of Allied troops in Brussels and the ouster of the German army. The child would be born in Antwerp on May 10, 1945, just at the end of the war in Europe. Less than a year later, in early 1946, she conceived a third child, who would be born in November of that year and be named Robert, after his paternal grandfather. Women like Marlene de Man and Nellie De Ligne usually avoided criticizing Anne, who returned to their world of Brussels in the 1990s, but about her having so many offspring during or just after the war (for conditions actually deteriorated after May 1945), they spoke. It was selfish, almost dangerous: Food was short, life uncertain, and their own husbands were either soon to be put on trial or were already in jail. No doubt they understood that with each birth, Anne tied Paul more tightly to the marriage.

The events of war pulled Paul de Man after them. After D-day, he immediately went to Antwerp and registered his residence as Langeleemstraat 2. This was the building where he had grown up (and where his mother had killed herself). He had to have an official residence, but declaring himself an inhabitant of Kalmthout—where he never admitted officially to living—would only have invited the threats and pursuit that resulted in De Ligne, De Becker, Jan de Man, and other collaborators being sent to jail or forced into exile, and these dangers grew much greater during this era as the Resistance gained strength.

Then even Paul, who usually simply ignored most inconvenient rules, had to deal with a most irritating law. It would have denied him his parentage of his firstborn son, Rik. He was pleased to be a father, and his son had memories of him as a good father—and one who once taught him that anti-Semitism was wrong. De Man was so proud of his child that he took him with him to show him to his formidable aunt Yvonne.[14] The situation of Rik's birth caused great merriment among Paul's friends, partly because so many of his transgressive tactics were in play. Little Rik had been named Henri Hrand Jäger, and there was no way to change that, for Belgian law forbade adopting one's own illegitimate child if that child was the result of an adulterous union. Thus in registering in Antwerp, Paul stated that with him was "Henri Hrand Jäger, born [in] Etterbeek [a borough of Brussels] January 11, 1941," the son of the first marriage of Anna Baraghian Deman.[15]

However, de Man was not going to tolerate the loss of his status as Rik's father, and he resolved the legal problem in what later became a characteristic way. Elements of the bureaucratic records are murky, but Paul's process was simple fraud. A birth certificate was issued in Antwerp on November 30, 1944, for the same Henri Hrand Jäger (little Rik), but he was now named Paul Hendrik de Man, and his date of birth was given as November 27, 1944.[16] On that date, Anne was already three and a half months pregnant with this boy's younger sibling, Marc. This would have made Rik, now almost four, only some five and a half months older than his brother, a biological impossibility. But what had happened to Henri Hrand Jäger? If an official began asking the wrong questions, a vile crime might be suspected. Anything like that must be prevented at all costs. Paul thought of a way around that too: He simply arranged for a death certificate to be issued for the same Henri Hrand Jäger by a Brussels doctor (sources disagree; some say the doctor was in Paris), so that the child could be "born again" under his true father's name.[17] How Paul managed this has not been determined, and friends suggested he bribed either the doctor or the registrar, or both. Georges Goriély summed it up succinctly: The son Paul didn't have, who came to birth in Brussels, died a death that did not occur in Paris, but was nevertheless reborn in Antwerp—and as an infant three years younger than he actually was. At least Paul had not lost him, like Aunt Yvonne's basket of linens, in transit.

For Paul, diddling the city fathers was a matter of indifference. There were still good things to enjoy. As they felt more secure, he and Anne made quiet trips to Antwerp and Brussels. Anne took a course in art history. In Kalmthout, Paul enjoyed a creative, idle life, brooding, letting ideas about his future cross his inner horizon like the clouds that drifted over the Flemish sky.

This was the period when he made the acquaintance of David Braybrooke, who attested that Paul was reading a great deal, especially American journals, such as Dwight Macdonald's *politics*, when he could get them (which Braybrooke supplied), undoubtedly with a view to accommodating himself to the eventual American presence on Belgian and French soil. In befriending Braybrooke, Paul acted with characteristic intuition and openness to new possibilities, ignorant of how deeply his impulsive act would affect his later life. He answered three funny little advertisements he noticed in a French Catholic newspaper, probably *La Libre Belgique*. They were placed by Braybrooke, a young American soldier newly arrived in Antwerp; "one for a mattress, one for a tutor in Greek and Latin, and one that said '*Jeune sociologue cherche cercle belge* [young sociologist seeks Belgian circle]'—rather pretentious." When Paul spotted the ads and replied, he and Braybrooke began what would become a deepening but complex relationship, both personal and professional. "He was, in my view, my best friend," said Braybrooke, who would play an important role de Man's life, for he knew him in the United States in the late 1940s and 1950s. Braybrooke was twenty-one, a corporal in the Signal Corps. He'd had a bare three years of high school French, and only a year of college before enlisting in the army, but he was a highly intelligent, good-looking lad who went on to have a distinguished career as a professor of both philosophy and government.[18]

Paul appreciated him as an intellectual, potentially useful as an American, and admitted him at once to his circle of friends. His new acquaintance was overcome by delight. The two talked about philosophy, but not of Heidegger or other philosophers de Man later pursued.[19] Gaston Bachelard at that time was foremost in de Man's mind. Braybrooke also met Bob de Man, whom he described as "a little man . . . passably friendly," although they "talked very little about him." He noticed that Bob was "a rich man" who drove a Studebaker. (Goriély remembered the same fact; that was the car of choice for rich industrialists of the era.) The young visitor, frustrated by his lowly status as a mere corporal, was vividly aware of the open sexual liaisons among the large group that floated between Antwerp and Kalmthout, and he recalled with pleasure "a bouncing blonde . . . the daughter of Paul's father's mistress. Said mistress was married to an army officer. The milieu of Kalmthout—it was lovely. I've always wanted to find another world like that. . . . No prospects."

He would "go with Paul and Anne to the local bar in the evening at Kalmthout and to concerts in Brussels." Braybrooke was attracted to Anne. "She was very fiery," he reported, repeating the words, "very fiery in temperament. Quick to anger but also quick to subside. She was explosive." He understood her frustrations: "She was impatient with lack of money" and the problems of motherhood and her new pregnancy. Given that he came from a country that Paul now considered important, Anne would have been at her most seductive and warm toward the admiring young man, who knew her only briefly, seeing her only on random occasions. Paul, he perceived, probably from the added perspective of his own later experiences with him, as "rather vaporous in the way of projects. What he [de Man] may have been seeing was a continuous series of optimistic ventures." "Vaporous" and "a continuous series of optimistic ventures" suggest that, like Anne's first husband, Braybrooke perceived Paul as a dreamer. Paul also entertained a lot while in both the village and Brussels, and Braybrooke remembered that: "There was always a little bit of food in spite of rationing." Inevitably, this meant purchases on the black market, which was for many the norm.[20]

READING AMERICAN TEXTS, Paul was especially drawn to Melville's *Moby-Dick*, which had been translated into French only in 1941 but at once received remarkable encomiums from several French writers, Camus and Sartre among them.[21] The latter wrote that only in Hegel's and Melville's worlds did the Absolute, "white and polished as a mutton-bone," appear to the reader, but only if one were ready to "lift the veils by which we hide its face."[22] What aspiring publisher of mystical bent could resist such a description? Translating *Moby-Dick* into Dutch and seeing it into print became de Man's project and the preparation for his next career. First, he would produce a handsome edition; then he would use the book to raise the money to set up a publishing house of his own.

The first job was to get Melville's English into Dutch. Later scholars would find errors in de Man's translations that sometimes seriously affected—or inflected—his assertions about the texts. Such misstate-ments may have arisen partly at least from Paul's indifference to being precise about his sources. He told many people, including Braybrooke and Pat de Man, that a translator did not need to know well the lan-guage of his source, but, rather, needed skill only in writing in the tar-get language. This was what might be called a principle of intellectual parsimony; Pat de Man understood this when she later repeatedly said that her husband "never read a book for which he did not have an immediate use." De Man did not add to his pronouncement that he did not care how many anonymous hands provided the work he parceled out to others. Walter Van Glabbeek remembered that Paul would tell Melville's story in the village to an audience of men old and young, who listened—and became so fascinated that they later carried on the discussion among themselves all over town, even in de Man's absence. *Moby-Dick* became their own. They had the same reaction to Paul's narration of his vision that Bob De Braey had had to his cousin's thrill-ing performances of *The Three Musketeers* or playing *Bolèro* on the pho-nograph many years before. The townsmen, too, must have "appreciated the way he made [them] appreciate life," and found that "he was the one who made things interesting." This ability passionately and sponta-neously to share ideas and fascinate audiences presaged Paul's later extraordinary power as a teacher, when he held academic positions and was able to acquire acolytes and move students even when they did not entirely understand him.

Van Glabbeek asserted he was "absolutely sure" that Paul had done the translating himself, as "I've seen him working on it with my own eyes." No doubt this was true. However, Paul also enlisted several different hands. Probably the lion's share fell to Georges Goriély, who asserted this, and whose testimony has consistently been shown to be correct. Georges was a scholar, fluent in several languages, and always ready to help Paul—as he had done at ULB. Translation is an arduous art if it is to be done well, but neither dealing with details nor sticking to his last was Paul's forte. It was easier to inspire others to do the work. The book appeared in 1945 under mixed, somewhat mysterious circumstances. The publisher was Helicon, N. V., the place Antwerp, but no date of publication appears on the title page, nor was credit given to the translators. It did have excellent woodcut illustrations in the fashion of the day by the well-known artist René de Pauw, who was credited. Unfortunately, however, the volume was printed on poor-quality paper, almost newsprint, which even at the time began to turn brown and shatter, as Van Glabbeek noted.[23]

Why the anonymity and inferior production? Paul, ever a lover of luxury, the prospective editor of that deluxe though aborted journal of Nazi art and ideology, *Les Cahiers Européens*, certainly knew what first-class production meant, but paper was in short supply, tightly controlled by the Nazis, who did not surrender in western Europe until May 7, 1945. Probably de Man realized that it would not yet be safe to identify himself as the source of the book, for the Repression, or the Purge, was in full cry in the period just after liberation. Jan de Man was tried and imprisoned early, spent two and a half years in jail, and worked as a salesman, unable to find substantial professional employment for the rest of his life. Until Paul was cleared by the postwar forces of the Repression, it was probably not safe for him to draw attention to himself. (Henri, said to be protected by an old socialist friend in the Swiss government, was never pulled out of Ardez in the Grisons to be brought to trial.)

Bringing out *Moby-Dick* was a major coup, and it must have given de Man a great surge of energy and determination. On the other hand, it was true that although he had worked in the media, he had had no direct experience in publishing. In his period at the Agence Dechenne and the Toison d'Or, something under two years in all, he had functioned not really in management of the business but primarily as an editor, an insightful reader, and a critic of books and manuscripts. One has seen what chaos his foray into the management side of publishing—that is, the purchasing of stock—caused. But of this experience, he needed to say nothing. Now Paul's habitual secrecy served him in good stead. None of his friends knew anything about his ascent in the world of the media, and so none knew of his disgrace beyond the relatively minor one of having reviewed for *Le Soir (volé)* and read manuscripts for the Toison d'Or. He could proceed at will in the turbulent and anxious years that followed the liberation. With Braybrooke and his other friends, he settled on the name for his company: Hermès, who was the messenger of the gods. The main thing was to find the money to send him on his flight.

19

HERMÈS

———

THE TWO YEARS IN WHICH PAUL CREATED, MANAGED, AND THEN ABANDONED the publishing house called Hermès were the most deeply buried part of his past, a matter of shame to his family and even more profoundly concealed by all than his wartime collaboration. For Paul's career as a publisher was a "desperate downward spiral" (to quote Christopher Ricks in another context), during which he committed major financial crimes: thefts, frauds, and swindles, for which he would be found guilty in absentia and sentenced to five years in prison with heavy fines. Although hushed up by Paul de Man's influential father as long as possible, Hermès was a significant scandal that damaged many, and it stained Bob de Man's reputation, severely damaged his finances, and changed his way of life. The de Man family wanted to forget it. To those who knew Paul de Man only in his late, mature years, the facts concerning his career of theft and swindling are so unlikely that they resist assimilation and seem absurd in the original sense of the word— without root, inexplicable.

SOMETIME IN THE WINTER of 1945–46 Paul met with his assembled investors in his apartment on Langeleemstraat in Antwerp. Outside the velvet curtains of the salon, under a cloudy northern sky, there was a gray light on the cobbles and the stones were covered with ice and grit, but indoors a coal fire was burning in the grate. De Man knew very well how slippery "Long Clay Street" was. He was living now just floors away from the apartment where he'd grown up, and the draperies had been his mother's, for his wife had removed them from Bob de Man's apartment. Anne needed them, she had told her father-in-law, so she took them. He did not protest.[1] Goods—food, fuel, clothing—everything was in short supply after the war, and Anne was not to be denied.

The season might be ominous, but Paul's mood was high, although an interrogation by the prosecutor was hanging over his head. At any rate, other avenues were closed: De Man could not return to the university even as an undergraduate, and he had no standing there. "Candidature" meant he had spent a few years there but had no degree. After the war, collaborators might not have been indicted, but some gates would still be closed.[2] It was commerce, or nothing. To Anne, that was desirable. She wanted to move to Paris after the war, for that was where the great world of real money and society showed itself.[3] There she could shine. But although Jan de Man regarded Paul as "the slave of his wife," on this one point, Paul refused.[4] He intended to stay in Belgium and, it appears, to favor his Antwerpen roots. No doubt his Flemish investors felt the same way.

Soon the young Belgian and his father opened their most opulent reception room to a group of men to whom Paul explained his aims. Jan Buschmann, Paul's wealthy young cousin, was one of several other Antwerpen businessmen who were clustered in that upholstered salon, their excitement rising and cheeks reddening as they listened to the brilliant Paul sketch his dreams of their future riches. The twenty-five-year-old who could get all the folk of a rural village to talking excitedly about *Moby-Dick* during wartime was an irresistible seducer. Present would certainly have been the biggest moneyman, the printer Jan Eeckels, whose name appears like a red thread in the fortunes of the de Man family.[5] Eventually, there would be nine investors.

Paul told them about the surefire project that would involve little risk but increase their wealth and no doubt their social prominence. Bob was to be *mandataire* (sleeping partner, or agent), and Eeckels *commissaire* (trustee or steward of the books and financial propriety of the company). Neither man paid much attention to the company. Hermès was Paul's project only, and he was managing director.[6] One may guess that Bob felt proud at this moment that his scapegrace son, who had proved in spite of everything to be a hard worker, was now creating such an enterprise, and that he, Bob, was able to place his wealthy old friend Eeckels in a position of honor and power, which, to be sure, he would not need to exercise. The printer-auditor brought along two other men, and the three supplied two-thirds of the original capital. Bob and Paul between them provided only 9 percent.[7]

The project again displayed de Man's intellectual parsimony. He would not publish original works at all, but would buy the rights to existing publications of high quality, translate, and then sell them to foreign markets.[8] Paul would choose books on art, including biographies and criticism of great artists and dramatists. Only the most elevated art was to be promoted: "commentaries on famous painters and dramatists," translations of "internationally well-known novels; musical compositions . . . from certain areas" only—that is, "pre-Bach and post-Ravel"—and monographs about various arts. Their list would include fiction—foreign best-sellers. Everything would be "sponsored"—not financially but bearing the invaluable imprimatur of a grand cultural institution, such as the Palace of Beaux-Arts (where Paul Willems was to find his permanent place). All would appear in the same elegant format, one that would give tone to the books and bespeak the buyer's taste in buying the works of Hermès, as they lay displayed about one's salon. No doubt Paul argued that his translations of popular books would be presold and would, if they were American in origin, inform Belgians about this newly important influence on their lives. Prestige was the key concept.[9]

Gathering the money proved easy. By the time all the meetings were over, Paul's supporters together pledged one-half of the company's projected capital.[10] They had no idea at all how de Man would actually use their money.

HERMÈS WAS OFFICIALLY SLATED to begin business on February 14, 1946, at a pleasant office in the center of Antwerp, 215, chaussée de Malines. Paul de Man, however, did not stand on ceremony. Ten days before opening the office, on a single day he defrauded two academics, Paul Fierens and Robert Guiette, to each of whom he promised advances of thirty thousand Belgian francs for new books, but paid each only half that amount, while pocketing for himself the balance of thirty thousand francs. On the fourteenth, he forged receipts and posted false entries in the company books to cover these thefts.[11] In later years, Georges Goriély learned of this when he happened by chance to be on a jury with Guiette, who told him the story of having been shown his own forged signature by the police when they were chasing down many of Hermès's false receipts.

De Man, who had not yet invested a franc of his own money in the company, was not yet done that Valentine's Day. His salary was eleven thousand Belgian francs per month, a very generous sum and approximately the amount he'd been getting at the corrupt Agence Dechenne, where greatly inflated incomes were normal. But that was not enough. On the same opening day, he paid himself an "honorarium" of 86,000 francs, which was more than three times the sum he eventually invested in his own company and was the equivalent of about two thousand dollars, an amount on which students still could live for a year in the United States (and was a year's income for many middle-class Belgians at that time). In short, in addition to the thirty thousand francs realized from the forgeries, he took out about ten months' salary on the first day he had control of the till.[12] These withdrawals and the amount of Paul's salary angered the auditor, F. Grimbers, who was appointed by the court after Hermès went bankrupt, because Paul de Man had not yet done a stroke of work to earn even his salary.[13] The timing of these frauds suggests that he had planned them in advance and was prepared to begin rifling the company's funds at the earliest possible moment.[14]

The two episodes with academic authors became a template for Paul de Man's practices, which caused the company to go bankrupt. It was actually not really a publishing company at all. The one thing this business—named, as it was, after the god of commerce, thieving, and juggling—did not really do was publish. That is a pursuit that requires, in addition to intelligence, great skill and attention to detail, but these were not de Man's strengths. The company that Paul de Man founded was almost inert, a kind of paralyzed victim of its creator, who drew off its capital while it remained lifeless. In the words of his first wife, Anne, "He just went in and took out the money."[15]

A clear narrative of the succession of events at the company is difficult to construct because after Hermès became defunct, but before Bob de Man and Jan Eeckels called in the authorities, an unknown person or persons entered the office, opened the company's safes and files, and stripped them, so that almost all the relevant papers that would be needed by a judicial inquiry were entirely missing and never recovered.[16] In theory, only Bob de Man and Jan Eeckels had access to the offices. When eventually Grimbers came to do his work of establishing the facts that would lead to the civil and later criminal charges launched against Paul de Man, he found the safes open—and empty. There were no assets or contracts, only the books and some receipts. Keeping the books was Eeckels's personal responsibility, and he would have been held liable if they disappeared.

From February 1946 until at least October 31, 1947, de Man signed numerous other documents that would prove worthless except to himself. Some were agreements for works men wrote but that never saw the light of day. At least one was a total fabrication, a forged contract for a book the supposed author had never heard of and which existed only to provide the basis for a a false entry in the company's books, with a forged receipt for moneys paid out. From others, friends and strangers, vendors and men richer than himself, in small sums and large, as "honoraria" or as loans, Paul embezzled and swindled indifferently, whether they were authors, friends, relatives, or investors. He kept the books himself, but he sent the outside auditor away, and he did not actually pay the bills for the telephone and other vendors, but, rather, forged receipts and kept the money he posted as expenses. He took money from everyone, and did not spare even his old nurse, Filomene, a family retainer who came to him and entrusted him with her entire life savings.[17] She, too, lost it all. Yet she had served the entire family all her life and Paul, as Madeleine's child, had been her favorite.[18] Paul's aunt Yvonne invested a significant sum, but he treated her as he did the others. Translations were a major channel for stealing from the treasury. He would often commission translations, using the names of personal friends (one was his mistress, to whom he promised a higher than usual fee), but keep for himself the moneys due them, in whole or in part, while entering payments for the full amounts in the company's books. Elsa Willems-De Groodt, Paul Willem's wife, was one of those whose names he used. Her supposed signature appeared on a receipt for five thousand Belgian francs. She refused all requests from the police to appear at the station and be deposed, but eventually the judiciary called on her at home, which was known as the castle of Missembourg, and got her reluctant statement that the writing was not her own. A forged signature of Marcel Slusny, a lawyer and the brother of the violinist Nahum Sluszny, was also found. Paul even listed the name of Georges Goriély's mother, Mme. Temmerman, stating she had received fifteen thousand Belgian francs for some translation. Paul also forged the name of his friend André Souris, the Belgian musician, on two receipts totaling ten thousand francs; this was the same man whose work he had planned to publish in the aborted issue of *Messages*. When contacted by the police, Souris said that he had neither received payment nor signed the papers. Paul swindled an American literary agent in Paris by paying her a trivial amount for six books, never publishing any of them, but using the contracts as assets against which to raise new money. In general, Paul's friends moved on, if they did not always forget, but the agent, Mrs. William Bradley, would sue.

In less than two years, de Man expended essentially all those assets. When the investors finally began to demand answers and none were forthcoming, their inquiries led first to the collapse of Hermès and then to de Man's criminal trial for forgery, swindling, and embezzlement. Long before the case of Hermès came to court, however, Paul de Man had disappeared.

The financial collapse itself is not the most remarkable fact about Hermès. What is most astonishing about de Man's company is that only one book appeared in Belgium under its imprint, and research shows that Hermès published at most two texts.[19] One was Hermès's Dutch version of *Un Portrait de Vincent Van Gogh*, by Jean de Beucken, but this handsome work had first appeared in France in 1938.[20] The other one was by Paul Haesaerts (a wealthy man who kept apartments in posh districts of Brussels and Paris), entitled *Renoir: Sculptor*.[21] De Man made these two attempts early on. In 1946, as other scholars have discovered,

Paul went to Sweden (a summer trip, for which he charged over 38,000 Belgian francs in travel expenses) and succeeded in selling Haesaerts's book to a publisher there for the sum of 135,000 Belgian francs. As *Renoir som bildhuggare*, the book appeared in Stockholm in 1948. However, it may have been in the same "damaged condition" that caused an American publisher later to reject it.[22] It did not sell, and the Swedish publisher did not pay for it.

By the summer of 1947, Hermès was scraping bottom, and Paul de Man flew to New York—an expensive way to journey—arriving in June and returning toward the end of July. He met with Braybrooke, made him his "American agent," and together they visited Prentice-Hall and two or three other publishers. This was a period remembered fondly by Braybrooke, for de Man "used to come out on weekends at this little lodge of ours on the Rockaway River. He used to say mildly shocking things to my mother—and she would protest and laugh." For years, Braybrooke considered Paul to be one of his best friends. But he could not sell the van Gogh book or Willems's book on Goya. "And yet, it wasn't crazy," Braybrooke noted. "The van Gogh book was printed. After that, I was busy with my studies at Harvard."[23]

Braybrooke did translate Willems's text and he gave Paul both his own manuscript and Willems's. Paul, however, lost both of them. That summer, Paul stayed at the Drake, a rather expensive hotel in midtown owned by Belgians.[24] Both manuscripts evidently disappeared at the hotel, for after he failed to pay his considerable bill, the hotel evicted him and destroyed everything he had left behind, including his passport, a cherished letter from Paul Valéry, which he always carried with him, and the manuscripts.

Paul did not pay Braybrooke for any of his work, including this translation. "He was quite irresponsible," his friend commented. "I was in expectation of being paid . . . for some years. . . . I was disappointed." In this instance, Paul basically killed two friends with one stone. Willems's manuscript was the second of three unique manuscripts that de Man "lost;" the first was the one given him to review at the Toison d'Or, and the third would be his own translation of *Madame Bovary* (actually the work of Pat de Man), which went missing "in the mail." De Man told Willems that he had "forgotten" his manuscript somewhere, and the author never got it back. Willems was an urbane man with many other options. After a passage of almost fifty years, this episode was undoubtedly the reason for Willems's remark that Paul had "thrown his treasures out the window," by which he said he meant "treasures of taste, intelligence, and connoisseurship. He was light; he threw his gifts away—his knowledge of art was a treasure. He carried his erudition too lightly. So much wasted knowledge. You could say that he just forgot it all as a kind of gesture. He destroyed what he had. He was a man one could not despise; one could condemn, but one could not despise him."[25]

De Man did manage to sell the English-language rights for *Renoir: Sculptor* to a small New York publisher, Reynal & Hitchcock, but he bungled the negotiations and they later returned the book as unsalable because the text "furnished did not correspond to the conditions" agreed upon, according to Bob de Man.[26] Back in Antwerp, Paul de Man charged his company 125,000 Belgian francs for travel expenses, a very large sum, especially in view of his failure to pay his hotel bill. Then he took his normal month's holiday in Kalmthout.

In autumn, the last he would ever spend in Belgium, Paul de Man was desperate. Perhaps he was losing his balance on the tightrope he had been walking for years, trying to satisfy Anne's demands as well as his own extravagant needs, while admitting to no one that there was nothing beneath his feet but an inch of hemp. Perhaps he wanted to fall. On October 31, 1947, he engaged in a deliberate swindle. His victim was Raymond Eeckhoudt, an insurance broker and family friend, whom he induced to lend him fifty thousand Belgian francs on the strength of his own signature only, saying he had the right to bind Hermès at that high level. He did not, and he never repaid the loan. When Bob de Man learned the facts later, he voluntarily accepted the obligation as his own, promised to repay the money, and did so, just as he met many of his son's other debts. According to Jan de Man and Bob De Braey, his own business never recovered from these losses.

At the end of 1947, Jan Eeckels finally studied the financial records of the company, in which he had personally invested 150,000 Belgian francs. He got a shock.[27] In less than two years, Paul had expended almost all the assets of the company, whose total capital had eventually risen to 1,450,000 Belgian francs. Yet it was in part his own fault, for Bob and Jan Eeckels should have pulled Paul up short much sooner. At the beginning of 1948, they began an "internal investigation." From that point onward, with the disastrous year-end results in view, the normally complacent Bob was forced to move with comparative swiftness. It was already too late. The more they discovered, the clearer it became that they themselves would be liable for the results of Paul's depredations, both legally as directors and especially ethically, as they had been guarantors among their friends of Paul's good faith, which now was irrevocably destroyed. It must have been a frightening time. Culpably, however, when the auditor and Bob grasped the problem, they did not advise others on the board that great sums of money had been lost. Undoubtedly, they were hoping to find exculpating facts or perhaps to somehow rearrange matters so that the results would be less damaging. Nevertheless, after all the lawsuits, claims, and counterclaims for precedence among the creditors, no one got anything; all the assets of the company had long been dissipated and only the derisory sum of 66,000 Belgian francs remained. Throughout, Paul paid himself a salary, including the final week of May 21, 1948.

By March, Bob realized that Paul must be secretly gotten out of the country, for he would certainly face going to jail once the facts were known. There was probably fraud involved: seeming forgeries, certainly swindling, evidently crooked dealings. The unexplained loss of close to a million and a half francs, with only two publications to show for the investment—one in unsalable condition—was not a small failure. At the very least, receivership was the next step for Hermès, and perhaps bankruptcy after that.[28] Even criminal charges might ensue. Bob got his son a visa for the United States, a document difficult to obtain, which led to rumors of bribery. In a way, the situation was much worse for Bob than for Paul. His reputation was far more at stake than his son's. Not only was his own money invested in the company but it was on his faith and credit that friends like Eeckels and others had supplied the capital his son had stolen.

When the de Man men did lose control of their tempers, it was terrifying. That month Bob for once was forced to confront his son and demand where the money had gone. The fact that Bob never saw Paul

again and refused to answer any letter or message implies how wounding that meeting or set of meetings was. What remained of the assets
Paul had purchased? Even if the imperturbable and secretive son tried
to turn aside the questions, it was impossible for him to conceal his pattern of falsification when the company's books were at hand and the
interrogators had the will to consult them. Did Paul reply at all? Was he
direct, admitting his acts, and indifferent to the inferences to be drawn?
Did he cite Anne's demands and his own needs? The turbulent postwar
business climate? Or did he merely shrug off the questions, refusing to
let them touch him? Whatever words were uttered, Paul must have
known that the reputation of everyone concerned was permanently
tainted, and that he would have to leave, and very soon.

It would be unnecessary and tedious to follow the details of the case
of Hermès through its two trials, which began in 1949 and did not end
until 1953. Bob de Man and Jan Eeckels were uncooperative and played
keep-away, sending the auditor, F. Grimbers, back and forth between
them when he appeared with questions about his list of creditors, whom
Paul had supposedly paid. In the end, the court prosecuted Paul for
swindling, forgery, and embezzlement in relation to five people, three
of them authors, one an agent, and only one a defrauded translator.[29]
After two court-ordered audits and the involvement of three more justices, Paul de Man was found guilty and was sentenced in absentia on
October 23, 1951, to a total of five years in prison, plus heavy costs and
fines. This kind of crime was taken seriously, and the judges ordered his
immediate arrest should he ever return to the country.[30]

20.

THE PALACE
OF JUSTICE

THE PALACE OF JUSTICE RESTS ON TOP OF A CLIFF IN BRUSSELS LIKE A great brown hawk surveying the city below, its stony bulk already a reproach to evildoers. The central hall, shadowed by an enormous dome, is known as the Cour des pas perdus (the Hall of Lost Footsteps). At three o'clock in the afternoon of July 30, 1946, just a day before the court would close for a month of vacation, Paul de Man crossed it for his interrogation by the prosecutor. The weather had been torrid, broken by storms. By midsummer, the stone of the building has absorbed months of sun, and the leaden roofs reflect their heat down into airless spaces. The office in which Paul sat was undoubtedly hot and the chair hard.

He cannot have approached his interrogation by the chief prosecutor for the Epuration with a light heart, however he acted. This was the most intense period of activity for the Epuration, or Repression, and Roger Vinçotte, the prosecutor, had racked up a string of successes. No record of Paul de Man's being questioned could be found in the period following the "revelations" of 1988, however, and therefore the argument was made that he had not been considered a collaborator at all. However, the critical document, de Man's procès-verbal (the record of his questioning) turned up in 1993, during the first year of archival research for this book, through the courtesy of the auditor-general of the Military Court. It shows that Paul was indeed interrogated by the same man who prosecuted almost all the major media miscreants for collaboration.[1] Vinçotte was a powerful, effective figure in the postwar judicial "cleansing" of collaborators and he had already sent both Paul's cousin Jan and his former boss Pierre De Ligne to jail. Paul's uncle Henri was being hunted by the Resistance. Only five days earlier, the prosecutor had successfully closed Raymond De Becker's criminal case, and the publisher of *Le Soir (volé)* had been found guilty of treason and sentenced to death.[2] Now he was aiming at Edouard Didier.

Paul de Man had known for a long time that he was liable to prosecution. Merely being his friend had already caused trouble for Frida Vandervelden and others who had endured the ominous interview in 1945, when a tribunal of the Epuration had called in the Dosognes and the Jaegers. Interest in trials for collaboration and war crimes was high, and during the same week that Paul was interrogated, daily press reports reflected intense public scrutiny. Only two days after de Man's interview, the mayor of Bruges was condemned to life in prison for having denounced to the Nazis seven of his fellow citizens, who had been deported to Germany, where one of them had died.[3]

Under those circumstances, it took a certain amount of courage to remain in Belgium and not flee to France, but de Man was a gambler. Immovable once he had made up his mind, he undoubtedly counted on his skill at persuasion to pull him through. He may also have calculated that his record was less egregious than that of others. Unlike Jan de Man and Pierre De Ligne, he had run no public agency, nor edited a major newspaper. His roots were Flemish, and his investors were Flemish businessmen. He chose to stay and take his chances.

Vinçotte actually knew a lot about de Man before he confronted him on that summer afternoon, for he was getting ready to try the entire Agence Dechenne as a corporation for collaboration, and he had received the report of the external auditor, Frans De Coster, on December 5, 1945. (It is a riveting document, although long, and throughout it Paul de Man's name, interwoven with those of Peeters, von Balluseck, and the others, appears frequently, his rise and fall between 1941 and 1943 chronicled in the detailed, dispassionate narrative.) In addition, Vinçotte possessed the papers of the Editions de la Toison d'Or, which had been seized by the Resistance in 1945, on the basis of which he intended to find Edouard Didier guilty of treason.[4] The penalty for Didier could—and would—be death (although, in fact, he lived and died in comfortable exile).[5] Moreover, the directors of the Toison d'Or, who included De Becker, Didier, and Pierre Daye, had become the usual suspects among the Belgian collaborating media, for they were knitted together by interlocking directorates. One by one, these men were being investigated and put on trial. Paul de Man's name appeared in all these documents, in the correspondence of the Agence Dechenne, and in De Becker's file at the Toison d'Or, where Vinçotte found the prospectus for the *Cahiers Européens*, the document that he would cite against De Becker as a perfect example of treason.[6]

In short, the record of interrogation shows that Paul de Man's role was noticed by the Repression, and that he was significant enough for the busy prosecutor to take the time to examine him. However, though revealing in its own way, it is brief, only two pages long (in comparison, for example, to the nine, closely-written pages demanded of Raymond De Becker in 1945–1946), and the questions posed to Paul were neither pointed nor hard to evade. In fact, Vinçotte put only seven questions to Paul, of which three were purely formal (for example, "Have you anything to add?").

De Man's answers give insight into his strategy and ability to elude traps and difficulties. His plan was not to deny everything, for he knew the facts could readily be checked, but instead skillfully to shade the truth, not contradicting what was self-evident, but rearranging evidence, hiding what was not sought, casting blame on others when possible, and lying when it would be useful and safe. He aimed to get by not by asserting his importance but by appearing as insignificant as possible. To that end, he came prepared and ready to give a brief description of his career. Especially, he aimed to forestall questions about how his uncle's influence could have helped him, for Henri de Man at that point was a focus of some in the Repression who tracked him across France and then Switzerland, hoping to catch him. Without being asked, his nephew asserted that he had begun to work at *Le Soir (volé)* through the influence of Pierre De Ligne, a colleague from university days. In fact, De Ligne vigorously denied this when interviewed, asserting instead that de Man had simply shown up one day in the office of the newspaper of which he, De Ligne, was a director. The inference the managing editor drew was that De Becker had hired him because he was the nephew of Henri de Man, and probably at the minister's request.

Vinçotte demanded an answer to only one question that was designed to give the former columnist much trouble: "Do you admit having had, when you were at 'Soir,' a favorable bias toward the New Order [as the Nazi regime was politely known], as some articles seem to show?" De Man handled it adroitly, and Vinçotte let the witness run on. Yes, he had written about German books, but he had not been biased; he had judged them strictly on their literary merit. He knew that the anti-Semitic article of March 3, 1941, was the real issue, and he explained it away at once.

> I can explain this matter because I am known as being the oppo-site of an anti-Semite. I have always had Jewish friends, I helped them during the war, and they have kept my friendship. Meule-pas [an editor at *Le Soir (volé)*] [7] showed me an article by Eemans violently attacking the influence of Jews in literature. I pro-tested to De Becker, who told me I could write another article. The article that you have before you aims to show that the Jew-ish influence in literature is benign, and above all it responds to Eemans's article. I know that it appeared on a page devoted to anti-Semitism, but I was never warned about that and was not responsible for it.

That article, a bombshell when unearthed by Ortwin de Graef in 1988, was responsible for the scandal, known as "the revelations," con-cerning Paul de Man and it led to the publication of innumerable essays in the press attacking him and, through him, theory and deconstruc-tion, the critical approach he and Jacques Derrida had by then so per-suasively adopted. It also evoked almost as many pieces defending him. "The Jews in Present-Day Literature," discussed in chapter 13, was entirely unknown in the United States, and had been largely forgotten in Belgium until forty-two years after this interrogation took place. What the procès-verbal shows, however, is that in 1946 the page of anti-Semitic attacks was still in the minds of patriotic Belgians. No doubt it was scandalous when first published, and it provided Vinçotte with his line of attack when he confronted Paul with the essay he had written, mentioned by de Man as "the article that you have before you." Paul clearly recognized that his contribution to the anti-Semitic campaign launched by his newspaper in 1941 was now radioactive if he could not explain it away. To avoid conviction on the charge that he had shown pro–New Order, or Nazi, bias, he had to begin by exorcizing this central issue.

One of the greatest elements of the scandal following the revelations of de Man's writing for Le Soir (volé) and his article "The Jews in Present-Day Literature" was the strong implication that he had actually been anti-Semitic himself, and from his early years. What were his real feelings? his friends in the United States and abroad must have wondered. Had they and everyone else been hoodwinked during the decades he had moved in his adopted country among Jews and non-Jews alike? Many, especially those closest to him, were torn by a sense of betrayal, but none had previously perceived in him any such prejudice. In fact, within the context of facts that can be established, it appears that de Man did not hold pronounced anti-Semitic views. His comments were essentially opportunistic and intended to strengthen his claims for a hoped-for elevated career under the Third Reich. He was one of the lukewarm, whom Dante condemned to sit eternally at the gates of Hell, men without principles or convictions who compromised with evil. De Man indeed did have Jewish friends whom he did not abandon during the war, such as Georges Goriély, Marcel Slusny, and Marcel's brother and sister-in-law, Nahum and Esther Sluszny, and his assistance in sheltering the couple, which has also been discussed previously, did carry certain dangers. Esther herself later insisted that de Man was in no way anti-Semitic. Anne de Man was truthful, according to her friend Nellie De Ligne, when she emphasized that she had given a musical soirée at which Nahum and his quartet had played during the war. Paul's eldest son, Rik Woods, also volunteered that his father was no anti-Semite and recalled being reproved by him strongly when he unwittingly repeated an anti-Semitic slur he had picked up from another child in Kalmthout.[8]

On the other hand, a certain level of casual anti-Semitism existed everywhere, was taken for granted, and it did not disappear after World War II. Earlier anti-Semitism was immeasurably more conscious and overt. Henri de Man wrote repeatedly of his "visceral" dislike of Jews, even though his second wife had been Jewish.[9] Without such widespread, deep-rooted prejudice and its encouragement by leaders and the press, there might have been no Nuremberg Laws in 1935, no Kristallnacht in 1938, and no passive acceptance of the campaigns that long preceded the Final Solution. Karl Schleunes argued in *The Twisted Road to Auschwitz* that Nazism differed from other fascisms essentially only by making central its doctrine of anti-Semitism.[10] One cannot, therefore, assume that Paul de Man was better than those around him in this regard. He was, however, no ideologue, but easygoing and tolerant in his relations with others, and he chose his friends where affinity, not social roles, took him. The shrug with which his essay dismissed Jewish contributions to European culture was typical of his indifference to issues that inflamed others, and was intended—like his other characteristic shrugs—to put himself above such matters.

That said, however, there is no truth at all in de Man's protestations to Vinçotte that his essay showed that Jewish "influence" was "benign." On the contrary, it proposed deportation of Jews (a "solution" considered earlier by the Nazis but then dismissed). All that he could have claimed for his essay is that while he denigrated Jewish writers in general, his tone lacked the viciousness of other writings that had been appearing in *Le Soir (volé)*. One may, for example, compare his words to those of Léon Van Huffel, an extreme anti-Semite and racist who in page-one articles only a few weeks before had described Jews as "liars," and "bastards" because they were of "mixed race" (like "the yellow and Negro races"), et cetera.[11] This colleague also issued what was essentially a call to genocide: "The days of brutal, spontaneous and instinctive antisemitism are over . . . we must now substitute an antisemitism reflective, systematic, and peaceable."[12]

It is uncertain whether de Man was lying or telling the truth when he said he had voluntarily written the article only because Eemans had written a worse one, which he wanted to neutralize.[13] If that was true, his statement shows how greatly opinion has changed, for many today will consider that negotiating to contribute an anti-Semitic article for any reason at all is as bad as writing it under duress. If de Man did volunteer to write his essay in March 1941, as he asserted to Vinçotte, it was a career move, and he calculated well, for it enabled him—who had begun only two months before as an occasional stringer—to join the club of insiders.[14]

Vinçotte let the question of de Man's pro-Nazi bias slide and did not pursue the matter. Instead, he posed three other questions touching upon Editions de la Toison d'Or. Was de Man aware of this publisher's connections to Mundus? This was important, because Mundus was the great Nazi publishing entity, supervised by von Ribbentrop at the German Foreign Ministry, that ultimately controlled both the flow of paper to Belgium and the Toison d'Or itself.

De Man's response was innocent, even humble in tone: "When I worked at Dechenne, I learned that there existed a firm called Mundus, which appeared to be interested in La Toison d'Or." In saying this, de Man represented himself as a minor figure who vaguely had heard something about two other companies. In fact, Mundus was a kind of octopus, a major Nazi invention that organized and controlled publishing at home and abroad, and it supported the Toison d'Or, with its directors as its straw men. When Paul and Lothar von Balluseck conspired to oust Didier from his position in 1942, their contact was with Herr Seidel at Mundus. De Man wanted to conceal his ambitions and close knowledge of the workings of the publishing world, particularly in regard to the Toison d'Or. His closest friends, Paul Willems and Louis Carette, had both published their first books with the Toison d'Or, and his uncle Henri's memoir, *Après Coup*, had been that company's first publication. Given Paul's intimacy with these active players and his own attempted coup, it was virtually impossible for him to have been ignorant of the activities of Mundus. Vinçotte, with all the files at his fingertips, must have known Paul de Man's answer was disingenuous.

Then he asked if de Man knew whether Lucienne Didier was active in the company and how he had come to work for that publisher. These were easy questions, and Vinçotte accepted de Man's simple answers: Mme. Didier—Paul had merely heard this—exerted considerable influence. As for how he came to work there, he had gotten his job there just "through friends"—men who'd worked there and recommended him as a translator. He had read books for the publisher and recommended some, but he'd never been given "precise" instructions about the slant he should take.

> If I wrote some articles on German books, it was without any political bias, without any preconceived wish to speak preferentially about German writers, and only in terms of their literary value. The article on the destiny of Flanders is the only one I may have written that went beyond the [bounds of] a literary column. This article attacks separatism directly, and I point out to you that it was violently attacked by the Flemish nationalist newspapers.

De Man was pleading that he had resisted the Flemish nationalists, who were generally regarded as having been pro-German, and who favored separation from Francophone Belgium. In doing so, he entirely ignored his several essays that had gone beyond extolling the deep myths and mysteries of Germanic culture to urging Belgians to get off the fence and support the efforts of their conqueror.

No matter what Paul told the prosecutor, he was not cross-examined, and none of his statements was followed up. The uninformed reader of his short procès-verbal would be left with the impression that there was nothing questionable about de Man's replies, although they contain numerous shadings of the facts and several outright lies. One must ask, then, why the interview was so short, moderate in tone, and lacking in difficult questions. After all, Roger Vinçotte had in his files hard evidence both that Paul de Man had been intimately involved in planning a media coup with a major Nazi leader at the Agence Dechenne and that he had equally been part of De Becker's scheme to publish what the prosecutor himself thought of as the essence of treason, *Cahiers Européens*. Paul de Man was actually named in both dossiers as the chief editor of each of these adventures.

It would be wrong to infer that Paul was judged innocent by Vinçotte, but he had not the time to prosecute every collaborator. He had to choose his targets and was after only the major players. Jan de Man and Pierre De Ligne were convinced that Paul de Man was just as guilty of collaboration as they were and should also have been jailed, but their views, of course, were affected by their personal sense of resentment.[15] Nevertheless, there is no question that de Man's interrogation was a mild endeavor. Even its timing—late in the afternoon of virtually the last day before the summer vacation, when it would be almost impossible to pursue new leads—suggests that Vinçotte was merely tying up loose ends rather than aiming at opening a new case. De Ligne, De Becker, and Didier were important figures, while from de Man he probably hoped for little more than additional information in those cases. The real direction of Vinçotte's questioning tended toward the operation of the Toison d'Or, and he showed no interest at all in de Man's plot to steal it from Didier. His target was that owner, and not the instigator of a failed palace coup that had been directed at Didier. As for de Man's work on *Le Soir* (*volé*), Vinçotte had already tried and convicted Raymond De Becker, who would spend six years in prison and then live in exile in France until his death in 1959.

Vinçotte was faced in 1946 by a good-looking man who looked younger than his years and who seemed (unless one troubled to add up his remuneration at the Agence Dechenne and the two other companies he worked for simultaneously) to have become a publisher who might perhaps bring some luster back to the tarnished world of Belgian letters. The prosecutor had already imprisoned one de Man—Jan—and Henri would certainly be condemned to death if he were captured. Was he to attack the entire family? Paul de Man's offenses did not rise to the same level of treason.[16]

De Man's luck held again. One wonders if he recognized the paradox that at this crucial moment he was saved not as much by his strengths—his charm and persuasive powers—as by his weaknesses. The stag in Aesop's fable thanks not his proud horns, formidable yet entangling, but his hooves, which let him escape. Had Paul been successful in his grand schemes and gained control of the Toison d'Or, or if as editor he had actually published *Cahiers Européens* and become a powerful figure, he would more likely have been prosecuted. But he had failed at plotting against Didier, and at the Agence Dechenne he had been so incompetent that he had been forced to quit in April 1943.

Paul undoubtedly left the Place Poelaert feeling like a victor, a wrestler who knew how to win by not resisting. Vinçotte certainly did not imagine that this gifted twenty-six-year-old would ever again preoccupy a Belgian prosecutor.

21

DESPAIR, RAGE, AND THE PURSUIT OF SHADOWS

———————

THE HERMÈS SCANDAL IS HARD TO UNDERSTAND IN A PURELY RATIO-nal way. Paul de Man's first wife, Anne, suggested that like some other members of his family, he was "crazy." This is an exaggeration, but perhaps de Man did live those two years in some kind of manic state, traumatized by the violent vicissitudes of the war. Was he in flight from the dead end his existence presented in 1945, when the war was over? Was the uncontrolled waste a sort of frenzy, or did it express "socio-pathic" traits? Even if any of these doubtful terms were applicable, they would remain mere labels.

Unquestionably, he knew that he had severely damaged, if not ruined, his life's prospects. Two major limitations hemmed him in. He lacked an undergraduate degree, but even if he had wanted to return to the university at the age of twenty-six, something adults rarely do, the doors were now barred. Anne wanted Paul to go into the antiques busi-ness with her father, preferably in Paris, to him an unthinkable alterna-tive. Apart from that, there remained almost no other vocation for him. What he loved and did best, intellectual work, solving the puzzles of language and art and laying them open for the pleasure and intellectual growth of others—everything at which he would have excelled in a university—was impossible in Belgium as a result of his collaboration during the war.

On a personal level, he was equally checked. The quiet world and home into which he had been born and which he later reproduced in his second marriage was the opposite of his life with Anne. His mother had been sensitive, intelligent, and averse to the kind of socializing he later derided as going out with "*les girls*."[1] She had been chronically depressed, but she created an atmosphere that was serene and well ordered, where voices were not raised and a semblance of peace prevailed. As a man, however, Paul had found himself dealing daily with cries, constant demands for money, and even abuse—physical as well as verbal attacks—which, to his own shame, he came to give as well as sustain. Anne may also have been jealous of his affairs, which would have added to her rages.

From Anne's point of view, her postwar position was very difficult, and she was obviously disappointed and frustrated. Their circle of friends had, like themselves, lost their social status; De Becker and De Ligne—at whose city hall wedding Paul had been the witness—had even gone to jail. The de Mans needed money and servants. They could regain their standing by entertaining—conspicuously—and by securing the clothes and furnishings that went with this. Yes, she was extravagant, but if she badgered Paul for funds, well, was that not what wives were supposed to do to make their husbands settle down and provide well for their families? Hermès was all right as a foundation for the new life they must create. It hardly mattered where the money came from—but it must be plentiful and enable her and her family to live the generous, open, enviable lives that would again make them cynosures, the observed and powerful people.

To Paul, however, things looked very different. We have no direct evidence of his feelings during these two years, but his actions, though puzzling, suggest reasonable inferences about his motives. Certainly in 1945 and 1946, immediately after the war, de Man would have had to fight despair, for many avenues were closed to him. His past was tainted, and his professional future very problematic. Yet at twenty-six, with a family of four to support—and his own tendency to spend freely to consider—he could not continue his education or enter a profession.

Only the commercial world seemed possible, and he took that route. Yet the only schooling in business Paul de Man had experienced was exposure at a young and impressionable age to the massive and systematic corruption of the Agence Dechenne. There, capital had been grossly plundered by seemingly respectable men who kept careful books but who, once they had the chance, had personally pocketed the millions of francs of company profits. De Man knew better, but he had been formed in terrible times, and his business model had been worse than unworthy. Nor was his father an example he cared to follow. On the contrary, he had been critical from his adolescence of Bob's weakness as a manager, as Minime De Braey's memory of their visit to Bob's factory showed, and Paul probably thought him timid, unimaginative, and risk-averse. Like Charles Peeters—who before the war had seemingly been a worthy secretary of a large and thriving company—once Paul de Man had charge of Hermès's treasury, he found the temptations posed by so much unguarded money irresistible.

When he began his enterprise, he might have made the argument to himself that if the cash was there, and he could raise it easily and set up a plausible business, why not revel in it? After all, one must spend money to make money. If he often pocketed half of the disbursements he controlled, why, it made life easier. Anne would quiet down. His own standing, too, would rise with every thousand francs he spread about, whether to his friends as "commissions" for nothing at all, or for translations, or to writers whose approval might increase his renown. As for the company's books, he might have asked himself who would care if they didn't balance. It was a private company, some of the money was his father's and his own, and once it was all up and running, the losses would give way to gains, and with profits everyone would be happy.

Beyond that, the actual process of publishing, even in his specialized, pass-through fashion, is highly detailed and requires endless, focused attention. Yet de Man had not thought to keep records even of the books he had bought at the Agence Dechenne. Running an actual business was beyond his scope. A show of activity—buying books here (Paris) and selling them there—was easier, and this would keep him in touch with his new friends in France, where he was establishing friendships with men like Georges Bataille.

De Man may also have felt a certain resentment at the hypocrisy of the Antwerpen business world. Perhaps he considered that these businessmen all had more money than they needed, those men from his father's circle who, like Bob, had profited from the war. Paul might have wondered if he had done worse than they. His friend Louis Carette, living in successful exile as a French playwright after his own collaborationist career in Belgium, commented much later that "everyone in Belgium collaborated a little bit." Paul might have shared that view. In the 1960s, he enjoyed a joke one day with the eminent critic Georges Poulet, when the two literary men, attending a conference in Geneva, were overheard as they sat on a wall in the sun, chuckling about "*ces sales belges*" (these dirty Belgians).[2] Perhaps he meant the businessmen who had gone on peacefully in their mercantile lives as brokers and agents of the capitalist economy.

As for the money, he could have had in the back of his mind Georges Bataille's theory of wasteful expenditure—potlatch. In his essay on potlatch, "La Notion de dépense," Bataille began by asserting the natural opposition of wasteful sons and controlling fathers, and Paul might have justified to himself the taking of money from Hermès as an act of rebellion. He had always hated bourgeois limitations: the binding words of its contracts, its prudential calculations. Revolt was, after all, in the air; postwar philosophy advocated rebellion, and de Man in many ways had embodied the zeitgeist of his era, living, from his undergraduate years on, as what Erik Erikson later called "the alienated man."

As for his personal life, if Paul de Man had yielded to temptation in managing his publishing company, he had done much the same in marrying Anne. Now he faced cruel conflicts. The reality was that he was trapped, legally bound to a woman he had come to dislike. His father had warned him against her, but he had ignored him. Yet divorce was impossible. In Belgium, men had mistresses, girlfriends, affairs with the wives of their friends. There were "open marriages," and one tolerated the same in one's wife if need be. But one did not divorce.

Except for a shared love of luxury, his personality and Anne's were completely incompatible. At twenty, he had imagined that he could live a purely hedonistic life and had enjoyed her salons and soirées. That phase was long past. She was not his intellectual equal, and the more his interests had developed, the less they had in common. He cultivated friendships with contemporary philosophers; she needed always to be surrounded by a bevy of friends. What had seemed exotic and sensual in her when he was a very young man now looked affected and self-dramatizing. Her seductiveness now seemed like manipulation, her sociability like social climbing. She had been a catch—in Georges Goriély's phrase, "one of the most beautiful women in Brussels"; now her demands for money had become boring and vulgar. He tried to be a good father, but his sons were his hostages in a life he despised. He had come to hate their existence, especially Anne's emphasis on material splendor and a competitive social life. She wanted more of everything. She even took his father's curtains. Perhaps he saw that at heart she was the daughter of what she thought of as a potentate from southern Georgia, whose family had stretched farther than the eye could see.

It is clear that in these years, de Man made false promises, even while knowing that people would eventually notice that he had published almost no books. He let them remain in the dark. Perhaps at some level, he also knew that when the day of reckoning came, while it would mean disgrace, he would be free. One day he would simply fall out of the orbit of the bourgeois world and disappear. It would all be over, and he would not take Anne and their children with him. He would find his freedom: a criminal maybe, a man of bad faith certainly—but finally released from the chains of his class and its moral and practical obligations.

By 1948, his existence had only deficits. Rage and feelings of impotence must have been deep. At twenty-eight, when his father insisted on shipping him away against his will, he found himself in a cage, and he knew that if he was passive—and passivity was never his style—that cage would get smaller and smaller. Yet he was not ready to part definitively from Anne. Whatever the state of his wallet, he wanted to arrive in New York and be able to present himself as a respectable, reliable man of personal substance; that meant he should be possessed of an attractive wife and intelligent children.

ONE SHOULD NOT UNDERESTIMATE in this regard the influence on de Man of Georges Bataille. In fact, the last and most interesting of Paul's encounters in Belgium was with this distinguished, if controversial, French writer. A sociologist and intellectual, a follower of Nietzsche and de Sade, a friend of Lacan (indeed, the two exchanged wives after a time), and a cherished author of the important editor Jean Paulhan, Bataille was one of those modernists who, as Jürgen Habermas has pointed out, used rational method to reject the rationality of human- ism.[3] His ideas exalted transgressing and bursting the normal limits of behavior in search of the "ecstatic." Sadomasochistic elements had a strong presence in his work, although that theme diminished after 1950.[4] He had been known to Paul for some time. Their last meeting occurred in Antwerp between May 15 and 21, 1948, as indicated by a letter Paul wrote Bataille about six weeks later. The French writer had journeyed to Antwerp, geographically close but culturally very differ- ent from Paris. Evidently, Bataille made the trip for his own purposes, but also to see the younger man, and perhaps give him courage for what lay ahead. Given the evident depth of their communication at the time and Bataille's help soon thereafter, this seems possible. Paul's letter addressed Bataille as "Cher Monsieur et ami," its elegant formal- ity expressing humble acceptance of leadership mixed with affection. He valued their talk, for it went to the bottom of what he was experiencing.[5]

In person, Bataille was an impressive figure. He was soon to become an editor of the highly influential journal *Critique* and an important member of the non-Marxist but left-wing literary establishment, highly respected as an original thinker among French intellectuals. He was well suited to sympathize with this younger transgressor. He had begun as a Surrealist, and papers preserved in the Bibliothèque Natio- nale in Paris show he had moved into a kind of fascism his colleagues called "*surfascisme*" during the 1930s, advocating a strange mixture of doctrines that are reminiscent here and there of Henri de Man's author- itarian social ideas, but drawing also on Nietzsche, de Sade, the Person- alism of Emmanuel Mounier, and to some extent Hegel.[6] Bataille and Paul de Man no doubt first met late in 1942 or early in 1943, when de Man was seeking writers for that aborted next volume of *Messages*.

De Man had cultivated Bataille on his trips to Paris. Perhaps in their shared attraction to excess and also in their rage against their fathers, there was some kind of intuitive understanding between them.[7] The Frenchman was already famous, especially for his essay on potlatch, a celebration of the idea of seemingly wasteful expense, written during the period when he named himself an anthropologist and interpreted the practice of some indigenes as explicatory of much that was practiced in cultivated Western society. Bataille, who was also described by some as cherishing an inverted or negative Christianity, valued the pushing of experience to its extremes, a doctrine of wastefulness for its own sake, holding that in going beyond limits, as in seeking pain or loss at their most intense, one might get an ecstatic glimpse of enlightenment or truth. He concluded an essay he wrote on the nuclear devastation of Hiroshima on a positive note, writing, not without scandal, that perhaps such ecstatic vision had visited the victims of that holocaust.[8] Such striving could prove man's innate superiority to material values.

It is clear that they talked in Antwerp in some depth, and in July, Paul wrote to thank the older man for giving him a completely new way of "thinking and being in the world," and a point of view through which he could make fruitful contacts with certain kinds of persons whom he could now recognize through Bataille's persona, a point of view Paul said he had made his own. In effect, he felt Bataille had given him a new lens through which to view life itself.[9] This was no small gift. What Paul meant by what he wrote, one cannot be sure, but it probably had something to do with confirming his acceptance of his own experience of excess—excess in spending, excess in defying the marital norms, excess in stripping his company of its funds and in using it for his personal desires, excess in rebelling against his father's values and damaging him in the process. Perhaps he now saw that Hermès had been his own act of potlatch, an unconscious, mystical ritual of letting go, a cleansing, revitalizing destruction he had invented for himself. Bataille may have had his own reasons for advocating the ecstatic joys to be derived through the mutilation of self and others, while Paul de Man had impulses toward self-destruction of a different kind; perhaps he and Bataille were drawn to each other by some unspoken but mutual recognition.

This last encounter between them in that decade was a helpful and cherished moment for the younger man. He continued to draw on

Bataille's thinking in moments of need, especially a few years later when, his old habits of wasteful expenditure having once again caused him serious trouble, he lectured to students at Bard College in terms essentially set by Bataille, defending wasteful expenditure as a process connected to all the ideas of nobility, honor, and glory. Bataille held that in wasting family money, such sons were reflecting a truer economic law, the laws of pleasure, of transgression, of "heterogeneity." Poetry and the arts, moreover, were connected with wasteful expenditure.

FOLLOWING BOB DE MAN'S "independent inquiry" into the affairs at Hermès, on March 27, 1948, he secured a visa for Paul to go to the United States. Then he booked passage for his son, not by air this time, but on a humiliatingly low-class, slow vessel, a cargo ship, the *Ames Victory*. It was ironic that a family whose fortune sprang from transporting emigrants to the United States now used a similar vessel to dispatch into exile one of their own. Many in the city knew about it, and there were hints of corruption in securing the visa.[10] Jan de Man said that Paul then took the ticket his father gave him and sold it "several times," so that Bob had to buy another—and another, until finally he bribed the steward not to let his son off the boat. Perhaps it was Paul's way not only of raising cash but also of making the point that his trip, so déclassé in style, would cost his father just as much as a good seat on a plane would have. The *Ames Victory* departed for New York on May 21, 1948.

Before he left, Paul visited Gilbert Jaeger, now remarried, and sent his wife, Josette, to find Frida Vandervelden. "Come quick" was the message; she did, they parted, and never met again. Although Frida said she remained ignorant of the reason for his unexplained disappearance, it is clear that the Jaegers and most likely Georges Goriély, an intimate friend of all of them and always on the alert for important information, eventually not only knew of de Man's secret departure but probably learned the cause. When all of Antwerp was abuzz with that scandal, well-connected persons like Paul's friends in Brussels would have had little difficulty picking up the gossip. As Georges later said, "He had to leave when he went to America because the earth was burning under his feet."[11]

Bob de Man also paid for the voyage of Anne de Man and her three sons, but they were not going with Paul to the United States. They sailed instead for Buenos Aires, where they would join Anne's parents. Mr. Baraghian had emigrated to Argentina and established himself in his old trade, the antiques business. Many folk—displaced persons, survivors, even some fascists on the run—were leaving Europe and seeking refuge elsewhere in those years (ironically, some of them were the people Gilbert Jaeger was to oversee at UNRRA). In classic immigrant fashion, Paul de Man was supposed to go ahead to the United States, get work, and prepare a home where his family could join him. Anne said she expected to be with him by Christmas. De Man would later tell his new acquaintances in the United States that he planned to bring his family to join him by the holiday. In fact, however, when they separated in Antwerp, it was the end of the marriage; Paul never lived with Anne or his sons again.

Setting out on the *Ames Victory*, Paul de Man headed toward a new world, possibly dogged by the same feelings of "despair, rage, and the pursuit of elusive shadows" that Bataille attributed to the poet "consumed by his art."[12] Perhaps Paul, a modernist in spite of himself, hoped to become like that thinker, able to use those emotions and throw them off as by-products of a re-created self.

PART TWO

THE AMERICAN YEARS

22.

"BOOKS ARE THE KEYS
TO MAGIC KINGDOMS"[1]

—————

Arriving in New York on May 29, 1948, the *Ames Victory*, a slow cargo vessel, carried only three passengers, including Paul de Man.[2] The eight-day journey had brought him to the United States penniless, with no introductions or any history he could afford to mention. Tell Americans about Henri de Man? Impossible, although he would soon be relieved to learn that the name meant little on these shores. Say that he had owned a publishing company called Hermès? Only a fool would do that. At the dock, he reported to the INS that he was bound for the home of a friend, David Braybrooke, in Boonton, New Jersey, that he was a publisher, married, and—knocking an inch off the height he had claimed a year earlier—that he was five feet, nine inches tall. He had come on business and "intended to return to the country whence he came" in five months. But to others who might inquire, he could not produce a résumé, since he was a fugitive from the judicial trials that were sure to develop in the country he had left behind.[3] Under those conditions, the sole job he could get was as a stock boy at the branch of the Doubleday-Doran bookstore at the bottom level of Grand Central Terminal. Later, he joked that he was visible there only as a hand thrusting books upward from a trapdoor in the subterranean depths of the basement shop.[4]

Yet, in spite of these disabilities, de Man would soon make a place for himself in the heart of New York's intellectual circles. Within five months, Dwight Macdonald had put his name on his "First List to be asked," a roster of people who would lead the Europe America Groups (EAG), a cause close to Macdonald's heart.[5] The editor, as one of the leading intellectuals of the American Left, founder of both *politics* and, before that, a founding editor of *Partisan Review*, was a powerful man in that world. His list, ratified by an EAG meeting on November 18, 1948, is virtually an "Intellectual Register: 1948," a political Four Hundred. Hannah Arendt and Bruno Bettelheim were among those representing Europe, while Lionel Trilling, Irving Howe, Harold Rosenberg, C. Wright Mills, and Melvin Lasky figured among the seventy-odd Americans.[6] If there was a definable group of the important left intellectuals of the era, this list consecrated them. Even the silent omissions—such as the absence of *Partisan Review's* two editors, Philip Rahv and William Phillips—spoke to the era's state of intellectual life and its squabbles. De Man's inclusion, moreover, signified other acceptance: In the wake of Macdonald's sponsorship came friendships, including one with Mary McCarthy, who was to be important in de Man's life, as well as other major figures in the world of the arts.

It was a stunning leap upward. Nonetheless, although he spent two years in New York, the academic world he later dominated knew nothing about this period of his life, and not even his second wife was told the whole story. What made de Man so interesting to such a group, an intellectual cadre who would surely have shunned him had they known of his wartime activities?

His purely personal qualities had a great deal to do with his success, but these alone would not have sufficed. He also filled a need, a cultural and intellectual role he was to play superbly, for he arrived at a timely moment, a shift in thinking that one might call the "construction of Europe." After the constricted life of the war years was past, American intellectuals were bent on finding a wider horizon, a "world elsewhere," searching for it partly out of hope, partly of ignorance, and mainly from an urgent need to know and experience life more deeply. The struggles of the Cold War were intensifying, and these were reflected by the internecine battles on the Left itself, especially between the Dwight Macdonald/*politics* crowd and the one surrounding *Partisan*

Review. Many wanted to strengthen their understanding of what was taking place overseas in ideas and art, and to engage with the great actors who embodied the changes they felt in the air.

For de Man, that ferment was an ideal environment. The paralyzing sense of amorphousness he had described to Frida Vandervelden in 1939, that fluidity of character that he had not yet escaped, now gave him a freedom from which he could profit. Today some celebrate—or at least accept—the right to reinvent oneself. In postwar America, however, concealing one's origins was precisely a practice one must conceal; it might have seemed like deception or imposture. De Man was a very good actor, always on, as his cousin and wife knew, and challenges and competition set him alive. All his many advantages of appearance, intellect, and role-playing were essential for his easy crossing of the cultural gap. Yet he also arrived on his cue, exactly when needed. If there was a "Europe" to be constructed, he could easily present himself as an expert.[7] To put it another way, de Man's long-term success in the United States was to be based on two things, intellectual capital, his ready knowledge of contemporary ideas, especially those from abroad, and cultural capital, in Pierre Bourdieu's sense: the perceptible aura surrounding him of the powerful class he came from, and the connections and insights his life had given him; all these worked toward making him seem from the beginning the right man, in the right place, at the right time.

Or at least he appeared to be. Alfred Kazin, de Man's contemporary, was an esteemed intellectual who wrote in *A Walker in the City* that he had found the two-mile transition from Brooklyn to Manhattan to be the longest journey he had ever made.[8] But Kazin, Jewish, poor, the son of hardworking but uneducated immigrant parents, carried with him the baggage of different traditions, one of which was the understanding that making oneself was an arduous and gradual process of integration and reintegration, punctuated by self-doubt and emerging mastery. De Man, by contrast, had seen himself from the age of twenty-two as one prepared to "raise the bad taste of the mass." In that spirit, he had named his publishing house Hermès, after the mercurial messenger of the gods. The sole print he created as a publisher was of Brueghel's painting *Landscape with the Fall of Icarus,* and according to his second wife, he made that legend his personal emblem: the son of the engineer Daedalus had been a falling star, but a brilliant one.

De Man found a place to live, but from this point on, his quarters were always provisional. Moving while skipping out on the rent became his best and probably his only budgeting technique. He located an apartment through an acquaintance at 110 East Sixty-first Street, just east of Park Avenue, then, as now, a posh section of town. The building was a classic brownstone, converted to walk-up apartments, where he stayed for a few months before moving to the low-rent Jane Street in Greenwich Village.[9] He would have two other addresses in Manhattan before he left the city, making a total of four moves in sixteen months.

This was only the first of what was to be a lifelong series of evictions or disappearances for nonpayment of rent. Even much later as a renowned professor holding tenure at both Yale and the University of Zurich, he and his colleague Geoffrey Hartman serially shared the teaching of a course at the University of Zurich and together rented a house outside the city. But de Man moved out without paying his share. It was typical of de Man's relationships that his colleague paid for the lease in full, and never mentioned it to de Man.[10] In the beginning, the defaults resulted from arriving without funds, but in the long term it became a question of never learning to manage what he had or caring what damage he left behind. De Man was amazingly skilled at handling interpersonal relations. Yet in an almost novelistic way, he would be tripped up by the two classic motivations for transgression: money and sex—or, more properly, attachments to women.

In the summer of 1948, however, women were not on his mind. Eating came first, and to that end he took the job at Doubleday. Though he made a good story later (only to Patricia) of his subterranean position, it was only partly true. After finding texts, wrapping packages (incompetently he said), and pushing a handcart through the streets, he was before long promoted to the sales floor.[11] Meanwhile, he looked up David Braybrooke. He'd already made use of the American in the summers of 1946 and 1947, and the younger man, admiring Paul, continued willingly to cooperate.[12] Braybrooke, by then a graduate student at Harvard, had already put considerable time and money into translating de Beucken's book on Van Gogh. Translation is slow work, and Braybrooke had expected to be paid, but he did not know it would be almost the only publication of Hermès to see the light of day. He had taken seriously Paul's charge that he function as his agent in the United States and was not yet estranged from him.

Braybrooke was to condemn de Man for "dastardly" behavior a few years later, but during that first summer in New York, he liked seeing him again. On one occasion, Braybrooke went into Manhattan to return a visit and found his friend up one or two flights of stairs, living in the back of a building facing south. "There was a window looking out to the back of lighted apartments," Braybrooke recalled, describing a scene that calls to mind the thriller *Rear Window*, Hitchcock's iconic film of repression and desire in the New York of that era. Paul was not hospitable on that occasion. During David's visit, de Man simply walked out and did not return. Alarmed, the American, who later made ethics and government central to his academic work, went to the police and was told that his friend had probably found a woman and to ignore the situation. "He turned up," the visitor recalled. "I don't remember what he said he'd done." Braybrooke did not know that this was typical behavior for Paul. His father had described his son's sudden departure from Antwerp just a few weeks earlier in the same terms. The young de Man came and went silently, at will, and without explanation.

THROUGHOUT THAT SUMMER, de Man pursued attempts to enter American publishing at a professional level. He had probably first heard of New York's little magazines, especially *Partisan Review* and *politics*, from Braybrooke in Belgium and would have grasped at once that their point of view paralleled those of the non-Marxist left he knew in France and Belgium. De Man had been in New York only a few weeks when he approached William Phillips, the powerful but somewhat distant editor of *Partisan Review*, which was then and for a long time the most important and widely read journal of leftist opinion in the United States. The founding editors—Phillips, Philip Rahv, Dwight Macdonald, and Fred Dupee—were all men with a strong history of political commitment. Some of them had once been members of the Communist party, but by the time they suspended publication of the journal in 1936—

they resumed publishing it in late 1937—all were communism's active opponents.[13] They were the more assertive due to the fact that they were the more informed of the Party's history of betrayal and duplicity. In publishing, they cast their net wide, focused on the arts as well as politics, and provided a rostrum for the best-informed, most talented writers of their era, a period that stretched for decades before the magazine lost its cachet as the climate of opinion changed in the 1960s and the Left became the Old Left, supplanted by the New.

De Man probably was hopeful when he succeeded in making an appointment with William Phillips in June, but it was not as good a sign as he may have thought. He did not yet know enough about the social nuances of the groups he would be dealing with when he presented himself in the socialist-spartan anteroom of *Partisan Review*. The magazine had its offices in Times Square, an odd place for an intellectual journal, but *PR* had recently found a Maecenas in Allan Dowling, a man of letters and a very wealthy real estate developer whose family holdings included Grand Central Terminal, and he had moved the journal uptown from the so-called Bible House on Astor Place to his own property at the corner of Forty-sixth Street and Broadway, which also housed the Victoria Theatre. The reception area contained only the switchboard; there were no chairs, books, or magazines: One had business with the editors, or one departed. The building was filled with shabby theatrical agencies, and the editors spent as little time there as possible.[14] Eve Stwertka, a protégée of Mary McCarthy, was the editorial assistant and kept the work flowing and the premises tidy, but her bosses did their reading at home and came to the office largely to pick up their mail and manuscripts, meet the occasional visitor, and file out together for lunch at the delicatessen downstairs or at Barbetta's, still there today, down the block.[15] Philip Rahv would have preferred either Greenwich Village or the East Side as their venue, but Eve loved her view across Broadway directly at the airy rings blown by the Smoker, a famous animated sign that advertised Camel cigarettes in the days when tobacco meant sophistication and not the threat of cancer. The walls were "landlord green," the floor dark linoleum. All the details Stwertka remembered suggest a film noir in which Humphrey Bogart, feet propped on his desk, keeps his hat on his head and his back to the window, glancing up only to discern the figures behind the frosted glass of the partition.

Phillips's reception of de Man matched the decor. Getting in the door of *PR* meant little, for although Phillips would receive unknown persons, a visitor without a sponsor had essentially no entrée at all. Faced with the good-looking blond young man, with his clear intelligence, self-deprecating smile, and worldly shrug, Phillips still remained unimpressed. De Man projected great intellectual passion during that era, and he spoke of writers and matters of which the editor probably knew little, but Phillips relied on associate editor William Barrett for his French connections. Giving voice to a new political point of view— for inevitably, French literary circles, like American ones, were implicitly political—would be dangerous if done in ignorance of the context in which the players moved. The big plate-glass windows of the old building might look out on a seemingly open world, but *Partisan Review* was very selective. The reason, Eve Stwertka said, was that "everyone knew each other. It was a very small circle, and if someone came from Europe, they would know Arendt and [Nicola] Chiaromonte or [Nicolo] Tucci or someone else. People who came from Europe . . . [and] needed a job . . . went to the New School, and somebody would just say 'Bring them over.' It was much more informal than it is now."

Perhaps it was just as well for de Man that he did not gain the entry he sought by this door. In fact, if he had known anything specific about the New School, he probably would have stayed away, for in many cases it was staffed by—indeed, had been created as a haven for—high-level professorial émigrés, such as Hannah Arendt and others with a European socialist background, who, unlike Phillips, would certainly have recognized his family name. Sooner or later, awkward questions would have been asked.

Phillips, moreover, like many of the other Americans in his circle, did not personally know Europe or speak any foreign language, and he would have had few points of reference with which to connect the newcomer. He proved to be one of the few people who were immune to de Man's charm. (In general, Phillips's friends found him more skeptical than welcoming by nature, and he was certainly very shrewd about people.) De Man, always optimistic and hard to discourage when he had set his mind on a goal, followed up his meeting with Phillips by phone calls, but these were not returned. Frustrated, he left Phillips a note at his office on June 22, 1948, submitting an article he had written on "an important aspect of french [sic] writing . . . which your review has not yet covered as it deserves to be." His imperfect command of vernacular English was evident as he explained:

> My contribution on this subject is in the same direction of /as/ a series of similar articles /I wrote/ on american [sic] literature, which will appear in the French review "Critique." It could eventually be followed by articles of french writers like Bataille, Blanchot, Michaux, etc., belonging to this movement and who all expressed me [sic] their willingness to contribute to Partisan Review. . . . I wrote the article in french, but included the first draught of my own english [sic] translation (of the first part). I suppose it sounds rather funny but might be of some use though, in case of a final editorial review.[16]

In fact, de Man had not written for *Critique* and would not publish there until five years later, but he would make the same claim later. He went on to tell Phillips that he meant to remain in the United States "permanently."

> The publishing business has become almost completely impossible in europe [sic] and my main commercial purpose here is to continue and develop the publication of illustrated books partly manufactured in Europe. In the meantime, I took a job at Doubleday bookshops in order, first of course to secure myself a living, and to get acquainted with the technique of american book distribution.

Undeterred by Phillips's silence, de Man added, "I shall go on calling Partisan Review in the hope of getting in touch with you."

Paul's flawed English was no recommendation to a reluctant editor. In his old age, Phillips remembered that "he didn't establish or pursue a relationship with Paul de Man because he wasn't particularly impressed with him, and [thus] didn't know what he could do for the magazine."[17] *Partisan Review* had already published an issue devoted entirely to France in 1946 (as *politics* would do in 1947).[18] Moreover, the authors whom de Man proposed were not from the same stable as those *PR* was fostering, led in this by William Barrett. Their special French issue had featured the best-known existentialists, such as Sartre, Camus, and others, in a sense the French mainstream, while Bataille, Blanchot, and their friends were barely known in the United States. De Man would have to wait until he found a better point of entry.

De Man did not give up, and his next attempt at entering the world of New York letters showed he had learned from his too direct approach to Phillips. Soon he tried what might be called a cushion shot, a different maneuver and one that would prove more successful. The almost equally interesting magazine *politics* remained a possible goal, and now de Man played his French connection more effectively. He wrote a significant letter to Bataille, previously cited but worth quoting, for it both shows Paul's perceptions of the French philosopher and throws light on de Man's future approach to some of his own problems. His tone was somewhere between respect and friendship; he addressed the master as "*Cher Monsieur et ami*" and offered the older man an encomium that cited the happy moment of their meeting. De Man's informal prose was usually simple and instrumental in tone, lacking personal reference. Now, however, he wrote to Bataille of the "great happiness" he'd felt in their encounter and of keeping "still fresh the impression of a way of being and thinking that you represent which will make my life here easier and perhaps more fruitful. . . . I can establish contacts with certain minds which I easily recognize through your image."[19]

To write of perceiving the right kind of people "through" Bataille's persona was more than flattery, for it implied that de Man had so internalized the Frenchman's point of view that he had appropriated it as a kind of lens. The impression the letter gave was that de Man was a disciple and felt their meeting was a kind of turning point, a moment of growth. Bataille was a leading member of the anticommunist Hegelian Left that had been spun off from the famous seminar given by Alexandre Kojève in Paris in the 1930s.[20] It was undoubtedly Bataille's ideas about politics, and not about sexuality, that de Man found useful, for there is no evidence that he shared the older man's special but not very private interests. Bataille had made himself the center of a group that included philosophers like Eric Weil and was identified with the Resistance.[21] A man of impressive presence, he had withdrawn from Paris to live in Vézelay and then Carpentras in the south of France. He kept an office for *Critique* in Paris. To be part of his world was important. In France, his sexual preferences did not conflict with his influence as a gifted novelist and thinker, and Jean Paulhan, the dean of French editors, chief of Gallimard, was for many years his friend.

Paulhan also had special tastes, and more than one mistress. Among these was his secretary, Dominique Aury, a pen name for Anne Desclos, who attempted to maintain her boss's flagging interest by writing the wildly successful and scandalous *The Story of O*, a sadomasochistic work. (Until she published that book at age forty-seven she had only edited her father's collection of seventeenth-century religious verse.) She remained the work's anonymous author for many years.[22] It gives the flavor of the contrasting cultures to recall William Phillips's story of his first visit to France in 1949, during which he called on Paulhan. He was taken aback to see that instead of leaving the office as he and Paulhan spoke, Paulhan's secretary not only did not leave the room but sat on her boss's desk and crossed her legs. No doubt he was looking at the seductive and versatile Mlle. Aury herself.

In his letter, de Man now offered to serve as Bataille's representative in New York and urged him to send whatever he was preparing for the United States' public. He insisted:

> I see more than ever the possibility and necessity of seeing you published here and I think of having ["*je pense avoir*"] the means (connections, etc.) to do this under the best conditions—financially and from the point of view of influence and making an impression.

To "think of having the means" did not commit the writer to actually producing those "means," but it gave a stronger impression than merely hoping to have them would have done. He closed by suggesting that he would like to write a study for *Critique* of Alfred Kinsey's *Sexual*

Behavior in the Human Male, recently published in the United States, which, he did not have to add, was enjoying an immense success fueled by its element of scandal. His approach would be "strictly sociological," he noted.[23] The indirect approach via his French connection worked, and Bataille responded to the call, although he appropriated the *Kinsey Report* for himself and published an article on it in *Critique*. He was persuaded of the younger man's good will and deservingness. Was he privy to de Man's unreliability as a man of business? If so, his philosophical stance would have permitted his young friend wide latitude for transgression.

Around this time de Man evidently found the opportunity to make himself useful and alert Bataille to a mistake Dwight Macdonald had made. Someone—perhaps de Man himself—noticed that the American editor had reprinted an essay Bataille had written about John Hersey's account of the atomic bomb attack on Hiroshima in August 1945, which entirely destroyed that city. This event was a subject of enormous international significance and had profoundly affected the Left. Hersey's monograph, describing the unprecedented destruction of the city in unemotional but unforgettable detail, took up an entire issue of *The New Yorker*. It was translated and reprinted worldwide and helped shape international fear of atomic warfare. In France, Bataille wrote a thoughtful and suave review of Hersey's piece for his own journal, not overtly faulting Hersey's empirical approach but replacing it with his own quasi-philosophical focus on suffering as he pointed to the "sovereign instant" afforded by extreme pain that permits one to go beyond it into enlightenment.[24]

When Bataille got wind of the fact that Macdonald had reprinted his essay without crediting him, Paul de Man benefited. Whether it was he who told Bataille is unknown, but as an avid reader of these journals and as one aware of his friend's interests, de Man may have noticed the omission of credit and offered to act on his behalf. When asked about this matter, Pat de Man said it would have been normal for Paul to "tip off" Bataille about Dwight Macdonald's use of his essay. "He knew this" practice to be useful, she said, and "the reason [was] that he could then tell those anecdotes to mean 'Hey, you know, I'm the one who tipped off so-and-so.' "[25] Being a source of good information put him in the loop. Bataille sent a polite letter of protest to Macdonald. He thanked him for reprinting his essay. "But is it indiscreet," he asked, "to remind you that you've failed to send me author's royalties? Could you send a check to M. Paul de Man [a name he first misspelled as Mann], 110 E. 61 St, New-York 21."[26]

De Man, if indeed he was active in the situation, handled this matter with aplomb, using the same process he had employed before in proposing projects to von Balluseck and De Becker in 1942: identifying issues that could profit his bosses and proposing to work toward their fulfillment, thereby gaining the aid of more powerful men who would open a door through which he could pass. In Belgium he had been stymied, but this time he was successful. His goal was simpler: to meet the *politics* crowd under Bataille's aegis, and with the sponsorship he had lacked in approaching Phillips at *Partisan Review*. He also had a great advantage: He had not yet created enemies.

Bataille's letter was key. In mid-September, Dwight Macdonald came back from Cape Cod, found the protest, and apologized in typically open style, blaming himself and saying, "I really have no excuse; it was very lazy and high-handed of me. I'm sending a check for $20 to M. de Man as you ask."[27] Macdonald met with Paul the next month and de Man was a hit with him. Macdonald wrote Bataille again, reporting on his contact with de Man, and in mid-November the French writer responded, "I'm happy that you've met Paul de Man, whom I like very much." It was a further endorsement, and Macdonald accepted it as such. By then de Man was already part of his inner circle.

Their first meeting undoubtedly took place in Macdonald's office in the used-book district of the city, for *politics* was published at 45 Astor Place, a busy crossroads in downtown Manhattan. Paul would have approached the building known as "Bible House" with high expectations. Receiving the $20 check gave him permission to call, and the two men would have encountered each other in a historic district, old and fusty but cherished in local history.[28] Literacy was the local specialty, and lower Fourth Avenue was lined with bookshops and stalls running from Twelfth Street almost to Cooper Union, an old, free university famous for containing the hall in which Lincoln had spoken before officially announcing his presidential candidacy. The old pile of

Bible House had been erected in 1853 and had seen a great deal of American publishing history pass through its doors: Whitman would have skirted it on his forays along Broadway, and Horace Greeley had edited the *New York Tribune* there. Bible House was contemporaneous with Melville, and its grimness could have sheltered the scrivening and melancholy Bartleby. *PR* too had once been a tenant. Michael Macdonald has described the antique, ill-lit, and incommodious space as a place with "wide halls and creaky floors," all in "one room—big—long, very tall ceilings, rather gloomy. . . . [It] had windows on an enormous air shaft, no courtyard." The builder had pinched pennies, but *politics* went further when Macdonald walled up the air shaft's windows to allow room for a small separate office.

The American journalist and editor whom de Man met when he entered his turf was friendly and commanding, argumentative and untidy. De Man, for his part, was agreeable, ironic, perceptive, and amusing, but younger and more pliable, not yet the austere, even paternal figure he later seemed at Harvard or the intense and passionate philosophical advocate of doomed freedom that he soon personified as a young instructor. Each man, however, would have recognized in the other an air of self-confidence based on intelligence, innate vitality, and a lifetime of connections shaped in affluence. Even in those days of poverty, de Man was well dressed. Macdonald was indifferent to appearances, but then less scruffy than later on, his son thought, and with or without the bow ties, "braces," and tweed jackets he occasionally wore, he carried the markings of class. With a journal to run, it was his business to have his finger in as many intellectual pies as possible, and informed men and women of the Left were what he hoped to find. If they came from abroad, so much the better. He and the Belgian were clearly a good fit. They agreed to keep in touch; in fact, why shouldn't Paul come to a party Macdonald was giving soon? It was the beginning of the season—he could be introduced around.

23

THE RADICAL GENTRY

THE NEW YORK THAT PAUL ENCOUNTERED WAS NOT THE PROVINCIAL and rigid city that Edith Wharton—who had died only a decade earlier—had known, but a great, chaotic, and yet comparatively peaceful world, where young children traveled alone on subways and buses and matrons phoned the grocer Gristede's in the morning for deliveries that arrived before noon. The long vistas of dull brown dwellings Wharton had hated were gone, and "slum clearance" had not yet begun. Only on the most expensive side streets of Manhattan were there a few struggling plane trees, still too small to meet overhead, and *gentrification* was a term not yet coined by a future generation. In central Manhattan, there were no sidewalk vendors, coffee stands, or street fairs. "Obstructing the public pathway" was an offense in mid-century New York, and only in the districts where recent immigrants had brought their culture was there true street life. The elevated subway still cast its shadows over Third Avenue and displayed to the passing cars the private lives of the occupants who lived alongside it.

The Village, where de Man lived when out of pocket, was less stuffy than uptown and a fashionable area for those Dwight Macdonald called "upperclassbohemians." It had been associated with the arts and the political Left since the days of Eugene O'Neill and Hart Crane in the twenties and earlier. Dwight Macdonald lived on East Tenth Street, opposite St. Marks-in-the-Bowery, Harold Rosenberg on a floor just below him, and William Phillips moved between East Ninth and West Eleventh Streets.[1] Before their generation, the Village had been the very proper neighborhood of figures such as Henry James, who set *Washington Square* where he had lived as a child. In the 1940s, Mark Twain's handsome redbrick house with its white marble steps still stood at the southwest corner of Eighth Street and Fifth Avenue, and the café terrace of the Brevoort Hotel was diagonally opposite, its tubs of spindly, unwatered privet languishing in the summer sun and a culture inhospitable to public dawdling. A few blocks away on Eleventh Street and University Place was the bar of the Hotel Albert, where Fred Dupee took Mary McCarthy one afternoon in 1937 to loosen her up before her first date with Edmund Wilson.[2]

Brevoort's café and Lafayette's were almost unique in a city where the concepts of "street furniture" or street life were either unknown or virtuously rejected. "New York is not a good liberty city" was a report cabdrivers gave to male passengers—meaning that for sailors, carousing in New York and the cost of finding wine, women, and song was too high. Privacy was important. Inside the same block commanded by the Brevoort and bounded by Eighth and Ninth Streets, there survived a large communal garden where residents' children and their dogs could roam in safety, but it was hidden, a remnant of a nineteenth-century experiment in urban design. The streets of the neighborhood between Fifth Avenue and University Place were lined with old buildings whose second-floor apartments had majestic high ceilings and marble fireplaces, and from their tall windows one still in the late 1940s heard the voices of old men calling out as they walked slowly behind their horse-drawn carts, hawking fresh vegetables or shouting for knives to grind.

This was Dwight Macdonald's world. His kind did not stay downtown to shop, except perhaps at Wanamaker's. For their clothes, they went uptown, for children to Best's and De Pinna's, taking the number 5 open-top bus with its wicker seats up Fifth Avenue. There they ate lunches or light dinners at Schrafft's—a restaurant chain favored by Mary McCarthy—whose chicken sandwiches Paul de Man came to like very much, as his widow recalled with amusement.[3] Schrafft's with its dark wood-paneled wainscoting and elderly waitresses was considered genteel. For children, exploring the windows of the coffee-houses on Macdougal Street, south of Washington Square, was adventure enough. These were still largely the realm of old Italian men, and the beautiful, dark old-world spaces with their polished brass urns adorned with shining eagles and flags were rarely visited by people from north of the square until the end of the 1950s, when an influx of students followed the Beats into the Village.

New York had long been a city of immigrants, but it was segregated and restricted against both African Americans and Jews. "Flight to the suburbs" had not yet been formulated as a phrase, and the riots that had rocked Harlem during World War II, of which James Baldwin, among others, wrote so powerfully, had not spread. In the Village, the Cedar Bar was already in business on University Place between Eighth and Ninth Streets, but local residents ignored this tumultuous hangout of unknown artists such as Jackson Pollock, Robert Motherwell, and the rest of a group that would become known as the New York School— men almost violently opposed to the gentility of the district where they gathered.[4]

Civic order was uppermost in the minds of those who controlled public behavior and opinion, but that civility was a two-edged sword, whose other side was repression. On the one hand, the city of seven million inhabitants was safe. Drug use was still limited, but alcohol addiction was widespread and very public. The same children who could ride the subways with impunity were cautioned not to walk along beneath the El on Third Avenue, where drunks lay with their bottles in pawnshop doorways, but to cross directly and at top speed. That addiction, however, crossed all class lines, and Macdonald's crowd and much of his generation drank heavily in comparison to people today. Some of their children, like his, walked to the private progressive school on East Eleventh Street, the Downtown Community School, whose lack of discipline, or "structure," was comical and whose "Stalinoid and fellow-traveling" parent-teacher meetings even Macdonald, the virtual dean of right-thinking leftists, found intolerable.[5] Others enrolled students at Elizabeth Irwin, City and Country, and the Little Red Schoolhouse. The "upperclassbohemians" who had created these schools had long rebelled against the repression of the narrow world in which they had grown up, and they wished their children to be more free. In neighborhoods less privileged, where people lived in closer quarters, "family discipline" could be enforced by as many blows as a parent wished: The matter was "private," no matter how loud the terror might sound, and neighbors would not intervene.

In this as in some other ways, this stratum of society bore a certain resemblance to the advanced circles in which Henri and Paul de Man had moved in the 1920s and 1930s, mixing sophistication and cultural capital with an indifference to bourgeois convention, especially a resistance to restrictive sexual mores. Their semiotic systems, which coded clothing and possessions, were often parallel. On both sides of the Atlantic, art was what artists and the critics who consecrated them said it was, and not what academies, the stuffier galleries, and most patrons wanted to buy. Personal adornments could be costly or inexpensive, but they must be handmade. One did not hang reproductions (except for posters, suitable for college dormitories) or wear synthetic fabrics, apart from nylon stockings, because these things were mass-produced and relatively cheap. The taste of the masses was suspect, per se, since it was assumed to be driven by commercial culture ("big business") and not to spring from folkways or individual art. "True" folk art was something else, with historic and aesthetic interest and a voice of its own; it was, like the songs of Leadbelly, to be hunted up and enshrined, more or less for the first time. The same headmistress of a girls' school who taught her charges how to write thank-you notes and when to wear white gloves also gave the occasional lesson in art appreciation, mentioning Brancusi but not Renoir. These were the modernists at home.

It was in many ways a world whose denizens were in flight from the hard boundaries and social roles drawn by an earlier age, and for people on the Left, it became a matter of self-definition to be at the forefront of those ready to shape the new cultural and economic developments. Not remaining what one had been born, one might think, was one of the keys to this new world, whether one was a European or an American. Some would have called the process a duty to be skeptical, to be a naysayer, to think for oneself. Macdonald was the son of an upper-middle-class New York lawyer and his socially ambitious wife, and in his young adulthood he had been as anti-Semitic and virtuously class-bound as any stereotypical Exeter and Yale man could have wished. At one point, as Michael Wreszin has shown, he wrote to the girlfriend of a classmate, whose contact with her Macdonald was determined to end: "And then there is the fact that you are a Jewess, and rather obviously one, to make me react unfavorably [to you]."[6] But with changing economic and personal conditions, he had evolved greatly in the 1930s in all senses of the word; he called the world he and his wealthy wife inhabited that of the "radical gentry."[7] Philip Rahv thought of his confrères as truants who would eventually be claimed by the practical reality they had left behind, and William Barrett echoed that idea in naming his memoir *The Truants*.[8] Yet they did not go home. They had altered themselves for good. Rahv, for example, who had emigrated to the United States in poverty, eventually married a rich woman and dwelled in her Sutton Place apartment. William Phillips was "very rich," according to Eve Stwertka. Mary McCarthy, a young girl from the provinces, of mixed Irish Catholic, Protestant, and Jewish descent, eventually became—in her fourth marriage—a diplomat's wife who presided with some formality for a decade over the American intellectual community in Paris.

Paul de Man understood these rules instinctively. His own social world, after all, was in some degree similar. Just as Macdonald had moved from the prejudices of the upper-middle class to membership, however temporary, in the Socialist Workers party, so Hendrik Deman had changed himself from scion of a hard-fisted, self-made capitalist father to the international socialist leader named Henri de Man, before eventually turning fascist. Macdonald had been a pacifist from the 1930s, just as Paul had been. The "third camp" position of Macdonald after the war was essentially an attitude critical of the engulfing power of industrialization, of corporate and state totalitarian dominance, and of the depersonalization that flowed from these forces. Paul de Man's Surrealism had also been rooted in a critique, if attenuated in his case, of capitalism.

A narrower band of people could have more influence than today: Print was almost everything. "Tastemakers" appeared in print, primarily in monthly journals, or the "little magazines." There was no television, no Internet, and the radio was considered trivial when it was not dangerous through the dire influence of men like Walter Winchell, considered a shill for J. Edgar Hoover. The "elitism" for which modernism has been faulted was taken for granted by the Left as well as the Right. Macdonald himself during the 1930s had been attracted to authoritarian forms of government, and this attraction was general.[9]

To be indifferent to politics was morally wrong and selfish. *Commitment* meant allegiance to social change, and it was linked, as Frida Vandervelden said, to liberation of oneself from "family ties and sentimental connections."[10] But while one might give money and time to leftist causes, one need not surrender all one's privileges. Rather, as Edmund Wilson, himself an inheritor of agrarian wealth, saw it, the target was American big business. With the crash of 1929, Wilson wrote, came exhilaration at the "sudden collapse of that stupid, gigantic fraud."[11] The right, if not the duty, of creative minds to astonish the bourgeoisie became a given, and the artist was their proxy, an avatar of the freedom to rebel. The result was a degree of what later came to be called "radical chic." Long before Tom Wolfe used that phrase in the 1970s, Macdonald, visiting his brother-in-law Selden Rodman on Martha's Vineyard, named the milieu that of the radical gentry.

Similar origins were shared by many of his circle, including Mary McCarthy, who was to become important in de Man's life. She and Macdonald had met at the podium as rebellious anti-Stalinists at the Second American Writers Congress in the spring of 1937. By then twenty-five, she was writing for *Partisan Review* and, as a Trotskyist, for *The New Republic*, at the time a seriously socialist review.[12] Yet although McCarthy felt poor almost always, she was, in fact, an heiress in a small way from Seattle, a 1933 Vassar graduate who ran with wealthier girls and had an income that, though smaller than theirs, amounted to about twelve hundred dollars a year even in her most impoverished days. Such were the prejudices of the times, however, that Mary's money, beauty, and brains did not protect her against the insults of her richer classmates, especially those who did not have a Jewish grandmother lurking somewhere in their background. Eve Stwertka remembered McCarthy's pain: "At Vassar, Elizabeth Bishop called her an "Irish Jew!"[13] Being partly Irish in those precincts and that era was another stain.

The imbrication of sexual, emotional, and professional life evident in these dramas would have seemed familiar to Paul de Man, himself a veteran of a ménage à trois and a family marked by sexual and marital adventures. These facts were readily accepted in their circle. In the world of New York intellectuals, de Man's "knowingness," his taste for irony, his low-key, almost self-deprecating humor, his little shrug, an attitude toward the world Braybrooke described as "one of patient acceptance—'What, me worry?'"—all the elements of a self-performance that demonstrated his capacity to veil much that was conscious but not discussed—these signatures of experience needed no direct language to reach their audience.[14] Men and women on the intellectual Left in the United States during that era were often as alienated from their roots—and as fruitfully—as de Man himself. If there was something in his aura, some indefinable tone that implied that he, too, was in flight from the past, that there was an epoch of his life on which the doors were closed, he would not have been alone in that group of changelings.

De Man knew all the socialist and "third camp" discourse he needed for this world. And in addition to his other qualities, Paul spoke French, was a socialist, and had contacts among the literati of Paris. Macdonald— whether he knew the names Paul dropped or not—would have been led to see him as a valuable addition to his circle of European contacts, one who might potentially strengthen his hand vis-à-vis *Partisan Review*.[15] Macdonald, with his flair for finding new ideas and forging friendships, made his new journal, *politics*, a center for European ideas and immigrant refugees, and according to Gregory Sumner's excellent study, that, in fact, was its main distinction. Hannah Arendt called *politics* a refuge for homeless radicals, a "focal point for many who would no longer fit into any party or group."[16] They were not alone in this. The rival editor and sometime friend Philip Rahv had said of his own *Partisan Review* that its "avowed purpose was to promote 'the Europeanization of American literature.'"

Europe was regarded as rightly the source of much of what was taught in the academy. But there was more to it. The impulse toward the construction by this particular group of their own Europe came from many sources, above all a deep desire to grow intellectually. Emerson had counseled his generation, "Do not ask the name of the country toward which you sail; only sail, and tomorrow you will know it by arriving there." Simultaneously, of course, he had told them that "too long have we listened to the siren songs of Europe." Listening to that sage, so often ambiguous, one could hear what one chose; our intellectual history has reflected the same ambivalence. There is a well-known tradition, going back to the nineteenth century and one of our most prominent early writers, Washington Irving, in which American authors not only travel abroad but for a time expatriate themselves. Sometimes, overwhelmed by what they are learning, they set themselves to study what Irving called "the great golden book" of Europe, telling his readers to imitate its virtues while avoiding its faults. This process of deliberate imitation was the temptation Emerson later warned against.[17] That pattern continued for generations among whom the best known today are such figures as Stein, Hemingway, and many others.

By the war's end in 1945, the far edge of the Atlantic was not only a country, a horizon toward which one might sail, but a state of being that would tomorrow tell not only its name but also one's own. Yet firsthand knowledge of Europe was rare among this group, as the Depression and the war had made it difficult to wander at will. Elizabeth Hardwick, who arrived in New York after the war, became a friend of Mary McCarthy, and ultimately married the poet Robert Lowell, explained, "People didn't go to Europe then. They had very little energy about going abroad. Mary never went until '47—'48 with Bowden.[18] I didn't go till '51 with Robert, my husband—his parents had gone in the thirties, but he had not—he didn't want to go to Baden-Baden or somewhere like that. The war cut you off . . . from '38 on."[19]

Others were more frankly ironic about their conscious provincial reluctance. Delmore Schwartz's biographer, James Atlas, doubts that he would ever have gone: "He had no money and hated traveling. 'How could I go to Europe when I can't even shave at home?' he used to say."[20] William Barrett, the point man on *Partisan Review*, a brilliant linguist whose translations introduced existential thought to a certain public, had to begin his important work of translation before he had even visited France, the land where French was actually spoken.[21] In the same way, Mary McCarthy translated Simone Weil's allegorical essay "The Iliad, or the Poem of Force" before she had left American shores.[22]

This hunger for wider experience made it more natural for Nicola Chiaromonte to have a major influence on this group. Slender, dark, and calm, with a tonsure-like bald spot and an almost priestly reflectiveness, Chiaromonte had trained as a philosopher but volunteered and fought bravely in the Spanish Civil War, becoming something of a legendary figure, whom André Malraux ennobled in his novel *Man's Hope*.[23] A warm and deep presence, the Italian had led a long hegira and was befriended by Albert Camus before departing via Casablanca for New York. Their friendship undoubtedly made him even more interesting to the group he met on the other side of the Atlantic.[24] His influence was particularly felt by Mary McCarthy, with whom his relations were deep, although not sexual. It was through his mediation and that of Hannah Arendt that she had found the ideas she summarized as "Europe": a "moral core" that had been lacking in her American friends and mentors, in Edmund Wilson as well as the *Partisan Review* people.[25] In 1945, after a tumultuous marriage to Wilson, who had encouraged her writing but who had also been abusive, she divorced him. Now she perceived that he and his kind were fundamentally formalists who, she thought, refused to consider a writer's ideas to be significant in judging their ultimate worth.

By contrast, she reflected later, "My friendship with Chiaromonte . . . I think was probably the crucial event in my life. Getting to know Hannah Arendt and Nicola Chiaromonte, and becoming very close to them—probably that was Europe!"[26] The term *ethics* had long been out of favor among Anglo-Saxon philosophers, but it was essentially an ethical point of view that men of Chiaromonte's stripe were reintroducing into literary and social thought. In the summer of 1946, Mary McCarthy was preparing for a new job teaching at Bard College, and she spent it on Cape Cod at Truro, where she deepened her friendship with both her Italian mentor and Hannah Arendt as they walked and talked on the beach throughout the long months. "What I was listening to on the beach," she said, "was Europe."

The idea for the Europe America Groups was started by the Macdonalds, especially by Nancy, Mary McCarthy, and others to assist European intellectuals who were impoverished after the war. It reflected Chiaromonte's agenda both in name and aims, but though short-lived, it became de Man's seedbed.[27] Chiaromonte returned to France after a nine-year-exile in the spring of 1947, and with his departure, some of the spirit leaked out of the EAG. Internecine warfare broke out within the managing committee. "The boys" of *PR*, as Rahv, Phillips, and others were derisively named by Macdonald and McCarthy, were part of the EAG, but there was a political split between the *politics* crowd and those at *Partisan Review*, based on their opposing attitudes toward the Cold War, with Macdonald holding to a "third camp" position opposed to the technocratic organization of all modern industrial societies. In March of 1948, McCarthy had been elected chairman of the EAG at a meeting that took place in Macdonald's Tenth Street apartment and had raised the sum of $2,500. Then, in the early summer of 1948, just as Paul de Man arrived in New York, the *Partisan Review* crowd tried to stage a coup, aiming to take over the EAG's treasury. They were foiled by McCarthy, who had learned of the plot and rallied her troops. She later recalled with pleasure the "faces of [Sidney] Hook and company when they looked around Rahv's living room and realized they were not in the majority."[28] The event was vividly described by Sumner.

It was in this heated atmosphere that de Man met Macdonald in late September 1948. His timing could not have been better. Macdonald had hoped to found a transatlantic journal, with Albert Camus as coeditor, but Camus had not taken up his duties. Macdonald was angry but could do nothing about it.[29] The young Belgian was certainly no substitute for the author of *The Stranger*, but there were few men around who came from the correct European background, spoke perfect French, commanded fluent, if accented, English and German, and had the personal attraction, ambition, intellectual subtlety, and experience that de Man displayed.

They decided to reorganize, and on October 21, Macdonald, still hoping to persuade Camus to be active in their endeavor, wrote the Nobel Prize—winning novelist:

Last night we held the first meeting of EAG since last spring: about 20 members came, including Sidney Hook, Elizabeth Hardwick, Barrett and Phillips of "Partisan Review," Paul De [*sic*] Man, Nicholas Nabokov, Mary [McCarthy] and myself. It was mostly devoted to discussing the Stalinist issue.[30]

And there Paul de Man was: some four weeks after meeting Dwight Macdonald, enshrined on the committee of the Europe America Groups, his name among the few Macdonald chose to mention to the Nobel Prize winner. Macdonald did know something about Henri de Man, but Paul would certainly have denied any adherence to his politics.[31] By mentioning de Man, however, Macdonald was perhaps revealing how little he understood the implications that compromised surname may possibly have had to a French Resistant and intellectual. But in New York circles, to be included in that company of intellectual leaders announced his ascension if not to the throne of kings, at least to the elect.

De Man would have to watch his every step and remark from now on, but he deflected inquiries easily, and his friends never felt free to question him. Nor were his hosts, typical Americans in this regard, suspicious of his antecedents. He also had one very great advantage: It seemed that no one in New York, or at least no one he could not avoid, knew anything much about Belgium, especially Belgium during the war. The ignorance even among these cognoscenti and willing students of what was foreign was the result of many forces: great distances, generations of indifference, and economic depression. It was also a measure of America's ongoing intellectual isolation. Here was a man whose surname had been made famous and then notorious by his uncle throughout the international socialist political circles in Europe—and in the United States, as well—and whose own byline had appeared for years in a major newspaper that was published under Nazi censorship and widely distrusted. Yet no one in New York thought to doubt him.

With caution and circumspection, de Man set about making friends. Twenty or more years earlier, as a child playing for hours at *The Three Musketeers*, Paul had liked to take the part of the dangerous and fascinating English spy known as Milady. He had recognized the best role when he saw it, even when very young. In a sense, Milady had reappeared, and s/he was still "something special." Now in New York, de Man was again performing. This time, however, he could not go home when he got tired. The game would play him, and he was in it for life.

24

MAKING FRIENDS

WHEN PAUL ARRIVED AT A PARTY DWIGHT MACDONALD GAVE IN THE EARLY fall of 1948, an observer could have seen in his face a combination of curiosity, detachment, and absence of judgment, all underlain by an indefinable air of knowingness. He was a very attractive man. His body was athletically built but slender, his countenance marked by the kind of masculine, prominent nose recognizable from Flemish paintings, and he radiated both intellectual and sexual intensity. Macdonald's gatherings were legendary, and this was a moment of unique opportunity. The editor was a generous, if argumentative, host, and through his quarters passed some of the most interesting people of the era. East Tenth Street was an inexpensive part of town, but known to the avant-garde, and the Macdonalds had chosen their neighborhood carefully. It was as liminal and diverse as they and their friends were. The old mid-nineteenth-century town house with spacious rooms and marble fireplaces contained three floor-through apartments that housed virtually an intellectual community.[1] They lived not in but on the margin of a working-class district. Just across Second Avenue lay a Lithuanian and Polish world of tenements, from whose butcher-shop storefronts rabbits, still in their white fur coats, dangled in the wind, but on the west side of the avenue the buildings on Tenth Street were older and more genteel. Across the street from their red-brick and limestone town house was one of the oldest churches in the city, where Peter Stuyvesant lay buried. The progressive school the Macdonalds' children attended was just around the corner; nevertheless, it was private and relatively expensive. Astor Place and the office of *politics* were two blocks away to the west.

If de Man paused to breathe in the smoky air, redolent of alcohol, food, and the perfume of charming women, loud with bonhomie and instant argument, he would have realized at once that he had come to the real New York, the place he'd been looking for. It was a rambunctious crowd, self-assured and very much alive; not staid, not genteel, and not at all Belgian. These were not men and women who had known each other since early days, or whose parents had financed each other's business ventures down to the second and third generation. On the contrary, the wooden floors creaked with the weight of newcomers—to the party, to New York, even to the country, like Paul himself. Some had met in college, others at political demonstrations, some knew one another only by name from the printed page. They were drawn together by ideas, and the same level of energy that had produced their thought was intensifying the noise and excitement of the evening. He would have observed Macdonald's classic mixture of Trotskyist socialism and upper-crust self-assurance, and he would instantly have registered the familiar marriage of things that marked origins and habitus: the big Steinway placed under the skylight beside the high modernist glass and metal table and Macdonald's big white desk, the walls painted in Art Moderne black and white, little family antiques mixed with contemporary pieces. These were the intellectuals who were giving kitsch its bad name on both sides of the Atlantic. De Man, himself the publisher of two handsome books, his failures behind him but not forgotten, must have understood the potential represented by this group and how important the occasion would be for him.

By the end of the evening, his success was a fact: He had been appropriated as a friend by the woman who was generally understood to be a leader of that circle, Mary McCarthy, who met him there for the first time and was to provide him with entrée not only to her group but to academic life in America. Yet although none of de Man's new friends were as close or did as much for him during his first year or so in the United States as she did, both de Man and McCarthy preserved a deep silence, which resulted in the lifelong obscurity of their relationship. That she got him his first teaching job at Bard was known, and it became well known after his death, when in 1992 David Lehman published a letter she'd written forty years earlier in which she had repudiated de Man and all his works.[2] Why she had helped him in the first place, however, and what their relationship was are questions worth pursuing, for their friendship was, in fact, pivotal in his life, and it may have been significant for her, as well.

Fortunately for de Man, ready money counted for little among the other guests at Macdonald's party, but "intellectual capital"—intellectual, social, and personal gifts, contacts, and information—mattered a great deal. Readiness to engage, charm, and be charmed was all. His host, a "wildly gregarious" man, might on any given night have had from thirty to eighty of his friends flowing through the big living room and into the main bedroom of his floor-through apartment. Many of the guests were stars or stars-in-waiting: T. S. Eliot had reclined on the chaise longue more than once; George Plimpton might arrive at midnight with his own entourage, fresh and ready to start the night, while the young Norman Mailer enjoyed all of it, especially the openness, the not knowing "if the evening would end in an acrimonious debate between two intellectual figures, or whether you would hear or learn something you never knew before, or whether you would just get drunk, meet a good woman and have a good time."[3] One brought one's own bottle and climbed the stairs, hoping for something new—and at Macdonald's, that included new men and new women, new flirtations. Sex and politics both were in the air.

Visiting European intellectuals—men and women like Marc Chagall, Jean-Paul Sartre, and Simone de Beauvoir—might turn up at either a *Partisan Review* or *politics* gathering, and to the younger writers, the chance to be admitted was precious. Saul Bellow remembered that as a novice he would gladly ride the thirty-six hours on the bus from Chicago to visit New York friends, and he was "wild with happiness to be invited to those parties. There was always something special going on, and there were people I simply enjoyed being in the presence of, like Delmore Schwartz, William Barrett, or Philip Rahv or Dwight Macdonald. And Dwight Macdonald's own place . . . he welcomed everybody."[4]

The intellectual competition at these gatherings was intense, a kind of testosterone contest, if you will, for the intelligentsia. Alfred Kazin said in effect that you had to come to a meeting of the *PR* crowd with your fists up: ready to "attack"—especially those not present—and be attacked. Macdonald, a ferocious debater, had famously been brought into the renewed *Partisan Review* in the early 1930s by means of an argument launched by William Phillips, Philip Rahv, and Fred Dupee, which ended only at the end of the day, when he was "backed up against the wall, literally" and finally conceded that they were right, the Communists wrong, and he would have to throw in his lot with his friends.[5]

A woman might have a place there, but she was rarely independent of men. Mailer and Diana Trilling reacted differently to the sexually charged atmosphere. To the young, highly macho author of *The Naked and the Dead*, Macdonald's were "the only literary parties where you could count on something flirtatious, a rosy hue so to speak—stealing into the salon."[6] To the far more conservative Diana Trilling, although with her "dark eyes and flaring nostrils," she was considered beautiful as a young woman,[7] "those parties were absolutely horrible if you weren't on the make, sexually. . . . Unless a man in the intellectual community was bent on sexual conquest, he was never interested in women. He wanted to be with the men. They always wanted to huddle in a corner to talk."[8] That was then normative in American—and other—intellectual circles until much later in the century: as Doris Lessing put it in *The Golden Notebook*, the only role in that era for a smart woman in a group of well-bonded men was that of "gun moll, or girlfriend of the leader."

Mary McCarthy, however, was not Diana Trilling. With her black hair, fair skin, and green eyes, she was strikingly attractive and, to many, beautiful, renowned as a critic and formidable as a person, a free spirit, sexually liberated long before feminism took hold, and ready to make her way both by and with men. Her younger friend Margaret Shafer remembered Mary arriving at a party at Bard College, where she taught in 1946, dressed in silver lamé and surrounded by a coterie of young Harvard men, one of whom thrillingly tucked a note into the décolletage of her clinging gown.[9] She had used her exceptional courage, intellectual talents, and sexuality to overcome the traumas of her orphaned and abused early years, but these had left their scars.[10] A close friend of Dwight, McCarthy was known and feared for her devastating wit; he famously said of her that when other young women smiled at him, he was flattered; when Mary smiled, he checked to see that his fly was closed. She had already been the drama critic for *Partisan Review* and had published numerous powerful stories in *The New Yorker*, as well as her debut novel, *The Company She Keeps*, and other works that can still startle with their edgy frankness. Dominant in the group, she was, in effect, its queen and well able to defend her position; it is not surprising if other intellectual women who were also used to admiration, such as Simone de Beauvoir and Trilling herself, disliked her.

At this time, McCarthy was already married to her third husband (she was to have four). By her own account, she was highly experienced, and her marriage was more or less open. Her current spouse, Bowden Broadwater, was reported by her biographers and the couple's friends to be bisexual, but in those closeted days, it would have been socially unacceptable and professionally dangerous to admit as much.[11] Sometimes employed as an editor and writer and later more permanently as a teacher, he loved his wife and was supportive of her writing and in domestic matters. Mary, who had no children with him, brought in the lion's share of their income. About McCarthy's many and complicated attachments to men and her pursuit of the younger Broadwater, her friend Barbara "Andy" Dupee said, "She was afraid to be without a man," and Andy's husband, Fred Dupee, had said the same. Moreover, Mary's "passions were intense—and passing."[12] Sexual freedom had always been important to McCarthy and she had taken it as she found it, and eagerly. As an adult looking back at her amorous career, she recalled one winter when "once I got started, I saw all sorts of men. One often led to another. Most of them I slept with at least one time." Her biographer Carol Brightman wrote that on the day in the 1930s when Mary realized she had slept with three men in succession, it made her " 'slightly scared,' but she 'did not *feel* promiscuous.' "[13] But Andy also knew that Mary's need for love had to be understood in the context of a childhood when, first, she lost her parents, who had died together in the great flu epidemic of 1918, when she was six, and then was handed off with her brothers for three years to the care of distant relatives, who appropriated the children's inheritance while abusing them physically. "It's about loss," Andy said. But Mary was also a figure of exemplary courage who wanted to care for others—a chosen few to be sure. She was also a good and generous fighter for the causes and people she believed in.

Mary McCarthy would not have overlooked Paul de Man that night. He was decidedly different from the noisy and contentious crew of New Yorkers who had made their way by wit, intellectual talent, and verbal aggressiveness. His habits were the little smile, the charming shrug, the accessibility in his glance of detached, interested intelligence. While he did not resemble the idealistic and austere Nicola Chiaro- monte, no one could have embodied the glamour of the Old World better than Paul. He knew people and wasn't shy about dropping their names. Mary would have been impressed. He used his information consciously with Mary, for he later told his wife Patricia that McCar- thy was interested in his gossip and information about French intellec- tuals, and that she would be "turned on" by these "sophisticated Europeans."[14] As Mary's friend and one of her literary executors, Eve Stwertka, remarked, "She had a romance with Europeans. De Man would have fitted that niche perfectly."[15] Margo Viscusi, who was at first her secretary in Paris and became a friend and literary executor, said the same thing and added that she thought an affair between them was possible, given Mary's preference for people who were "adrift" and needed help, especially if they were blond and European.[16]

Still twenty-eight, de Man was younger than Mary McCarthy by about six years, but he was actually the same age as Mary's husband.[17] Margaret Shafer, who met Paul a year later at Bard, found him "*extremely* handsome," with a melancholy air that reminded her of Paul Henreid in *Casablanca*. Even a child, Mary's son, Reuel Wilson, noticed that he had "*very* good manners" and that he dressed well.[18] The intensity of his gaze, especially when he was excited by ideas, was a striking feature; photographs taken a year later caught the laserlike intensity of his body and gaze as he taught. With his northern European appearance, he was also obviously not Jewish. To someone who was ambivalent about Jews, as McCarthy was, that added to de Man's attraction.[19] In short, he was catnip to women, embodying a certain kind of highly attractive, well-brought-up European intellectual male. He might be working in Doubleday's as a stock boy, but he fitted his adventuresome new friend's ideas to a tee. In that gendered atmosphere, while the big guns were politicking together in a corner, an intelligent, good-looking, and sophisticated foreign male who to all extents and purposes was functionally single would have had his choice of women to flirt with. He admitted freely to a wife and children, but they were more than five thousand miles away in South America, and his new friends probably regarded him as an available man.

From that night forward, the friendship of de Man and McCarthy progressed. Within a month or less, she and Dwight placed de Man on the roster of the sponsoring committee of the EAG, where his name appeared along with Hannah Arendt's, Bruno Bettelheim's, and Albert Camus's. He also gained both a social life and, equally important in that group, a new political identity. Mary loved entertaining and invited Paul to her frequent parties and all the big holidays, usually reserved for close friends—Thanksgiving, Christmas, and Easter. Through these steady contacts, he came to know and was befriended by two distinguished figures: the art critic Harold Rosenberg, who occupied a privileged place of influence among those intellectual leaders, and the sculptor Alexander Calder, who, after a long residence in Paris, had returned full of honor to the area and was living in Connecticut. De Man visited him there—and gave all these people the expensive art books that Mary later, although without evidence, accused him of having stolen. It was a pity that he could not have shown them the art books he had published himself.

Elizabeth Hardwick remembered meeting de Man at these gatherings; more dimly, Eve Stwertka did also. She, younger than the others, had been McCarthy's student at Bard.[20] An émigrée born in Vienna, she alone in that circle did not really trust her mentor's new friend, a perception for which McCarthy later gave her credit.[21] Eve was suspicious. Shy, "not part of the drinking crowd," she was highly intelligent, levelheaded, and not naïve. Her traumatic teenage experience of being ripped from a comfortable world in Vienna to flee the Nazis and then coming as a stranger to live in New York's émigré community gave her a different and in some ways a deeper perspective on people, and she knew that something about Paul de Man was not quite right. "I was not much taken with him," she recalled. "He was very evasive with me. He was not a child, and I was a young teenager [when each had left Europe]. I feel he wanted to make sure that we did not get to talk with each other—I was very shy. . . . He did not want me to know who he had been or where he came from. Refugees at that time would discuss who you left behind and how did you get out. . . . That's something I would have noticed. I don't like people who are not straightforward."[22] Eve knew that her older friend had been fooled by other people who were poseurs or fakes, but it was not for her to press the matter.

De Man probably did not know at first that this was a difficult season for Macdonald, who was hoping against hope to maintain *politics* and the EAG before both sank under the waters of debt and political sea changes. Engaged with but always at sword's point with the *Partisan Review* boys, who drew with greater success on a similar body of readers, Macdonald had been getting discouraged, and *politics* was a money pit. As Gregory Sumner has shown, the little magazine, which never had a circulation much above three thousand, had been the couple's personal creation, financed largely by Nancy, and she was its actual publisher.[23] Macdonald still hoped to stem the rising tide of problems, and he began his new campaign in September, when he wrote to Albert Camus, who had lectured triumphantly in New York in 1946, when Nick Chiaromonte had introduced them. Heartened by what he thought was Camus's support, Macdonald tried to go forward again, and a month later he typed up a list for an important meeting, "EAG— First List to be asked." It contained some seventy names in all, and Paul de Man was on it, listed after Fred Dupee and David Dellinger and just before James T. Farrell and Clement Greenberg. The typescript is docketed by Macdonald's typewriter at the top: "voted on, Nov. 18, 1948."[24] No doubt about it, de Man was in. Certainly he hoped, as other activities would show, to be included among Macdonald's stable of writers and reviewers, and he was, in fact, by far the most qualified among them to comment on a certain strand of current European ideas. Unfortunately, this was the last gasp of the Europe-America Groups. Camus did not respond. When the little group sank, de Man's hopes for a long-term international connection for *politics* went under also, and Macdonald closed the journal down at the end of the year. Over the next two years, he returned to employment as a journalist, increasingly alienated from American anti-Communists.[25]

Paul was probably not aware of these developments when he slipped away from New York at the end of December 1948, briefly to visit David Braybrooke's home and be best man at his wedding. He had a stake in that union, for he had encouraged his friend to marry his fiancée, Alice, over her family's objections.[26] De Man hadn't met her, but he gave his opinion anyway. Meanwhile, his friendship with Mary McCarthy had grown close, as a trip he took with her and Bowden in a few months implies. Her life was changing, too, and perhaps partly under Broadwater's influence she had begun to distance herself from the *Partisan Review* crowd, which was based almost entirely in New York. Just before meeting de Man, she had begun to write *The Oasis*, a satire on that circle of socialist intellectuals in which she had moved for over a decade. This roman à clef was published in June 1949 and infuriated her friends. Simultaneously and probably with its proceeds, she purchased a little farmhouse near the coast just north of Newport, Rhode Island, evidently to serve as a base for her move into higher social circles. Interestingly, she took de Man along with her when they traveled up to Rhode Island for the actual closing on the purchase, which took place on June 15, 1949. This was a sign of real trust, for one does not decide on serious financial matters in the presence of random acquaintances. He reminded her of their trip a month later, when he took up her invitation to stay, saying he would be "delighted to spend two or three days with you up in Portsmouth, in the new house of whose acquisition I happened to be a very interested spectator."[27]

Several months before that trip, de Man, unwilling to let go all hopes for some connection with Macdonald and *politics*, had come up with a couple of new ideas, one for an ambitious publishing venture and another for an essay on Arthur Koestler. He visited the newlywed Braybrookes in Geneva, New York, up at Hobart College in the Finger Lakes district, in April 1949. From there he wrote Dwight of a new plan. Still seeing himself as a potential businessman, he now suggested a publishing venture modeled on French lines to Macdonald. The concept was simultaneously to publish a line of books and a literary maga-

zine, each feeding the other with personal contacts and cash.[28] Buoyed
by questionable self-confidence, he argued for—without naming—the
"many advantages, commercial and intellectual" of his plan. These
were "too obvious to require enumeration."[29] This was typical of de
Man's intellectual style, and in later years it would lead to criticism of
his habits regarding literary argument, as well. "Too obvious to require
enumeration" has the flavor of what physicists call a "hand-waving
experiment": One could prove great things if one but took the time. As
for the practicalities, he was offhand: "Production and distribution are
no problem, if you happen to know that business."[30] The making and
selling of books were, of course, precisely what de Man had failed to do
with Hermès. Evidently, in spite of having worked for nine months or
so at a commercial bookshop, he did not understand that in his new
country, publishers sold books through jobbers and did not twin them
with distribution of serials, especially not with intellectual journals
that lost money. "Little magazines" in Europe might be carried for their
prestige as loss leaders, but in the United States they had to find independent backers willing to sink their own money in such an endeavor;
publishers sought profits. De Man was being wishful, and it was the
luftmensch speaking. One notes that, as in the past, he proposed to
move forward under the sheltering mantle of a much better known and
established older man, offering ideas but drawing on the other's credit,
reputation, and connections.

Undoubtedly, some of the impulse to press forward came from his
Belgian and bourgeois family's tradition, which, in a classic double
bind, favored a cultured existence but also demanded material success.
Having money was essential, but to keep a certain distance from gross
matters, to establish a zone buffered by aesthetic values, was part of the
game. As Paul de Man's oldest son said many years later, both parents
had taught him that "you were supposed to . . . be a teacher, or artist,
[and] don't ever soil your hands making money, yet the chronic refrain
was, 'Where's more money?' . . . My last conversation with my father
had to do with 'If I had to do it all over again, I would have done it as a
wealthy man.' "[31]

To persuade Macdonald, de Man offered to "abandon all other professional alternatives and turn it into the 24 hour a day, low-payed [sic]

job in which I am most at ease, and I think, rather usefully experienced."
He went on: "I can think of some people who have money and might be
interested in such a project." Just to get started, thirty thousand dollars
would do, providing they were "extremely cautious and modest." The
implication that he could raise or help to raise $30,000 among his friends
was pure fantasy, but it may not have been taken as such by Macdonald,
who apparently asked his younger friend to show him something more
concrete. Three weeks later, de Man wrote, "I am working on a rather
long and detailed report on the possibility of operating an economically
sound but intellectually decent publishing firm in this country," and he
would show it to Dwight before the editor left for Cape Cod. These
letters underscore his other limitation, an uncertain grasp of English
grammar and usage. De Man's written style is clear but awkward. His
discourse was more than adequate for normal purposes, but a higher
level was requisite in publishing. Dwight Macdonald had a superb ear
for colloquial diction and would have recognized that the young émigré
was not ready to edit English texts. As for the money, he probably also
realized that if de Man really had even indirect access to the sums needed
to start a new publishing venture, he would not have been working in
an underground storeroom in Grand Central Terminal.

No more came of this proposal than from the essay he proffered, a
revised article on "Koestler's book." The Hungarian intellectual was no
favorite in Macdonald's crowd. De Man reported that he had retained a
"somewhat tedious abstract argument against Koestler's system in order
to have some basis on which to found the second, more concrete part."[32]
The essay wasn't accepted, and the editor sent back the draft in December 1949, when he was closing up shop. The bottom line was that whatever projects de Man could propose now were likely to be long shots,
for he did not bring enough to the table. He was too much an outsider
to be a publisher or editor on American terms, and he had not brought
with him, as such other émigré publishers as Helen and Kurt Wolff or
Jacques Schiffrin had done, a European reputation and stable of writers.[33] No doubt that is why he sometimes substituted pure bluff. Even a
friendly man like Dwight Macdonald could not help him. By then,
however, it didn't matter. Mary McCarthy had come to Paul's rescue.

25.

RECOMMENDED
BY MARY

ON JUNE 9, 1949, MARY MCCARTHY WROTE TO ARTINE ARTINIAN AT Bard (a small college in Annandale-on-Hudson, New York) about Paul de Man. She had taught there in 1946–1947, leaving behind a vocal group of admirers, and had influence with the professor of French, who was Bard's sole instructor in that language. Mary was getting ready to leave New York, and it was time to take the question of Paul's future in hand. Having heard that her former colleague was leaving for Paris on a Fulbright fellowship and that his job would be open, she introduced de Man, a "young friend," who was just the person to fill the post Artinian was temporarily vacating. She wanted to "recommend him . . . to recommend him in fact, very highly. He is a Belgian intellectual, very much au courant in literature and also in politics, sensitive, intelligent, cultivated, modest straightforward."[1]

Not only was Paul de Man qualified in French and German, with very good English as well, she wrote, but he was also something of a paragon of virtue, for he had "a genuine superiority of mind and spirit that should mean a great deal in the Bard teaching system." She and Bowden had "seen a good deal of him" since meeting him through Dwight Macdonald. She enclosed his "prospectus which he got up at my request."

There is little in McCarthy's published biographies that explores this friendship or explains her later about-face, probably because with a couple of exceptions she told no one about it. She was not normally secretive about herself, but in this case, she was silent from the beginning. Yet she played a pivotal role in de Man's life and was directly responsible for his breaching the doors of the academy, which would have been closed to him without her sponsorship. Recent research shows that there is good reason to believe that the relationship she had with Paul was much closer than she later wished to admit. Their connection benefited him, but it left her angry, resentful, and without closure, so that even at the end of her life, she was exploring from her hospital bed the bad news that had recently turned up regarding her onetime friend's buried past.

At the time Mary first wrote Artinian, she had been misled by Paul about numerous facts, among others that he'd already been offered a job at the remote Hobart College, where Braybrooke was then an instructor in history and literature.[2] His prospectus, which she submitted along with her letter, evidently contained other dubious assertions. If, as is no doubt the case, it was the same as the CV he gave Bard in person a few months later, the man who had left ULB after just over two years, having tried but given up on three different majors, never to return because barred by his work as a collaborator, now claimed to hold the "equivalent of your Master's degree," to have been "an editor of Editions de Minuit, in Paris, a firm born out of the literary resistance movement," and to be the grandson, not of Adolph Deman, the butcher's son who had risen to become head of the provisioning department for the Red Star Line, but of a "founder of the University of Ghent."[3] Paul's only academic forebear was Jan Van Beers, a poet and professor, late of the teachers' training college in the provincial town of Lierre, who was his maternal great-grandfather, and who had not founded the University of Ghent.[4]

McCarthy could not know these facts, of course, but by May 1949, the number of de Man's failed projects must have been discouraging to his friends and probably even to himself, optimist though he was. After a year in the United States, he was still working as a salesman in a basement bookstore in Grand Central Terminal. He had been lonely and uncomfortable and was probably ready to try anything that would move him forward. No doubt he enjoyed Mary's friendship and also cultivated her friends, but these encounters were occasional; he did not live with or among them on a daily basis, as he had done with his circle in Belgium.

Nor did he like New York: It was noisy, dirty, and crowded. He could be out of Brussels or Antwerp and deep into the country in a few minutes by train or in his roadster, but this city felt uncivilized, and the Village, where he had fetched up after moving again and again, was, he said, "infernal." Clerks like himself in that period punched time clocks, an indignity to someone who had run his own company, or, if they were in more cultivated businesses, signed in on arrival at work; their activities were monitored all day. He was undoubtedly ill-paid, and one may be sure that he spent what he had on books, entertainment, and especially on clothing, for he always dressed very well. Did he even know how to cook? There was no take-out food then, and except when Paul dined with Mary and one or two others, he probably took his meals at coffee shops. He was living on Jane Street, then far west of the better parts of the Village, and at one point had even stayed at the Hotel Marlton, an establishment frequented by writers and others, which has been somewhat glamorized in memory but by then was a broken-down sort of place on Eighth Street that his second wife later described as a "fleabag."[5]

Paul de Man had only just begun to reflect on what had gone wrong in his life at home; it would be some years before the work of self-scrutiny began to inflect his actions and behavior. In 1949, he was still just on the brink of thirty, and on this side of the Atlantic, he was gradually discovering that for all his advantages, he could not readily walk into a job in which his talents would be well used. Being taken up by Mary was a great stroke of good luck. Did he recognize in her both a temptation and a danger? She was striking, sexually vibrant, intellectual, generous, and witty—in all ways a catch and Anne's superior. But she was also commanding, even domineering, and was used, even in that antifeminist era, to having her own way. Did he wonder if he might be drawn in further and find himself again a useful man being managed by a woman rather too clear-sighted about how she would move ahead? Yet what were the alternatives? There were worse things than being a planet in Mary McCarthy's orbit, at least for a time.

The concentric circles radiating from Columbia University and New York City were still tight in those days. Artinian had once been a student of Fred Dupee, of the Columbia English Department, and later the onetime student had brought Dupee to Bard as a visiting professor. Then Dupee had placed Mary there. As it happened, Artinian had an interest that was not intellectual and much more than a sideline: He had become a serious collector and trader of prints. A Bulgarian immigrant who had arrived in the United States at the age of thirteen, he was a self-made man who had entered the academic world strictly by his own efforts and the help of scholarships. He was alert to issues regarding money and gave no lip service to the conventional academic scorn for material profit. Instead, during the 1950s he made a fortune by buying and selling French drawings and prints of writers. He picked these up on vacations, study periods, and sabbaticals; this was a genre he appears to have invented for himself. Eventually, he was able to sell his collection at a handsome profit and retire early to Palm Beach, where he continued his activity into his nineties. He was a bluff, hearty man, able easily to dismiss the comments he heard from his students, who sometimes complained or joked that he was inattentive to them when he escorted them abroad, favoring the Paris booksellers.[6]

That focus irritated some of his colleagues, who thought their profession should be a full-time pursuit and that the hours not actually spent teaching should be devoted to deepening one's knowledge by study. In return for the time and ability to call their minds their own, academics were tacitly understood to accept their genteel poverty, avoid all contacts with trade, and rise above their near indigence by maintaining high-minded principles. (Some also held it against him that he subscribed to the middlebrow *Saturday Review of Literature*.) The professor of French did not follow their path. Characteristically, Artinian kept all his papers and notes concerning McCarthy and de Man, even the scraps and lists they exchanged. He retained, therefore, not only the well-known letter that Mary later sent him denouncing her former friend but also her first and very different missive recommending him.

Artinian responded positively but not definitively to Mary's June 1949 letter, and the matter remained open until the end of the summer. He may have been negotiating with the college and the Fulbright Committee about terms of service: In the long run, he arranged to leave six weeks later than planned, continued teaching until mid-October, and thereby retained 20 percent of his salary. Nevertheless, with her letter, Mary had set her young friend's life on a new course, and from that date their relationship took on a greater intimacy. Indeed, de Man was on her mind so much that she mentioned him in almost every letter she sent to her close friend Elizabeth Hardwick over the summer, drawing the three ever closer and creating a little vortex of secrets within secrets that would bind them together. In doing this, she broke Elizabeth's confidence when she told Paul that her friend had secretly married the poet Robert Lowell, who was not yet ready to tell his mother, justifying herself by saying of Paul, "he has so little, as Bowden says, that he needs a secret to enrich him socially."[7] This was a witty remark, but typical of Broadwater's ambivalence toward de Man.

Summers in New York are hot and steamy, as its denizens know all too well, especially brutal in the era before air conditioning. In July 1949, a classic heat wave set in, and by this point, de Man had worked at Doubleday for a year, normally long enough to merit a two-week vacation. On July 11, he proposed that he visit Mary for two or three days, evidently acting on a prior suggestion, and that became an invitation to spend the whole of his vacation with the couple in their new house just north of Newport.[8] The journey by train would have been beautiful, worth the hours it took for the train to wind its way up the coast of Long Island Sound as it crosses the high bridges over the wide Housatonic and Connecticut Rivers, skirts their estuaries, and runs along vivid green salt marshes edged by blue water, where white egrets pose in the grasses and ducks bob on the waves. Summer people from Boston and New York had made their homes along that coast since the nineteenth century, and de Man arrived during the short, sensuous weeks of New England's summer, which Emerson described as the refulgent, luxurious season of gourds and vines expanding in the sun. On these wide, flat horizons softened by ocean light, the Luminist painters had seen eternity itself, the soul at peace. Here one let go and took the days as they came, like the quiet waters lapping ceaselessly toward the white sand.

In moving up to Portsmouth, Rhode Island, with Broadwater's encouragement, Mary was trying out her hand at entering society, as defined by Newport, Carol Brightman has suggested. On June 15, less than a week after writing to Artinian and settling de Man's problem of vocation, she invited Paul along for the journey when she and Bowden traveled to Portsmouth for the closing on the house they had bought. For Paul, taking days off in the middle of the work week implied a certain indifference to the rules, but no doubt he felt the game was worth the candle.

The farmhouse, set on fifteen acres of land bordering St. Mary's Pond, needed a lot of repairs, but it was the era of do-it-yourself renovation, and Mary worked hard. After more than a month of labor, the house was ready. Everything was polished, the walls in the kitchen were painted a glossy blue and bright red and those in the parlor a pale yellow and white, the windowpanes were newly glazed, and the place was furnished with antiques picked up at local sales, all shimmering in the extraordinary light of the coast. It was meant to please the senses, and Mary was very happy there for a time.[9]

Although the cottage had only two bedrooms and one bath, she invited many friends, who stayed for short visits. De Man, who had not left New York and his series of lodgings for more than a few days, visited for just under three weeks, for he had obtained an unusually long vacation, from July 23 through August 12. He good-naturedly helped with the washing up, scythed the fields, stripped off old wallpaper, and pitched in wherever he was needed. He also read the couple's mail, Bowden let it be known, when once they had gone into town and left him behind.[10] That was a mere detail they ignored at the time. Even Broadwater seems to have found him attractive. He remembered de Man's eyes some fifty years later, saying, "He wowed the students [and they felt a kind of] fascination." To Broadwater, de Man's accented voice was "uninteresting," but he had "very pale coloring—like an articulated ghost. Very blue eyes. Attractive in a sort of Dutchy way. [He] must have been rather sexy. The concept of sex more than sex itself. Sturdy. Sturdy."[11] Broadwater repeated "Sturdy," as if to emphasize the physicality of his subject.

Paul showed how much he responded to the magic of the place and was moved by it. In a long, unpublished letter he sent Mary after the visit, he wrote:

I will remember your house as one of those delicate landscapes of happiness which always stay with you. It takes a number of rare virtues to build such a landscape, a combination of light, water and land with a certain pattern of activity, above all the human quality of the hosts who made it all. From now on, my vision of happiness will inevitably include images of the quiet horizon of your pond, of Martinis [sic] on your porch, of wallpaper scrubbing in your rooms, and, most of all, of your presence in that decor.[12]

To the contemporary eye, that pond set in scrub is not one of the prettier spots found along the coast, but perhaps de Man was moved by his feelings.

If Paul and Mary had an affair, it would certainly have partly occurred during this period in that "delicate landscape of happiness" whose "rare virtues" included not just the "light, water and land" but the "human quality" of his friend who "made it all." His flattery was effective, and to say that henceforth "my vision of happiness" would include not only the "quiet horizon" of her pond but also helping her scrub off old wallpaper and drink martinis on her porch undoubtedly touched an echoing chord in Mary. He probably meant it at the time. He had undergone fifteen hard months alone, and the place and their natural impulses all invited greater intimacy.

His second wife, Patricia, reported that she "always thought there may have been something. Because she wrote letters to journals about Paul, about burning Paul's books before the revelations [of 1988]. He spoke of her very lightly."[13] She also knew from Paul, although she never personally met McCarthy's husband, that "Broadwater didn't particularly care whether she was up to anything or not."[14] This was a general assumption, and Eve Stwertka interpreted Mary's act of hanging a douche bag on the back of the bathroom door in the Portsmouth house as being her way of advertising to her friends, who supposed that the couple found satisfaction with others, that they were wrong and that she and her much-talked-about husband did indeed have sex.[15] But having simultaneous partners had never inhibited Mary, as her own anecdote of enjoying three men in twenty-four hours demonstrates.

Cramped quarters were not important; there were, after all, fifteen private acres all around them, and although the house was small, both were used to limited space. Frances Kiernan records Mary's almost total lack of sexual inhibition in a story told by a younger friend who unexpectedly had to spend a night with Mary and her first husband in their one-room apartment on the Upper East Side. The beds were placed head to head in an angle of the room, and the visitor was awakened in the middle of the night by hearing the couple, lying only feet away, having sex. The young woman came to a mutual acquaintance "in a state of shock. . . . She was terribly upset."[16]

Reuel, Mary's son by Edmund Wilson, was ten that summer and staying with Mary and Bowden at the time. He was a few years older than Paul's firstborn son, Rik, who was living with his mother in Argentina. Fifty-odd years later, Reuel remembered several of de Man's visits, not just the one to Portsmouth, where he stayed in the guest room. Interestingly, although he retained none of their conversations, he recalled those markers of class that de Man displayed so distinctly in dress and behavior. The guest, whom he knew from the preceding winter as well, was "very quiet, shy, rather well dressed, wearing one of those sleeveless blue . . . sweater[s] and a tie." Even he, as a child, was impressed by the visitor's "*very* nice manners" and his soft-spokenness. He also recalled both that Paul brought "magnificent art books"— welcome gifts that his parents discussed out of their guest's hearing: "They loved these presents and they would wonder how he could afford them."[17] De Man himself recalled later that Reuel would stay up late, unwilling to let go of his mother while she had an interesting visitor, as he and Mary continued talking late into the night, long after Bowden had gone upstairs. Reuel would hang on until finally Bowden padded downstairs, complaining that if no one else would do it, " 'maybe I should put the kid to bed.' " That vignette, told by de Man to his second wife, was one of the several remarks that eventually made her suppose that the two had had an affair.[18]

Of all his remarks about his visit to Portsmouth, however, the most telling was his comment to Mary in his letter of August 13, 1949, that what was most painful on returning to New York and what he missed most was "the casual conversation of friendship, the restful pleasure of just being oneself in the presence of others. To which was added, in my particular case, the delight of rediscovering this experience; the acquired habit of unconfortable [sic] solitude had made me forget that such a thing was possible."

The English psychoanalyst W. D. Winnicott expressed a profound insight in an often-quoted aphorism: that what he called the "good enough mother" was one "in whose presence her child can be alone." De Man was recognizing in this letter the distinction between the "unconfortable solitude" of loneliness and that deep restfulness of "being oneself in the presence of others," an intimacy that is closer for its silence.

Paul did not return directly to the city at the end of his visit, but took a long detour to Cape Cod to visit the Macdonalds, where they reigned in the "backwoods" section of Wellfleet. They were renting an enormous Victorian summer place from friends. There was no electricity, and oil lamps served for lighting. In the evenings, no doubt a romantic gloom pervaded the atmosphere.[19] In spite of his own youthful indiscretions, de Man was now strictly bourgeois about maintaining appearances, and he found that the Macdonalds lived in a state of very disagreeable freedom. When he arrived, Paul, always very modest about showing his body, discovered that a naked cocktail party was being held at the pond below the house, and he had to join in.[20] Throughout the visit there was a decided "absence of pants," as he described it in his letter to Mary, and he objected to the nude parties there, which were the order of the day, and night as well. "The sight of that crowd practicing nudism on the beach is a pretty horrible vision," Paul wrote. In Macdonald's presence, however, one followed the leader. The guests could not have been a pretty sight, given that they were middle-aged in an era when exercising was not popular. Saul Bellow later satirized his host in *Humboldt's Gift*, where he described his character Orlando Huggins, summering in Wellfleet, as sitting buff naked astride a log in one of the ponds, arguing at full strength with a guest, while his penis jumped "back and forth like the slide of a trombone" at every dialogical emphasis of its master. The worst of it was, Paul reported, that this seemed to be Dwight's real and most comfortable lifestyle. The crowd was "bohemian" and "vulgar" in their manners, and while he exempted Macdonald himself, he could not forgive this upper-middle-class man for being "desperately well at ease" among such people. "He actually takes them seriously! They are his real crowd!" He was also disappointed by Dwight in the vagueness of his plans for *politics* and "his consistently inconsistent personality. . . . a pure waste of a wonderfully adventurous curiosity." Macdonald was at loose ends, depressed, and drinking more heavily, but he managed to produce "a baseball game, a night picnic on the beach, with strange looking and tasting hamburgers and every clan jealously watching its own bottle, the preparation for a collective discussion of Whitehead's Science in the modern World . . . etc." "Pseudo-libertarian nitwits," "obscene," "every clan jealously watching its own bottle"—the outpouring of scorn in de Man's language reflects an element of snobbery, but it also reflects the newcomer's social bewilderment. The American delight in mixing the high and the low, Whitehead's philosophy with beach picnics—even boozy ones—it was all Whitman's "barbaric yawp," it was Thoreau on the beach (and Thoreau had walked and lived on those very dunes), and everyone there but the immigrant knew and took pleasure in it. What was worse, Macdonald did not despise these "bohemians," but shared their proclivity for mixing the high and the low, for following their woodsy pursuits with philosophical musings. Paul de Man would never get used to "peanut-butter and jelly sandwiches blended with sand from the beach," and he recommended Wellfleet to Bowden if he wanted material for "his Book of bohemian Etiquette."

After that weekend, "New York seemed quiet and peaceful." He'd had a stroke of luck. The father of a friend from Paris, Oscar Nitzschke, was leaving his apartment at 255 East Seventy-second Street. It was cool, big enough for his "reunion with my wife and children," and "astonishingly cheap." De Man was no "proletarian" and was glad to escape from the Village.[21] Meanwhile, however, there was no word from Artinian. Mary was counting on Bard. In late September, trying to distract Elizabeth Hardwick from the troubles of her new marriage, McCarthy wrote her friend that Paul de Man would likely be in her neighborhood.[22] "Another possible diversion for you," she wrote, "is that Paul De Man may have a job teaching French at Bard; perhaps he already has it and this is no news to you; or again, the whole thing may be a chimera."[23] In fact, he did not quite have it, but it was in the works, as McCarthy knew. De Man had waited through the summer but had heard nothing. On August 29, he sent Artinian both a special delivery letter and a "cable," repeating the message that "I would still welcome an opportunity to teach at Bard."[24]

His timing was right. A week later, he was having an interview at the college with the president, telling him a thoroughly falsified narrative of his life. Edward C. Fuller was impressed and took careful notes.[25] The strategy behind the life story de Man provided was analogous to the exculpatory tale he had told Vinçotte in Antwerp in 1946: keeping to the broad outlines of his actual life, he modified or directly lied about facts at every level to produce the narrative his audience wanted to hear. Elements of this tale were the basis of what others would hear in future years, to the extent he told them anything about himself. As time passed, he was able to say less and less, especially as he learned what claims not to make. At the moment, his two years at ULB, in which he had unsuccessfully studied chemistry and engineering, became four years' work on literature and philosophy, for which he claimed a "License" in 1941 that was "(M.A. equivalent)." It would have been unwise to name any of the three collaborating companies he had worked for from 1941 to 1943, for the leaders of two of them had been sentenced to death, exiled, or imprisoned. A letter of inquiry from Bard might have had fatal results. Instead, Fuller's notes record "1939–41 wrote criticism but had to cease this activity." As for Hermès, the Belgian claimed to have founded it in 1944 (thus accounting for his two years in hiding)[26] and told Fuller that he was "connected with Editions de Minuit as editor for American literature. Still has both publishing connections." This would have been news indeed to the French publisher, which was founded as a Resistance and clandestine press. Its publisher, Jérôme Lindon, who was already at work there, attested to an utter ignorance of Paul de Man at the time.[27] No doubt de Man was trading on Georges Lambrichs's position as an editor there. On the other hand, he did affirm to Fuller, as to his friends in New York, his marriage and three children. The family was now "in Europe but would like to come here within the next three months." For that reason, he wanted to rent Artinian's large house. In fact, his wife and children were in Buenos Aires, but "Europe" had a better ring than Argentina, which had a somewhat louche connotation in an era when Nazi sympathizers were finding easy refuge throughout South America.

De Man was properly modest about his lack of teaching experience and was happy to follow Artinian's outlines for two courses in French. Fuller was pleased to note that he had "an approach that seems to me both sound and interesting." The prospective hire told the president that he had decided to make a career of teaching, since an American publishing house could not offer him the opportunities he sought for "creative writing and scholarly work." Creative writing was in good odor at Bard, although at other, less progressive colleges, it would not in that era have been a password to success. "He has not yet begun writing in English," Fuller reported, "but he has written some fiction in French." (No evidence of such writings has survived.) Despite this, de Man claimed elsewhere in his written dossier to have published an essay entitled "A European Looks at American Publishing" (in *Publishers Weekly*, October 1947) and another, "Censorship Under Occupation" (in the *New York Times Book Review*, also in English, in November 1947). Since both of these journals could have been readily checked in Bard's own library and no such essays have been found, Paul's nerve in making these assertions was extraordinary. As for Uncle Henri, "Uncle, Hendrik de Man, was a professor at the University of Frankfurt."

The résumé (as the CV was then known) was the document McCarthy had overseen, and its rich and smooth style shows her good hand. He inflated much, but now he did not mention his great-grandfather Jan Van Beers, who had taught at a teachers' college in Lierre and become known to a few as the "Flemish national poet." His father's factory for manufacturing X-ray tables disappeared, and the large night school Bob ran part-time became a "technological university" and Bob's sole occupation. Paul mentioned his Dutch translation of *Moby-Dick*, and also claimed to have produced a bilingual—German-French—edition of Goethe's *Faust*, of which no trace has been found. He had written "several articles of literary criticism which appeared in French and Belgian newspapers and magazines." Here, as with the names of his employers, he omitted identifying titles. This was all the notice as he gave of his two years' work and the nearly two hundred essays later collected in *Wartime Journalism*.

The major misrepresentation occurred on a form that asked specifically for "War Service (civilian or military)." To this, de Man responded, "Belgian Army in 1940. Demobilized 1941—Resistance Group under Occupation. 1943–44 Front de l'Indépendance (F.I.)" Paul of course, like so many others, and on the government's advice, had run away from conscription, and the Front de l'Indépendance was the major group among the several "armies" of the Belgian Resistance and heavily inflected by its Communist members. They would have made short work of the youth who had been smeared by the denunciation of him at ULB. Usually allied in small groups, members of the Resistants were distinguished from one another by the regional, political, and/or social backgrounds of their members. Claiming membership here was no mere embellishment of the facts, but a major lie: The FI could well have been one of the Resistance armies that scoured the countryside for men like de Man while he was taking refuge in northern Flanders, near the border of Holland, and benefiting from the protection of its Nazi civil government. Since no one at Bard could have decoded such a name, perhaps wrapping himself in FI colors was one of de Man's private jokes. The titles he concocted for his alleged M.A. thesis and Ph.D. dissertation were also grandiose, but they illuminate his fantasies of intellectual attainment. His putative master's study was "The Bergsonian Conception of Time in the Contemporary Novel," an up-to-date topic, as both Bergson and phenomenological approaches to time had been in vogue in France since Husserl and Heidegger had become intellectually fashionable in the 1930s. As for his doctoral dissertation—which he specified was "interrupted"—he claimed it bore the title "Introduction to a Phenomenology of Aesthetic Consciousness."[28]

Paul de Man was appointed an instructor, with an annual salary that was theoretically $3,000 but had been reduced by Artinian's negotiations to $2,400 (due to Artinian's arrangement to retain 20 percent of his annual salary by teaching till mid-October).[29] De Man did not take up his position until Monday, October 17. Paul was probably glad to have the job on any terms. In this case, as often happened with de Man,

Maria Sophia Deman-Van Aytmael, great-grandmother of Paul de Man. Wife of Jacob Deman-Van Aytmael, Antwerp.

ERIKA TILLEMANS-DE MAN

Jacob Deman-Van Aytmael (1816–1866), butcher, Antwerp.

ERIKA TILLEMANS-
DE MAN

Jan van Beers, known as Flemish national poet, painting by Jean Bertou, 1850.

ARCHIEF EN MUSEUM
VOOR HET VLAAMSE
CULTUURLEVEN

Adolph Léo Deman
(1859–1936),
passport photo,
ca. age sixty-five.

Madeleine De Braey (1893–1937),
fourth from left, studio photo,
Ostend, ca. age twenty-one.

Simone De Braey-De Haeck
(sister-in-law of Madeleine
de Man-De Braey, aunt of
Paul de Man), washing their
laundry when the two
women, both pregnant,
were evacuated to England
during World War I.

*Robert (Bob) de Man
(1890–1959),
father of Paul de Man,
age sixty-seven.*

BOB DE BRAEY

*Paul de Man, age four, with cousin
Minime (Micheline) De Braey.*

BOB DE BRAEY

*Paul de Man (then nicknamed
"de Pol"), with ice cream soda
at the shore in Holland, 1934–35.*

BOB DE BRAEY

Six members of the editorial board of Cahiers du libre examen, *1938–39 (Paul de Man not yet a member): from left, third, Nelly Blockx (later De Ligne-Blockx); fourth, Jean Burgers, hero of the Resistance; sixth, Georges Lambrichs.*

EDOUARD COLINET

Five members of the editorial board of Cahiers du libre examen, *1939–40: from left, second, Gilbert Jaeger; fifth, Paul de Man, ca. age nineteen.*

EDOUARD COLINET

Detail of photograph above: Paul de Man, ca. age nineteen.

EDOUARD COLINET

Henri de Man
(1885–1953),
late 1930s.

Paul and family in Kalmthout, 1945:
Anne de Man (née Baraghian,
1919–2000), Marc de Man (b. 1945),
Paul de Man, Hendrik (Rik) de Man
(later Hendrik Woods, b. 1941).

Paul de Man,
Renée Weiss,
Ted Weiss, ca.
December 1949.

Irma Brandeis, tutorial with unnamed student at Bard, ca. December 1949.

BARD COLLEGE
LIBRARY
ARCHIVES;
HAMILTON
WINSLOW

Artine Artinian, ca. December 1949.

BARD COLLEGE
LIBRARY ARCHIVES;
HAMILTON WINSLOW

Pat de Man (1927–2004) with infant Michael de Man (1950–2000) in basket, taking a break while picking straw-berries, May 1951.

PATRICIA DE MAN

Pat de Man with Michael and dog, in shallows of Loire River, France, 1955.

PATRICIA DE MAN

Paul, Patricia, and Michael outside Hôtel des Grands Hommes, Paris, 1955.

PATRICIA DE MAN

Vendage: Paul (first on right) and Pat de Man (second on right, holding basket) joining grape harvest, France 1955, with farm family.

PATRICIA DE MAN

Paul de Man with infant Patsy de Man, Massachusetts Avenue apartment, Cambridge, Massachusetts, 1960.

Paul de Man with daughter Patsy (on left) and son Michael (on right) aboard the Normandie, *returning to the United States from France, 1964.*

Hendrik (Rik) Woods with his first child and father, Paul de Man, who was in the last year of his life, already ill with a terminal brain tumor. Woodbridge, Connecticut, 1983.

confirmation of his position proved to be a cliff-hanger. The letter from Fuller went astray because—despite the "astonishingly cheap rent"—Paul had skipped out and taken shelter downtown in the Hotel Marlton, his fifth address in sixteen months. Fuller's offer finally found its way to de Man on Saturday, October 15, eleven days later. De Man, however, thrived on crisis, and—in spite of delays—here was success at last. He could take in his stride the fact that in exactly two days and without preparation he had to meet his first classes—and these would literally be the first he had faced in his life. Once again, he had the thrill of being saved by pure luck. The mail came in the morning, and after ripping open the letter, Paul stopped only long enough to reply and accept the job before hopping on the next train north. Undoubtedly, he first called Mary, whom he had kept au courant. She had arranged for herself a writing assignment that took her to nearby Vassar College, in Poughkeepsie. He reached the Rhinebeck station in time to meet his benefactor. They had previously coordinated their meeting, a visit she mentioned in passing to her husband.[30]

It was a very happy reunion. After over a year of hand-to-mouth existence, undignified work, and constant removals to ever smaller and dingier lodgings, de Man, whose previous homes, even during and after the war, had featured libraries and grand pianos, now moved into a large and handsome six-bedroom house that coincidentally bore a certain architectural resemblance to his grandfather's home in Kalmthout, possibly because they had been built in the same era. To de Man, it must have seemed only natural.[31] Paul, always characterized by what his widow called his "open hand," thought this prestigious dwelling, set in the best part of the campus, among tall pines and grassy slopes, was appropriate for himself and his family. Yet he was now committed to paying close to 40 percent of his small income in rent, and that was something de Man avoided whenever he could. This time, his habit would become a very serious problem.

That, however, was still in the future. He arrived at Bard on a sunny day, and he and Mary wandered about the charming campus, running into her friends as they walked. These included the writer David Bazelon and others. One could do worse at Bard than be introduced to one's colleagues under McCarthy's aegis. Mary also had something important to look forward to. She was now pregnant with a child she wanted. She'd had miscarriages, but at thirty-seven she wished for another child and would not have much more time to conceive one. She referred to this coyly as "our Secret" when writing to Bowden, but it was not so great a secret that she had not already told one of her former teachers at Vassar and perhaps others, as well. Keeping news to herself was not her strong point. Since her condition was not evident, she was probably still in her first trimester, and her pregnancy would have begun in July or August.

By now, Paul had prepared for her as a special gift an essay that he had written especially to celebrate one of her recent publications. *The Oasis* was an easily pierced roman à clef on the political and personal follies of her New York circle, whom she showed as retreating from the threat of the A-bomb to an ill-conceived and doomed experiment in communal living in Vermont. McCarthy's friends were either outraged or just hurt.[32] The novel won a prize in England but had gotten only mixed reviews in the United States.[33] In a sense, *The Oasis* was another of Mary's acts of leave-taking or breaking off, this time not only from a lover, but from a whole group or epoch in her life.[34] (Philip Rahv, once her lover, was a special target of her satire, and he prepared to sue for libel—until Macdonald reminded him that in order to win his case, he would have to prove in court that he *was* the uncouth ex-Communist Will Taub, at odds with a thinly veiled Macdonald.) De Man's appreciation of the satire remained a kind of billet-doux between himself and Mary, and was never published. However, she thought it was wonderful, and during their rendezvous at Bard, he read it to her aloud *in French*—a transporting experience. She wrote to Bowden two days later:

> Then P. read me in French his article on *The Oasis*, not a bad one, really, but like Cyril [Connolly] he felt he had to modulate his praises in deference to his audience—why? Off the record, he told me that he had read it a second time and that it was a work of exquisite craftsmanship, a perfect *conte philosophique* and even better than I realized (this I refuted by joining in the the eulogy myself).[35]

Kiernan, who printed the letter to Broadwater in her biography of McCarthy, commented, "Ever after, she would refer to *The Oasis* as a *'conte philosophique.'*" As for the relations between them, her biographer commented, "If anything further passed between her and Paul De Man, it went unreported."[36] McCarthy also told her husband that she was staying at a two-dollar-a-night boardinghouse run by a Mrs. Thomas—who did exist. But since her tastes, like Paul's, were for the more rarified things of life, and the lodging smelled of cabbage, she reported, while de Man's luxurious new home clearly permitted—with its six bedrooms *invited*—their joint exploration, it is likely that "if anything further passed" between them, it was in those quarters. (She carefully reported to Broadwater that Paul slept elsewhere, in a "barracks.")[37]

McCarthy once remarked that a woman never leaves one man until she knows she has another waiting in the wings. De Man, as Margo Viscusi said later, was her new European. He wrote her that he took her work as a jumping-off point from which to criticize by way of contrast the general "mediocrity" of American writing, with its "rigidity of convictions." There was a "crisis": American culture was prey to "a rigidity of convictions which does not tolerate the inherent insecurity of real invention" and thus produced a "prevailing mediocrity." (The reproach that American culture rejected internal criticism of its conventional ideas was a classic European position.) De Man would ignore the "worst examples of American naturalism" or "primitivism" (meaning Steinbeck, perhaps, or even Hemingway, who was regarded by some French writers as refreshingly "barbaric").[38] He would target only the real enemy, the reviewers for the *New York Times*, *The Saturday Review of Literature*, and so forth. It was an easy promise to make, of course, but it was probably all de Man had to offer.[39]

The encounter they shared at Bard was happy, but it was the last enjoyable meeting the two ever had. Thanksgiving came five weeks later, and during that time the two friends should normally have been in touch. The Macdonalds were going to visit Mary, and she would certainly have invited de Man to the party she gave that year. Yet, despite all she had done over the past year to put him where he was, he did not visit her, but instead stayed on at Bard. She must have been disappointed. He did not visit at Christmas, either. Indeed, he would never contact her voluntarily again, and they would meet only once more.

ON OCTOBER 17, PAUL WALKED across the campus toward his first classes, enjoying the fall morning by the Hudson River, when the leaves are often brilliant, the sky intensely blue, and the wind brisk. When his teaching was over and he had seen the eager faces of the students looking up at him in those well-worn old rooms, he probably knew that his existence had changed for good. He had arrived at his work virtually unprepared, yet from the beginning he had held his audiences in the palm of his hand, and he would do so again and again: Teaching would be his profession for the rest of his life. Whether as a boy in Kalmthout, when "he was the one who made life interesting," or as a novice businessman who could raise large sums from older and hardheaded merchants, Paul de Man was a storyteller who could instantly excite his audiences, make them share his ideas and passions, and accept him as their leader. (When he later wished to obfuscate his theories, no one was less comprehensible.) He had failed repeatedly when he had dismissed the facts and acted out merely imaginary successes, but now he had a forum where his erudition and talents for communication and intellectual play were what counted and where his flights of ideas did not make him seem "light," but, rather, intensely interesting, illuminating, even deep.

Involvement with teaching—staying ahead of his students by at least one chapter in the syllabus—was not, however, the only thing that kept Paul de Man from calling Mary or responding to the invitations she undoubtedly extended. In the third week of October, Patricia Lightfoot Kelley, a tall, slim senior of twenty-two, walked into Paul's office. Fair-haired, with a gentle, musical voice, high intelligence, and a perceptiveness that always seemed to take in much more than she needed to utter, the French major had stopped by, hoping for a conference about her future. She was not Paul's student, but her mentor, Artinian, was away, and she thought his replacement could advise her on how to get a Fulbright. The afternoon sun was streaming through the windows, reflecting off her hair and the old brown woodwork as

Paul stood up, shook her hand, and began to listen. Perhaps as he sat down, his knees were shaking a little. For at that moment, he fell immediately and completely in love, and he would remain so, possessively and passionately, for the rest of his life.[40] Always intuitive and impulsive, he probably guessed that if he could seize this woman at this point in time and bring her into his life, everything that had happened before, and much that might go awry in the future, now could be transformed. "All . . . changed utterly: A terrible beauty is born." So Yeats had written, and it applied to Paul de Man and Patricia Kelley. It was beautiful because they were young and on the brink of what Patricia called "a forty-year love affair." It was terrible because many people would be damaged in the process.

26

FINDING PAT

PATRICIA WAS NOT LIKE THE OTHER WOMEN PAUL DE MAN HAD KNOWN.
She shared his origin in the upper-middle class as the daughter of a
wealthy woman lawyer from an old family in Washington, D.C., where
her grandfather had been a rich and fashionable doctor. Pat said she had
dreamed of his mansion on California Avenue for many years. Yet her
childhood, although less traumatic than de Man's, had been bad enough.
Her mother, Lucy Lightfoot Kelley Woods, was a lawyer working at a
high level of the National Labor Relations Board, but she was "volatile." Her life was turbulent, and her daughter's youth was marked by
divorces, repeated abandonments, and neglect.[1] Pat had been left unvisited for months in a sanitarium at age six, abandoned by her caretaker
on a ranch in the West at age seven, and exposed to instability when at
home. As Lucy got older, she drank. Pat grew up to admire her mother's attainments and charm, but she did not want to be like her.[2] By her
senior year at Bard, Pat was a pretty woman with a high forehead and
regular features, but she wore no makeup, preferred long skirts and
thick socks to the waist-cinchers and crinolines of the fashionable New
Look, and pulled her long, thick blond hair away from her face into a
ponytail. She was also highly intelligent, gifted in languages, and possessed of courage. Unusually athletic, she had, at age eighteen, cycled
for months with a few friends on a rough trip through Central America, climbing from sea level over the six-thousand-foot crests of the

Pan-American Highway to Nicaragua. An illness she picked up en route had put her a year behind her classmates, but with her varied talents, her future was promising. She only knew that she did not want to live as her mother had. Cheerful and positive, rather than depressive, she might yet have struck Paul as being like his mother in some ways, for she preferred reading to becoming one of "*les girls*" as Paul said Madeleine had done; perhaps Pat was like her, too, in a certain detachment, gentleness, and capacity for irony.

His attraction was instant, but she did not respond immediately. "I was not a dating type of person," she recalled. She had no current boyfriend, was not especially interested in Paul, and when early on, in the era before faculty-student relationships were formally forbidden, he asked for a date, she refused. Nor did she respond to his phone calls at first. Her friends, hearing of his determined interest, told her she was "crazy," she said much later. "All my roommates were saying, 'Oh, bring him to supper,'" but she did not warm up so quickly. She had early recognized in Paul a tendency to say what "would sound good. He always wanted to seem solid. He wanted the appearance." Pat sought honesty. Lucy cared for appearances also, and her daughter had "determined from the beginning that I would not be like my mother—absolutely not."[3]

Pat did not, in fact, hold out for very long. She may have been aware that he was married, as it was not a secret, but he probably minimized that attachment. Paul was immensely "ardent" and "absolutely determined" to win her, and he had already proved irresistible to far stronger and more experienced men and women than she. Much later, she described him as competitive in everything, "carried away by his ideas," fixed on them, and able to persuade virtually anyone to see things his way, from herself to a dean, when he had chosen a goal. She recalled, "He would sit there and kick up sand. Like an ostrich. It was clear that he wanted it that much. [Later in his life,] he would go into a dean's office and they'd come back smiling—he got [what he wanted.]"[4]

De Man, although he was juggling two other relationships at the same time, began a campaign that fall to help Pat get her Fulbright to France. On November 3, he wrote a flattering letter to Artinian, promising the rent, offering to forward his *Saturday Review of Literature*, and telling his landlord that all was well, the house suited him marvelously, the courses he was teaching interested him, and it was as Artine had promised: Some students were better, and all were honorable. "It's easy to replace an excellent predecessor." Two weeks later, he wrote again, but now he used his tried-and-true method to gain Pat's advancement by asking a senior man to intervene and help. This time, he focused entirely on her, "our shared advisee," whom he was encouraging in her wish to apply for a student Fulbright because he believed "she could develop into a very good student and in any event [applying] will do her good psychologically and raise her sense of self-worth."[5] He urged Artinian to send the report to him by return mail. He also approached Jean Wahl, an eminent French philosopher with whom he had corresponded but not yet met. (Pat's proposal was denied, not by the Fulbright Committee but in an office of the college, where an ill-disposed woman, jealous of their relationship, Pat believed, asserted it was too well written and that Paul must have done it for her.[6] This was ironic, for Paul needed Pat's help for some years in revising his English.) In assuming the task of helping Pat, de Man was showing his protective side. Since he was habitually, fatally indifferent to planning ahead for his own future, his attention to her needs indicated his growing care for her. There is also a buried tenderness in this businesslike letter to Artinian, with its unusual number of emotive adjectives and adverbs (*good, very good, immense, extraordinary, best, perfectly, complete*), that speaks for the love that was fast developing between the first-year instructor, still twenty-nine, and his twenty-two-year-old student.

Paul de Man's other commitments, however, were problematic. He told Artinian in his first letter that he intended to bring his family to the United States by the Christmas holidays, and Anne reported that he wrote about their long hoped-for reunion, telling her to buy expensive clothing because he meant to show her off to Mary McCarthy, a fashionable woman, and to Peggy Guggenheim, as well.[7] He neglected to say that he was out of touch entirely with Mary McCarthy.

In Portsmouth, life was going forward for Mary also, but very sadly. A week before Thanksgiving, on November 17, Mary fell down the stairs of her cottage and had a miscarriage. Three days later, she wrote to her friend Dwight Macdonald that it had been "the classic fall down

stairs" and that she was still in the hospital because they feared complications, a statement suggesting that the pregnancy was advanced, perhaps to its second trimester.[8] She had been planning a big dinner for the
holiday on the twenty-fourth and had invited the Macdonalds, who
were going to make the long trip to Portsmouth. In spite of everything,
she gave her party four days later. Paul, however, did not come.

Had Mary invited him? It would have been surprising if she had not
done so. After all, they both had a lot to be thankful for, and Mary by
rights could have expected to receive a good deal of homage from the
man she had placed in such a desirable position. The rest of the year was
a dark one for Mary McCarthy. Losing the unborn child sat heavily on
her spirits. In December, she wrote Elizabeth Hardwick, "We are a little depressed . . . for obvious reasons." She hadn't been able even to look
at her new novel for six weeks (this one became the well-received satire
on Bard, *The Groves of Academe*), and she didn't see how "the human
race" could "endure itself much longer."[9]

Paul had stayed at Bard while Pat went home for the holiday. When
she returned around November 30, they consummated their relationship, a day they regarded thereafter as their true anniversary. Pat said
that he had proposed marriage at once.[10] Something, probably his conquest of Pat, put Paul in high spirits. A letter survives that he wrote five
days later and sent to Dwight Macdonald. A sudden change of mood
was evident in its exceptional cheerfulness. Gone was his normal dry
style; the operative word was *fun*: Teaching was "great fun"; a visit by
the Macdonald family would be "lots of fun." "Some of the students are
interesting and all are very pleasant." Macdonald had returned an anno-
tated version of "[his] article" and he was grateful for the comments: "I
had forgotten all about it but it was kind of fun to read it over again."[11]
But he was not yet ready to identify the source of his new American
spirit of fun—nor had he yet officially ceased to plan for the arrival of
his wife and children. On the contrary he wrote to Macdonald, "I live
in a large rather comfortable house just of [*sic*] campus, perfectly suited
for my family which will be here possibly just before Xmas and certainly soon after. As soon as they are installed (which won't take long)
you must come up with your family." He found the atmosphere of Bard
during vacations "remarkably quiet" and recognized that "I wouldn't

mind staying here for 2–3 years (not more), time to get some-what rested from 10 hectic years and to finish a book I start [*sic*], a few years ago, on aesthetics."

There is no evidence that he worked on any such study in 1949, but to write about aesthetics seems to have become a private fantasy he would realize much later. Perhaps at some level de Man had now begun what would be his lifelong attempt to turn back the clock, wipe out everything to do with Anne, bury the war and collaboration, and erase his crooked dealings with Hermès. He would start life afresh in the United States, and he would create a new self purely as an intellectual. Yet in mentioning his family but not Patricia to Dwight, Paul was still keeping his options open.

Things moved fast, however, and he and Pat decided to spend Christmas with her mother and stepfather in Washington. The visit was an unqualified disaster. Lucy Woods "never approved of Paul," since her daughter had "come home for Christmas with a married teacher. I was her great favorite," Patsy recalled, and this socially prominent woman had imagined for her daughter a very different future. She quickly got out of Paul his personal status, and however transgressive her own private life had been, she would not countenance the intimacy she saw between them, much less Pat's marriage to an older, foreign, penniless substitute instructor of no known family or social background, who was already saddled with a wife and three children, and *not* divorced. It is also possible that she, worldly and experienced, may have been one of the few people who instinctively distrusted Paul de Man. "Mother got her way all the time," Patricia remarked—but then, so did her lover.

After a bad start, Mrs. Woods created havoc just before New Year's Day, a melodramatic confrontation complete with alcohol, shouts, slamming doors, and a pistol. They hadn't told her of their plans to wed, but Lucy "beg[an] to see our relationship was more intimate [and] came down strongly against it." They were taking down the Christmas tree when Pat said something about the tree going to waste. Typically, her mother tempestuously "decided to have a scene," entering the living room dramatically declaiming, "'You feel sorry for the tree when the heart of a mother . . .'" Then her "stepfather pull[ed] a gun" and shouted at Paul to "Get out of this house!'" Paul complied at once—and "slammed the door so hard, I thought there was a shot. 'You've shot him! you've shot him!'" Pat cried. With parents like those, an unaggressive young woman might well be attracted to a seemingly protective man on whose "strong ego," as she once put it, she knew that others could "break themselves."[12]

Evicted from her mother's house on a snowy night without money, mercy, or clothing, they found their way on foot through the dark streets to her father's home and spent what was left of New Year's Eve with him. Ogden Kelley was employed at the Library of Congress. He was very sympathetic to the couple, both then and later.[13]

More drama lay ahead of a more serious sort. On the first or second of January, en route to Bard, they passed through New York City, spending the night at the "dark and awful" Hotel Marlton. It was there that the normally healthy and resilient Pat, though buoyed by the adventure of her romance, suddenly fainted. Paul did not take that lightly. Possibly alerted by his years of marriage and fatherhood, he took her next morning to a doctor he knew. As Pat was lying on his examining table, the physician told her that she was pregnant. How he divined this so early and without the normal tests is unknown, but he was right. She was about one month along, and by mid-April, she was showing. They did not consider abortion, just as they had taken no precautions against pregnancy. They were "both too innocent," she recalled. Of herself, at least, that was true. She went back to Washington in April for the Easter holiday, and "made up with mother. . . . She decided to support the marriage." The support was unenthusiastic and qualified always. Lucy Woods never got over her resistance to de Man and always refused the couple material help until the very end, when they did not need it.[14]

It may have been on that eventful day when he knew he would again become a father and be a family man that Paul made his decision. He wrote Anne that he wanted a divorce. He had already determined to marry Pat, come what might, and in sending the letter, he showed characteristic decisiveness and what was to become an ever stronger trait, a capacity to hold on stubbornly to his goal. That he was already married, that his connection to Patricia would certainly mean the end of his friendship with Mary McCarthy and her influential circle, that Pat's pregnancy itself would involve serious embarrassment throughout their life at Bard—none of this mattered. It was a blow, however, to his wife, separated now from him for almost a year and three-quarters, who received the letter in Buenos Aires on January 11, 1950, a day she did not forget, not least because it was the birthday of Rik, her eldest son, conceived in wartime Brussels in an era and a world that was very far away.

It would also matter to Mary McCarthy. In January, she knew nothing of what had transpired in the three months since she and Paul had strolled the campus and explored his new home, but his silence was ominous. It was time to get to the bottom of things. Knowing where they stood at least would help lift her depression. She arranged to meet Paul on January 22 at the home of Fritz and Margaret Shafer, friends from her days of teaching at Bard, when Frederick had been the college's intellectual chaplain.[15] Now he had a new pulpit in Cold Spring, not far away. They liked to invite guests over for Sunday dinner after Fritz had given his sermon, the high point of the week. "Fritz would mix them martinis," Margaret recalled, and they could relax with intimates. Margaret remembered that the house was drenched that day with winter sunlight reflecting off the snow that covered the grounds outside, and that the very handsome "Paul was sitting with the light in his eyes."

For the first time in years, Paul de Man was at the top of his form. He had just turned thirty, and life had spun around, suddenly opening before him with new possibilities: a fresh start, a true vocation, and a new person, who was entirely unlike the women he had known before, with whom to share it. His students saw him as "ardent" and "hot": He gave off energy, and photographs taken at the time show the laserlike focus of his body and gaze as he addressed a group. The intensity of his gaze, especially when he was excited by ideas, was a striking feature. While Paul was holding the floor that Sunday after dinner, a delighted Mary commented to Margaret, "Now Paul's eyes are in full cry." Margaret remembered some fifty years later that phrase and that his eyes were very blue. The comment was made by a woman who had internalized Paul's look. But whatever Mary's feelings, it was on that day, January 22, 1950, that de Man told her of his liaison with Patsy Kelley, his plans for a divorce, and his intention to marry the younger woman.

He had known, of course, when he received Mary's invitation—or rather, summons—to meet her at the Shafers' what lay ahead: She was going to want to know where they stood and why she had not heard from him. The generous friendship offered, the work she had done to get him his job, the CV she had written, the strings she had pulled, the friends she had mobilized, and the reputation she almost alone had vouched for should have counted for something. The trip he had accompanied her on when she purchased her cottage in Rhode Island, the long vacation spent in intimacy as he labored on the house, the encomiums on her writing, the year of invitations and holiday visits, the long hours of talk into the night, not to mention other aspects of their relationship—where had they all gone? Mary was tough, and she would not have been shy about demanding an accounting. From his point of view, however, it had been fun while it lasted, but it could not go on forever. Now thirty, he had at last a fully grown man's relationship to a younger woman who had quickly come to adore him, and a surprisingly bright future, in which he would need no capital and could live free of the irritating constraints of records and budgets. Best of all, Patricia was pregnant. He would be a father and a husband and could start over in a new country.

Did he owe it all to Mary, or much of it? From the point of view of a man intent on his own needs, not those of others, he probably supposed he owed her thanks for helping him along, but no more. After all, she was married, but even had they both been single, she was not for him a long-term companion. Perhaps he had had enough of women with a public life. He had disliked the "worldly" Lucienne Didier for just that quality, and with Anne, he had been living with a very socially ambitious woman eager to move in high society, a woman whose extravagant entertaining had brought him to ruin. He and Mary had been good friends, but she did not understand what he really could do—and he was only now discovering his real talents. Moreover, for all his failures and acts of malfeasance, he himself had been the center of attention in Belgium, the gatekeeper, the man with influence who made connections for himself and others. The modest and quiet demeanor his New York friends had seen was partly natural under the circumstances, but he was a good actor, and it was also a cover for his own intense ambition and competitiveness. With Pat behind him, he could start over. Fresh from a triumphant public lecture he had given at Bard in December, he knew that his underground days were over.

McCarthy remembered with precision the date of their final meeting when its anniversary came up. As she wrote to Artinian in 1951, "We last saw him almost exactly a year ago when he told us about a divorce, a girl named Kelly (I think)—all rather confused. Since then, we've heard nothing from him and have no idea, even, where he is."[16] Evidently, after his lively spate of talk, he had waited till after lunch that day to tell her of his new situation—and therefore, inevitably, of her changed status in his life. After that, he sought no further contact, and neither did she. Being the one to leave and not the one abandoned was McCarthy's preferred role.[17] Just as bringing her friends together was healing for her, being discarded by them was deeply wounding and reawakened old vulnerabilities. As her letter of a year later showed, she was furious. She had done a great deal for him. One may justifiably presume that harsh words passed between them. She was never at a loss for barbed and painful language, and devastating criticism was her métier. If this was spoken it would account in part for the mutual hostility of their subsequent comments about each other. For de Man, any wound to his narcissism undoubtedly was hurtful, given what he knew he owed to Mary. He could be withering, and the contemptuous indifference that his widow later said he expressed in regard to McCarthy would have been his weapon. De Man had considerable personal power face-to-face when he turned it on: a famous shrug that dismissed what he disliked; a laying down of the law that students never got over. He undoubtedly felt that since both of them were married, McCarthy should not have assumed any long-term commitment, and that whatever he did to change his marital status was no concern of hers.

That afternoon was decisive. Nothing could be recaptured of their friendship. A year later, however, in January 1951, when de Man had fallen into disgrace at Bard College, Artinian, who by then was his open enemy, responded to an inquiry from Mary about de Man's various defalcations. She replied, and this letter, although couched in terms of sorrow rather than anger, actually expressed venomous criticism. It was written exactly a year after her disastrous last meeting with her former friend, and the anniversary date had carried a burden, as the anniversary of loss often does. The professor of French had let McCarthy know that his former tenant had caused him financial grief by not paying his rent and was embroiled now in a different scandal of his own making. Her reply was long and skillfully composed, deprecating everything—the whole affair, her part in it, her bad judgment of people, but mostly, of course, Paul de Man himself.[18]

The tone avoided revealing personal pique but was devastating. She made a point of "feel[ing] sorry" for the "poor fellow" who had left "so many points of no return behind him." Clearly, she wished to distance herself from further connection with this problematic figure whom she had sent up to Bard. Yet the language also reveals how deeply she had thought about Paul de Man, closely and coldly analyzing the tendencies of his character. Gone was the "straightforward" and "honest" man she had recommended to Artinian in June 1949. Now he was given to "lying, evasion, fantasy, greed, possibly even theft." She saw him now as habitually using up one friend after another:

> Everyone has had the same experience . . . he has come . . . sponsored by a first friend, become an intimate or regular guest of the second household, asked finally for a recommendation of some third sort (employer, lawyer, etc.) then disappeared, leaving an eddy of slight wonder behind him. . . . It was the fluidity of the relation that was slightly disconcerting; one felt one was part of a very soft cord or chain going, one knew not whither.

"An eddy of slight wonder . . . fluidity . . . slightly . . . soft cord . . . one knew not . . .": This language stressed her perception of de Man as weak, unstable, and unworthy of attention, suggesting not so much an active schemer or opportunist as something wormlike, slipping from one position to another, a nonentity, beneath notice. With all that, he was also a liar and probably a thief. She admitted that she could not fault him for borrowing money, but she added, "I must say I begin to wonder about those expensive books he bought us—were they pinched from Doubleday's?" This was not a justified inference, as she spoke neither from experience nor evidence. Yet one need not take at face value her assertion that de Man had not borrowed money, since that was habitual with him. McCarthy had been generous with others, and she may have helped de Man out, as others had loaned him money in Belgium. But it would not have been good for her image to admit as much to people at Bard.

She revealed herself most in her demands for information. She and Bowden were egregious backbiters in a circle famously given to slander, and she pressed for information: "But, Artine, if you have a spare moment, do write me at least one lurid detail. . . . And where can the poor fellow be now? . . . Please . . . let me know. Is he remarried, has the girl money, was that the point, what about his first wife, and what were the lies he told?" It is possible to read McCarthy's letter as simply a writer's skillful character analysis of one who has caused her embarrassment, a detached observation of an "adolescent" man, "plastic and formless" but not "really a bad person," and others have done so. But although the tone is controlled, the structure of the letter, its length, care, and detail carry the message that she had been hurt and that a year after he had let her down she was still interested in de Man to a significant degree. "She did not even let it be seen as anger, but as disdainful amusement," Richard Rand said of her tone when she spoke to him years later of her onetime friend. The pressure of that anger weighs heavily on the ponderous nonchalance of this letter to Artinian.

Thereafter, except for a few passing but always negative remarks, de Man avoided referring to McCarthy for the rest of his life. She followed the same course, though less rigorously and with a tinge of bitterness. Rand, a student of de Man at Harvard from 1956 to 1960, was fascinated by and devoted to him. Meeting McCarthy on a social occasion in 1959, he asked her what she thought of his professor. She was brutally dismissive. " 'Oh yes, Paul de Man,' " she said. " 'He always reminded me of a poor little Dutch boy without shoes.' And she didn't hesitate to mention his employment at the Doubleday store in the basement at Grand Central."[19] Like Broadwater and her friend Macdonald on a similar occasion, she affixed an ethnic label—Dutch—and in stressing his poverty and low status added an element of class contempt. She also repeated to Rand the slander about the art books de Man gave his friends: "I always surmised that he stole them." On another occasion, according to Pat, Mary included a passing reference to de Man's works in the course of an essay in *The New York Review of Books*, suggesting that his books should be burned.

Yet his name was on her lips at the very end of her life. An inquiry from Ortwin de Graef, the scholar who first uncovered de Man's wartime journalism, started her on a quest that lasted intermittently for the next two and a half years, producing numerous documents and many hours of personal discussion.[20] Even at the very end when she was dying of cancer in a hospital bed in Maine, she brought the discussion with her close friend Elizabeth Hardwick back to the subject of Paul de Man. According to Hardwick, who had seen de Man frequently in 1949 when visiting the Broadwaters, his name had never come thereafter. McCarthy had suppressed the subject but had never forgotten him. "All these years. She was my closest friend and it never came [up.] . . . [In the hospital] she told me about the wife thing. It was very amusing the way she told it," Hardwick recalled. She continued as the scene came back to her: "I was talking to Mary before she died. . . . We were up in Maine. We were in the hospital. We were sort of laughing about Paul de Man. Because [he had become] so famous at Yale. [She said], 'God I would never have thought this.' All of the Nazi stuff had come out. . . . She did not survive. This was the summer. We were laughing about the wife thing. She said, 'Well, he was a trimmer always.'

"Then she went into how dreadfully he treated his [first] wife. Very amusing. He left her. They [Paul and Pat] had a child. What did he do?"[21]

Inevitably, the question arises as to whether de Man and McCarthy had an affair. Paul's widow thought they did. Thinking over the several episodes he had recounted, Pat thought such a liaison quite likely. Paul told her, she reported, that McCarthy had "come onto him" but that he had not accepted her advances—a proviso undoubtedly meant to forestall marital discord, she thought, for Pat and Paul were jealous of each other. She reasoned that McCarthy's belated "dislike for him came after she was somewhat a woman scorned."[22] Given the other crucial information de Man concealed from his wife—including even the bigamous status of their own marriage—to allude to McCarthy in several small but personal anecdotes was, for him, exceptional.[23] Margo Viscusi, who knew Mary better than anyone, thought that an affair between Paul and Mary was possible. He was "attractive, blond, and especially because he was European: She had a weakness for Europeans." More than that, McCarthy "was attracted to people who were adrift—physically adrift, who needed help and whom she could help."[24] For such a rescuer, this brilliant and good-looking European, an athletic, sexually attractive but impoverished young immigrant, struggling far below his social and intellectual level, would have exactly fitted the profile of a person to whom she would want to give help.

Some of the women close to Mary McCarthy at the time initially conceded only the possibility of an affair, although none of them knew the scope of their private contacts or correspondence. Eve Stwertka decided finally that an affair was possible, but only if "*he* found *her*" attractive.[25] Elizabeth Hardwick said she had no knowledge of any such relationship. But middle-class women in that era—and later also—married or single, feared for their reputations, however daringly indifferent McCarthy might have been to scandal. Moreover, to presume the existence of an affair with a man whose reputation was subsequently so damaged would reflect very badly on their friend. Younger women tended to be more open on the subject. "She was very fond of him," said Margaret Shafer, who was more than a decade younger. Remembering Mary's subsequent anger at de Man, she reflected that possibly a love affair might explain both that animus and Broadwater's hostility to de Man, which Margaret had been aware of over time.

Men, on other hand, who knew de Man at the time tended to bring the subject up and to insist on an affair as virtually certain. David Braybrooke, thinking over the sequence of events, remarked in his logician's mode, "You should have to make an argument why they were *not* lovers"—that is, he found the affirmative case so strong that only a careful counterargument could begin to deny what was obvious.[26] Richard Rand, whose parents were part of McCarthy's circle, went further and concluded from the bitterness of her tone both in her second letter to Artinian and in personal remarks to himself that "she was mad as hell. She was slow to recover her sense of humor. Mary was terribly in love with Paul, and he walked away. . . . I think they had an affair."[27] Rand inferred from her ongoing anger something further, that she had hoped for marriage: "She was so mad at him. She sounded like a rejected, spurned lover. . . . I'm sure she thought that this was going to be a bond . . . and that they would be married. . . . She did not even let it be seen as anger, but as disdainful amusement. Another person who used the words [poor little Dutch boy] was Dwight Macdonald." The Broadwaters' contemptuous phrase had been picked up by Dwight, which suggests that, in the way of friends, he had closed ranks with them. De Man was banished from their world, as a later rebuff from Fred Dupee would show.

No one in their circle has connected McCarthy's miscarriage to her friendship with de Man, but if an affair took place and she had reason to think him the father, that would go far to explain both her devotion to his interests and her subsequent ongoing bitterness, especially if, as Rand thinks, she hoped to marry him herself. Certainly the dates of his visits to her in Portsmouth—the days in mid-June when she closed on the house, followed by the long visit in July and August—coupled with the miscarriage in mid-November, make such an inference possible. If she was four or five months pregnant in mid-November, that might explain the seriousness of the miscarriage and the fear of complications that put her into the hospital.

Whether he and Mary had an affair cannot be established with certainty. However, given the many facts of the history, habits, and social world of each person, there is no plausible reason why they should not have had one, and more than enough need on each side to bring it about. The weight of the evidence suggests that they were indeed lovers as well as intellectual compères, for as Hardwick said in another context, "The conjunction of romance and the events of the day is characteristic of Mary at all points of her life."[28] That, of course, was much easier to assert publicly forty-odd years later than it would have been at the time.

It takes a certain amount of mental gymnastics to recognize that the austere leading professor of de Man's years at Cornell and Yale had been a ladies' man, and in the conventional sense, he was not one. Almost ineluctably, women came to him. Until he met Patricia Kelley in 1949, he was not the pursuer. Simply by existing in the aura of personal glamour he exuded, he attracted, one after the other, the most desirable and intelligent women wherever he found himself. (And in so doing, he undoubtedly increased his prestige among men.) Frida, Anne, and Mary all wanted to "bring him happiness." If he and Mary did have an affair, its dynamics were the classic ones of that era, with all its secrecy and gendered asymmetry in terms of social power. It was the 1950s, and from de Man's point of view, a fling, a brief romance with an experienced woman eager to help him, would have been normal. So would dropping people from his life: He would go much further in that direction in the next few months, when he turned away from his own children. McCarthy gave much more, but had little power to hold, control, or retaliate, because she could not speak. It is not surprising, then, that when, drawing toward death, she was asked about de Man in the late 1980s, she cast a cold eye across forty years, laughed about him with Hardwick, and began to resettle her memories before closure came and she could let it all go.

At the time, she handled the matter with a certain amount of grace. She let her friends know of Paul de Man's misdeeds—the reading of her mail, the alleged theft of books, his habitual use of friendship to gain his private ends—and then turned her own page and got on with the rest of her life. For her, the real Europe, which de Man had embodied with illusory glamour, still lay ahead.

27.

BARD

D E MAN GOT OFF TO A BRILLIANT START AT BARD, "WOWING THE STUDENTS" and his colleagues. By mid-December, he was a celebrity, asked to give a campus-wide lecture, made literally a so-called poster boy in a photo shoot for Bard's publicity, and interviewed about his opinions by the student newspaper. The college where he made so quick an impression lies on the slopes of the upper Hudson River, a hundred miles north of New York, and was founded as an Episcopal seminary in the nineteenth century by old New York families that had their Dutch and English roots there. It is a classic small American liberal arts college, established to fill religious pulpits but now secular in spirit, "progressive" in educational philosophy, and open to the arts. Dominated by "the River," a broad and shining ribbon in places almost a mile wide, it was a region of orchards and berry farms.[1] In that Anglophilic era, John Bard, the college's founder, and his descendants had at different times renamed their land "Blithedale" and the village Annandale, in tribute to Walter Scott's romances and in veneration of his own Scottish and English antecedents. The neighboring properties, owned by Roosevelts, Livingstons, Schuylers, Astors, and Beekmans, had produced an "estate culture," which a hundred years ago permitted the owner of Bard's campus to raise his own "light infantry"—in a time of peace—and drill the men of Rhinebeck and Red Hook (probably his employees) in situ.[2] This was Edith Wharton country; in *The House of Mirth*, Lily Bart came to just such a manor as the Vanderbilt home when she aimed to snare a husband but instead lost too much at bridge.[3]

The prevailing mood in the area was conservative. Dutchess County was home to the presidential candidate Thomas Dewey—supporter of Joseph McCarthy—over whom Harry Truman had just triumphed in 1948. J. Edgar Hoover was far more welcome to the local newspaper than Democrats or leftists from the college like Fred Dupee and his friends. The head of the FBI visited and gave a talk locally in early 1950, and months later the *Rhinebeck Gazette* was still vibrating: "The FBI is as near to you as your telephone. . . . This is vitally important now. The forces which are working to undermine us are not always easy to identify. If any fact of any nature comes to your attention which suggests sabotage or espionage, report it at once."[4] In fact, the weather and berry festivals were page-one news. Fillers dealt with "Getting work horses into top condition," and jail was reserved for a peeping Tom or a fight among migrant workers.

At Bard, de Man could recognize the signs of settled wealth, comfortably shabby perhaps, but taken for granted. The fortunes created in nineteenth-century America that had given birth to this college had sprung from the same worldwide industrial forces of expansion that had enabled the Demans on the other side of the Atlantic to rise in two generations from artisans and teachers to become de Mans, company owners and international political leaders. Because Bard had always been seriously underfunded, the college had become expert in struggling with its church-mouse status among wealthy patrons, and the older faculty tended to identify with the problems of the college. When Paul de Man arrived, one of his colleagues, Felix Hirsch, had spent years befriending the college's neighbor, Christian Zabriskie, son of the plutocratic drillmaster, and together they took a walk every morning. In 1951, the efforts of Professor Hirsch and President James Case were rewarded when Zabriskie decided to move down to New York City and leave his immense estate to Bard.[5] Most faculty tended either to possess some private funds, however small, or to come from intellectually elite backgrounds. The college might have been poor, but its mission was to pass on its store of knowledge and social values. Self-made men, immigrants from the working class like Artine Artinian, were rare. Students agitated for unlimited visiting hours in the dormitories, but they did not get their wish. During World War II, the pool of male students had shrunk, and in 1944, Bard had become coeducational. However, far from welcoming women as equals, *The Bardian* now expressed the postwar sentiment that pressured women into gender-specific behavior: A male columnist in the student paper complained in "Jeans and the Jane," for example, that now that women had been admitted, they were not dressing like "ladies," but wearing jeans: "Come on girls, give us a chance. Make *us* gentlemen and we will treat you like ladies."[6]

Along with its new women students, Bard had welcomed a new set of instructors, among them several German-Jewish émigrés, not famous but reasonably distinguished intellectually and in the arts. Some were highly sophisticated and well-trained. In the ten or fifteen years following the war, these included Heinrich Blücher, who was a political scientist and the husband of Hannah Arendt, Felix Hirsch, Kate Wolff, and others. Fred Dupee, who had brought Mary McCarthy to the campus in 1945, had only just left for Columbia. Another leading figure was Irma Brandeis, professor of Italian, described as a "fierce, proud, angelic figure," and the lover of the poet Eugenio Montale, a Roman who had made her his muse.[7] Ted Weiss, a poet, critic, and editor of the *Quarterly Review of Literature*, was head of the Literature Department and was to become de Man's titular boss and an important friend. Under his influence, the campus became a magnet for some of the era's most distinguished American writers: In the 1950s, Saul Bellow, Anthony Hecht, and Ralph Ellison arrived there. In short, in spite of its conservative underpinnings, Bard prided itself on being a place where unconventional talents and credentials were sought after and welcome.

De Man found the quiet of Bard's green campus, dotted by Victorian Gothic stone buildings and shaded by conifers, very agreeable. The place was serene, the people well mannered and some highly sophisticated, and the atmosphere agreeably old-fashioned. "The church was in the middle of the village," de Man used to say with nostalgia to his second wife when trying to describe Belgium, meaning that life was centered there and social oppositions equably balanced by the weight of traditional values. Paradoxically, things were not so different at Bard.

The college is perhaps best known in literary terms for being the setting of Mary McCarthy's roman à clef, *The Groves of Academe*, a political satire on the "anti-anti-communist" backlash among intellectuals of the era. The novel turns on the attempt by a dismissed faculty member to retain his position by manipulating campus sentiment and falsely representing himself as the victim of an anti-Communist purge. Its joking premise springs from a given: that the liberal faculty was so automatically opposed to Joseph McCarthy and committed to defending the Left that they became forced to support their colleague, a disagreeable, duplicitous, whining father of three, who was not the victim he claimed to be. If McCarthy had Paul de Man in mind, it was only in the details: De Man was indeed duplicitous and the father of three, but charm, not whining, was his style, and he stayed strictly away from all political issues.

De Man knew how fortunate he was and undoubtedly recognized that this was a moment when he could change the direction of his life. In accepting the Bard appointment, he wrote Fuller on October 15, 1949, that he hoped "Bard College will be as pleased with my teaching as I am with this opportunity of working in such pleasant, congenial and stimulating surroundings. I could conceive of no better place to start an academic carreer [*sic*] in this country."[8] "Pleasant, congenial and stimulating" were not words de Man could have used to describe the emotions aroused by much that had happened to him over the last ten years. He needed Bard. The cultural capital he brought with him had opened doors in New York City, but it was not the same thing as moral depth: He did not have the exceptional moral insights or intellectual experience of a Nicola Chiaromonte or Hannah Arendt, and it was probably those limitations, and not his imperfect English, that stymied him. In addition, he might also have realized that to the friends he had made in New York, apart from Mary McCarthy, long-term acceptance would depend on demonstrated talent. With his acute social perceptions, he probably grasped that if he did not establish his worth on equal or nearly equal footing, he would soon lose his cachet. In the competitive scrabble of New York, no one had cared that he worked as a clerk, but de Man undoubtedly sensed that ultimately acceptance would be based on fulfilling his implicit promise to be much more.

Real fitting-in would depend on his writing, but his attempts, whether on Koestler or French contemporary literature, had not struck the right note with the right people, and neither Phillips nor Macdonald had put him into print.

Bard, however, was another matter. A sense of excitement probably began five minutes after he first opened a classroom door. It was here that he excelled, and here that he began to recognize his true métier, for here it all came together in a blazing talent: subtlety, intelligence, intuition, love of language, and the glamour of obvious but tacit European origins were enacted in a performance such as these young adults had not seen before. He could interpret and communicate what words meant and what they did not; what mattered and what didn't; who was educated and who was not. Experience and social skills gave him authority; self-assurance and imputed foreign credentials gave him weight. The charm he had been born with now mingled with authority.

De Man's teaching duties were heavy. Bard prided itself on its highly individualized system of instruction and assigned him seven tutorials in addition to two courses. Theoretically, conscientious professors like Mary McCarthy could find themselves preparing seven distinct topics for each of their tutees in addition to teaching two courses. Not all the instructors actually met these demands at a high standard, and some doubled up hours, or skipped some; the poet James Merrill arranged his schedule so that he could be in New York four days out of seven.[9] These shortcuts were frowned on by the administration, and Eve Stwertka reported that the students noticed and resented them. De Man skimped in his first semester, and he had to promise the president that he would reform. The next year also, excuses were made by others on his behalf.[10] Not adjusting well to Bard's "system" was the phrase used to cover this kind of deficiency.[11] He, however, relied on his ability—described by his student and later his colleague Peter Brooks—to sit down in front of a text and make it magic. "He could follow and sustain a very coherent argument for a couple of hours" not in a "dramatistic sense," but with a "power of the mind dealing with texts that you knew were important but didn't quite know why. He was always going to the heart of the processes of meaning and signification."[12] In addition, de Man was always a hard worker who could produce under pressure. He used

Artinian's outlines, dug out what he needed to teach his students, and, above all, relied on his years of reviewing and reading literature as resources.

He had been on campus less than three months when Bard produced a set of images for publicity purposes. Among the photographs, which include Irma Brandeis—and also Artinian posing in a beret before a plaster bust of a French writer—there is one of de Man sharing a classroom with his chairman, Ted Weiss, as he leans forward to address a group seated around him and at his feet. His youthful features ardent, he is intensely focused on a distant point, his hand gesturing slightly for emphasis as the others drink in his words with their eyes. De Man glows in the light, emanating an almost palpable sense of presence. The vivid eyes, pale skin, and the laserlike intensity of his gaze are all evident—he is even wearing the sleeveless sweater that Reuel Wilson, son of Mary and Edmund, recalled much later.

That moment in the spotlight was emblematic, and December 1949 was particularly heady. Less than two months after de Man first set foot on campus, excited students felt that he was changing their outlook on the world, that he was a great man. *The Bardian* interviewed him and reported on a public lecture he had given on philosophy,[13] and Patricia remembered that the next year a group of her fellow undergraduates actually went to the dean in a body and asked that their new instructor be hired as a permanent replacement for Professor Artinian, whom they found less interesting. "Paul was considered just slightly too hot. Students would say [to Artinian], 'Why aren't you fascinating like Paul de Man?'"[14] The next year, a student wrote on an evaluation report, "If I have known a great man, it is Paul de Man." Others were still saying the same thing twenty and more years later. In December 1949, the Literature Department, sharing the students' enthusiasm, reappointed him for the following year, an act that because of its timing and in spite of all subsequent disasters was probably the single most decisive encouragement of his intellectual career. He and Patricia meantime had become lovers and probably conceived their first child in the same week. De Man must have felt himself riding a powerful wave toward success—the first such triumph since Lothar von Balluseck had befriended him in 1942.

Ted Weiss began attending his colleague's classes when his wife, Renée, who was then studying for her B.A. degree, started bringing home her notes and reports. (Romances between professors and students in academic life were then tolerated, although probably not encouraged, and not infrequently led to marriage.)[15] The course Paul taught dealt with the novel, and he used Weiss's reading list. What Ted was hearing was interesting but unorthodox. The students were excited, the ideas new, and he was curious about what de Man had to say. It became something of a three-way conversation. Weiss was the first of the many visitors who would come to sit in on de Man's classes over the years. Only three years older than Paul, he became a close friend. He recalled that a "major component" of the syllabus was Stendhal's *The Red and the Black*,[16] a text that Columbia's Lionel Trilling had, through his influence, made important all over the country.[17] Trilling's approach was humanistic, but Paul hadn't been trained in the United States—hadn't been trained in the literal sense at all—and he had given up the "humanitarian" point of view he had embraced in his adolescence. Weiss could not recall his friend's exact words, but he said that "Paul was concentrating too much in one perception. . . . He was the kind of man who wanted to write one small thing that would change the world. As a teacher he was immediately successful."

As for Paul's character, Weiss found him "a very charming person. He was very winning." If he had a fault, Weiss added, "if I had to say anything critical of Paul, he was a temporizer. He went with the situation, and made the most of it. He was pretty wily and managed to land on his feet." Nevertheless, he found de Man's approach interesting. At one point, they lived on different floors of the same house, and de Man would stop in after classes to talk and argue, intensely wrapped up in his own ideas and eager to express himself. On one issue, Ted and Renée Weiss went out of their way to make a point: De Man was no anti-Semite. Weiss was not only certain of this but, having brought up the subject, added, "We were Jewish and very close friends. [There was] no sense of discomfort or uneasiness." In this, to be sure, he was echoing what every other person said who knew de Man in the 1940s or later, whether in Belgium or in the United States.

What did Paul de Man teach? He published nothing during this period, but one can gain a general idea of his position from a detailed front-page article written by one of his students in *The Bardian* about the lecture he had given on philosophy: "Mr. Paul Deman: he evaluates Surrealism." While he discussed Surrealism, essentially his talk was an attack on Jean-Paul Sartre's ideas from the point of view of the anti-Marxist Left and the existentialism of Georges Bataille and his circle, but de Man avoided mentioning this alliance or using the controversial label *existentialist*. He was to continue the attack for many years and in print as late as 1964.[18] De Man represented himself as engaged on two fronts: working out his own relation to ideas—which embraced Surrealism, aesthetics, and ethics—while taking aim at Sartre and his Marxist materialism, which de Man also avoided naming.

He had entered a new phase in his development, one in which he not only struggled to think philosophically about art but had begun to identify himself with its process. He did not bother to explain to this audience that Bataille and Sartre were avowed enemies, nor did he mention his friend Bataille except in passing. Sartre, he held, had appropriated a number of American naturalistic writers—Dos Passos, Wright, Hemingway, Faulkner, Farrell, and Steinbeck—essentially to serve "his intention to use art as a social phenomenon to further his social aims." Sartre's pet American novelists, de Man believed, were chosen essentially as counters for his own political views. De Man had already informally claimed a critical position toward this philosopher when in his interview with Fuller, Bard's president, he falsely said he had "replied" to Sartre.[19] Now he stated that the writer had shown "a lac[k] of esthetic quality," and his "ideals"—the American writers he favored—reflected his "political purposes." As for the genre of American naturalist writing, he dismissed it: Naturalism took root as an American stance because of the country's particularly "secure" history: "Americans do not have that sense of defeat and failure common to most Europeans due to defeat in wars, particularly in the recent one." The reasoning was simple. Europe had a tragic history that amounted to broken lives and defeat, and these gave rise to Surrealism (a process that, of course, ran parallel to de Man's own experience). The United States was secure, had experienced only victory, and thus had produced naturalism. De Man's deployment of this common cliché lacked depth and was of a piece with his unnuanced reaction to American intellectual assumptions on the beach in Wellfleet when, to his disgust, sand got into the sandwiches and Whitehead got into the discourse. *Crisis* was already a favorite term of de Man's, but he didn't grasp that American thought resisted the excesses and leaps of his form of Surrealism essentially because this culture did not share its underlying, implicit notion that "crisis" and madness are the givens of the human condition.

Surrealism, on the other hand, de Man represented, according to the article, as a philosophic movement motivated by "an attempt to provide writing with 'an awareness of its purpose.'" Its exponents were "The poetry of Elouard [sic] and Breton, [which was] written with the realization of this conflict in mind." The exponents of "good art" in contemporary France de Man identified as "Blanchot, Ponge, Michaux, Georges Bataire [sic] and some of Camus." (With the exception of Camus, these were essentially the same group in which de Man had tried unsuccessfully to interest William Phillips.) De Man explained that Surrealism recognized that while "the sole end and aim of art" was objectivity, achieving objectivity was an impossibility, for "'art can never be perceived as a total object.'" Surrealism had its origins in the insensate slaughter of World War I and its aftermath, but de Man paid almost no attention to its historical context, mentioning only in passing the general intellectual revolution, "of Relativity . . . the discoveries of Einstein" and their "refut[ation] of Newton's theories." From 1918 on, figures like André Breton, Paul Eluard, and Georges Bataille campaigned violently and with deliberate scandal against the shibboleths of the established Order that had created the Great War, but Paul presented their Surrealism not as a turn toward the irrational or as part of a historic continuum of rebellion, but as a freestanding philosophic movement.

Already de Man's subject was fundamentally the relation of literary movements and writing itself to philosophy. Works of art "are unavoidably products of a subjective consciousness." False nineteenth-century notions of "Realism" were the enemy. It was consciousness and its conflicts that preoccupied art. Serious modern artists knew that achieving objectivity was an impossibility. A realistic representation of life was impossible. What art reflected was, rather, the human condition of yearning to know itself, and being frustrated in that search.

What did he have to say that made him so influential? Reflecting on how de Man later became so important a critic, Ted Weiss pointed out that it had been through "developing the philosophic and literary direction he had already taken in Europe" and mixing that with the New Criticism he found first at Bard.[20] That is certainly true, but only part of the phenomenon. De Man transmitted a worldview, a sense of what only was valid, tragic, and inescapable about being human. His persona was persuasive and the subject on which he touched was both fundamental and in general ignored in this country. Given the time, the man, and the place, however one-sided his views were, his success was not surprising. Paul found an audience because he was both unique and a forerunner of broader studies that came afterward. Popular magazines like *Life*, which ran a memorable essay on the oddity of Colin Wilson, a young English philosopher, were just catching up to these new European ideas. But about existentialism's roots in German philosophy, about the teachers of Bataille and the writers whom de Man followed—or the debt of this approach to Heidegger, Husserl, or the Hegel mediated in the 1930s by Alexandre Kojève—little or nothing was known. De Man was careful not to name these forerunners. Instead, his procedure was to present ideas as if they were fresh, original, and without previous history. What de Man expressed therefore had freshness and power, and if one accepted his premises, there were few complexities of history and context to master.

One can also see even through this secondhand account in *The Bardian* several early expressions of themes that were to be ongoing, not only the focus on Surrealism itself but also his attention to the particular process of literature, which uses an "abstract medium, words. Words . . . tend to become the essence of things themselves rather than a representation of the subjective state of describing things." Later, he made the slipperiness of meaning in language a major element of his thought. And one sees him also stressing his already-chosen group of contemporary writers, whose case de Man continued to press throughout the next two decades.

Weiss was undoubtedly right that de Man had a "narrow focus," but he brought something new to the campus and later, more broadly, to American aesthetic thought. What this European, theoretically an atheist, later renowned for the "rigor" of his thought (a rigor subsequently found open to question), brought to considerations of literature was, in fact, something else: an essentially metaphysical focus, for issues of "ontology," or the nature of being, can only be grasped in a context that meditates on the nature and purpose of existence. Metaphysics had for some time been dismissed from the American philosophy syllabus—even more from the literary canon—as impossible to define or discuss rationally. Undergraduates had nowhere to turn for the discussions that arise among young adults about their nature and purpose on this earth. They were, in a sense, as famished as those whom Emerson had addressed over a hundred years earlier when he told Harvard divinity students that the dead doctrine they were learning would cause a moaning in the heart of their future congregations. "Deal out to the people your life," he urged, "life passed through the fire of thought." De Man had nothing else in common with the Transcendentalist, but in this one issue, both were ultimately concerned with what Heidegger (himself a failed priest) had taught generations to call authenticity. Paul de Man caught the attention and enthusiastic support of young adults in large part because he seemed to point a way by which thinking could gain "an awareness of its purpose." When he presented himself before them, intense and ardent, it was he who was seeking that awareness. Long afterward, he continued to gather followers enchanted by what was often called his "aura"—a mixture of intellectuality, deep commitment, austerity, and vision with a peculiar personal charm. His defenders said the seductive impression he gave was unwilled; his critics more sourly asserted that the performance was conscious and his confusing and inconsistent use of language an easy cover-up for a lack of substance. It was said in the 1960s among some Cornell humanities professors, when de Man taught there, that one did not teach the text; one taught oneself. De Man had great insights into texts, but he also possessed an actor's ability to project his own passionate image and inspire others with ideas that were less than transparent. It was not accidental that "performance" became one of his bywords in later years. Evidently, both his own performance and the impression he gave of deep engagement with a quest were being shaped in his first months at Bard.

De Man projected wordlessly, tacitly, a true paradox his students were in no position to apprehend rationally but could probably perceive in other ways: Behind the supposed "rigor" and the austere mask of the man devoted to thought alone was a figure they found exemplary, someone who was wrestling with what it was to be human in a world defined by tragic limitations. He believed this about himself, and they believed in him. Had he begun to think about the historical and personal questions he faced, and privately to take responsibility for his own mistakes? Clearly that "sense of defeat and failure" he attributed to Europeans in general was his own, and the deep furrows of anxiety and tension later so visible in his face must have begun to show their traces around this time. It is clear, however, that he was following an existential path in the Sartrean mode in "fleeing forward" and leaving behind past anguish. With Pat Kelley, he would move toward a new family and a new life; he would look only ahead, and she would learn nothing of his problematic career in Belgium. He was not ready to overcome those failures and defeats by confronting or admitting them even to those closest to him, and he never would be. His path would be erasure and repression of the past.

28.

"LIES, AND LIES, AND LIES"

———————

PAUL AND PAT RETURNED TO BARD IN EARLY JANUARY 1950 TO A PER-petually improvised existence. Paul had already found his salary too meager to maintain his way of life and pay the rent, and this from the beginning he failed to do. Much less could he support a wife and child. Moreover, his reappointment at Bard was not yet technically complete. He had, however, chosen well in Pat, who was the opposite of Anne in every way. Innately attractive, she was indifferent to clothes and social status, much less money. Life with her wealthy but unstable mother had taught her that securing a place in society was a worthless pursuit. Paul was her first real attachment, and once won over by him, she was passionately in love and remained so. With a bent for study and scholarship, she was a natural member of the academic community and felt no need to claim a place as a matron in the class she had abandoned.

As for Paul, although he had willingly entered into collaboration in Belgium, he now wanted to forget the downward spiral of his life there and to bury that past far out of sight. His years with Anne had been toxic. In another time, their affair might have been a passing relationship between two young people. Or had he been in a less turbulent period of his life and less resentful of his father, he might have broken off the relationship before he was totally committed. Instead, it had been cemented by the pressures of war and, above all, Anne's determination. Now, however, he had found—and seized on—a highly intelligent, cultivated woman who loved him, made no demands, and was amazed and delighted by his talents. Foolish in so many things, when he encountered Pat, he was wise enough to determine not to lose her. Pat recognized his emotional commitment, and it sustained her in the difficult months of her pregnancy and throughout their marriage. She came to see his faults, but early on she learned to close her eyes to many of them. For his part, he clung tightly to her: There is no doubt that in a real sense she became the hero of his story. Without her, the next ten years of his life were unlikely to have ended as well as they did, for it was a decade that only a very strong woman convinced of her husband's genius could have endured.

Their first year together was operatic in its drama. Having proposed marriage to Pat and written to Anne demanding a divorce, de Man had another woman, Mary McCarthy, to break off with. This he effected in late January 1950. Anne, however, was a different matter. Neither she nor her parents were prepared to let this marriage go. The couple had lived together for eight years, been married since 1944, and had three sons to bring up. She was an attentive mother, if a difficult one, and everything in her determined, emotional character was prepared to fight for the continuation of her legal alliance.

By March 1950, Paul and Pat were essentially living together. She had entered her fourth month of pregnancy, and he wanted her near him, so she stayed in his large house—ill-heated, for fuel was expensive. The snow that fell on the late winter morning of March 5 was the least startling event of the day. Pat was in class and Paul was asleep when the phone rang. Anne de Man was calling from La Guardia Airport, where she had arrived in a snowstorm with twenty dollars in her pocket, no command of English, and three children in tow. She had in her luggage the expensive new dresses that Paul had told her to buy, so that he could show her off to high-society women such as Mary McCarthy and Peggy Guggenheim. She had planned this unexpected arrival to surprise her errant husband; it was her response to his notice that he wanted a divorce. As she recalled, "He didn't show up. Nobody came. . . . He was with her [Patricia]. I arrived with twenty dollars in La Guardia. The stewardess called him. They took him out of the bed."

The redoubtable Anne then found Grand Central Terminal, boarded the train with her children and luggage, and arrived in Rhinebeck. Of course she had received his letter. But unlike Mary, she had legal claims and was not prepared to go quietly.[1]

"I came by surprise," she said later. "He picked us up—he came with his small smile: 'Everything will be all right.' And then he was very nice. But he was in such a situation. This woman . . ."

There was his "small smile" again, always disarming. She had waited in Argentina for a year and a half to be summoned to join him. And then on January 11, 1950, the birthday of their oldest son, Rik, she received the letter she had been waiting for ever since she had heard about Paul's new job. She supposed it would contain money and the tickets for her passage with her sons to the United States. Instead, she found his demand for a divorce. "Cruelty," she said. The unhappiness and violent fights, his failures in business, the collapse of her own ambitions and plans, the ever-looming threat of postwar prosecution, whether for collaboration or for fraud—even their secret flight from the threatened trial—these were not now the issue. She had no adequate source of funds and three children to provide for.

Neither saw the other as they saw themselves. De Man believed that her parents were rich and could well support her. She reported that, on the contrary, her life in Buenos Aires since June 1948 had been difficult; money was short, and she had lived crammed into a single room of her parents' apartment, sleeping with her three boys, who ranged in age from nine to four. Her middle-aged father had emigrated after the war, but he was not equipped to begin over at his former level. Paul also knew that she had become involved with a Romanian businessman named Peter Brajatuli, who was supporting her. Anne described Brajatuli as politically dubious and personally repulsive, a "double agent" who had raped her, she reported, but her mother refused to inform Anne's father and had instead pressed her to accept his protection for her children's sake. Once under his control, she was put to work by him in a cottage industry he had begun, making yogurt in the apartment where they lived. Moreover, although not divorced from de Man, she first married and later divorced Brajatuli "in Mexico," but without having gone there. She later described the marriage as "illegal."[2] Brajatuli, although not faithful to her, was good to her two younger sons, who came to like him.[3] When de Man's ultimatum arrived in January, Anne's father had advised her to take the long journey to New York, confront Paul, and try to salvage their union. "I did not want to go," she recalled, but "my father said it was my duty."

Once Anne arrived on that snowy day and entered his house with their children, Paul insisted—over Pat's strenuous objections—on spending the night with his wife, perhaps the better to try to persuade her to leave. A month of extreme tension followed, with confrontations, screams, and threats on both sides. Anne was shocked and furious, for she soon found mortifying evidence that another woman had been living in the house. Paul, displaying even more than his normal secrecy, wanted Anne to stay out of sight, and for a time he quit the Artinian home. It was untenable for Anne. "We had nothing to eat," she remembered, but she conceded that "he sent a grocer finally with food." Had he known she was coming, he might have laid in supplies, but that would have disrupted the dramatic entrance she had planned.

Dealing with Anne over the divorce while trying to conceal her presence in Annandale became for Paul a return to one of the worst periods of their lives together, a dance of despairing aggression. He kept Patricia in the dark about the facts to the full extent of his powers of mystification. That she put up with and turned a blind eye to some of the confusion suggests both her commitment to her companion and her vulnerability: Pregnant and unmarried but not wishing to "trap" him, certain of her lover's devotion, she let things take their course. The arguments between Anne and Paul became even more extreme than they had been in Belgium. "We were very emotive," Anne said of herself and her family, but the de Mans' habits were low in key, and Paul hated to fall back into the pattern of shouts, blows, and threats. He demanded that his wife not leave the house. "He convinced me he would be in the street [if she did not grant the divorce]. He want[ed] to strangle me. He said, 'If you want to make me difficulties, I will kill you and I will kill myself.'" Gesturing, she described how her eldest child, Rik, was across the room, and asserted that he recalled the scene in Annandale. (Asked about this, Rik Woods did not remember it.)[4] She had not understood how utterly incapable Paul was as a businessman. Trapped in her own imperfect vision of his capacities, she wanted him to return with her to Argentina and go into the import-export business with her father.

Everything about their supposed divorce is murky and confused, except for the fact that it did not take place. Paul de Man was determined to stay in academic life with Pat in the United States. He had already been cleared by the Literature Department for reappointment, and he could reasonably expect promotion and tenure in those days when such privileges were more readily granted. His wife, on the other hand, was equally determined to hold on, and she had plenty of reason to do so. She, too, was trapped. Paul's basic reason for keeping Anne and the children out of sight was almost certainly that March was the month when the reappointments already recommended by the faculty would be ratified by the president and his council, and Anne had arrived at the critical moment when the letters of reappointment or dismissal were being prepared. If a scandal had broken out at this delicate point, it could have ruined him. Fortunately, on March 22, 1950, President Fuller sent de Man a letter of agreement, renewing his contract as an instructor in literature for the year beginning July 1, 1950, at a salary of three thousand dollars. This was heartening news. It meant that if things went smoothly, he at last had a career ahead of him, the very pathway that in Belgium had been closed by his acts during the occupation and his lack of a degree. The president significantly added in a postscript that he would take up the matter of a promotion "later this spring" with the trustees.[5] De Man was favored and on the fast track.

With his contract in hand, Paul was in a stronger position to negotiate with Anne. Now he had proof that he had a real future in the United States. He argued that he was determined to live with Patricia and end his relationship with Anne, and that she would fare better with her parents in Argentina, where the money de Man promised to send would go much further. Somehow, in the process she had secured legal counsel, and after the shouting ended, she, exhausted, signed a contingent agreement to divorce. Her conditions were stringent: a lump-sum payment of $5,000 and a monthly allowance of $250. "Paul gave me a very good settlement," Anne reported. This was another of Paul's fantasies, yet she believed his lie, as she had often done before. De Man had neither the capability nor the intention of paying any part of the money: The promised monthly allowance was ten dollars more per month than his gross salary before taxes; the lump sum was even further out of his reach. Anne could not have known this, but he did, and his indifference to reality at this point was to have devastating results on his future freedom, not to mention the condition of all his dependents, of whom he would soon have six. As for Anne, she actually had little choice. She could see that for Paul holding on to his new job was crucial. It was obvious that his future—and thus her income—depended on it. She allowed herself to be persuaded that for as long as he was able to keep the job at Bard, she could hope for support. On the other hand, if she made a public stir and he lost his job, they would both be worse off. What he did have was an increasingly and soon visibly pregnant wife-to-be, whom he had already promised to marry, and not enough income even to meet the rent.

Anne never met her rival, but she knew a child was on the way. Whether or not she believed Paul's threat that he would kill himself, she knew that her husband was immovable when he had set his mind on a given course, however impractical it might seem. Very reluctantly, she agreed to the proposed settlement. On April 5, eight days after he had signed his copy of the letter of agreement with the college, she departed with her two younger sons for South America. She had never worn her new gowns for Mmes. Guggenheim and McCarthy. The couple borrowed one thousand dollars from Pat's father, Ogden Alfred Kelley, to pay for Anne's tickets, but she did not go quietly. In a last, dramatic, and very public act, she took Rik, her firstborn son, to the campus green, where, with the community standing about and without prior notice to anyone, she handed the ten-year-old boy over to his father, abandoning him to a man she knew did not want to keep him. Those who witnessed this scene were astonished.[6] Then she and the two younger boys departed. Rik felt then and later that her motive was to use him to keep Paul tied to her, and he instantly understood and resented the manipulation even as a child. Anne reported that it was understood that Rik would remain in the United States with his father for the school year, visit Argentina during the summers, and that on alternate years she and her sons would journey to the United States to be reunited with Paul.[7]

The only part of the arrangement that was realized was Rik's continued and permanent residence in United States. It was actually a relief to be free of his mother, who he already knew was charming, but temperamental and difficult, and "could turn on a dime" from good nature to blows. "I was a mess," he recalled as a grown man and successful executive.[8] Energetic and intelligent, he made friends at school and learned English quickly. Annandale was a welcome haven, and he liked Patsy.

Anne soon found that the settlement Paul had agreed to was meaningless. He did not pay what she needed to feed, clothe, and educate their children. Instead, he "sent twenty dollars, thirty dollars." Even the first check he gave her for $250 proved "faux." For Anne, the months and years of stress, disappointment, and pain had culminated in total loss. "What stories he did with the divorce. He did lies, and lies, and lies without any shame."[9] The memory was still fresh in her mind more than forty years later as she exclaimed against his treatment. In the years following this agreement, she turned to all the means she could find to enforce it and to pressure him into compliance.

PAUL AND PAT WERE trammeled by multiple difficulties after Anne departed. They had with them young Rik, and by April, Pat's pregnancy was beginning to show. In an era when even married women were often forced out of employment once they were seen to be with child, a college student usually was not permitted to marry at all, much less to appear on campus in a pregnant state. Anne's visit had not really been kept secret, and her dramatic departure had added to the scandal and instability of the situation. Paul de Man could face that possibility: For him, it was one more crisis.[10] Part of his charismatic appeal for his followers was the sense he projected of one who lived face-to-face with infinitely important ideas and decisions—which they might not even have thought of—and who had stripped himself bare and was ready for the engagement. The state of inner conflict became something he drew on; in a sense, he thrived on uncertainty in his life, as he later did in his linguistic philosophy. As Patricia said much later, "He was insouciant" when he made mistakes or took on more than he could manage. "That was his great strength. I just had the feeling that people would break themselves on that," on his strong ego.[11]

There was much more damage to come regarding Paul's supposed divorce, however. Patricia believed that after giving Anne written notice of his intention to seek a divorce, he procured one in Arkansas.[12] His story was made of whole cloth, however, and research has shown both that no divorce occurred and that de Man could not even have filed for one. Although Arkansas had once been a state where divorce was easy, Arkansas after 1947 had required that anyone filing for divorce must appear in person as plaintiff, and that this must be followed by two months of residency. Case law has revealed that judges looked askance at one who thought he could "come into this state, pay three months' board, leave the state, and then return to prosecute his suit upon the theory that he has resided in the state for three months." Similarly, a man who in January 1946 had rented a hotel room in Arkansas by the week and then filed for divorce two months later lost his suit for lack of "bona fide residence."[13] This ruling is crucial in understanding Paul de Man's subterfuge, for it would have been impossible for him to have been absent from his teaching duties for two months between January and June, and he was not. If he left Annandale at all, he could only have gone down to New York, stayed a few days, and turned around. At some uncertain date, de Man also told Patricia that his divorce had failed because the Arkansas law had been changed between the time he had started his supposed trip and the final judgment, but that was also false.[14]

In this matter, de Man was deceiving both his wife, Anne, and his fiancée, Patricia. He had no means or intention of paying his wife's settlement and knew that no agreement he signed with her would be valid; it was only a means of getting her out of the country. He was certainly lying when he told Pat in 1950 that he had secured a divorce in Arkansas.

Patricia de Man reported that the couple was married in June 1950, in Yonkers, New York, a suburb adjacent to New York City on the Hudson River, with her mother and stepfather in attendance as wit-nesses.[15] According to her, this was not an unclouded occasion. Paul had told her of his resentment at being "trapped" by Anne into marriage because of her pregnancy, and the young American woman did not want to marry her lover under the "forced" circumstances he blamed on Anne. "I had told him the opposite, that I did not want to marry him under any sort of forced arrangement, and he said, 'Oh no. This is what I want.'"[16] In this case, it appears that Paul was the one who was pressing for the ceremony. Yet when they were at the marriage license bureau, Paul instructed his bride, " '[Where it asks] if you've been married before, don't fill in that I have been married before. The lawyer told me that this would hold it up.' " As it turned out, Lucy Woods had reconciled with her daughter after the quarrel over the Easter holiday and attended the ceremony, but she refused permission for Pat to be wed from her home in Washington. Although a veteran of numerous affairs herself, she intended to keep up appearances and protect her daughter's reputation

The second Mrs. de Man reported that she had no inkling that she was living in bigamy for a decade because her marriage in 1950 was invalid. She later pointed out that this lighthearted attitude and indifference was typical of Paul's behavior and character. He did not, for example, secure a driver's license until they moved to Boston in late 1951, although he had been driving for at least two years in New York. He also had numerous difficulties with his passport that resulted from disregard of the regulations. This unresolved issue concerning the supposed divorce had consequences that would fester and powerfully affect him and his family.

Pat had an evident patience, more like a talent for taking things as they came. So far as she knew during that summer of 1950, her life was on track. She spent the last three months of her pregnancy peacefully reading in Annandale while Paul prepared for the fall semester. His standing at the college had already been questioned by some, but now that they were married, the couple hoped that Pat's mother would in some way come to their aid. This she did when she proposed in August 1950 to take nine-and-a-half-year-old Hendrik off their hands. Mrs. Woods and her husband found the boy very attractive, and she was prepared to educate him in Washington in the style to which her family was accustomed. Pat had no reason not to agree to this, and Paul turned his back on his paternal obligations without hesitation. Hendrik was adopted by Mr. and Mrs. Charles Woods, and he took the surname Woods a few years later.

From then on, Paul de Man saw nothing of any of his sons, not even Rik.[17] It is hard to understand why he avoided his firstborn son, an intelligent and talented boy. With a baby on the way, he could not support Rik, but he didn't even call, write, or permit visits; even many years later, he did not return a phone call from the adolescent Rik.[18] No doubt de Man felt that any contact would link him to an earlier, disgraceful life and feared any threat to his fragile new existence. He also believed, according to both Patricia and Rik himself, that Anne had manipulatively left Rik behind as a kind of Trojan horse, abandoning her son in the hope of maintaining contact with Paul.[19] This, de Man was absolutely determined to thwart, and if Rik had to disappear from his life, he willingly made that choice. De Man's early writings show a debt to Heidegger and his search for authentic selfhood, but, in developing deconstruction, he came to attack the notion that there is a stable self or any stability to language itself. He would later, as a teacher, speak of the "*abîme*," the abysm of existential life. In view of his personal history, his theory, or philosophy, became a rational explanation of the life process. Gaps—*aporia*, to use the term he made current—were all around him, fissures in the melting ice floe of existence. It is an understatement to say that fatherhood was not de Man's strong suit, as this example of extreme self-regard painfully demonstrates.[20] Eventually, Rik Woods got past those difficult years and forgave his father. Whether de Man forgave himself, or indeed whether he ever blamed himself, is impossible to know. Anne, who had many faults but was very attached at least to her younger sons, later commented, "He was always when you saw . . . with guilt." She filled in the lacuna by drawing her hands over her face, gesturing as if drawing the deep lines that appear in the later photographs of her former husband.

Patricia liked Rik but was glad her mother took responsibility for him, for she would be a mother herself very soon. She was trustful of Paul and content with her new life, as she worked at home on her translation of Molière's *L'Ecole des femmes*, "The School for Wives." This was a senior project she had started with Artine Artinian and that, reliable even in difficult times, she finished. Paul was also working from home.[21] Sometime in August, a few weeks before her first grandson was born, Lucy Woods arrived to pick up young Rik. She did nothing further for the couple, neither visiting nor helping with hospital expenses. They were on their own. Paul, however, was probably more at peace than he had been in many years. He had a wife, would soon be a father, had friends and supporters in Ted Weiss and Irma Brandeis, and once more had found a place in society. Above all, a career to which he was perfectly suited seemed to lie before him.

29

BAD WEATHER

———

From the week in April 1950 when Anne departed until the couple very quietly and without notice to their friends left Annandale in July 1951, they endured what was perhaps the most disastrous period of their lives together, one that tested and changed them both. Literally and figuratively, it was the year the roof fell in. Yet it was also the year when for the first time another de Man began to emerge: a man credited by one colleague with "unostentatious brilliance," whom some students thought was "a great man"; a man also who for the first time could use the word *serious* in a positive sense.

The weather was fierce on a Saturday in late November when Paul and Patricia, needing kindling for the antiquated coal furnace of their rickety cottage, stepped outside into a violent storm, which was referred to locally as a "land hurricane." It battered the area as it drove up through the Northeast, felling trees, disrupting traffic, and bringing down power lines. Snow was falling, their two-month-old baby was inside, and they needed heat.[1] They were in the woodshed when a tree fell onto the roof and trapped both of them in the wreckage. Pat clawed her way free, but Paul could not move; he was immobile. She was alone and couldn't budge the heavy beams holding him down. The wood broke his collarbone, slightly crushed his skull, and damaged a nerve. He was taken to the hospital, his right arm temporarily paralyzed.[2] The experience was emblematic of their existence at Bard.

Paul's reputation had continued to grow during the previous spring, but his impressive public persona as the unconventional, witty law-giver, the dashing lover with grand ideas and a grand house to match, was very different from the private man. Pat and he had been living together openly, but she was in an ambiguous position as her pregnancy advanced. Shy by nature, she did not well sustain the occasions when they had to appear in public. In the eyes of the older faculty, the couple were suspect, and they did not, it seems, believe Paul's assertion that they were married. No one challenged them publicly, but they were closely watched, especially by friends of Artine Artinian. The college community could not know that when Anne left, de Man had merely swept the problem out of sight. In fact, by being unable to pay her what he had promised in writing, he was turning Anne into a determined enemy, even more so than she had already become. He had lived with her for eight years and might have anticipated the nature of her anger, but her feelings were irrelevant to him, a serious error both pragmati-cally and ethically.

It was the same fatal lack of imagination about others' needs and probable behavior in the ensuing months that would help destroy his career at Bard, for he was soon up against a much stronger and more entrenched enemy than Anne in Artine Artinian, his theoretical bene-factor and actual landlord. He and the professor of French had begun their relationship with seeming warmth, and de Man gave him a list drawn from his own circle of friends as potential contacts for Artinian's stay in Paris—but it was useless, a list written on a scrap of paper with-out addresses, nothing like the letters of reference he knew how to write.[3] Artinian would have to make headway there on his own. The fundamental issue between them once again was money, although de Man was also much less tactful in his early years, before he came under the "tutelage" of his second wife, as she put it, and he made enemies. He was "abrasive" toward his older colleagues, his wit was "harsher," and he alienated some people unnecessarily.[4] In spite of the obvious need to remain on good terms with this man, from the beginning he had not paid even part of his rent. He had a modest but reasonable salary, one on which other instructors not only lived but raised families, albeit in straitened circumstances. Annandale was not an expensive community, and while there wasn't a great deal of surplus wealth, there also wasn't much to splurge on: both Teddy Artinian, Artine's wife, and Margaret Shafer, Mary McCarthy's friend, testified to the common practice of passing around clothes, not only for the benefit of the children but themselves, as well. That was decidedly not Paul's style, which was munificence, not careful penny-pinching.

Indeed, Paul sent Anne nothing. Money slipped through de Man's fingers at the best of times, but Artinian had set the rent at seventy-five dollars per month for his capacious and well-furnished dwelling, one that he rented from the college for approximately forty dollars. Since faculty housing was subsidized, it was forbidden to sublet at higher rates, and some later felt that the extra thirty-five dollars was excessive. Artinian believed that his furnishings, books, and the like added value to the property.[5] If de Man had paid the rent in his first year, he would have had only about $125 a month after taxes left for all his other needs. Undoubtedly, he had large initial expenses, and these included buying the old Ford he still drove sans license some two years later, for one could not live in Annandale without a car.[6] Those needs were immediate and his landlord was far away. From the beginning, he gave Artinian only promises. He was already in arrears when, only two weeks after moving in, he wrote the older man on November 3, 1949, that his failure to pay his debt was due to an "administrative contretemps" that had delayed his receipt of the money he was "expecting from Europe"—a mythical sum, since no one in Europe had any idea where he was, and if they had known they would have been seeking funds rather than sending them. Paul said he had deposited $100 into Artinian's account in Red Hook, and he promised to pay the following $210 he still owed "as rapidly as possible," but he did not.[7]

It had happened before in New York, as his five removals in fifteen months suggest. He was now being dunned for rent on the East Seventy-second Street apartment, which he owed to Oscar Nitzschke, father of a French friend, as Artinian discovered from a letter de Man unconcernedly left behind.[8] Once again, as in his dealings with the De Vos family in the Hermès affair, Paul de Man had used the father of a friend to bankroll his life, but the elder Nitzschke was not a knowing contributor and could not afford it.

By April 1950, Paul was about six months in arrears—that is, he had not paid the rent at all. Artinian kept in touch with his friends on campus, and money was very important to him. That month, writing from abroad, he took vigorous steps to recover his funds. Soon he would be an open enemy, and with that, de Man's position, already made shaky by the marital scandal and Pat's pregnancy, began to fall apart. De Man normally could talk his way around his creditors, but in Artinian he was dealing with a sharp businessman, who by the next semester came to feel he was fighting not only for money owed but for his professional life. Artinian believed he was grossly underpaid by the college, but his entrepreneurship in collecting and selling prints was not appreciated by many, including the students whom he tended to ignore while chaperoning them in Paris. When he started to campaign against de Man in the fall, his actions divided campus opinion.[9]

Artinian corresponded with Willi Frauenfelder, the professor of German at Bard, who along with Artinian had been on the committee that had hired de Man and was an old friend. Frauenfelder knew about Anne de Man's visit and the breakup even before she left Annandale in hyper-dramatic style, and in late March he was already sending news to his absent friend about the scandal:

> I will report briefly and factually on the deMan [sic] affair. Mrs. deMan arrived apparently unexpectedly with the 3 children. . . . Paul spends a great deal of time in New York, settling, I presume, what is to be settled. He has not offered any information and I have not asked him. There are all sorts of rumors. The whole thing is very unfortunate.[10]

Bard faculty members were very aware of one another's practices: When even the popular Mary McCarthy, teaching for the first time, paused in her discourse, Artinian, listening in the next room, noticed long silences in her classroom.[11] As of March, de Man had missed six months' payments, and Artinian laid out a strategy and wrote Frauenfelder on April 3. On May 9, Frauenfelder reported, "I spoke immediately to Paul and he told me without a moment's hesitation that he had just written to you and explained and settled everything." Now he concluded that "either he is telling fibs, or he is so absent-minded and unsettled that he doesn't know what he is doing." Probably at his friend's request, he had "given the facts to Ernest Hayes and he will try to pin him down and do for you what he can short of using a sheriff's badge and stick."[12] Ernest Hayes was the college bursar, and while his powers did not include garnishment of Paul's salary, which was a legal action, he carried much influence. He could and did suggest garnishment to Artinian, and in the long run became the agent of an equivalent action, which had an equally disastrous effect on the couple.

Willi Frauenfelder was a hospitable Swiss-born man, recently appointed counselor to foreign students, and he passed on to Artinian details of the younger instructor's behavior at a reception he had recently given. Paul and Patricia were living together with Rik and "they are supposed to be married. No announcement has been made of any sort," but although "the Dean suggested something to that effect to Paul . . . nothing has come of it yet." Frauenfelder evidently felt it incumbent on the community to help integrate the couple by organizing some kind of reception, but they'd decided to do nothing for them "as long as Pat is a student." She was scheduled to graduate that spring. Pat, he added, "never look[s] you in the face and giv[es] you no chance to speak to her. At the International Student weekend I introduced Paul to a Belgian from the U.N.; Pat stood somewhat apart, but Paul made no effort to introduce his wife, walked away with the guest while Pat strode off in a different direction."

It was a critical moment. Even to admit to this functionary that he was a member of Henri de Man's family could have been explosive. A well-connected man from the upper levels of Belgian society who questioned him in Patricia's presence might be capable of revealing to her and the assembled party information about de Man's antecedents and the de Man family's wartime position. He might even elicit from Patricia facts that he could pass back to officials in Belgium, where de Man's case was still open and he was a fugitive from justice. Paul had to live in fear of denunciation throughout his life in the United States. One cannot know what he might have whispered as he walked away with his arm around the shoulder of his compatriot, but Paul was always fertile in invention and persuasive. At any rate, it was enough to keep the other man silent. Still, Frauenfelder was critical of Paul's behavior. "I have rarely," he reported, "seen such an ultra-bohemian couple as they are." As for Rik, he wrote, "The boy Henry is a nice kid, self-assured and aggressive and, of course, running quite wild."[13] For Patricia, it must have been painful to appear in public, five months pregnant, and be rendered invisible by her companion when he had to deal with a compatriot.

Troubles accumulated. Garnishment of Paul's small salary began to loom. In May, Ernest Hayes became directly involved. He wrote the absent professor that de Man had responded to a note and told him that he thought he had paid $250 in bits and pieces, whose dates he couldn't recall, but that maybe he hadn't paid in full, that he'd pay it all by month's end, and that thereafter he'd pay Hayes the seventy-five dollars' rent directly. Hayes's polite skepticism was muted. He merely transmitted the information this time, and "no bones broken at all, at all." But at the end of June, he reported that de Man hadn't ponied up. "It may be that's the way he does business," he said (with a copy to de Man), and "short of a garnishment" he could do no more—that would be Artinian's role. He pointedly referred to "all the campus gossip," which his correspondent would already have "picked up from émigrés to Paris." Finally, on August 1, Hayes received another missive from de Man, predated by a month. The instructor was again talking of "still expecting daily the arrival of money," but in the meantime he had paid nothing toward the debt. In consequence, evidently he planned to avoid formal garnishment by authorizing Hayes to withhold a portion of his salary: "Starting from October," Hayes was to "withhold $75.00 from his pay check until the complete amount is paid."[14]

De Man was supporting Patricia now, and he would soon have the costs related to their new infant, who was expected in early September. There would be hospital expenses and doctors' fees, as well as the cost of furnishings, clothing, and the like. All of this would have to come out of a monthly income that, after deducting the monthly rent due to Artinian, would have been perhaps $160. This would mean real indigence. The couple didn't have enough money to keep themselves going. They stayed in Artinian's house till mid-August, then moved to an unfurnished gardener's cottage on the Merritt estate. Mrs. Woods arrived to take Rik away that month. She was not even present when Pat gave birth on September 7. They named the baby Michael.

Young Rik had been in good spirits when he departed with Lucy Woods in August. He recalled, "I was not all that unhappy with what had happened. I liked the company of Patsy and Paul. I was having a good time, you know, as a child at Bard. [It was] a congenial place, and the notion of going to Mr. and Mrs. Woods was quite appealing to me." After living with his "very volatile, very emotional and physical" mother, Lucy Woods's home "was a kind of a haven," and he was also aware that he was a pawn in Anne's game: "By remaining with Paul, I represented her link to Paul."

Rik, who would later take the surname Woods, knew that his mother would eventually seek contact with him, but she was silent for more than a year after leaving him without notice. That is, to put it mildly, a very long time for a child. In his own view, his mother wasn't deeply involved: "I don't think my mother made such extraordinary efforts to reach me, either. There may have been a letter or something," but the attempt was not "pro-active."[15] It is on this issue of Paul's abandonment of his children that even his onetime close friends, such as Georges Goriély—who as a Jew himself defended de Man strongly against charges of anti-Semitism—simply shook their heads in profound disapproval.[16]

THE COTTAGE WHERE THE COUPLE lived from September 1950 on had not been refurbished since the end of the nineteenth century. The rent was low, and they had electricity and running water, but the heating system was primitive. It was unusual even for that era that water for the cottage was furnished by a windmill.[17] There were essentially no furnishings, and the couple scrounged for what they needed at flea markets. Paul took a loan to buy a washing machine, one so old that it came with a mangle. Health insurance was a rarity and the couple had none. By November, the bill for Pat's uncomplicated delivery and for Paul's injuries in the storm amounted $324—a sum approaching two months' take-home pay. But the child, Michael, was healthy, and when the students returned at the end of the month, they showed their favorite teacher their support by running a notice in a box in their newspaper at the top of page one:

> Son born to Mr. and Mrs. Paul De Man [*sic*]. On behalf of the entire Convocation the BARDIAN would like to express a warm welcome to Michael De Man the very latest addition to the Bard campus. We're sure he'll find everything to his liking.[18]

By mid-August, Artinian had returned to Bard and his home, and its condition was not to his liking. He had put the bursar to work and eventually recovered all the arrears of rent, approximately $750. Then he had a new complaint: De Man had damaged or lost some of his belongings.[19] Artinian presented de Man with a list of the items, for which, he claimed, he was owed $93. De Man gave him $10 for a missing iron and returned some of the other items. Artinian, ever a collector, kept the list.

When miseries gather strength together, it is common to say that things cannot get worse, but in fact they did. In December, while de Man was still convalescing and in bed, three men, all wearing identical tan raincoats, knocked on the door. They were agents from the Immigration and Naturalization Service, and they were there to deport him. He had entered the country in 1948 with the stated intention of remaining five months; in 1950, he probably changed his status on the grounds of his marriage to an American citizen. His widow believed that someone had advised the INS that his marriage was invalid, jeopardizing the status of his visa. A handwritten annotation on the manifest of his ship, the *Ames Victory*, shows that on November 18, 1950, in New York a "W/A" was issued; the code is unclear, but some official action was taken, no doubt in connection with the interview a few weeks later. De Man eluded this trap in his usual way—by persuasion and charm. He pleaded his injury, the men demanded to see his scars—which he readily exhibited—and they went away.[20] He had eluded Vinçotte, and an interrogation like this one, with all the evidence of his suffering written on his body and the signs of his normal, indeed prestigious, professional status around him—the wife, the infant child, the books, the dog Patsy could never live without, the professorship itself—was hardly a challenge. It would be years before he heard from the INS again.

Artinian's hostility, however, did not diminish, and their relations were the antithesis of cordial, as together they formed a department with only two members and had to confront each other at receptions and on campus. It was during this period that, according to Pat de Man (as mentioned earlier), a group of students went to the president and asked that de Man be appointed to replace Artinian. No doubt this contributed to Artinian's action when he publicly attacked Paul de Man and called on other faculty to be his judges. Ted Weiss reported that "Artinian brought charges against Paul even though he had not broken or taken things. It's my impression—I assumed he cooked up a case against Paul to get rid of him. Understand, he was the only teacher of French."[21] Patricia de Man believed that Artinian was jealous of Paul's success with the students and that he worked to influence the administration and other faculty against her husband. This opinion was shared by Ted Weiss and Irma Brandeis.

Unfortunately, de Man was still incurring other debts, and in December everything came to a head—the money he had owed Artinian and its aftermath of hostility resulting from the professor's public campaign against him, the large bills he owed the hospital for both his own injuries and Michael's birth, other essential expenses, and, of course, underlying it all, the marital scandal. De Man had purchased a refrigerator and the washing machine from the Haen Jewelry Store, which doubled as an appliance store. He had used the installment plan, but although essential, his purchases were beyond his means. He was completely unable to manage his medical costs.

The final blow came in the midst of all this when, perhaps spurred by Artinian's campaign, the administration of the college turned dramatically against its instructor. President Fuller had resigned in mid-year due to ill health and had been replaced by James Case, an urbane, wealthy man who did not in the long run prove popular with the faculty. Born rich, the son of a deputy governor (later chairman) of the Federal Reserve Bank of New York, he was very well connected, but his decade as head of Bard did not go smoothly.[22] The new president decided to get rid of the offending instructor unceremoniously. Without notice, he, the bursar, Edward Hayes, and the dean—the three chief officers of the college—appeared in a body at Paul's bedside at home, where he was still recuperating from his injuries. On the spot and in Patricia's presence, they fired him. Later in the month, the president held a "three-cornered conversation" in his office among himself, Hayes, and de Man, a meeting at which de Man presented "a plan to apply for a bank loan" to settle his bills.

Ted Weiss thought it wrong of the college to have made Paul suffer in this way: "As a teacher [de Man] was immediately successful. In normal circumstances, Bard was open, so that even without needing a man, they might [have kept] him."[23] Rightly or wrongly, Pat believed that the president had also influenced the other faculty to shun the de Mans socially.[24] Whether the impetus came from Case or whether the faculty had their own reasons, the de Mans were ostracized by the community. This was hard to bear, especially for Pat, who was isolated in the cottage and a first-time mother. Lucy Woods had withdrawn into unforgiving silence, and Pat's classmates had graduated in June. She found herself entirely alone, without friends. Moreover, she couldn't drive, and she also had been impaired in the accident. Merely visiting the seriously injured Paul in the hospital without a car was almost impossible for her.

Not everyone was cowed. Twice in December, Irma Brandeis confronted James Case. She was an associate professor of Italian, earlier the mistress and muse of the Italian poet Eugenio Montale, a firm friend of Paul and a courageous woman, and, like many of de Man's closest friends, Jewish. But for all her presence, she got nowhere when she tried to appear in defense of de Man. Both in passing and then in a formal meeting in Case's office, she was "cut short." On January 3, 1951, she tried a third time, writing him a "postscript" to that discussion, urging that she was "very strongly in favor of reappointment."[25] Since this is the first contemporary written record of a colleague's response to de Man as an intellectual, it is worth quoting:

> The things we do know of this young man are much to his credit, while nothing opposed is verified. The college needs his easy, unostentatious brilliance, his youth, his ability to reach and stir

his students. It needs people trained and interested in more than one field of study.

She allowed that "the questions that have been raised must, of course, be answered" but wished that Case would "raise them directly with Paul himself." Clearly, even in January, Case had not told her or the wider college that the dismissal was a fait accompli. It gives insight into Paul's habitual secrecy that almost a month after he had been so devastatingly fired, even his friends did not understand its finality. Case replied a week later with a curt nine words: "Let's discuss the situation when I see you next."[26] The news by then was out, and on January 21, Mary McCarthy, in New York, responded to a letter from Artinian. It was in this letter, written a year after her and Paul's last meeting and discussed previously, that she at last requested information about him, his whereabouts, and a "lurid detail" or two.

Case was not affected even by the remarkably positive student evaluations de Man received for his English 67 seminar, the "Criticism of Literature." The fourteen students in the course were already aware of their professor's imminent departure and asserted that his loss was "great" and "tremendous." In numerical evaluations, they were almost unanimous in praising the course, de Man's preparation, the value of the discussion, papers, and oral reports; all but one of the group affirmed his openness to other points of view. Two felt the level of the course was somewhat above "the general class level." The written comments, however, were extraordinary and prefigured de Man's emergence into that iconic status that developed around him at Harvard a few years later:

> It is difficult to say what Mr. Deman has given me, for it is so great. It is a way of thought, an approach and a coherent frame-work philosophically. He will continue to be of value to me, even if I never see him again. This coupled with his intellectual honesty, makes his loss deplorable, un-excusable. If I have known a great man, he is Paul deMan.

The "great man" theme thus emerged spontaneously among his students during his first years of teaching. Some felt that contact with him was formative and "inspiring": "To me, he has been the most helpful teacher I have had in four years at Bard. My thinking and creative ideas have advanced greatly under his direction. I have known no finer teacher."

One tentatively hoped for "more actual practice of the theories presented" but was sure the theory "has been worked out." Another, perhaps replying to a naysayer, was sure one could apply de Man's critical point of view also to works written "before the birth of the particular school of poetry and philosophy from which this theory of criticism has come."[27]

ON MAY 21, 1951, thirteen months after flying back to Argentina, Anne wrote to Artine Artinian for help in contacting Paul's lawyer on her behalf.[28] She did not know what had happened to Rik. Having received nothing from Paul, she understood by then that the man who was still technically her husband was now her enemy, and she would treat him as such for the next decade. From then on, Anne, though still in Argentina and married to Peter Brajatuli,[29] began to use the bigamous state of de Man's new marriage and her own abandonment to bring pressure on him for payment of his obligations. Artinian, the enemy of her enemy, had become her friend. He replied at once, telling her that her son was "in Washington D.C. with new grandparents," and he promised to look up the lawyer. Paul de Man had already been dismissed, but Artinian had been criticized for his campaign against him, and he was glad to assist the rejected wife and the additional complaints she provided. Anne also now wrote of her unhappy story to both the Belgian consul and to the president of Bard.

Artinian was also in touch with David Braybrooke, then a graduate student at Cornell. Much taken in Antwerp by Anne's seductiveness and "fiery temperament," he, too, had been disappointed by his one-time friend, for he had never been paid either for his two translations or his work as de Man's agent in the United States. He decided that Paul had been "dastardly" to Anne, and from Ithaca he found her a New York City lawyer, whose name he gave Artinian, the firm of "Cascal [sic; probably Kaskell] and Schlesinger." This was invaluable, for from this date Anne was able to use legal channels to follow her husband to Boston and demand payment of her promised funds. Since Paul did not have the money, he met the demands barely or not at all, but they were felt by him and Pat as torturesome. By mid-August 1951, when Paul and his family had left Annandale, Artinian dropped the matter. He was satisfied: He had recouped all his rent, and his rival had been driven in disgrace from the scene, not entirely by his landlord's enmity.[30]

The students, however, were still on Paul's side, and they asked him to speak at the graduation ceremonies. It was Saturday evening, June 2, 1951, when de Man again addressed the Bard community. He was defiant and unapologetic. His convictions about the falsity and hypocrisy of societal norms had only been strengthened by his treatment at the college, and now more than ever he drew on what he had learned from Bataille, that lens through which he had learned better to see his relations to others. His divided audience, according to *The Bardian*, "either became more 'entrenched' in their antithetical convictions, or gave themselves joy upon hearing his words."[31] His subject was "The Morality of Literature," and it constituted an attack on conventional morality, a justification of art as superior to other productions of the economic system, and a defense of wasteful spending. It was everything his young admirers would have rejoiced to hear. Exemplifying what was understood in that era as the existential position, it also dismissed history, mixing a variety of philosophic concepts, whose sources he did not name, into a strong brew of rebellion.

There was a "crisis," and "Man," as the student reporter wrote, "in an attempt to organize the chaos of his existence formalizes his activities in moral systems composed of invented values." All values were invented values. The one that counted was "the aesthetic act" because it rebelled against the false conventions of capitalist "acquisitive behavior." Art was "scandalous" and "could not be integrated into the productive system": the man—the philosopher—who perceived these relationships was on the side of the angels, the scandalizing rebels. True to his devotion to Surrealism, de Man asserted that literature was "necessarily wasteful," and to invoke "constructive 'communication'" was merely "hypocritical," an attempt to cover up the "essential alienation of art from this system, its deep rebellion against it."

It is hard to escape the sense that the "scandalous" object, which refuses appropriation by the "system," was the speaker himself, one who had cauterized the wounds inflicted by this world through alienation and "deep rebellion against it." There could be no art, he went on, that did not stand outside that system in a posture essentially alienated from it.[32] He found a perspective Bataille would have accepted on morality itself:

> Like the aesthetic act, moral systems are wasteful in that they acquire to spend. Moral systems are by their very nature destructive. They are unserious in that they are liable to change, and in order to certify themselves are forced to travel to their limit expending energy value on the way. Upon arriving at their limit moral systems decay and become stagnant.

As Bataille said later, "Scandal is the same thing as consciousness." If de Man had caused a scandal, so much the better. Without citing Hegel, he appropriated the concept of the unhappy consciousness. Moral conventions had been invented only adventitiously to account for the "chaos" and "present panic" of actual life. They were "unserious," destructive, and liable to change. (One notes this first use of "unserious" as a pejorative.) His conclusion was determined by his premises. "Therefore history is not continuous, but a discreet system in that there must be a rejection of the past in order to invent the validity of the different present."

This was an important issue, bearing on freedom itself. There could be no freedom as long as we let history look over our shoulder. That had been Heidegger's lesson, and Sartre's, and for de Man it was of prime importance. History was a sore spot for existentialists, and breaking its grip was a precondition of freedom. One felt "anguish in the face of the past," Sartre granted in addressing his countrymen during the occupation; that was inevitable, but one's task was to move forward and get over it.[33]

It was certainly himself that Paul de Man was talking about passionately when he invoked the destructive nature of morality and its "drive to travel to [its] limit and burn [it]self out" as it went. Behind the smile, the shrug, and the real indifference, there may have hovered an image of a comet traveling on some tangent into the void, burning out and disappearing. He was describing his own position. As one who must be moral on his own terms, who lived in a "different present," it was he who must reject the past—his past—in order to meet the actual world. He had already "traveled to the limit," expended his energy value, and been "unserious" in his inconstancy and liability to change.

Engaged in a struggle with American hypocrisy while secretly and hypocritically concealing his own wartime activities, deliberately wasteful of funds in his refusal to be trammeled by the corrupt morality he saw about him and had seen since his youth, he was justifying his actions to himself by attacking not only the system that victimized him at Bard but also the hypocrisy that had putrefied the air around him in his first Belgian home, with its secret history of suicides, buried lives, familial violence, rapes, infidelities, and early deaths. It had tainted the air of Belgium itself in his father's circle due to the accommodations that they and the country—not to mention himself—had made to the New Order and its commands to get rich quickly, and young. Now again, he felt it in the failed morality of a dead marriage still wound tightly around him but from which he was determined to escape.

It was surely the speech of a man in pain striking back. Yet it is possible that it marked a real turning point, a true crisis. He knew that he stood alone and in a short time was going to have to leave his home once again in silence—very much as he had to scurry away from Antwerp. He would be forced once again to try to start over somewhere else. He had liked shocking the bourgeoisie, but this was real failure. For his words reek of disgust. Perhaps there are buried in this language signs of the nascent change, a note suggesting subtly that he had begun to recognize for what it was the compulsion that drove him overtly to offend, destroy, and fly. He had had hopes at Bard, but now he had added another weight to the burden of concealments he carried with him. He had a family he wished to support, but could not, and a career he wanted to pursue, but the way was barred. Now a system he disapproved was "destructive" and "unserious." These terms had never been part of his own frame of reference, but they had been applied to himself by both friends and foes—Willems and Peeters, for example—who had judged him culpably "light," frivolous, and reckless of consequences. Now he appropriated these terms and they entered his vocabulary in their gravity for the first time. De Man was getting bored with lightness.

DESPITE HIS NEW ENTANGLEMENTS and disasters, he now had one advantage he had not had before: Pat, who also stood outside "the acquisitive framework." Where his mother had been depressed, and Anne had shopped, his young wife, Patricia, would edit Paul's ongoing attempts at English translation and would learn without complaint to make ends meet on very little cash. Already their lives together, although harassed and trying, had produced a welcome infant, a new life with nothing hypocritical about it.

In a literal sense, Paul worked that summer of 1951 at getting grounded. Together, the couple spent the next month working in the local fields as "stoop labor," picking strawberries. Patricia parked the baby in the shade of a nearby tree and harvested beside her husband. They were paid by the quart box, and very badly. "Everyone else was a migrant laborer."[34] (This was the source of the opening chapter of Henri Thomas's roman à clef, Le Parjure.)[35] Their interim lodging was an apartment over the Weisses'. In the evening, Paul played duets with Renée; he was "not especially good," she recalled, but playing music expressed intimacy for him, as it had done with Frida Vandervelden and his father years earlier. Under the circumstances, being able to play an instrument at all after days of field work speaks to his resilience.[36] Paul would drop in at the kitchen door, and he and Ted would talk about his literary ideas, engrossing the conversation, to the disgust of the twelve-year-old Ros, Renée's cousin, who was visiting.

Ted advised Paul that he must go to Boston, get into Harvard, and work toward the formal education and degrees that he lacked. On Paul's behalf, he wrote to Harry Levin, who later that decade would publish The Power of Blackness. He was the head of the Comparative Literature Department at Harvard and a man of great influence in the field.[37] Around the beginning of July, Paul de Man packed himself, Pat, and the baby into their unreliable car and left Annandale silently, giving no forwarding address and telling no one except the Weisses. None of the others was likely to be of help, and anyone who pursued him was certain to want money. It was the flight from Antwerp all over again. In lieu of rent, he left behind the new refrigerator he'd bought on credit from Haen's Jewelry Store but had not paid for.[38]

Nevertheless, it was a real turning point. Money would continue to be a problem, and meeting the rent was always problematic. Yet from that point on, de Man began to live in a way that appeared "austere" to his colleagues. Clothing, books, and travel apart, he and Pat spent little on appearances or material goods; their rented apartments and even their eventual home outside New Haven were simple in style. They did not entertain much, and Paul, a European bourgeois, not only refused to let Pat take a job, he would not permit her even "to dance."[39] He focused on her jealously, guarded their privacy, and established a pattern of marital fidelity that was the opposite of what he had seen as a child. De Man's philosophic tenets may have served more to obscure his missteps than to deal with them, but he was not again a bankrupt, and in the most private aspects of his life he was aiming at change. As to why he fell in love with her in particular, Pat reflected that he was "not articulate about why," but all their lives he was possessive and jealous of her attention. "He never wanted to be away from me. It would worry him immensely. He would call every night and write in between if we had to be separated at the beginning and end of the semester."

In spite of everything, the couple were happy with each other, and if one seeks the missing element that helped de Man gradually evolve into a more stable person over the next decade, an evolution that did not begin at once, it was this marriage, begun under such doubtful circumstances, that proved to be long and deeply nurturing. Those who later knew him only as an austere, self-disciplined figure on some sort of barely discerned "spiritual quest" would hardly have recognized the highly domestic and possessive husband who was always, in a way, very proud of his love. "He would tell me about it," Pat recalled. " 'Look, I love you so much, and we've been married so long.' There was a poet . . . [he would quote] who wrote poems to Ilsa, a series of love poems throughout their married life, and [Paul] was touched by someone else who was married with so much passion and fidelity."[40]

With the other women he had known, he had been a young man engaged in an Oedipal triangle. With Patricia, seven years his junior, an innocent dependent on him, he was taking on finally the man's role as his era knew it.

30.

BOSTON

———————

ON A TORPID JULY DAY IN 1951, DE MAN, HIS WIFE, BABY, AND DOG were still ten miles outside of Boston when their rattletrap Ford broke down completely. They abandoned it by the side of the road, as the Okies had done with their own jalopies on the way to California, and with the infant on Pat's hip and luggage in their arms, they struggled on. It was a desperate situation, typical of Paul at his lowest ebb. His string of previous failures at ULB, the Agence Dechenne, Hermès, and as a Belgian citizen in flight from the law, or with his scattered family—none of these had seemed fundamentally to change him. Now, however, the stakes were different.

They fetched up as houseguests of the Jack Kotiks, friends of Pat. Pat remembered their kindness at the beginning of what she called "our bohemian period. . . . [We] drove in a falling-apart car—like *The Grapes of Wrath*—Michael in my arms—Paul had no license . . . had none in Belgium. Michael started crying at two in the morning. [We] lived at first with kind friends—[we had] not a penny."[1]

For a while, it had seemed as if things were looking up. Having fired de Man in December, James Case, perhaps out of belated sympathy or in response to appeals like Irma Brandeis's, tried to get de Man a job at Columbia, where the dean was Harry Carman, who was also head of Bard's board of trustees. Carman was impressed by de Man and wrote Case that he would "do everything I can to place him." That sounded promising.[2] But a dean can only do so much; a candidate must also be acceptable to the prospective department, and despite the dean's backing, de Man did not get the job. Pat believed that Artinian, in addition to acting on behalf of Anne by putting her in touch with Bard's administration, translating her letters to Case, and finding her other supporters, had directly blocked Paul from getting the job at Columbia by writing ahead to Fred Dupee to warn him off.[3] "He went to speak to Fred Dupee, but Artinian had written ahead to Dupee and poisoned the water." Dupee, of course, had long ties both to Artinian and Mary McCarthy, who continued to speak slightingly of de Man when the occasion arose.

De Man was more successful when he boldly presented himself at the offices of Kaskell and Schlesinger, the law firm that Braybrooke had found for Anne. Calling cold and speaking to an associate, he told the lawyer about his injury the year before and promised to begin payments in September, when his new job at Columbia—which did not exist—would begin.[4] She was impressed, friendly, and persuaded.[5] Visiting Anne's lawyer was a defensive move, damage control only. The couple was at the bottom of their fortunes, and they were glad to move on to Boston. Their stay, though recalled as pleasant by Jack Kotik, involved a new and painful episode for Pat. She was again pregnant that summer, but she miscarried early. Lucy Woods appeared around this time, determined to locate another dwelling for the couple but not to assist them financially. Jack Kotik remembered her visit sardonically: "One of the events that stands out in association with their visiting us was the appearance of Pat's mother. The idea was that they were incapable of finding a place to stay. I remember driving her in a blue Chevrolet convertible with the top down in areas of Boston where I'd never been. She projected the feeling that she felt she had to help them."[6]

For Pat, it was a nightmarish visit. Having neither money nor health insurance, she had not been able to go to a hospital at the time of the miscarriage. Yet instead of paying for medical treatment, Lucy dragged her daughter on foot, her body not yet recovered, through the sweltering streets of mid-summer Boston, determined to find them an apartment and locate secondhand furniture at a Goodwill store.[7]

In times of ill fortune, however, de Man was never passive. When he reached Boston that summer of 1951, he aimed at Harvard, across the Charles River, but to earn his keep, he turned to Berlitz, a popular, internationally based language school that advertised even in the subways. The institution had supported his family before in times of need, for Henri de Man, long before he had been a political leader, had made his living through teaching at Berlitz in Germany and in London.

The school had its headquarters in Boston, near the Massachusetts Avenue Bridge. From then on, the de Mans located themselves in a series of inexpensive apartments nearby. Tutoring adult students in French and German was not prestigious work, but it brought in better money than Paul would later make as a teaching assistant. He would later get special permission to teach at Berlitz while also working as an assistant at Harvard (usually forbidden), and therefore he would actually have a much a higher income than the average graduate student. By October 1951, he had established himself at Berlitz as "a terribly popular teacher," their star, setting his hours as he chose and working sometimes more than twelve hours a day while keeping himself on call from nine in the morning till ten at night.[8] He worked full-time for Berlitz throughout the next decade, according to his widow. Once he was at Harvard, his supervisors did not know all the facts, and they also turned a blind eye and bent the rules for this excellent student.[9] In fact, his annual income over the decade—before deducting money for payments to Anne—may have been as much as a tenured professor would have been earning at some colleges.[10] Those arrangements, however, were still in the future when, in 1951, he told his colleagues at the language school that he would soon be teaching at the university across the river. They, of course, disbelieved him.

Another source of income came from the most notable among his students, Henry Kissinger. A German immigrant three years younger than Paul, at twenty-nine he was already a powerful figure in Harvard's Department of Government.[11] Completing his M.A. that year, Kissinger felt the need to improve his French and hired de Man as a private tutor. Although instructors at Berlitz were not supposed to work privately with the students they encountered at the school, de Man agreed to Kissinger's proposal to accept more money than the school gave him, and less than Kissinger paid the school, an arrangement that was to their mutual benefit. In addition, Kissinger saw another use for de Man as their relationship flourished, and by December 1952, the Belgian was regularly being published as a translator in Kissinger's journal, *Confluence*.[12] Actually, although the translations were officially done by Paul de Man, in fact many of them were secretly the work of Patricia de Man, for whom translation had been a specialty since her college days. Paul worked for the German-born scholar for about two years, and not only as a translator. It was on a Christmas Eve that Kissinger, "lonely," according to Pat, called her husband on the phone and demanded that he come to his home and provide a French lesson. Although she "protested vigorously . . . Paul said we needed the money." De Man also complained to Pat and others that the German émigré had offered him a job but had not paid him in full.[13]

He had many pressing reasons to change. Poverty, responsibility for a growing family (his wife's second pregnancy must have given him a jolt), and awareness of his own advancing years were burdensome. Pat's influence helped, as did the fact that his cohort of other graduate students were also living on a shoestring. He was not alone in his straitened circumstances. Meantime, there were both sticks and carrots to drive him on: The unbearable prospect of a lifetime at Berlitz on the one hand and on the other the chance of a career via a Harvard degree. Modifying his habits was becoming a habit.

Paul did not, however, completely change his stripes, and he remained spendthrift to the end of his days. "For the thirty years [they] were married" Pat could never understand why her husband "could not manage his spending." She recalled, "When we were in Boston, he was paid by the week. We spent everything Friday—we went out to a modest French restaurant the first night. We practically spent everything and the rest of the time we lived on cheap wine and hamburgers. No matter how much money we had, it seemed to slip through his fingers."

Then and later, he kept their finances to himself, paid or did not pay the bills, and provided Pat only with such funds as she made clear were necessary. Throughout their lives, she dreaded the arrival of dunning letters, although she chafed at being kept ignorant about the actual state of things. She had to accept it even when it involved "a certain kind of frighteningness [*sic*]—he never let go of the reins, but he wasn't steering us." He wasn't exactly extravagant and did not buy "fancy things," but nevertheless the funds he possessed got wasted; he was "reckless."[14] They were perpetually short of money, sometimes even for food for Michael.

Throughout the decade, Paul continued his habit of moving frequently. Between September 1951 and the summer of 1960, his transcript at Harvard and his own correspondence show that he inhabited six or seven different dwellings, ending up in his last year on Massachusetts Avenue in Cambridge.[15] Yet they took vacations: In the summer of 1952, they spent time on Nantucket, then inexpensive and charming, as a photograph showing his smiling face and that of his little boy testifies. Although there were the financial issues, Pat said, "It's very corny. He was the love of my life. Except for some stubbornness. [We] shared so much. We enjoyed each other's company so much. [We] never seemed to have enough time to say what we had to say to each other."[16] The only consolation after his death—and it was very slight—was that at last she had control of the checkbook.

The greatest of all the fears under which they lived was the threat that Anne would reveal to the authorities the true state of his marriage. Anne had to be pacified. Far off in Argentina, she had nothing to lose by doing so, and she threatened via a series of letters he received from a local law firm, Foley, Elliot and Hogg, to expose his bigamous status. In addition, Paul, although not Patricia, knew she could also reveal his collaborative work during the occupation. Yet, as Mme Ipsen herself volunteered, after returning to Argentina, she herself married again—to Peter Brajatuli—while still legally wed to Paul de Man. She added that she both married and later divorced Brajatuli in Mexico, and that neither the marriage nor the divorce was legally valid. She held that she had remained Paul's legal wife throughout. As an adult, her son Rik stressed that she was indeed married—and legally so—to Brajatuli.[17]

De Man hid everything from his companion, who was theoretically in the dark throughout. Yet although Pat was ignorant about the underlying facts that made her husband's "divorce" and her own "marriage" of 1950 a rigmarole, she did know that something very serious was wrong and spoke of her feelings of dread each time she saw another envelope addressed to Paul from the Boston lawyers. She also understood that Anne was demanding funds even from Canada, where later in the 1950s she had followed Brajatuli from Argentina.[18] These threats were characterized by Patricia as "blackmail" and were deeply disturbing because the couple did not have the money and lived in poverty.

Nevertheless, in spite of—or perhaps to some extent because of—these difficulties, life settled down, and slowly and gradually Paul de Man began to adjust his way of life. The "austere" man his American friends knew from the 1950s onward began to form as his stable character during this year. Pat recognized this. One of the first things she remarked on later when discussing her late husband was that "Paul the personal man was very different from the public one." Perhaps privation turned out to be valuable to him. Pressed by poverty and the fear of being unmasked, he had his back against the wall. By one means or another, he managed to avoid those debts that could have brought down his reputation. His recklessness with money meant that cash not just for rent but even for baby food might be lacking. However, though merchants might dun him, his salary was not attached; and while his changes of address were frequent, they did not result in garnishment. He took nothing that did not belong to him. With Pat beside him, he was able to accept a minimal standard of living. Money still slipped through his fingers, but there was no pressure on him at home to bring it in, and the world he now inhabited did not measure a person's worth by his spending.

With Pat, he would never again move in a sea of money, with his children bustled away by servants, his food prepared by cooks, his social life enjoyed in a salon kept by an ambitious and extravagant wife. Nor did he want to. De Man had accepted a new American existence. He had come to hate Anne and the facade they had maintained of a happy couple. From Pat, on the other hand, he could expect not only unconditional love but also intellectual companionship. In addition, she could and did manage everything alone: cooking, cleaning, shopping, and caring for first one child, then two. But Paul engrossed her attention, always talking about his ideas. Being with her was his own time, not family time.

His sense of purpose began to harden during this decade and his capacity for discretion grew stronger as he began to learn from his mistakes. In December 1951, he turned thirty-two, and the old excuses were worn-out. He might once have seen himself accurately as misled in his youth by his uncle into collaboration, or unmoored emotionally by his mother's and brother's deaths, or pressured by Anne into wild spending. Yet in the last two years, he had again gotten in over his head and had turned both New York and Bard into places to which he could not return. He was aiming at admission to a seminar at Harvard on some terms or other in January 1952. He knew that essentially this was his last chance.

In the stead of the Antwerpen playboy, there began to appear another figure, a grave, clever man who spoke rarely and only to the point but who did not lose the arguments he engaged in and whose jokes, when he made them, could change the tone of a discussion and put him on a level above the competition. Instead of the memorable parties he had given in Belgium, de Man entertained almost not at all. He had colleagues and friends, but invited very few home. Although he was technically once again an unwed father, this time he actually wished to be married, and he acted the part of a legal husband, using all his powers to keep up that appearance. A decade earlier, he had lived in a ménage à trois, refused to marry his companion until their son was four years old, and had permitted himself one or more affairs. Now he lived with his spouse in mutual fidelity. He could not afford his former style of life, but he also did not want it; it was in this period that his reputation for "austerity" was born.

Psychoanalysis did not interest him. What he summoned to his aid was main will and the capacity to imagine and summon up a new persona behind which he could both modify some behavior and hide from sight what he could not or did not wish to change. In prior years, his friends had recognized his indifference to consequences. Now he was inventing a different mask. At Bard, his malicious wit had made enemies, and at the end he had found he had too few real friends there. At Harvard, he began gradually to limit, though not eliminate, his open derision of others. Pat later credited herself with teaching him to be less abrasive and defiant; by now, he could see for himself the result of having used his wit against men whose friendship he might need.

Paul loved to gossip, but henceforth a relative form of discretion became his watchword. His American friends consistently and with amusement mentioned his quickness to disparage whatever friend or student had just left the room, but he usually did it only after the door had closed.

He was fundamentally a social and highly competitive man and never ceased privately to love the best food, the feel of "good English tweed" under his fingers, or the luxury of superior accommodation on the ocean liners when he and his family traveled later. Outwardly, however, he seemed self-denying in his habits, and his habitual secrecy now became even deeper.[19] A veil of impenetrable silence and mystery began to descend about him. One could not successfully ask him questions about himself, and friends, colleagues, and superiors all accepted the noli-me-tangere aura he projected. In Cambridge, a community chockablock with intellectuals who spoke with foreign accents, Paul fitted into that niche and went unquestioned as one more European, like all the others, who had come to work and enjoy the relative freedom and prosperity the country offered. He made this secrecy a conscious program that he would follow for the rest of his life. Henceforth, he would avoid anyone from whom he could not learn. Already five to ten years older than other graduate students, burdened with multiple jobs, he had learned from his last three years that he could manage well enough with only a few friends. The good times were over. If in Milton's terms, life is a "vale of soul-making," Paul walked there alone.

Except of course for Pat. In fact, he drew on his new wife's attention so unreservedly that she knew their children were being slighted, and, according to her, she had "to fight" to give them her time, yet they "would get only a certain amount. . . . He enjoyed doing the dishes because he could control the time we would be together. [Yet] he was sweet-natured always and liked to work at home and be with his family. . . . He was a family man."[20] One might conclude that their marriage was a good example of what some family psychologists call "fusion," a union in which he could enjoy virtually exclusive possession of his wife's time and affection in a tight, exclusionary bond. It might not have been everyone's idea of a satisfactory life, but the more de Man and his family kept to themselves, the less they had to do with others, the safer he would be. Getting his degree and entering a profession were now the only essential things.

It would be a mistake to think that in the 1950s de Man suddenly internalized conventional moral standards, but the new circumstances of his life in this new world helped him adjust. Gradually, he put into practice the recognition that had begun to come to him in the last months at Bard. He did not abandon Bataille's ideas, but his acts and commitments show that the "creative act" of life became for him something other than that of a spent atom or particle of debris from outer space. Georges Bataille would remain a valued contact, but the extreme way of life his writings explored (but which he did not himself practice in any way comparable to de Man's early self-immolating career) had little to do with the world in which de Man was now engaged.

31.

PRINCE IN EXILE

I T TOOK DE MAN ONLY THREE MONTHS TO GAIN ADMISSION TO A HAR-
vard graduate seminar, remarkable in that he lacked even an undergraduate degree in any subject. Not much later, he became officially a
graduate student in the Department of Comparative Literature, attaining a normally impossible goal, and achieving it through the kind
offices of Harry Levin, first of all, and then of Renato Poggioli.
Undoubtedly Ted Weiss had written to Levin, who would become the
Babbitt Professor of Comparative Literature, and on October 4, 1951,
Paul himself wrote the man who was to help him a great deal in the
next few years, requesting an interview and saying that "for the last
year" he had been "working on a book on poetical theory, taking
french [sic] symbolism as a starting point."[1] He was seeking, he told the
professor, "to evolve a critical language that would fuse the recent
european with the american [sic] critical vocabulary." He didn't have a
phone, he said, but he would follow up.

Levin replied, and they met and talked at some length. By now, de
Man had moved in American intellectual circles for more than three
years, and he knew precisely what line to take—what to emphasize and
what to omit. Levin was impressed, and in January 1952, he admitted
de Man on a nonmatriculated basis to a special seminar he and Renato
Poggioli, who had succeeded Levin as the chair of the Department of
Comparative Literature, had organized for a handpicked group of

senior graduate students. (The field, reanimated by Levin and Poggioli, was actually more American than European, as it was little studied abroad.)[2] Undoubtedly, part of de Man's success in gaining this favor was that those who met him encountered an arresting man of thirty-two, handsome to the point of beauty, with interesting features, a voice that was deep, accented, and shot through with an amused sense of irony, and a glance that was piercing but not hostile, open to what he might learn, and accepting. The seminar he joined met at Levin's home, and admission was a mark of great favor. It was after one of these sessions that de Man sent Levin a note on April 16, 1952, thanking him for an evening invitation and his "kind interest." Levin reported that the seminar was one he and Poggioli were proud of, for its members included George Steiner, John Simon, and others from whom they expected great things.

In that group, Levin said, de Man had more than held his own.[3] He made a success of it, and in the course of the semester, although he was not required to write for the colloquium, Paul asked Levin to read "a chapter of the essay on symbolism on which I am working." Then, making another overture, he wondered if "Mr. Poggioli may want to see it?" This step, normal for a newcomer, reflected what Mary McCarthy had noted as Paul's way of using one friend to make contact with someone important. He was fortunate in gaining Levin's protection, for the professor provided the basis for de Man's career at Harvard, which looked so extraordinary in the beginning, and for years he supported his continued standing there in spite of de Man's shortcomings. Paul de Man was his protégé. Levin was later blamed by de Man and his circle for damaging his career, supposedly out of jealousy, but, as will be discussed further, the facts do not support that allegation. Paul de Man approached Poggioli a few months later by walking in cold without an appointment. He won his support also, and in the fall of 1952, de Man was admitted as a matriculated graduate student and teaching assistant.

"Old Mother Harvard," as some institutional veterans refer to the university sardonically, was not an easy place in which to launch or maintain a career, but it was the epicenter of American literary work at the time. It prided itself on its three hundred–odd years of unbroken institutional existence, its Puritan origins, and its high intellectual standards. It was particularly known for its sovereign ability to produce a plethora of literary, political, and commercial leaders. Graduates of its programs could—and did—expect to be placed in good jobs at other institutions, essentially without competition. Indeed, the archives show that when contemporaries got a bigger plum than did another man newly "on the market," the latter might feel entitled to complain. It was not a warm place, and although it sometimes took Oxford as a model for particular programs, Harvard was neither donnish nor cozy.

One of de Man's earliest friends was the twenty-three-year-old George Kateb, an idealistic young man who was then writing his dissertation on utopias and later became a professor of politics at Princeton. He regarded both Paul and Pat as "two of the kindest people I had ever met in my life. Their kindness," Kateb said, "stood out all the more clearly against the background of Harvard, where warmth was scorned and self-possession was alone admired."[4] Yet for all that, to many of its graduates, acceptance by Harvard tended to become integral to their sense of identity. As Paul de Man told Peter Brooks much later when he was urging him to reject a teaching offer from their alma mater, "One never entirely gets over that place. But you have to. You must." Brooks, Harvard class of 1959, had been de Man's student as an undergraduate, and he later had a distinguished career at Yale. "One didn't get over Harvard," Brooks said, "because of its enormous and self-assured arrogance. [It's] the Mount Everest of American education. You have to climb it because it's there. You don't get over feeling it's the place to be."[5]

Harry Levin, the man Paul de Man chose as his protector, was a powerful, if not legendary, figure on the Harvard stage, and within the humanities he exercised great influence. Slender in build and emotionally cool, he was exceptionally erudite, wrote with great clarity, and had a fundamentally conservative, driving energy that he devoted to bringing the Department of Comparative Literature into prominence. The field had once been a gentleman's career, attracting highly intelligent men but also some talented amateurs. Graduate education, however, was becoming professionalized in the 1950s, and Levin wanted his students to be able to compete on a level with those in other disciplines. One of his aims was to ensure that the doctoral program was a rigorous one, and the students the university placed in the best positions all over the country had therefore been required to show mastery of course work, examinations, multiple language requirements, a weeklong general examination, and had written a book-length dissertation of noteworthy quality. Highly effective in university politics, he got his way. Richard Poirier said that Levin "stationed himself at all the key points [and] where he couldn't block an appointment [from] English, he would block it . . . in the humanities or comp lit. And when promotions came . . . he might be defeated in one of these places, [but] then he succeeded in others."[6]

Levin was loved by some, but he also attracted resentment. He was a midwesterner, trim, Jewish, and well dressed—too well dressed, some thought. Jews were then very much in the minority at Harvard, and many around him would have preferred a more rumpled look, a recognizable figure who did not affect English tailoring or place the stress in his surname on the second syllable—who had ever heard of a Levin becoming a Le*vin*?[7] He defended himself with a sharp tongue and deployed a lethal verbal shrug. Peter Brooks remembered that Levin had said of Yale, "Oh, I think they've someone good in the eighteenth century," and that he also commented about Cornell, "Why, Ithaca is a lovely place to bring up children." De Man himself was notorious for similar remarks, but his circle found it amusing or shrugged it off as part of his natural competitiveness. Why one person is forgiven transgressions forbidden to another is one of the mysteries of personal power.

Paul possessed exactly what Levin lacked, the thing John Hollander and others called his "aura." To be sure, this was based partly on the falsified story of his origins that de Man had told his mentors, the glamorous, bewildering, tragic personal history that he himself refused to talk about but which everybody had heard, but "not from him."[8] Hollander believed he comprehended and sympathized with Paul's history, which he remembered clearly: De Man had the "burden" of being Henri de Man's nephew.[9] The surname was unknown even to these sophisticated Americans. They were given to understand that Paul's uncle had been the Belgian prime minister during the war and complicit in the occupation: his soiled reputation had damaged

Paul's life there. Nevertheless, according to this fabricated story, Paul de Man had been a "*maquisard*"—a member of the Resistance—during the war. Afterward, he had gone into art book publishing in Paris (not Antwerp). He had emigrated to the United States to escape the shame of his uncle's behavior (Hermès, with its forgeries and embezzlements, never took place). Paul also had a South American connection, something vague, but one that provided him with an older son who was living there (not two other sons, nor an undivorced wife, nor Rik, invisible and unvisited in Washington). Perhaps to others, de Man added what he told Pat: that his publishing venture had been crushed by the machinations of Gallimard (sometimes she remembered the name as Hachette), the dominant French house determined to destroy Belgian competition.

Because of its vagueness, the story was the more readily absorbed as the truth, for it was never the newcomer who disseminated the myth, and one could not successfully ask de Man personal questions, even of the most basic and ordinary nature. "Distance is powerful," as Emerson said. "Touch me not" was mixed with attractiveness, and with the seductiveness of his eyes and smile, supported by a tone of calm authority, while over his person there played a nimbus of devastating wit and an outspoken sense of superior access to inside, arcane knowledge of the world and its great minds.

Georges Goriély in later years commented on the brilliance of his former friend's manipulation of the facts concerning his relation to Henri de Man. By citing the connection and then refusing to talk about it, Paul had benefited from the role of crown prince in exile: "Henri was compromised during the war. It would be very indelicate to ask questions—as to ask a prince about his father who lost his crown. On the one hand he had the prestige of being the prince, and on the other hand one was not longing to hear news about it. But how is it possible to be capable of such a lie?"[10] Goriély was clearly aware of one of the central ironies of Paul de Man's American reputation: The man who later, as a theorist, taught his students to suspect all narrative, and biography in particular, had built his career on a false one, for this impression he gave of himself as a "prince in exile" became part of his résumé. Colleagues from his Harvard days carried the story with them, and in the next decade, it was current at Cornell, where de Man taught and began to attract an ever-widening circle of followers.[11]

Renato Poggioli was the administrative half of the comparative literature team, and it was Levin who dealt with the students.[12] Poggioli was a warmer man than Levin, colorful and kind, but out of the fray. Burton Pike, a favorite of Levin who later became a long-term, close friend of de Man, knew Poggioli well before de Man arrived. He recalled the chairman fondly as a careful administrator but also unbuttoned, playful, and witty, a short, round, balding, and tonsured man with a cigarette permanently stuck in Continental fashion to one side of his upper lip. As he taught, his students made mental bets on how long the ash could grow before he swept it away.[13] For a long time, Poggioli was increasingly generous to de Man. The chair got him a scholarship, and by the spring 1953, he was arranging for him to draw one hundred dollars in advance for the summer.[14] He even later persuaded the dean to waive a normally inflexible requirement and allowed de Man to attend the university part-time, thereby letting him continue his full-time work sub rosa at Berlitz.

De Man's relation to Poggioli is paradigmatic of his career both in and out of the university. Again and again when constricted by normal requirements—even for making an appointment before showing up at the door to gain admission—he persuaded the men in power to waive them. This pattern raises a central question. Both Levin and Poggioli were sophisticated people; Levin had lived, studied, and traveled much abroad, and Poggioli was born and educated in Italy. One must ask why they were so ready to take de Man at his word and accord him, as will be seen, so many special favors. Pierre Bourdieu's concept of cultural capital and the "skeptron" is possibly relevant to these dynamics at Harvard and even more relevant in de Man's later period of great influence. The French sociologist posited that a group selects a spokesperson, grants him or her an emblem of authority that permits the chosen one to address the group, and called this emblem a "skeptron"—a rod held in the arm by such a speaker in a supposed Homeric ritual. The delegated speaker must already have access to those in power, but once given the skeptron, symbolizing command, that person, by his or her speech, exercises power over an audience, which, by the very act of listening, has granted that command. In modern terms and in academic settings, the skeptron of authority is given to chosen speakers who have permission and the capacity to use an arcane "discourse" peculiar to that setting. Only the use of that special language (skeptics would denigrate it as "jargon") marks him or her as an authorized spokesperson and not a mere imposter in masquerade. "The spokesperson," Bourdieu mordantly summed up, "is an imposter endowed with the skeptron."[15] In de Man's case, both his apparently high social background and also his claims for philosophical sophistication made through his use of special language, about which his friends could not challenge him, may have allowed him the authority by which he successfully presented himself as a unique person whose gifts deserved privileged treatment. Bourdieu ironically stressed the element of sheer acting, of performance per se in authoritative discourse. Paul de Man, for whom *performance* came to be a central term, held the skeptron because he knew very well what tale the New World wanted to hear and was ready in his "discourse" to define American ideas about Europe and European thought; his audience, perceiving the power granted him, legitimized him as their speaker. The issue of the kind of personal power Bourdieu analyzes is hard to pin down, but one thing is clear: From the time Paul de Man matriculated at Harvard, those around him, from undergraduates to the dean, almost always accepted or agreed to his requests. Perhaps it seemed almost a favor to be allowed to help him.

The day Paul came home with the news that he could attend Harvard was an extraordinary moment of triumph. On the strength of it, he behaved in character: He borrowed money and took his family that summer for a vacation on Nantucket. It was then a charming but not yet a fashionable retreat; a photograph shows him there, happy, young, and handsome, his curly blond hair windblown, as he holds his bicycle—and the dog—and leans against a wharf with his bicycle in the sun. Pat laughed, recalling the episode: "It took us a year to pay one hundred dollars to Home Finance. Even Paul had to pay it—and we did, ten dollars a week."[16]

Harvard University, unlike Bard College, did attempt to check de Man's academic credentials, and it contacted ULB. This was a moment of silent but real crisis. If ULB proved too forthcoming, de Man knew that he could be dismissed. He must have awaited the reply with some anxiety, and perhaps hung around the department office in order to be present and able to examine the document when it arrived. In fact, ULB sent accurate and damning information, showing that de Man had failed the relevant examinations and that his record of studies, marked by failed or missed requirements, made this almost inevitable. Nevertheless, de Man got around the procedure that an official transcript is intended to guarantee, and Harvard's effort was in vain. Someone—judging by the handwriting, it was probably de Man himself—subtly but importantly emended the central document after it reached Harvard. The reply had been sent on September 5, 1952, and signed by the head of the Office of University Information—in effect, the registrar—who attested that de Man had failed his first-level examination for a "licence" in social sciences in October 1941: "*a été déclaré 'ajourné'*" by the jury. "*Ajourné*" may mean either failed or "postponed," and the finding may be awarded as a result of not appearing. However, since the document specifies that he had appeared—"*Monsieur Paul DEMAN s'est présenté aux examens pour ces matières*"—he clearly took the examination but failed it. This was not surprising in view of the fact that the letter also specified some fourteen social science courses in which de Man had also enrolled and which would have prepared him for the test. In addition, the transcript showed the failure in his first year's studies of engineering and the middling work he did the following year in chemistry. De Man was already hard at work at *Le Soir (volé)* and his other jobs by March 1941, and according to his first wife, he had made only pro forma appearances at the university. Evidently, he last sat for the social sciences examination in October 1941 on the off chance he might pass it, but since he had been preoccupied since December 1940 with earning a living and supporting his child, it was merely a wasted few hours.

ULB's letter was in French, however, and foreign technical academic jargon is never fully decipherable except by an informed native. Moreover and significantly, there appears at the bottom of the document, written in English in what appears to be de Man's hand, the crucial statement: "took and passed the actual 'Licence' exam before a State Board in 1942."[17] That note nullified the negative message of the typed letter. Perhaps the department showed Paul the letter for clarification, permitting him to append what was essentially a self-certification, or perhaps he asked to look at it and simply added the note of his own accord. The handwritten note asserted an impossibility, however, because ULB had famously closed on November 25, 1941, for the dura-tion of the war—one of the few Belgian institutions to shut its doors as a matter of principled protest against German interference. Harvard officials would have been ignorant of that. By 1942, of course, de Man was at the height of his career as a collaborator, furiously juggling work for the three media companies favored by the Nazis who employed him. Even if "a State Board" had existed or functioned, he could not have passed any examination given by it. In fact, there was no "State Board" that gave such an examination, and a "licence" in that context at ULB was automatic; it meant merely completion of the first two years of study without regard to progress or quality of performance. The invention of the "State Board" was a little like his earlier assertion that his grandfather had founded the University of Ghent, or that he himself had fought with an army of the Resistance. Apparently, how-ever, the authorities at Harvard were satisfied.

The main thing was gaining access to Harvard. Once he was in, he met with immediate admiration. De Man's first years at Harvard, though poverty-stricken, were a personal triumph, and he made many friends who were to help him throughout his life. As a teaching assis-tant, he found that his peers looked up to him, and his students were sometimes enraptured. Ten years older than his cohort, vastly experi-enced, he was a married man with an unknown but tremendous and complex past, and came from a closed but fascinating world. They were, in Hollander's words, "just terribly impressed"—by "what he knew" and above all by his "aura."[18] Years later, Helen Vendler, who was never part of de Man's coterie but was his coeval at Harvard, remembered him from Cornell in the early 1960s, when both were teaching there. He would read "genially, advisedly, meditatively aloud something he found enchanting. [There was something] provocative, especially in [his] attitude—the assumption of a communal medita-tion." The same lack of side, a rejection of the defenses powerful people often employ, came out in his way of looking at others. His regard, she said, indicated a "willingness to be amused. It was very ruefully self-ironic," and there was implicit "the assumption of equality." It was "as far as possible from the mandarin imposition" of ego common among the professoriat.[19]

Such seeming accessibility coupled with presumed wisdom was enchanting to the young. Paul had read so much that they had not—philosophers who were to them literally closed books—Husserl, Heidegger, and Hegel. His own cohort of friends and colleagues, who were all younger and almost all men, were dazzled by him. They, too, had not read these German philosophers, then important in France, and they felt their lack of knowledge.[20] Nor had they come to Puritan Harvard with such a fascinating and glamorous—if rather indefinite—past. "Austere" in habits, yet good-looking, attractive to women (and some men), and seemingly modest until engaged in the cutthroat dogfights at a Harvard seminar table, from which he generally emerged the victor, he was at once a figure of authority, exotic, and amusing.

Pat recalled vividly the "jostling among contemporaries" that existed at Harvard, and Paul's almost inevitable triumphs. He was basically *hors de concours*. Later, he aroused jealousy, but he was not being abrasive, only competitive. After a lecture "among [his] contemporaries, someone would come up and say, 'You made all the others look . . .'" or 'We should never have had you first.' . . . He was sweet enough that very few resented him."[21]

Moreover, he stood up to and against the very conservative powers that were in charge of the humanities at Harvard. Eventually, he represented himself as their victim, although the facts do not fully support that inference. At the time, however, John Hollander reported that he had "warmed to him immediately" and part of that feeling was based on their shared sense of opposition to the powers that ruled them. "I was tremendously fond of him and terribly impressed by what he knew and interested in [the way he was] framing his position at Harvard because he was so totally unlike anything in the Harvard English Department or even in the Harvard Comp Lit as governed by Harry in the totalitarian way."[22] Hollander, while respecting Levin's erudition, disliked him for the heavy hand with which he governed, and when de Man later blamed his academic troubles on Levin, his circle was ready to hear and believe. De Man still enjoyed challenging authority, but from the time he entered Harvard, he began to channel his defiance into more acceptable, more symbolic forms. He was dealing profession- ally now with language, and the breakage would be the egos of his competitors rather than the destruction of lives or fortunes. Only after his later problems arose, especially those related to his doctoral disser- tation and the failure of examinations, did his position at Harvard become problematic.

To some younger men, de Man seemed "avuncular."[23] When he began teaching, undergraduates flocked to him. Richard Rand, then a freshman, asked him about sex. "Go to a bordello and find out," de Man told him. A few years later, in response to Rand's question "What should I do?" de Man was equally terse and unillusioned: "Go to New York and grow up. . . . The people who succeed are the people in trou- ble."[24] He would not judge, he could not be shocked, and he would certainly understand. He performed from a stance that made his new acquaintances eager to hear and believe him, and authorities who were empowered to guard the gates and reject intruders tended to become his supporters, eager at some level for acceptance by him.

Not everyone shared the enthusiasm, however. Richard Poirier, although a friend and himself a popular teacher, took a somewhat jaun- diced view. De Man was "brilliant," but at staff meetings of those teaching in Reuben Brower's influential Humanities 6 course, Paul "was always anxious to show off, because he was, you know . . . in the higher spheres." He thought him a "showboat." In particular, he recalled a half-hour lecture de Man had delivered on Yeats that ended with his saying, " 'Come dance with me in Ireland,' and big applause from these kids. And we all, the staff, thought, you know, who the— who the hell is he bullshitting?"[25]

For two years, de Man followed the standard course of study in the Department of Comparative Literature, although attending only part- time, courtesy of one of the favors Poggioli won from the dean.[26] He got A's in everything, as indeed he could have expected, given his life- long immersion in various languages. At some point, he began teaching in Reuben Brower's famous Humanities 6 course. Brower, a professor of English, was widely loved, and everyone agreed that he had great influence on de Man, both in terms of the close reading he famously stressed and disseminated and personally as a friend and supporter.[27] Reuben Brower is universally credited with introducing de Man to the American style of "close reading" and to the special kind of attentive, sensitive analysis of a piece of writing that is the foundation of what Peter Brooks called de Man's capacity to "sit in front of a text and just pluck magical things out of it."[28] Such interpretations were what Barbara Jones Guetti called "leaps"—that is, readings that seemed completely right and yet might have little clear evidence for them in the apparent text.[29] She was part of the circle surrounding Reuben Brower and sometimes had coffee with her mentor de Man at the university café. She met Pat and saw their baby, Michael, but never visited him at home. "We couldn't go to his home," she recalled. "They were too poor. He told me they lived in a really dilapidated house with white cockroaches that crawled up out of the drain."[30]

Richard Poirier, a devotee of Reuben Brower from undergraduate days, when the latter had taught at Amherst, points out that de Man credited not his study of philosophy but Brower for teaching him the "'critical, even subversive power of literary instruction.'"[31] Brower's method and that of Hum 6 (which he carefully taught to his graduate assistants in teaching sessions of their own) insisted that students not carry the shibboleths of cultural values into their reading of a work (what Hemingway would have called the "big words"—or Poirier thought of as "Big Talk"). It was a method that aimed to release students from "illusions about 'meaning'" and make them focus instead on the way words worked in relation to one another.[32] The "work in itself," as some professed, was alone what counted. Was this style of reading actually possible? Perhaps, perhaps not, but such was the aim. Biographical and contextual questions were dismissed out of hand.[33]

Although he learned a great deal of practical value from Brower, de Man also thought his approach "philosophically naïve and uninformed." He did not teach by the standard American discussion method. According to Peter Brooks, "His was not the ordinary American way of teaching a seminar—and not the European way, either. [He had a] powerfully rhetorical mind and he could follow and sustain a very coherent argument for a couple of hours. [He did not lead] a discussion, but people did interrupt and he would answer at length and pursue [the question]. But as time went on, de Man naturally developed his own style."[34]

The judgment of naïveté was rooted in de Man's European preference for beginning from a philosophical given (stated or unstated), from an assumption that certain issues or crucial points are worthy of being addressed, and then demonstrating their play throughout a given work (proceeding, that is, "from an abstract or theoretical position down toward a text"). The "uninformed" approach, which Brooks called the "American style of reading from the text upward toward (perhaps) abstraction" and which de Man rejected, would focus first and foremost on the pattern of language and meaning on the page before—if ever—attempting to relate that self-referential formal whole to broader "philosophical" issues. In a sense, this is one of the older conflicts about reasoning, reembodying the distinction drawn by Bacon between deductive and inductive reasoning: In England, induction, or reasoning from observed facts upward, had long dominated what came to be called "the Anglo-Saxon approach" to philosophy, and eventually underlay American pragmatism. On the Continent, and especially France, where philosophy was called on to fill the teleological gap so rudely torn open by the Enlightenment, it was and remains an unacceptable notion that valuable thought can arise from observation not shaped by an underlying aim, or telos. Of course, in preferring a European approach, de Man was also following his own earliest intellectual training—indeed his only formal instruction in how to think—provided by his study of mathematics, which is always directed by its goal and cannot begin without knowledge of what is to be demonstrated.

IN THE SPRING OF 1954, Levin and Poggioli were so impressed that at the end of de Man's second year of course work, they nominated him for membership in the Society of Fellows. This was a plum indeed. To have been a Junior Fellow was a distinction that followed the holder's reputation into his later life. The Society of Fellows was founded by President Abbott Lowell in the 1930s, and its grants were originally meant not to support the doctoral dissertation, but, rather, to subvert the dogged specialization produced by doctoral programs.[35] After World War II, however, Harvard and the United States were no longer isolated from competition, and Harry Levin, whose antennae were highly tuned to the contemporary world and academic politics, wanted his students to attain the doctorate—although he himself had not needed it—and he pressed them sometimes against their will to use their three years of the fellowship toward that end. Some in de Man's circle of friends, such as John Hollander, a Junior Fellow who was already becoming known as a poet, chafed over a pointless requirement, but Paul did not. Their crises were not his. On the contrary, a Harvard Ph.D. would be a major buttress of his new identity, the only postsecondary degree he possessed. Election as a Junior Fellow was the highest honor any department could give, and together with Hollander, de Man enjoyed choosing the wines for their luxurious weekly dinners, then held in Eliot House, when guests came to the Society's wood-paneled dining room for good talk and high-level companionship. Only six to eight fellows were chosen each year, and many, like Stanley Cavell, Noam Chomsky, and Marvin Minsky, coeval with de Man, became internationally known as creative thinkers. Fellows were paid a handsome stipend of three thousand dollars per year, a sum that matched the salary of some junior professors at lesser institutions. There were no teaching or other duties; lodging was provided to the single men. One could not apply; membership descended like grace by election. The fellowship was the opportunity of a lifetime. Three years earlier, Paul de Man had reached Boston in a state of dire poverty; now he crossed that privileged threshold and joined the club. His days as an embattled junior faculty member struggling for tenure at Bard were clearly behind him.

32.

DENOUNCED

Y THE SUMMER OF 1954, PAUL DE MAN'S PERSONA HAD EVOLVED. No longer the impassioned firebrand of the Bard years, or the supple, agreeable young immigrant who had been Mary McCarthy's friend, he had become an older man, wise, charming, and deeply cultured. He was already a father figure to some students and a cherished ally of other doctoral candidates, who rejoiced in his knowingness, acerbic wit, his tone of unshakable, indifferent self-confidence, and his charisma. In December 1953, he had published his first academic essay, "Montaigne," in *Critique*, an important step both because it foreshadowed his future intellectual development and because publication before completing—much less beginning—one's doctoral dissertation was a signal achievement. Then, a few months later, he had been elected a Junior Fellow. And with that, a high-flying tone began to appear in some of de Man's correspondence, a bit of swank or boasting that must have felt justified. That summer was the first time he rented an inexpensive cottage on Gotts, a remote island off the coast of Maine; it lacked running water and electricity but was covered in pine forests and romantic mists. There, he wrote Levin, he was "reading nothing more frivolous than Plotinus and Husserl," and Harry was welcome to join him "if Wellfleet becomes too worldly."[1]

In the meantime, while continuing to teach fulltime at Berlitz, de Man had also been assisting Henry Kissinger. It was in his office and in the same exuberant mood that de Man may have made a nearly fatal mistake when he spotted a letter from Georges Goriély, who by then was a fully accredited historian at ULB. The young professor had applied in the spring of 1954 to join a seminar that Kissinger was running at Harvard in international studies. Paul saw the application, and in April he wrote Georges that chance had "put him in the presence" of it. Kissinger was a "friend," Paul had a "tiny" influence, and if the "decision depended only" on Kissinger, then "your chances of coming here would be considerable" (the implication being that Kissinger trusted de Man's judgment). After his ignoble flight in May 1948 and the following years of enforced silence, anyone in de Man's position would have been gratified now to reappear in so desirable a role. Then de Man asked Goriély to pass on to Gilbert Jaeger—the third member of the ménage à trois—a letter that had "a certain importance." As a "phantom from the past," de Man said he'd been out of touch too long to have Jaeger's address.[2] He added further news of his own success, mentioning his doctoral project as a summation of symbolism, "whose philosophic echoes interest me ceaselessly." He saluted "destiny" for this encounter with Georges.

The letter was written in an elevated mood, and it may have been a mistake to send it. Undoubtedly, Paul had long wished to return to Belgium in a favorable light, and this must have seemed the right moment to prepare the way. Yet de Man was boasting to Goriély about his connections: He had been admitted to Harvard as a Ph.D. candidate and now had some "influence" on Kissinger, a figure who was now important to Goriély. He did not know that Goriély had by coincidence that very spring served on a jury with Robert Guiette,[3] one of the men whose names de Man had forged while stealing funds from Hermès, and that in talking about their mutual friend, Georges had learned for the first time about Paul's acts of fraud, embezzlement, and forgery while at Hermès and his subsequent conviction in Antwerp. The historian was shocked, and the letter from Paul de Man that followed this encounter doubly amazed him. Goriély did not get the grant, but he did get de Man's address and learn of his status at Harvard, information that until then no one in Belgium had possessed. From there those facts were intended to go elsewhere, and they did.

Thus by disseminating his address while still a fugitive, de Man had emerged into full view, possibly of Belgian jurisprudence and certainly of his former friends.

De Man was hoping to return to Belgium, regain legal status, and somehow make amends for his misdeeds.[4] He told Patricia that because he felt secure in his status as her husband and as a student at Harvard, he had gone to the Belgian consulate in Boston to get a visa for his return to Europe. Suddenly, however, on the very day they returned from Maine, September 7, the agents of the INS once more showed up without warning at his home, again in the midst of violent weather. The de Mans had planned both to celebrate Michael's birthday that day and also to move to a better apartment on McLean Street. Instead, Paul now faced deportation. The Immigration and Naturalization Service knew that he had arrived on a brief visitor's visa in 1948. Six years later, they had run out of patience. His position as Pat's husband would no longer shelter him, and the agents were no longer interested in the scars and injuries he had shown them at Bard in 1951. De Man would have to leave the country. He had only two choices: to be deported, or to leave via "voluntary departure," which permitted him the possibility of returning under the sponsorship of his wife.

He chose the latter. Returning to the States would be the problem, however, for he would need a Belgian visa on his expired passport— but that he would face when he had to. Yet to get a visa in Europe was highly problematic, for, given his notorious surname, if he visited any of his nation's consulates, whether in France or Belgium, he would be only a phone call away from the Antwerpen judicial system, and should a zealous attaché discover his fugitive status, de Man might even be arrested. It was a chilling thought, but there was much worse to come.

Sometime between the day the agents descended and September 28, when the Service gave de Man its ruling, Poggioli suddenly called him in. The Society of Fellows had received a detailed and deeply damaging denunciation of their protégé. Wide-ranging accusations showing considerable knowledge of de Man's past came in the form of a letter, whose writer, according to de Man's widow, was never revealed to him. She never saw the letter herself. However, it was clearly from someone who had precise information about the émigré, not only in Brussels under the occupation but also in Antwerp postwar. In addition, the writer both knew that de Man was at Harvard and raised questions about the circumstances of his admission there. This meant that every invented story de Man had told the university about his background was now either controverted or in question.

The authorship of this denunciation was kept secret at the time and has never been admitted by any person able or willing to respond. There was wide speculation but no agreement about who might have written it. De Man told his wife the unlikely story that it was not composed by anyone who had been close to him and that he guessed that when he had gone to the consul's office in Boston, some Belgian national had recognized him from across the room. Others speculated to this writer long after the fact, naming a specific person. Perhaps they were correct, but their hearsay information was always thirdhand.[5] However, the letter certainly contained Belgian information, was relatively up-to-date, and clearly came from someone with both detailed knowledge of de Man's former life and a motive to attack him. Noticeably, it did *not* mention de Man's bigamy.

The authorities could not ignore the denunciation; they wanted clear and specific answers. A roof had actually fallen on him in 1951. Now, if Poggioli and the others were allowed to believe the accusations, if de Man did not find some way of dismissing them so entirely that none of his American friends and superiors would even dream of mentioning them to others, more than his collarbone would be broken. He would lose all he had created: His profession, family, and residency in the country would all vanish. He would have no future. For four months, de Man delayed replying to the accusations, but eventually he responded to Poggioli in a letter dated January 25, 1955, which until this point has been the only known document he produced with regard to this matter. Some of the words in this letter later became notorious when they were published in *Responses: On Paul de Man's Wartime Journalism*, a posthumous compilation of essays by his friends, critics, and former students intended to make accessible the facts and arguments on both sides of the controversy.[6]

De Man's reply dismissed the accusations, explaining them away inventively and with odd plausibility. His argument was that he was the victim of being the *son* of "Hendrik" de Man, a "controversial" Belgian politician (he avoided the word *fascist*) and a man evidently still so problematic that his *son* Paul, although living in self-exile, was now victimized even overseas and made the hapless target of baseless attacks. This assertion that his uncle was his father, quite as much as his essay of March 1942 critical of Jewish writers, outraged de Man's Belgian readers and quondam friends; it both confused and profoundly puzzled his American supporters in 1992. What could it mean that a man they had so respected—loved, and some would say idolized—could have lied to this extent? Some wondered if it was conceivable that he actually was his uncle's son.

Two hitherto-unpublished manuscripts open a new window into Paul de Man's thinking at this time. Both were long separated from the typescript that was printed in *Responses*. The second, shorter one will be discussed below. The first is the actual manuscript of the published self-exculpation, a nine-page handwritten document marked by many revealing changes.[7] It shows that de Man actually wrote the letter he sent in January much earlier, beginning it on September 25, 1954, just before the INS offered him the choice between deportation and "voluntary departure." Between that date and late January, he revised the manuscript, redating it January 28, 1955. He had it typed the same day, after the second semester had already begun and months after he should have sailed for France. In the long-meditated manuscript emendations, one can see what issues gave him trouble and second thoughts. At least one of the changes he made is of central importance.

As to what he was accused of specifically, until now we have had only de Man's printed replies to them made available in *Responses*. Lacking the actual denunciation, we must approach these with caution. He began with a set of rubrics to which he must reply, but the manuscript variants permit us to see that he decided to ignore or minimize at least some of what he did not wish to address. He summarized the points on which he stood accused, listing these as: "(1) the modalities" of his admission to Harvard and election to the Society of Fellows; (2) the conditions under which he entered the country and "my present status with the Department of Immigration"; "(3) my political past, particularly under the German occupation"; and (4) "legal charges brought against me as a result of the liquidation of a publishing firm to which I was attached."

The most revealing difference between the published and unpublished texts of his reply is the presence in the early draft of an accusation that his final version omits entirely. At the beginning, he set himself to discuss "(3) my legal status as the adopted son of my uncle." Later, he crossed this line out. However, this rejected rubric is the first time one sees de Man make this yet more bizarre claim that he was the son of Henri de Man, *not* Bob de Man's son, but, rather, his nephew. Henri was far from being forgotten by Paul; in fact, he seemed, perhaps in spite of himself, to be reliving aspects of his uncle's ever-changing career. Indeed, many aspects of their lives, from their early rebellions to the complexities of their sexual and marital adventures—even to their exile and work at Berlitz—followed a parallel trajectory. There was undoubtedly a deep strain of identification with that mentor. (Henri, however, had claimed his children—by kidnapping them—rather than abandoning them, and it was ideology and a longing for power, not money, that brought him down.)

It is a strange and baroque fantasy for a grown man to entertain, but under pressure, one regresses. Paul de Man was a swan in a family of geese. His parents' marriage was dubious—they were first cousins— and had been disastrous. Why should not another cousin, Henri, Bob's sibling, older and better, have become his father? It is clear, in fact, from a last letter he wrote to Poggioli, that Paul not only wondered about this, but asserted it again. That de Man himself was uneasy about the assertion is evident from the fact that he struck it out, and it did not appear in the typescript or printed versions of this letter. Nevertheless, he saved it, so to speak, and did return to it in another text, as will be apparent in the second manuscript to be discussed below.

Some of the language in de Man's four headings is obfuscatory. "Modalities" of admission, for example, can mean anything, but the original accusation may have related to de Man's record of failure in or abandonment of three different majors (engineering, then chemistry, then social science) at ULB. Obviously, his enemy knew that de Man lacked a postsecondary school degree and knew that it mattered, that entering Harvard without a college degree might have been a matter of deceit. Paul handled this issue by evasion, admitting only that at ULB there had been "a change in my academic field, from science to the humanities," and that he had said so in applying. Telling Poggioli about a "change" of course was not the same thing as admitting he had no degree at all or that he had entirely failed his first year and spent only two at the university. In this first letter, he did not renew the claim he had made two years earlier on his transcript that he had been "licensed" by a state board, having probably written that phrase at the bottom of ULB's letter of September 5, 1952. That particular document had gotten him into Harvard, but the body of the letter from ULB also attested in French to his failure of the social science examination, and it would not bear scrutiny well, especially if his emendation were now reconsidered. (Renato Poggioli, trusting de Man as always, went on believing in this phantom license and still accepted it when, trying to help his student, he edited de Man's curriculum vitae in his own hand in 1959.)[8]

The second attack in the denunciation related to de Man's status as an immigrant. Here he replied that he was "married to an American citizen" and thus "was allowed to stay here, and I started naturalization proceedings." This was doubly untrue, for they were not married, and Pat later attested that he had never applied for citizenship. He could not have done so, of course, if it had meant producing a marriage certificate or undergoing background checks in Belgium. After 1952 or 1953, even Pat came privately to realize, she said, that the marriage was invalid; yet she could not confront Paul about it, and he told her only in 1960.[9] The vague but portentous term *moral turpitude* hovered over them; for anyone, but especially a Junior Fellow, to live in a bigamous relationship with an illegitimate child would at that time have meant dismissal.

De Man told his superior, "Up to the moment when I was notified that there were restrictions on granting me a passport, I never knew that anything was wrong." This was a lie in so far as his contacts with the INS went. Interestingly, however, he found a way to make a strong argument out of this supposed status as candidate for citizenship by asserting that when he had applied, his "entire history, here and abroad, was investigated and found to be satisfactory."[10] Of this process, there is no remaining evidence, nor could there be, as he never applied, and of course the threatened deportation implied the opposite of any putative "satisfactory" investigation. Nevertheless, by claiming that he had applied for citizenship, de Man could also assert he had passed a rigorous investigation—all without proof. It was a kind of piggybacking, a leveraging of an assertion that rested on a narrow and plausible but unsupported claim into a ringing defense. To the end of his days, de Man did not become an American citizen, although in 1959, he again told Poggioli he was making an attempt. This method of establishing as it were a first-stage, or foundational, lie and building upon it a bigger narrative edifice—all untrue—became a technique de Man used later on.

The third accusation was probably the one he considered the most damaging: charges "about my political past, particularly under the German occupation." Here he faced a much bigger threat. Matters of immigrant status or academic degrees were one thing, technical in nature, but political allegiances had obvious implications and were potentially far more dangerous. In reply, he reached for the broadest assertion he could make and claimed to be the son of "My father, Hendrik de Man," whom he described as "former Minister and Chairman of the Belgian social-democrat party." Here and elsewhere, de Man has focused on details of language: The POB, the Parti Ouvrier Belge, or Belgian Workers' party, of which his uncle had briefly been head, was not the same as the nonexistent entity he invented as the "Belgian social-democrat party," but the latter provided a more winning title than one with "Workers" in it would have done, for in mid-1950s America, that word had a red-tinted connotation.[11] In this role and "because of [Henri de Man's] attitude under the occupation he was sentenced in absentia after the war and died in Switzerland, in exile, last year. His case remains an extremely touchy issue, which, for reasons that go to the roots of internal Belgian political problems, arouses extremely strong feelings at least in some Belgians, apparently still today." Nevertheless, the man showed "devotion to his ideals," not "machiavellism [sic]" and "did what he thought was best for his country and his beliefs." Far be it from this son "to pass judgment on him." One notes that de Man gives nothing away: If someone ignorant of "Hendrik's" actual career and work under the Nazis should read this letter, he would learn nothing here, for the language gives us instead an idealistic politician suffering unto death from the unfortunate political infighting of his country.

It is special pleading: a mixture of untruths, half-truths, and evasions that achieves a tone that is mature, thoughtful, forgiving, and yet moral, the voice of a man who is able to separate himself from wrongdoing, disliking the sin but not the sinner. Yet the fundamental assertion was false. He was not Henri's son. During the war in Brussels, he had made the same claim (or let the story flourish) when it gave him prestige. Now he used it in reverse, but he was still sheltering under Henri's powerful aegis: Being a fallen and hunted leader's "son" would explain at once why he had fled Belgium and why, as Goriély's "prince in exile," he should not be pressed on the subject.

In the light of de Man's later theoretical assertions as to the slipperiness of language, one must acknowledge that he knew what he was talking about. Grand lies had their place and must be provided, but the details were crucial. In comparing the first and revised texts of this self-exculpation, one notes that many changes center on his uncle, with significant minor variants indicating that the writer was aiming to smooth away the more negative references. For example, a reference in the first draft to the leader's "ambiguous" attitude under the occupation loses its qualifying adjective in the second version. An initial assertion, "He remains an extremely debatable figure," which Paul let stand in the second version, he altered before it was typed, so that it read, "His case remains an extremely touchy issue."[12] The "figure" becomes the "case"; a hot argument about a human being becomes an issue that is "touchy." De Man moved the language toward the instrumental and impersonal because he aimed to minimize and detoxify the accusation. It was best to use a rhetoric as cool as possible, suited to the administrative committee that would review it.

As to the specific charges of collaboration, he denied everything. "I wrote some literary articles [but] I stopped doing so when nazi [sic] thought-control did no longer allow freedom of statement." Gone was his closeness to the Nazi Lothar von Balluseck, the Belgian Nazi Raymond De Becker, and Louis Didier, the Nazi-paid publisher of Editions Toison d'Or, men condemned to death postwar and forced into lifelong exile. Gone were the Nazi-funded publishing enterprises he had proposed to run—and to use to disseminate Nazi doctrines. Forgotten were the years of high pay from multiple collaborating companies, of toadying to the infamous Paul Colin, and of looking forward with Anne to a role as "minister of culture" in the embassies of the pan-European German Reich that would dominate Europe after the war. Instead, he stated that "during the rest of the war I did what was the duty of any decent person." Not only had he acted "decently," he had passed a postwar "severe examination of his political behavior" and gotten a certificate of good conduct to boot. This was reference to the brief interrogation by the prosecutor Roger Vinçotte in 1946, from which he had emerged unpunished and certainly with no certificate by dint of the falsehoods detailed in a previous chapter. One notes that in this argument, too, as in the one about his status as an immigrant with the INS, his strategy was to leverage a first and false claim (the lie that his behavior had been officially approved postwar) into a broader one, the assertion that there was not "the slightest reproach against me" and that he had actually received a "certificate of good conduct."

In similar fashion, he denied and swept away whatever questions were raised about Hermès. Yes, he had published art books, but although in fact he alone had had access to the company's funds, de Man spread the blame around to "three other" managers and asserted that he had merely left Belgium to pursue business interests in the United States. He knew nothing, and had heard nothing. Paul de Man had done "nothing dishonest." His "address ha[d] always been known in France and in Belgium." This, too, was false. The one incontrovertible statement in this letter was that he had "devoted the last seven years of my life to building an existence entirely separated from former painful experiences."[13]

Finally, more in sorrow than anger, he deplored the motives behind the attack. The false information was "calculated to cause me a maximum of harm." Made in secret and "behind my back," it was caused not by "viciousness, but merely because of the connotations of my name." This heavy burden of history had rendered him "weary and exhausted." The "dammage [sic] which all this has cost me" would be extensive; he had "no illusions" about that. He hoped now only to be able to "prove the truth of what I have stated" by keeping his fellowship and "letting the future depend on what will happen in Belgium." Keeping the fellowship indeed was everything.

Paul's effort succeeded. It was hopeless for Americans in their field, living in Massachusetts, none of whom spoke Flemish or were literate in Dutch, to penetrate the arcana of a Belgian lawsuit, bankruptcy, or whatever the denunciation asserted, and de Man knew it. It was lost in the murk of the postwar years, and de Man gambled accurately that no one really wanted to wade into it. The Society of Fellows, after all, wanted not to convict him, as the tone of his letters to Poggioli suggests, but to keep its skirts clean and have a document that would fully justify keeping him on.

There was criticism of Paul's delay in sailing for France, but very likely he was working overtime at Berlitz to earn extra money to spend on his return to Europe, where a dollar went almost twice as far as in the United States. Simultaneously, he was also thinking deeply—and creatively—about how to strengthen his reply. He came up with an added element to his response that, by its very oddity, perhaps made it more plausible. In private conversations held perhaps in January with Poggioli and evidently with Roger Shattuck, at the Society of Fellows, he shared with them in deepest confidence a profound family secret: He was not only the actual son of the disgraced minister; he was also the adopted son of his merely putative father, known as Bob de Man. Robert de Man had adopted his brother's love child.

In a letter of January 20, 1955, addressed to Shattuck, he modified his application for travel, asserting that he must go to Belgium for several reasons. (Belgium was not the home of any of his three subjects of study and travel there needed justification.) His visit there would be in connection "to adoption," to "liquidation of a publishing firm," to "finish naturalization" and to "see documents" for his work.[14] All four explanations were either outright lies or wild improvisations. There had been no "adoption," his publishing firm had long since disappeared, and he could not afford even to be seen by any of his creditors. Thus it was highly unlikely that he could solve his visa problems on the Belgian end of things. And with regard to his work, documents about Stefan Georg, a German, or de Man's French and Irish subjects would also not be found in his homeland.

Shattuck accepted the story, and so would the Society of Fellows in general, under the friendly influence of Harry Levin and Renato Poggioli. Eight days later, to secure his position yet more tightly, after having his official response typed, de Man composed a two-page handwritten letter (dated January 28), a somewhat eccentric communication. In it, Paul confided in Poggioli that he had "mentioned the political aspect of my father's career [sic]" but hoped that "the matter relating to my adoption by my uncle, Robert de Man, could not [sic] remain unstated." He went on to say:

> You could mention it orally to the Senior Fellows, but I would prefer not to put it in a letter which is, to some extent, a part of a public record. It has no direct bearing on the case, since it has nothing directly to do with any of the charges and, really is strictly an internal family matter. Also, I think that when it was done in 1938, some legal corners were cut, and this would involve my uncle whom, certainly, I want to keep out of this. So, unless you think it better otherwise, I would prefer to leave this unstated.[15]

Now Bob de Man was not only displaced as Paul's real father but he had cut "legal corners" in adopting this love child of his brother. Having told the lie about his family history successfully to Poggioli and Shattuck, Paul de Man now ensured that it would get around, requesting that it be disseminated orally, but in secret.

Why assert the adoption? And why choose that date? In 1938, the nineteen-year-old Paul had been still mourning for his mother, was estranged from his father, and was growing closer to his uncle Henri. Perhaps he hit on that date because it was then that his ties with his uncle had flourished and he had shared the minister's family dinners and Jan's flat. As to why he claimed not only that he was Henri's son but also that he actually had been adopted by his own father, one is powerless to imagine what good he thought it might do him. To be sure, the official records, if ever checked, would show that Paul had enrolled at ULB as the son of Robert de Man, but official records going back to his birth on December 6, 1919, would also show that Robert was his father.

Perhaps by giving a false date to a false adoption, de Man thought to give the narrative verisimilitude. The weird detail of a brother's adoption of a sibling's illegitimate child added the disagreeable whiff of deep family scandal. Having had to deal with his own son's illegitimate status, he already knew that in Belgium it was illegal to adopt one's own illegitimate child. (One recalls that he had made young Hendrik first disappear and then return to life four years younger via a false birth certificate.) It is likely that, knowing this, Paul may have created this convoluted narrative: Bob had adopted his own brother's bastard because Henri could not legally do so himself. It also mirrored the story, part of the family myth, of Bob de Man's informal adoption by his aunt Ida when he was substituted for her institutionalized, supposedly dead son, Adolph Kemna. One thing is clear: In its many falsities and multiple levels of confessions that are not confession (and as such is proleptic of de Man's later investigation of Rousseau's confessions), the narrative testified most of all to how deeply de Man was committed to this strange fantasy.

Mary McCarthy's memory may be apposite. She replied to Ortwin de Graef, quoting her onetime friend:

> He used to talk quite often with me about his uncle, Henri de Man—the Belgian socialist who . . . became a Fascist. This weird transformation which took place in his own family greatly interested Paul and said something to him probably about his own nature.[16]

Perhaps Paul felt that he and Henri shared a tendency to move and change their shape, as well as sharing an ability to please and move others, that gift for charismatic appeal. In many ways, the wandering "socialist who became a Fascist" was deeply embedded in his nephew's psyche. And so, no doubt, was his unhappy death as a stateless man who most likely committed suicide at a railroad crossing in Switzerland. This was a fate Paul did not wish for himself.

"But how is it possible to be capable of such a lie?" his onetime friend Georges Goriély wondered when he contemplated Paul's claim to be his uncle's son. Goriély was a man of strong family feeling and intellectual integrity and could ask that question without irony. The American poet James Dickey, on the other hand, who in private life was no exemplar of morality, once commented insightfully, "The manner in which a man lies, and what he lies about—these things and the *form* of his lies—are the main things to investigate in a poet's life and work."[17] De Man was not a poet, but he was a master of concealment and invention, "a wonderful liar," as his cousin Li said, and Dickey's words are apropos. In later years, de Man often used the word *mystification* in his theories in no creditable way: It was, he thought, what texts and writers and all of his contemporaries must inevitably do. But the blame was not theirs; it rested on the nature of language itself. De Man was not seriously out of touch with reality. He was not his uncle's son, and in promulgating this lie, he was not living a delusion, but using it to mystify others.[18] Part of his indifference to what others would call truth was part of his family's culture. Among that generation of de Mans, this sort of storytelling was what was known as "kicking up sand." His cousin Jan laughed about the process when he described it as a family skill, part of the de Mans' inherited "dominance" of character, and Paul's second wife remembered the phrase also.[19] His cousin Li had laughed when remembering Paul's skill at the practice.[20]

De Man sent his long-withheld official letter of defense, four typed and single-spaced pages in its final draft, to Poggioli on January 28, 1955, along with the manuscript previously discussed. Then with his wife and son, he boarded the French liner *Liberté* on February 5. He loved the luxury of the great ships, and it was a well-earned rest. Icarus was returning to earth, where, guided by Jean Wahl, he would become a philosopher; he would stay at the Hôtel des Grands Hommes. Under the circumstances, it was not a bad address.

33

RETURN TO EUROPE

WHEN PAUL DESCENDED INTO THE LOBBY OF HIS HOTEL IN THE MORN-ing, as he wrote Harry Levin, it was so packed with American professors on Fulbrights that the minuscule space reminded him "of an MLA meeting that [has] suddenly become light-hearted and elated."[1] The Hôtel des Grands Hommes, once home of "André Breton's illicit and scandalous amours" was a "modest but dignified" address across the street from the Panthéon and a stone's throw from the Sorbonne. A convenient but not an inexpensive lodging, it had an elevator, but its upper floors were reached only on foot, and the higher one climbed, the lower the rent. It was a token of their chronic poverty that by the end of their fourteen-month stay, the de Mans were living on the seventh floor, and Pat had learned a new skill: how to cook three dishes stacked one on the other in the steam generated by a single, illegal alcohol burner.[2]

It was not a lighthearted moment, however, when de Man opened the letter he had been awaiting from Louis Joris, long his family's solicitor in Antwerp. De Man had a scrap of paper on which he had written a list of names and things he must do: register with the police, write to Kenneth Murdock and Henry Kissinger back at Harvard, and contact the man who served his father as legal counsel and had known Paul since his childhood.[3] He had written him from the States, hoping that this old friend could sort things out with the authorities in Belgium and enable him to go home and reconcile with his father. It was essential to secure a new passport and regularize his legal status. Until now, he had been at best a nonperson. This would be the right time to revise his status. He was a man of thirty-five, a good age to return under the aegis of a rich fellowship provided by Harvard to a Europe that was still recovering from the damages of the war. His role would be that of a professor well connected in Paris and under the wing of the leading philosophers of the French intellectual world. Some might raise questions, but his new American wife and child would certainly make him seem more stable. Anne was far away, the "divorce" he would claim was no longer rare, and he could hope that the failure of Hermès would be overlooked. De Man had kept his circle in Brussels ignorant of his business dealings in Antwerp, and he might have imagined that these and his journalism during the occupation—for only that had been public—might be forgotten in the excitement and warmth of renewed friendship.

The lawyer, however, was worse than discouraging; on the contrary, his letter of February 17 strongly warned de Man to stay away. Joris told de Man that in spite of his representations to the Foreign Ministry, the prosecutor in Antwerp had recently ruled against issuing de Man a new passport. Nothing further could be done about it.[4] The underlying issue was the trials in 1949 and 1950 for crooked dealings, forgery, and embezzlement. A verdict had been rendered against him. In fact, the judgment had been handed down provisionally in his absence, on February 10, 1949, and this had been made final in the second case in 1951. The advocate wrote at length and pulled no punches. In both French and Dutch, he quoted from the opinion of the Antwerpen courts, discussed in a previous chapter, summarizing the multiple counts of forgery and of the seven other analogous crimes of taking money in the names of various clients or associates of the company. De Man had been convicted of sixteen acts of forgery, the amounts totaling 287,754 Belgian francs, or roughly $5,755, the equivalent of a little less than two years of his salary from Harvard at the time. The lawyer also summarized the separate and more damning charge of having made false entries in the books of the company to the tune of hundreds of thousands of francs. Finally, he informed de Man that he had been

judged guilty of taking money from other persons under false pre-
tenses.[5] He wrote him also of his very severe sentence of five years of
imprisonment and of the fines levied against him. Paul had asked Joris
about paying off his creditors, but this was "out of the question," he was
told. Bob de Man had repaid Raymond Eeckhoudt, but the court's
judgment stood no matter what. This voluntary reimbursement for one
of his son's thefts was evidently one of the several payments Bob de
Man made, which had severely damaged his financial standing and,
many said, had bankrupted him.[6]

Joris used the familiar *tu* in addressing the younger man, but the
letter was harsh. Above all, he said, Paul should not expect to be able to
return to Belgium, for if he did, he would be immediately imprisoned:
"If you see any means whatever (and I stress that) not to have to come
to Belgium, use it. For there is little chance, as I've said, of an acquittal.
That's equally true for your return to the United States."

If Paul did decide to risk returning, he'd be thrown immediately in
prison. Were he to decide to return to Belgium, he must obey Belgian
law, register with the police, and launch his appeal against the judgment
of 1951. This, however, would lead to his immediate arrest, and it
would be a "devil of a job" to meet even his personal needs in the
"establishment"—meaning the prison—in which he would find himself. Joris counseled de Man precisely on how to prepare himself. First,
he must send money ahead to the lawyer so that some cash would be
available, because anything he had on his person would be seized and
held on deposit. And second, he must arm himself with two letters,
written in advance but "NOT SEALED," as he would have to prove to
his jailers they were written only to his lawyer. One of these would
notify Joris of his arrival and the other would assert his legal appeal
against his conviction. No other message could be included in the texts.

The trial, he said, would be "important." He did not have to explain
why, given the family's association with Henri de Man, who had also
been judged guilty in absentia—for treason. Added to that were the
circumstances of Paul's crimes and Bob's position in the business world.
Under these clouds, the trial would become notorious. And it would be
Paul, not Bob, who would have to pay his fees.

If the lawyer meant to frighten de Man away, he succeeded. Yet there was also a deeper and sadder implication in his letter. Obviously, Paul's father knew and approved of the lawyer's advice. The tone of absolute rejection, the absence of any expression of sympathy, undoubtedly originated with Bob. As a result, Paul did not go to Belgium on that trip, and he would never see his father again. A gentle, conventional man of ordinary tastes and ambitions, Bob de Man had seen his life destroyed by one tragedy after another, with the long illness of his wife, followed by her suicide, the probable suicide of his admired brother, Henri, and the death of his son Rik also. But of all Bob's disappointments, Paul had been the greatest. A brilliant and promising child, he had rebelled against his father as an adolescent, lived openly in a ménage à trois, fathered an illegitimate child, married his consort against advice, and then turned crook and swindler. Bob had saved his son from jail by sending him away, but Paul had then abandoned his wife and the grandsons Bob had loved. By repaying Paul's thefts, Bob had bankrupted himself. Now after seven years of total silence, the prodigal sought reconciliation.

Bob would have none of it. He could not forgive his son, and he did not want to see him. The humiliations had been at once public, private, and deep.[7] After a journey he made to Ardez, Switzerland, in 1953 to claim Henri's body, he did not travel again. He had been close to Paul's children in Antwerp, but he never saw these grandchildren after 1948, and by 1954 he ceased his long practice of inviting Jan de Man's sons for their Sunday lunches.[8] It was a sad and lonely end for a well-liked man whose life had been unfortunate from the beginning. Already ill, Bob lived out what was left of his life with a young companion who had once been his nurse; he died in Antwerp of cancer of the throat in 1959.

In spite of their estrangement, Paul had been close to his father in his youth, closer than to his mother, and was deeply affected when he died.[9] The letter from Joris, severe as its warning was about legal consequences, therefore contained another message, silent but even more painful. Bob had nothing to say to his son. For Joris might have added, "In spite of these legal obstacles, your father wants to hear from you." Bob now knew where Paul was and could easily have visited him in Paris, only a couple of hours away by train, even if his son could not come to him. But he did not send such a message. Paul, whether or not he knew of his father's illness, would certainly have understood the meaning of his silence. When Paul and Pat's second child, a daughter, also named Patricia, was born in 1958, her mother wrote a letter to her father-in-law, although Paul advised her not to bother. His father, he said, "would see a relation with us as trouble." Bob did not answer. Yet he placed the letter in his safe, where it was found, Patricia reported, after his death. It had touched him, but he had kept it locked away with other memories he did not want to revisit.

With nothing he could do on that front, Paul de Man turned his energies elsewhere. He never lacked courage, and less than a month after reading the lawyer's discouraging letter, he approached the Belgian embassy in Paris after all. Perhaps he had learned from one of his countrymen in Paris, a group whom the Resistance poet Jean Lescure called "the Belgian Mafia," the fact that he had there a potentially useful contact. De Man looked up one of Anne's lovers from the war years, a man named A. Wendelen. They discussed Paul's problem, and although the other man at first had balked, he came around. "Paul felt there was some kind of resentment," Pat recalled. Noticing de Man's address at the Hôtel des Grands Hommes, in fact, Wendelen commented, "I might have known," referring to Paul's self-esteem, but nevertheless, "He said [to Paul] he didn't 'particularly like it but I'm doing it anyway.' "[10] On March 15, Wendelen, who was the economic counselor to the Belgian embassy in Paris, returned to Paul his formerly outdated passport, reporting that he had "the honor" of enclosing it, "extended to June 14, 1955," and politely requesting the considerable sum of 380 French francs in fees.[11] This was important progress: De Man had legal standing at last, at least in France. De Man's role of complaisant husband was not entirely without its merits, at least retroactively. Once again, he had risked much, but connections and boldness had carried the day.

These months, however, became a turning point for de Man, both intellectually and personally. He knew now that he could not resolve the impasse, that the break could not be repaired, and if not with his father, then not with his culture or country. He would later return to Europe, and after 1960, his visits would professionally be in triumph.[12] But all the conflicts with the world of his birth would have to remain unresolved. The impasse was probably one of de Man's deepest disappointments; it became, one surmises, a wound that would not heal. The feelings James Joyce called "the agenbite of inwit," and the lines of sadness and anxiety in his face, now began to show themselves.

There are passages in life that one comprehends fully only as one grows older. The finality of Paul's remark accepting his renunciation by Bob would gain greater resonance in his thinking. It was at about the same time that de Man, working his way through contemporary theory in company with Heidegger's writings, addressed the question of the past in his critical writings. In an essay on André Malraux, he dismissed conventional ideas about history, sweeping away tradition as mere "sediment" and innately toxic. At some level, Paul de Man was most certainly banishing his own relation to his father and his homeland in every sense—to his family ties, to Belgian society, and to his own grand ambitions under the occupation: "He would see . . . us as trouble" was the epitaph de Man would pronounce not only over his father but over his former life itself.

34.

HEIDEGGER:
A PLACE TO STAND

————

E MAN WAS GLAD TO HAVE JEAN WAHL AS HIS GUIDE IN PARIS, FOR the philosopher was not only a friend but also an editor who put him quickly into print, and under his aegis, Paul became unusually productive as a scholar. Wahl was a short man, so diminutive that he "came up only to the chin of his tall, red-headed wife," but he had cast a long shadow in French intellectual life even before he helped generate the excitement for Camus's *The Stranger* in 1942. By the time Paul joined him, he had become the major French force promoting the ideas of Martin Heidegger and editing two journals, *Le Monde nouveau* and *Deucalion*.[1] He was also a highly sociable man of sixty-seven, white-haired and slight of build, with blue eyes that "pierced and pierced."[2] People loved him for his generosity and enjoyed his eccentricities. Susan Sontag, who was taken to one of his parties, described what she encountered there:

> . . . a tiny slim birdlike old man with lank white hair and wide thin mouth, rather beautiful . . . but terribly distrait and unkempt. Baggy black suit with three large holes in the rear end through which you could see his (white) underwear. [He lived with] a tall Tunisian woman, [many children] and ten thousand books . . . [in] a rather beautiful disorder.[3]

Pat de Man thought of Wahl as a "true intellectual" both "immensely serious and immensely nice," whose apartment could scarcely be entered because one had to climb over the piles of books that were stacked to the ceiling and encroached on the door.[4]

It was partly through his guidance that the de Mans enjoyed an active social life, but they also had their own contacts. One resource was Ogden Kelley, whose love for his eldest daughter, Patricia, is evident in the photographic portrait he made of her, long-legged and tranquil, looking down at her small son as they stand together at sunset in the shallows of the Loire River. Kelley now lived permanently in France, and the couple visited him and his second wife as often as they could. Another outing enjoyed in the fall was to join in the *vendage*, a jolly harvest holiday in France, when students, normally forbidden to engage in manual labor, worked with farmers at gathering in the ripened grapes.

Paul knew Wahl already from his postwar days at Hermès, and the philosopher in 1949 had supplied a transatlantic letter of support for Pat's ill-fated application to the Fulbright Committee. He and de Man shared an enthusiasm for Melville, and Paul would certainly have given him a presentation copy of his handsomely illustrated Dutch translation of *Moby-Dick*. For de Man to have started work during the war on Melville's novel, with its blinding vision of being, "white as a mutton bone," in Sartre's words, was a real commitment; to have brought his translation out soon afterward was an impressive achievement. Melville had been in vogue among French intellectuals since Sartre had written about him in the 1930s, and Wahl could have known from that publication alone that de Man was a potentially valuable friend, a quick study with intellectual flair and a sense of timing for current ideas.

Wahl was a French Jew who had fled the Nazis (unusually late and reluctantly after imprisonment at Drancy). To Americans, it may seem ironic that this French philosopher's main role was to promote German existential thought within French philosophy,[5] but German philosophy had long been highly respected in France, Germany's neighbor and often its enemy. He took Paul under his wing at once, and his encouragement helped de Man release an intense surge of creative energy. The letter from Joris had been a shock. Paul de Man would have to live in a

state of permanent exile from Belgium, its citizen but always threatened by imprisonment should he return. In effect, he would be stateless.
It was too intimate a pain to discuss even with his wife, who remained
ignorant of the correspondence. He dealt with it using the same defenses
by which he had put his mother's death out of mind two decades earlier.
Admitting nothing, he turned the page on a great loss and focused
instead on his work, a driven man. During his two years abroad, he
would write and publish nine papers, extraordinary in number and
original in approach.[6] Never again would de Man be so prolific. His
father's silence both rendered him mute and forced him to find another
voice. When he cleared his throat, the tone that emerged was different.
He might privately have felt guilt, but he would never be able openly to
express remorse or seek forgiveness; he would be saved from public
shame, but he would never experience reconciliation. For he did reply
to his father, if indirectly, repairing nothing but finding a way to wipe
the slate clean as he worked through contemporary ideas earlier posited
by Bataille, Blanchot, and others that denied language's capacity to
communicate and denied to history the power to hold us accountable.
This era was the beginning of de Man's exploitation of ideas that would
save his intellectual balance and give him a place on which to ground a
renewed sense of self-respect. The permission to "flee forward," implicit
in existential thought, not to escape the anguish of memory but to
refuse to let it determine present action, would allow him to justify and
accept what he had been and done, and would point him toward a new
destination. But this stance and the new language he adopted with it
also put him on a course that would ultimately lead him into open and
serious intellectual collision with his mentors at Harvard. Increasingly
in what de Man wrote and how he lived, he would become again the
"the hero of the story," but this time the performance would be a philosophic narrative, conceived on Heidegger.[7]

Like Paul Simon's singer who couldn't run, but could walk away
very fast from disaster, de Man moved from his problems at the steady
clip of controlled anxiety, swallowing his guilt and turning it into a
song. It is not within the scope of this biography to discuss the literary
influence of Paul de Man's writings, but it is essential to mention the
general direction his thought was taking, for whatever his mentors at

Harvard expected, to him the purpose of his journey became a process of organizing his thoughts and shedding the ideological entrapments and personal errors of his past life. He had other plans for his dissertation than the kind of research the Society of Fellows expected on W. B. Yeats, Stéphane Mallarmé, and Stefan Georg. Paul produced very little on them while abroad, and he soon dropped the German poet entirely in a unilateral decision he made without consulting Levin, and this would rankle when his mentors learned of it.

Instead, de Man immersed himself in the dominant philosophy of his era, existentialism as defined by Martin Heidegger. (The term, *existentialism*, was shrugged off by both Sartre and Heidegger, but it was eventually accepted by both for want of a better one.)[8] Two of de Man's nine essays from this period deal directly with the philosopher, while his thought energizes the approach and language of the others. De Man was calling philosophy to his aid in finding a way to put a coherent ideology under his vision of both life and art. De Man knew that by his own acts he had lost all the dense network of memories, voices, and affections that had made up his earlier life. The least thoughtful of persons would have flinched at the sound of such heavy gates closing in his face, and the exclusion would bite deep. It was in this context that the impossibility of "direct contact" with being became one of Paul de Man's themes in the 1960s. It is not surprising that the approach that emerged in his writings brought into focus art's repressions—the eloquent gaps and silences of art—for which one could use his own term, *aporia*. Silence and secrecy constituted his own mode of dealing with difficulties or mistakes, and in adopting Heideggerian concepts, de Man's guilt would become human guilt, universal, and it would go unnamed. One would shoulder it and move on. Neither while he was at Harvard nor later did he ever reveal his past complicity with the German occupation, and there is no printed trail that would bridge the period between de Man's last wartime reviews in 1943 and his writings of the 1950s. Simultaneously, he adopted at this time a philosophic attitude that defined literature not in social or political terms but in its relation to being, Heidegger's master concept, while avoiding any reference to the German philosopher's questionable past or his politics.

Heidegger was popular among French intellectuals in spite of a dark political history. A failed priest who had abandoned the seminary to marry and become an influential philosopher, Heidegger joined the Nazi party in the early 1930s and became rector of the University of Freiburg. There, among his early duties, he had acted to purge Jews and other opponents of Hitler (including Karl Jaspers, a personal friend, who was married to a Jew) from the faculty. Even after resigning from the party around 1941, he projected his belief in Hitler's fantasy of the "Thousand-Year Reich," and justified the rule of the strong over the weak. During the de-Nazification period in 1945, he was put on trial at his university, found guilty, and dismissed from his professorship. Debating with Sartre at the time on the subject of his past commitment to Nazism, Heidegger called history "evanescent," a concept de Man eventually profited from. Hannah Arendt, a Jew, had been both his student and much younger lover (in 1924, she was eighteen, he thirty-five), but she fled Hitler and went into exile in the United States in the 1930s. Later, Heidegger, seeking rehabilitation, did not hesitate, in spite of his Nazi history, to badger her for help, as she had become an internationally influential intellectual. Reluctantly, she eventually complied, although he seemed to her like "a dog with its tail between its legs." With similar aid from others, he regained his chair in 1952 and continued the teachings that had become immensely influential, especially in France.[9] His existentialism was highly inflected by his history as a Catholic, and long after he had developed as a philosopher, he could still insist to a group of seminarians at Marburg, where he had trained, "I am a Catholic theologian." His followers welcomed the depth of his thought and his attempt to express the ineffable longings of humans toward a higher consciousness. He himself insisted to Karl Löwith that the " 'factical' or existential immediacy" of his own life shaped his philosophy. One of his critics, Richard Wolin, does believe that Heidegger's life shaped his ideas to an important degree and concludes that "the circumstantial aspects of Heidegger's thought, far from being . . . tangential, are . . . fundamental . . . to understanding his philosophy."[10] This is undoubtedly equally true of his follower, Paul de Man.

In spite of his wide influence, Heidegger's ideas and especially his terminology became highly controversial. Critics accused him of using terms (especially *being*) in contradictory and undefined ways in order to import into conventional philosophic discourse fundamentally religious ideas. To some critics, this murky terminology gained acceptance essentially because he offered hope for the future and, by the ambiguity of his language, provided a way of sidestepping or ignoring past deeds, not only personal ones but those of history itself as it is ordinarily conceived. The darkness of his language only added to the mystery he seemed to represent in his persona, which was charismatic; he reminded Walter Kaufmann, who studied with Heidegger and translated his work, of "a wizard." George Steiner considered Heidegger "anti-intellectual" and thought that the "*mysterium* of being"—the term most privileged by the philosopher but also most disputed—was used by him to negate rationality. In *Sein und Zeit* (*Being and Time*), being was, according to Steiner:

> A lofty abstraction that result[s] in a systematic anti-intellectualism. The rational self is negated in the name of its possession by the *mysterium* of being, even as the human instrumentalities of language are obfuscated by Heidegger's famous dictum that it is "language that speaks."[11]

Or, as the materialist Philip Rahv growled in response to one of Paul de Man's followers, "What's the address of being?"[12]

For de Man, Heidegger was important especially on two counts: first, his freeing of the human agent from guilt over one's own and others' history, which the philosopher expressed as the necessity of living "forward," of not being shackled by the notion of past selves; and, second, in his emphasis on poetry as a path not to an actual vision of the sacred but to dwelling, meditating on, and yearning for it. There are some confusing contradictions evident in the use of the past as de Man refers to it. Early on, it was de Man's ideal that one must privately confront the "painful consciousness" that one concealed from others; one's mind must not be "seeking protection from" such bad memories, but, instead, "trying to expose itself completely to a total awareness." Such a mind must "live in a balance of extreme tensions," a "drawn bow [that] achieves immobility when it is bent to the point of breaking."[13] He also mentioned in passing the connection between writing philosophy and living during the war when he wrote that Heidegger's "commentaries were thought out just before and during World War II, and are directly linked to an anguished meditation upon the historical destiny of Germany."[14] Apart from that, de Man ignored the philosopher's political past and endorsed his idea that history was not the narrative of mere facts. Rather, what mattered was one's intention in shaping the narrative of being, or *Sein*. This permission to turn away from the merely "real" past is relevant to a contentious issue, for de Man has often been criticized, although sometimes reluctantly, for not confessing to his wartime collaboration even by such a friend as Harold Bloom. But he had reasons for not doing so, and Heidegger's ideas undoubtedly helped him escape responsibility of the kind that Philip Watts stresses in his critique of Derrida and thereby of de Man by implication.[15] However, such confusion was beyond Paul de Man, either philosophically or in terms of his character.

On the other hand, the creative, poetic spirit needed the past and was "concerned with the past to reassure itself that there were times when it could be."[16] The poet looked backward only so that, knowing a former time of fruition, of feelings of having intuitions of being (or in Catholic terms of living in a state of grace), he could go on creating. Apparently, memory could pick and choose. One defined oneself in the present and without reference to whatever difficulties, mistakes, or profound errors lay behind. For Heidegger, in a phrase that de Man picked up and echoed, the "real force of the past is in the present and future."[17] The closest he came even to alluding to his political past and the ideas that had fueled him during his work as a collaborator under the occupation was the passing comment he made in "Montaigne and Transcendence":

> The wretched myths that surround us are no sooner born than they degenerate into sclerotic bureaucracies. They must appeal to the most factitious loyalties—those to race and nation . . . to gain any vitality at all. [Montaigne] in such circumstances . . . would be on the side of the rebels.[18]

"Myths . . . [of] race and nation" sums up nicely and with no unnecessary precision the fascist ideology that de Man had been taught and that he had, in turn, purveyed as a collaborating journalist.

Heidegger's importance to de Man was evident even before the latter reached Paris, appearing in two essays he published while he was still in Cambridge ("Montaigne and Transcendence" and "The Inward Generation").[19] By history, neither he nor Heidegger meant history in the ordinary sense of the word. *Being and Time* taught that history was not a static or absolute set of facts whose outline intellectuals set themselves to discover and interpret, but, rather, that it was what persons living in the present constructed in order to shape their future. One was to live forward, not backward, and one should look behind only in the process of constructing an idea of what lay ahead.[20]

Undoubtedly after the war, this concept was helpful in dealing with relevant, anguishing, but not widely proclaimed issues. The period of the Cleansing (or Repression, as it is called by Flemings) was soon recognized as having been too harsh, but how to deal with it philosophically, how to justify to oneself or one's society the problems of guilt and the desire either to purge oneself or punish others was difficult. Sartre occupied a different camp, and in 1945 he insisted on the ideas of individual agency and responsibility, and he was a critic of the "destiny" and "truth" of Heidegger's own recent past, which, as his trial showed, to his chagrin, had refused to evaporate and disappear into Being.[21] Heidegger, however, turned his back on such issues and insisted that history was far more elevated and essential than "the evanescent past," which was composed only of mere events, detritus. Real history, he wrote, "occurs essentially as the destiny of the truth of Being and from it."[22] It was more a teleology than a record of where human beings had been and what they had done.

Some thirty years later, the work of the Chilean scholar Victor Farías drew attention once more to Heidegger's Nazi past with detailed research that created widespread controversy.[23] Since then, other writers have pointed out that existentialism was in part a response to its era, and Philip Watts and others have more recently looked again at the process as raising questions that have not been settled.[24] For de Man in the 1950s, however, Heidegger's approach to history was immensely liberating, and under his inspiration he wrote one of his earliest and perhaps most lyrical essays on Michel de Montaigne, an ego ideal who lives only in the present and forgets the past, a Heideggerian *avant la lettre.*[25] The skeptic, having freed himself from the past, from doubt and failure, had abandoned the dangerous world of religious and political conflicts swirling below him to live in serenity and gaiety of spirit, secure in his mountaintop château in seventeenth-century France. Knowledge, ethics, and even aesthetics had failed the French essayist, but with grace he "moves unceasingly on the narrow ridge where no temporal density can accumulate." De Man attributed a Heideggerian consciousness to this French subject when he said that "history is introduced [by Montaigne] as a determining force in the present only," for "his tense is exclusively the present . . . the past collapses straightaway into oblivion." Getting free of a determining past and living removed from ordinary time was important for de Man.

Montaigne wrote from the perspective of one "who is already dead," from "the point of view of death." That is why de Man's Montaigne never reread himself, never "refers to his previous declarations. He had forgotten them . . . and lives beyond failure" on that narrow ridge where the winds of being blow unimpeded on the "pure beauty of his sentences . . . the entrancing sinuosity of his art . . . the tranquil irony" of his regard.[26] One of Paul's puzzling phrases is his praise that in Montaigne's writing the "tense is exclusively the present," "the past collapses straightaway into oblivion," and the writer "escapes from his subjectivity" and "never refers to his past declarations" because "quite literally he has forgotten them." This becomes more transparent in light of the remarkable fact that Paul after he arrived in the United States, literally forgot Flemish, his mother tongue—a repression that became inconvenient when he eventually did meet again some of his Flemish relatives.[27]

Once in Paris, de Man dusted off his hands and began to clear the ground of competing and misinformed thinkers some then considered important. J. Hillis Miller, who had preceded Paul at Harvard by a few years and later became a friend, was one of the few American critics then seriously interested in "Continental" philosophy. Miller commented that de Man tended to write "against" writers whom he had previously favored and that it was precisely those who had been important to him whom he criticized.[28] While still in the United States, he had already attacked some of the great names among contemporary writers—Gide, Hemingway, and Pound—who, he asserted, were alienated from being and suffered from "unhappy consciousness" because their politics had been "too facile" and they had avoided "the ontological question." The pot engaged with the kettle: Their "convictions proved so frail that they ended up by writing off this part of their lives altogether." Their condition could be remedied only by awakening to the "prophetic vision" of Nietzsche and Heidegger.[29]

Now he attacked writers he considered either naïve or ignorant, such as Maud Bodkin, a Jungian critic who wrote on archetypes, and the novelist and essayist Nathalie Sarraute. He showed more respect for A. O. J. Lovejoy, then renowned for his book *The Great Chain of Being*, but accused him of "pluralism" and the use of "historical common sense."[30] Lovejoy also erred in publishing in what de Man called "eclectic journals" that did not pursue a firm preestablished line. De Man took these writers to task for not grasping the importance of what was transcendent or for misunderstanding the crucial relationship of art to the divine. But poetry could only long for a glimpse of being, never achieve it: "Art does not imitate the divine or repeat it; it is an endless longing for imitation."

A novelist more important than Sarraute whom de Man attacked was the influential André Malraux. This hero of the Spanish Civil War would be minister of culture under Charles de Gaulle for a decade and had iconic status as an intellectual, but the anti-Marxist Left was his enemy. (Bataille had written a mocking satiric squib against him.) De Man attacked Malraux for his belief that history provides essential traditions that nourish culture and must be handed on. Such history or culture was, according to de Man, mere "sediment." In the novel entitled *The Walnut Trees of Altenburg*, "where the principal character receives the revelation of the permanence of man by seeing the ancient trees of the ancestral manor," Malraux had rendered himself a "nihilist."[31] To de Man, it was wrong to invoke the authority of the dead past to shape an agenda for the living. One must engage in a "struggle for being," and in spite of his "discontinuities," Heidegger should be one's guide.[32]

Perhaps the most valuable thing de Man learned from Heidegger was to regard poetry not as a pathway directly to the divine or to a glimpse of being—for that was forbidden to mortals—but as a mediate way to dwell upon being, or to lift one's consciousness toward, if not into, transcendence. Poetry could compete on a level ground with philosophy of history and speak equally as well about the "ontological question." Heidegger's work on the German Romantic poet Hölderlin was immensely valuable, for in the early nineteenth century, Hölderlin had been a soaring creator who had fallen into madness and been forgotten. Yet Heidegger had understood that Hölderlin was a "true philosopher" and must be rediscovered.[33] To demonstrate the connection between this poet and Heidegger's visionary insights would elevate both. To this end, de Man evoked an additional image of the philosopher, bringing Hölderlin—who was simultaneously Icarus—back to earth: "For the promise of Heidegger to be realized, Hölderlin must be Icarus returned from his flight."[34] Since de Man had chosen Icarus as his own emblem, he seems to imply here that Heidegger needed to have him at his side as well as the poet. De Man's trope is tightly wound, a secret allegory with more than a grain of his old hubris. Paul lived in exile, but he would bring back something wonderful, and in good company.[35]

The mystical tendency of his adolescence had not disappeared entirely, but was returning under another guise. Undoubtedly the tacit ardor of de Man's interest was part of his intense appeal to young and searching minds.

Poetry might ascend, but accuracy did not have to nip at its heels. De Man also gained from Heidegger a dispensation from ordinary standards of fidelity to one's sources (although given his liberties with the records of the Agence Dechenne and Hermès, he might have found his freedom independently). Paul's practice of misquoting or distorting his sources was noticed early by some of de Man's bemused students. Later, as Ortwin de Graef has shown, de Man knowingly misrepresented Rousseau's language when it suited him in order to make a point that the text would not sustain of itself. (The scholar, however, believed that de Man could not honestly have done otherwise.)[36] In the latter part of the 1950s, Richard Rand was disappointed by his mentor's indifference to accuracy and recalled their conversations. "An example: '*L'Impasse de la critique formaliste.*' I checked as a sophomore his comments on Marvell and Empson on Marvell. De Man's comments on Empson did not jibe.

And I said to de Man, 'This is not what Empson was saying.' And he looked at me and said, 'I know that.' I said, 'This guy is not [concerned with] what he can get away with. It's that he knows what matters and he knows what . . . doesn't matter [in] what you get away with, what doesn't count.' "[37]

Barbara Johnson, who went on to become a respected feminist scholar, was another friendly witness to her professor's misquotations: "It's as if literature was telling him stuff and it was of the utmost urgency to transmit the message, and it was like he was on a cell phone that kept breaking up and he would just stick in something that had to be there. The argument he wanted to make was stronger than the evidence—but it *came* from evidence. . . . About [his] making up quotations. Saying what Melville should have said but didn't. What he said was less important than what Melville should have said but didn't."[38]

The occasional irritation and arrogance de Man might show when challenged did not disqualify him for the devotion and love many of his students felt for him. Without saying it directly, de Man seems to have implicitly demanded and gotten from his followers essentially the same antinomian dispensation from the disciplines of scholarship that he had granted to Heidegger.

In 1955, de Man had already been amused by the German philosopher's practices, which were "far from scientific philology," marked by "apparent excesses," and able even to "reverse the thought" of the poet's meaning. He justified them on the grounds that while such readings might express the direct opposite of Hölderlin's intention, they had the "great merit" to have brought out "precisely the central 'concern'" of the work. Heidegger was defensible, guilty only of "direct adherence" to "the ineffable"—to God or being. "The blind or violent passion with which Heidegger treats his texts" was, given his mysticism, understandable. Evidently, de Man saw Heidegger as an antinomian, guilty of violating merely human laws of rationality in the name of a higher law.

Many of Paul's older colleagues, however, took exception to such practices. John Hollander, contemporary with Paul at Harvard and not his student, noted the same transgression, but not forgivingly. He had a stronger complaint: that de Man disregarded and devalued the canon of literature itself, teaching and caring only for those texts he personally preferred. Such a colleague might like de Man personally while resenting a betrayal of the fundamentals of education. Yet evidently, none could stand against the tide of his sweeping success. In a certain sense, Paul de Man treated the literature that had preceded the Romantic era as he did his personal history. Paul's second wife said more than once that he "never read a text for which he did not have an immediate use." What was past for him was not prologue, but a shackle. He and some of his students (though undoubtedly not those quoted above) wanted liberation from it.

De Man's philosophical approach to literature would cause him trouble after he returned to Harvard, and one of de Man's students reported that being a Heideggerian made him "suspect."[39] Yet in 1955, he was choosing a wide-open field, and his timing was excellent, for literary criticism in the United States had become hidebound. With his keen sense of what was in the wind, he already knew that the philosophical currents then sweeping the European Continent were fruitful, and also that New Criticism was ready to collapse from desiccation. He had quickly absorbed its methods of close reading as taught by Reuben Brower, but a great deal of literary analysis had by then become formulaic, formalistic, and stale. Under its aegis, all discussions of content or context were essentially banned, as were "value judgments." Some departments of English considered philosophy to be "extrinsic" to the work—as Cynthia Ozick told Lionel Trilling (see p. xx). Often professors stressed philology and the kind of literary history that focused on facts at the expense of ideas. J. Hillis Miller, who was a few years ahead of de Man at Harvard, got his Ph.D. there in 1952. He cited his general examination in 1950, which "stopped with Thomas Hardy": "There was no twentieth century. This is 1950. We were halfway through the twentieth century. . . . It was questions like, 'There was a famous bonfire in the 1590s,' and you were supposed to say, 'Yes, that was the burning of the books.' And they would say, 'What books were there?' and you'd say, 'Well, Green's *Groatsworth of Wit* was one of the books that was burned.' They would say, 'Thank you,' and go on to the next question. . . . Then you wrote a dissertation that was philological or whatever."[40]

In Western Europe, by contrast, although literary studies had their own burden of pedantry, to separate the social or political implications of a written work from its language would have been unacceptable in the polarized spheres of intellectual debate. For a French intellectual journal or publisher, it would be essential to have begun by at least tacitly locating a text in terms of its philosophical and political orientation. Jérôme Lindon, who became publisher of Editions de Minuit—where Paul had falsely claimed to have worked[41]—made a point of saying that he had favored authors who represented the post war, more "democratic" ethos, and not that of Jean Paulhan, a high bourgeois.[42] For that reason, he had dismissed, among others, Paul's old friend Georges Lambrichs[43] as chief editor and installed instead Alain Robbe-Grillet, who told him he was "stupefied" by the lack of "line," the "eclectic" point of view in the journal 84, which Lambrichs had acquired for the company.[44] Lindon did not have to say that in French publishing there was no self-delusion about value-free writing or analysis.

IN THE LONG RUN, what Heidegger meant to de Man changed. He would internalize his message and turn his attention elsewhere. But in this period, he was wrestling with conflicting needs. On the one hand, he endured his own destructive and anguishing memories, which probably became increasingly real and deep as he became more mature; they were truths that must, in Lear's words, "to the kennel be whipt." On the other, he had, in a certain sense, found a way and a life. In his longest and most Heideggerian essay from this period, he quoted the philosopher on the relationship of God to poetic metrics, or measure. There can be no "measure," de Man wrote, without "an entity against which one measures" and that entity is God: "the sky, or God, pure and absolute transparency. Thus God is the invisible, the unknown; poetry is thus the measure of the invisible, and that is why it speaks in 'images.'" De Man admitted in "The Temptation of Permanence" to feeling Heidegger's "seduction," to being "carried along" by a movement of thought so "captivating" that one may ignore its "discontinuities." "The seduction is effective," he concluded, "as it requires a great vigilance finally to resist it. Perhaps that is its end, for vigilance is the very weapon of the struggle of being."[45] It seems clear that for de Man, this "struggle of being" was a quasi-religious one, not unlike the Augustinian struggle that sought belief through unbelief.

In de Man's effort to find a lever long enough to shift the burden of his guilt to a more bearable position, Heidegger had done him service. His being was not precisely a Christian God, but if poetry was indeed "the measure of the invisible," then to dwell on the "pure and absolute transparency" of metrics would be time well spent. With all the denials to which de Man was now committed, the doors he must keep shut, and the faces he must remember to forget, it was useful at least in imagination to stand somewhere in nature on a little hill under the bending dome of the sky and dwell on transparency. The grimness and austerity of de Man's life during the late 1950s were partly due to overwork and his eventual academic failures. Between poetry and memory, he would struggle to find peace.

35.

"*EXCUSEZ LE JARGON*"

Ⅰ NTELLECTUALLY, THE TWO YEARS THAT PAUL DE MAN SPENT ABROAD in the mid-1950s were extremely successful, the beginning of a rich era. He had plenty of work, and his remarkable social skills and ability to assess and enter into whatever was most new and promising were vital to his success. With friends like Wahl, Bataille, and others, he had excellent entrée. At a conference in Geneva in the summer of 1955, he met the venerable phenomenologist Georges Poulet,[1] and an observer remembered the old Belgian critic and the young one sitting together in the sun on a wall.[2] His friendship with the poet Yves Bonnefoy began when they met in Wahl's seminar that spring, a course Bataille also attended.[3] Paul spent a good deal of his time in the St. Geneviève Library at the Sorbonne, preparing the essays he would soon be publishing.[4] Eric Weil, a translator of Hegel and an editor of *Critique* serving under Bataille, gave a seminar that Paul attended at the Sorbonne in addition to Jean Wahl's. He did not, however, make any new acquaintances in Weil's group because, as Pat recalled, "It was so small that it was attended only by Paul, Weil's family, and a few *clochards* [drunkards] off the street coming in from the cold. A minimum number of students was needed for it to run. It was Eric Weil who told Paul that this was why his family came."[5]

When Paul de Man was getting ready to decamp to the country for the summer of 1955, he summarized for Harry Levin his satisfaction with the three and a half months he had passed in Paris. In the tone of a cultural reporter sending bulletins from the scene, he reported that it was a "captivating" place, but he found it easy to avoid the "sins of commitment" that involved almost everyone else in a "ceaseless mood of polemics and '*prises de position*'" (public taking of sides), which had become for Parisians a "vicious circle and second nature."[6] He introduced the subject of the Marxism prevalent among French intellectuals, together with a seemingly casual but stunning lie about himself, tossing it in as if in passing while shaking his finger at the childish and belated Marxists who surrounded him:

> Their main obsession remains, of course, political—but in a way which, after the U.S. seems rather childish. The long and painful soul-searching of those who, like myself, came from the left and from the happy days of the Front populaire, seems to have made less headway than in the States. It still takes on the form of an embarassed [*sic*] and apologetic criticism of orthodox marxism [*sic*]. . . .

This was an outrageous claim. Paul was asserting that he felt himself at one with those Americans and Belgians of the Left who during the mid-1930s had banded together with the Communists to fight Hitler— Charles Dosogne, for example. De Man not only was falsely claiming partisanship in the Front populaire (Popular Front)[7] but was inventing for himself a "long and painful" period of "soul-searching" by which he had cleansed himself—like his American brothers—of deluded socialist notions and had emerged a mature thinker. In fact, he had been only a schoolboy during the era of the Popular Front and had shared no "happy days" with its members in that period when he had been most influenced by his uncle, who was turning into a fascist and leading Belgium into appeasement. In fact, he himself was trying to keep his head above water in a family that was struggling with young Rik's crimes and his mother's descent into depression and suicide. The only position of his own Paul could have pointed to was the short piece he had published in *Le Rouge et le Noir* in Belgium at sixteen, in which he had urged a form of appeasement and taken a middle ground.

Why did Paul de Man bother to lie to Levin about the Popular Front, such a minor matter? Probably, it was out of habit, but largely to shore up the persona he had been creating since he had first presented himself at Harvard in 1951. He probably recognized that in communicating with Americans who were living through the Red Scare, it would not do if he seemed to move too easily among Communists and Marxists. Better to embroider a bit on his preexisting story. Already he had fabricated a tale of life in the Resistance as a member of the Front de l'Indépendence. Now he also created an adolescence to go with it.

This enriched personal narrative left Paul free to report on what his new circle argued about: mainly politics, especially Marxism, its literary practitioners (Sartre, Merleau-Ponty) and its ancillary topics (Algeria, Tito, Mendès-France), and the baccalaureate degree, along with details of the hidebound, inward-looking habits of the scholarship practiced at the Sorbonne. He took a sardonic tone: "More restless minds," he wrote, "drift toward philosophy," mentioning Wahl, Weil, Hyppolite, and Kojève. He also claimed to have "written [an] article . . . for [Wahl] which will appear in the *Revue de métaphysique et de morale*," but he had not—although Levin himself did publish a paper in this highly prestigious journal a year later.[8]

De Man played down the issue of work on his dissertation, mentioning it only briefly. It was not necessary to reveal any sooner than he must how different his own direction now was. How Levin took this, one cannot know. He was an experienced and shrewd man, used to the tergiversations and delays of students facing the blank page of the largest work they had yet undertaken, but de Man was still the favored and perhaps the most promising student in the department, and only the affair of the denunciation, now dismissed, had blotted his record. Undoubtedly, his mentors had decided to give de Man a long leash.

That spring was a good time for him. His passport problem was at least temporarily under control, his first essay had appeared under Wahl's sponsorship, and, best of all, he was far from Anne's lawyers and her incessant demands for money and contact. By his own wish, he was entirely out of touch with his three sons. Rik was being raised by Mr. and Mrs. Woods, but Paul knew nothing of his life, as he had refused all contact with his child, while on her side, Mrs. Woods had no use for her spendthrift son-in-law and misguided daughter.

With the coming of summer, Paul and his family left Paris for the Loire Valley and Pat's father, with whom they stayed into the late fall. It was a good time to relax in the countryside. France and Europe had not yet fully recovered from the war, and to someone coming from the United States, French apartments and hotels seemed cramped, cold, and ill-lit. The *minuteries* that measured the seconds of electric light provided on the stairwells gave barely enough time to get from one floor to the next before plunging the visitor into darkness, and less affluent travelers brought their own soap, face cloths, and sometimes towels to those hotels they could afford. French food was almost always good, but before the arrival of espresso from Italy, French coffee was surprisingly bad, almost as bad as American. The smell of French cigarettes was everywhere and appreciated by some. Clothes cost so much and rents were so high that few Americans understood how the French could live at all. But it was France, and the language sounded as delicious as the daubes tasted, and enchanted as easily as the way French persons with a little shrug and a small smile could move through a crowd and leave no eddy behind. All the men looked, as a young American woman remarked, as if they knew how to dance.

In the country, the family went fishing, and Ogden Kelley took pictures of the daughter he loved but had seen little of since his divorce. There was Pat—already adept at picking strawberries—at the grape harvest; Pat, long-legged and clad in shorts, with her son and husband, standing in the shallows of the Loire, lit from behind by the setting sun as she looked down with a sense of repose at little Michael wading beside her. At the harvest in autumn, they all lodged with a peasant family, working, eating, and drinking together in jollity if not comfort as they clipped the vines, filled the baskets, and trudged through the vineyard. Working at the *vendage* was one of the few manual tasks that custom and issues of social class permitted students and academics to enjoy. The three generations remained together until All Saints' Day, November 1, when Paul took Pat and Michael, now five, back to the old hotel near the Sorbonne.

Most of the time, de Man wrote. By that fall, he had four articles either published or coming off the press, and he probably knew or sensed the shape of his next three or four essays. He was preparing the ground—rather, clearing it—for the work that he would define for himself in the future and moving steadily toward an intellectual goal. This was probably evident to those few who attempted to follow him. One of these was the philosopher Stanley Cavell, also that year a fellow of the Society of Fellows, who met de Man in Paris during his own year abroad. He reported that he read the essays that appeared in *Critique*, found them interesting, and got in touch with Paul. They spent a day together at a picnic they arranged in the country near Paris, with Pat and Michael present. He found their exchanges "oddly friendly," and they kept in touch partly out of his impulse of friendship. Later, when Cavell was teaching at Harvard and the Philosophy Department had been stymied for some years in making an appointment, he was "impressed enough about him" to suggest that his colleagues resolve their impasse by appointing two new people: one would be Paul de Man for a joint professorship in the history of philosophy and nineteenth-century literature.[9]

Of immediate importance to Paul de Man was to determine his strategy in writing to Renato Poggioli. His aim was to stay on in France for another year, continue writing, and put off the day when, instead of producing a considerable portion of his dissertation, he would show him and Levin essays that dealt with two Germans, one a sublime Romantic poet who had died mad (the Hölderlin essay) and the other, Heidegger, a living and very controversial philosopher—but nothing at all on Stefan Georg and very little on Mallarmé and Yeats. To that end, de Man created a series of stories, one building on the other and turning on a David versus Goliath drama of an innocent but determined man fighting for his rights against not one but two governments. In December 1955, after a year's absence from teaching commitments, Paul appealed to the chairman to extend his grant for another year.[10] This was against the rules: other fellows—Stanley Cavell was one—also had wanted a second year abroad but did not ask for or get it. This letter was the first of a new series in which de Man would write falsely about his status and, once that was established, piggyback another tale onto it until he had gained his end. The stories he invented focused on

getting a new passport and settling the finances of his unnamed publishing house. Both he knew to be impossible, but they undoubtedly
expressed a deep wish. The process was a kind of autobiographical
Ponzi scheme.

His first invention was a lengthy description of an imaginary trip
made in November to Belgium in order to regain his passport, a fanta-
sized journey he reported in language loaded with legal jargon, as if he
had just returned from deep immersion in the life of the courts, an
impression he stressed by noting parenthetically, "*(excusez le jargon).*"
His tale was all good news, and he its hero. In Antwerp with his
"lawyer-friend," he had confronted "the official who handles my
'case'" and succeeded in having his passport "extended to normal travel
in all countries." In fact, he had not returned to Belgium and could not,
for the reasons discussed previously. The actual case against de Man had
been couched largely in Dutch because the courts sat in Antwerp, but
for his own reasons, de Man chose to develop a particular diction
derived from French legalisms to detail his consideration of proposed
alternate procedures. Perhaps he would pursue a "countersuit" to
"obtain a non-lieu" but—and this was a path proposed by the mythical
"*juge d'instruction*" himself—there were two alternate procedures, each
diverging and leading to "two possibilities . . . a passport . . . without
more ado," or a "hearing," which would lead to "the same result." In
either case, he would triumph. The acquisition of the passport, however, was unfortunately to be delayed until "January, or early February
at the very latest." It was not an accident that this date would be too late
for Poggioli to put de Man on the teaching roster for the spring of 1956.
De Man allowed that he would prefer "to return around April"—"or
perhaps simpler, at the end of the Spring term altogether."

Paul de Man did not have a passport or any prospect of getting one.
In fact, he had to travel on Pat's documents as her spouse for the rest of
his life. He could not apply for U.S. citizenship, she said—for obvious
legal reasons. This was a problem that would not go away. But it was
also a fact Poggioli must not learn. The passport narrative was the distraction, the smoke and mirrors, of the four page-letter, whose other
purpose was to secure the funds to stay abroad another year. Referring
to the false story he had told about having lost his publishing business

through the unspecified misdeeds of others, he closed his letter by expanding on his character as the hapless but undaunted victim of "bookkeeping irregularities" and the technicalities of the Belgian legal system. It was these and not dishonesty, he said, that had caused the failure of the company he had run with his partners. Gone were his massive forgeries and embezzlements; instead, he wrote that the failure of his company had nothing to do with any dishonest act of his own, but merely with problems concerning regulations about foreign money exchange rates and licenses. No one had pressed charges against his company because nobody had been hurt financially. Yet he had been refused a passport because at some unnamed time a judicial warrant had been issued against him—an act that had never been followed up on. However, all that was in the past, and his passport had been normalized for travel abroad.[11]

No one had been hurt financially. So much for the tens of persons—including his father, aged nurse, and most of his social circle—who had lost over 500,000 Belgian francs due to de Man's own depredations. He closed with generous words of sympathy for Poggioli at having to read so long and boring a letter.

De Man was receiving a generous three thousand dollars a year from the Society of Fellows, at a time when an American instructor could live on such a salary and when abroad the dollar went almost twice as far as it did at home.[12] Moreover, Ogden Kelley undoubtedly had footed most of their expenses for the four months while his daughter, Paul, and Michael stayed with him. Yet Paul could not afford, he wrote in opening this same letter to his supervisor, to have a carbon copy of his manuscript made for Harry Levin, or indeed to pay the additional postage that a "folder" for the loose sheets he was enclosing would have entailed. Thus he entrusted his only copy of the Mallarmé material to the vagaries of the transatlantic mails. De Man had lost unique manuscripts before and would do so again, at great damage to himself. What was he doing with his funds? No one, including Pat de Man, ever understood Paul's finances. Was this poverty? Or was he once again "throwing his treasures out the window," to use Paul Willems's phrase? Unquestionably, he was again tempting fate.

His story paid off, and Paul stayed abroad for a second full year, until the end of 1956, by which time he had eight new essays in print. Clearly, whatever faults de Man had, his work showed him to be both an exceptionally productive and highly original thinker. Yet Paul did not keep spinning those variations on his theme for Poggioli and Levin merely to prolong his stay. There was a deeper and more dangerous issue at stake. If he ever admitted to them that he could not get a passport, the jig would be up. Inevitably, his superiors would have to ask him why, and anything he might say could be readily checked at the logical place, the Belgian consulate in Boston, or even at a governmental office in Belgium. His continued status as a student at Harvard required a foundational lie: that he had gone to Belgium to secure a new passport, and onto that he laid the superstructure of falsehoods about the judicial hearing, the alternative routes to success, the delay in issuing the document, his innocence of false charges against him, which ultimately had simply fallen away and should never have been brought, the new and inappropriate delay by the American officials, and so on. Each tale rested on the previous one, each addition seemed to strengthen the initial assertion, and a problematic story became accepted as a motivational part of his persona. In later years, when de Man had become what he called a "theorist," he drew attention to the suspicious nature of all narratives, the need for the reader to examine them closely for the lies they told and the underlying motive or character they inevitably revealed for what was "at stake." That emphasis stemmed at least in part from his own intimate knowledge of how successful one could become at constructing plausible tales, how gullible most people were in the face of them, and how much one could profit by telling the right story, in the right way, to the right people. Levin and Poggioli were highly intelligent men, but as long as they wished to believe Paul and had no reason to doubt him, he knew that they would trust and see him as he wished to appear.

HAVING WON PERMISSION, PAUL remained in Paris until April 1956, a pleasant time to travel. Then, again accompanied by Ogden Kelley, the family departed by train for England via Holland. Pat remembered seeing the tulips in bloom as they approached the Hook of Holland for the ferry to England, where de Man planned to carry out his research on Yeats. It was probably around this time that he began to realize that he would have to drop Stefan Georg as the third focal point of his dissertation. Only a few months remained for research, and he had not visited Germany. Given his intense schedule of writing on other topics, the thesis had gotten very little of his attention. He'd done a limited amount of writing on Mallarmé and had looked around a bit for material on Yeats, but that was all. He must have recognized that with time so short, it would be hopeless at this late date to try to cram in research on the German poet; this was a decision Harry Levin decided later was based on the political taints that were attached to Georg's name.[13] It was time to tour Great Britain at leisure and meet such great men as he might encounter. His first stop was Oxford University, charming in the spring, the golden sandstone of its buildings weathered to gray, its college gardens green and brilliant with flowers, and its high tables surrounded by dons whom de Man would take pleasure in meeting. Oxford was not Yeats country, but the poet had been given an honorary degree by the university, and Paul planned to find manuscripts and make such contacts as would benefit him. He stayed for a couple of months and met whatever intellectual celebrities opportunity offered. Writing Levin at the end of May, he reported that he had "seen" Isaiah Berlin and W. H. Auden, the two great lions of the university community, and he also met Maurice Bowra, the locally famous classicist, influential in academic politics for both his judgment and wit.

Good as Paul was at making social and professional contacts, however, he was inept at the conventional business of accurate scholarship. He was, after all, the same person whose indifference to all limits and record keeping had allowed Peeters to trip him up—and push him from—the Agence Dechenne in 1943. Now he complained to his mentor:

I am a little staggered by the immediate confusion that sets in as soon as one touches upon something connected with Yeats. Fortunately, there are a limited number of precise points about which I want to find some information, for I pity anyone engaging in extensive research on that subject.[14]

Original research based on unedited manuscripts inevitably means sorting through immense amounts of chaff before finding a grain or two of wheat, and that classical approach to scholarship was tedious and probably impossible for de Man. He was obliged, however, to make a real—if highly abbreviated—effort at finding the manuscript material on Yeats that had provided the justification for going abroad on the Society's ticket. He made the best of it, and proceeded across England and through Wales, where, having left Ogden Kelley behind, he and his family took ship for Ireland on Midsummer's Eve, or Saint John's night, June 21. Before long, he found a cottage on Rosses Point, in County Sligo, on the west coast of Ireland, the region where Yeats had lived most happily and an area famous for its beauty. Ben Bulben, near which Yeats wrote that he wanted to be buried, was the haunt of hawks, which perched on its crest and hovered over the fine blue bay and green fields bordering the county seat of Sligo. Their dwelling had a thatched roof and lay between the low mountain, Knocknarea, and Ben Bulben, the focus of Yeats's poem "Under Ben Bulben." It sounded idyllic ("how conventional can you get?" Paul asked happily about his choice), but it was uncomfortable, and Pat remembered that the peat fire, their only source of heat, smoked vilely. Her husband found the poet's widow (who referred to her late husband by his initials) to be "spirited, uninhibited . . . very funny . . . mischievous, and a bit tough," with "an explosive witch-laugh."[15] But although they got along well, Paul was oppressed by the massive quantity of the texts he was supposed to have spent most of his time studying. A few months later, when he had settled in Dublin, he let Levin know that he needed still more time there. He wrote:

> [T]he amount of unpublished Yeats material is staggering. The widow Yeats had that day lent me very graciously all early versions of the Player Queen, in which I have a special interest: all in all eleven fat envelopes of notebooks and typescripts, more than 500 pages of Yeats' difficult handwriting.[16]

Like many literary executors, Mrs. Yeats had probably been hoping that just such an intelligent and personable young scholar would present himself, without quite knowing what his particular talents would turn out to be. But she picked the wrong man. Since he planned to embark for home in two weeks, it was obviously hopeless to do more than tentatively survey, perhaps with a sinking heart, this new and unmanageable mass of papers. He was undoubtedly fortunate that in that era it was functionally impossible to make photostatic copies, and making microfilms was an expensive and slow process. De Man had exceptional talents, but he had little for the disciplined gathering, study, and analysis of masses of data; he infinitely preferred that intelligence which arrived quickly and by intuition to the tedious processes of induction. Constructing a thesis upward, as it were, from the facts was exactly what he eschewed; creating or grasping a theory and demonstrating it by finding facts to fit, as needed—that was for him real thinking. When eventually he wrote the section of his study that dealt with Yeats, he used elements of the manuscripts he had found in Ireland, but those sources were in no way central to his arguments.

He had written Poggioli that he would return at the end of spring semester 1956, but that was not his goal.[17] Apparently, he had realized that the tale of the passport would yield yet another semester abroad if he exploited it anew, albeit from a different angle. Now the story ran that he did indeed have this important document (secured, as he had promised, from those recalcitrant judicial authorities in Belgium), but it was the American services that were delaying a visa from the United States. Once again, he was constrained to wait until the end of the year.

Yet the time came when he could delay his departure no longer, and at the end of November 1956, he booked passage for himself, Pat, and Michael on a cheap freighter, which took two weeks to cross the stormy Atlantic. In doing so, he was taking a great risk, for he did not have a scrap of official papers, not even a visa. They sailed from Cork, on the west coast of Ireland, experiencing "an amazing departure" on a small Greek vessel staffed by a Greek crew that was sailing under the Nigerian flag on a ship overflowing with Hungarian refugees who had just escaped from the Communist army's crushing of the revolution in their homeland.[18] The ship was crowded, the crew raucous, and everyone drank to relieve the tedium and celebrate freedom. Paul had reason for anxiety, for since he had left the United States "voluntarily," a merely technical way of avoiding forced deportation, he had good reason to fear that his alleged status as the so-called spouse of an American national would not see him through the thickets ranged against him by the INS, his old enemy. If the Service's records held good and de Man could not persuade the agents otherwise, he might be sent back at once—and in Europe, to be without papers was very serious. He might well find himself transported precisely to the prison in Antwerp that the lawyer, Louis Joris, had warned him about in 1955.

The crossing was rough, the weather bleak and dark, and it was Christmas Eve when they finally arrived in New York Harbor and sailed up the Narrows. Pat remembered the chaos and how when "the INS boys came on board" as the ship docked, she was "waiting, and thinking, and waiting, and wondering if this was it." As they reached the dock that night, everyone was drunk, and when the Immigration Service boarded the ship, they were confronted by a soused, unruly Greek-speaking crew, an air of confused holiday festivities, and a loud and nearly ungovernable group of Hungarians, few of whom spoke English, men and women very excited at having successfully reached their safe haven. The Hungarians were the victims of the Soviets, but the INS would inevitably suspect the immigrant group of secretly harboring Communists, who were forbidden entry to the United States and would require utmost vigilance. In this brouhaha, the officials had too much work on their hands to pay attention to a well-mannered little academic family returning from sabbatical. De Man's extraordinary luck held good, and the very oddness the agents found on the overloaded vessel conspired to pull him through. The de Mans were waved through and disembarked without questions. Once more, Paul was home safe. Safe, at least from the INS.

36

THE MIRROR

―――――――

PAUL DE MAN RETURNED TO HARVARD IN JANUARY 1957 AND OVER THE next three years transformed his public image into an iconic one: an extraordinary man and an exciting teacher, fascinatingly distant, austere in habits, but magnetic, the embodiment of the European intellectual. To some, he was simply "a great man." Privately, however, those were also years of major new failures, about which even his closest friends knew nothing. In 1960, he would escape from his troubles at Harvard fast and silently, just as he had done from Antwerp and later from Bard ten years earlier. Only two or three other people ever knew the true facts, for his mentors concealed them out of kindness and a sense of professional honor and obligation. For years, they sympathized with his apparent poverty and economic struggles. Nonetheless, de Man let it be known that he blamed at least one of the same men for his failures.

As a married man and a father, almost a generation older than most of his colleagues, he now appeared a benign and "avuncular" figure to George Kateb, whom he befriended. He was benign because he applied no conventional moral standards to others, but simultaneously his charm, good nature, the warmth when he was pleased and the invincible shrug of indifference to hostile criticism, the poise, the indefinable accent—all the elements that had won Mary McCarthy and so many others—were still apparent. He now possessed something harder to describe but instantly felt, a reserved sense of authority, a consciousness that emanated from the language of his body that he was a man to be reckoned with but not engaged. At seminars, he always carried the day, according to what Pat heard. Outside those gatherings, he sought no fights and left aggression to others, making his funny, often malicious comments only later.

De Man could be as obscurely monotonous as the next professor when he lectured on formal occasions—as at MLA conferences—but as a teacher, he attached himself to poetry, and at his best he was pulled upward by it. This was the more true because the poets he chose, Yeats and Mallarmé among them, often had a numinous or mysteriously spiritual quality very appealing to the emotions of a young audience. It was in this period that he gave the extraordinary lecture on Yeats remembered sourly by Richard Poirier but also long afterward by more than one of those present. His younger colleague William H. Pritchard, also one of Brower's teaching assistants, has described how de Man's "artfully delivered lectures were organized so that each began with one of the four stanzas of Yeats's difficult late poem, 'The Statues,' and he used them as springboards into various aspects of Yeats's poetry."[1] In particular, Pritchard recalled the dramatic moment when, at the end of his final lecture for the course, de Man read aloud one of the last poems, emphasizing the last lines, which end with the invitation to come and "dance with me in Ireland." At the end, "the entire student population of the course burst into spontaneous applause. . . . De Man gave his modestly winning, slightly embarrassed smile, acknowledging the tribute." This was the occasion that Poirier later recalled, saying his own reaction was, "Who the hell is he bullshitting?" And he added, "I thought he was sort of fake."[2] Pritchard, younger and not a rival, recalled that what Poirier had actually said to him during the tumult was, "Next time I'm going to lecture on poetry."[3] Poirier also gave de Man credit, however: "Part of the aura was that he . . . had a wonderful face. He was gentle; he was charming [and] warm."[4]

The years from 1957 to 1960 were also the period when de Man began attracting a set of students, some of whom remained devoted to him for the rest of his life. Without overtly attempting to draw others in he was immensely seductive, and it was not surprising that among

others the children of American college presidents, visiting aristocrats, and scions of wealthy families were captivated by him. Some of
these themselves became professors of literature, or translators of significant French works. Another word chosen by three unlike wit-
nesses was *magic*. Edgar de Bresson, half-French, half-American in
origin, reflected on his memories of Harvard as he stood in his Paris
apartment overlooking an ancient enclosed garden in the Eighth
Arrondissement that was once part of an immense pre-Revolutionary
convent. He recalled, "We were getting something no one else could
give us. It was magical."[5] Peter Brooks, who succeeded de Man as
Sterling Professor at Yale, said of his mentor that as he "would just sit
in front of . . . whatever text it was . . . and would sort of pluck magical things out of them."[6] Ellen Burt, the student who had picked up
her goods and followed literature from Johns Hopkins to Paul's classroom in New Haven, used the same word about his process of teaching: His whole reading of Mallarmé, she said, meant that one must
find a representational moment—and fill in the gaps![7] His approach,
she said in an interview, was essentially intuitive.

Barbara Guetti, had experienced his teaching earlier. She "used to
have coffee at the university café" with de Man because he was her
mentor, and he and others "gave me tips on who to read." Guetti spoke
of having learned the "moves" of de Man in his readings of poetry.
These were evidently unpredictable but persuasive leaps of intuitive
understanding of difficult passages: "It was about close reading and
making moves," she said. "It was part of . . . class performance" and had
to do with an interpretative leap that was more (or less) than logical.[8]
For her as a young woman, " 'Making moves' was impressing my teachers in the right ways. It was all those guys."

She also volunteered that de Man was skittish and conventional
politically. (Ellen Burt also mentioned de Man's reluctance, even anxiety, when in the 1970s she brought up matters relating to World War II
and the Holocaust.) Guetti was dating an African American, but both
de Man and Richard Poirier, another of her favorite instructors, tried
to persuade her not to, going so far as to suggest a wealthy but unat-
tractive man they considered more eligible. Race prejudice was, unfortunately, a matter of course in the 1950s, and Barbara and her friend

"were getting yelled at in the streets. I was lying to my parents, who'd have taken me out of school." Guetti admired de Man, but she never forgot that her celebrated professor, whose favorite she had been, *always* said bad things about people who were away. " 'Oh, Barbara Guetti—she's very far-out. Sometimes she's almost too far-out. At Harvard, she almost married a Negro.' " Late in the 1970s, Guetti taught at Yale, in part she said through her friendship with de Man, and she also became aware of the anxiety her comments about anti-Semitism and the Holocaust aroused in him, for after many years of being a suppressed nightmare, the latter had finally begun to receive ever-growing public attention. De Man may have become increasingly aware, therefore, as he grew older, that his writings and collaborationist work in World War II constituted a real danger should they ever be discovered.

As to the actual process by which de Man made such a deep impression on his students, one might, at the risk of oversimplification, say that at least a part of his gift was the deployment not only of his own intuitive powers but the capacity to infuse the class with a willingness to join him in his severely focused condition of attention on the chosen text. Simone Weil wrote that to give true attention is to give love; de Man it seems, without directly invoking emotive values, was a leader able to call on his students to focus their minds in a devoted way and to evoke from them an effort of perception modeled on his own. It may have been this sense of shared and rewarded effort that caused that class on Yeats to burst into spontaneous applause. Undoubtedly, it was partly what students meant in speaking of de Man's "charisma."

Paul was not his uncle's misbegotten son, whatever he told other people when it suited his needs, but he deeply admired Henri, had studied and identified with him. Whether temperament can be inherited is an ambiguous issue; but within families, the tones, mental habits, and intellectual tendencies of others are often internalized; certainly Paul in his early, impressionable period had many years to observe and incorporate the comportment and ideas of this figure who was known as "a great man." Undoubtedly, he would have liked nothing better than to have appeared to have the same kind of magnetic force, and as he had confided in Mary McCarthy, he saw traits of Henri reborn in himself.

He and Henri shared the quality of charisma, and it served him well when he established his international reputation in later years. When his cousin Li, though long estranged, heard in the 1970s that Paul was giving a lecture in Geneva, she rushed to attend it, and she discovered at this conference that the intellectual academic audience looked on her younger relative as "a god."[9]

Ellen Burt reflected on how de Man taught in a way that was at once earnest and ironic. Thinking took place somewhere else; the classroom was for the performance of their respective roles, he as leader (even in the somewhat anarchic days of the 1970s), the students as persons whose part was to get beyond the formulae of interpretation. She also recalled with great respect and precision that she was amazed by his facility. Whatever his faults, de Man was a powerful intellectual leader who formed the ideas of generations of men and women, one whose ideas and terminology eventually found their way even into popular culture. (For example, the term *deconstruct*, now in common usage in both verb and substantive form, was rarely employed before de Man and Derrida adopted it.)

Yet for all his maturity, some of de Man's habits had not changed. If anything, his need for money and the flatteries of bourgeois life deepened as his years increased. One of the odder relics of his past in this regard is a letter he sent to a private school in Boston, inquiring about admitting his son Michael, then around eight years old, as a student (and not on scholarship). This was wishful thinking, for there was no possibility that Paul could have afforded the fee, and private schooling was not usually regarded as essential for an academic's child, especially for the son of a teaching assistant and at such an early age. It was only a fantasy, one that left almost no trace behind; perhaps it was Frédéric Moreau, the would-be "ambassador or minister of culture," showing up again.

Narcissism, of course, in the broad sense was at the root of much of this ungovernable need for the trappings of class and material wealth, just as it promoted such particular habits as the ongoing and hours-long practice of mirror gazing, which amused but also puzzled his wife This predisposition—or personality disorder—was one his colleague Peter Brooks commented on, remembering the power of his teaching and, in particular, his discussion of Yeats's poem, "The Indian to His Love," on which he spent "a lot of time." In it the poet evokes a beautiful but impotent, angry bird caught in a paradise that is too still to endure:

> *The island dreams under the dawn*
> *And great boughs drop tranquility;*
> *The peahens dance on a smooth lawn,*
> *A parrot sways upon a tree,*
> *Raging at his own image in the enamelled sea.*

That figure of a marvelous bird gazing in helpless rage at its own image was a strange and potent one. There was, Brooks pointed out, a connection between his friend's teaching of this work by Yeats, subject of his dissertation, and his own unspoken but powerful sense of imprisonment in his own consciousness, a link to the insight Paul showed also at other times into the nature of narcissism. Had Paul de Man begun to see himself in that "enamelled sea," frozen in a world in which at least a part of himself was captured? When he taught Yeats so intently, did he understand that the exquisite but angry bird was "raging" because the island and the reflecting waters in which he gazed represented something of his own relation to language? And that from this stasis, this condition of dreams and tranquillity, the mind could neither escape, change, nor grow?

His influence also rested in part on his sense of himself as a free being, one who had not internalized the obligations that tied others down. For de Man, the teachings of Heidegger as he understood them, or of existential thought in a more general way, the tendency of his own nature, and the pressures of his personal role in actual recent history, all converged in the late 1950s. He wished to operate from an insouciance that permitted no questions and wordlessly denied external limitations. Some graduate students complete their work late or not at all, but they are generally not the same people to whom special favors have been granted and on whom the highest hopes are pinned. De Man was such a cynosure, but he did not feel the need to produce the results in a timely way or to follow the regulations of his institution. Others felt harnessed to a round of scuffling with their mentors, while longing for just that self-evident and fundamental lightness that de Man seemed to embody. He emanated a sense of freedom that was enchanting, even liberating to the young men and women who surrounded him.

Supporting his position was the news that had gotten out about his numerous published articles, which added greatly to his renown. To publish anything before receiving the Ph.D. was considered exceptional. His cohort knew of their existence, although, as two of his friends testified, they did not read them at the time.[10] No one was aware that some were written while he was working at three jobs. Secretly and against the university's rules, de Man always taught full-time at Berlitz, not part-time—the story he told Poggioli and Levin—and in addition he taught a normal assistant's course load at Harvard, even while tutoring or working privately, as he did with Kissinger. These demands were in addition to his studies toward the degree. Yet with the exceptional income he gained from all this activity, he nevertheless continued always to overspend so freely that in the summer of 1958, when his second child was born, he was forced to take a job on the production line at the nearby General Electric plant in Lynn.[11] (This was a fact Pat volunteered with embarrassment, for it was a crossing of class lines that had been painful to them both.)

Perhaps as de Man learned to exploit his own resources and those of the classroom, the teaching of poetry became for him a vital source, not only an "enamelled sea," but a privileged space in which his mind could move and, at least momentarily, feel free. There was too much he could not discuss: so many lives—and deaths (of his mother, father, brother, and uncle); so many complex issues—his own collaboration, and then Hermès and his thefts from it, his flight before trial, his abandonment of his sons, even the political issues much debated in the 1950s—all were buried. For de Man, there was so large a field of human experience that he must protect from the world's view that he must have been driven inexorably back into his own consciousness at every turn. Psychoanalysts who study narcissism have stressed the element of repressed rage that motivates this disorder. Missing intimacy from the earliest age, prevented early from developing feelings of power, and overcome by "uncontrollable feelings of helplessness, anxiety, and rage," for some the sense of identity itself becomes alienated. Otto Kernberg believed that out of a sense of inner emptiness, narcissists may need to "attach" themselves "to someone, living in almost 'parasitic' existence"—a formulation that casts light on Paul's great dependency on his second wife (if not indeed previously on Frida and Anne). Others write of the sufferer as he or she deals with the distance between the self perceived and the wished-for self—a discrepancy that is virtually a gloss on Paul de Man and his mirror.[12]

In his maturity, Paul de Man found both in real life and in the virtual mirrors of poetry that he could deploy a vision still fluid and creative, but sharpened by many years of introspection.[13] Perhaps he also began to see old patterns of behavior as just that—archaic, disused, and better left behind. Committed to his marriage and profession, successful in many aspects of these, but disciplined by the fear of exposure by Anne—even of imprisonment in the Belgium to which he could never return—de Man appears in this era to have accepted many existential limitations. He was approaching forty, had been immersed in academic culture for ten years, and simply began to settle down. He lost none of his penchant for unpredictability and grand assumptions of invincibility, but in Pat he had another kind of mirror, someone on whom he leaned, an other on whom to ground his sense of being. Such a life lacked the glamour for which he had once aimed—but he knew that new ideas can have a profound impact on the world that they interpret, and by now he knew what he thought. Undoubtedly he believed that it was within his power to influence the minds of his era.

37.

MENDING THE NET

Boston has cold winters, so cold that the Charles River, although it is tidal and salty, sometimes freezes solid, and ice floes cake and pile up like remnants on the table of a jumble sale. After a blizzard, the temperature falls again, the air is calm, and the snow-filled roads are empty. A skier, slipping out into the frigid morning, may reach a bridge where, pausing on the span, suddenly she feels an unmistakable rush of warmth. It is a vapor hovering in the air, heat visible, left behind by a half-naked runner.

Renato Poggioli was no runner, but he had put in a long bout of wrestling with his student, Paul de Man, and he was used to the climate. The temperature had already plunged to minus 12 degrees F. when on a quiet Sunday he entered his chilly office, sat down, and pulled out the file on Paul de Man. He had waited until he could be alone, when the semester and holidays would be over and his mind clear, to write a difficult letter. The result, typed in a small font by the departmental secretary, Betty Ann Farmer, was a two-page single-spaced document that ran almost to the margins.[1] Word had gotten out that he and Harry Levin had decided to let Paul de Man go and that Harry's animus—even jealousy—was the reason. Reuben Brower, the much-loved head of Humanities 6, an experimental interdepartmental course, in which Paul was a valued instructor, had written Renato and Levin more than once, most recently a week earlier, begging him to keep de Man on.[2] Poggioli's work that morning was finally to explain de Man's problematic history in the Department of Comparative Literature, which until then had been kept secret, and to tell Brower why he and Levin were determined to part with him. What is most interesting about the letter is less his long and expert exposition than the two postscripts he added at the last moment.

The story dates back to January 1957, when Paul had reappeared at the university, fresh from the Greek vessel whose return to New York Harbor had been so adventitiously chaotic. Their star pupil had shown up in the departmental office, cheerful and smiling, but unencumbered by anything like a dissertation. In addition, because it was precisely to enable Paul to acquire legal status as an immigrant that he had been granted funding for the unique extra year in Europe, Poggioli must certainly have inquired about that—and just as surely, Paul had evaded the question once more. He was overworking, became sick that season, and ulcers were mentioned in one document. The chairman was willing to pass over the bureaucratic issue of his status as an immigrant. The real question he and Harry Levin posed was, where was Paul's dissertation? De Man had sent them only some pages on Mallarmé and not anything like the dissertation per se.

He was behind in everything, and undoubtedly Poggioli would have brought up the issue of the general examination, a major hurdle. But that was something whose resolution they put off for another day. Paul went back to teaching at the end of the month and, unknown to Renato, to his three jobs. Anne's demands for money via her Boston lawyers were becoming more onerous. By the middle of the decade, she, never a patient, accommodating woman, had had enough of Peter Brajatuli. Details of her hegira vary, but, leaving behind her parents, by one means or another she made her way from Mendoza, in western Argentina, to the United States and then continued to Canada. Throughout this period, her two younger sons, who had remained with her, were growing fast, becoming adolescents, and were more costly to feed, clothe, and educate. Anne was difficult to live with, but no one suggested she was indifferent to these sons or lacking in courage. She was in her late thirties, and no doubt she had her eye out for their future as well as her own. In Canada, she intended to find a wealthy husband, and sometime around 1955 (dates are uncertain), she had moved on, with or without Brajatuli, to forge her own future. Meanwhile, the dunning letters Paul received continued and probably increased in their demands.[3]

At the end of the spring semester, Poggioli tracked the progress of his current cohort of graduate students. Chivvying his students forward was where a chairman earned his salary, for after completing their course work, the men and the small number of women were largely on their own, but some got lost in the next stage, the unstructured tasks of passing the difficult general examination and then completing the doctoral dissertation. The danger from the point of view of the department was that once students completed their course work, they might disappear into the limbo of part-time or substitute teaching, or accept a lower-level appointment at a minor college, from which some might never emerge. Harvard was proud that it accepted only the best applicants, and the institution did not want a lot of A.B.D.s—"all but dissertations"—populating the faculties of local junior colleges. It would be bad for the university, which had invested time and money in the students, and bad for the individuals, who, after having been at the top of their cohort most of their lives, would become literally déclassé, certainly ill-paid, and perhaps personally frustrated. On rare occasions, a student completed everything in a single year. At the extreme, it could take most or all of a decade; this was not a good idea. That person would not be offered one of the better appointments among the many the department could arrange.

Poggioli read de Man's responses to one of his questionnaires carefully, and evidently shortly thereafter he called Paul into his office.[4] Renato's cigarette habit was legendary, and he may have smoked more than usual. A round, erudite Italian, he was an easygoing man who spoke nine languages, although with so pronounced an accent in English that the benign Burt Pike kept a diary of "Poggiolisms," one of which was Renato's description of a novel with "ze heroine vhipping on ze nack, bosom of ze hero."[5] But there was no weeping on anyone's neck that June day, and de Man was ceasing to be a hero.

Poggioli insisted that de Man take the general examination on October 10, some four months away. By then, de Man would be entering his sixth year as a student at Harvard and would have had plenty of time to prepare for a test that was essentially based on the work of the first two years, plus whatever extra study the subject wished to give it. Many postulants took extra time off, ranging upward from a month or two, to prepare. The general examination was a monster: a six-hour, three-part ordeal spread over a week that required the subject to show mastery—both breadth and depth of knowledge—of all the literature in the major and minor fields; that is, it included both texts one had studied and those one had avoided in one's course work. On day one, the student wrote a two-hour essay; on the second, two essays of an hour each; on the third, the person was questioned orally, again for two hours, by three examiners. Paul's interlocutors would be Poggioli, Levin, and Henry Hatfield, a Germanist, whom Paul did not care for. When that obstacle had been passed, normally the students were on their own to define and complete their dissertations.

To his mentors, the time had come for their investment in de Man to show results. Gifted students usually moved through quickly, but at this rate de Man might be around for another couple of years, perhaps longer—not a good record, especially for a man who had been treated so well. Quite apart from their foreign philosophical focus, discrete essays published in French journals were all very well, but to Poggioli and Levin, they were only a garnish on the platter; the academic entrée was a coherent book-length study of some issue that supervisors hoped would be significant but must at least deal with a subject that was part of the mainstream and of interest in the field. The Department of Comparative Literature at Harvard was in the business of producing scholars and critics who would populate and eventually lead similar departments all over the country. The major criterion for "placing" graduates, as the hiring system was delicately known, was the quality of their first book, normally a revised version of the dissertation. De Man was always adept at thinking sharply in the short, focused essays which would become his forte, but the writing of a book-length study was beyond him, and he never produced one. When Geoffrey Hartman wanted to bring his friend to Yale in 1969, he said that he and other friends had helped overcome Yale's inflexible criterion that a high-level appointee must have a published book by working with de Man to pull together the articles that became his very influential work, *Blindness and*

Insight.[6] Many people around him at Harvard expected that de Man would be offered the holy grail there—that is, immediate appointment to a full-time line with good prospects for tenure at the university. He let his friends and students hear of these wishes, and they agreed with him, George Kateb and John Hollander among them.[7]

In his questionnaire, de Man had written that his dissertation was more than half-finished. That was untrue. If in fact he had written anything new on Mallarmé, or done more than take some notes on the wealth of documents Mrs. Yeats had shown him and which he had found confusing, he would have mentioned this, but evidently he did not.[8] It would be two more years before, working together under great pressure, they could force together parts of his study, as Poggioli would write, into a whole. In addition, there was a third, important problem with his work. He had nothing at all to show on Stefan Georg. His silence on that subject was a thorn in the flesh of his mentors, and he did not inform them that he had dropped a third of his project entirely until he was actually submitting parts of the dissertation at the end of 1959.[9]

Georg had been a leader of pre-Hiterlian German right-wing literary thought (and Heidegger had been a strong supporter of Georg and his focus on Hölderlin).[10] Levin may have been right that de Man had recent political history in mind in omitting him, but the strongest reason for cutting this corner was undoubtedly that de Man simply wanted to save time and effort. Levin also disliked the philosophical tendency of what de Man did show them, specifically about the French poet. He said that neither he nor Poggioli were pleased with de Man's handling of Mallarmé. It wasn't close to the poet's language, and it used words that were impenetrably metaphysical, philosophic, or jargonistic, rather than couched in normal critical terms. They understood where he was heading, but did not approve. "Opaque," as Georg Steiner has pointed out, was a desirable quality for language in Heidegger's view, for he was engaged in a game of "existential bluff."[11] De Man not only achieved opacity himself but he also once praised a student's paper as "impeccable—and opaque."[12] Learning to manipulate the "special language of the discipline," as some called it, was part of the course. In fact, however, Levin said he and Poggioli had most objected to the omission of Georg, because by definition the discipline of comparative literature required high competence in three languages from different language groups, and de Man, by omitting German, had employed only two.

In that era of literary criticism, with its non-contextual approach to works studied and its rejection of any move to draw on "extrinsic" ideas, whether political, philosophical, or even biographical ones, his supervisors had by now seen enough of de Man's work to be aware of its strong bias toward existential thought. Already in 1955, Levin had written Paul of his reservations: that he occasionally felt that de Man's use of metaphysical language interfered with his work, but that he, unlike de Man, was little attracted to Heidegger.[13] He was referring to Paul's article attacking André Malraux in "The Temptation of Permanence" (see p. 376) The existential philosophy itself was more than questionable: It was concerned with ontology, "being"—and that was not real philosophy from the "Anglo-Saxon" point of view. It was—like Nietzsche—"poetry." Levin was proud of having gone to Cambridge University to study with Alfred North Whitehead, the mathematician and philosopher who wanted to found all thinking on rigorous logic. Faced with the existential approach so overt in de Man's recent French articles, his professors were displeased. Harry Levin said later that he had studied with Whitehead and considered himself well trained in philosophy. De Man, on the other hand, was an autodidact: Where had he studied and with whom? De Man meant well and had many insights, but his sort of thinking was merely literary philosophy, Hegelian and poetic, not the serious sort.[14]

That abrupt characterization, though accurate, was dismissive. George Kateb, as a mature political philosopher, believed something quite different: that de Man's real contribution was to be deeply concerned about meaning. "De Man is an interpreter more than a theorist. . . . One cannot read *Blindness and Insight* and [the] essays of [the 19]50s and '60s and come away thinking Paul de Man is uninterested in interpreting life. His pursuit of inconsistency [was making the point that] life can't be encompassed."[15] To Kateb, de Man was a "literary philosopher," an honorable position. Other literary philosophers, such as Hannah Arendt, Isaiah Berlin, and Lionel Trilling, were not abstract in their thinking, but, rather, richly conceptual. On the other hand, to Kateb reading Levin was "like biting on colored glass."

Both Levin and Poggioli made a point throughout that period and long afterward of maintaining a correct professional silence in regard to any aspect of de Man's work and their reasons for dissatisfaction with it. It was not from them that news of de Man's troubles reached the Harvard community. How much either man knew of what de Man told his friends to keep his own reputation in the clear, one does not know. Probably his mentors heard little directly, or they would have been forced to reply. As it was, honor-bound by the ethics of the profession, they kept their disappointment to themselves. It was better not to wash the dirty laundry of the department in public. Others heard from Paul the story of his battles with Harry Levin, but no one knew the crucial facts or the several fronts on which he failed to meet the department's expectations. Unfortunately, this discretion left Levin in particular open to slurs and to the widespread impression that when Paul ran into trouble with the department, it was the result not of his own shortcomings, but of professional jealousy, or being caught in "political cross fire," as Pat de Man believed.

Paul de Man, however, did not refrain from laying the blame for his ongoing troubles at the door of his mentor. Kateb knew from Paul, who insinuated rather than said it, that Levin was alone the source of his troubles. "Paul made it unmistakably clear that Levin brought him some animosity. . . . He was not forthcoming at all except to say, as much in tone of voice or expression on the face, that it was Levin that brought disappointment and horror."[16] De Man did not tell Kateb about his own literal failing of the General Examination, and his friend was shocked more than forty years later when he learned of that. John Hollander remembered something similar, the remark made in sympathy, "Ah, Harry is a scoundrel," spoken lightly.[17] Others may have heard the same sort of thing from him. Kateb's own doctoral dissertation, about opposition to utopias, profited from his discussions with Paul, but he recognized that de Man was amused by his speculations "about what it meant to prefer a world in which, say, there was vice, to a world where there was only virtue. . . . He may have thought that the very idea of a world without vice or weakness or violence was so far-fetched that at most it was a thought-experiment."

Paul was very fond of his younger friend, but enlightening him was not his job. The challenge was handling Poggioli and keeping him at bay. In his letter of August 1957, Paul did tell Poggioli that "all in all, I am sure to be ready in time with what I hope to be a coherent and solid study." "Coherent" and "solid" might indeed be all that de Man aimed at, but these terms may have echoed the demands of his supervisors for greater clarity and fewer abstract arguments. From de Man's point of view, he had invested his time supremely well: By digging into new ideas, he undoubtedly hoped to have laid the foundation for his own career and a new approach to literature. He would not have argued these larger matters with the powers that watched over him, for he knew they were already rejecting his approach, implicitly a radical critique of normative literary criticism, and more openness would only have deepened their opposition. A smile and a shrug were likely his defense in this unequal contest.

Paradoxically, for all the misstatements and even lies he offered during the 1950s, it was perhaps precisely in these years of struggle with Harry Levin and Renato Poggioli that de Man's mature character developed. Stubbornness he had always had; now that stubbornness merged with his intellectual commitments and gave him strength of purpose. The fecklessness and lightness of his youth, and the willingness to resort to false and desperate dodges that he had displayed in owning Hermès, began to fall away. He knew that his ideas were not accepted by Levin and Poggioli, and perhaps he guessed that they would eventually make him unwelcome, but nevertheless he pressed on and did not give them up. The Paul de Man who later came into wide view, who stood for something and changed the cultural map with sweeping and influential concepts, would probably not have come into existence but for this period of testing when he had to grow strong—or give way.

Nevertheless, he was going too far. Levin and Poggioli had invested their own prestige in supporting him. In failing to use well his privileged time, he reflected badly on them and even their standing, for if they had misjudged their man, their colleagues at the Society of Fellows and elsewhere might be critical. Wasting the prestige of the prize was no small thing.

However, Poggioli's and Levin's resistance to de Man's thesis was not merely personal or basely primarily on his dilatory, sometimes misleading assertions about his work. What they most disliked were his ideas, those philosophical attitudes that he put forward without regard to history or context—as Poggioli would write Brower on January 20, 1960, in a letter discussed below—those fundamental assumptions that de Man would forever after drop into his writings as if they needed no grounding or explanation. Paul, on the other hand, and especially from 1955 onward, was defending his ideas at a visceral level and fighting for them in a true defense of his thesis, one that was far more real than most ritual "defenses." At stake for de Man, beneath the text of his work on Mallarmé and Yeats, was his commitment to an intellectual position that he had developed gradually over the decade.

Gradually, by fits and starts, de Man sought and put to use ideas that almost imperceptibly were to change the course of his life. Such deeply rooted developments often move only slowly; changing the consciousness of oneself takes place in silence, thought, and growing seriousness—qualities that de Man had not possessed in his twenties, when he had lived under the multiple influences of his own ambition, his uncle's example, and the pressures of the occupant. Later in his teachings, Paul de Man would develop aspects of this growing philosophical approach, specifically in his stress on the incommunicability of human meaning through language, and his devastating skepticism—which would evolve into his stress on irony—both of which underlie deconstruction. Behind that profound skepticism was Paul's recognition of how fatally and easily he had allowed himself to be misled by "sclerotic and wretched myths," those nationalistic and racist ideas that in his era he had accepted (as he ruefully recognized and acknowledged in passing in his essay of 1953 on Montaigne).

By the late 1950s he knew that he could not repair the damage of his past life and writings, but he could adopt another position toward history, however negative, that would deny valency to all assertions of supposed truths—especially those that are conventionally considered humanistic ones. That this combination of deep skepticism and acceptance of human mutism, of our inevitable and eternal silence, also allowed de Man to sweep his own past misdeeds out of sight as merely "factical" history was another benefit existential thought provided its followers.

These were not assumptions he could expect Harry Levin or Renato Poggioli to sympathize with; far less could he articulate to them or anyone else the experiences out of which his new intellectual approach to language had sprung. Perhaps not even to himself did he fully acknowledge how much his own experiences—that narrative of his life, precisely that autobiography which he would later dismiss as impossible and merely a fiction—had shaped his intellectual and philosophical point of view. Perhaps he wasn't a very good philosopher, as Harry Levin remarked in 1992, but merely one in the Hegelian mode— the poetic, not logical sort of philosophy. Yet reading Levin, as George Kateb remarked, was "like biting on glass." Over one hundred years earlier, Emerson had told his group of young ministers to "Deal out to the people your life, life passed through the fire of thought." As a teacher, Paul de Man, although he had entirely secreted and concealed his own story, was so perceptibly speaking from deepest convictions that this young instructor's even younger audiences responded to his authenticity, even if they were not yet good judges of his intellectual skills. Whether or not one accepts de Man's approach, it was in this long decade of struggle to assert and defend his ideas that Paul de Man insensibly left behind the feckless, "light" youth he had been and grew gradually into a powerful polemicist who became known to the cultural world as the source of wide influence and a man who formed generations of thinkers.

However, his older audience, Levin and Poggioli, had reached a point (like Peeters at the Agence Dechenne, Hayes at Bard College, and Bob de Man) where they had had enough. From now on, they would help Paul de Man, but their perception of him began to change and, with that, their hopes for him. For his part, Paul, overworked and not in good health, believed he deserved to spend the summer of 1957 in the sun and fogs of Gott Island, the wonderfully primitive spot, cheap and difficult of access, which he and Pat had found off the coast of Maine. The water was too cold for swimming, and "Gotts," as they called it, could be reached only by a boat that arrived once a week, if the weather held.

A couple of years later, Paul invited a French friend, Henri Thomas, to the island. (A friend of Lambrichs from Paris, Thomas had his own ambiguous history, having attached himself in occupied Paris to the entourage of Ernst Jünger, the German army officer and writer stationed there during the war.) Paul wrote Thomas of how he and Pat inhabited a little cabin that faced the Atlantic, where he liked to sit quietly on the rocks, studying the endless two-way traffic of cormorants that used "the sea as their boulevard," and watching the dense mists cling to the tops of the pines, burn off, and gradually lift to reveal "almost forgotten horizons." Time slowed down there, and he and Pat warmed themselves by cutting the firewood they would burn at night.[18]

Other friends visited in the summer of 1957, making a long and difficult trip that showed the depth of their affection for him. He even invited Levin and Poggioli, teasingly suggesting that he was reading "nothing more serious than Plotinus" and writing airily to Renato that he'd had so many guests that "you must get the impression that half the academic world spends the Summer coming and going to Gott Island, which fortunately is far from true."[19] De Man had "all of next year's problems well in control," he asserted. What de Man did not do was prepare for the generals. For most graduate students to spend the summer in a library getting that done would have been disagreeable but inevitable, an obligation best gotten rid of as soon as possible. Paul, however, never fitted himself to the expectations of others. Throughout, he remained an autodidact. As his written work already showed, he liked to dig into a self-chosen subject; reading many books in which he felt no interest would have gone totally against the grain of his character. His good friend and later his department chairman at Cornell, Burton Pike, said that one thing that amazed him about de Man was that although he "knew a fantastic . . . just incredible amount," he didn't own books.[20]

De Man, however, was ahead of his mentors and formal obligations in one regard: He wrote his first paper for the annual conference of the Modern Language Association that September. Reading an essay there was then an important opportunity, one that brought prestige and potentially renown. Paul enjoyed surprising Renato with news of this invitation, for he did not tell him until August 26, when he wrote from Gotts that he would be "in Cambridge on September 6th (Friday) en route to Madison (Wisc.) where I have to read a paper at the MLA meeting (on Yeats)." He would return, he said, in mid-September.[21] De Man had, of course, been planning the appearance in Madison since early the previous spring, for the program was announced by the MLA at that time.[22]

Geoffrey Hartman later said that it was at this meeting and on hearing his paper that he first encountered Paul de Man.[23] This was a turning point in Paul's career and would prove life-changing, for from that moment, their friendship began. Soon they were close friends. What they shared, the very young German-born professor of comparative literature at Yale said, was a committed critique of American literary criticism and the absence from it of any true philosophical grounding. Hartman had been one of the Jewish children removed from Germany and sent to England by the *Kindertransport* movement in 1939 (and detained once there for a lengthy period in a camp for enemy aliens—a fact, one would add, that is often omitted from popular histories of that well-intentioned movement). Hartman was something of an intellectual prodigy, and after a prolonged, difficult journey, he fetched up eventually in the United States. Politics or the history of the war never came up between him and de Man, he said. He simply assumed that Paul was an émigré, like himself.[24]

Poggioli was certainly pleased to learn of Paul's new venture, and the younger man undoubtedly used the opportunity of his visit to the MLA conference to extract two new and valuable favors from his boss. The first was an extraordinary act of financial assistance, and it involved quietly breaking an ironclad and important rule. The records show that on September 27, 1957, de Man was given a "corporation appointment," which, among other things, relieved him from paying registration fees as a student. Asked to explain, the living person most qualified to understand this, Betty Ann Farmer, secretary of the department, replied that this meant Paul de Man was still a Junior Fellow.[25] Yet his three years had expired on June 30, 1957. He had gotten the money, if not the official status, for a fourth year. How Poggioli managed this is unknown. Perhaps he had enough influence and power simply to assign another three thousand dollars to Paul from the Society of Fellows' treasury. Certainly there was no public extension to him of a fourth year as a Junior Fellow, but no doubt de Man could simply appear when he wished for the society's dinners as an alumnus of the group. No one need know that he was secretly still on its payroll.

But the most extraordinary favor Poggioli did for de Man, intellectually and academically far more serious, was that in early October, acting on what can only have been de Man's own pleading, the chairman canceled two-thirds of Paul's general examination at the last minute, leaving no reasons in the records. This wiped out the two days of written essays and left only the oral examination at the end, a Thursday. All that remains of Poggioli's decision is a memo in which he asserted his unorthodox ruling and named the examiners, Levin, himself, W. Frohock, and Henry Hatfield. Unfortunately, while Paul did not like Hatfield, the professor of German had written his own thesis on Stefan Georg, the very figure on whom de Man had produced nothing and would soon drop entirely. Hatfield may have gone into the examination room already miffed and ready to call the upstart to terms. In addition, the careful chairman got the others to sign off on the change: on the printed form of the undated memo appears, "Thurs, Deman 10" and "OK Frohock"[26]

Paul was thus excused from taking all written examinations in the three fields in which he was supposed to demonstrate mastery. The decision is a shock, as bizarre as it was unexplained. Why Poggioli should have granted this unheard-of favor is unfathomable. He liked Paul. He knew the man was suffering from overwork and family responsibilities. Paul must have recounted a moving tale of his serious poverty, which was real in spite of his significant earned income. Had the chairman decided at some level just to move him ahead at almost any cost? Did Paul tell him that he went to pieces when faced with writing an examination, especially in a foreign tongue? Obviously, he must have drawn on all the levers of persuasion at his command, citing his superior standing and the long years in which he had demonstrated his mastery. Poggioli's decision stood, but from the result, it became clear that everyone concerned lived to regret the outcome. The oral exam, the remaining hurdle, is usually considered the easiest of the trials, for one can divagate, throw out glittering new ideas, and, as ancient wisdom among acolytes has had it probably since medieval times, ideally set the examiners to arguing among themselves. Yet, when de Man took the examination on October 10, 1957, he failed it, and not by a little. He stumbled miserably, as Poggioli informed Brower in January 1960, and Paul himself wrote essentially the same thing in a follow-up letter to Levin at the time. (Although he had done brilliantly at the Athenaeum, not studying, or being too traumatized to be able to study, for his engineering examination at ULB was precisely where Paul de Man's university career had first gone wrong in 1938.)

His problem in the oral examination, the only one he had to take, came in the German section, conducted by Henry Hatfield. De Man had studied German as a high school student at the Athenaeum, and he had been reading Heidegger, perhaps in that language, though possibly in Wahl's French translation or previously in the Dutch version by de Waelhens.[27] No doubt he judged that he was in adequate control of the subject. Hatfield decided to press de Man on Schiller. Evidently, de Man preferred to avoid reading German writers he did not care for, whether or not they were on the syllabus, and this one had dropped beneath his horizon. De Man floundered, but the professor of German doggedly pursued his line of questioning. He was at an impasse and could not respond as Hatfield wished. Eventually, Harry Levin, sensing a looming debacle and acting as chair of the examination, stepped into the breach and announced that as Paul's mentor, he declared the session adjourned.[28] Technically, Paul had not failed, and he could sit the exam again without prejudice. Privately, everyone present knew what was at stake, and what had been lost.

Paul told his wife that night that Hatfield, who did not like him and whose courses he seems to have avoided, had pursued him and would not let go. His brain, he told Pat, had "turned to mush." Interestingly, Paul reacted to this crisis as he had done before, for his second child with Pat, their daughter Patsy, was born July 8, 1958, exactly nine months after the disaster of the examination.[29] Life was performance, as he knew—but not all performance was intellectual.

The failure was kept secret. George Kateb was shocked to learn much later that de Man had failed his generals; any of his friends would have been equally stunned.[30] Yet this was the period when the gossip about de Man's supposed victimization at the hands of his mentors grew. No one, however, knew the story of the death by a thousand cuts Paul had inflicted on himself in this failure through avoiding other, previous requirements. All the friendly colleagues interviewed thought that de Man had passed this and other hurdles without difficulty and completed his dissertation satisfactorily when he was unfairly let go by Harvard later.

There can be no question of Levin's help. Eleven days later, Paul wrote Harry an apology, saying that he had not prepared at all:

> This is a good opportunity to apologize for my inability to perform last week. I discovered to my horror that, at present, my mind and memory refuse to function even under the gentlest and most considerate kind of pressure. I have no doubt about my ability to redeem myself, but since I realize now that I can not always depend on what I have previously known, I will not be able to present myself without previous preparation—as lack of time obliged me to do in this case. The delay does not come at a propitious moment, but I certainly have only myself to blame for that.[31]

He closed "With thanks for your interest and assistance," words he would not have chosen if Harry had not indeed saved his bacon by adjourning the session, as the professor later reported.

In this private message, Paul was temporarily grateful to Levin, but over the next two and a half years, his mentor nevertheless became known among de Man's friends as the cause of de Man's problems and a jealous enemy. Yet in spite of all, Poggioli did one more thing for Paul before the end of that October. Far from withdrawing the new "corporation appointment" or the fellow's stipend he'd given de Man in September, the chair canceled on September 18, only a week after the failed examination, yet two more courses that de Man was required to take.[32] (Paul had completed yet another questionnaire, again denying having outside employment.) He was now free to make his way toward retaking the generals, but this time he would have to present himself and respond to all three days of questioning.

Whatever the reasons for Paul's collapse—his inability or unwillingness to prepare, that invisible "self-destructiveness" Pat mentioned, bad health and fatigue—his outward demeanor was impeccable. Colleagues who met Paul only after he returned from France, Neil Hertz among them, were awed, seeing in his "aura" a mixture of seeming asceticism and high European culture, emanating from a person with a handsome face deeply marked by care. They hoped to be touched by, to absorb by osmosis the charm, wit, and buried sympathy that surrounded him. Above all, however, the key to his magnetism—and with few exceptions his friends insisted that he did not try to attract others—was undoubtedly his virtually unique knowledge of the new ideas that were emanating from abroad and for which he would make himself the conduit.

De Man's economic problems actually grew over the next two academic years. In the following spring of 1958, before his daughter was born, he took the déclassé job on the production line of the GE plant in Lynn. Meanwhile, he continued to write essays not directly related to his dissertation, but to Heidegger and his ideas, and cultivated the valuable friendships he had been establishing, as with Hartman. One article was a translation of an essay by Heidegger entitled "Hölderlin and the Essence of Poetry," which the loyal Ted Weiss published in his *Quarterly Review of Literature*.[33] If Levin or Poggioli heard of it, it might have seemed to them yet another example of wasted time. Yet for de Man, that effort would have been not merely homage to an intellectual master but also a raising of the flag, a defiant reassertion of where he stood, as well as a notice to American intellectuals of what Heidegger might offer them. His other essay was to become far more important, a long piece called "The Intentional Structure of the Romantic Image," as it was known when translated later. It eventually became known by some as "the most Xeroxed essay ever circulated among English graduate students."[34] It was published in France in 1960, but it must have been composed earlier, probably in 1959.[35]

De Man always "wrote against" someone, to quote Hillis Miller, and de Man liked to see Sartre as a starting point and an antagonist. His title threw down the gauntlet: He wanted his challenge to be known. Two points might be mentioned here. As was his usual practice, his essay did not acknowledge its origins, one of them Sartre, at all, except indirectly. Whatever one believes about this nonstandard approach, it became a habit; by obscuring the genealogy of his ideas, Paul created both mystery and the mystification he has been widely accused of. In addition, de Man took an original approach to the idea of imagery, stressing that the Romantic image created in poetry (by which he basically meant the human consciousness) "yearns" for its nothingness. The flower, the rock—all natural phenomena evoked by the Romantic poets—are identical with nature; they are, ontologically speaking, being. However, when these are used as images, they express not nature, or being, but the poet's own deep wish for it and for ontological insight, which is tragically forbidden and impossible.

DE MAN RESISTED POGGIOLI'S pressure to retake the general examination soon, but eventually he was forced to sit for it in May 1959. He passed, but even with this delay, his work was mediocre. That, for Poggioli, seems to have been a clear and decisive signal as to what he must do. Finally disabused and feeling betrayed, the chair apparently felt de Man's work was weak enough that it meant he must make the long-delayed but now immediate decision to end his career at Harvard.[36] Paradoxically, it was not the thin-skinned and sharp-tongued Harry Levin who took this stance, but the steady and balanced Renato Poggioli. His patience had given out. The genial chairman alone knew how many expensive favors he had done for this man, and he had reached the end of his rope. He may even still have been sitting in the exam room when, after reading de Man's essays and presiding over the oral examination, he picked up a blue book and used it to draft a letter to the dean, McGeorge Bundy. In his letter, he set forth the department's new position. De Man was to get only a two-year, terminal reappointment because he was "older" than other students. Trying to sound fair, Poggioli noted that both Harry Levin and Reuben Brower, who employed Paul as an instructor in Humanities 6, "enthusiastically" supported de Man's retention. However, the disfavor with which he now regarded Paul was reflected by the proposed salary, which he wrote could be set as low as the dean wished. Poggioli's ambivalence is evident in the manuscript itself, for he first proposed an "average" rate of pay, but then lowered that to read "at least the minimum" for the rank. The chairman acknowledged Paul's "contributions" but stressed the long series of delays with his dissertation, which was obviously already a sore point—and this was many months before Poggioli knew that this lecturer was dropping Stefan Georg. He still expected Paul to submit his material by the following October, but by now, that hardly mattered.[37]

This period was yet another low point in de Man's life. Henri Thomas[38] had a certain amount in common with Paul, for he was a French writer who, like de Man, had been close to the occupant during the war and was a friend of both Lambrichs and the entourage that surrounded Ernst Jünger in Paris, from whom he secured translation work and social contacts. Thomas was spending a year in Cambridge, and Paul's growing sadness was perceptible to him. Thomas's voluminous notebooks record that Paul admitted that it was hard living in exile and confided that even after ten years he was still not used to American ways. Thomas, himself a perpetually unhappy man, noted the Belgian's austere style of life: "An apartment with high ceilings on Massachusetts Avenue, sparsely furnished," he wrote, "is the new home of Paul de Man, his wife, their two children."[39] In a roman à clef that Thomas published a few years later, he used many central facts of Paul's life—his impoverished exile, the unlikely but romantic marriage to Pat, and even a version of their summer of strawberry picking (which Thomas rendered as a season of plucking chickens in a factory, to Pat's annoyance), as well as the underlying melancholy he perceived in the forty-year-old exile, in creating the protagonist of *Le Parjure*, published in 1964.[40]

Yves Bonnefoy, the renowned French poet, visited Harvard in 1959, and early that summer he first met Paul and in a sense fell in love with him on sight when he first saw him crossing the green Yard, coming toward him in "the light" of the sun and of his own blue eyes, as the poet put it. That summer, de Man invited him to a picnic on the shore, and Bonnefoy remembered that it was sundown when in "the clarity of a fire which one perceives in the distance, on a beach . . . [one] senses that someone is repairing his net down there, is sewing back together the earth and the sky."[41] This is not an earthly vision. During the following winter, Bonnefoy caught the same feeling Thomas had experienced surrounding de Man in that Massachusetts Avenue apartment when he photographed him holding his infant daughter on his lap.

Bonnefoy's lyrical words at Paul's memorial service celebrated a Paul de Man who was himself a source of light. The image he had caught in the chill winter, lit by the high window of the same apartment, shows not the handsome and glowing youth women had loved in Brussels, or the charmer who had penetrated the New York circles a decade earlier, but an inward, tired, and very complex man who has known defeat and pared away a great deal from his needs.

DE MAN, AS USUAL, spent much of the summer of 1959 on the island off Maine. Yet unknown even to himself, the steep tides of Maine were turning, and now were moving fast in his favor. Suddenly, Anne announced the first change: She was ready to let go. The "blackmail" of the last nine years was over. She had met the right man, one who fulfilled her needs. Gerhard von Orland-Ipsen had been an officer in the German army, but not a Nazi, she always added. Postwar, he had emigrated to the States and, she said, had some connection with her sister, who lived in Los Angeles. He had gone into business, possibly construction, made a good deal of money, and by the time Anne met him, he was living in or around Montreal, where she had settled with her two younger sons. He had added his mother's family name, the Danish Ipsen, to his own, and after marrying him, Anne called herself Madame Ipsen (or von Orland, or von Orland-Ipsen). By the summer of 1959, Gerhard wanted to marry her, and she needed a real divorce.

De Man, no doubt happily, sped off to Reno. From Nevada, he sent Pat a love letter, which was normal—she said that when they were separated, he wrote her every day. As he insisted even on washing the dishes with her nightly so that he alone could continue to engross her attention, that assiduity was typical. Lyrical, happy, and lonely for her, he was waiting the six weeks required to establish residency and get a valid divorce. Addressing the letter to "My sweetest loveliest darling," he told her how he longed to hold her in his arms, shower her with "thousands of kisses," and was measuring the days between her own daily letters and their arrival, which he counted with an accuracy he had never given to the Agence Dechenne or Hermès. He remembered their bed, evoked the rising moon that had shone over them in Gotts, and described the hotel guests in Reno who had gone to church that Sunday morning "wearing amazing combinations of hats."[42] He said he would spend the day in a park, reading.[43]

Then something much more exceptional happened. Geoffrey Hartman had been at work on Paul's behalf at Cornell, and in the fall of 1959, he let Paul know that he was being considered for an appointment there. The master of literary studies at Cornell was M. H. Abrams, author of *The Mirror and the Lamp: Romantic Theory and the Critical Tradition* (1953), which has had a long life as a classic, influential discussion of the shifting world view behind Romantic literature. Abrams, known to all as Mike, was keenly interested in the philosophical underpinnings of literary criticism and told this writer that he had picked up de Man's essay "The Intentional Structure of the Romantic Image," then available only in the French journal that published it in 1960, in his normal course of reading. Hartman reported that he was the one who had called Abrams's attention to it. Both were probably true. Abrams said that from that moment, he had wanted to hire de Man to build up the department. His word was powerful at Cornell. Comparative Literature was not a strong field there at the time, and the respected professor of English, held in affection by many, had the clout to make such an important appointment a reality.

De Man kept the tentative offer very quiet, undoubtedly hoping to use it for leverage with his discontented mentors. Abrams had been a classmate at Harvard of both Levin and Hatfield and had good-enough relations with Harvard, but Ivy League colleges compete for talent, and professors know one another very well; Abrams had gotten his degree at Harvard, and no doubt he knew about Levin's dismissive words concerning Cornell ("It's a nice place to bring up children"), which was an institution Mike loved deeply. A modest person, he liked to tell the story that in the days when men could be hired without having published much at all, he was eventually asked if he had anything he could produce for publication, and on that cue he had gone to his desk in Goldwin Smith Hall and pulled from a drawer the manuscript for *The Mirror and the Lamp*, which he had finished but had not yet bothered to send into the world.

Once things had reached the stage of a clear offer, Paul let his friends know that he was prepared to leave Harvard if it did not meet Cornell's approach. News that Harvard was letting de Man go was a shocking ending to his meteoric career, and word spread rapidly. Consternation and blame were widespread and directed particularly at Harry Levin. Reuben Brower sprang to his assistant's defense. Brower was in the English Department, however, not Comp Lit, but there he was rather an "isolated" figure among his colleagues, Peter Brooks said, adding that in fact the close reading Brower stressed so heavily, Paul considered to be "naïve though pedagogically useful."[44] Brower wanted deeply to keep Paul at Harvard and he spoke and wrote repeatedly to Poggioli on the subject. The issue was almost decided when, in mid-January 1960, he sent a letter to Levin and Poggioli one last time, an encomium on de Man, in which he deliberately went a little beyond the bounds. The warmth of his language suggests how much he cared about the younger man and perhaps implies by its disregard of caution his knowledge that this last attempt was doomed to failure. In Brower's eyes, Paul had deeply valuable qualities.[45] Of course he should have completed his dissertation, but his history of poverty, fatigue, and ulcers must be recognized. Brower admitted that personally he could not always grasp what de Man had to say about Yeats (a comment often echoed by de Man's followers), but his knowledge so greatly surpassed his own that Brower was moved by Paul's capacity for unique insights. The other tutors attended closely to his words when he spoke, and his influence on younger men was powerful. Harvard called out for men of his kind. Finally, he wrote, Paul possessed something deeply spiritual—soul. Couldn't the university for once take a god-given opportunity and gamble on this man? Yes, Paul could occasionally be off-putting, but so could all the best men, and—a particularly interesting remark—to de Man, the aesthetic and the moral were one and the same thing, and could not be separated. What could this last comment have referred to? That Paul became abrasive when faced by opposing opinions? Or did Brower truly believe that Paul felt that ideas about art must be grounded in the thinker's moral nature? If so, that was probably true of the humanist Brower himself, and was perhaps a projection.

Poggioli's reply of January 20 gave Browder a point-by-point time line of the lecturer's failures: his miserable showing on his first general examination, only mediocre work on the second, the endless promises, given only to be broken, for submitting his dissertation, and the inadequacy of that once it arrived piecemeal, not even in time for a February 1960 degree.[46] Moreover, in December—and not until then—de Man had informed them that he had dropped Stefan Georg entirely, a unilateral decision they perceived as a betrayal of trust. Harry Levin testified that this was de Man's major default and prominent among the reasons he and Poggioli had lost faith in him.[47] What de Man presented to them—and only in the last weeks—was scarcely worth showing, and yet he had been excessively late. He'd had three years in the Society of Fellows, the old scholar recalled, and he and Poggioli had understood all along that de Man had finished his work; yet Paul had come home without his thesis and had continued on at Harvard with nothing to show. In the end they accepted the dissertation without the section on Georg because de Man had done a good deal of work on Yeats and Mallarmé, but although they agreed to accept the dissertation, they appointed him only to a lectureship.

Levin wondered later if his former student had not found the poet a hot potato. He suggested that Paul had dropped Georg because if he had included him, perhaps some latent sympathy with Nazi ideology—its myths of blood and soil—might have surfaced in his own writing.[48] Georg, by exalting such themes, might have betrayed de Man into political indiscretions. That seems unlikely, but Levin's remark was uttered with the hindsight of thirty-five years. For de Man, dropping the German section was certainly a matter of saving time, but it is also true that Stefan Georg had been one of the avatars of German nationalism, a poetic precursor of ideologies that were later taken up enthusiastically by the Nazis. (Somewhat bewilderingly, for a man who had just floated the idea in discussing Paul's thesis that writing on Georg might have betrayed de Man's latent Nazi sympathies, Levin added that he deprecated the use of de Man's life to criticize his theories.) Poggioli did not cite, though he probably implied, the distaste he and Levin felt for the philosophic approach Paul took, writing to Brower that he and Harry felt that de Man's work had omitted all context, and that it presented his ideas without relating them to anything that had come before. He did not acknowledge the necessary connections of his work to history and criticism. What Poggioli implied was that Paul's ideas, lacking any underpinnings for his unconventional approach, were therefore unsupportable.[49] One might note in passing, for that is not the focus of the present work, that the dissertation does indeed read as if its terminology and underlying point of view had come to the writer directly and without parentage, as is true of some of de Man's later writing. Many readers at the time of his great influence did not object, and only the small American audience already knowledgeable about the unspoken source of those ideas would have recognized their intellectual genealogy.[50] On the other hand, naming such ancestors would no doubt have created annoyance or hostility in some.

Poggioli said nothing about how he himself had twisted and stretched the rules to give Paul extra stipends, excused him from course requirements, excused him from examinations, and turned a blind eye for years to his work at Berlitz. Drawing to a close, he added the crucial sentence that his department would let Paul de Man go without discussion if he received an offer from another institution. Obviously, they all had heard about Cornell's intended offer. Poggioli ended his long letter by insisting that further help for de Man would be unfair to other superb students, and he named four rivals who could "get the goods," when de Man could not. None of whom, it is fair to say, ever achieved the renown won by de Man.[51] It was a bureaucrat's letter, heavily emphasizing missed deadlines and lacking references to de Man's "soul" or other intangible qualities. The tone was not like Poggioli in his normal mode. But he was a boss, and firing as well as hiring were essential parts of his job.

We have no direct record of de Man's own feelings during these last three years at Harvard, but with his real burdens, he probably expected to mug his way through the requirements—doing enough to get out with the degree and to write the dissertation his own way. What he did not compromise was his ideas. Especially the essay "The International Structure of the Romantic Image" was deep, heartfelt, and eloquent. Unburdened by the need to document or substantiate its assertions, it was de Man at his most persuasive, and that was a high standard.

Poggioli was twice surprised by Paul de Man shortly thereafter. After his long letter had been typed by Betty Ann Farmer and signed, the paper was rolled back into the platen, and at the bottom Poggioli squeezed in two postscripts. The first noted that Paul had phoned saying he couldn't meet his February deadline for his dissertation after all, and also that Cornell would make him a clear offer almost at once. In the second, even more surprising postscript, Poggioli added that Paul had just told him that Cornell was offering $9,000 and an associate professorship in comparative literature. He intended to accept. That was an enormous leap. Within the space of a month, Paul de Man had gone from being one of Harvard's near failures, a meteor about to fall into the oblivion of "Slippery Rock University" (a conventional joke name but a real institution), to achieving an important position at an Ivy League university—and at a high salary.[52]

Paul de Man went to Cornell in the fall of 1960 and was elevated to a full professorship just four years later. Moreover, by then he held tenure both there and at the University of Zurich simultaneously, because within a couple of years he had gained the secret approval of the deans of both universities, who agreed to lop off a few weeks at each end of the semester at each department. Thus each university could "benefit," it was said, by his presence. That was why no one except those intimately involved knew about the arrangement until after de Man's death. Literary criticism is sometimes accused of using a "Procrustean bed"—a torturing of language when a commentator stretches or shortens a helpless text to suit his or her intentions. Paul had now put the device to use on the academic calendar itself. But as he said to his son Rik toward the end of his life, if he had it to do over again, he would live it as a rich man.

With Cornell's offer in hand, Paul could look forward to a new existence. Still working feverishly against a deadline that Betty Ann Farmer remembered, he finally submitted his dissertation in May of 1960, and one of her colleagues feverishly typed it up. Then in August, he packed himself, Pat, and their two children into a car and drove westward across Massachusetts, New Hampshire, and almost half of New York State. The couple stopped briefly in Lancaster, New Hampshire, and there they were married on August 11 by a justice of the peace.[53] Double to the end, he repeated the marriage once they had reached Ithaca and Cornell. They were wed again there, Pat said, perhaps because, as usual, he had done things en route the quickest but not most correct way. Still, it got done. The couple had legal status; he could always travel as her husband, and his future was assured. There were no extramarital affairs for either partner, and no lawsuits.[54] Paul continued to manage his role among his colleagues and academic superiors skillfully, and they lived happily for the next eight years on the edge of Ithaca, a small and charming upstate college town, in a small and inconspicuous house. As Paul de Man's name gathered renown, Johns Hopkins called in 1968; then Yale demanded his services, first as professor of French and then also of comparative literature; ultimately he ascended to the Sterling Professorship. From 1971 on, de Man doubled back and forth, crossing the Atlantic in grand liners like the *Normandie*, and living perpetually on both continents in a continual state of gratifying disequilibrium. He was continually in demand as a speaker and examiner of Ph.D. candidates all over the country and abroad, while almost single-handedly making irony, the essence of doubleness, into a watchword. Traveling so much, he and Hartman were sparing of their time, and often away from the campus at New Haven. The lines in his face grew deeper, the lines of his writings more and more doubtful of the capacity of words to communicate stable meanings. "Double in all things," as Hans-Jost Frey called him, he exerted, through the "deconstruction" he and Derrida promoted, enormous influence on his students, colleagues, and the art and culture of his age.

EPILOGUE

PAUL DE MAN IN SOME WAYS WAS AN ANTI-HERO OF OUR TIMES, ONE WHO lived not only a double life, but several. The deconstructive philosophy that he later taught with its emphasis on doubleness and irony seemed to echo the tortured narrative of the first part of the twentieth century. The thirties, that "low dishonest decade," as Auden called it, with the catastrophic years that followed, found their reflection in the early life of this theorist. De Man's supremely selfish political choices, along with his other nefarious dealings, embody just part of the madness. He was pulled into history both by his uncle's preeminence and his own thirst for opportunity, money, and a stage that could accommodate his very real talents. In many ways, his academic rehabilitation well after the war seems to mirror a larger world righting itself after decades of self-destruction.

It was no accident that from 1943 through 1945 the work in which de Man immersed himself was the anonymous translation and publication of *Moby-Dick* in its first Dutch edition—even while in those same three years he was arranging for the simultaneous creation and collapse of Hermès. One may speculate that even before he opened the doors of his company he had begun to see himself through the lens of Melville's own vision, as a man afloat, far from land, carried onward by a foundering ship that would ultimately pull its crew to the bottom of the sea.

Later he would long to return to Belgium, but like the *Pequod*, would never make it back home.

How did he reach that point? Born in Europe, a brilliant schoolboy from the high bourgeoisie, he was gifted with beauty, charm, and perceptiveness, but equally cursed by a family that for all its wealth and prominence would be destroyed by suicides, deceits, and in Henri de Man the results of soaring ambition gone wrong. When World War II arrived during his youth, Paul was a man beloved by women, but he was also a college dropout; secret in every way, he rolled the dice and became a high-flying collaborator, and at war's end a publisher who, unable to resist the lure of his company's cash, stole it without concern for the friends and relatives whose money it was. Facing certain conviction and a long jail term as a felon, and with "the ground burning under his feet," never again able to hold a passport or return to Belgium, at twenty-eight this once most promising and talented man fled to exile in the United States.

There, the immensely seductive but tragically fluid and undisciplined Paul de Man continued to reinvent himself, a process his lifelong habits of complete secrecy allowed him to carry off. In New York, he became known at first as a new member of the circle of New York intellectuals, but again as a result of his own acts, this era became another closed chapter of his life. Once more he fled forward. Chastened, burdened, and, not incidentally, at length happily married—or living as a married man—the Paul de Man known by others began to emerge in 1950 as an admired young academic who at Bard College, Harvard, Cornell, and Yale established himself as a stunningly important intellectual, seemingly austere and almost unapproachable, with a cult following, and wide international influence, gained by his new ideas and personal authority.

Yet behind his mask of high seriousness and respectability, his personal life had been chaotic. In the course of enacting his several selves—or "performing" them, to use his term—de Man had lived his early years in a ménage a trois, had married—both validly and bigamously—two wives, and fathered five children in two families, two of whom were born out of wedlock, keeping all of them ignorant of their half-siblings' existence. This was messy, and the consequences led to a decade of blackmail. Through it all de Man lived on two continents and held tenure at two universities.

His was an extraordinary life, and the questions we want to ask are less about his misdeeds than how de Man so transformed himself from the 1950s onward. Certainly it was a conscious effort. His devoted cousin Li, when asked, said Paul had changed through "the love of a good woman"—Patricia de Man. Undoubtedly there is truth in this. Equally, however, it was crucial that in the United States this cultural critic was able finally to escape the crippling pressures of family, class, and, indeed, European history and his own youthful participation in the war as a collaborator. Had he not been Henri de Man's nephew but a middle-class youth like Gilbert Jaeger or Georges Goriély—or even the well-born Paul Willems—had he been someone who had to make his own way, he probably would not have taken the job at *Le Soir* (*volé*), for he alone in his circle had collaborated with the machinery of propaganda. Had he not been born into wealth and social prominence, he might still have flunked his boring courses in chemistry, but he would have found his way, guided by his talents, into literature as his friend and ally Georges Lambrichs did. With necessity driving him, Paul de Man would not have been slow to learn that keeping a job in any enterprise meant not merely charming his superiors, but also mastering its tedious demands. And without Paul's high political connections, his mistress, the beautiful and extravagant Anne Baraghian Jaeger, might still have fallen in love with the feckless youth, but she was unlikely to have abandoned an indulgent and forgiving husband who had plenty of money and was clearly marked for great success in favor of a youth who could not pass his examinations and had no profession.

Indeed, we know that de Man himself wondered what effect Henri's life had had on him, as he once confided in Mary McCarthy. And it was that connection, more than any other that seems to have stung when he replied to the denunciation in 1955 by writing to Poggioli that he had given the last seven years—meaning his entire life in the United States—to creating an existence totally separated from the world of his birth.

Yet the puzzle remains: In what cauldron of experience was deconstruction born? Of course, his ideas were developed in conjunction with Jacques Derrida, and today it is the French writer who is understood by many to have developed them, but this is essentially because de Man's life has been occulted by scandal. Derrida, after writing a lengthy discussion of his relationship with de Man, rationally enough refused to open the subject ever again. However, it was de Man who helped pave the way for his friend's reputation in the United States, for the other man was little known in 1967, and de Man's reputation had been growing throughout the 1960s; when they met he was approaching the great renown he achieved after 1971 when he went to Yale.

Essentially, the thinking of this anti-hero came not only from Heidegger and Hegel but from everything de Man had known and lived through: From the aftermath of World War I, from the rise of Hitler in the 1930s and the turn by political leaders from Socialism to fascism in that decade, their procession during World War II into collaboration, and then to the desperate, downward spiral of many careers as they plummeted to earth in 1945.

De Man decried biography—and autobiography—for obvious reasons. Undoubtedly, however, the complex story of his many lives is tightly imbricated in his theory. The branches of literature may indeed reach heavenward, but the roots of language are deep in those forces that Lionel Trilling named: psychology, biography, society, and history. De Man's ideas, so often negative in import, turn on dismantling false perceptions more than finding our way through them to what he once called the light. In the view of this writer, those ideas were born not only out of a desire to penetrate and disturb false notions about the sufficiency of discourse, but also to allow himself the ability to deny—to himself above all—the stability not just of words but the stains of character, of history, and of personal responsibility.

DE MAN BECAME AN eminent figure, although not readily approached. His friends were possessive. When he chose to invite a junior person to lunch with him at Cornell, one of his circle might stop him as they left the faculty club and ask, "What did you talk about?" The enormous social and intellectual upheavals that culminated in 1968–1969 were already under way, and de Man, with his new ideas, was the man of the hour. When Georges Poulet returned in 1971 from visiting de Man in the States, he reported to Hans-Jost Frey that their much-traveled friend had "checked in his luggage with the structuralists."[1] Paul knew the insiders and passed on the information, Patricia said. Chat floated about Father Ong, but no one mentioned Heidegger, or Jean Wahl, at least in public, although names of mediators were tossed about. De Man's stance could well have been summed up in the comment he made on a graduate student's paper, quoted earlier: "impeccable—and opaque." His past was invisible.

Early on, students followed him from Cambridge to the remote town above Cayuga Lake in upstate New York, and then others arrived. He stayed at Cornell until 1968. Hired as an associate professor, he was promoted to full professor in 1964, after the minimum period of four years. Keeping a low profile, he and Patricia entertained infrequently. This helped ensure that the cloak of secrecy that guarded his prior life could not be penetrated, but no doubt it also sprang from a determination not to repeat the mistakes of his first marriage, with its flamboyant and extravagant lifestyle, which was pursued by both Paul and Anne. He still had to juggle his finances, and he alone held the checkbook. His widow reported that the bills might go unpaid, and on at least one occasion he ran out on hotel charges in Switzerland, even while the suits he wore to his public lectures were superbly tailored. But there were no more scandals. In the 1950s, he had endured uncertainty, afraid at all times of further devastating denunciations, whether from Anne or some other unknown person. With every passing year, he felt a little more safe, but the stakes were high and the anxiety never left him. At a deeper level, he undoubtedly did not want to lead the life of "gallantry" his father had pursued with its parties, late-night romances on the lawns, and the musical mistress who had displaced Madeleine. He had a happy life with Patricia and was wise enough to hold on to it.

Paradoxically, this would have been just the time for such antics, for in the 1960s and 1970s all around Paul de Man at Cornell and later at Johns Hopkins and Yale, there boiled the political and social turmoil that had begun in the early 1960s with the Free Speech Movement in Berkeley: black liberation, protests against the war in Vietnam, feminism, and sexual liberation. He lived apart from it, and his reputation for "austerity" certainly was related to his deliberate decision to keep a distance from easy sexual conquests. For the first time, women felt free to express their own sexuality openly, and behavior changed. It was an era when a woman student at one college or another might appear at the desk of a male professor—married or single—whom she, not he, was pursuing, literally panting from the exertion of running down her object, and the men left notes with scandalized secretaries to pass on to their pursuers. (Paul did report to Pat about one woman student—who later became a theorist—who was bent on seducing him. "She seems demure. But she is *naughty*," he told her.) The real abuse of sexual freedom by both male and some female professors toward their students came to be the subject of criticism and regulation on the heels of this period. But de Man had nothing to do with such sexual intrigues. When he wanted a change of air, he either retreated to Gott Island or sailed back to Europe on a good liner.

Throughout the period from the late 1960s until his death in 1983, de Man's fame grew. He became nothing short of a star. Morris Dickstein was only one of many aspiring young literary scholars who, hearing about de Man from friends, made the trek to New Haven to sit in on his classes. By then, according to Dickstein, he had a cult. Politically, however, de Man was visibly skittish and unwilling to engage in discussion on the subject. Barbara Guetti remained a favorite of de Man, and later she taught with him at Yale from 1976 to 1980, a position she said she could only have held if he had helped her get it. In that era, she remarked, "I had a few interchanges with [de Man] about anti-Semitism. I was teaching 'Modernism'—Proust, Freud. I had a lot of smart Jewish students, and we talked about anti-Semitism. I told Paul it was becoming an interesting discussion. . . . He gave me this look. He used to get angry if you mentioned politics. I thought it was anger, but later I thought he was . . ." She did not finish the sentence. Paul de Man's friend Juan Marichal, the historian and literary critic, noticed the same anger when he attempted to broach political issues in the 1950s.[2]

Before long, de Man's ideas were attracting the attention of those at many other institutions. In 1967, as Jacques Derrida has said, the two men met and struck up a friendship at a conference in Baltimore. It was during the 1960s that de Man began publishing in the prestigious *New York Review of Books*, then early in its run but already a forum for voices that were important before the term *public intellectual* was coined. In 1968, de Man moved briefly to Johns Hopkins and its Humanities Center through the influence of Charles Singleton and the good offices of his friend John Freccero, who had preceded de Man in leaving Cornell for Baltimore, but Paul accepted Johns Hopkins's offer only after arranging for a paid sabbatical year abroad *before* he took up teaching duties. It was a signing bonus, perhaps one of academia's first, and proof that de Man never lost his skills at negotiating.

Almost simultaneously, Geoffrey Hartman, who had visited de Man at Cornell earlier, was working, along with Victor Brombert, then chair of the French Department, to bring de Man to Yale. In 1970, Yale lured him by also promising him a year's sabbatical before he began teaching. The only sticking point for Yale was that de Man had not published a book, a matter on which the university stood firm. Hartman and Brombert reported that they were determined to get him as a professor of French, and so the three of them "cobbled together" the essays that formed de Man's first collection, *Blindness and Insight*, published in 1971 by Oxford University Press.[3] They persuaded Yale to accept this as satisfying the requirement, which it wisely did, for the book established de Man's reputation and became widely influential very quickly.

Over the next several years, Paul de Man published three more collections of his essays in book form.[4] Two others were edited and published by his students after his death.[5] His fame continued to grow, and he became the central figure in defining the new model of literary studies and American high cultural life before Jacques Derrida, whom de Man befriended and helped become known, appeared on the scene. De Man remains a major example of cultural influence and how it may grow (a subject illuminated by William Clark's interesting study of how "charismatic professors" in Germany had also once managed their careers).[6] Speaking engagements and sitting on extramural examination committees were normally rewarded with cash, and this was always important to de Man. He did not always live up to expectations, but no one criticized him.

———

AFTER A SECRET and disappointing visit to Belgium in 1962 de Man did not go back; he would never see his friends again. Frida Vandervelden said she was "haunted" all her life by his memory, and missed him. When she learned he was teaching at Yale after 1971, she asked her daughter, who was visiting there as an academic herself, to get in touch with him—but the younger woman could not get through to de Man. On the whole, those in de Man's university circle in Belgium had note-worthy careers, and they kept in touch with their early friends. Gilbert Jaeger, in particular, rose high, becoming the director of protection for the United Nations High Commission for Refugees, an important and valuable worldwide service headquartered in Geneva. Frida continued her career as an industrial chemist. Georges Goriély became a highly respected professor of sociology and political science, as well as a histo-rian and specialist in contemporary German history. Fortunate in choosing his wife, Simone, he was father of several children who achieved significant intellectual careers. Charles Dosogne and Frida remained friendly, while he married again and thrived as an engineer. Paul Willems, novelist, playwright, and lawyer, took a different tack, rising to the top of Belgium's cultural life, and presiding for many years as president of the Palais des Beaux-Arts, the premier arts institution of the country. In the last decade of her life, Anne von Orland-Ipsen, a wealthy widow, left Paris and rejoined her circle in Brussels. Almost all his former friends survived de Man, living into the 1990s or into the next century. When they heard about Paul, they were interested, but not critical: the ménage à trois was a kind of joke. They thought his collaboration had been limited to his work as a book reviewer. If they knew about de Man's embezzlements from Hermès, they did not say so. Certainly Jan de Man and Georges Goriély were informed to some extent (he had to leave Belgium "because the earth was burning under his feet" was Goriély's comment), but it was not good form to expand on that topic.

I had moved on from Cornell, but continued from a remove to observe Paul de Man's career with interest, but little insight. Matters became more clear later when I began to study his essays of the 1950s.

In the beginning I merely wondered if tracing the development of de Man's early career in Belgium might yield the insights that direct confrontation with his writings had not produced. A number of Paul de Man's American friends, meanwhile, feared that a biography would mean a merely journalistic inquiry, something superficial and possibly false. The reality was the opposite. The facts could not be grasped without a much deeper understanding of the world he had come from and of the tortured era that had formed him, his uncle, and the tragic events of the de Man family.

Eventually, however, it became clear that de Man's career encompassed subjects too disparate and required too much time in too many archives and locations all to be contained in one volume. Belgian history, the war, the occupation, a profoundly convoluted and concealed story of commerce, bankruptcy, and the dual-language records of Belgian courts, U.S. immigration regulations, the laws governing divorce in Arkansas—not to mention the quantity of the personal testimony of the many friends, colleagues, and relatives of de Man—it was all essential, but it was not at all the life of theory or deconstruction. That topic certainly resulted in part from the internalization of Paul de Man's experiences, but it drew on completely different materials, was written work on which he had long meditated, and was connected to his previous life only by the years when he created the essays he published between 1953 and 1960. The end of that important period of transition became the right place to end my study.

Others, I hope, will take up the challenge. De Man's theories about his "linguistic philosophy" have been the subject of many articles, but very little has been written that would place them in the context of his life. Yet his terms did not come to him through the ether or by revelation, although they appear to do so. We need to know more precisely what, in fact, he took from Blanchot, from Hegel, from Heidegger, from Barthes. Philosophy as it used to be taught existed in a vacuum, isolated from the general life surrounding its exponents and their origins. It was understood to have developed through the influence of one thinker on another, but—like literature itself—in the Anglo-Saxon tradition it was presented as if untouched by the politics and history of the eras in which it was formed. It was pure. Yet we no longer believe in that kind of parthenogenesis. The links and connections that impacted de Man's writings after 1960 need to be established, not merely from the influence of one philosopher on another, but from era to era, and from life to thought and back again.

That work remains for others to take up. One hopes that it will be traced in detail and depth, and with some skepticism, from a position that recognizes that the choices we make among philosophical perceptions or explanations are not inevitable, but represent in part human experiences, and are inflected by what we and our epochs have lived and endured.

A FUNDAMENTAL QUESTION REMAINS: What are the differences and what are the connections between the life and ideas of Paul de Man's first twenty-eight years of life and those of his maturity? There is no single or simple answer, for he was a moving target, and his thinking developed and changed over time, sometimes reversing course, but always remaining in motion. To be brief, one can say that the real difference between the early period of his life and the late one is his invention of theory, and that this strongly reflects and responds to his real-life dilemmas.

De Man had many personal and intellectual conflicts to dwell upon and resolve when he began to think of himself as a "linguistic philosopher." From 1948 on, a strategy was essential to conceal his past history and protect the new life he was creating in the United States. In this, he was successful. Yet, as Emerson wrote, "we go abroad to travel, and we take ourselves with us." De Man brought his memories with his baggage on his flight from Antwerp, and with maturity came a deeper, more biting understanding of what his relations had been, how these had looked to others, if not to himself, and what roles he had played in the world. Yet there was no going back: He was exiled not only from his homeland but from speaking about his deepest roots and emotional ties. In fact, he lost all his command of Flemish, as he told both Patricia and Geoffrey Hartman: He calculated mentally in his native tongue but could not speak it. He might tell Pat he was nostalgic for the days when "the church was in the middle of the village," but that metaphorical church, with its ideology of trusting belief and social stability, had been reduced to rubble even before the war. Paul de Man needed a way of thinking that, even if it could not be justified, could at least provide distance between himself and the history in which he was formed.

What de Man produced instead was a kind of Ypres before its reconstruction, for between 1914 and 1918, that Gothic city in Flanders became a site where only the blackened stumps of old, glorious buildings stood as dire reminders of what civilization had once created, and how in four years it had eaten itself alive. Today, that Ypres is unrecognizable; to the visitor, it is a Belgian Williamsburg. Its museum alone reminds one of its history, for the city itself has eliminated World War I, and along the streets that cover over its rubble rises what appears to be an unweathered Gothic town of no certain date or origin. Deconstruction, in a sense, denies the possibility of rebuilding Ypres as a solution to the pain of history. While de Man himself would never be so indiscreet, his practice insists that, on the contrary, there is no constructive way to dissolve painful memory. The job of thinking is to reveal the complex processes of the war, its damage, and its aftermath. At its best, deconstruction would say clearly that we cannot and we must not wipe away the lies and false beliefs that produced such devastation.

This, I would venture to say, was, metaphorically speaking, the matrix of Paul de Man's "philosophy of language," which began with contemporary existential ideas and went on not only to hold that communication was impossible but to assert eventually that speech among human beings, alienated as we are and living on the brink of the *abîme*, the abyss of nothingness, was no more to the point or useful than a picture of a waterfall; it was a mere representation, not a source of power. His premise was that words (in which we store and recapture memories) are innately unstable and that the language of whatever we have written—political or personal, abstract or confessional—is merely a representation whose unreliable "meanings" are always "slippery" and subject to "hermeneutic suspicion," to be distrusted and taken apart in a process that demonstrates their inevitable self-contradictions.

De Man had seen a great deal that would have conduced to this position. In his youth, his home environment was filled with an air of mystery, a place where bereavements had prevailed and where hypocrisies in both private and public life seemed necessary for survival. In adulthood, he experienced the results of accepting in his uncle a model of behavior that had led him, as nephew—and imaginary son—to adopt and try to advance Nazi doctrines, as in his proposed *Cahiers Européens*. As a young reviewer, after feeling himself shipwrecked, rudderless, and at the mercy of changing winds and waves, he had sought power and money, but his move into pro-German propaganda probably satisfied not only opportunism but a need for the presumed stability promised by the Thousand-Year Reich. No wonder, when his career and then Germany itself fell apart and de Man retreated for almost three years to Kalmthout, that the great book he took up there was *Moby-Dick*, the tale of another exile afloat on a sea of uncertain identity. He was still morally at sea when he landed at Hermès, perpetrated acts of fraud on its first day of existence, and continued his thefts until all its considerable treasury was exhausted.

Undoubtedly, his exile in the United States led him gradually to begin to rethink what his life had been and how he could rescue self-respect from its ruins. There had to be a way to stitch together the many layers of the persons he had been and had become. Perhaps it was this process of reintegration that Yves Bonnefoy had perceived in his friend when, having lived under the German occupation himself, he observed that the charismatic but deeply tired, inward man he saw on the beach holding close to his small family was repairing his net. De Man was, in fact, very earth-oriented, as he showed in his annual retreat in summer to a remote island without running water or electricity. His low-key existence in Boston and New Haven was not merely strategic; it also expressed his new wish for seriousness, for a balanced, loving, and predictable life with a wife who was the same person she had been the day before and would be again tomorrow, and who would help him maintain his equilibrium.

It was from this position of exile and silence that de Man, after he reached Cornell, began to develop what became an approach to literature that took as its bedrock a subversive doubt concerning the truth-telling power of language. Language itself and its limitations, rather than the choices of the individuals who used it, became the focus, if not the culprit. That approach continues to interest some followers, but it is part of a still lively battle, for scholars like Carlo Ginzburg believe that far from being separate, in de Man's case "a close relationship exists between the mask that he wore for forty years and his work as a critic."[7] Years ago, David Lehman took this position when he concluded that there was a "problematic relation" between de Man's "guilty silence" and his "theories about guilt and speech" that must be addressed.[8] More friendly comments come from figures like Geoffrey Hartman and Peter Brooks, his colleagues at Yale, who have tried to defend de Man's ideas, calling them "reparative."[9] They, like many others, had loved him, in spite of what they thought they knew to be his mistaken but early anti-Semitic political stance as a reviewer—a stance they understood was limited to a single article. They infer that de Man came later to understand that the political philosophy he had embraced in the 1930s and 1940s had so badly misled him that he developed deconstruction as a fundamentally doubting response to the authority of words, a stance of "hermeneutic suspicion."[10]

One may sympathize with their effort to justify their friend, but this ameliorative vision was formed with no inkling of how far and actively Paul de Man had entered into collaboration, or how creatively he sought to support Nazism, as in his proposed journal. At the time of this writing, de Man is still generally understood to have been merely a dubious book reviewer in Belgium. In the same way that his Belgian friends knew nothing of his brother Rik's death, his mother's suicide, his own thefts at Hermès and convictions for fraud, those in the United States knew nothing of his abandoned wife and three sons, the decade of bigamy, his lack of an undergraduate degree, his failure with regard to the general examination at Harvard, his lack of a passport and why he could not acquire one—or, indeed, of his double-dipping with respect to tenure and his short-changing of students on two continents. He dealt with facts whether of his life or of the texts he examined insouciantly, by secrecy, and from behind what Ginzburg called a "mask."

Yet, even should one hypothetically grant that it was Paul de Man's intention to make "reparation," it seems unlikely that by later developing theory, de Man was making amends, giving satisfaction for a wrong, or expiating an injury, as the word *reparation* is understood to mean. Rather, it is more evident that he was shifting the blame. "He was the kind of man," Ted Weiss had recognized in 1950, "who wanted to write one small thing that could change the world," and who "went with the flow." In his ideas about language, Paul de Man evidently found a lever long enough for his purpose. For one may argue that theory was an argument shaped not to address or repair past misdeeds but, rather, to turn away from them and make them irrelevant. The deconstructive process he developed of demonstrating over and again that language is unstable and may not be relied upon, that one may pick apart virtually any text and find its "seams," where other, contradictory meanings are concealed, is not only essentially negative but potentially a way of putting out of sight whatever the statements in question seem intended to convey. In his daily life, de Man dealt with his dilemmas in the same way, and always had done so: by turning away, covering up, and moving on from them to something else.

"AUTOBIOGRAPHY AS DE-FACEMENT," an essay de Man wrote late in life,[11] is a revealing work and very personal, for the "de-facement" of the title is, of course, shadowed by the suppressed image de Man lived with: the image of his hanging mother, Madeleine, whose distorted visage, literally defaced, hung over his consciousness, as his friend Paul Willems insisted, for the rest of his life.[12] The muteness of the world was both hers and his own. De Man's essay focuses on the Dalesman, a deaf and mute figure in The Excursion, by William Wordsworth, who lives alone in the woods because he cannot communicate. To the poet who created him, the isolated woodsman was guarded by the sun, which follows its course across our lives, rising and setting below what Wordsworth called our "horizon of sorrow and of tears."[13] That sun, a figure of light, represented "absolute sovereignty upon itself," a form of being or God. De Man, however, professed no belief in the soul, and rejected all "transcendental authority." That is the fundamental reason that "Autobiography as De-Facement" asserts that autobiography is impossible: it is indistinguishable from fiction, for without a subject able to speak with authority, there can be no adequate summing up of a life.

In the suffering of the Dalesman, however, de Man recognized a buried aspect of himself. In using language, de Man tells us, we are all condemned to muteness, and his meditation on the woodsman of *The Excursion* is suffused with pity as well as horror, recalling some of de Man's earliest and most lyrical writing. Yet as philosophy, linguistic or otherwise, it raises certain questions, for it allows him at once to move us with his lifelong sympathy and yearning for transcendental contact while stepping aside to deny not only the possibility of communication but, by implication, the fact that he himself has been the agent of our response. Nietzsche famously wrote in *Beyond Good and Evil* that all philosophy is "the personal confession of its author and a kind of involuntary and unconscious memoir." However imperfectly, language does communicate, and words, as Emerson said, are acts.

This has been understood by all who seek social change or influence, as censorship itself demonstrates, and it was grasped by the political movements that gathered power in the 1970s and welcomed the potential power of deconstruction to "undo" the rhetoric of their enemies and strengthen the attack on oppressive political processes. Architects of feminism, black liberation, and gay rights all found support in theory as they sought to overturn the forces that had so long used slogans and the abstract concepts behind "gender, race, and class" to subvert the rights of minorities or the powerless. In that battle, however, theory was only an heuristic tool in what was basically a defense of another abstraction, democracy itself, an Enlightenment value if ever there was one. It was not de Manian irony, but deep commitment, that moved those struggles forward, for de Man avoided politics, grew annoyed and perhaps frightened when discussion of anti-Semitism was pressed on him, and did not and could not vote.

One is again reminded of the poet James Dickey, who wrote that one must consider "the manner in which a man lies, and what he lies about." Paul de Man employed many lies in many forms in his lifetime. Jacques Derrida—although with his friend and coadjutor of deconstruction, he inevitably distrusted biography—astutely said of de Man that mourning is an important "motif" in de Man's work, an especially insightful comment given that he wrote this before he knew about de Man's own experiences of loss.[14] Derrida hedged by calling this de

Man's "irony," but nevertheless, he clearly believed it, and in the same
essay he wrote of de Man's life after 1950 as a time of "exile, radical
reconversion . . . an enormous suffering, an agony that we cannot yet
know the extent of." He also quoted a comment de Man made in an
interview that ideology and politics were "always uppermost in my
mind," and "I don't think I was ever away from these problems."[15] That
is probably true, and it supports the argument that for de Man, deconstruction, rather than existing apart from ideology, was deeply impli-
cated in dealing by denial with the valency of past, compromising acts.

De Man's suffering, which his friend perceived, showed itself in his
visage more and more clearly as the years went on, and Derrida's words
suggest how, like it or not, theorists, critics, and biographers alike draw
inevitably on similar material from which to weave their arguments.[16]
The endless complexities of any human life are difficult to deal with,
but to paraphrase Lionel Trilling, in the long run literature—and philosophy, as well—have everything to do "with psychology, with biography or society or history." The relationship is not determined by
simple causality, but one must know the facts and the contexts from
which lives and ideas spring as we seek to understand them.

After the scandal of 1988 and its aftermath, de Man, though dead
for five years, became a pariah. If de Man's "extreme skepticism," a
term Denis Donoghue used with respect to deconstruction, contributed anything to moderating American "naïveté," he is unlikely soon
to be given credit for it. His ship has sailed: The great transatlantic ves-
sels he preferred, like the *Normandie* and the *Ile de France*, have disappeared over the horizon. Holiday cruises make other trips with a
different clientele. Faith, not modernist doubt and skepticism, has
become the order of the day, and whatever the vessel, there will be new
card parties on the decks, and new winners will take all, at least for a
while. Yet at the end of his life, Paul de Man would not have joined
them. Reckless and a gambler in his early years, he removed himself
from the self-destruction into which he had leapt as a young man. Paradoxically, when he evoked the Dalesman, who was unable to hear
even the storm that existed for him only as a picture might hang on a
wall, de Man both illuminated the nature of alienation and gave tongue
to what is mute. Yet his awareness of his own contradictions showed in

his face as well as in his sympathies, his wit, and his intention not to give up.

A senior professor, who had once been a candidate for a position with de Man and Hartman, told of speaking to the two men of "the magic" at Yale. "Yes," de Man had answered, "we are magicians. And when you get here, we will all disappear." Disappear he did, and his secrets went with him for a long time. Many have now come to light, but Paul de Man left behind another mystery, embedded in the roots of this book but still unresolved. What makes people follow what they don't understand? Why are so many, whether educated or not, cultivated or operating only on instinct, ready at times to follow the leadership of men and women whose teachings and doctrines they and their friends cannot explain? That it happens, we know. New and chaotic eras call for new beliefs, and new messiahs spring up and gain adherents. Perhaps Paul de Man was right at some level when he wrote to a bemused faculty in Zurich that he must "go to Yale because he was needed in the US [,where] the political situation was difficult and his presence was required." Hungry for a leader, we follow the self-proclaimed. The dynamics of that process resist rational explanation, and reason is limited. The skeptic David Hume said that the Christian religion not only was founded on a miracle but could not be believed without one. Mystery is attractive, and magical thinking is seductive.

Perhaps for de Man, even a negative theology was better than none. He did his best to change the course of his life after he reached the United States in 1948, and to a large extent he succeeded. He did feel the anguish of the past, he did "live forward," and over the next thirty-five years he did reinvent another and better self. There was more hopefulness in the turn he was able to take in his actual life than in the philosophy he taught. Movements for social change found strength in his ideas even though de Man himself eschewed all political links. Deconstruction became integrated into the discourse of the day. If Paul de Man was something of a Pied Piper, among his adherents were those able to discard what they did not need and discern what was germane in his teachings, using it not to turn away from the world, but to reshape it. If we judge others less by their words than by their acts—and the fruit of their acts—perhaps de Man, however imperfectly, communicated a certain hope almost in spite of himself, providing ideas that became vital and generative to those who, without irony, followed in his stead, seeking to challenge the conventions that surrounded them and make their convictions real. Among the younger generations who have learned from Paul de Man, it may be that some perceive on their own horizons not the smoke of his disappearing vessel, but an indestructible hope against hope for a "world elsewhere."

The world,—this shadow of the soul . . . . lies wide around. Its attractions . . . make me acquainted with myself. I run eagerly into this resounding tumult. —I grasp the hands of those next to me, and take my place in the ring to suffer and to work; taught by an instinct, that so shall the dumb abyss be vocal with speech.[16]

ACKNOWLEDGMENTS

I AM GRATEFUL TO THE FOLLOWING INSTITUTIONS FOR FELLOWSHIP and other support during the years while this book was in preparation: the National Endowment for the Humanities; the Fulbright Commission; the National Humanities Center, where Kent Mullikin, its executive director, was a particularly kind and valued leader; Edmond L. Volpe, president of the College of Staten Island, City University of New York; the Faculty Awards Program of the City University of New York.

Debts to individuals and colleagues are pleasant to acknowledge. In the United States, early encouragement and support came from M. H. Abrams and Alfred Kazin. To Patricia Kelley de Man I owe a great debt, for her warmth and active interest in the project lasted through the decades; without her active encouragement I could not have written this biography. Other valued colleagues have been Warner Berthoff, who read more than one version of this manuscript and encouraged it always with erudition, tact, and patience, and Ann Berthoff, whose warmth and intelligence are a special gift. Morris Dickstein and Fred Kaplan have been valued colleagues and advisers. So were Robert A. Ferguson and Priscilla Parkhurst Ferguson; Michael Macdonald, who allowed me to consult his unpublished memoir about his father, Dwight; Ed Margolies, a longtime colleague and friend; Conor Cruise O'Brien and Máire Mhac an tSaoi O'Brien, who early on showed they believed in my work. I have a special debt of gratitude to the German historian Fritz Ringer: I gave him code and he made it history. Michael Wreszin was a superb historian and guide. I am grateful also to Michael Adams, librarian, Graduate Center, City University of New York. For useful suggestions I thank also Christopher Benfey and Barbara Louis. Many members of the Women Writing Women's Lives Seminar in New York City have for a decade enlightened my work as a biographer, and the Biography Seminar that was begun by Aileen Ward, sponsored by New York University, and has continued under the guidance of others has been helpful from the beginning of this study. I am especially grateful to the editors of Paul de Man's *Wartime Journalism* and *Responses* for their groundbreaking work: Werner Hammacher, Neil Hertz, and Thomas Keenan.

In Belgium I had invaluable help and suggestions from Jacques De Decker; Frans De Haes, chief librarian at the Royal Library of Belgium, who led me to unique material; Paul Aron; Ortwin de Graef, who shared archival material with me; and the noted historian Jean Stengers. At the Military Court, N. Van Winsens, an officer of the Military Court and military auditor showed me special courtesy in providing his copy of the missing procès-verbal on July 20, 1993. Also in Brussels my research at the Military Court relied for years on the patience of the librarians Andrée de Raet and Olivier Longevin. For their personal testimony I want to cite with warm appreciation Bob De Braey, Micheline De Braey, Edouard Colinet, Marlene de Man-Flechtheim, Gilbert Jaeger, and Frida Vandervelden.

To the late Anne de St.-Pierre-Fontaine, I am tied by memories not only of her friendship and hospitality but also of her deep historian's love of her country and its byways. In the learned historian Georges Goriély I found a greatly respected source of information and insight; he and Simone Goriély were and are cherished friends. To Hendrik ("Rik") Woods I am grateful for sharing with me both invaluable information and the insights he had gained over many years.

Bob Weil, editor in chief of Liveright, was the superb editor of this book; he deserves the wide renown his name has gathered. Georges Borchardt, my agent, and Will Menaker at Liveright have been greatly valuable in bringing this book to the public.

Over the years I have been fortunate in having the assistance of special persons, including Brenda Levy, Taneka Martin, Steven Dost, and Adrián Montúfar, who have gone on to higher but not more appreciated callings.

NOTES

LIST OF ARCHIVES AND ABBREVIATIONS

Below are listed the names of frequently consulted archives together with their abbreviations. Professors Harry Levin and Artine Artinian provided the author with photocopies of their files, which were used in this biography. The original materials were later given to their respective depositories; these are cited below. Some documents not placed in those depositories are cited as author archive.

AA	Artine Artinian Collection, Harry Ransom Humanities Research Center, University of Texas at Austin
ADPC	Auditeur Militaire Agence Dechenne—Documents (Pièces Annexe) supporting the Report of the Expert
ADRP	Auditeur Militaire Agence Dechene—Report of Expert for the tribunal prosecuting the Agence Dechenne
AM	*LSv*: Auditeur Militaire: *Le Soir (volé)*. This was the informal name of the journal when it was published under German censorship. Before and after the war the title was *Le Soir*.
AM	TdO: Auditeur Militaire: Toison d'Or
BC	Bard College archive
BNF	Bibliothèque Nationale de France
CB	Commune of Bruxelles
CE	Commune of Etterbeek—Etterbeek is Flemish for Ixelles, a borough of Brussels
DB	Bob De Braey papers
FV	Frida Vandervelden papers
GG	Georges Goriély papers

GK   Gemeente/Commune of Kalmthout

HL   Harry Levin papers (bMS Am 2461), Houghton Library, Harvard University

IMEC   Institut Mémoires d'Edition Contemporaine

INS   National Archives, Immigration and Naturalization Service of the United States Department of Justice

KA   Koninklijk Athenaeum—Royal Athenaeum archive, Antwerp

MdMF   Marlene de Man-Flechtheim papers

MLB   Musée Littéraire de Bruxelles—Literary Museum of Brussels

REA   Rechtbank van Eerste Aanleg—First Court of Appeal, Criminal Division, Antwerp

RL   Robert Lowell papers (MS Am 1905), Houghton Library, Harvard University (correspondence between Mary McCarthy and Elizabeth Hardwick)

RVK   Rechtbank van Koophandel—Commercial Court, Antwerp

SAB   Stad Antwerpen Bewolking—City of Antwerp Population Register

UCI   Paul de Man papers, Special Collections and Archives, University of California at Irvine

ULB   Université Libre de Bruxelles—Free University of Brussels

VC   Mary McCarthy papers, Archives and Special Collections Library, Vassar College Libraries

Yale   Dwight Macdonald papers (MS 730), Manuscripts and Archives, Yale University Library

INTRODUCTION

1. Interview, December 29, 1990.
2. In 1970, when news got out that he was leaving Hopkins after a brief stay, one Bennington undergraduate told another that literature had gone to Yale.
3. Henri Thomas, a French poet and novelist who met de Man at Harvard in the late 1950s, made him the subject of *Le Parjure* (Paris: Gallimard, 1964), and some three or four other novels have included figures based on him since then. Jacques Derrida examined the term *parjure* closely, with some shifting of its common usage. See *Without Alibi*, ed., trans. Peggy Kamuf (Palo Alto: Stanford University Press, 2002).
4. Elise ("Li") LeCocq-de Man was almost the only member of his estranged Belgian family to retain her affection for him. Interview, June 30, 1990. The other was his cousin Minime (Micheline).
5. Interview, March 8, 1993. De Graef went on to publish two studies of de Man: *Serenity in Crisis* (Lincoln: University of Nebraska Press, 1993); *Titanic Light* (Lincoln: University of Nebraska Press, 1995).

6. The photograph used by the magazine had no relation to Paul de Man himself.

7. Georges Goriély, "A Personal Testimony," typescript 6 ll., with emendations by the author, given at an international conference: "Paul de Man (Antwerp—New Haven)," University of Antwerp, Department of Germanic Philosophy, June 24–25, 1988.

8. Personal discussion with the author, 1992.

9. James Atlas, "The Case of Paul de Man," *New York Times Magazine*, August 28, 1988, 36–69.

10. David Lehman, *Signs of the Times: Deconstruction and the Fall of Paul de Man* (New York: Simon & Schuster, 1991).

11. Paul de Man, *Wartime Journalism*, 1939–1943, ed. Werner Hamacher, Neil Hertz, and Thomas Keenan (Lincoln: University of Nebraska Press, 1992); Werner Hamacher, Neil Hertz, and Thomas Keenan, eds., *Responses: On Paul de Man's Wartime Journalism* (Lincoln: University of Nebraska Press, 1992).

12. Interview with M. H. Abrams, June 24, 1992; interview with Hans-Jost Frey, June 29, 1991.

13. A young American graduate student and socialist, Alice Cook, later a leading sociologist, took a prestigious fellowship to Germany to "sit at Henri de Man's feet . . . at the new university in Frankfurt" in 1930. De Man's study, *The Joy in Work*, she said, was "a very interesting book that really became the basis of industrial psychology." When she later learned that he had become "a complete fascist," she was severely disappointed. Interview, August 11, 1992.

14. Mark Mazower discussed the meaning of collaboration in *Inside Hitler's Greece: The Experience of Occupation, 1941–44* (New Haven: Yale University Press, 1993) and in other works; as a historian, he discounted the term's use because it was freely employed by opposing political groups to attack opponents. Philippe Burrin points out that the word *collaborate*, used positively by Pétain after meeting Hitler in 1940, soon became pejorative, expressing instead flat "condemnation . . . of a policy found controversial right from the start"; see Burrin, *France Under the Germans: Collaboration and Compromise*, trans. Janet Lloyd (New York: New Press, 1996), 4.

15. Gérard Loiseaux, *La Littérature de la défaite et de la collaboration: D'après Phönix oder Asche? (Phénix ou cendres?) de Bernhard Payr* (Paris: Publications de la Sorbonne, 1984), 501.

16. MLS from Jan de Man to Evelyn Barish, February 3, 1994: "Where do you/I think you are from? Many thousands of years in desert nomadry shape a people, *biologically*. . . . Remember . . . that your ancestors have, for *many* thousands of years, lived as nomads in the desert/steppe (here I should write a whole treatise on the socio biology of cultures)." He added that an "ant" cannot understand "irrational human beings," and that hence the researcher's efforts are pointless. A Jew is an "ant" here not only because of the connotation of verminous life, but presumably because ants exemplify the one-track-mind, merely cerebral, and lower form of intellect, known as *Vernunft*, unlike the superior Nazi *Verstand*, which in Nazi doctrine connoted superior, instinctive perceptions. This letter, written in the last year of his life, with its undisguised anti-Semitism, came out of the blue in response to a request for information, part of a correspondence over the years that was neutral or pleasant in tone. Perhaps, knowing his life was ebbing, Jan de Man felt free at last to express what previously was not in his interest to communicate.

17. McMurtry wrote that he shared this "deepest conviction" with his friend, the

editor and writer Barbara Epstein. See Larry McMurtry, "Barbara Epstein," *New York Review of Books*, August 10, 2006.

18. Nietzsche, if mentioned at all to undergraduates in the 1950s, might be referred to as a "poet," while Marx was not studied, but regarded as a dangerously misguided "political economist." The ideas of both would have been heresy to assert, for supposedly the study of literature had no philosophy or politics, but sprang instead from timeless values. Ozick was a graduate student seeking admission to Trilling's seminar at Columbia in the 1950s; see Cynthia Ozick, "The Buried Life," *The New Yorker*, October 2, 2000, 116–27.

19. In the early 1960s, the idea of deconstruction had not yet been formed. Jacques Derrida was little known in the United States until after he gave a well-received lecture late in the decade.

20. In the 1980s, two prominent academics in the humanities lost their jobs in New York and another state because they had secretly been teaching at other than their primary universities. The career of one was ended.

21. In the words of his widow, "He would go into a dean's office and they'd come back smiling and rubbing their hands." She added, "He got [what he wanted]." Interview, December 29, 1990.

22. In later years, an archive at UC-Irvine was established with materials that at first focused on the years after 1950.

23. One crucial document, for example, was the record of de Man's postwar interrogation by the Commission d'Epuration (the commission investigated collaboration, and was called "the Cleansing" by Francophones, but called "the Repression" by Flemings). It had escaped prior search by a Belgian scholar. Was de Man interrogated after the war for collaboration with the occupant? Because no file was found by Belgian researchers working for the American editors, some argued that he had not been suspect and was therefore not blameworthy. It did exist, but the office of the Military Court, which kept collaborators' files, was not easy to access. See chapter 20.

24. Many excellent studies of France and World War II have, of course, been published. See, for example, Robert O. Paxton, *Vichy France: Old Guard and New Order, 1940–1944* (New York: Knopf, 1972); Robert O. Paxton and Michael R. Maurras, with a foreword by Stanley Hoffmann, *Vichy France and the Jews* (Palo Alto: Stanford University Press, 1995).

25. This was the comment of both Harry Levin, who then offered me his file on de Man, and of Paul's friend who was the other man in the ménage à trois mentioned on page 104.

26. Paul Aron and Cécile Vanderpelen wrote about a friend of de Man, also a collaborator, in "Félicien Marceau, la mémoire et l'histoire," Centre histoire de la literature belge de langue française, ULB, Brussels. See also Paul Aron et al., eds., *Leurs Occupations: L'Impact de la Seconde Guerre mondiale sur la literature en Belgique* (Brussels: Textyles; CREHSGM, 1997).

27. For a general study, see Jacques Willequet, *La Belgique sous la botte: Résistances et collaborations, 1940–1945* (Paris: Editions Universitaires, 1986). Two other excellent works are by Jules Gérard-Libois and José Gotovitch, *L'An 40: La Belgique occupée* (Brussels: CRISP, 1971); and Jean Stengers, *Léopold III et le gouvernement: Les deux politiques belges de 1940* (Paris: Duculot, 1980). For a detailed and useful study of a major collaborator, see Martin Conway, *Collaboration in Belgium: Léon Degrelle and the Rexist Movement 1940–1944* (New Haven: Yale University Press, 1993).

28. I shared this information, and it has since been published in Belgian sources not now available to me.

29. MSLS from Bob de Man to Yvonne De Muynck-de Man, June 2, 1948. Paul had just secretly left the country for New York; his family was going to Argentina. Letter translated by Marlene de Man-Flechtheim and the author, author archive.

30. Interview with Geoffrey Hartman, December 2, 1997.

31. Interview with Hans-Jost Frey, June 29, 1991. "I would call this his irony—his thoroughly ironic way of looking at everything including himself. He had a completely cynical view of the world and life in general," said Frey, adding, as if in solidarity with the man who had been both teacher and friend, that he himself also was "cynical."

32. Cf. Marc Redfield, ed., *Legacies of Paul de Man*, Romantic Circles Praxis Series, available at http://www.rc.umd.edu/praxis/deman/index.html.

1. THE BUTCHER'S BOY

1. "Paul spent immense amounts of time looking in [the] mirror—not out of vanity—not combing his hair—as though he were interested in himself or looking for some mystery. He once said, which was totally untrue, 'Perhaps I'm schizophrenic.' In so many ways he was one piece of cloth." Interview with Patricia de Man, December 29, 1990.

2. Jacobus Philippus Deman married Maria Sophia Van Aytmael (1816–1884) in the town of Merksem in 1844. Information taken from the family tree composed by great-grandson Jan de Man and Marlene de Man-Flechtheim, February 2, 1993.

3. For discussions of the fascist ideology, see Ze'ev Sternhell, with Mario Sznajder and Maia Asheri, *The Birth of Fascist Ideology: From Cultural Rebellion to Political Revolution*, trans. David Maisel (Princeton: Princeton University Press, 1994), 24, 28, 32.

4. Interview with Bob De Braey, November 18, 1992.

5. Interview with Jan de Man, June 28, 1992.

6. With about ten million citizens, Belgium has a population approximately one-sixth that of France. The Netherlands has half again as many people as its southern neighbor.

7. The aristocratic mother of Charles d'Ydewalle, living in Flanders and born of Flemish stock, was unable to communicate with her cooks and servants because she spoke only French; *see La Cour et la ville, 1934–1940* (Brussels: Editions Libres, 1945), chapter 1.

8. The roles have now been reversed, Flanders is ascendant, and the country is close to dissolution.

9. Transcript of the contract establishing Etablissements de Man, dated July 6, 1920; archives of Bob De Braey. Spelling even in official documents reflected the fluidity of cultural boundaries. When Bob asked his father-in-law to design a country house for him, the drawings were registered as "Request to build house *for R. De Man*"—still a Flemish name—by the architect, "Michel De Braey & Fils, 124, avenue du Margrave, Anvers," on October 24, 1924. The village of Kalmthout was spelled "Calmpthout" by Michel De Braey.

10. Henri de Man, *Après Coup* (Brussels: Editions de la Toison d'Or, 1941). For studies of Henri de Man, see Henri Brélaz, *Henri de Man: Une Autre Idée du socialisme* (Geneva: Editions des Antipodes, 1985). See also Peter Dodge, *Beyond Marxism:*

The Faith and Works of Hendrik de Man (The Hague: M. Nijhoff, 1966); Dan W. White, *Lost Comrades: Socialists of the Front Generation: 1918–1945* (Cambridge: Harvard University Press, 1992).

11. Queried about whether this was considered a legitimate reason to change one's name at the time, a young Belgian historian reflected that, given Henri's status as the lover of the queen mother—a story she accepted—it was justified.

12. Ruling of the colony was brutal. See Adam Hochschild, *King Leopold's Ghost: A Story of Greed, Terror, and Heroism in Colonial Africa* (Boston: Houghton Mifflin, 1998).

13. A leading collaborator, Henri addressed both the Belgians, who were chafing under the boot of the Nazi occupant, and his German bosses by presenting his homeland as being culturally in accord with "Germanic" social views. For general discussions of the Germanic ideology, see George Mosse, *The Crisis of German Ideology: Intellectual Origins of the Third Reich* (New York: Grosset & Dunlap, 1964); Fritz Stern, *The Politics of Cultural Despair: A Study in the Rise of the Germanic Ideology* (Berkeley: University of California Press, 1961); Fritz Ringer, *The Decline of the German Mandarins: The German Academic Community 1890–1933* (Cambridge: Harvard University Press, 1969).

14. Interview with Jan de Man, June 28, 1992.

15. Hervé Hasquin, *Visages de la franc-maçonnerie belge du XVIIIe au XXe siècle*, (Brussels: Editions de l'Université de Bruxelles, 1983). For a satiric view of both the Church and Freemasonry itself, see André Gide, *Les Caves du Vatican* (Paris: Gallimard, 1914).

16. Interview with Bob De Braey, November 18, 1992.

17. In the words of Jan de Man, Felix was "nutty and locked up somewhere." He added that Felix was "pleasant, of course," but institutionalization suggests he was not easy to manage. Interview, September 18, 1992.

18. Interview with Elise ("Li") LeCocq-de Man, June 30, 1990.

19. Archives of the city of Antwerp, Bewolkingsregister, give the birth certificate of Adolf Kemna as April 23, 1877, and the date of his departure to Godhuis de Cellebroeder in Mechelen (Malines). He died on June 6, 1909, at Katenijnevest 1, a street in Mechelen that no longer exists. It was reported by the monks Engelbert Van Swygenhoven and Gummarus Van der Auwera, who gave as Kemna's home the family's address at Van Schoonbekestraat, 12, Antwerp. See number 481, Overlijdensregister, Burgerlijke Stand (City Register of Deaths, Mechelen).

20. Henri and Bob de Man's sister, Yvonne, also wrote a family memoir, *Our Daily Bread*. Her text stresses how the clan excluded others, recalling that on the single occasion they admitted a visitor to share their games, the girl had run crying from the home.

21. Interview with Anne Ipsen, July 4, 1991. For a discussion of Down syndrome, see www.gpnotebook.co.uk/cache/-1509556190.htm; comments by Len Leshin, M.D., at www.ds-health.com.

22. Interview with Anne Ipsen, July 4, 1991. She married four times, and thus her name changed at various periods in her life. Except when the context demands otherwise, this text will refer to her as Anne Ipsen, the name she used with this writer in 1992; she also used von Orland-Ipsen as her postal address in Brussels at that time.

23. Ida Kemna, b. May 11, 1878, d. April 19, 1897; archives of the city of Antwerp. Henri's son, Jan, Paul's cousin, simply denied that Ida and Adolph Kemma-de Man had had children.

24. Madeleine de Man-De Braey was the daughter of Maria Adolfina De Braey-Van Beers, the third of the four Van Beers daughters. Customarily, married women and their husbands appended the wife's maiden name to their married names, so that, for example, Jan de Man and Marlene Flechtheim became as a family the de Man-Flechtheims. Their children, however, took their father's name only.

25. Her father, Michel De Braey, was an alderman of the city of Antwerp; interview with Jan de Man, February 15, 1993.

26. Postcard addressed to M. P. Buschmann, postmarked August 27 (probably 1902), DB.

27. Interview with Anne Ipsen, June 30, 1993.

28. Her full name was Simone De Braey-De Haeck.

29. Jan de Man said of Paul's mother that she was "brought up in perfect peace and harmony [and was] just a nice girl. A peaceful bourgeois." His cousin Paul experienced "complete harmony" with his "mother, brother, and father. [There was] absolute peace [and] no problems. Because [the family was of] higher intelligence." Interview, June 28, 1990.

30. Interview with Anne Ipsen, June 30, 1993; interview with Li LeCocq-de Man, June 30, 1990.

31. Rik (Hendrik) died June 20, 1936.

32. Interview with Micheline "Minime" De Braey, July 27, 1994.

33. That was the memory of Bob De Braey, Paul's younger cousin; interview, June 2, 1993.

34. Interviews with Micheline De Braey and Patricia de Man, who reported her late husband's comment, July 27, 1994.

35. Paul de Man's widow testified that her late husband was far from the austere figure others imagined. For discussions of this narcissistic trait, see works influenced by Jacques Lacan: Peter Brooks, *Body Work* (Cambridge: Harvard University Press, 1993); Christopher Lasch, *The Culture of Narcissism: American Life in an Age of Diminishing Expectations* (New York: W. W. Norton, 1979; rev. ed., 1991). Technical, earlier studies include Otto Kernberg's classic *Borderline Conditions and Pathological Narcissism* (New York: Jason Aronson, 1975), 283; Heinz Kohut, *The Analysis of the Self* (New York: International Universities Press, 1987), 16, 62, 172.

36. Interview with M. H. Abrams, June 24, 1992; interview with Bob De Braey, November 18, 1992.

2. KALMTHOUT: THE RULES OF THE GAME

1. Interview with Bob De Braey, June 2, 1993.

2. Interview with Patricia de Man, quoting her late husband, January 17, 2003.

3. The plans show the house was built "for Robert De Man," but since Adolph lived there and died there in 1936, he probably financed it. GK (municipality of Kalmthout).

4. Interview with Patricia de Man, January 17, 1993. Patricia said he deprecated his aunt's origin.

5. Interview with Patricia de Man, December 29, 1990. Burt Pike spoke of his "killer Ping-Pong game"; December 8, 2001.

6. Interview with Patricia de Man, December 29, 1990.

7. Ibid.

8. Interview with Micheline de Braey, July 27, 1994.

9. Interview with Bob De Braey, November 18, 1992. This and subsequent quotes are from this interview. The name Pijnenberg refers to a mound in the big back garden of the house in Kalmthout.

10. "I only remember him once referring to a very special girl—Madeleine—for whom he may have had some admiration. But it could have been because of intellectual or literary interest. No mention of her physical attraction," Bob De Braey recalled.

11. Interview with Patricia de Man, January 17, 2003.

12. "[Paul's] grandfather . . . founded the gymnastic society in Antwerp—and that was unconventional at the time in this period. Emotionally, Rik, [Henri de Man], Bob, and Yvonne were unconventional too. Very independent and a little bit bohemian. [Kalmthout was] sexually liberated." Interview with Marlene de Man-Flechtheim, July 7, 1991.

13. Interview with Bob De Braey, November 18, 1992.

14. Testimony of Micheline and Bob De Braey.

15. Interview with Micheline De Braey, July 27, 1994.

16. Interview with Patricia de Man, December 29, 1990.

17. Interview with Anne Ipsen, June 30, 1993.

18. Interview with Frida Vandervelden, July 8, 1991.

19. The business was owned by two investors, probably friends of Adolph. Bob was paid fifteen thousand Belgian francs a year, and owed them all his time, profits, and patents. He could be fired without notice for failing to fulfill any part of the fifteen-year contract; DB.

20. In addition to being interested in music, he also founded a technical college for workers; interview with Micheline De Braey, July 24, 1994, and interview with Bob De Braey, November 18, 1992.

21. GK (municipality of Kalmthout).

22. The original address was Putsesteenweg 260A; in 1931, the number was changed to 363 and finally renumbered 25. Bob De Braey remembers sharing a bed with Paul's grandfather. TSLS, May 15, 1994, population registry of Kalmthout to author.

23. Jan de Man, Paul's older cousin and the son of Henri, remembered sleeping three to a bed with his grandfather and Paul in the bedroom over the kitchen; interview, September 18, 1992.

24. Interview with Bob De Braey, November 18, 1992.

25. There was a gendered distinction within the family as to who knew—or could admit—what her condition was. Madeleine's nieces or female cousins could speak of it later (Li, Minime, and Marlene de Man-Flechtheim, wife of Jan de Man). Bob De Braey and Jan de Man professed themselves ignorant of the situation even late in life.

26. Interview with Elise ("Li") LeCocq-de Man, June 30, 1990.

27. Interview with Micheline De Braey, July 27, 1994.

28. Patricia de Man reported, "They wanted to take her out shopping, and it would irritate her"; interview, January 17, 2003.

29. Archives GK.

30. Interview with Micheline De Braey, July 27, 1994.

31. Interview with Bob De Braey, November 18, 1992.

32. Interview with Micheline De Braey, July 27, 1994.

33. The members of both families—the six de Mans and the six De Braeys—would have known, and so inevitably would their servants, as well as the doctors and staff at the hospital.

3. PAUL AND HIS TEACHERS

1. Interviews with Herman Schoeters and Thomas Coppens, October 24, 1992.

2. Henri de Man, *Après Coup* (Brussels: Editions de la Toison d'Or, 1941), 35.

3. A friend of Bob's also served on the board, the wealthy Jan Eeckels, an accountant who was later to be a director of Paul's publishing house. Both men had been "added" to the board, not elected, which meant that "they knew people who regarded them highly"; interview with Thomas Coppens, headmaster of Royal Athenaeum, October 16, 1992.

4. He belonged to the Dutch-speaking class; there was also a Francophone ("Wallonne") class of ten. *Onderscheidingen Behaald Door De Leerlingen Van Het Koninklijk Athenaeum te Antwerpen* (1932–1937), KA.

5. A Belgian friend of de Man from the university said that his own German was better, while Hans-Jost Frey reported that de Man spoke German fluently but with a heavy Belgian accent that was sufficiently nonstandard that it alienated significant numbers of students; interviews, June 21, 1991.

6. In the 1930s, philosophy was not taught; the curriculum was different in this way from that in France. See Fritz Ringer, *Fields of Knowledge: French Academic Culture in Perspective, 1890–1920* (Cambridge: Cambridge University Press, 1992), 43.

7. It was not an exclusively Christian environment, but students with Jewish names tended to cluster in the French-speaking classes, and few or none were to be found in the Dutch-language class. Students in different curricula mingled very little. Herman Schoeters, who later became headmaster of the school, did not even know his age-mate Paul de Man; they were members of the same cohort but in different courses; interview, October 16, 1992.

8. Interview with Julien Vandiest, October 24, 1992. Subsequent quotes are from this interview.

9. Interview with Robert Tillemans-de Man, a physician and relative of Paul de Man by marriage, October 16, 1992.

10. The term also connotes petty feudalism. In *A European Past: Memoirs 1905–1945* (New York: W. W. Norton, 1988), 148, 51n, Felix Gilbert defines "Elbian Junkers" more generally as "agrarian-conservative circles which had been strong under Hindenberg."

11. On rare occasions, their teachers read to them from their own writings. Perhaps this implied they had serious intellectual interests that were frustrated by the official curriculum.

12. See Ernst Benz, *The Mystical Sources of German Romanticism*, trans. B. R. Reynolds and E. M. Paul (Allison Park, Pa: Pickwick Publications, 1983), 1, 6–8, 21; James M. Clark, *The Great German Mystics* (New York: Russell & Russell, 1949; reprint, 1970), 1–35. Vandiest specified that de Man didn't like the mystics in general, or figures like Saint Teresa or Saint John of the Cross because "they smelled too much of religion."

13. Milton he "couldn't imagine without a long beard," and Shakespeare was, in the Flemish, a "*veelschryver.*"

14. Paul-Henri Spaak, *Combats inachevés*, vol. 1 (Paris: Fayard, 1969), 25–26.

15. Kazin's remark was made to the author in 1991.

16. *Zur Psychologie des Sozialismus* was first published in Jena in 1926 by Eugen Diederichs.

17. Henri de Man, *Après Coup*, 21. He omitted this passage from the edition he pub-

lished three years after the war, when Germany had been defeated and France was again free.

18. "I had four mothers," Henri wrote; *Après Coup*.

19. Interview, July 16, 1990.

20. Eckhart's doctrine, reconstituted from fragments and the accounts of his trials, had recently been published as his collected works by Eugene Diederichs. The medieval theologian was valuable as a potentially foundational German thinker useful for German nationalism. Hegel reported of Eckhart, "That is exactly what we want, that is the whole of our ideas, of our intentions"; Benz, *The Mystical Sources of German Romanticism*, 1, 6–7. See Theodore Kisiel, "Heidegger's Apology: Biography as Philosophy and Ideology"; Otto Pöggeler, "Heidegger, Nietzsche, and Politics," in *The Heidegger Case on Philosophy and Politics*, ed. Thomas Rockmore and Joseph Margolis (Philadelphia: Temple University Press, 1992), 121.

21. See John Hellman's excellent *Emmanuel Mounier and the New Catholic Left: 1930–1950* (Toronto: University of Toronto Press, 1981), 58, 72.

22. Vandiest compared Paul with the French collaborating writer Drieu la Rochelle, whom he had met in 1943: "I can very well imagine . . . the *Herren* [master] race [and] . . . his aristocratic demeanor would have appealed to him. . . . Drieu . . . reminded me of Paul in mentality."

4. *LE ROUGE ET LE NOIR*

1. Paul Deman [*sic*], "L'Humanité et l'homme," *Le Rouge et le Noir*, September 9, 1936, 139. A strongly pacifist editorial by Fontaine appeared on the same page. See also J.-F. Füeg, "André Baillon et *Le Rouge et le Noir*," *Textyles* 6 (1989): 21–28. The journal's name was chosen by the editor to connote a positive kind of anarchy and openness to all shades of opinion. Politically, the colors were associated with the anarchists and syndico-anarchists of the late nineteenth century, but, in addition to Stendhal's novel *The Red and the Black*, there are many other political, religious, and literary associations with those colors. Pierre Fontaine wanted his journal "to be open to everything and everyone." See J.-F. Füeg, in Pierre Fontaine, "Naissance du *Rouge et Noir*," in "Souvenir d'entre-deux-guerres," special number of *Porquois pas*, February 2, 1967, 139. Paul later claimed, accurately, that he had begun publishing politically quite early, but the article could not be found, probably because, although written in French, it was published in Belgium.

2. Bob De Braey remembered the distance as twenty-five kilometers, or about fifteen miles. Interview, November 18, 1992.

3. His death was reported to the registrar by his uncle, Madeleine's brother, Jan De Braey, and two other men on June 22, 1936. The event was entered into the register on June 29, 1936.

4. Interview with Patricia de Man, December 19, 1990.

5. Robert O. Paxton, "The Jew Hater," *New York Review of Books*, November 16, 2006, 26–29, especially p. 28, reviewing the history of denying the existence of anti-Semitism in France. For subsequent letters about Hungary and Bulgaria, see the *New York Review of Books*, January 16, 2007, p. 66.

6. Bianca Lamblin's *Mémoires d'une jeune fille dérangée* (Paris: Ballard, 1993), 83–102, is a chilling narrative of the attitude of people she thought her close friends, Simone de Beauvoir and Jean-Paul Sartre, toward herself and other Jews.

7. Mosley, too, like both Henri de Man and Mussolini, had been born to privilege, had joined the Left, and had been prominent in the Labour party throughout the 1920s, but he found his inner bully as the Nazis rose to power. See www .spartacus.schoolnet.co.uk/Lpublic.htm.

8. *Le Rouge et le Noir*, September 9, 1936, 139.

9. Quoted by Armand Charpentier, "La Belgique et le désarmement unilateral," *Le Rouge et le Noir*, September 9, 1936, 139.

10. John Hellman, *Emmanuel Mounier and the New Catholic Left: 1930–1936* (Toronto: University of Toronto Press, 1981). Mounier promulgated what he called a "Third Way," especially through his intellectual journal *Esprit* and a monkish community he established, and this was adopted for a time by Henri de Man. Another Christian movement appealing to the upper classes was Moral Re-Armament, created by an expatriate American missionary, who was "thankful" to Hitler for preserving civilization from communism.

5. MADELEINE'S DEATH

1. Interview with Jan de Man, June 28–29, 1990.

2. Paul de Man, "Criticism and Crisis," in *Blindness and Insight* (New York: Oxford University Press, 1971), 18.

3. Interview with Patricia de Man, December 19, 1990.

4. Ibid.

5. Paul thought the movie greatly affected her; interview with Patricia de Man, December 19, 1990. Bob De Braey recalled, "I was told by my parents that it was Paul who found her. On the top of the apartment building were rooms to dry the linen. There was a lift [in which] you [could] see your own face. . . . Paul went upstairs to the top and he found his mother hanging there"; interview with Bob De Braey, June 2, 1993. Patricia reported that "Paul said she did not find fulfillment in what was expected of a woman of her society. 'There must have been *something* wrong.' He would try to analyze the '30s. He would speak with some irony of their life"; interview, December 29, 1990.

6. Discussion with Neil Hertz.

7. Interview with Patricia de Man, December 19, 1990.

6. "MY FATHER, HENRI DE MAN"

1. King Léopold proclaimed himself neutral, but neutrality became identified with appeasement. Léopold's "neutrality" eventually led him to visit Hitler at Berchtesgaden during the war, where he was photographed sitting beside the Führer on the terrace, wearing the uniform of a Nazi officer. Image found by Jean Stengers; see *Léopold III et le gouvernement: Les Deux Belges de 1940* (Paris: Duculot, 1980). André Gide agonized at length in his journals and letters in the 1920s and 1930s whether he should "go to Russia," or "go to Berlin"—or later, during the Occupation, to Paris—because as a public figure his voyage would mean he approved of the regime.

2. The term *charisma* was coined by Max Weber as a quasi-religious quality possessed by some leaders, whose followers give them almost cultic status; see William Clark, *Academic Charisma and the Origins of the Research University* (Chicago: University of Chicago Press, 2006), 14–19. Clark glosses Max Weber, *Wirtschaft und Gesellschaft: Grundriss der verstehenden Soziologie*, ed. J. Winkelman, 5th rev. ed. (Tübingen: Mohr, 1985).

3. Paul-Henri Spaak, *Combats inachevés*, vol. 1 (Paris: Fayard, 1969), 25–26. In spite of the policies favoring Germany that he shared before the war with de Man, Spaak retreated from them once the occupation occurred, decamped for London, where he became a minister in the government in exile, and lived to find international success after the war.

4. Raymond De Becker, *Le Livre des vivants et des morts* (Brussels: Editions de la Toison d'Or, 1942), 183. He described the apartment as dark and small.

5. Henri de Man, *Cavalier seul: 45 années de socialisme européen* (Geneva: Editions du Cheval Ailé, 1948), 19–20. He replied to enemies who criticized his upper-class athletic pursuits by framing the argument in anti-French ideology, which held that country to be degenerate, frivolous, and sunk in sensuality, while he chose the higher, austere ideal of Germany; see Henri de Man, *Après Coup* (Brussels: Editions de la Toison d'Or, 1941), 21.

6. Jules Gérard-Libois and José Gotovitch allude to the rumored romantic connection when they refer to his access to the king through Queen Elisabeth. See *L'An 40: La Belgique occupée* (Brussels: CRISP, 1971), 217.

7. Interview with Alice Cook, August 11, 1992.

8. In his frequently unreliable wartime memoir, he took pains to distance himself from the social democrats, enemies of the Nazis.

9. One of the many romantic stories he told about himself was that he and Vandervelde were deputed by Great Britain to accompany Trotsky in a sealed railroad car through Sweden back to Russia at the time when the fighting had erupted during the Russian Revolution. He did not accompany Lenin—who returned from Switzerland—as some accounts have it.

10. Henri de Man, *Après Coup*, 189.

11. Asked about the banning of "decadent" art imposed by the Nazis, Alice Cook continued, "The Socialists and later the Communists were trying to develop a complete lifestyle that would engage everything. If you played chess, you played it [with] with other Socialists or Communists—'worker culture,' it was called. The Party included all kinds of leisure-time groups. It had schools, camps, et cetera, and so did the Communists. . . . One who was identified with [orthodox] socialists would not, therefore, even [have] thought about the decadence of literature." To a socialist, the approved literature of her or his party would by definition have been free of "decadence." Interview with Alice Cook, August 11, 1992.

12. Henri de Man, *Après Coup*, 189.

13. Passed on September 15, 1935, the Nuremberg Laws stripped Jews of citizenship and forbade all sexual intercourse between German Gentiles and Jews. Following the objections of Hjalmar Schacht, economics minister, however, the regulations did not forbid Jews from doing business, as this would damage Nazi economic interests. Aryanization (spoliation) of Jewish property took place in 1937–1938.

14. This was the opinion of Louis Carette, a friend of Paul de Man interviewed October 14, 2002. He broadcast the news daily for the German propaganda office. Carette would later be known in France and internationally as Félicien Marceau, a very successful writer of farces. See chapter 16.

15. Henri de Man, *Après Coup*, 178.

16. De Man's version of the battle is given in *Après Coup;* see especially "Le Plan du Travail," 221–47.

17. Henri de Man, *Après Coup*, 131.

18. Henri was attractive to women, although "harsh," according to his daughter-in-law, Marlene de Man-Flechtheim, who came from a Jewish family that had lived in Germany for over four hundred years. As the daughter of a Gentile mother and a Jewish banker who had converted to Christianity under the Nazi regime (only to find his act considered meaningless), she was told by her father in 1933, when she was eighteen, to emigrate to Belgium because on coming to power Hitler had excluded all Jews from the universities, including those from "mixed" marriages.

19. Henri Brélaz, *Henri de Man: Une Autre Idée du socialisme* (Geneva: Editions des Antipodes, 1985), 158.

20. Paul de Man told his second wife, Patricia, that Elvire Lotigiers was also Jewish, but other evidence for this is lacking.

21. Brélaz's information came from Lotigiers's brother after her death. The biographer accepted the date de Man gave of 1929 for his divorce from Lily Reinemund. Evidently, after marrying Lily in 1922, as Marlene de Man asserted, and finally securing a divorce from Elvire Lotigiers in 1928, Henri de Man reversed himself and divorced Reinemund only one year later. (Henri de Man, *Après Coup*, 182; Brélaz, *Henri de Man*, 159.) Brélaz gave no date for the marriage of Lily and Henri, a delicate subject, for the marriage was apparently bigamous.

22. Henri de Man, *Après Coup*, 182.

23. The name Reinemund is German-Jewish, and some half a dozen persons of that surname were buried in Germany between 1897 and the 1960s. See New Mt. Sinai Cemetery death register, available at www.mtsinaicemetery.org/Death%20Register%20for%202DD.pdf.

24. Marlene, once she was established in Belgium, trained first as a nurse and then became a clinical psychologist and was well informed about the relationships within her husband Jan de Man's family. Jan and his sister, Li, lived with their stepmother, Lily, together with her two daughters, who were the same age as Henri's children; interview with Marlene de Man-Flechtheim, September 10, 2000.

25. "Truth's a dog must to kennel; he must be whipped out, when the Lady Brach may stand by the fire and stink"; see *King Lear*, act 1, scene 4.

26. Henri de Man, *Après Coup*, 206.

27. He minimized the attack as resulting from a bad diet and fatigue, but his son, Jan, described to this writer an extended coma that brought his father near death.

28. Interview with Alice Cook, August 11, 1992.

7. A BROKEN RUDDER

1. The term *patriot* had multiple connotations, including love of country and/or resistance of some kind to the occupant.

2. Henri de Man, *Cahiers de ma montagne* (Brussels and Paris: Editions de la Toison d'Or, 1944), 84.

3. While Jan denied that Henri provided Paul with money, his sister, Li, insisted that, in fact, he made Paul such gifts; interviews with Jan de Man and Elise LeCocq-de Man, June 30, 1990.

4. Interview, July 8, 1991.

5. Jan was already employed by a utility company as an electrical engineer. He never forgave Paul de Man's dismissiveness and, much later, refused his attempt at reconciliation, rebuffing him with the question, "Where is my map?"

6. Paul recounted to Patricia his uncle's salty reaction to Jan when his son was hovering around him on a fishing trip and Henri set Jan to picking the fleas out of his fishing trousers, a demeaning task.

7. Henri Brélaz, *Henri de Man: Une Autre Idée du socialisme* (Geneva: Editions des Antipodes, 1985), 149. Paul once recommended Georges Goriély in a note to his exiled uncle, whom he addressed as "Mon cher Rik." Goriély, an intimate of Paul de Man from the beginning of his college years, understood Henri de Man to be his colleague's uncle and certainly not his father; GG, Anvers, May 15, 1948.

8. "Engineers are stupid," Paul told Jan, politely excepting his own father—but not, it seems, his cousin.

9. Interview with Frida Vandervelden, July 8, 1991.

10. Patricia de Man reported he was 5', 8½" a median height for American men at that time and close to her own.

11. Subsequent quotations and information from Frida Vandervelden come from interviews of July 6–8 and July 16, 1991, and numerous other contacts.

12. One of her nieces visited the same inn and sent her the card from it.

13. Named by Paul in a letter to Frida from the spring or summer of 1938 and dated by her; ms. letter, n.d., Jaudervelden MSS.

14. It was owned by a Russian-Jewish émigré who was a friend, an engineer by training but not able to practice because of tuberculosis.

15. He refused to let her travel with her classmates to Italy. She had agreed without argument but also vowed she would never go to Italy—and she never did.

16. Frida asserted that she had joined the Party and then resigned at an unspecified date, but her ex-husband, Charles Dosogne, insisted that while he had abandoned the Party after the German-Soviet Pact of August 23, 1939, Frida did not leave until the upheavals of 1968.

17. The "Schors did not take everyone, just a few people."

18. "He wrote me after the exam [took place] that he had not presented for the exam. . . . 'And I shall take another direction and I shall take your subject, chemistry.' "

19. She visited Paul at home when he was recovering from an appendectomy, an operation that left him with an ugly scar. They played Mozart duets, with Paul on the piano and Bob with his violin.

20. January 3, 1939, quoted by Ortwin de Graef, "Aspects of the Context of Paul de Man's Earliest Publications," Werner Hamacher, Neil Hertz, and Thomas Keenan, eds., *Responses: On Paul de Man's Wartime Journalism* (Lincoln: University of Nebraska Press, 1992), 97.

21. The term could mean utter failure or failure due to nonappearance. The latter was the case with this first year-end test in civil engineering.

22. MSLS (fragment) from Paul de Man to Frida Vandervelden, May 29, 1939. FV.

23. Martin Heidegger, "Hölderlin and the Essence of Poetry," trans. Paul de Man, *Quarterly Review of Literature* 10, no. 1–2 (1959): 79–94.

24. Ortwin de Graef, "Silence to Be Observed: A Trial for Paul de Man's Inexcusable Confessions," in *(Dis)continuities: Essays on Paul de Man*, ed. Luc Herman, Kris Humbeeck, and Geert Lernout (Amsterdam: Editions Rodopi, 1989), 51–73; de Graef also defends de Man in his refusal to make "excuses."

25. His "*ce qui*" is ambiguous in its referent.

26. TSL from Frida Vandervelden to the author, including extracts of letter from Paul de Man of spring to summer 1938; see also de Graef, *Responses*, 96.

27. It appeared a year later, in 1939, in *Jeudi* (Thursday), another journal sponsored by Frida and Dosogne.

28. *La Nourritures terrestes* and *La Porte étroite* were especially influential.

29. Scarcely a year later, working under Nazi censorship at *Le Soir (volé)*, Paul de Man was far more critical of Gide and of all French literature. In the 1960s, he dismissed him: "Whatever Happened to André Gide?" *New York Review of Books*, May 6, 1965, 15–17.

30. Hamacher, Hertz, and Keenan, eds., *Responses*, 96.

31. Edouard Colinet: "He was a character. The administrative people at ULB . . . feared him. He was really brutal. A Trotskyist. He went to Spain during [the] Spanish Civil War with a couple of lorries—just when Communists were killing all the anarchists. He was threatened there and happy to come back"; interview, October 13, 1993.

32. Interview with Charles Dosogne, July 8, 1993. Dosogne's friends liked to describe him—not without affection—as a bit of a "brute." Dosogne said he was "not a brute but . . . very violent, a bit of an anarchist, a defender of the United Marxist Workers' party (Parti Ouvrier Unité Marxiste). . . . I was surrounded by cultured students. The others drank a lot of beer and despised the intellectuals. . . . It was I who had the idea of creating a review to defend the intellectuals. It had a collective editorial board, and it had a very big success. . . . In addition to that, I had to earn money. I got scholarships from various sources and I published memoed course outlines—and sold a lot of them. Mineral chemistry and then inorganic chemistry."

8. UNIVERSITY: TAKING SIDES

1. The song "We're Marching Against England" was a Nazi propaganda song. Interview with Bob De Braey, July 24, 1994.

2. Interview with Jan de Man, 1992.

3. Paul Aron, "1942: Pierre Peyel remporte le concours littéraire du *Soir*: Les Ecrivains belges et l'occupation: Entre engagement et indifférence," in *Histoire de la Littérature Belge Francophone: 1830–2000*, ed. Jean-Pierre Bertrand et al. (Paris: Fayard, 2003), 401–410.

4. Werner Hamacher, Neil Hertz, and Thomas Keenan, eds., *Responses: On Paul de Man's Wartime Journalism* (Lincoln: University of Nebraska Press, 1992), 469, trans. by author.

5. Their manifesto, published just four weeks after the invasion of Poland, attacked anyone in France or Belgium who would permit troops or other aid to cross Belgium and bring support to Poland, because the future of Belgium was entirely at risk without such conciliation; see Jules Gérard-Libois and José Gotovitch, *L'An 40: La Belgique occupée* (Brussels: CRISP, 1971), 36–43.

6. Those who signed a counterresponse published in mid-October wrote that without wishing to dispute the neutralist policy or break with the silent majority of the country, they affirmed their anguish at the current position, as well as their right to remain faithful to their country's historic ties to Britain and France, who had defended Belgium in 1914 against Germany; see Gérard-Libois and Gotovitch, *L'An 40*, 43.

7. See Alan Sharp, review of Anthony Lentin's *Lloyd George and the Lost Peace: From Versailles to Hitler 1919–1940* (Palgrave, 2001); available at www.history.ac.uk/reviews/review242.

8. That aphorism actually dated from after the war, in a House of Commons speech he made on November 11, 1947; date credited to Kurt Gaubatz.

9. Interview with Esther Sluszny, November 15, 1992.

10. This person wished to remain anonymous.

11. Interview with Charles Dosogne, July 8, 1993.

12. "The Medical Examination of Students," *Jeudi* (March 23, 1939), in *Wartime Journalism*, 2–4.

13. "What Do You Think of the War?" *Jeudi* (January 4, 1939), in *Wartime Journalism*, pp. 13–14.

14. Ibid.

15. Colinet identified the members of the editorial board shown in his original print, but the cropped photograph he supplied shows only some figures on the right-hand side. Sluzny would survive the war and become a lawyer; Goriély became a professor of history. Sluzny's brother, Nahum Sluszny, a violinist, entered the Resistance, as did his wife, Esther, and both were college friends of Paul de Man; see chapter 16.

16. Interview with Pierre De Ligne, October 19, 1992, and AM: *LSv*, Summary of Charges and Sentences, vol. 8, 1946, pp. 1–41, especially p. 20.

17. TLS from Paul Jamin, September 19, 1994, concerning JIB.

9. THE DIDIER CIRCLE: SERVANTS TO POWER

1. Paul Willems stated the relationship with Didier as a fact; interview, April 26, 1993. Henri de Man's son, Jan, when questioned about it, neither affirmed nor denied the relationship, but asserted that Lucienne Didier had remained a staunch friend of himself and his family during and after World War II, assisting them materially with goods she brought from France and carrying messages from his father, who was in exile there. Having access to such free travel was a sign of her good standing with the occupant, especially after she began her friendship with Ernst Jünger.

2. Léon Degrelle, *La Cohue de 1940* (Paris: Avalon, 1991), 380. Degrelle was intrigued by Lucienne's sexuality, but her social dominance and closeness to his rival, Henri de Man, kept him at a distance.

3. Moulin is quoted in Fabrice Schurmans, *Introduction à la Collaboration Intellectuelle en Belgique Francophone*, 2 vols. (Liège: Mémoire: Univ. de Liège, 1989–90), 44–46.

4. Michel B. Fincoeur discusses the Didiers in his excellent essay, "Le Monde de l'édition en Belgique durant la Seconde Guerre mondiale: L'Exemple des Editions de la Toison d'Or," *Leurs Occupations*, 21–47, especially 31–34.

5. Paul Aron, "1942: Pierre Peyel remporte le concours littéraire du *Soir*: Les Écrivains belges et l'occupation: Entre engagement et indifférence," in *Histoire de la Littérature Belge Francophone: 1830–2000*, ed. Jean-Pierre Bertrand et al. (Paris: Fayard, 2003), 401–410.

6. "The Belgian publishers have no chance. The French put a kind of embargo on Belgian books. If one writes a good book in French and lives in Belgium, one has no chance of it being reviewed in France. I had a painful experience of this with Gallimard [regarding] *La Ville à voile*. . . . [Gallimard's] editor said it was the beginning of a career in France, would play in [the] best theaters. A year later I asked about it and he said I would have to move to Paris, live there. If I did, I'd meet French reviewers, be part of that world. Otherwise he could not

help me. But I am Belgian; my roots and life are here. I could not do it. Would not." Here Willems, sitting on his patio, gestured around him to his baronial mansion and small moat. Interview, April 26, 1993.

7. This was stated repeatedly by her friends, among them Nellie De Ligne, but the subject was not pursued by this writer. Interview, April 26, 1993.

8. "Two of my books were published by Editions de la Toison d'Or." They were *Tout est réel ici* (1941) and *L'Herbe qui tremble* (1942), interview with Paul Willems, April 26, 1993.

9. Interview with Pierre De Ligne, October 19, 1992.

10. AM: TdO, Case 3265.

11. See Bernard Delcord, "A propos de quelques 'chapelles' politico-littéraire en Belgique (1919–1945)," *Bijdragen Cahiers*, November 10, 1986, 153–205.

12. André Molitor, *Souvenirs: Un Témoin engagé dans la Belgique du xxᵉ siècle* (Gembloux: Editions Duculot, 1984), 161–62.

13. John Hellman, *Emmanuel Mounier and the New Catholic Left: 1939–1950* (Toronto: University of Toronto Press, 1981), 125.

14. Interview, June 1993. Léo Moulin, also a member of the circle, said its organizational style was "simple enough: 'It consisted of looking forward twice a month to a brief exposé by one of the guests and then of allowing exchanges of opinions and of private conversations to develop freely.'" In fact, almost all the exposés turned around the theses of Henri de Man, "'for whom Mme. Didier avowed a certain admiration.'" In effect, it resembled a seminar as well as a purely social gathering. Schurmans, *Introduction à la collaboration intellectualle en Belgique Francophone*, vol. 1 (Liège: Université Liège, 1990), 45.

15. See Ortwin de Graef, "Notes on Reading Paul de Man's Flemish Writings," in *Responses: On Paul de Man's Wartime Journalism*, ed. Werner Hamacher, Neil Hertz and Thomas Keenan (Lincoln: University of Nebraska Press, 1992), 121, n. 29.

16. Willems told Fabrice Schurmans that Didier was a "dilettante. He had taste and an instinct for quality. . . . He was elegant and worldly. He and his wife spent a lot of time with the French aristocracy. Toward the '30s, they were celebrated in the French fashionable magazines. Completely correct in business, he was neither stupid nor intelligent. I don't think that he would have had precise political ideas. He believed in the German victory and believed in the necessity of an accord with that country. If he had been French, he would have been a Pétainist. He never talked to me about his opinions. He never suggested that I should write a politically committed work that one might call 'New Order.'" Schurmans, 91.

17. Extracts from *Les Mémoires de Pierre Daye, Le Dossier du mois*, no. 12 (December 1963) Delcord, "A propos de quelques 'chapelles' politico-littéraire en Belgique (1919–1945)," 167–69.

18. Interview with Pierre De Ligne, October 19, 1992.

19. Jules Gérard-Libois and José Gotovitch, *L'An 40: La Belgique occupée* (Brussels: CRISP, 1971), 46.

20. The secretary of Edouard Didier, Simonne Waslet, was questioned about this "serious insinuation" by the Military Court, but she said that although she had heard it at the time, she had paid no attention. AM: TdO, Case 3245, information file V, Item 46, deposition of witness.

21. Hellman, *Emmanuel Mounier and the New Catholic Left*, 88.

22. Otto Abetz, *Histoire d'une politique franco-allemande: 1930–1950: Mémoires d'un ambassadeur* (Paris: Libraire Stock, 1953), 12–13.

23. "Le Dossier Bousquet,"*Libération*, July 13, 1993, supplement 3776, 8; Hellman, *Emmanuel Mounier and the New Catholic Left*, 6.

24. AM: TdO 3245, information file V, items 41, 43, procès-verbal of Otto Abetz, July 1, 1946, Cherche-Midi Prison, Paris. When tried for war crimes in France, Abetz recalled meeting Henri de Man at such a conference, when they had had a conversation, he said, about the French Enlightenment icon, Reason—whom de Man had represented as bedraggled and of easy virtue, but a "great goddess" nonetheless. As a tale told in a prison cell, one should not overcredit Abetz's anecdote, for he was trying to show himself de Man's friend by representing the other more as an anti-Marxist than as a pro-Nazi, but it gives the flavor of his style. In the same document, he asserted that he had tried to protect Henri de Man from hostile forces in the Gestapo by describing him as not a left socialist but as an opponent of Marx. "Le Dossier Bousquet," 8.

25. Raymond De Becker mentioned his excitement at attending these meetings in his autobiographical *Le Livre des vivants et des morts* (Brussels: Editions de la Toison d'Or, 1942).

26. The journal was called *Deutsch-Französische Monatshefte (Cahiers franco-allemands)*. A shrewd reader, it was Abetz who plucked the term *New Order* from the Personalist journal of that name, edited by Alexandre Marc, and presented it to von Ribbentrop for wide use. He was also responsible for the plan to greatly increase the number of Jews to be exterminated by having the Vichy government expel foreign Jews and other refugees from the free zone to the occupied zone; once there, they could be deported to the concentration camps. According to Robert Wistrich, Abetz was tried for war crimes in 1946, convicted, and was released in 1954. Four years later, he burned to death in an "accident" when the steering wheel of his car failed—an event that some saw as "revenge . . . for his role in sending French Jews to the gas chambers." Robert Wistrich, *Who's Who in Nazi Germany* (London: Weidenfeld & Nicolson, 1982), 4.

27. Barbara Lambauer holds that Abetz's anti-Semitic orders, especially for deporting Jews, expressed both his personal views and the wish to strengthen his hand against enemies in the Foreign Office and Berlin; *Otto Abetz et les Français, ou l'envers de la collaboration* (Paris: Fayard, 2001). See also Abetz, *Histoire d'une politique franco-allemande*, 43; Hellman, *Emmanuel Mounier and the New Catholic Left*, 6–7. For a discussion of Abetz's journal, which he edited with Fritz Bran, see Michel Grunewald, "Le 'Couple France-Allemagne' vu par les nazis: L'Idéologie du 'rapprochement franco-allemand' dans les *Deutsch-Französische Monatshefte/ Cahiers franco-allemands* (1934–1939)," in *Entre Locarno et Vichy: Les relations culturelles franco-allemandes dans les années 1930*, vol. 1, ed. Hans Manfred Bock, Reinhart Meyer-Kalkus, and Michel Trebitsch (Paris: CNRS, 1993), 130–46.

28. Daye's career received a boost in 1932, shortly before he was elected to the Académie française, by the publication of a special issue of the Belgian journal *La Nervie* (No. 4). It is illustrated with an unironic representation of Daye mastering the world, represented as the globe, which he holds in his hand as he studies it. The text was composed of short paragraphs written by literary friends puffing his talents. Among his much-praised qualities were his athleticism, particularly skill at tennis, and his readiness—obviously based on multiple residences—to drop in and out of Paris and Brussels at a moment's notice, requiring only a change of shirts.

29. Stanley G. Payne, *Fascism: Comparison and Definition* (Madison: University of Wisconsin Press, 1980), p. 7.

30. Brasillach's sexual orientation is implied by William Tucker when he writes repeatedly of Brasillach's admiration for the "bare-chested torsos" of the German youths at the Nuremberg games, or his attraction to "the muscular young men of the Rexist security guard" (William R. Tucker, *The Fascist Ego: A Political Biography of Robert Brasillach* [Berkeley: University of California Press, 1975], 112, 100). De Becker was described as gay by his second in command, Pierre De Ligne (interview, October 19, 1992). It was considered a known fact, as Delcord noted. De Ligne added that, at work on *Le Soir (volé)* during the war, office romances included the reporter—and novelist—Louis Fonsny's unrequited love for Paul de Man (who was not gay), and De Becker's infatuation with another staff member (interview with De Ligne, October 19, 1992). Henri Bauchau and Christian Roy, defenders of De Becker, denied his sexual orientation in interviews of June 26, 1998, and September 29, 1998, respectively. Bauchau reported that De Becker was in "violent" conflict about the matter, but not sexually active.

31. Bernard Delcord and José Gotovitch, *Fonds Pierre Daye* (Brussels: CREH and Musée de la Littérature, 1989), 15. Section III, "Belgique Occupée, 1940–1944." Pierre Daye to Paul de Man, Brussels, s.d. 1 sheet. CREH, Brussels, Correspondance Générale, no. 352.

32. Interview with Pierre De Ligne, October 19, 1992; interview with Paul Jamin, February 4, 1993. Christian Roy, who has written on De Becker, doubts this origin. Léon Van Huffel, "Pour un antisémitisme racial," *Le Soir (volé)*, January 29, 1941, and February 11, 1941, both p. 1. De Becker's autobiography reflects his racist hatred of a Jewish employer of his youth (*Le Livre des vivants et des morts*, op. cit.). Both De Ligne and Jamin stressed De Becker's "Semitic" features, which Jamin said made him "ugly." Like many of those convicted of collaboration, Jamin opened an essentially correct interview by volunteering that he was "not-anti-Semitic." As I left, he asked this writer, "And are you Jewish, Madame?" "Yes," I said. "I thought as much," he replied.

33. Hellman, *Emmanuel Mounier and the New Catholic Left*, 93, 106, 92. For De Becker's version of his contacts with Henri de Man, see De Becker, *Livre des vivants et des morts*, 178–184. Like Spaak, he also used the word "seduced" to describe Henri de Man's influence on such figures as Marcel Déat (p. 186)—as well as on a gathering of some forty students, initially doubtful of Henri de Man, one of whom concluded by remarking after a lengthy discussion with him, " 'What a pity that such a man should have arrived in Belgium so late! He alone might have been able to become the master of our generation. But we are a generation without masters' " (182).

34. Hellman, p. 93.

35. Gérard-Lebois and Gotovitch, *L'An 40*, 45; for friendship with Paul, discussion with Félicien Marceau in November 2004, and telephone interview of November 15, 1992, with Esther Sluszny, who cited Carette's presence in her friend's circle one of the reasons she withdrew from it. Félicien Marceau, *Les Années courtes* (Paris: Gallimard, 1968), 320–24.

36. Marceau, *Les Années courtes*, 198–99.

37. De Becker, *Livre des vivants et des morts*, 172–78.

38. The thirty-three guiding principles of De Becker's proposed community have been described as "authoritarian, hierarchical, elitist, and undemocratic." De Becker wrote that frequent guests of the Didiers were such men as the critic, filmmaker, and fascist journalist Robert Poulet, half-brother of the phenome-

nologist critic Georges Poulet, and, from France, Bertrand de Jouvenel and others. Probably the Belgian publisher Paul Colin showed up as well; De Becker, *Livre des vivants et des morts*, 185.

39. In addition to De Becker, others from the paper *L'Avant Garde* appeared at the Didier salon. One found there also the Seigneur brothers, Auguste Marin, and the militant Catholic Henry Bauchau (who later became an adviser to Paul de Man in his publishing business after the war, according to the Military Court's findings). Moulin remembered also the journalists from *Cassandre*, *La Nation belge*, and of *L'Ouest* (another of De Becker's journals). Joris Van Severen, leader of Verdinaso, an extreme right-wing political group, would be present, and also José Streel, the Rexist second in command to Degrelle, who himself went only once. Moulin also saw there Robert Brasillach and the right-wing writers Henri de Montherlant and Albert Fabre-Luce (a leading historian who notoriously was to write a famous four-volume history of France, the first two volumes of which were pro-German, while the second two, written postwar, took the opposite position).

10. ANNE

1. Interview with Anne Ipsen, July 4, 1991.
2. Marriage certificate of Jaeger and his second wife, issued by the city of Brussels, August 2, 1944, gives information about his first wife, Anaide Baraghian.
3. Georges Goriély also commented that she had enjoyed a happy childhood in a privileged position; interview, June 29, 1990.
4. It was primarily Romania's oil that interested Hitler. Gerhard Weinberg, *A World at Arms: A Global History of World War II* (Cambridge: Cambridge University Press, 1994), 20.
5. He was also an authority on international law, although not a lawyer; interview with Gilbert Jaeger, July 16, 1990.
6. Paul Willems, for example, went to Austria to study marine law in 1940, although it was a touchy period spanning the Phony War and Germany's invasion of Belgium, a journey about which he was interrogated postwar, he said; interview, April 26, 1993.
7. Interview with Georges Goriély, June 29, 1990.
8. "[Paul] was [under] the influence of his successive wives. He was not a *coureur* [womanizer]. She [Anne] was completely in love . . . and still now I think she never forgot him"; interview, June 29, 1990. One of Goriély's friends testified to his feelings for Anne.
9. Willems eventually became the eminence grise of Belgian culture and described himself as a cultural entrepreneur and the person responsible for starting the Queen Elisabeth Competition and bringing most of the great artists of the West to Belgium. He was close to the couple during the war; interview, April 26, 1993.
10. Interview with Hendrik Woods, March 14, 1998.
11. The excuse for the state-sponsored riots was the assassination of Ernst vom Rath, an act committed by a German-Jewish student named Herschel Grynszpan, who saw that Germany's deportation of thousands would mean they would be left stateless.
12. Two years later, deposed by oil-hungry Hitler, King Carol fled on September 6, 1940, escaping to Switzerland with what William L. Shirer called "ten carloads

of what might be described as 'loot' "; *The Rise and Fall of the Third Reich: A History of Nazi Germany*, 30th ed. (New York: Simon & Schuster/Torchlight, 1990), 800.

13. Interview with Anne Ipsen, July 4, 1991.

14. Ibid.

15. MSL (fragment), January 3, 1939, dated by Frida Vandervelden. Significant parts of these fragments, redacted by Frida (she blacked out portions of the photocopied manuscripts), from whom this writer received them, were first published by Ortwin de Graef, in *Responses: On Paul de Man's Wartime Journalism*, ed. Werner Hamacher, Neil Hertz, and Thomas Keenan (Lincoln: University of Nebraska Press, 1992).

16. Letter of May 29, 1939.

17. *Satisfaction* would accord with an American grade of C; *distinction*, a B (approximately 18 percent of the cohort); *grande distinction*, an A (10 percent of the cohort); *la plus grande distinction*, an A+ (approximately 2 percent of the cohort). Statistics are based on consultation with five senior ULB professors, July 1990.

18. Frida reported that she and Paul both were reading Gide, who "had a very deep influence on our generation. *L'immoraliste*. The man who has the courage to liberate himself [from] family ties, or *ses liens sentimentaux*. Paul read Gide and yes I think he loved him. Yes. Perhaps he made investigations [into real philosophy], but I really don't know." She agreed that he was self-taught: "Essentially he was formed by himself—his reading, his spirit of curiosity." When the two friends met they spoke about "books and music," especially English novels, which they read in the original language, works "good, bad, and indifferent," but some of which were considered "very brilliant." She cited A. J. Cronin, Charles Morgan, Rosamond Lehmann, and Aldous Huxley, but "no American novels" except perhaps "some Fitzgerald." Interview, July 8, 1991. Other friends of de Man, including Nellie De Ligne, echoed the names of these writers.

19. Interview with Patricia de Man, December 29, 1990.

20. Ibid.

11. EXODUS

1. Willems, facing prosecution postwar, successfully defended himself by holding that his management of the Fisheries Department was apolitical and beneficial to his food-starved country, and that wearing the army uniform was required; interview with Paul Willems, April 23, 1993.

2. See, for example, Paul Willems, letter to the editor, in *Responses: On Paul de Man's Wartime Journalism*, ed. Werner Hamacher, Neil Hertz, and Thomas Keenan (Lincoln: University of Nebraska Press, 1988), 472.

3. His mother, Marie Gevers, a highly popular novelist, published in several overtly collaborating journals; interview with Paul Aron, July 7, 2004.

4. The English soldiers were pushed off the Continent by the German army in May–June 1940 during the famous rout, or evacuation, at Dunkirk.

5. This is a repeated theme of the wartime memoir written by the journalist Anne Somerhausen; see *Written in Darkness: A Belgian Woman's Record of the Occupation, 1940–1945* (New York: Knopf, 1946).

6. To Paul, "papers [a legal union] did not matter"; interview with Jan de Man, June 28, 1990.

7. A remnant took refuge in France and wandered from Limoges to Poitiers, and

then to Bordeaux, while some eventually joined their French counterparts collaborating in Vichy.

8. Jules Gérard-Libois and José Gotovitch, *L'An 40: La Belgique occupée* (Brussels: CRISP, 1971), 235.

9. Jean Stengers, *Léopold III et le gouvernement: Les Deux Belges de 1940* (Paris: Duculot, 1980).

10. Gérard-Libois and Gotovitch, *L'An 40*, 238–45.

11. Ibid., 234–35.

12. Sarah Fishman, *We Will Wait: Wives of French Prisoners of War, 1940–1945* (New Haven: Yale University Press, 1991), 25.

13. Jean Vidalenc, *L'Exode de mai–juin 1940* (Paris: Presses Universitaires de France, 1957), 32–60; on p. 364, Vidalenc cites Marius Leblond, *Redressement* (Paris: Editions Denoël, 1941), 85.

14. Jean Vanwelkenhuyzen and Jacques Dumont, *1940: Le Grand Exode* (Paris-Gembloux: Editions Duculot, 1983), 153.

15. Many, including Paul Valéry, a poet Paul greatly admired, described this epic suffering. The poet, himself fleeing along the road, saw wagons like hayricks moving infinitely slowly, overstuffed with people, tools, animals, with the heads of blond-haired children sticking out from the straw. Paul Valéry, *Cahiers*, vol. 23 (Paris: Centre National de la Recherche Scientifique, 1960), 307.

16. Gérard-Libois and Gotovitch, *L'An 40*, 220.

17. This was a famous evening, subject of much speculation by historians, who wonder if the Germans wanted to bring together the intellectual Henri de Man with Degrelle, a Belgian Nazi and an extroverted, bellicose man. See Fabrice Schurmans, *Introduction à la collaboration intellectuelle en Belgique francophone*, vol. 1 (Liège: University of Liège 1990), 49 ff., citing *Le Soir*, November 11, 1946. See also Martin Conway, *Collaboration in Belgium: Léon Degrelle and the Rexist Movement, 1940–1944* (New Haven: Yale University Press, 1993), 34–35.

18. Léon Degrelle, *La Cohue de 1940* (Paris: Avalon, 1991), 380.

19. Interview with Esther Sluszny, November 15, 1992; Interview with Frida Vandervelden, July 16, 1990.

12. PAUL COLLABORATES

1. See Jacques Willequet, *La Belgique sous la botte: Résistances et collaborations, 1940–1945* (Paris: Editions Universitaires, 1986).

2. The child, registered as Hendrik Hrand Jaeger, was named after Henri. The boy's surname would be changed in a few years to de Man by a bureaucratic sleight of hand managed by his father, as discussed in chapter 18.

3. Transcript supplied by the Université Libre de Bruxelles; interview with Georges Goriély, June 29, 1990.

4. Alexander von Falkenhausen, *Mémoires d'outre-guerre (Extraits): Comment j'ai gouverné la Belgique de 1940–1944* (Brussels: Editions Arts & Voyages, 1974), photograph facing 92.

5. Jan de Man said that late in the war he voluntarily went to work in a German factory (where he spoke the language, having lived there until 1933) because he needed the money—another fact held against him during his trial for collaboration; interview, June 28, 1990.

6. Els De Bens, "La Presse au temps de l'occupation de la Belgique (1940–1944)," *Revue d'histoire de la deuxième guerre mondiale* 80 (1970): 4.

7. It is conceivable that this undated event may have occurred during the period when Henri de Man was losing favor with the occupant before he fled into exile; interview with Anne Ipsen, July 4, 1991.

8. See chapter 13, n. 17.

9. Raymond De Becker, *Le Livre des vivants et des morts* (Brussels: Editions de la Toison d'Or, 1942). This was published a year before Fonsny was assassinated. It should be noted that a partisan of De Becker, Christian Roy, does not believe his subject was homosexual, or that if he was, that he did not express it in practice; interview with Christian Roy, Sepember 29, 1998.

10. Interviews with Pierre De Ligne, October 19, 1992, and June 19, 1993.

11. Pierre De Ligne implied that this angry bias sprang from the fact that De Becker's businessman father, for whom his mother had worked in a low-level job, did not support—or, as it appears, even acknowledge—his offspring; interview with Pierre De Ligne, June 19, 1995.

12. Later Jamin lived on in Brussels. He joined the Rexists in 1936. Without being asked, he offered this writer the standard excuses: Mussolini made the trains run on time. Degrelle and Rexism were not anti-Semitic. The BBC London broadcasts were responsible for the assassinations. Everyone in Belgium collaborated. The good collaborators were the ones who were attacked (postwar, like himself); the bad ones were left alone. Good collaborators helped people. Von Falkenhausen saved many lives; he deserved a medal after the war. José Streel was "a very moderate" man. Jamin was loyal to the end to Léon Degrelle, who published and paid him very well. (Here, Jamin gestured to a large sideboard, which his first bonus from the fascist leader enabled him to buy.) The vivid anti-Semitism of his work was not held against him by the judicial system. In a personal discussion in 1993, Jean Stengers considered him "something of a genius," credited him with making Degrelle's paper profitable, and thought him probably too harshly punished. Interview with Paul Jamin, February 4, 1993.

13. De Becker, *Le Livre des vivants et des morts*, 23.

14. Facing prosecution after the war, De Becker tried to minimize his anti-Semitism by asserting that his racism was strategically adopted to give a basis for claiming that the Belgians were a "sub-Nordic" race and thus deserving of consideration as Aryans. De Becker fled to France after the war and lived there in exile, while being condemned to death in absentia for treason. AM: *LSv*, arrest September 30, 1949; Case 7259, item 44; information file V, folder A, item 28, procès-verbal of Raymond De Becker, questioned by Roger Vinçotte, October 13, 1945, 10:00 A.M. Picard was instrumental in the construction of the "Belgian soul," according to Jean-Marie Klinkenberg. This was built on the exaltation of Flemish culture, rejection of the leprosy of republicanism and the evils of foreign customs, and "special reverence" for German Romanticism—all the while rejecting the use of Flemish in favor of French. "La Production littéraire en Belgique francophone," *Littérature* 44 (1981): 33–40, 42.

15. *Le Soir (volé)*, October 1, 2, 5, and 11, 1940. *Völkisch*, a politically sensitive term, meant literally folkish, or of the people, but it actually implied the strong Nazi doctrine of "blood and soil," the teaching that truth and purity resided instinctively in the German peasantry and only in those of so-called Aryan blood; anti-Semitism was intrinsically a part of the *Völkisch* movement.

16. *Le Soir (volé)*, November 28, 1940.

17. Rents were lower at the beginning of the war but picked up by early 1941, and the numerous advertisements reflect this. See also Anne Somerhausen, *Written in*

Darkness: A Belgian Woman's Record of the Occupation, 1940–1945 (New York: Knopf, 1946), 27, 61. Later still, however, rental advertising shrank to a minimum, suggesting that with renewed bombings and intensifying poverty, the market had collapsed.

18. *Le Soir (volé)*, December 1, 1940, November 3, 1940, and January 30, 1941.

19. Interview with Nellie De Ligne (the wife of Pierre De Ligne), October 19, 1992. Anne, who took Ipsen and von-Orland as her surname late in life in Brussels, explained that her last husband's name was Ipsen-von Orland because there were many Ipsens, while his "old" family came from the island of Orland.

20. Philippe Burrin, *France Under the Germans: Collaboration and Compromise, 1940–1945*, trans. Janet Lloyd (New York: New Press, 1996).

21. AM: TdO, Case 3245, item 47, information file V, procès-verbal (marked "copy" in ink, dated July 30, 1946, at 3:00 P.M.), of Paul-Adolf-Michel De Man, living in Anvers, Longue rue d'Argile, no. 2 [2, Langeleemstraat].

22. Interview with Pierre De Ligne, June 19, 1993.

23. As this involved reporting weekly on internal developments in Belgium, it was partly for collecting this information, which De Becker passed on to the German authorities, that both were prosecuted; AM: *LSv*, "Summary of Charges and Sentences," Council of War, vol. 8, 1946, 1–41, especially 14. De Ligne was sentenced to five years of hard labor and served two.

24. The term *collaboration* evolved over time from the relatively neutral meaning of working with the occupant, as theoretically required, to the "bloody" connotation it had by 1944 of spying, betrayal, and the voluntary wholesale adoption of Nazi policies. See Burrin, *France Under the Germans*, 4. In 1940, Gaston Gallimard wrote to Jean Luchaire, a prominent French Nazi, addressing him as "collaborating publicist, director of *Les Nouveaux Temps*," and announced that his publishing house now was ready to "collaborate with Dr. Kaiser of the Propaganda Squadron." Olivier Todd, *Camus: Une Vie* (Paris: NRF/Gallimard, 1996), 180, n. 25, commented that Gallimard's term was "a dangerous word but not then used in the full and bloody sense it expressed in 1944" (n. 25: Archives de France). Even José Streel, a leader of Rex, parsed the word; see Martin Conway, *Collaboration in Belgium: Léon Degrelle and the Rexist Movement* (New Haven: Yale University Press, 1993), 162.

25. Interview with Frida Vandervelden, July 16, 1990.

26. Interview with Pierre De Ligne, October 19, 1992.

27. See chapter 16.

28. Interview with Anne Ipsen, June 30, 1993.

13. "THE JEWS IN PRESENT-DAY LITERATURE"

1. Interview with Paul Jamin, February 4, 1993. By 1940, the drawings of Jamin, whose humor turned on representing Churchill, Roosevelt, Freemasons, and Jews as one indistinguishable band of enemies, appeared regularly on the front page of *Le Soir (volé)*.

2. The embassy tried to compete with the army by also supplying funds directly to publications, *Le Soir (volé)* included. See Els De Bens, "La presse au temps de l'occupation de la Belgique (1940–1944)," *Revue d'histoire de la deuxième guerre mondiale* 80 (1970): 4, 5, 2. For De Becker, see Archives of the Military Court (Brussels), procés-verbal, May 9, 1945, October 15, 1945.

3. Liebe, quoted in De Bens, "Le presse au temps de l'occupation de la Belgique (1940–1944)," 4.

4. According to De Ligne, censorship was too time-consuming for the Propaganda Division's inadequate personnel. Finally, De Becker arranged to have instead a German journalist, a *Sonderführer*, come "from time to time to discuss problems." Later, the German civilian censors were much more rigorous.

5. *Le Soir (volé)*, October 1940, 1.

6. Paul de Man, *Wartime Journalism, 1939–1943*, ed. Werner Hamacher, Neil Hertz, and Thomas Keenan (Lincoln: University of Nebraska Press, 1988), 45.

7. Interview with Anne Ipsen, July 4, 1991.

8. See www.breendonk.be/EN/index.html.

9. Gerhard Weinberg, *A World at Arms: A Global History of World War II* (Cambridge: Cambridge University Press, 1994), 298.

10. The latter had written a brief review of *De Familie Klepkens* on January 31, 1941, and an article on Bergson (recently deceased) on February 4 and February 11, 1941, for the cultural page.

11. See Stephanie Barron, ed., *"Degenerate Art": The Fate of the Avant-Garde in Nazi Germany* (Los Angeles: Los Angeles County Museum of Art, 1991).

12. George Mosse, "Beauty Without Sensuality: The Exhibition *Entartete Kunst*," in *"Degenerate Art*," ed. Barron, 8, 24.

13. Pierre Drieu La Rochelle, *Journal: 1939–1945* (Paris: Gallimard, 1992), 105–7.

14. Interview with Nellie De Ligne, October 19, 1992; interview with Frida Vandervelden, July 16, 1990.

15. De Man, *Wartime Journalism*, 230, 232, 207, 208, 321–22.

16. Max Brod, *Franz Kafka: A Biography*, trans. G. H. Roberts and R. Winston (New York: Schocken Books, 1960), 110–11.

17. Degrelle wanted more exposure than he could get from the small circulation of *Le Pays réel*. Reeder resisted, however, arguing with the high command that *Le Soir (volé)* neutralized attitudes, especially among the old military and church circles. It influenced "realists" among the business and bourgeois class and was gradually detaching them from their Anglophile mentality. It should win for the Germans a practical collaboration. *Le Nouveau Journal* and *Cassandre* (both very small-circulation publications managed by Paul Colin, whose bills the Germans were paying), and *Le Pays réel* were sufficient to give Degrelle's ideas expression, Reeder judged. The Belgian Schraenen, Reeder wrote, who administered *Le Soir (volé)*, was a "Germanophile of long date," and this "constitutes a guarantee that a stronger political influence can always be exercised on the newspaper when it appears opportune." In fact, De Becker told the prosecutor that he made all his personnel decisions working in tandem with Schraenen, with whom he had few disagreements. AM: *LSv*, "Summary of Charges and Sentences," Council of War, vol. 8, 1946, Information file V, folder A, item 28, procès-verbal of Raymond De Becker, questioned by Roger Vinçotte and others, May 9–October 15, 1945.

18. Gérard Loiseaux, *La Littérature de la défaite et de la collaboration: D'après Phönix oder Asche? (Phénix ou cendres?) de Bernhard Payr* (Paris: Publications de la Sorbonne, 1984), 501.

14. THE YOUNG WOLF

1. In addition to the 186 articles in *Le Soir (volé)* and ten articles in *Het Vlaamsche Land*, an Antwerp paper, he also wrote one hundred brief *comptes rendus* (book

summaries) for a monthly called the *Bibliographie Dechenne*, a publication of Belgium's largest distributor of books and journals.

2. The first index was named the "Liste Bernhard." Perhaps because the German ambassador, Otto Abetz, liked the idea, the second, more notorious index, "Liste Otto," was named after him. Focused on non-Germans, it appeared in September 1940 and banned the publication of some 842 Jewish or "anti-German" authors, and contained more than two thousand titles. See Gérard Loiseaux, *La Littérature de la défaite et de la collaboration: D'après Phönix oder Asche? (Phénix ou cendres?) de Bernhard Payr* (Paris: Publications de la Sorbonne, 1984), 21–35, 44, 50, 60, 66.

3. Gérard Loiseaux discusses the work of Bernhard Payr, a subordinate of Alfred Rosenberg and the censor in charge of French literature. Rosenberg was an extreme anti-Semite and regarded Hitler as a quasi-religious figure. See Loiseaux, *La Littérature de la défaite et de la collaboration*, 21–35, 44, 50, 60, 66 passim.

4. Interview with Ted Weiss, May 14, 1991.

5. One could probably assimilate his ideas to a Johnsonian rejection of painting the streaks of the tulip—that is, to a neoclassic emphasis on the universal and eternal.

6. Paul de Man, *Wartime Journalism, 1939–1943*, ed. Werner Hamacher, Neil Hertz, and Thomas Keenan (Lincoln: University of Nebraska Press, 1988), 64.

7. She correctly made notorious Brasillach's mandate that "It is necessary to separate the Jews as a group and not to save the little ones," the last words of which, *"ne pas garder les petits,"* often connote the offspring of animals; Alice Yaeger Kaplan, *Collaborator: The Trial and Execution of Robert Brasillach* (Chicago: University of Illinois Press, 2000).

8. Alice Y. Kaplan, "Paul de Man, *Le Soir*, and the Francophone Collaboration (1940–1942)," in *Responses: On Paul de Man's Wartime Journalism*, ed. Werner Hamacher, Neil Hertz, and Thomas Keenan (Lincoln: University of Nebraska Press, 1988), 266–84, especially 271. In her memoir, Kaplan has also published an interesting discussion of Paul de Man at Yale and her reflections on his thought; see *French Lessons: A Memoir* (Chicago: University of Chicago Press, 1988), pp. 147–74. Gilbert Joseph, *"Brasillach ou la trahison du clerc*, by Michel Laval," *La quinzaine littéraire*, no. 616 (1993): 23.

9. De Man referred also to Brasillach's memoir, *Notre Avant-Guerre*, in *Wartime Journalism*, 130–31.

10. Loiseaux, *La Littérature de la défaite et de la collaboration*, 151.

11. Jean Paulhan, *Les incertitudes du langage* (Paris: Gallimard, 1970), 145; cited by Loiseaux, *La Littérature de la défaite et de la collaboration*, 111.

12. See Pierre Drieu La Rochelle, *Notes pour comprendre le siècle* (Paris: Gallimard, 1941).

13. De Man, *Wartime Journalism*, 170–71.

14. In April 1942, de Man agreed with Friedrich Sieburg's book, *Dieu est-il français? [Is God French?]* (Paris: Grasset, 1930). "We enter into a mystical era, into a period of faith and belief, with all that that implies of suffering, exaltation, and drunkenness. The very notion of happiness has been modified and draws near to the norms that many authors have believed they could compare with those of the Middle Ages." German technology was inspired by a "strong spiritual current attached to the origins of the Germanic genius, glorifying the constant elements of that spirit" and keeping its organizational principles free of American sterility. See de Man, *Wartime Journalism*, 227, 226.

15. De Man, *Wartime Journalism*, 196, 345.

16. The old building where Jews were collected was connected by an underground tunnel and railroad spur to the main railroad line close by. Perhaps this was to spare the citizenry from watching the departures—or to prevent reaction. The building had been repurposed by the 1990s and was an archive.

17. *Het Vlaamsche Land*, August 20, 1942.

18. De Man, *Wartime Journalism*, 325.

20. George Mosse, "Beauty Without Sensuality: The Exhibition *Entartete Kunst*," in *"Degenerate Art": The Fate of the Avant-Garde in Nazi Germany*, ed. Stephanie Barron (Los Angeles: Los Angeles County Museum of Art, 1991), 25–31.

20. Payr reported that Grasset blamed problems of capitalism on "the exclusive taste for money and profit" and "this taste is an essential racial characteristic of the Jew." Payr evidently shared Rosenberg's interest in founding a new sort of anti-Christian religion of Nazism; Loiseaux, *La Littérature de la défaite et de la collaboration*, 213–14.

21. De Man, *Wartime Journalism*, 87.

22. Grimm, on Hitler's orders, had personally taken from prison Herschel Grynspan, the man whose assassination of von Rath was the excuse for Kristallnacht. See Loiseaux, *La Littérature de la défaite et de la collaboration*, 57, 98–101; Robert O. Paxton and Michael R. Maurras, *Vichy France and the Jews* (Palo Alto: Stanford University Press, 1995), 65–66.

23. Alexander von Falkenhausen, *Mémoires d'outre-guerre (Extraits): Comment j'ai gouverné la Belgique de 1940–1944* (Brussels: Editions Arts & Voyages, 1974), photograph facing 192.

24. De Coster pointed to the article "The Literary Congress at Weimar" in *Bibliographie Dechenne* (1942): 31. His attribution is supported by both extrinsic and intrinsic evidence: Two other short items appear on these two pages, one praising the increased reading of philosophical works, the other citing both Maurras and Brasillach in discussing the changing of literary style. This didacticism was beyond the competence of Bauwens, a low-level employee whom Paul had largely supplanted. Its place of publication, style, and content all suggest that it should be added to Paul de Man's bibliography; *Rapport d'expertise comptable: En Cause de l'Agence Dechenne S.A.*, 2ème volume. Frans De Coster, Expert-Comptable, près les Tribunaux, 13, rue Paul Bossu, Woluwé-St-Pierre, telephone 33-45-97 (p. 281). (This volume is marked III in red crayon.) The tribunals (tribunaux) were part of the Military Court that prosecuted collaborators. Only four volumes of De Coster's audit concern this study and are referred to as ADRP (Agence Dechenne Report) and ADPC (Agence Dechenne Pièces-Annexe). The Report is a two-volume narrative summary. The Pièces-Annexe, also in two volumes, contains the documents that support the narrative, and each element is numbered.

25. According to Hedwig Speliers, the meetings were meant to show the "the close tie between writers" and the Nazi office in charge of literature, but its supposed purpose, spontaneous discussion of "the spiritual problems of the time" was a "pure fiction." All German writers had been selected by the minister of propaganda, and only "nationalist writers, faithful to the Party, were admitted." See Speliers, "Le miracle de Weimar," in *Leurs Occupations: L'Impact de la Seconde Guerre mondiale sur la littérature en Belgique*, ed. Paul Aron et al. (Brussels: Textyles; CREHSGM, 1997), 157–70, especially 165.

26. Loiseaux pointed out that in spite of collaborative activities, Jacques Benoist-Méchin and Jean Giono did not go to Weimar; Loiseaux, *La Littérature de la défaite et de la collaboration*.

27. Things had reached "such a degree of decomposition and degeneration that, above all, the will to change must exist." Daye provided "fundamental truths" in "clear and simple terms" that should "govern the action of men of goodwill." De Man, *Wartime Journalism*, 138.

28. Werner Hamacher, Neil Hertz, and Thomas Keenan, eds., *Responses: On Paul de Man's Wartime Journalism* (Lincoln: University of Nebraska Press, 1988), 193.

29. Letter of Pierre Daye to Paul de Man and Louis Fonsny, Royal Archives, vol. 3 (1942), 3, 2.

30. De Coster, *Rapport d'expertise comptable*, vol. 2, 280.

31. "Pierre Peyel remporte le concours littéraire du *Soir*: Les Écrivains belges et l'occupation: Entre engagement et indifférence," in *Histoire de la littérature belge francophone: 1830–2000*, ed. Jean-Pierre Bertrand et al. (Paris: Fayard, 2003), 401–10. Peyel was the pen name of Louis De Becker, author of *Hohenmoor*.

32. Léon Van Huffel was also a jurist.

33. Personal communication with Paul Aron, July 7, 2004.

15. DRINKING FROM THREE SPOUTS

1. See AM: TdO, Case 3245, Information file V, items 48 and 4; item 48 is the HMS procès-verbal, dated September 12, 1945, a statement by Roger Vinçotte, the substitute attorney general, listing the annexes he was including in the file. Vinçotte wrote, "attachments 17 and 18: memo on 'les Editions de la Toison d'Or' and on a project for a review. Attachment 18, which constitutes the draft of this memo, is in the handwriting of De Becker." Note that Vinçotte erred in attributing it entirely to De Becker. The first sheets (11–17) of the holograph manuscript, attachment 18, which is the document underlying the typescript (attachment 17), are in the handwriting of Raymond De Becker. However, the last two sheets are in the hand of Paul de Man.

2. Interview with Anne Ipsen, July 4, 1991.

3. By retreating from Brussels after April 7, 1943, de Man avoided what became a dangerous connection during the period of the Epuration/Repression. See Court of Appeal, Agence Dechenne Le Soir, Information file V, folder A, sub-folder 44 (De Becker), items 16–17.

4. The Nazis created "*Reichskammeren*," or "chambers," of the Reich, trade groups that listed all their members, reporting on and regulating their actions, and excluding enemies of the Reich. Membership was a privilege. The prosecutor's files on *Le Soir (volé)* show that De Becker may have been one of the most influential of Belgian collaborating journalists. He got control of the Association of Belgian Journalists, wrote its regulations for the Propaganda Division, and drew up lists of potential members. He tried to block the appointment of Paul Colin as leader, preferring the amiable Pierre Daye, but ultimately he had to nominate his enemy, who was assassinated by the Resistance only a week later. See AM: *LSv*, "Summary of the Charges and Sentences," Council of War, vol. 8, 1946, 1–41, especially 14. Information file V, folder A, subfolder 44 (De Becker), items 11, 14–15.

5. This writer understands that an essay (citation unavailable) was produced by a student in Belgium.

6. This writer found the prospectus in the De Becker files at the offices of the Toison d'Or of which he was a director; AM: TdO, Case 3245, Information file V, attachments 13–15.

7. Ibid., items 17–19.

8. The document exists both as an original holograph manuscript and as a carbon copy of the typescript that was submitted to Mundus. De Becker typically used pencil on sheets torn vertically in half for his drafts, as he did here. Information also available in an interview with Pierre De Ligne, October 19, 1992.

9. See note 6 above.

10. Gerhard Weinberg, *A World at Arms: A Global History of World War II* (Cambridge: Cambridge University Press, 1994), 292–93.

11. Information given to José Gotovitch.

12. ADRP, vol. 1, 135: "The bimonthly *Bulletin* is a publication aimed solely at its clients (bookstores and periodical shops)." The German-headed management of the Agence Dechenne created a publication aimed at the public. It was called *Bibliographie*. Five issues appeared in 1941, twelve in 1942, and twelve more in 1943; thus de Man joined a preexisting enterprise when he began writing for the *Bibliographie* in early 1942.

13. ADPC, item 400.

14. "One must stress that, contrary to the rule that only the director, the secretary-general, and the adjunct-secretary [Albert Pletinckx] should sign their correspondence, Paul de Man constantly signed the mail of his department"; ADRP, vol. 2, 276.

15. Letter from Paul de Man to M. Lonnoy, Secrétaire du Cercle Belge de la Librairie, August 24, 1942; ADPC, II: 402.

16. I am indebted to Fritz Ringer for reading this section of the manuscript and interpreting the German acronyms and allusions. He found it code and made it history.

17. Berlin Document Center, 26.

18. The secret file on von Balluseck reports that a "business contact," a Mr. Bräutigam of Leipzig (perhaps the agent who was "running" the director-general), said that on several occasions, the Leipzig man reported that von Balluseck often missed meetings with him, probably because he was in multiple other countries managing the sales of *Signal*. Berlin Document Center, 26.

19. Regarding Charles Peeters, see ADRP, vol. 1, 69.

20. ADRP, vol. 1, 46.

21. ADRP, vol. 2, 414, Conclusion: "Peeters, dead in May 1944 [*sic*], bears the greatest part of the responsibility for the collaborative activity of the Agence Dechenne."

22. ADPC, vol. 2, vol. 1, item 17F.

23. ADRP, vol. 1, 31; vol. 2, 246–47. De Haas spied for the Germans (was "under German jurisdiction" in 1940) and briefly ran the Agence Dechenne in the summer of 1940. A visitor observed him gathering the staff, haranguing them *en termes*, and whipping them up against their former employers by displaying a chart showing their salaries.

24. Eagerness to disseminate *Signal* and initiative in meeting German needs were taken by the examining expert postwar as factors contributing to a recommendation to prosecute; Agence Dechenne, court militaire, vol. 5, judgment, 7.

25. He would "call him on every occasion favorable to augmenting [the] circulation" of *Le Nouveau Journal*, De Coster noted. Colin also published the journal *Cassandre*, in addition to running his Nouvelle Société d'Edition. All of these activities were said to be subsidized by the Nazis.

26. ADPC, vol. 1, 272.

27. "A situation can be created which is contrary to the signed nomination at the time of the creation of the Order of Journalists and by which I engage myself not to receive any remuneration from a publicity organization of any sort." The ambiguity of this sentence, especially surrounding the word "nomination," is typical of Paul de Man's locutions when matters were murky. Possibly he believed that he would yet achieve nomination and membership once the AJB was formally established.

28. José Gotovitch, "Resistance Movements and the 'Jewish Question,' " in *Belgium and the Holocaust: Jews, Belgians, Germans*, ed. Dan Michman (Jerusalem: Vad Yashem, 1998), 280. See also Anne Somerhausen, *Written in Darkness: A Belgian Woman's Record of the Occupation, 1940–1945* (New York: Knopf, 1946), 86, 10. For other views of Colin, see a journalist on the Left, Jo Gérard, a royalist, and Fernand Demany, *Mourir debout: Souvenirs du maquis* (Brussels: Editions Germinal, 1945), 44, 59–61.

29. Pierre Daye, *Les mémoires de Pierre Daye, 1936: l'apogée du Rexisme: 1940: la Collaboration, Le Dossier du mois* 12 (1963): 28.

30. ADRP, vol. 2, 288. Paul de Man was paid the following amounts: "*année* 1942 [after June 29, 1942], BF 39,400; *année* 1943 [until April 9, 1943, plus three months' notice], BF 60,000."

31. If the other jobs each added between 10 and 15 percent to his regular salary, then he was doing exceptionally well. Pierre De Ligne began at *Le Soir (volé)* in 1940 at BF 1,500 per month, and at the end of three years—1943—he was receiving BF 7,500 monthly, or BF 90,000 per year, and considered himself very well paid. De Ligne had a law degree, was six years older than Paul, and had a major responsibility in running the newsroom of one of the country's largest daily papers. Jan de Man, an Echevin (alderman), in charge of Brussels's electric system, earned about BF 7,000 per month.

32. Archives Générales du Royaume de Belgique, state prosecutor, incriminating evidence 1940–1944; item 149—S.A. Nouvelle Société d'Editions (n 653), Services, payroll book—shows that in July 1943, the last month entered, a cleaning woman was paid BF 400 once a week for six days' work. Previously, in November 20, 1940, a janitor received only BF 100 for a five-day week, which may indicate the presence of inflation. A messenger usually got BF 100 less.

33. Interview with Georges Goriély, August 9, 1995.

34. Interview with Georges Goriély, June 29, 1990.

35. ADPC, vol. 2, 405, dated by contents.

36. Lambrichs was employed by the Agence Dechenne by December/January 1942–43, when Peeters blamed him as well as de Man for the debacle in the French Book Department; ADPC, item 412, January 20, 1942, Peeters to von Balluseck; de Man was known by his friends merely to have gotten Lambrichs started in Paris in some unspecified way.

37. She said she dropped the *k* from Stuckx, her maiden name, unlike her sister Georgette ("Josette"), who eventually became Gilbert Jaeger's second wife. The absence of the *k*, Mme. Lambrichs said, showed that the family name was French and not Flemish. However, Josette had also adopted the French spelling by the time she married. Administration Communale de Bruxelles, August 2, 1944, marriage certificate of G. Jaeger and G. Stux; interview with Gilberte Lambrichs, June 16, 1998.

38. Interview with Jean Lescure, June 15, 1998.

39. ADPC, vol. 2, 7, item 405.

40. Letter from Lothar von Balluseck to the home office of Mundus, GmbH in Berlin W. 35. Tiergartenstrasse 10, October 12, 1942; ADPC, vol. 2, 8a, item 37.

41. Interview with Paul Willems, April 26, 1993; interview with Pierre De Ligne, October 19, 1992.

42. See note 40 above.

43. A contract had been drawn up to that effect, dated June 1, 1942, by Mundus.

44. The Toison d'Or's accountant, Désiré-Joseph Tollet, testified that the bill from Mundus for supplies of paper, amounting to millions of francs, was never paid. Capital was often advanced in this factitiously correct fashion, rather than through outright funding; AM: TdO, item 52.

45. ADPC, vol. 2, item 37, 9a.

46. The name Seidel was also spelled "Seydel"; ADPC, vol. 2, 10a, item 37.

47. Ibid.

48. ADPC, vol. 2, 11a, item 37.

16. THE BOULEVARD HAD TWO SIDES

1. The building was replaced postwar by a new structure at 88, boulevard Louis Schmitt, the street having been renamed for a political leader shot by the Gestapo, who had maintained their headquarters there.

2. Interview with Paul Willems, April 26, 1993.

3. Paul was Pierre De Ligne's witness when he and Nellie married in January 1943; interview with De Ligne, October 19, 1992.

4. See Israel Shirman, "Un Aspect de la 'Solution Finale': La Spoliation économique des juifs de Belgique," *CHSGM* 3 (1974): 65–83. See also Maxim Steinberg, *L'Etoile et le fusil*, 3 vols. (Brussels: Vie Ouvrière, 1983–1986).

5. Interview with Bob De Braey, November 18, 1992.

6. Hubert Mansion, an engineer from Antwerp, had registered himself as dwelling in an apartment he owned in that building on November 17, 1937. He deregistered on May 5, 1942, theoretically returning to 168 Markgravelei, Antwerp, the same elegant street on which Michel De Braey, Paul's architect grandfather, had once lived; CE, Brussels.

7. Advertisements in *Le Soir (volé)* and comments in Anne Somerhausen, *Written in the Darkness: A Belgian Woman's Record of the Occupation, 1940–1945* (New York: Knopf, 1946). The real estate market shifted from the beginning of the war, when people fled the city, to a later period, when prices rose. Still later, the market virtually disappeared.

8. More than once in the next decade, de Man absconded when rent was due, so that his landlords either evicted him and threw away his belongings (including his passport and manuscripts) or, in one life-changing case, pursued him relentlessly, destroying all hope of his continuing in his academic job.

9. Interview with Nellie De Ligne, October 19, 1992.

10. Jean Paulhan, who was in no way a Nazi, was a leading example. The powerful Parisian editor at Gallimard, publisher of Camus, Gide, and others, might in the evening attend dinners at the home of the wealthy American Florence Gould with men like Gerhard Heller, the Nazi chief censor in Paris. Then on occasion, he might return to his office to support a clandestine press. Camus's biographer considered Paulhan a "subtle manipulator," although not, at the bottom of his several Russian-doll personalities, pro-Nazi. See Oliver Todd, *Albert Camus: Une Vie* (Paris: Gallimard, 1996), 275. With regard to Paulhan's activities, see

also Ernst Jünger, *Paris Journals* (Paris: Juillard, 1951), and Jünger, *Second Journal parisien: Journal III, 1943–1945*, trans. Frédéric de Towarnicki and Henri Plard (Paris: Christian Bourgois, 1980).

11. Marcel, who spelled his surname both Slusny and Sluzny, became a lawyer and practiced all his life in Brussels. He had been on the editorial board of the *Cahiers du libre examen* at the same time as de Man; interview, November 19, 1992. His brother Nahum spelled his name Sluszny.

12. Telephone interview with Esther Sluszny, November 15, 1992.

13. Interview with Anne Ipsen, June 30, 1993.

14. She added that Lambrichs was not himself actively in the Resistance; interview, June 16, 1998.

15. The pay there was higher and he needed to feed his family, but this was held against him at his trial, he reported.

16. Interview with Bob De Braey, July 17, 1994.

17. Interview with Micheline De Braey, July 27, 1994.

18. She told her story, which she deprecated, only at the insistence of her admiring younger brother, Bob; ibid.

19. David Braybrooke, interview, July 18, 1999.

20. Discussion with Frans De Haes, June 16, 2004.

21. "Between 1935 and 1942 she published eight short stories and two novelettes in Colin's *Cassandre*." (Rolin would pay a consolation call on Colin's widow after his assassination.) Frans De Haes, "Dominique Rolin et La Belgique: premier jalon," (46 typescript pages), 18.

22. This document was something between a work permit and a passport that could allow travel outside the country. Two Dutchmen wrote, "An *Ausweis* was a work permit that allowed them more freedom of movement and excused them from the labor camps. The *Ausweis* didn't include a picture or fingerprints, but only included a name with an official German stamp and signature of the local commandant"; see http://www.koornwinder.org/Genealogy/data/ps01/ps01_021.htm.

23. HMSLS from Robert Denöel, July 14, 1942, on the letterhead of Les Editions Denöel. 19 rue Amélie, Paris, VII; Bibliothèque Royale, Brussels.

24. Even the German censor in Paris, Gerhard Heller, thought Denöel went too far in his anti-Semitism and "vomiting" over enemies of the Reich. See Gerhard Heller, *Un Allemand à Paris, 1940–1944* (Paris: Editions de Seuil, 1981), 132–33. (Heller's autobiography was certainly self-serving.) Fouché reported that Denöel was one of only two French publishers to go so far as to accept German ownership, or "Aryanization." He became the publisher not only of *Comment reconnaitre le juif*, by Georges Montanden, but also of Hitler's *Discours*. See Pascal Fouché, "L'Edition, 1914–1992," in *Histoire des droites en France*, vol. 2, *Cultures*, ed. Jean-Francois Sirinelli (Paris: Gallimard, 1992), 273–74.

25. Interview with Anne Ipsen, June 30, 1993.

26. Interview with Dominque Rolin, February 2, 1993.

27. ADRP, vol. 2, 282. After Paul's departure from the Agence Dechenne, there remained unsold 6,000 calendars, of the 12,000 he purchased in two orders from the Union of Manual and Intellectual Workers (UTMI), which according to his son, Jan, was inspired by but not literally founded by Henri de Man; interview with Jan de Man, June 4, 1993. The company would lose fifty thousand francs on them (ADPC, vol. 1, 412). De Coster wondered pointedly if "in this circumstance, P. de Man did not wish simply to favor U.T.M.I., in whose creation his father [*sic*] had a role."

28. Interview with Hendrik Woods, March 14, 1998.

29. After this episode, the Slusznys understood that they must leave Brussels and flee into the maquis, where they worked with the Resistance, supplying food to the *"refracteurs,"* rebel outsiders like themselves. Telephone interview with Esther Sluszny, November 15, 1992.

30. Ibid.

31. Although Marceau defended those actions as harmless work in which he had merely continued a job he had held before the war, Paul Aron and Cécile Vanderpelen have shown this was untrue. See "Félicien Marceau, la mémoire et l'histoire," from the Centre histoire de la littérature belge de langue française, ULB, Brussels, author archive. See also Paul Aron et al., *Leurs Occupations: Impact de la Second Guerre mondiale sur la littérature en Belgique* (Brussels: Textyles; CREHSGM, 1997).

32. See *Le Soir (volé)*, March 19, 1942.

33. Interview with Félicien Marceau, October 14, 2002.

34. Ibid.

35. Interview with Frida Vandervelden, July 6, 1991.

36. Interview with Frida Vandervelden, July 16, 1990.

37. For this, he was given credit by Lambrichs, whose scheme it originally was; see Werner Hamacher, Neil Hertz, and Thomas Keenan, eds., *Responses: On Paul de Man's Wartime Journalism* (Lincoln: University of Nebraska Press, 1992), 470–72.

38. Thomas Keenan (one of the three editors of *Responses*) published groundbreaking research in his dense recapitulation of what could be discovered before 1992. See Keenan, "Documents: Public Criticism," in *Responses*, 470–71. Jean Lescure stressed to this writer the use of "de" rather than "du" in the volume's title, indicating its wider grammatical implication.

39. Lescure, who said he was 87 when interviewed, misremembered the volume published in Brussels as the third; interview, June 19, 1998. Lambrichs described the publishing of this volume in a letter to Neil Hertz, March 28, 1988. See *Responses*, 469–71, especially 470.

40. *Messages* was controversial among some on the Left (and attacked, of course, by Colin's journals), but to Lescure, the crucial point among those in the Resistance was whether to hate all Germans or only the Nazis; the poet defended the second position. Paul's review of his journal, he thought, reflected a mind that "took the position of fidelity to non-Nazi civilization." Interview, June 19, 1998.

41. Lambrichs wrote to their mutual friend André Souris that "Lescure would like to read [your notes]. And de Man leaves for Paris Monday the 18th." MSLS, January 14, 1943, n.p.; Musée Littéraire [de Bruxelles], B. R. 5550/144.

42. Several of these writers were a part of the intellectual circle led by Georges Bataille, with whom de Man would later associate himself. Gisèle Sapiro's excellent study has called them "dissidents of Surrealism," who shared with Lescure and one another "interests in the new studies of psychoanalysis, sociology and ethnology," which had taken form in the College of Sociology created earlier by Bataille and others. See Sapiro, *La Guerre des écrivains, 1940–1953* (Paris: Fayard, 1999).

17. ICARUS FALLS

1. He signed his letters at the Toison d'Or as "Administrator-Director"; AM: TdO Case 3245, Information file V, item 48, and documents, vol. 23.

2. AM: TdO, Case 3245, documents, vol. 23. Correspondence [of De Becker] from July 1, 1941; found in his office at *Le Soir*. Rubric D.

> Report to M. R. De Becker about the work of Mr. Paul de Man, appointed by the company as a reader of foreign literature and translator. S/ L. Didier, Brussels, Dec. 4, 1942; Administrator-delegate (executive officer).
>
> . . . On the contrary, in regard to translations, we haven't had reason to find ourselves particularly satisfied. The first books translated by P. de Man, "The Double Visage" of Alverdes, and "Soldier John," of de Pillecyn, received, and properly, laudatory criticism, but the texts that were published are not the ones this translator originally provided.
>
> The latter were unsatisfying, encumbered with linguistic faults and more particularly with Germanisms. They required numerous changes.
>
> "The Spirit of Nations," by Brinckmann [*sic*], which should have been published this summer, is still not ready now. Paul de Man advised us on August 11 that his work was ended and asked at the same time for twice as much payment as we had originally agreed on. We consented, but after having examined the text more closely, it appeared that the latter still needed deep revisions for which we have had to employ another translator. [This book was discussed in *Bulletin de la Toison d'Or*, February 1943, 7–8.] This translator perceived that several chapters were not even translated by P. De Man, which the latter had carefully hidden from us.
>
> As to the book by Leemans, "Political Sociology," this case was still worse. After having announced to us that the work was finished as of August 11 and having requested payment for it, at a rate above that originally agreed on, Paul de Man has not yet sent us his manuscript as of October 20, in spite of our repeated protests.
>
> At that point, the author asked us to find out the facts about the translation, and when we demanded of de Man that he return the text immediately, he let us know that he had sent it directly to Mr. Leemans.
>
> Because of this assertion, we did not concern ourselves further with it, but Mr. Leemans has just advised us that he has never received the translation, and as a result we find ourselves in a ridiculous situation in regard to him.
>
> Paul de Man has roundly insisted that it has been lost in the Post Office. I am, for my part, convinced that there is nothing to this and that the translation was never completely finished. . . .

3. Interview with Patricia de Man, December 19, 1990. After discussing her work with this writer, she contacted colleagues and then asked the book's publisher, W. W. Norton, for title-page credit as translator in the 1992 edition of *Madame Bovary*, which she received. She stressed, however, that her late husband alone had written the notes. He also told both her and David Braybrooke, translator of another manuscript de Man intended to publish, that a translator must be able to write his or her own language well but need not be adept in the language of the source.

4. ADPC, vol. 1, 412, January 20, 1943.

5. See chapter 20 regarding de Man's narrative to the prosecutor postwar, which contained fabrications with respect to important details; Military Auditor,

procès-verbal, July 30, 1946. De Man exculpated himself to the Military Court attached to the War Council in Brussels; AM: TdO, Case 3245.

6. ADRP, vol. 2, 278.

7. Martin Conway, *Collaboration in Belgium: Léon Degrelle and the Rexist Movement 1940–1944* (New Haven: Yale University Press, 1993), 176.

8. Gerhard Weinberg, *A World at Arms: A Global History of World War II* (Cambridge: Cambridge University Press, 1994), 361.

9. ADPC, vol. 2, vol. 1, 412; and ADRP, vol. 2, 282.

10. ADPC, vol. 2, 1, item 413.

11. Ultimately, said Lescure, he had the next volume of *Messages* printed in Switzerland.

12. ADPC, vol. 2, 1, item 414.

13. ADPC, vol. 2, 1, item 415.

14. ADPC, vol. 2, 1, item 416.

15. Sometimes de Man had listed the wrong book entirely, or he might have recorded the right book but his figure for the number purchased would be wrong by from one to three thousand copies. He also omitted some three or four texts that the vending publishers asserted de Man had, in fact, requested.

16. ADPC, vol. 2, item 418. Holograph manuscript, written in ink on stationery: "Paul de MAN/ Boulevard Saint-Michel, 151/ BRUXELLES," n.d. [April 7, 1942, per date stamp of Agence Dechenne].

> *Cher monsieur*
> *Suite à notre entretien, je vous confirm le décision dont je vous ai fait part de cesser ma collaboration à l'Agence Dechenne. Je me trouve, en effet, dans l'obligation de poursuivre certains travaux d'ordre littéraire que mes occupations actuelies [sic] avaient complètement interompus et que je ne puis abandonner. Comme il m'est possible de reprendre un travail qui me laisse la liberté dont j'ai besoin, j'ai dû me résoudre à vous demander l'autorisation d'abandonner mes functions présentes.*

17. ADRP, vol. 2, 287.

18. ADRP, vol. 2, 278, 279.

19. ADRP, vol. 2, 268, 263.

20. ADRP, vol. 2, 280, 282–83: "One finds among them the most collaborationist of publishers and others who are among the most controversial in point of view of patriotism, but to my knowledge (and after a rapid examination of two or three titles), no work that merits being qualified as subversive or able to serve the policy of the enemy. . . . On the other hand, many bad purchases, both in France and Belgium, heavily injure the results of the company during a very long period."

21. ADRP, vol. 2, 279. His expense account gives no dates. But since he sent a letter to the secretary of the Cercle Belge de la librairie, dated August 24, 1942, one can assume August 25, 1942, as a *terminus ad quem* for the trip. The next item by him is dated September 23, 1942, to von Balluseck—so the *terminus a quo* is September 23, 1942. Probably he took his Paris trip during the first two weeks of September 1942, wrote it up shortly thereafter, and would not have purchased stock before the trip.

22. ADRP, vol. 2, 281. It was in this context that he analyzed the review of Fonsny's novel. "Not content to extol books in the French language, for which he

had the sale rights, P. de Man also acted as critic for books published in Flemish, notably 'De Vleeschauwer—Humanistische Kultuur' (Bibliographie XIX, 5)."

23. The piece alludes to literary influences in the eighteenth century, goes on to discuss Bellesort, Brasillach, and Maurras, speaks of the ties between German and French literature, and generalizes about revolutionary eras. These little essays could only have been written by de Man, given the limitations of his colleague.

24. ADRP, vol. 2, 284–86.

25. Other reports give the place of execution as above a bookstore.

26. Interview, October 19, 1992.

18. HIDING IN PLAIN SIGHT

1. "Strahlungen," Ernst Jünger, *Second journal parisien: Journal III, 1943–1945*, trans. Frédéric de Towarnicki and Henri Plard (Paris: Christian Bourgois, 1980).

2. MSLS from Paul de Man to Henri de Man, "Mon cher Rik," Anvers, May 15, 1948, author archive.

3. Henri de Man drove his car down the mountain from Ardez every morning to the post office, crossing a railroad track. He died, as his namesake nephew, Rik, had done, in a collision when his car stopped on the tracks in the path of the oncoming train that arrived every morning at the same time. His young wife (or companion) died with him. His son, Jan, as well as Paul and others, believed his death was a suicide, given Henri's knowledge of the train's schedule and his years of isolation and depression.

4. MSLS from Paul de Man to Marlene de Man[-Flechtheim], November 6, 1945, from Kalmthout.

5. CB, August 2, 1944, copy of marriage certificate of G. Jaeger and G. Stux. This document refers to the divorce of Jaeger and Baraghian on July 1, 1943.

6. General Göring wanted to keep German industry free to produce armaments; as a result, manufacturers of "medical equipment" in particular experienced a "considerable increase" in sales to the Germans. The will to work with the occupant was unequal, but "the common denominator was a desire for business to prosper, for utilitarian aims, and pragmatic reasoning." See Philippe Burrin, *France Under the Germans: Collaboration and Compromise*, trans. Janet Lloyd (New York: New Press, 1997), 236, 229.

7. Interview with Walter Van Glabbeek, September 29, 1990.

8. Interview with Micheline De Braey, July 27, 1994.

9. Interview with Hendrik Woods, March 14, 1998.

10. Interview with Bob De Braey, November 18, 1992.

11. Interview with Micheline De Braey, July 27, 1994.

12. Marlene de Man-Flechtheim said that he gave the "impression" of being happy, repeating and stressing "impression"; interview, September 10, 2000.

13. Interview with Walter Van Glabbeek, June 29, 1990. Henrietta Van Beers married twice, the second time to Jan Buschmann of Antwerp. Her money would be controlled by her son, also named Jan Buschmann. He was Paul's first cousin once removed and some six or seven years younger.

14. At age six or seven, Rik had repeated a casual insult toward Jews, a comment he had picked up at school, and Paul de Man told him never to make such remarks; interview with Hendrik Woods, March 14, 1998. Marlene de Man-Flechtheim commented about the infant Rik's status, "Yvonne was not at all shocked"; interview with Marlene de Man-Flechtheim, September 10, 2000.

15. SAB, TSLS, July 13, 1993.
16. The birth certificate for Paul Hendrik de Man, born November 27, 1944, in Antwerp, was issued November 30, 1944; SAB, information July 13, 1993. Bob De Braey attested to the facts as "godfather," but not in good faith, he said, as the child was the same Henri Hrand Jäger ("Rik") who had been born in Brussels in 1941 (interviews with Bob De Braey, winter-spring 1992–93). That some irregularity occurred is certain, given that the birth certificate states that an "infant was produced and shown to" the recording officer.
17. No such document has been located. Edouard Colinet, one of the old *Cahiers du libre examen* crew, reported the tale of the death certificate emanating from a doctor in Brussels; interview, October 13, 1992. Georges Goriély alluded to a false death certificate having been issued in Paris.
18. Braybrooke described himself as being, in academic terms, "an ordinary language analyst of the British school"; interview, July 18–19, 1999.
19. De Man's philosophical interests did not then exist, according to Braybrooke. Discussing the linguistic and other divisions that marked de Man's life and mind, Braybrooke said, "He told me himself he did arithmetic in Flemish but higher math—calculus and algebra—in French." Later in the United States, Paul de Man forgot his spoken Flemish, according to Patricia de Man.
20. Jan de Man asserted that he himself made no black-market purchases. That was rare self-denial. Anyone who drove a big car—a Studebaker, for example—needed not only money but access to gasoline.
21. Jean Giono was one of three translators of the novel in 1941, the others being Lucien Jacques and Joan Smith.
22. "Sartre rushed into print in a collaborating journal, *Comoedia*, on January 21, 1941, against the advice of Simone de Beauvoir, so great was his eagerness to publish on the work." Annie Cohen-Solal, *Sartre: 1905–1980* (Paris: Gallimard, 1985), 244, cites as her source Michel Contat and Michel Rybalka, *Les Ecrits de Sartre* (Paris: Gallimard, 1970), 634–37.
23. Interview with Walter Van Glabbeek, June 29, 1990. See booklist of Archief en Museum voor het Vlaamse Cultuurleven in Antwerp, where the book is accessible.

19. HERMÈS

1. Interview with Jan de Man, September 18, 1992. In 1947, Jan de Man was released from prison and stayed for a time with his uncle Bob. He wrote his exiled father, Henri, that Bob "doesn't seem to get much pleasure from his son and daughter-in-law who tend to exploit him."
2. His friends and contemporaries stressed this point in discussion, especially Georges Goriély.
3. Interviews with Anne Ipsen, July 4, 1991, and June 30, 1993.
4. Interview with Jan de Man, September 19, 1992.
5. Bob De Braey spent his life in Antwerp as an insurance broker and knew the business world there, including Eeckels.
6. TSLS from Robert de Man and Jan Eeckels to the *procureur* (district attorney) in Antwerp, February 7, 1949, denouncing Paul de Man as guilty of the crimes of swindling and forgery.
7. Among them, they invested BF 675,000. Then in October 1946, Paul and his father almost doubled the capital. Paul had inherited money from his mother's

estate, which had taken years to be settled, but he invested only a little of it. Other investors joined and were named as directors also. In less than a year, the total capital of Hermès rose to BF 1,450,000. This in dollars was $32,952, no small sum at the then-current rate of BF 43.83/$1; Report by F. Grimbers to the court, for trial of Hermès by the Rechtbank van Eerste Aanleg (First Court of Appeal, Criminal Division), Case 3891, first report of March 28, 1950, hereafter Grimbers. Eeckels brought in J. and L. Lebrun, who shared his office. Bob de Man pledged much less, only BF 125,000, but, in fact, he prudently supplied only BF 45,000. Paul himself pledged the same amount, but in the end he placed only BF 25,000 in his own company. Walter Van Glabbeek, who met Paul "dozens of times" during the Kalmthout period, was a friend of both Paul and Jan Buschmann and aware of the loss of money in Hermès; interview with Walter Van Glabbeek, June 29, 1990.

8. Paul was advised by one of the Didier circle, Henri Bauchau, a writer, aesthete, and onetime publisher, who said he considered de Man "brilliant" but had nothing to do with Hermès; interview with Henri Bauchau, June 26, 1998. According to Grimbers, however, Bauchau received BF 5,000 in honoraria.

9. In addition to the Lebruns, other investors included Vladimir Woronoff, a member of a distinguished and very rich Russian family that had immigrated to Belgium in an earlier century. Jan Buschmann contributed the large sum of BF 250,000 in January of 1947 and became a partner.

10. They aimed to raise BF 1,350,000 in a year but started, as was customary, with half that amount, BF 675,000.

11. De Man commissioned Paul Fierens to write a book on Corot. Robert Guiette was supposed to write a book on Berlioz. Three years later, Fierens told the police he had delivered his manuscript, but Hermès never published it, and the writer never saw another franc of the fifteen thousand owed him. Guiette did not submit a manuscript.

12. Bob De Braey reported being in Paul's office and said, "I never saw anyone there. He worked hard on translation. He couldn't live from the [publishing of] works of art"; interview, November 18, 1992.

13. On November 8, 1949, Judges F. Kockx and J. Cornette, of the Rechtbank van Eerste Aanleg, decided to open the Hermès case, no. 3891/180 / 1949.

14. On March 28, 1950, F. Grimbers made his first report.

15. Interview with Anne Ipsen, June 30, 1993.

16. Almost everything that is known about the collapse of the company was reconstructed by court-appointed auditors from the random documents they found in its empty offices, interviews with Paul's father and Jan Eeckels, interviews with vendors or creditors, and by police work. Case 3891 began after Bob de Man was forced by his former friends, the other investors, to denounce his son to the police, for he was titular head of Hermès. Had he not done so, they would have made him party to the crime. After this act, he produced a narrative history of Hermès entitled "Exposé des Evénements" (Explanation of Events), written for the receiver October 11, 1948 (cited hereafter as "Exposé").

17. Several family members told this story, including Bob De Braey and Jan de Man. De Braey reported, "He even went to the servant of my grandfather [Michel De Braey, an architect]. She gave him her life savings—sixty thousand Belgian francs. Filomene. She cared for [both Bob's father and Madeleine]." This servant had lived with and worked for them from the late nineteenth century to around 1960, when she retired to a village, where she died in reduced circumstances. Interview, October 18, 1992.

18. Patricia de Man said that on a secret visit back to Belgium in the early 1960s, her husband "thought" of repaying Filomene, but he could not (perhaps because she had died); interview, October 18, 1992.

19. There is no book listed in any Belgian catalog as emanating from Hermès except for de Beucken's text, which the busy author recycled yet again in the 1950s. The chief librarian of the archives of the Royal Belgian Library and Museum, Frans De Haes, reported the same negative finding.

20. Jean de Beucken, *Vincent Van Gogh: Un Portrait* (Brussels: Hermès, n.d. [printed at J. E. Goossens, S.A.], pp. and 18 plates); interview with David Braybrooke, July 18, 1999. De Beucken must have demanded more than the writers Paul had previously dealt with. They agreed on Paul's normal price of BF 30,000, and the author actually received BF 25,000, but Paul was later charged with swindling him by withholding BF 5,000 from his advance payment, having promised to give that small sum to a creditor of the writer but instead keeping it for himself. Unlike de Man's other writers, de Beucken was not willing to overlook a minor loss, and he was one of those who later sued Hermès. He did not get his money back, but his complaint became one of the counts of abuse of confidence against de Man for which he was ultimately penalized.

21. Approximately three thousand copies of a book referred to by Bob de Man as "Renoir d'Anvers" and "Renoir franc" existed in "stock" in 1949, when Bob wrote his "Exposé." The bemused Bob de Man noted that Paul had also bought and warehoused four hundred kilos of shipping carton.

22. The Swedish publisher was P. A. Norstedt, of Stockholm; the translator was Dr. Hugo Hultenberg. The book was first noted in Werner Hamacher, Neil Hertz and Thomas Keenan, eds., *Responses: On Paul de Man's Wartime Journalism* (Lincoln: University of Nebraska Press, 1992), xxi. De Man could not sell the French version in France, nor the English edition in England. Like many books Paul had bought while at Dechenne, the Haesaerts text was a "nightingale." The National Library of France does not list a copy, although a copy is in the Bibliothèque Royale in Brussels. The Belgian national register of published books does not include it, however, perhaps because it was published in The Hague by a company called Daamen, whose imprint shows it was working in concert with Hermès.

23. Interview with David Braybrooke, July 18, 1999.

24. Patricia de Man said that this was her husband's choice of hotels a year later, in 1948.

25. Interview with Paul Willems, April 26, 1993.

26. Paul agreed to a low price, had nothing in writing, and the other company concealed its intention to go out of business and merge within weeks with the much bigger Harcourt, Brace. The ninety-two-year-old Gerald Gross reported that, as an editor at Reynal & Hitchcock, he had acquired *Renoir: Sculptor* from the "attractive" young Paul de Man, who "came knocking on my door" in 1947; interview, October 21, 2013. In his "Exposé," Bob de Man blamed a weak business climate for the company's bad sales on a weak business climate, but he also acknowledged Paul's "lightness" and lack of business sense.

27. At the end of 1946, Eeckels had already noted that the books did not balance, but he and Bob de Man ignored the problem.

28. For that they would have to assemble the other directors and lay out their losses, a humiliating step they began in September 1948, when a series of angry meetings ensued.

29. He was also found guilty of making false entries in the checkbooks to cover other false entries, and of falsely entering profit and loss amounts, from BF 100,000 to 307,000, in the books.

30. On July 17, 1950, Grimbers had made a second report in responding to a new judge, J. Cornette, who then commissioned another auditor, M. Dielen. Cornette wanted deeper searches into the forged receipts, and he cited a "commission" paid to André Souris "in the guise of an honorarium." Three more justices, Bossyns, De Bee, and De Kepper, all from the commercial court, also dealt with the matter.

20. THE PALACE OF JUSTICE

1. Procès-verbal of Paul de Man, dated July 30, 1946, responding to Roger Vinçotte. Photocopy provided by N. Van Winsens, auditor-general for the Council of War; on July 20, 1993, he told this writer he had the original in a file in his office.

2. "Statement of Facts," Court of Appeal, and AM: *LSv*, "Summary of Charges and Sentences," Council of War, vol. 8, 1946, 1–41, especially 28.

3. This was the policy even of a right-wing daily, *La Nation Belge*, which had welcomed to its columns the "young wolves of the corporatist, Maurrassian right" (Jules Gérard-Libois and José Gotovitch, *L'An 40: La Belgique occupée* [Brussels: CRISP, 1971], 40). The mayor, or *bourgmestre*, was Germain Gallant, tried along with another man for the crime. The Nuremberg War Crimes trials were ongoing and also in the news (*Le Soir*, August 1, 1946; see p. 4).

4. Vinçotte had deposed Didier's assistant, Simone Waslet, only the day before he met with Paul de Man. Military Auditor, Council of War, concerning the trial of the Agence Dechenne (Editions de la Toison d'Or et le Soir), Nr. Not: 4196/46: deposition of witness Simone Waslet [July 29, 1946, 3:30 P.M.].

5. The sentence, like most death penalties, was not carried out, although more people were executed for treason in Belgium than in France.

6. De Man claimed that he voluntarily left *Le Soir (volé)* in December 1942 because he had received a better offer from the Agence Dechenne, and he told George Lambrichs and others the same. De Man also told Vinçotte that he had gotten along famously with his "dear friend and colleague" at the newspaper when they had worked hand in hand on what Vinçotte considered "treasonous" material, but de Man hid why he and De Becker had parted. By then, the publisher of *Le Soir (volé)* was in prison.

7. Joseph Meulepas, secretary of the editorial board from September 1, 1940, until November 9, 1943, was eventually condemned to four years in prison; "Summary of Charges and Sentences, *Le Soir*," Council of War, vol. 8, 1946, 1–41.

8. "I can recall an incident [in Kalmthout, 1945–46, when Rik was six or seven] . . . I told Paul the story, and he . . . acted with horror over this whole incident in a way that was unmistakably in opposition to [the slur]. [He felt] . . . that this is . . . terrible, the implication being that people should not do something like that, behave that way. . . . I construed it as the opposite of anti-Semitism on his part." He thought Paul "was sort of pleasant as a father"; interview with Hendrik Woods, March 14, 1998.

9. Henri de Man, *Après Coup* (Brussels: Editions de la Toison d'Or, 1941), 132–33, 187, passim.

10. A similar though less virulent prejudice prevailed in the United States. Even the

iconically liberal Eleanor Roosevelt was for many years caustic about Jews until her political activities drew her into friendship with many of them. See Blanche Wiesen Cook, *Eleanor Roosevelt*, vol. 2: *1933–1938* (New York: Viking-Penguin, 1999), 315–17. See also Karl A. Schleunes, *The Twisted Road to Auschwitz: Nazi Policy toward German Jews, 1933–1939* (Urbana: University of Illinois Press, 1970; reprint, 1990).

11. See Léon Van Huffel, "Toward a Racial Antisemitism," *Le Soir (volé)*, January 29, 1941, p. 1, and his review of Edmond Picard's *Synthesis of Antisemitism*, February 25, 1941.

12. See also Léon Van Huffel, "Is There a Jewish Race?" *Le Soir (volé)*, February 11, 1941, p. 2.

13. Marc Eemans was a Belgian Surrealist painter and writer who became an active supporter of the campaign against "degenerate art." He had edited the literary journal *Hermès* from 1933–1939 but shut it down and turned further right as a follower of Robert Poulet (brother of the critic Georges and son of an army general) and the right-wing, pacifist, pro-German group he helped to lead. Eemans was not a regular member of the staff of *Le Soir (volé)*, but he received occasional assignments and made at least one contribution to the culture page. When in 1942 De Becker considered de Man for membership in the Association of Belgian Journalists (the AJB), Eemans was not on the preliminary list.

14. Always competitive, de Man, as a youth, had liked the irrationality of Surrealism and undoubtedly knew Eemans's Belgian journal, *Hermès*. It may be relevant that he adopted the same name for his own company, which similarly emphasized art publishing. De Man exculpated himself by pointing the finger at Eemans, now a weaker rival on the newspaper.

15. Jan de Man quoted Paul as having told him that his interrogation had been a "mere . . . pleasant conversation . . . a tap on the wrist."

16. Geert Lernout discusses a debate that compares Holland's greater zeal in prosecuting collaborators, and quotes Wolfgang Holdheim, who wrote that "in Holland in 1945, Paul de Man could indeed have been 'a moral, political, and probably social outcast,' but not in Belgium where in 1944, in the midst of an exceptionally violent repression, Paul de Man's 'crime' did not even make it to court." Luc Herman, Kris Humbeeck, and Geert Lernout, eds., *(Dis)continuities: Essays on Paul de Man* (Amsterdam: Editions Rodopi, 1989), 13.

21. DESPAIR, RAGE, AND THE PURSUIT OF SHADOWS

1. Interview with Patricia de Man, December 19, 1990.

2. Georges was the brother of the talented collaborator and strongly pro-Nazi writer Robert Poulet, who described himself as a royalist; quotation from interview with Peter Hughes, June 28–29, 1991.

3. Jürgen Habermas, "Modernity vs. Postmodernity," *New German Critique* 22 (1981): 3–14; cited by Richard Wolin, "Left Fascism: Georges Bataille and the German Ideology," *Constellations* 2 (1996): 397.

4. Jean-Michel Heimonet, "Bataille, Camus, Baudrillard: Révolte contre l'histoire et contre-terrorisme," paper delivered at the Maison Française, Columbia University, March 26, 2003.

5. MSLS from Paul de Man to Georges Bataille, July 3, 1948, BNF (Paris), NAF collection; discontinued from the catalog for unknown reason. I am grateful to Jeanine Plottel for a copy.

6. BNF (Paris); NAF 15952, documents concerning Georges Bataille. In text folio 38, Bataille proposed eleven axioms that elevate fascism to quasi-religious status— "*Organized* existence as reconstituted by fascism is the closest to God . . . accept crime and perversion as human. . . . Destruction and decomposition are achievements."

7. Bataille is usually referred to as "controversial" in reference to his exploration of sadomasochism. His biographer Michel Surya originally did not accept Bataille's testimony of having been grievously violated and abused by his father; see *Georges Bataille: La Mort à l'oeuvre* (Paris: Libr. Séguier: F. Birr, 1987; new ed., Paris: Gallimard, 1992), 1–34. However, the gifted writer's testimony may be true, and subsequently Surya modified his interpretation. (Bataille reported that he had been kept in a cellar for sexual use by his crippled father, a man whom he and his mother abandoned, Bataille said, on the road—still in his wheelchair— as they fled from the bombardment of Paris during World War I.)

8. See chapter 22.

9. In 1946 Georges Bataille founded the influential journal *Critique*, and he would publish four of de Man's essays between 1953 and 1957. Later, in October 1957 after failing his general examination, Paul would send Harry Levin a copy of his article on Faust (*Critique*, May 1957). In the 1960s he corresponded about potential submissions with Jean Piel, by then *Critique*'s editor. MSS IMEC, MAN, Paul (de), 1966–1969.

10. "We know people in Antwerp and elsewhere" who knew all about "the circumstances in which in 1947 [*sic*—it was actually 1948] PdM obtained permission papers inaccessible to other people to go and study in the USA . . ." M. V. B., "Scholarly Nonsense about Paul de Man," *Pallieterke* (Antwerp), November 10, 1988. Jan de Man said the same; interview, June 28, 1990.

11. Interview with Georges Goriély, June 29, 1990.

12. Georges Bataille, "La notion de déspense," in *Oeuvres Complètes*, vol. 1, *Premiers Ecrits, 1922–1940*, ed. Michel Foucault (Paris: Gallimard, 1970).

22. "BOOKS ARE THE KEYS TO MAGIC KINGDOMS"

1. Motto painted on a wall above the bookstalls of Fourth Avenue; on an opposite wall appeared Archimedes' cry: "Eureka! I have found it!"

2. Ship's manifest, *Ames Victory*, INS.

3. INS.

4. Interview with Patricia de Man, July 10, 1992.

5. For a detailed discussion of Dwight Macdonald, see Michael Wreszin's excellent study, *A Rebel in Defense of Tradition: The Life and Politics of Dwight Macdonald* (New York: Basic Books, 1994). I am grateful to Professor Wreszin for useful discussions. See also Gregory D. Sumner, *Dwight Macdonald and the politics Circle: The Challenge of Cosmopolitan Democracy* (Ithaca, NY: Cornell University Press, 1996), 224. This chapter and the next have benefited greatly from Sumner's work.

6. Dwight Macdonald Papers, MS 730, Manuscripts and Archives, Yale University Library, New Haven, Connecticut.

7. For a general study, see Richard Pells, *Not Like Us: How Europeans Have Loved, Hated, and Transformed American Culture Since World War II* (New York: Basic Books, 1997).

8. In an interview for television, later included in the documentary film *Arguing*

the World, Kazin credited Daniel Bell with this remark. In an interview with Carol Brightman, he attributed it to Norman Podhoretz; see *Writing Dangerously: Mary McCarthy and Her World* (New York: Clarkson Potter, 1992), 319.

9. Interview with Patricia de Man, July 7, 2000.

10. Interview with Geoffrey Hartman, December 5, 1997. The dual tenureships were permitted by the deans of the two universities but were not known to most of de Man's colleagues. Each university was persuaded that the transatlantic linkage was helpful, although each lost two weeks of his services, out of about thirteen, at the beginning and at the end of their semesters. Normally, in the United States, this practice was forbidden and was punished in some cases by dismissal.

11. Interview with Patricia de Man, July 10, 1992.

12. Interview with David Braybrooke, July 18, 1999.

13. Sumner, *Dwight Macdonald and the* politics *Circle*, 10.

14. Interview with Eve Stwertka, June 4, 1999; "*PR* had just then gotten this wonderful angel sponsor [Allan Dowling]. His brother owned Grand Central Station. He was a poet, a fine-looking poet and gentleman. [He] did not work [and was] very rich. Under his sponsorship, *PR* reached its best period. It moved to Times Square, and had an office in the Victoria Theater building . . . opposite the Smoker. At that time, he hired Bowden [Broadwater] [there were four editors] . . . a business manager, and an editorial assistant." (Macdonald subsidized *politics* with his own money and the private income of his wife, Nancy Macdonald, and the magazine, with only about three thousand subscribers, always lost money.)

15. Interview with Eve Stwertka, January 19, 2001.

16. MSLS from Paul de Man to William Phillips, June 22th [*sic*] 1948, 110 E. 61St., NYC, archives of *Partisan Review*, Boston University. See also Paul de Man, *Critical Writings: 1953–1978*, ed. and with an introduction by Lindsay Waters (Minneapolis: University of Minnesota Press, 1989), xii.

17. TSLS from Edith Kurzweil (editor, *Partisan Review*) to the author, May 10, 1999, paraphrasing William Phillips's response to my written question.

18. The French issue of *Partisan Review* appeared in 1946 (vol. 13, no. 2: 143–265) and was edited by William Barrett.

19. BNF, NAF Papiers Georges Bataille #526, 1584, July 3, 1948. "Je tiens à vous dire le grand bonheur que j'ai eu de vous rencontrer à Anvers quelques jours avant mon depart et d'emporter ainsi l'impression toute fraîche d'une manière d'être et de penser que vous représentez— . . . Je vois plus que jamais à la possibilité et à la nécessité de vous voir publié ici et je pense avoir les moyens qu'il faut (relations, etc.) pour que cela se fasse dans les meilleurs conditions— financièrement et du point de vue influence et retentissement." See also Paul de Man, *Critical Writings: 1953–1978*, ed. and introduction by Lindsay Waters (Minneapolis: University of Minnesota Press, 1989), lxiv, which printed the manuscript in 1989 but gives "peux avoir" for "pense avoir." Waters credits Alan Stoekl for discovering the letter.

20. Tony Judt, *Past Imperfect: French Intellectuals, 1944–1956* (Berkeley: University of California Press, 1992), 75–98; Raymond Aron: *Memoirs: Fifty Years of Political Reflection*, trans. G. Holoch (New York: Holmes & Meier, 1990), 65–67.

21. BNF (Paris), NAF 15952, documents concerning Georges Bataille. See also Suzanne Guerlac, *Literary Polemics: Bataille, Sartre, Valéry, Breton* (Palo Alto: Stanford University Press, 1997). The French Left was split in multiple ways on

a spectrum between the center-left and the Communists, and in this very small world, it was virtually impossible to avoid internecine attacks.

22. Dorothy Kauffman, "The Story of Two Women: Dominique and Edith Thomas," *Signs* 23, no. 14 (1998): 883, n. 3; see also Geraldine Bedell, "I Wrote the Story of O," *The Observer*, July 25, 2004.

23. Bataille was a founder of the "College of Sociology" in Paris in the late thirties, when sociology was a new and cutting-edge subject, and one could read and debate with friends and declare oneself a sociologist, as Henri de Man had made himself a professor of psychology.

24. Georges Bataille, "A Propos de récits d'habitants d'Hiroshima," *Critique: Revue générale des publications françaises et étrangères* 2, no. 8–9 (1947): 126–40.

25. Interview with Patricia de Man, July 17, 2002.

26. He added that he intended to send some articles to his New York agent and offered Macdonald his further work; MSLS from Georges Bataille to Dwight Macdonald, July 31, 1948, written from Vézelay on *Critique* letterhead at Calmann-Lévy; Yale, MS 730, box 12, folder 300.

27. BNF, Georges Bataille, Letters Received, 15854, #529, TSLS, September 14, 1948, on *politics* letterhead. One can assume that Bataille intended Paul de Man to benefit, knowing his impoverished state.

28. It is described by Michael C. D. Macdonald, Dwight's son, in his detailed, unpublished memoir, "My Father," author archive.

23. THE RADICAL GENTRY

1. Carol Brightman, *Writing Dangerously: Mary McCarthy and Her World* (New York: Clarkson Potter, 1992), 143; Gregory D. Sumner, *Dwight Macdonald and the politics Circle: The Challenge of Cosmopolitan Democracy* (Ithaca, NY: Cornell University Press, 1996), 7.

2. There, in order to be able to face the important man to whose desires she was preparing to yield, she began a memorable drunk, from which she awoke next morning in a strange hotel room, drawing a blank on the preceding events. (She awoke in fact in the presence of another woman editor.) See Brightman, *Writing Dangerously*, 131–33.

3. Interview with Patricia de Man, December 19, 1990.

4. Lionel Abel, *The Intellectual Follies: A Memoir of the Literary Venture in New York and Paris* (New York: W. W. Norton, 1984), 210–16.

5. The Downtown Community School believed, like many progressive institutions, that children left to their own devices in an unstructured social setting would eventually develop inner controls without adult discipline. Some did; others did not, and the atmosphere was seldom tranquil. Patrick Dennis, the pseudonym of Edward Everett Tanner III, author of the supposedly fictional, very popular novel *Auntie Mame* (New York: Vanguard Press, 1955), probably did not exaggerate the atmosphere of heady freedom at his real-life school.

6. In his campaign against the girl named Miriam Isaacs, the college student added, "For I dislike rather violently the Jews as a race." He also was contemptuous of "niggers," the Irish, and others in this early stage of his life at Exeter and Yale. See Michael Wreszin, *A Rebel in Defense of Tradition: The Life and Politics of Dwight Macdonald* (New York: Basic Books, 1994), 10.

7. Wreszin, *A Rebel in Defense of Tradition*, 46.

8. William Barrett, *The Truants: Adventures Among the Intellectuals* (New York: Anchor/Doubleday, 1982), 12–13.

9. Wreszin, *A Rebel in Defense of Tradition*, 158, citing Jean Malaquais's letter to *politics*, September 1945, 283–84.

10. "That was why Gide had a very deep influence on our generation. *L'Immoraliste*. The man who has the courage to liberate himself [from] family ties or *ses liens sentimentaux*. Paul read Gide and, yes, I think he loved him." Interview with Frida Vandervelden, July 8, 1991.

11. Edmund Wilson, "The Literary Consequences of the Crash," in *The Shores of Light: A Literary Chronicle of the Twenties and Thirties* (New York: Farrar, Straus and Young, 1952), 498–99, cited in Wreszin, A *Rebel in Defense of Tradition*, 28.

12. When McCarthy was interviewed in 1984, she described her politics from the 1950s and onward as "left of *The Nation*" and not as "middle of the road" as others had said. Carol Brightman, "Mary, Still Contrary," in *Conversations with Mary McCarthy*, ed. Carol Gelderman (Jackson: University Press of Mississippi, 1991), 234–35.

13. Her parents having died in the flu epidemic of 1918, McCarthy was raised by a successful Presbyterian lawyer who had married a wealthy Jewish heiress. Stwertka recognized the ugliness of the prejudice Mary had faced in college: "She tried to conceal her Jewishness by any means possible. There was great snobbery there. At Vassar, it was a class issue as well." Interview with Eve Stwertka, June 4, 1999.

14. Interview with David Braybrooke, July 18, 1999.

15. Paul's widow, Patricia, said, "Paul would say, 'Bataille said this, and Bataille said that,' and his audience was impressed."

16. *Sumner, Dwight MacDonald and the* politics *Circle*, 20.

17. Emerson avoided imitation, but he twice traveled extensively abroad, profiting intellectually but also putting himself on guard. See Evelyn Barish, *Emerson In Italy* (New York: Henry Holt, 1989), photographs by Evelyn Hofer, passim, and *Emerson: The Roots of Prophecy* (Princeton: Princeton University Press, 1989), 229–49.

18. Hardwick's dating of this event is incorrect. McCarthy followed her husband-to-be, at his suggestion, to France in the summer of 1946; VC.

19. Interview with Elizabeth Hardwick, January 27, 1998.

20. James Atlas, *Delmore Schwartz: The Life of an American Poet* (New York: Farrar, Straus and Giroux, 1977), 123. Others had to wait. Mary McCarthy's trip in 1946 was a brief summer visit. Alfred Kazin got to England during the war, when he served as a private in the army. Phillips first arrived in Paris in 1949, when he was in his forties. Lionel Abel, although a confirmed Francophile, had gotten there only a year or two earlier.

21. Barrett, *The Truants*, 29.

22. McCarthy's translation was published in the November 1945 issue of *politics*; see Brightman, *Writing Dangerously*, 276–78. Of them all, only Dwight Macdonald seems to have had the cash actually to have crossed the ocean. He spent six weeks in Italy on his wedding trip in the early 1930s. He did not, however, much like travel, and he did not go back until the 1950s.

23. Chiaromonte had been a member of Malraux's squadron, and the French writer modeled the character of Scali, the Italian philosophical idealist and warplane navigator in *Man's Hope*, directly on him.

24. Herbert Lottman, *Albert Camus: A Biography* (Corte Madera, CA: Gingko Press, 1997), 250–51.

25. Brightman, "Mary, Still Contrary," 249, 242.

26. Ibid.

27. The most detailed discussion of EAG appears in Sumner, *Dwight Macdonald and the* politics *Circle*, 192–214. See also Wreszin, *A Rebel in Defense of Tradition*, 214–15.

28. Sumner, *Dwight Macdonald and the* politics *Circle*, 206–7.

29. Yale, box 10, folder 214.

30. "We all condemn Stalinism," Macdonald continued, "and most of us believe it to be 'the main enemy' in Europe today; but some of us—Hook and the *PR* editors notably—put more emphasis on fighting Stalinism and less on more general matters (such as the war issue and socialism) than others do (notably Mary and myself)." TL from Dwight Macdonald to Albert Camus, October 21, 1948, Yale, box 10, folder 214.

31. Gerald Gross (see chapter 19, n. 26) said that in 1948 he was present at a party of Macdonald's when the two men discussed Henri de Man; interview, October 21, 2013.

24. MAKING FRIENDS

1. Interview with Michael C. D. Macdonald, November 20, 2000.

2. The letter from Mary McCarthy to Artine Artinian (January 23, 1951) describing her reaction against Paul de Man was first published in large part by David Lehman in his article "Paul de Man: The Plot Thickens," *New York Times Book Review*, May 24, 1992, and as the preface to Lehman, *Signs of the Times: Deconstruction and the Fall of Paul de Man*, 2nd ed. (New York: Simon & Schuster, 1992). Artinian contacted Lehman and offered him McCarthy's letter, but he stressed, "only after Lehman's book and many critical articles had already appeared." Artinian had not wished to attack McCarthy's reputation by printing this link to Paul de Man. Interview with Artine Artinian, April 2, 1998. TSLS author archive.

3. Norman Mailer, quoted by Michael C. D. Macdonald, "My Father, Dwight," unpublished memoir, 32, copy, author archive.

4. Joseph Dorman, *Arguing the World: The New York Intellectuals in Their Own Words* (New York: Free Press, 2000), 101.

5. Ibid., 70.

6. Michael C. D. Macdonald, "My Father, Dwight," 33.

7. Mary McCarthy described her thus, thinking that "she looked like Katharine Cornell"; see McCarthy, *Intellectual Memoirs: New York, 1936–1938* (New York: Harcourt Brace Jovanovich, 1992), 73.

8. Dorman, *Arguing the World*, 102.

9. Interview with Margaret Shafer, December 9, 1997.

10. McCarthy admitted her own use of sex when she criticized Simone de Beauvoir as a mere hanger-on of Jean-Paul Sartre: "How dare she talk about injustice to women when she has put herself on the map solely by attaching herself to Sartre, *solely*. . . . She made it through her sex by attaching herself to this man, and many others of us have made it through our sex; but it's most ungrateful in her case [laughing]," Carol Brightman, "Mary, Still Contrary," in *Conversations with Mary McCarthy*, ed. Carol Gelderman (Jackson: University Press of Mississippi, 1991), 246.

11. Before they met, Bowden had had an affair with a female editor [Katharine White] at *The New Yorker*, but Brightman remarks that his "latent homosexuality was known to at least some of their friends," and she quotes many sources, including Hannah Arendt, Mary Meigs, and Daphne Hellman. Their consensus was that Mary repressed the information, and her biographer wrote that "The sheen of heterosexual life . . . appeared relatively unruffled by anything other than a few extramarital affairs, mostly Mary's"; Carol Brightman, *Writing Dangerously: Mary McCarthy and Her World* (New York: Clarkson Potter, 1992), 434, 435, 445, 446. See also Frances Kiernan, *Seeing Mary Plain: A Life of Mary McCarthy* (W. W. Norton, 2000), 243.

12. Interview with Barbara Dupee, May 10, 1999.

13. At age thirteen, she said, she had willingly given her virginity to a man of twenty-six in the seat of his Marmion roadster; McCarthy, *Intellectual Memoirs*, 62; Brightman, *Writing Dangerously*, 55–60; Carol Brightman, ed., *Between Friends: The Correspondence of Hannah Arendt and Mary McCarthy: 1949–1975* (New York: Harcourt Brace, 1995), 127, citing *Interview*, February 1988.

14. Interview with Patricia de Man, July 17, 2002.

15. Interview with Eve Stwertka, June 4, 1999.

16. Interview with Margo Viscusi, January 26, 2001.

17. Brightman, *Writing Dangerously*, 287.

18. Interview with Reuel Wilson, March 13, 2001.

19. McCarthy had numerous affairs with Jewish men, but she did not marry them, identifying herself instead with her Protestant grandfather Preston. Stwertka recalled that "Fred Dupee once said in my hearing that 'Everybody is anti-Semitic' "; interview, June 4, 1999.

20. Eve had the job at *Partisan Review*, an ill-paid one previously held by Broadwater, and arranged by McCarthy in each case.

21. Letter from Mary McCarthy to Artine Artinian, January 21, 1951: "Eve Gassler [Stwertka's maiden name] interestingly enough, was the first person to point out a discrepancy about him. I must write her . . . that her misgivings were founded," AA.

22. Interview with Eve Stwertka, June 4, 1999.

23. A strong leftist like her brother Selden, she was devoted to many causes and was de facto the publisher of *politics*, which she personally collated and mailed—no doubt including the copy Braybrooke had given Paul de Man in Antwerp; interview with Michael Macdonald, November 20, 2000.

24. Camus, although he was already overemployed as an editor at Gallimard and also had a public role to fill as a distinguished writer and Nobel laureate in Paris, strangely wrote a very enthusiastic "Yes" to Macdonald's idea of a transatlantic journal on October 6, 1948. Letter from Albert Camus to Dwight Macdonald, October 6, 1948, Yale. See Gregory D. Sumner, *Dwight Macdonald and the politics Circle: The Challenge of Cosmopolitan Democracy* (Ithaca, NY: Cornell University Press, 1996), 192–207 and Michael Wreszin, *A Rebel in Defense of Tradition: The Life and Politics of Dwight Macdonald* (New York: Basic Books, 1994), 191–210, for excellent discussions of this period in Macdonald's career; TL from Dwight Macdonald to Albert Camus, October 21, 1948, Yale, box 10, folder 244; Sumner, 209–11.

25. The collapse came when Macdonald learned only indirectly that Garry Davis had become internationally notorious when he sat down on the steps of the American embassy in Paris and renounced his citizenship, making himself a

"citizen of the world," to protest American foreign policy. The French Left was delighted, official America was appalled, but Macdonald was furious, not at Davis but at Camus's failure to alert him. See Sumner, *Dwight Macdonald and the politics Circle*, 14.

26. Interview with David Braybrooke, July 18, 1999.

27. MSLS from Paul de Man to "Mary and Broadwater," July 11, 1949; VC. The date of the purchase appears in the archives of the town clerk, Portsmouth, RI, Grantee Index: 1647–1949, book 42, p. 258.

28. In France, Gallimard had long published the *Nouvelle Revue Française* (NRF), and Georges Lambrichs was now overseeing the prestigious *Critique* at his post at the avant-garde publisher, Editions de Minuit. Barney Rosset would later do something like that in the United States in the 1950s with the *Evergreen Review* and Grove Press, but that was exceptional.

29. TSLS from Paul de Man to Dwight Macdonald, April 18, 1949, Yale, box 33, file 808. I am grateful to the late Michael Wieszin, biographer of Macdonald, for providing a copy of this letter from the Yale University Macdonald Papers, cited above.

30. De Man denied "thinking a moment of Sidney Phillips' plans in relation to this; his intentions and ambitions are incompatible with this project and I see no possibility of contact between you two. Personally I would prefer this alternative as being more useful, more alive and altogether more rewarding than the rather dull, semi-technical line which Phillips wants to develop." Sidney Phillips had "started a publishing house called Criterion Books," according to William Phillips (MSLS from Edith Kurzweil to the author, June 4, 1999). This was confirmed by Jenny Van Horn Greenberg, whose late husband, Clement Greenberg, had been a friend of Sidney Phillips; interview, July 22, 1999.

31. Interview with Hendrick Woods, March 13, 1998.

32. MSLS from Paul de Man to Dwight Macdonald, April 9, 1949, 20 Jane Street. Which book by Koestler he meant to write an essay about is not clear. *Darkness at Noon*, Koestler's most famous work, had been published in 1941 in the United States, and it is unlikely that Macdonald would have encouraged de Man to comment on a book published so far back. In 1943, Koestler had brought out *Arrival and Departure*, and he had published a well-known essay in the *New York Times*; see Sumner, *Dwight Macdonald and the politics Circle*, 15. Both Koestler's political "oasis psychology" and his sexual predations were held against him; see Sumner, 14, and Brightman, quoting McCarthy, *Writing Dangerously*, p. 301.

33. See André Schiffrin, *The Business of Books: How Conglomerates Took Over Publishing and Changed the Way We Read* (New York: Verson, 2000), in which Schiffrin deals with his father's experience.

25. RECOMMENDED BY MARY

1. TSLS from Mary McCarthy to Artine Artinian, June 9, 1949, author archive. See chapter 24, n. 2 , above.

2. De Man had visited Braybrooke in April 1949; later, Braybrooke guessed that de Man might merely have met some of his colleagues; e-mail to author, December 1, 1999.

3. CV, late summer 1949 (dated by address, 255 East 72nd Street) but probably the same as the one McCarthy sent to Artinian in June 1949; BC.

4. The University of Ghent was founded in 1817. Jan Van Beers was born in 1821 and died in 1888.

5. Interview with Patricia de Man, June 1, 2000.

6. Interview with Margo Viscusi, January 26, 2001.

7. MSLS from Mary McCarthy to Elizabeth Hardwick, July 20, 1949. RL, 1755.

8. MSLS from Paul de Man to "Mary and Broadwater," July 11, 1949, VC.

9. When McCarthy later began her gradual move to Europe, they sold the house in 1952 and lost a good deal of money. The property was purchased for sixteen thousand dollars on June 15, 1949, by Bowden Broadwater and sold by him "et ux" (and wife) on October 10, 1952, for thirteen thousand. Broadwater, sad to leave it, retained possession of the "dolphin weather vane"; MSLS from Mary McCarthy to Elizabeth Hardwick, July 20 and August 22, 1949, RL, 1755, 1756; Grantee Index, 1647–1949 and Record of Sales, book 44, p. 107, archives of the town clerk, Portsmouth, RI.

10. Interview with Margaret Shafer, December 9, 1997, and telephone interview with Bowden Broadwater, January 11, 1998.

11. Telephone interview with Bowden Broadwater, January 11, 1998.

12. MSL from Paul de Man to Mary McCarthy, August 13, 1949, VC, f. 344.17. The letter is unsigned and breaks off after leaf 5. I am grateful to the executors of the Mary McCarthy Trust for sharing this text with me.

13. Interview with Patricia de Man, July 7, 2000.

14. Interview with Patricia de Man, June 1, 2000.

15. Interview with Eve Stwertka, June 6, 1999.

16. Frances Kiernan, *Seeing Mary Plain: A Life of Mary McCarthy* (New York: W. W. Norton, 2000), 95.

17. Interview with Reuel Wilson, March 13, 2001.

18. "Broadwater was cooking and cleaning and doing all the work around the place. [Paul] said that they would complain when [her] son came back from the Wilsons about how [Reuel's] clothes were torn and dirty"; interview with Patricia de Man, June 1, 2000.

19. Interview with Michael Macdonald, November 20, 2000.

20. De Man, his widow recalled, didn't like the idea of nude bathing, but he would have complied; interview with Patricia de Man, July 2, 1992.

21. The apartment belonged to Oscar Nitzschke, father of Riton Nitzschke. It was near Second Avenue, in what was then a modest district of artisanal shops and dealers in secondhand furnishings.

22. The newly married Robert Lowells had taken a house nearby, but the poet had suffered a violent mental breakdown and was at the Payne Whitney Clinic in New York.

23. MSLS from Mary McCarthy to Elizabeth Hardwick, September 23, 1949, RL, 1757.

24. Paul de Man to Artine Artinian, author archive.

25. BC.

26. He mentioned a trip to New York in 1946 to arrange "joint publication ventures with his European firms and Reynal & Hitchcock, as well as Harcourt, Brace."

27. Interview with Jérôme Lindon, June 28, 1998.

28. His literary forebear, Flaubert's Frédéric Moreau, had also imagined that he would write a "History of Aesthetics."

29. Artinian affirmed his arrangement in an interview, April 2, 1998. Top professors earned only $4,500 at Bard. In early October, the Literature Section met de Man and gave him its enthusiastic endorsement and on Tuesday, October 4, Fuller wrote to engage his services; BC.

30. Kiernan, *Seeing Mary Plain*, 23, and VC.

31. Interview with Artine Artinian, April 2, 1998; interview with Margaret Shafer, December 1997.

32. For excellent discussions, see Gregory D. Sumner, *Dwight Macdonald and the politics Circle: The Challenge of Cosmopolitan Democracy* (Ithaca, NY: Cornell University Press, 1996), 212–14; Carol Brightman, *Writing Dangerously: Mary McCarthy and Her World* (New York: Clarkson Potter, 1992), 312–17; Kiernan, *Seeing Mary Plain*, 300, 304, 312–13.

33. Brightman, *Writing Dangerously*, 313.

34. In the summer of 1948, she had felt guilty for letting down Chiaromonte by not writing him after a separation he had initiated by returning to Europe; see Kiernan, *Seeing Mary Plain*, 295–96.

35. Kiernan, *Seeing Mary Plain*, 323.

36. Ibid.

37. MSLS from Mary McCarthy to Bowden Broadwater, October 18, 1949, VC, box 353.14.

38. See Pierre Drieu La Rochelle, "Hemingway," in *Sur les écrivains*, 2nd ed., ed. Frédéric Grover (Paris: Gallimard, 1982), 108; see also his *Journal: 1938–1945*, ed. Julien Hervier (Paris: Gallimard, 1992).

39. "Obviously, one cannot speak with comprehension about this present <american> literature without referring to the general crisis of the <american> intellectual, as dealt with in your novel. This oasis is a necessary explanation for the prevailing mediocrity. For the sake of the judgment of american writing on the Continent, it seems more fair to try to describe this crisis, to explain what a serious writer here has to surmount (not commercial pressure, but the pressure of a certain rigidity of convictions which does not tolerate the inherent insecurity of real invention), rather than to provide the worst examples of <american> naturalism as curious specimens of primitivism." MSLS from Paul de Man to Mary McCarthy and Bowden Broadwater, August 13, 1949, VC, box 344.17.

40. "I couldn't say anything about a man without him leaping [to a negative stance]—and the . . . his motive was jealousy. I think he felt that our bond was very tight [and that] anything that might at[tack] it or throw some [shadow] on it [would be threatening]"; interview with Patricia de Man, July 7, 2000.

26. FINDING PAT

1. Married three times, twice to the same man, Charles Woods, who was also unpredictable, Lucy could be "volatile, bad-tempered, and given to hysterics"; interviews with Patricia de Man, December 29, 1990, and February 9, 1991.

2. Ibid.

3. Interview with Patricia de Man, June 1, 2000.

4. His unbounded competitiveness was epitomized to Patricia by the first time he played baseball, when his son Rik was visiting in 1950. Patsy was fielding at first base, Paul was at bat—and literally ran her down, knocking her off her feet. She thought it was funny, but since she was pregnant, she didn't play baseball with him again. Interview, December 19, 1990.

5. MSSLS from Paul de Man to Artine Artinian, November 3 and November 16, 1949, AA.

6. Interview with Patricia de Man, July 22, 2003.

7. "He was already in the States and because I had to come and stay and he had to

show me to Peggy Guggenheim and the other one, who was Mary McCarthy, I had to be very well dressed, very chic"; interview with Anne Ipsen, June 30, 1993.

8. Letter from Mary McCarthy to Dwight Macdonald, November 20, 1949, Yale, box 31, f. 779.

9. MSLS from Mary McCarthy to Elizabeth Hardwick, December 13, 1949, Harvard University, RL, III, 1758.

10. Interview with Patricia de Man, June 1, 2000.

11. Probably a reference to Paul de Man's essay on Koestler. There is no evidence that de Man placed the essay for publication. MSL from Paul de Man to Dwight Macdonald, December 5, 1949, Yale, box 33, folder 808.

12. "He was insouciant. That was his great strength. I just had the feeling that people would break themselves on that [on his strong ego]"; interview with Patricia de Man, December 19, 1990.

13. As a friend of Archibald MacLeish, the chief librarian, who would come under fire from Senator Joseph McCarthy, Kelley, too, would be hounded from his job and would leave voluntarily to live in France.

14. In the 1970s, when de Man was already prominent, Lucy Woods began sending the couple "bits of stock" in companies she owned; interview with Patricia de Man, June 1, 2000.

15. Frederick "Fritz" and Margaret Shafer had been part of the leading circle of Bard's younger group of faculty. Margaret, who was a poet and junior in the group, adored and was "awestruck" by Mary's wit, looks, and style; interview with Margaret Shafer, December 9, 1997.

16. MSL from Mary McCarthy to Artine Artinian, January 23, 1951. See chapter 24, n. 2.

17. A psychoanalyst told her that she had made it her business to leave the men in her life so that they could not abandon her first, as her parents had done. See Mary McCarthy, *Intellectual Memoirs: New York, 1936–1938* (New York: Harcourt Brace Jovanovich, 1992), 38.

18. Letter from Mary McCarthy to Artine Artinian, January 23, 1951.

19. Interview with Richard Rand, August 28, 1999.

20. The issue involved some seventeen documents: McCarthy wrote nine extant letters concerning the matter, plus one whose existence is implied by her own reference; Ortwin de Graef wrote four letters to her, plus another hypothecated by reference. She received one actual and one hypothecated letter from Michael Wreszin. In addition, she made inquiries of Nancy Rodman Macdonald, Andy Dupee, Eve Stwertka, and Elizabeth Hardwick. Copies of manuscripts from Artine Artinian, Ortwin de Graef, Michael Wreszin, VC; Yale; and interviews with above subjects.

21. "I said to Mary, 'I think I should take this down,'" Hardwick said, referring to their conversation, "and we thought we would. She thought he was a very shady character and not because of what had been found out about his wife." Interview with Elizabeth Hardwick, January 27, 1998.

22. De Man was groundlessly jealous, and comically so—for example, he derided her for admiring a picture of a male model in a magazine. He assumed she felt the same about him. Interview with Patricia de Man, June 1, 2000.

23. Interview, June 1, 2000.

24. Interview with Margo Viscusi, January 26, 2001.

25. She cited Mary's imperfect figure ("wide hips") as the obstacle. Interview, January 19, 2001.

26. Braybrooke had encountered McCarthy "when I was younger and much better-looking" at the Yale Faculty Club and had felt "from across the room" the pull of her attraction and interest. Interview with David Braybrooke, July 18, 1999.

27. Interview with Richard Rand, August 28, 1999.

28. Frances Kiernan, *Seeing Mary Plain: A Life of Mary McCarthy* (New York: W. W. Norton, 2000), 104.

27. BARD

1. On its banks still grow the "trees, vines, flowers and berries" that early explorers could smell from their ships far out at sea. See Reamer Kline, *Education for the Common Good: A History of Bard College—the First 100 Years (1860–1960)* (Annandale-on-Hudson, NY: Bard College, 1982), 2, 3.

2. Ibid.

3. The Vanderbilt estate in Hyde Park, with its long vista down to the Hudson below, may have been Wharton's model for Bellomont.

4. *Rhinebeck Gazette*, August 17, 1950.

5. Kline, *Education for the Common Good*, 34–35; interview with Eve Stwertka, June 4, 1999.

6. Richard Amero, "Jeans and the Jane," *The Bardian* 1.8, April 1949.

7. *Eugenio Montale, Collected Poems: 1920–1954*, ed, and trans. Jonathan Galassi (New York: Farrar, Straus and Giroux, 1990), 484.

8. MSLS from Paul de Man to Edward Fuller, October 15, 1949, BC.

9. Frances Kiernan, *Seeing Mary Plain: A Life of Mary McCarthy* (New York: W. W. Norton, 2000), 242.

10. MSLS from Paul de Man to Edward Fuller, March 25, 1950, BC.

11. He was later to prove vulnerable on this score, both at Harvard and elsewhere.

12. Interview with Peter Brooks, September 18, 2000.

13. R.S.S. "Mr. Paul Deman, Interview," and Debi Sussman, "He Evaluates Surrealism," *The Bardian*, December 10, 1949.

14. Interview with Patricia de Man, December 19, 1990.

15. Two of this writer's senior professors had married students at the college she attended. One wife, by then white-haired, still attended her eminent husband's lectures—and took notes. College women in the era before contraception was easily accessible were not expected to be—and often were not—sexually active, or to provide sexual favors to the men they dated, and if they did so without intending to marry, this was generally concealed. Falling in love with instructors or having a crush was normal, and not all faculty-student contacts were exploitative.

16. Interview with Ted and Renée Weiss, May 15, 1991.

17. Weiss had studied at Columbia with Lionel Trilling, the great exponent of the "liberal imagination," which had become a central tenet for the humanism then dominant in the United States. Norman Podhoretz, another student, wrote that Trilling had made Julien Sorel of *The Red and the Black* the prototype of what Trilling called the ambitious "Young Man from the Provinces," a theme much discussed in college work throughout the 1950s; see Podhoretz, *Ex-Friends* (New York: Free Press, 1999), 84–85.

18. Sussman, "He Evaluates Surrealism." This lecture evidently expressed the ideas of the meditated but unpublished essays he claimed in his résumé to have already published: "The Crisis of Naturalism in the American Novel" and "Sartre's Literary Motives," both supposedly published in *Critique*.

19. Part of de Man's handwritten list of publications that he submitted to Bard read "January 1948 Mobiles littéraires (a reply to J. P. Sartre) CRITIQUE [illegible] PARIS January 1948"; BC.
20. Interview with Ted and Renée Weiss, May 15, 1991.

28. "LIES, AND LIES, AND LIES"

1. Interview with Anne Ipsen, July 4, 1991; interview with Nellie De Ligne-Blockx, October 19, 1992.
2. Her oldest son, Rik, insisted that they were indeed married. Interview with Hendrik Woods, March 14, 1998.
3. Ibid.
4. Ibid.
5. He specified that in the coming year de Man must be willing to serve on faculty committees and that his pension benefits would begin; TLSC from Edward Fuller to Paul de Man, March 22, 1950, BC.
6. Letters from Bard about the drama reached New York, and the widow of Fred Dupee, Barbara ("Andy") Dupee, remembered that "Irma [Brandeis] said de Man's wife came and they divided up the children on the lawn (across from the chapel)"; interview, May 10, 1999.
7. Interview with Anne Ipsen, July 4, 1991.
8. Interview with Hendrik Woods, March 14, 1998.
9. Interview with Anne Ipsen, July 4, 1991.
10. *Crisis* was the term de Man used regarding the "State of the American Novel" in an article he purported, in 1949, to have published in *Critique*. It was also Sartre's failure to "recapture the quality of an inner crisis" that marred his autobiography, *The Words*, de Man wrote when he reviewed it in 1964; see "Sartre's Confessions," *New York Review of Books*, November 5, 1964, 13.
11. Interview with Patricia de Man, February 1, 1990.
12. Pat reported, "The first divorce was [invalid because of a] technicality. [We were] married in June of that year, '50. [The] first divorce was in Arkansas, with her [Anne's] consent in 1950 or [the] end of '49. He had to go to Arkansas—they were allowing it—and I think it was declared illegal." I am indebted to Professor Toni Clarke of the Department of Family Law, University of Arkansas at Little Rock, for pointing out that Patricia de Man's use of the term *illegal* is not accurate. A divorce can only become "illegal" once it has been granted and then successfully challenged, as by a defendant living in another state.
13. *Carlson v. Carlson*, 198 Ark. 231, 128 S.W. 2d, 242; *Cassen v. Cassen*, 211 Ark. 201 S.W. 2d, 585.
14. In fact, none of Arkansas's divorce laws were changed between 1947 and 1953. The Arkansas statutes had only recently been revised, and a new compilation was published in 1947. The next Session Law regarding divorce was not passed until 1953.
15. This writer was unable to discover documents relevant to this marriage either in Yonkers or White Plains, cities where Patricia De Man believed the civil ceremony may have taken place; a search of the New York State records also yielded no results.
16. Interview with Patricia de Man, July 7, 2000.
17. He lived in Washington and later put himself through college; interview with Hendrik Woods, March 14, 1998.

18. A colleague, Burt Pike, took a puzzling message from de Man's "son," of whom he had never heard. Rik Woods reported that at age fifteen he had telephoned his father at Cornell from Canada; interview, March 14, 1998.

19. Rik's mother demanded that he send her "*colis*"—packages of goods from the States, a request the child knew he could not meet; he recognized it as a way to "keep her hooks in him." Interview, March 14, 1998.

20. A colleague, Richard Poirier, who liked Paul and visited the family in Switzerland in the 1960s, thought him "unloving and unfriendly" toward his fourth son, the child he had with Pat in 1950. De Man "was very tough. He was . . . I wouldn't say he was brutal, but very, very unloving and unfriendly." Interview, December 11, 2001.

21. Interview with Patricia de Man, June 1, 2000.

29. BAD WEATHER

1. *Rhinebeck Gazette*, November 30, 1950 (Thursday), refers to the storm of Saturday—that is, November 25, 1950. "Storm Fells Trees . . . Electric Power Suspension Greatest Hardship . . . Wind and Rain: 'Land Hurricane.' . . . Saturday's high wind and driven rain has been called the hardest storm to hit this area in many years."

2. Interview with Patricia de Man, December 29, 1990.

3. Author archive.

4. "Some took a dislike [to Paul] . . . because he hit their amour propre. That became better under my tutelage to some extent. I'd say it was 'a bad habit, not doing you any good. Some of these people are more hurt than you realize, and some of the trouble [after the birth of their son] coming from that.' Paul's jokes were less witty in the early days, and harsher." Interview with Patricia de Man, July 7, 2000.

5. The normal rent was "at most forty dollars," according to Margaret Shafer; interview, April 17, 1998.

6. Of its breakdown just outside Boston in the fall of 1951, Patricia de Man said that in this detail Henri Thomas's roman à clef based on de Man, *Le Parjure*, was correct; interviews, June 1, 2000, and Dec. 29, 1990.

7. "My administrative difficulties have delayed my receipt of the money I've been expecting from Europe. I've deposited $100 into your account at Red Hook, and I'll deposit the remainder, about $210, in the fastest way possible. I am sorry for this unexpected problem which I hope won't cause you too much trouble. If you'd rather that I sent the funds to Paris, let me know." MSLS from Paul de Man to Artine Artinian, November 3, 1949, author archive. Artinian testified that all the deposits de Man described were mythical.

8. From Paris, Riton Nitzschke wrote in February 1950 that de Man had "never cleared up the unsettled piece of business" and that he was losing his friendship because of the harm Paul had caused the older Nitzschke; author archive.

9. Interview with Ted Weiss, May 15, 1991; interview with Barbara Dupee, May 18, 1999.

10. TSL from Willi Frauenfelder to Artine Artinian, March 27, 1950, author archive.

11. "McCarthy would be silent for the longest time and then grope around for words. [She was] not very articulate"; interview with Artine Artinian, April 2, 1998. McCarthy's friend Eve Stwertka pointed out that students were silent

because they were intimidated: no one wanted to say something stupid in front of her. Interview with Eva Stwertka, June 4, 1999.

12. TSL from Willi Frauenfelder to Artine Artinian, May 9, 1950, author archive.

13. Ibid.

14. TSL from Ernest Hayes to Artine Artinian (then living on rue Bonaparte, 47, Paris 6), May 17, June 27, and August 1, 1950, author archive.

15. Interview with Hendrik Woods, March 14, 1998.

16. Interview with Georges Goriély, June 29, 1990.

17. Interview with Patricia de Man, June 1, 2000.

18. *The Bardian*, September 30, 1950.

19. Missing were a steam iron, wastebaskets, a heater, a chopper, gloves, a sweater, a child's hat and pants for a snowsuit. Two rugs had been chewed by a dog. De Man had forced the lock on the garage and used up the wood stored there.

20. Patricia de Man reported that she did not know who the informer could have been and that she was unaware of the bigamy until Paul informed her of it in 1960; interview, December 19, 1990. Annotation reads: "W/A-iss. at N.Y. 10-18-50;" National Archives, U.S. Department of Justice, INS, roll 7605, pub. T 715, cab. 44–48.

21. Interview with Ted Weiss, May 15, 1991.

22. Case had arrived knowing Bard had a budget deficit, but he was not aware it was one and a half times greater than he'd been told. No doubt he was digesting that problem when confronted by the de Man affair; see Reamer Kline, *Education for the Common Good: A History of Bard College—the First 100 Years, 1860–1960* (Annandale-on-Hudson, NY: Bard College, 1982), 132–39.

23. Interview with Ted Weiss, May 15, 1991.

24. Interview with Patricia de Man, June 1, 2000.

25. TSLS from Irma Brandeis to James Case, January 3, 1951; BC.

26. Brandeis asked Case to give de Man "advice" and time "to adapt his ideas of teaching to Bard's demands. I think his value far outweighs his errors." She added, "Consider, too, that he has without doubt ruffled personal vanities here and there. When this happens odd judgments sometimes result," an obvious reference to the personal element in Artinian's attacks. TSLS from Irma Brandeis to James H. Case, January 10, 1951; BC.

27. One student wrote, "I consider this course to be of highest calibire [*sic*] of any I have ever taken. I do not think that there is any teacher at Bard who has more to offer us; nor is there anyone from whom I have gained more. Regardless of arguments with him on critical questions the method and clarity of his thought and expression are inspiring to me, and I believe, to most others who have come into contact with him." And another described "an intensely searching mind . . . . an aura of intimacy existing between Mr. DeMan and the class—a course which cannot be discussed in terms of academic values . . . there is much more that transpires in these hours." A third wrote that having "now taken three terms with Mr. De Man" he or she had "just begun to use the material adequately. I need another term with him." BC.

28. AA includes the following letters and other documents: Anne de Man to Artine Artinian from Mendoza, Argentina, May 21, 1951; Artine Artinian to Anne de Man, May 31, 1951; one check on First National Bank, May 1951, and one note to Lucy Woods, June 9, 1951, found by Artinian in a drawer, signed by Paul de Man (Patricia de Man later said her husband had intended to repay her loan for his hospital expenses); Anne de Man to Artine Artinian, June 10, 1951; David

Braybrooke to Artine Artinian, June 15, 1951; David Braybrooke to Artine Artinian, August 20, 1951. Author archives.

29. Interview with Hendrik Woods, March 14, 1998.

30. Artinian reported that he received his seventy-five dollars' back rent on every payday; interview, April 2, 1998.

31. "De Man Draws Analogy Between Moral System and Aesthetic Act," *The Bardian*, June 5, 1951.

32. This was the ground on which he had praised McCarthy's *The Oasis* for its willingness to be critical of and "inventive" in an American literary world marked by "mediocrity."

33. "Freedom is the human being putting his past out of play by secreting his own nothingness . . . not just at a particular moment . . . consciousness continually experiences itself as the nihilation [*sic*] of its past being because anguish was innate to our condition of being separated in daily life from our sense of being, from our essence, and thus anguish as the manifestation of freedom in the face of self means that man is always separated by a nothingness from his essence." What lay in the past was essence; the work of life was to move forward toward the future: "This *self* with its *a priori* and historical content is the *essence* of man. . . . "The flight before anguish" he perceived, "is not only an effort at distraction before the future; it attempts to disarm the past of its threat." See Jean-Paul Sartre, "The Problem of Nothingness," in *Being and Nothingness*, trans. Hazel Barnes (New York: Philosophical Library, 1956); Sartre, *Essays in Existentialism*, trans. Wade Baskin (Secaucus, NJ: Carol Publishing Co., 1999); Sartre, *The Philosophy of Existentialism*, ed. Wade Baskin (New York: Philosophical Library, 1965), 118, 125, 129, 140.

34. Interview with Patricia de Man, February 9, 1991.

35. Henri Thomas, *Le Parjure* (Paris: Gallimard, 1964).

36. The Weisses had been among the few who had met Anne. Renée said that the justified criticism of Paul was the abandonment of his children: "If anything had been said it would have been, 'What kind of person is this taking up with a student, and he has a family.' " They pointed out that other faculty had married their students, and "the people who were most outraged—we were a progressive college—were people who themselves had been very loose. If any place would have been able to take it, it would have been Bard." Interview with Ted and Renée Weiss, May 15, 1991. In a similar case, a faculty member had run off with someone else's wife and child. (That Bard's faculty was less than a troop of celibates was a theme echoed by other of de Man's defenders.)

37. Levin later became the Irving Babbitt Professor of Comparative Literature at Harvard, and his important study *The Power of Blackness* was published in 1958 and widely acclaimed.

38. Interview with Patricia de Man, June 1, 2000.

39. It was "part of bourgeois tradition of protecting you. He didn't want me to cook. He didn't want me to dance even. He felt a woman was exhibiting herself—it would have meant [the] end of marriage." Interview with Patricia de Man, December 19, 1990.

40. Interviews with Patricia de Man, July 7 and 10, 2000.

30. BOSTON

1. Interview with Patricia de Man, February 1, 1991.

2. Dr. Harry J. Carman, Moore Professor of History and dean emeritus of Columbia

College, was elected chairman of the board of trustees at Bard College October 24, 1950; *Rhinebeck Gazette*, Oct. 26, 1950; Jacques Barzun, "Reminiscences of the Columbia History Department," *Columbia: The Magazine of Columbia University* (Winter 2000): 24–31; TSLS from Harry Carman to James Case, April 4, 1951, BC.

3. Interview with Patricia de Man, July 10, 1992.

4. TSLS from David Braybrooke to Artine Artinian, Nov. 19, 1951, author archive.

5. He attributed his nonpayment of support to his heavy hospital bills, which he would be able to meet once he was again at work. These expenses had been met by Lucy Woods. The lie about having a teaching job at Columbia put the firm off the track, suggesting that he would be accessible in New York; memo by Kaskell and Schlesinger, author archive.

6. Interview with Jack Kotik, June 22, 1999.

7. In fairness to her mother, Patricia recalled that Lucy Woods's marriage and health were then both stressful, but the failure of support cut deep; interview, June 1, 2000.

8. Interview with Patricia de Man, July 10, 1992.

9. His heavy but largely secret workload was a major reason why later de Man had to persuade his department at Harvard to let him reduce the number of courses he took at a time.

10. By the end of the decade, Paul would be earning seven thousand dollars at Harvard as an assistant without tenure. Pat reported that his income from Berlitz equaled his college salary; fourteen thousand dollars per year would have been acceptable pay for many full professors at the time.

11. Walter Isaacson, *Kissinger: A Biography* (New York: Simon & Schuster, 1992), 68–74; Harvey Starr, *Henry Kissinger: Perceptions of International Politics* (Lexington: University Press of Kentucky, 1984), 2–25. Dr. Kissinger declined to be interviewed for this study.

12. Some fifteen translations were credited to de Man between December 1952 and June 1955; the original texts were written in a variety of languages, including Spanish and Italian. Authors included distinguished figures such as Alberto Moravia and Jules Monnerot, a Surrealist from Martinique. Pat de Man, however, did a portion of this work, some of it, as she admitted, "from languages I barely knew"; interview, February 21, 2001. Given her husband's early uncertainty about some grammatical points, she probably also edited his work. *Confluence: An International Forum* was published in seven volumes, from March 1952 to the summer of 1958, under the auspices of the Summer School of Arts and Sciences and of Education at Harvard University. It provided Kissinger with an opportunity to make contact with a wide variety of European statesmen at a high level, who produced brief essays for him in their own language, which he had translated into English.

13. Both Pat de Man and John Hollander remembered de Man's complaint, but whether the default was for lessons or translations, de Man did not specify. Interview with Patricia de Man, June 1, 2000; interview with John Hollander, June 11, 2001.

14. Interview with Patricia de Man, June 1, 2000.

15. He lived successively at 10 Blossom Street, 27 and 30 Maclean Street, 41 (and possibly 20) South Russell Street, 40 Irving Street, and 1679 Massachusetts Avenue in Cambridge.

16. Interview with Patricia de Man, June 1, 2000.

17. Interview with Anne Ipsen, June 30, 1993; interview with Hendrik de Man, March 14, 1998.

18. Interview with Patricia de Man, June 1, 2000; interview with Anne Ipsen, July 4, 1991. Anne offered a different account, reporting that she had traveled independently to the United States with only her two younger sons in the mid-1950s, and then gone on to Canada, where she made friends and eventually met her fourth husband, Gerhard Ipsen-von Orland, a former German army officer. In an interview on March 14, 1998, her eldest son Rik stated, on the other hand, that his mother had left Argentina with Brajatuli and his two brothers, but abandoned Brajatuli once they reached New York, putting his clothes out on the street.

19. In New York, he had spoken openly with Mary McCarthy about his wife and family and even discussed his problematic uncle, speculating on Henri de Man's motives, while he had lied about his own wartime activities.

20. Interview with Patricia de Man, June 1, 2000.

31. PRINCE IN EXILE

1. MSLS from Paul de Man to Harry Levin, October 21, 1951, HL, I, A, 240.

2. The comparativist Lilian Furst found English universities indifferent to her proposed field in the 1950s; only Harry Levin in the late 1960s "was "enthusiastic" about her proposed subject. See Furst, "A Travel Rug for Graduate School," *Sewanee Review* 117, no. 2 (2009): 248–67, especially 262. Hans-Jost Frey reported that comparative literature was not popular in Europe, particularly in Switzerland; interview, June 29, 1991.

3. TSL from Harry Levin to Georges May, April 8, 1970, HL, I, M, 660.

4. Kateb discussed his dissertation with Paul and found him "encouraging. . . . He had a mobile . . . well-stocked mind." Kateb posited to Paul "what it meant to prefer a world in which . . . there was vice to a world [where] there was only virtue." De Man "may have thought that the very idea of a world without vice or weakness or violence was so far-fetched that at most it was a thought experiment to imagine the world otherwise. . . . But he was encouraging. . . . He had a mobile . . . well-stocked mind." Kateb thought de Man showed himself a good "moral philosopher" in his first collection of essays, *Blindness and Insight*; interview, June 27, 2001.

5. Interview with Peter Brooks, September 18, 2000.

6. Interview with Richard Poirier, December 11, 2001.

7. Interview with Richard Poirier, December 12, 2001.

8. In a letter written in 1988, Levin remembered Paul as the politician's son, but this recollection was probably based on a self-justifying letter Paul de Man wrote Poggioli in 1955. See chapter 32, n. 7.

9. Interview with John Hollander, June 11, 2001.

10. Interview with Georges Goriély, June 29, 1990. Goriély met the exiled Henri de Man in 1948, having been given a note of introduction by Paul. He long took Anne's side in the marital dispute, and later, at a conference in 1988 in Antwerp, he offered a paper outlining de Man's misdeeds. De Man's American circle did not publish it.

11. This writer, then an assistant professor at Cornell, was told this story around 1966 by one of de Man's colleagues, who indicated that one must not discuss the subject with him.

12. Interview with Richard Poirier, December 11, 2001.

13. Interview with Burton Pike, December 28, 2001.

14. TSLC from Renato Poggioli to Dean Phelps, September 25, 1955, and May 5, 1953; HL, I, 792.

15. Bourdieu emphasized that it is not language alone that makes for authority in discourse, but also the social setting whereby the speaker is accepted and recognized by his audience; see Pierre Bourdieu, *Language and Symbolic Power*, ed. and with an introduction by John B. Thompson, trans. G. Raymond and M. Adamson (Cambridge: Harvard University Press, 1991), 109.

16. She mentioned at this time that Paul always had a secret cache, "some stock in the Red Star line—that his grandfather gave him as a gift"; interview, January 17, 2003.

17. TSLS from R. De Vreese, head of the Office of University Information, September 5, 1952; received by the Graduate School of Arts and Sciences, Harvard University, September 11, 1952. Author archive.

18. Interview with John Hollander, June 11, 2001. This and subsequent comments are from this interview.

19. Interview with Helen Vendler, November 29, 2000. She was a graduate student in English at Harvard from 1956 to 1960.

20. J. Hillis Miller, who preceded de Man at Harvard, reported that he had become interested in Husserl independent of his mentors years earlier; interview, February 18, 2001.

21. Interviews with Patricia de Man, July 7 and June 1, 2000.

22. Interview with John Hollander, June 11, 2001.

23. Interview with George Kateb, June 27, 2001.

24. Interview with Richard Rand, August 28, 1999.

25. He remembered de Man's comment on Spenser's *The Faerie Queene*: "In Book Two everything blooms, dies, and is reborn, and . . . life ends: It's sad, and immortal." Brower asked Paul if it bothered him. De Man replied, "It bothers me no more in Spenser than it does in Plato." Poirier had rolled his eyes, thinking it unhelpful to young students. Interview with Richard Poirier, December 12, 2001.

26. From the fall of 1952 through the spring of 1954, de Man took three courses each in French, German, and English, and five in comparative literature. Among others, he studied with John Kelleher (emphasis on Yeats), Jackson Bate, W. M. Frohock, and Douglas Bush (Keats), in addition to Poggioli and Levin.

27. Interview with Patricia de Man, February 9, 1991.

28. Interview with Peter Brooks, September 18, 2000.

29. Interview with Barbara Guetti, September 10, 1999. Barbara Guetti, daughter of a college president, was one of several students coming from elite backgrounds who were attracted by Paul de Man. Others included children of wealthy writers and foreign aristocrats.

30. Ibid.

31. Richard Poirier, *Poetry and Pragmatism* (Cambridge: Harvard University Press, 1992), 178.

32. Poirier distinguished "close reading," as developed by Brower, from New Criticism, promoted under the aegis of John Crowe Ransom, which he characterized as a "heady mixture" of "science-bashing . . . Christianity . . . and . . . political emphasis" that reinforced the concepts of coherence and order. The term New Criticism was "inexact," but it represented a backward-looking ideology whose "enemy" was rationality, abstraction, and "northern, big-city capitalism." It was "a Southern regionalist mutation" of I. A. Richards's ideas.

33. The favored awful example was a nineteenth-century flight of fancy, an essay

famously titled "How Many Children Had Lady Macbeth?" ridiculed by L. C. Knights in the twentieth.

34. Interview with Peter Brooks, December 11, 2001.

35. Lowell wanted to produce Emersonian "whole men" and original thinkers on the model of the fellows of Trinity College, Cambridge, a mixed group of select intellectuals, unlike those created by American graduate schools, where specialization, not socialization, was the point; see George C. Homans and Orville T. Bailey, *The Society of Fellows*, ed. Crane Brinton (Cambridge: Harvard University Press, 1948).

32. DENOUNCED

1. MSLS from Paul de Man to Harry Levin, July 29, 1954, author archive.

2. MSLS from Paul de Man to Georges Goriély, April 3, 1954, (year dated by content: the last two digits of the date are reversed in the original); GG.

3. See chapter 19, no. 11.

4. TSLS from Louis Joris (a lawyer in Antwerp) to Paul de Man at the Hôtel des Grands Hommes, Paris, February 17, 1955, UCI.

5. This writer was told by more than one person that the identity of the writer was known to Poggioli and Levin but that they dismissed the letter because the writer was "a woman scorned" and had too patent an interest in damaging de Man's career. The two academics were said to have confided in Henri Peyre, who much later was chair of de Man's department at Yale when he was appointed there in 1971, and Peyre is said to have confided the denouncer's identity to various academic friends. Anne had already twice denounced Paul, although not anonymously, in 1951, addressing the "Recteur" of Bard to detail Paul's behavior with Patricia and to provide details of his financial malfeasance. She had also at that time written to the Belgian consul. Given these indisputable facts (the letters are in AA), facts unknown to Levin and Poggioli, it is conceivable that she could have done so again, directly or through an agent. However, Poggioli, Levin, and Peyre are all deceased and there is no way to corroborate the story. Hearsay apart, documents show that de Man's address and connection to Harvard were known from April 1954 to Georges Goriély, who was a close friend and defender of Anne; to Anne, who had retained legal counsel in Boston; to Gilbert Jaeger; and undoubtedly to others in Belgium and Argentina. Paul de Man had asked that his address be made known to Jaeger and had placed no reservations on disseminating the information.

6. Werner Hamacher, Neil Hertz, and Thomas Keenan, eds., *Responses: On Paul de Man's Wartime Journalism* (Lincoln: University of Nebraska Press), 1992.

7. MSLS from Paul de Man to "Dear Professor Poggioli," dated "Sept. 28th, 1954" in upper left corner and "Jan. 25th, 1955" in upper right corner. For the purposes of this discussion, I am taking the revisions as constituting the second draft, although de Man may have worked on the letter between the two dates. The third text is the printed letter, which de Man redated January 28, 1955; box 16, f. 1, UCI; Hamacher, Hertz, and Keenan, eds., *Responses*, 475–77. *Responses* gives January 26, 1955, erroneously.

8. By 1959 de Man's changing CV read "Candidature en Sciences, Free University of Brussels, 1941. Courses completed for Licencée en Sciences Sociales (Philosophie) at Free University of Brussels," technically true but misleading. To this last sentence Poggioli thoughtfully added punctuation and the date: ", 1942." He thereby provided de Man with the license that in this case he did not claim;

Poggioli may have derived the date from de Man's amendment to ULB letter of September 5, 1952, cited in chapter 31, n. 17.

9. "Paul had a way of double-talking. . . . It was the only time I can say for myself . . . I wasn't quite satisfied with Paul's explanation"; interview with Patricia de Man, February 1, 1991.

10. See note 7 above.

11. For example, the *Daily Worker*, the slogan "Workers of the world, unite," and the IWW all employed this word.

12. TSLS from Paul de Man to "Dear Professor Poggioli," Boston, January 28, 1955/ 30 McLean Street, on Harvard University letterhead. This is the letter printed in *Responses*, except that the typescript letter is dated January 28, not January 26, which is the date given in the printed text.

13. See note 7 above.

14. TSL from Paul de Man to Roger Shattuck, January 20, 1955; MS-C004, box 16:14, UCI.

15. MSLS from Paul de Man to "My dear Renato Poggioli," January 28, 1955, Boston, on Harvard University letterhead; box 16, f. 1, UCI.

16. TSL from Mary McCarthy to Ortwin de Graef, March 17, 1987. I am indebted to Professor de Graef for sharing this communication from McCarthy.

17. Dickey quoted in Henry Hart, *James Dickey: The World as a Lie* (New York: Picador, 2000), xii.

18. He cast Henri's name as Hendrik, its Flemish/Germanic version, underscoring the damage this Teutonic relative had done him.

19. Interview with Jan de Man, June 28, 1990; interview with Patricia de Man, December 19, 1990.

20. See chapter 1 for a discussion of Henri de Man's erasure from family history of the lives of his two cousins, Ida and Adolph Kemna.

33. RETURN TO EUROPE

1. MSLS from Paul de Man to Harry Levin, February 23, 1955 (written from Hôtel des Grands Hommes, Paris); bMS Am 2467 (240), HL.

2. Interview with Patricia de Man, July 7, 2000.

3. *"A faire: telephoner, aller police. écrire à Moredo[k] Kissinger, Bodeck, Joris,"* MS note, UCI.

4. Pat de Man said that while Paul did not "talk about . . . Hermès . . . Joris was a family friend"; interview, January 17, 2003; TSLS from Louis Joris (Antwerp) to Paul de Man, February 17, UCI.

5. He detailed the swindling, which included BF 5,000 taken from Jean Carol de Beucken and the swindling of BF 50,000 from Raymond Eeckhoudt, the insurance broker. Joris figured his own fee by calculating that one dollar equaled BF 50; thus this theft alone would have been $1,000, a very considerable sum in that era. Joris, who had already invested considerable time and effort, said his fee would be a conservative and especially favorable BF 25,000, or $500.

6. This reimbursement was expected of Bob. When he died in 1959, he had little or nothing left from Etablissements de Man; testimony of Bob de Braey and Jan and Marlene de Man, 1990–1995.

7. The stress had resulted in the "radical exhaustion of my wallet," Bob wrote, adding that his morale also left "something to be desired." MSLS from Bob de Man to Yvonne de Munck-de Man, June 2, 1948; MdMF.

8. Interview with Marlene de Man-Flechtheim, June 2, 2002.
9. Interview with Patricia de Man, December 19, 1990.
10. Interview with Patricia de Man, January 17, 2003.
11. TSLS from A. Wendelen to Paul de Man, March 15, 1955; UCI.
12. Bob De Braey, executor for Bob De Man's estate, met Paul and Patricia de Man in Antwerp and turned over certain family objects to them in 1962, four years after Bob's death. According to Patricia, Paul first returned to Belgium with her and the two children that year, when he was abroad teaching at the University of Zurich. They also then met Louis Joris, who gave them both the violin of Paul's father and an oil portrait of his mother. Paul had wanted to pay off some of Bob's remaining debts, "including one to an old servant long since dead, and the lawyer was sure she had been paid, but no receipt had been given and her heirs wanted to collect on it, and did." This suggests that Paul's debt to Filomene was paid to her heirs by Bob de Man's executors. Interview with Patricia de Man, January 17, 2003.

34. HEIDEGGER: A PLACE TO STAND

1. The prolific scholar was credited with at least ninety-one entries in the Bibliothèque Nationale de France.
2. Lionel Abel, *The Intellectual Follies: a Memoir of the Literary Venture in New York and Paris* (New York: W. W. Norton, 1984), 165; Olivier Todd, *Albert Camus: Une Vie* (Paris: Gallimard, 1996), 289, 407; Jean-Paul Sartre, *Search for a Method*, trans. Hazel Barnes (New York: Knopf, 1963), 19, cited by Ann Fulton, *Apostles of Sartre: Existentialism in America 1945–63* (Evanston, IL: Northwestern University Press, 1999), 16.
3. Taken to his apartment by "the disgusting Allan Bloom," she found beautiful drawings by both children and artists everywhere on the walls, "a man who looked like Sartre," and "lean old ladies in fur hats." Susan Sontag, *Reborn: Journals and Notebooks 1947–1963*, ed. David Rieff (New York: Farrar, Straus and Giroux, 2008), 188–89.
4. Interview with Patricia de Man, July 10, 2000.
5. For some details of Wahl's ambivalence toward Germany, see Hamilton Basso, "Profile: Philosopher," *The New Yorker*, March 12, 1945, 27–41, especially 31. During Wahl's imprisonment, he wrote a set of short poems, dated "Paris, aôut, septembre, octobre 1941, prison de la santé," one of which is titled "Croyance," affirming his belief in Jesus. See Jean Wahl, *Poèmes*, illustrated by André Masson, introduction by Marcel Raymond (Montreal: Editions de l'Arbre, 1945); Wahl, *L'Idée de l'être chez Heidegger* (Paris: Centre de Documentation Universitaire, 1951), and Wahl, *La Pensée de Heidegger et la poésie de Hölderlin* (Paris: Centre de Documentation Universitaire, 1952).
6. Within a month of de Man's appearance at Wahl's twice-weekly seminar, the philosopher published de Man's essay "Poetic Nothingness: On a Hermetic Sonnet by Mallarmé," and in the next two years he printed three more of his articles. Three others appeared in *Critique*, Bataille's journal, and in the United States, one was published in *Comparative Literature*, which Harry Levin placed for him (Levin was on its editorial board), and another in the *Cambridge Review*. In all cases, editorial power lay with de Man's close friends or colleagues, but that does not detract from his achievement.
7. As others have shown, notably de Graef, Lehman, and Rossi, sometime between that date and 1955, Bataille's influence gave way to Heidegger's. See Stefano

Rosso, "An Interview with Paul de Man," in Paul de Man, *The Resistance to Theory* (Minneapolis: University of Minnesota Press, 1986), 115–121, especially 119. In Belgium, Alphonse de Waelhens published his dissertation, *La philosophie de Martin Heidegger* (Louvain: Editions de l'Institut Superieur de Philosophie, 1942). For a deconstructive and Heideggerian discussion of de Man's essays in this period, see also Ortwin de Graef, *Serenity in Crisis: A Preface to Paul de Man, 1939–1960* (Lincoln: University of Nebraska Press, 1993).

8. Rüdiger Safranksi credits both Jean Wahl and Gabriel Marcel for having introduced the term in the 1920s. See Safranski, *Martin Heidegger: Between Good and Evil*, trans. Ewald Osers (Cambridge: Harvard University Press, 1998), 342.

9. He appeared, Arendt wrote to a friend, "opinionated, remorseful, and embittered" and complained that " 'the devil' had egged him on"; see Safranski, *Martin Heidegger*, 332–52; 375–76.

10. Richard Wolin, *Heidegger's Children: Hannah Arendt, Karl Löwith, Hans Jonas, and Herbert Marcuse* (Princeton: Princeton University Press, 2001), 210.

11. George Steiner, "Writing to Music: Adorno at the Midnight of History," *Times Literary Supplement*, October 10, 2003, 3–4.

12. Interview with Richard Rand, August 28, 1999.

13. Paul de Man, "Montaigne et la transcendance," *Critique* 79 (1953): 1011–22; reprinted as "Montaigne and Transcendence," trans. Richard Howard, in Paul de Man, *Critical Writings: 1953–1978*, ed. and introduction by Lindsay Waters (Minneapolis: University of Minnesota Press, 1989), 3–11. "Montaigne and 'The Inward Generation,' " *Cambridge Review* 1 (1955): 41–47.

14. Paul de Man, "Les Exégèses de Hölderlin par Martin Heidegger," *Critique* 100–101 (1955): 800–819; reprinted as "Heidegger's Exegeses of Hölderlin," trans. Wlad Godzich, in Paul de Man, *Blindness and Insight*, 2nd rev. ed. (Minneapolis: University of Minnesota Press, 1983), 246–66.

15. Philip Watts, *Allegories of the Purge: How Literature Responded to the Postwar Trials of Writers and Intellectuals in France* (Palo Alto: Stanford University Press, 1998), 202–3.

16. See note 14, above.

17. Joseph P. Fell, *Heidegger and Sartre: An Essay on Being and Place* (New York: Columbia University Press, 1979), 170; Fell did not link their thinking to the war or to the events of the period.

18. Paul de Man, *Critical Writings*, 10–11.

19. Paul de Man, "The Inward Generation," *Cambridge Review* 1 (1955): 41–47; reprinted in de Man, *Critical Writings*, 12–17.

20. Fell, *Heidegger and Sartre*, 101, discussing *Sein und Zeit*.

21. Watts has pointed this out in discussing Sartre's criticism of Flaubert and the Goncourts for "not writing a single line" opposing the Commune. See Watts's discussion of Sarte in *Allegories of the Purge*, 202.

22. Martin Heidegger, "Letter on Humanism," in *Basic Writings*, ed. David Farrell Krell (San Francisco: HarperCollins, 1993), 239.

23. Victor Farías, *Heidegger and Nazism*, ed. Jos. Margolis and Tom Rockmore, trans. Paul Burrell et al. (Philadelphia: Temple University Press, 1989). The Chilean writer's findings met strong resistance, followed by a number of parallel discussions; numerous critics since have attacked Heidegger on both philosophic and political grounds, not only on his membership in the Nazi party but also on the totalitarian quality of many of his pronouncements.

24. It is polemical but probably true to say, as Philip Watts and others have done, that

certain existential ideas about history function to put out of sight the issues of guilt and responsibility. (Existentialism was, in fact, resisted at the time by orthodox philosophers, in part because it was perceived as too much a reply to merely contemporary events—war in particular.) "The spirit of the trial continues to haunt us as it haunted writers and readers . . . years ago." Watts, *Allegories of the Purge*, 204. Nevertheless, Heidegger's concepts and influence remain widespread.

25. De Man, "Montaigne and Transcendence," in *Critical Writings*, ed. Waters, 3–11.

26. This was probably the source of a mystifying ban on "rereading oneself" that emanated from de Man's circle at Cornell in the early 1960s.

27. "When we would go back and meet [certain relatives] who had spoken nothing but French—now they spoke only Flemish"; interview with Patricia de Man, December 29, 1990.

28. Interview with J. Hillis Miller, February 18, 2001.

29. De Man, "The Inward Generation," 41–47; reprinted in *Critical Writings*, ed. Waters, 12–17.

30. De Man, "Thematic Criticism and the Theme of Faust," *Critical Writings*, ed. Waters, 80–84, 86–89.

31. De Man, "The Temptation of Permanence," *Critical Writings*, ed. Waters, 31.

32. Ibid., 39.

33. "The poetical act is the quintessential historical act: that through which we become conscious of the divided character of our own being, and consequently, of the necessity of fulfilling it, of accomplishing it in time, instead of undergoing it in eternity"; de Man, "Keats and Hölderlin," *Critical Writings*, ed. Waters, 48. See also de Man, "Heidegger Reconsidered," *New York Review of Books*, April 2, 1964, 14–16; reprinted in *Critical Writings*, 102–6.

34. De Man, "Heidegger's Exegeses of Hölderlin," trans. Wlad Godzich, *Blindness and Insight*, 255.

35. If Heidegger's promise required the company of Icarus as well as Hölderlin to be realized, then Paul was helping to rehabilitate his own master.

36. Ortwin de Graef examined de Man's manipulation of Rousseau's language in detail, asserting that in dealing with the complex issue of confession, de Man could not honestly have written differently. See de Graef, "Silence to Be Observed: A Trial for Paul de Man's Inexcusable Confessions," in *(Dis)continuities: Essays on Paul de Man*, ed. Luc Herman, Kris Humbeeck and Geert Lernout (Amsterdam: Editions Rodopi, 1989), 51–73.

37. When Rand told Paul de Man of Rahv's terse comment, his professor responded, "Rahv doesn't count." Years later, Rand talked with de Man after his onetime mentor had given the prestigious Gauss lecture, at Princeton, on Rousseau and "The Purloined Ribbon." Rand recalled that "the subject of Austin came up. He had mentioned Austin (leader of the 'ordinary language' school of philosophy) and speech acts in relation to Austin—and I said, 'That's not exactly what Austin is saying' (about felicity conditions) and he said, 'Who cares what Austin thinks?' " Interview with Richard Rand, August 28, 1999.

38. Interview with Barbara Johnson, November 17, 2000.

39. "People very on-the-make, and nothing stood in their way, and gossip was rampant. . . . [Paul de Man] was very suspect [because of] what he was teaching. If you mentioned Heidegger, you were kicked out [of] Emerson Hall. [The accepted position was] analytic philosophy: Quine, Ayer, Peirce. The blasphemer was Heidegger, Jaspers, and Husserl. John Wise only taught [them]. De

Man was a wild Hegelian for these people." Interview with Edgar de Bresson, May 26, 1998.

40. Interview with J. Hillis Miller, February 18, 2001. This writer was also taught by a member of the philological school, who turned aside questions of "meaning" in Shakespeare's *Lear* or *Hamlet* in favor of studying "hard readings," such as decoding the crux "lipsbury pinfold"—a famously indefinable place of banishment to which Lear threatens to send Kent. Warner Berthoff has pointed out that other curricula, such as American literature, were more flexible and that Levin both wrote a major study of James Joyce and gave a famous course on Joyce, Proust, and Mann.

41. Lindon prided himself on publishing Alain Robbe-Grillet, Michel Butor, Claude Simon, and Samuel Beckett, the last two of whom later became Nobel laureates. Before the war, writing in France had been a preserve, Lindon held, for the upper classes of the literary world and was largely closed to outsiders. No writer could live by writing alone. There were no "bestsellers." That changed after the war.

42. Paulhan, a centrist and occasionally a royalist, was the "most important person" at the receptions of the famous Florence Gould, a woman who made a point of receiving all the Nazi generals, as well as the French social, literary, political, and economic world. Gerhard Heller attended frequently as the German censor under whom all French publishing passed in review. Gould had a history of personal alliances that spanned both sides of the war, but she was eulogized when the French government awarded her a medal more than fifty years later. See Gerhard Heller, *Un Allemand à Paris: 1940–1944* (Paris: Editions du Seuil, 1981), 62, 64, 191 ff.

43. Interview with Jérôme Lindon, May 28, 1998.

44. Lindon's enmity was both personal and political, for he wanted postwar writers of a different political stamp than those favored by Jean Paulhan, to whom Lambrichs was still tied. Lindon would, he said, enter Lambrichs's office, sit on his desk, and take away manuscripts that were lying there, in a gesture deliberately rude; interview with Jérôme Lindon, May 28, 1998. Anne Simonin's richly detailed study offers a more impersonal account of the rupture; see *Les Editions de Minuit, 1942–1955: Le Devoir d'insoumission* (Paris: IMEC, 1994), 428, 430, 451, 452.

45. De Man quotes from Martin Heidegger, *Poetry, Language, and Thought*, trans. Albert Hofstader (New York: Harper & Row, 1971), 226. See also Paul de Man, "The Temptation of Permanence," *Critical Writings*, ed. Waters, 39.

35. "EXCUSEZ LE JARGON"

1. MSLS from Paul de Man to Harry Levin, November 14, 1955, (written from Hôtel des Grands Hommes, Paris), HL, box 277, f. 791. Georges Poulet did not share his brother's fascism, but his sibling, Robert Poulet, was an artist, critic, and editor who worked under the protection of Paul Colin and edited Colin's *Le Nouvel Journal*.

2. Jean Starobinski, then Georges Poulet's assistant, also became de Man's friend at this time.

3. Interview with Yves Bonnefoy, c. 1990.

4. De Man went to the courses being given by Merleau-Ponty and saw him in private, as well. Interview with Patricia de Man, July 7, 2003. MSLS from Paul de Man to Harry Levin, June 6, 1955, HL.

5. Interview with Patricia de Man, July 7, 2000.
6. MSLS from Paul de Man to Harry Levin, June 6, 1955, HL.
7. The Popular Front began in 1934 but fell apart a few years after it helped Léon Blum take office in 1936.
8. Harry Levin, "James Joyce, un individu dans le monde," *Revue de métaphysique et de morale*, nos. 3–4 (1956): 346–59.
9. The other man Cavell suggested for a joint professorship in history of philosophy and history of science was Thomas Kuhn because, Cavell thought, "Kuhn will revolutionize the study" of both. Interview with Stanley Cavell, November 7, 2003.
10. TSL marked "COPY" from Paul de Man to Renato Poggioli, December 3, 1955, HL.
11. Ibid.
12. Six years later, a prestigious fellowship in New York City allowed $2,200 per year; and the Fulbright Commission in 1962 provided $2,500.
13. Interview with Harry Levin, July 8, 1992.
14. MSLS from Paul de Man to Harry Levin, May 31, 1956, HL.
15. MSLS from Paul de Man to Harry Levin, July 16, 1956, HL.
16. MSLS from Paul de Man to Harry Levin, November 28, 1956, HL.
17. In his letter to Levin of November 28, 1956, he remarked, "You have probably heard from Renato Poggioli that my re-entry visa in the U.S. was longer in coming than I expected—hence the delay in my return. This is all settled now and I will make it back into Cambridge a few days before Christmas."
18. Interview with Patricia de Man, December 19, 1990.

36. THE MIRROR

1. William H. Pritchard, *English Papers: A Teaching Life* (St. Paul, Minnesota: Graywolf Press, 1995), 101–2.
2. Interview with Richard Poirier, December 11, 2001.
3. Pritchard, *English Papers*, 101–2.
4. He was "incredibly learned, brilliant," but he "exploited . . . his appearance and his aura . . . very consciously," said Poirier, adding, "I've always had a great fondness for outrageous people, as long as they don't try to pull their fast ones on me." Interview, December 11, 2001.
5. De Bresson believed that in his late work de Man "killed what he loved most," meaning the "sensual" pleasure he took in reading. He recalled also "the backbiting and intrigues of the English and comparative literature departments." Interview, May 26, 1998.
6. Interview with Peter Brooks, September 18, 2000.
7. Interview with Ellen Burt, February 2, 2001.
8. Interview with Barbara Guetti, September 10, 1999.
9. The conference was run by Jean Starobinski. Li recalled, "I took a room in a hotel nearby—and I went there. . . . I went to dinner with everyone—[there was] very animated conversation. . . . Later we stayed and talked. I asked him if he ever said he was the son of my father and he said 'no.' . . . And I have seen that he was the god of all these professors." Interview with Elise ("Li") LeCocq-de Man, June 30, 1990.
10. Neither Richard Poirier nor Neil Hertz, contemporaries at Harvard, read those

essays at that time; interview with Poirier, December 11, 2001; interview with Hertz, May 8, 2002.

11. His income after 1957 was approximately fourteen thousand dollars, according to his widow's calculations; see chapter 30, n. 10.

12. "It seems to us that the basic form of unpleasure in disturbances of narcissism is an affective experience of mental pain. Mental pain . . . reflects a substantial discrepancy between the mental representation of the actual self of the moment and an ideal shape of the self." See Walter J. Joffe and Joseph Sandler, "On Disorders of Narcissism," in *From Safety to Superego: Selected Papers of Joseph Sandler*, ed. Joseph Sandler (New York: Guilford Press, 1987), 189.

13. Peter Brooks has written insightfully: "Relation to one's own body . . . frequently has its symbolic manifestation in a privileged visual moment: self-reflection in the mirror. . . . Our early experiences of our own bodies may be not necessarily those of oneness or unity, but rather those of otherness and alienation: our selves as they are for others, a relation of displacement which notably affects relations of erotic love to others." Brooks refers to Jacques Lacan, *Ecrits* (Paris: Editions du Seuil, 1966), 93–100, adding that "The 'anecdote' of the infant in front of the mirror need not be literal: the mirroring can come from other people." See Brooks, *Body Work: Objects of Desire in Modern Narrative* (Cambridge: Harvard University Press, 1992), 14.

37. MENDING THE NET

1. TSLS from Renato Poggioli to Reuben Brower, January 20, 1960, author archive.

2. TSLS from Reuben Brower to Harry Levin and Renato Poggioli, January 13, 1960, author archive.

3. Interviews with Anne Ipsen, June 30, 1993, July 4, 1991, and interview with Hendrik Woods, March 14, 1998. Pat de Man attested that the pressure for payments, failing which Anne would reveal Paul's past, were what kept her own family in poverty.

4. Two notes from de Man to Poggioli, June 21 and August 27, 1957, imply a recent meeting.

5. Interview with Burton Pike, December 28, 2001.

6. See *Blindness and Insight: Essays in the Rhetoric of Contemporary Criticism* (New York: Oxford University Press, 1971); interview with Geoffrey Hartman, December 2, 1997.

7. Being kept on as an assistant professor rarely occurred, although Richard Poirier was given that rank from 1958 to 1962; interview with Poirier, December 11, 2001.

8. Jean Wahl had published de Man's essay on Mallarmé almost as soon as Paul arrived in Paris, but none of the dissertation per se was advanced.

9. De Man had reported that the last portion of his thesis was nearly complete and that he liked it. However, he did not care for what he had produced about Georg, and this material would require changes. MSLS from Paul de Man to Renato Poggioli, August 27, [1957], dated by contents. Author archive.

10. Rüdiger Safranski pointed out that Hölderlin was made an icon in the twentieth century and that "the real renaissance occurred through Stefan Georg and his circle just before World War I. . . . The Georg circle viewed Hölderlin as the inspired precursor of 'symbolism,' not of an artistically playful one but of an

existentially urgent one. 'It is as though a curtain had been raised from the holiest of holies and the unutterable offered itself to the gaze.'" This was the tenor of the 1920s and 1930s: "Among the youth movement, Hölderlin was considered a genius of the heart," and Heidegger was the mediator. See Safranski, *Martin Heidegger: Between Good and Evil*, trans. Ewald Osers (Cambridge: Harvard University Press, 1998), 282.

11. Steiner was harshly critical: "To mouth Heidegger's indefinable, immaculate *Sein* as if the mere term carried mystical guarantees of existential sense is to fall into the trap of metaphysical autism, of self-referential bluff. . . . This opaque imperative allows Heidegger to avoid answers to that which matters most for man: the existence of God and the question of freedom. Thus there is in Heideggerian doctrine, as there was in his politics, an archaic submissiveness to mysteries beyond any individual, argumentative (dialectical) reach." See "Writing to Music: Adorno at the Midnight of History," *Times Literary Supplement*, October 10, 2003, 3–4.

12. A student of de Man at Harvard, who requested anonymity, took his course in French Symbolism in 1957 and quoted a younger student who told her that she had written a paper for de Man at Yale on which he had commented, "impeccable—and opaque." Interview, May 23, 2010.

13. TSL from Harry Levin to Paul de Man, December 2, 1955, HL.

14. Interview with Harry Levin, July 8, 1992.

15. Interview with George Kateb, July 7, 2001.

16. Interview with George Kateb, June 27, 2001.

17. Interview with John Hollander, June 11, 2001.

18. MSLS from Paul de Man to Henri Thomas, July 5, 1959, IMEC.

19. MSLS from Paul de Man to Renato Poggioli, August 26, [1957], HL, I, A, f. 791.

20. Interview with Burton Pike, December 28, 2001. Posthumously this had changed when Ellen Burt and others helped Patricia organize de Man's materials; by then de Man had an extensive library.

21. MSLS from Paul de Man to Renato Poggioli, August 26, [1957], HL, I, A, f. 791.

22. His paper was probably entitled, "W. B. Yeats and the French Symbolists." A prospective paper was announced in *PMLA* 73 (1957), "72nd Annual Meeting," Comparative Literature 5: "Anglo-French and Franco-American Literary Relations," chairman, Hugh H. Chapman, Jr., Pennsylvania State University; secretary, James K. Robinson, Northwestern University.

23. Interview with Geoffrey Hartman, December 2, 1997.

24. Ibid.

25. Cancellation form dated September 26, 1957, for registration as student because of "corporation appointment," archives of Harvard University's Department of Comparative Literature, provided July 24, 1992, by Betty Ann Farmer, on instructions from Harry Levin.

26. Ms memo [dated October 1957 by contents] from R. P[oggioli] to J. A. [?] Schwartz [with phone number EL4-5720]. On address line, circled, is "Thurs, Deman 10" and Frohock's OK appears in RP's hand. Author archive.

27. Alphonse de Waelhens, *La philosophie de Martin Heidegger* (Louvain: Editions de l'Institut superieur de philosophie, 1942).

28. Interview with Harry Levin, July 8, 1992.

29. "Patsy was born in a Cambridge hospital, July 8, 1958"; interview with Patricia de Man, December 19, 1990.

30. Interviews with George Kateb, June 27 and July 12, 2001.

31. Interview with Harry Levin, July 8, 1992; MSLS from Paul de Man to Harry

Levin, October 21, [1957], HL, I, A, f. 240. He also sent him a "copy of an article on Faust which appeared in Critique and in which you were kind enough to express interest when I mentioned it to you last year. It is a sequel to another article (on formalist criticism) and it is to be followed by a third one in which I intend to deal with the necessary and difficult synthesis between thematic and formalist criticism. With thanks for your interest and assistance."

32. On November 4, the dean agreed with the cancellation; author archive.

33. Martin Heidegger, "Hölderlin and the Essence of Poetry," trans. Paul de Man, *Quarterly Review of Literature* 10, nos. 1–2 (1959): 79–94.

34. Paul de Man, "Structure intentionelle de l'image romantique," *Revue internationale de philosophie* 51 (1960): 68–84; de Man's translation of this essay, "Intentional Structure of the Romantic Image," appears in Harold Bloom, ed., *Romanticism and Consciousness* (New York: W. W. Norton, 1970), 65–77, and in Paul de Man, *The Rhetoric of Romanticism* (New York: Columbia University Press, 1984), 1–17.

35. The title alludes directly to a much earlier essay by Sartre, "The Intentional Structure of the Image"—which had been noticed by Jean Wahl—material incorporated by Sartre into *Being and Nothingness* (1943), but which originated in his "La Structure intentionnelle de l'image," *Revue de métaphysique et de morale* 45, no 4. (1938): 543–609.

36. Poggioli himself gave de Man an A+ and A- on a major and a minor exam, and Hatfield an "a"—in a hand written very small and faintly. Evidently, more was expected. It may be that the oral exam was again de Man's stumbling block.

37. HL, I, C, f. 1275.

38. See Henry [sic] Thomas, *L'Etudiant au village* (Cognac: Le temps qu'il fait, 1998).

39. Henri Thomas, "Carnets," November 8, 1959; manuscript, IMEC. By 1948, Thomas was editing a journal called *84*, and he had grown close to Georges Lambrichs, who took over the journal at Editions de Minuit; see Anne Simonin, *Les Editions de Minuit: Le Devoir d'insoumission* (Paris: IMEC, 1994), 354.

40. Jacques Derrida discussed *Le Parjure* in his essay " 'Le Parjure,' *Perhaps*: Storytelling and Lying ('abrupt breaches of syntax')," in *Acts of Narrative*, ed. Carol Jacobs and Henry Sussman (Palo Alto: Stanford University Press, 2003), 195–234. See also Jacques Derrida, *Without Alibi*, ed. and trans. Peggy Kamuf (Palo Alto: Stanford University Press, 2002), 161–201. After the Siege of Stalingrad, when it was immediately widely surmised that the Germans were losing the war, Thomas calculated in his unpublished journal of January 3, 1943, that now the advantage would shift to the other side, which was better nourished and more numerous, and that if he maintained his balance in both camps at once, he would be able to maintain himself at a fairly high level of existence— or at least would be able to exist.

41. "Paul de Man," *Yale French Studies* 69 (1985): 17–21, especially 18.

42. MSL from Paul de Man to Patricia de Man, July 10, [1959]; the letter continues beyond the two photocopied pages provided to the author by Mrs. De Man; author archive.

43. The book was probably E[rnst] R[obert] Curtius's *European Literature and the Latin Middle Ages*, trans. Willard R. Trask (New York: Pantheon Books, 1953).

44. Interview with Peter Brooks, September 18, 2000.

45. TSL from Reuben A. Brower to Professors Harry T. Levin and Renato Poggioli, January 13, 1960, author archive.

46. His dissertation was later written against the deadline in May 1960, according to Betty Ann Farmer; interview, July 24, 1992.

47. "He was very slow," the old scholar recalled. "With three years in the Society of Fellows we assumed his thesis [*sic*] was near completion. (And at end of the fellowship, he became a lecturer.) Finally we forgave him Georg. He had written quite a lot by then on Yeats and Mallarmé, which we considered substantial." Interview with Harry Levin, July 8, 1992.

48. The words blood and soil, or race and land, connote the supposed mystical relation of Germans to territories they claimed as exclusively their own. Influential on younger men, Georg opposed all that modernism stood for: progress, commerce, political democracy, etc. Georg disliked Hitler and left Germany in 1933, but posthumously he was made a national poet by the Party.

49. Levin was asked by Paul almost as soon as he got to Cornell to support his application for a Guggenheim Foundation grant. His response was measured and positive in part, but it specified his own disagreement with de Man's approach. Author archive.

50. At Cornell, inquirers might be referred without further explanation to Gaston Bachelard or Roman Jakobson's essay "Le Chat," neither of which illuminated the basic issue of intellectual provenance.

51. Ironically, Icarus falling from the skies, Paul's own emblem, of which he had published a print while at Hermès, was the image central to a thesis written by one of these rivals.

52. This salary was three times what the Department of Comparative Literature at Harvard was contributing to Paul's annual seven-thousand-dollar salary, which was shared among three departments. When Harvard made an offer to Lionel Trilling of Columbia, he replied to Jackson Bate that he would not consider going there for less than fifteen thousand—a sum that Bate reported without comment and without sequelae.

53. "Verification of Vital Record," New Hampshire Department of Health and Human Services, provided to the author July 9, 2000.

54. Sharing a year of teaching at Zurich with Hartman, Paul de Man took a house outside Zumikon and proposed to Hartman that they use it successively, but he left without paying his rent. Hartman assumed the whole cost but did not mention this to his friend; interview with Geoffrey Hartman, December 2, 1997. Pat de Man recalled more than one episode of fleeing a hotel in Switzerland with the bill unpaid.

EPILOGUE

1. Interview with Hans-Jost Frey, June 29, 1991.

2. Interview with Barbara Guetti, September 10, 1999; TSLS from Warner B. Berthoff (a friend and colleague of Marichal) to the author, April 19, 2004.

3. Victor Brombert reported that he had encouraged de Man to publish this collection but noted that initially the Department of Comparative Literature did not want an unconventional theorist of the sort that he, as chair of the French Department, was seeking; interview, August 27, 2012.

4. Published or compiled by him during his lifetime were: *Blindness and Insight* (New York: Oxford University Press, 1971); *Allegories of Reading: Figural Language in Rousseau, Nietzsche, Rilke, and Proust* (New Haven: Yale University Press, 1979); *The Rhetoric of Romanticism* (New York: Columbia University Press, 1984); *The Resistance to Theory* (Minneapolis: University of Minnesota Press, 1986).

5. Compiled and edited after his death by former students from de Man's lectures

and other publications were: *Aesthetic Ideology: Paul de Man*, ed. and introduction by Andrzej Warminski (Minneapolis: University of Minnesota Press, 1996); *Romanticism and Contemporary Criticism: The Gauss Seminar and Other Papers*, ed. E. S. Burt, Kevin Newmark, Andrzej Warminski (Baltimore: Johns Hopkins University Press, 1993).

6. They gained special favors by "learn[ing] to fish for extramural academic offers [so as] to extort more money from the . . . ministry" and by attaining fame also gained "recognition of it by a minister and his select circle of supposed cognoscenti"—all of which reinforced their "charisma"; William Clark, *Academic Charisma and the Origins of the Research University* (Chicago: University of Chicago Press), 2006.

7. Carlo Ginzburg, *History, Rhetoric, and Proof* (Hanover, NH: University Press of New England, 1999); cited is de Man's *Blindness and Insight*, ix, 16, et seq. Ginzburg attacks the deconstructive position that historical fact and conflicting readings of evidence render historical fact in principle undecidable. He also objects to the movement's misappropriation of Nietzsche: It was "unscholarly reasons that, from the mid-1960s, led to reading Nietzsche in a new light" (18).

8. David Lehman, *Signs of the Times: Deconstruction and the Fall of Paul de Man* (New York: Simon & Schuster, 1991), 229.

9. Ortwin de Graef also used this term in 1989. Later, he demonstrated de Man's pattern of twisting or misquoting language and acknowledged de Man's habit of "'dubious translation'" and "twisted paraphrase," yet he defended his subject because de Man had aimed to make a confession "in a negative fashion" by "refusing to make excuses." See de Graef, "Silence to Be Observed: A Trial for Paul de Man's Inexcusable Confessions," in *(Dis)continuities: Essays on Paul de Man*, ed. Luc Herman, Kris Humbeeck, and Geert Lernout (Amsterdam: Editions Rodopi, 1989), 72 n. 18. For Allan Spitzer's critique, see "The Debate over the Wartime Writings of Paul de Man: The Language of Setting the Record Straight," in *Theory's Empire: An Anthology of Dissent*, ed. Daphne Patai and Will H. Corral (New York: Columbia University Press, 2005), 271–86, 285 n. 16.

10. De Man's son Rik Woods shared this view, believing that his father's "authority" came from his experience of falling into quicksand but recovering himself: "What he's saying is 'I was really seduced by some of this stuff and I should have known better'"; interview, March 14, 1998.

11. See Paul de Man, "Autobiography as De-Facement," *The Rhetoric of Romanticism* (New York: Columbia University Press, 1984), 67–81, 80. For a different discussion, see Neil Hertz, "Lurid Figures," in *Reading de Man Reading*, ed. Lindsay Waters and Wlad Godzich (Minneapolis: University of Minneapolis Press, 1989), 82–104.

12. Interview with Paul Willems, April 26, 1993.

13. De Man was quoting William Wordsworth, "Essays Upon Epitaphs," in *Wordsworth's Literary Criticism*, ed. W. J. B. Owen (London: Routledge & Kegan Paul, 1974).

14. Jacques Derrida, "Like the Sound of the Sea Deep Within a Shell: Paul de Man's War," *Mémoires: For Paul de Man*, rev. ed. (New York: Columbia University Press, 1989), 235–37.

15. Ibid., 245.

16. Ralph Waldo Emerson, "The American Scholar."

INDEX

Page numbers beginning with 448 refer to notes.